Studies of the Max Planck Institute Luxembourg for International, European and Regulatory Procedural Law

edited by
Prof. Dr. Dres. h.c. Burkhard Hess
Prof. Dr. Hélène Ruiz Fabri

Volume 9

Loïc Cadiet/Burkhard Hess/Marta Requejo Isidro (eds.)

Approaches to Procedural Law

The Pluralism of Methods

Nomos

Max Planck Institute
LUXEMBOURG
for Procedural Law

The Deutsche Nationalbibliothek lists this publication in the Deutsche Nationalbibliografie; detailed bibliographic data are available on the Internet at http://dnb.d-nb.de

ISBN 978-3-8487-4309-4 (Print)
978-3-8452-8512-2 (ePDF)

British Library Cataloguing-in-Publication Data
A catalogue record for this book is available from the British Library.

ISBN 978-3-8487-4309-4 (Print)
978-3-8452-8512-2 (ePDF)

Library of Congress Cataloging-in-Publication Data
Cadiet, Loïc / Hess, Burkhard / Requejo Isidro, Marta
Approaches to Procedural Law
The Pluralism of Methods
Loïc Cadiet / Burkhard Hess / Marta Requejo Isidro (eds.)
552 p.
Includes bibliographic references.

ISBN 978-3-8487-4309-4 (Print)
978-3-8452-8512-2 (ePDF)

1st Edition 2017

Table of Contents

Foreword

The first IAPL-MPI Summer School was held at the premises of the MPI in Luxembourg in July 2014. The success of the experience, crowned by the publication of the collective book *Procedural Science at the Crossroads of Different Generations* (B. Hess, M. Requejo Isidro, L. Cadiet eds, Nomos 2015), has encouraged the organization of a second edition. Two years after the first one, the second Post-doctoral Summer School in procedural law took place at the Max Planck Institute Luxembourg in July 2016. Organized by the International Association of Procedural Law and the Max Planck Institute for Procedural Law, the school offered to young researchers specializing in procedural law an opportunity to discuss their current research topics with fellow colleagues and law professors coming from different jurisdictions. In this way, the school implements the wish and the policy of the IAPL to diversify its activities towards young proceduralists.

The idea to organize the summer school was inspired by two complementary reflections that we explained in the aforementioned *Procedural Science at the Crossroads of Different Generations*. On the one hand, modern procedural law is characterized by its openness to comparative and international perspectives. On the other hand, the aperture of procedural science requires a new approach of research, which has to be based on a comparative methodology. Against this backdrop, the IAPL and the Max Planck Institute for Procedural Law decided to support contemporary research in procedural law by organizing the school, since immediate discussion with scholars coming from different jurisdictions is the best way to practice legal comparative research.

The general topic of this second summer school was: *Approaches to Procedural Law. The Pluralism of Methods.* "Pluralism" and "methods" are the key words.

Procedural law is no longer a purely domestic topic. The recent tendencies characterizing the field, such as Europeanization and harmonization, mark the evolution towards a new, cross-border dimension of this area of law. In addition, the growing importance of transnational legal relations in all spheres of civil and commercial dealings makes it unavoidable to face the new challenges of procedural law across national borders. The traditional approaches of national dogmatics, which have for a long time guided the reflections of scholars operating in the field of civil procedure, can no longer capture the increased complexity of the so-called postmodernity. Furthermore, the techniques and skills of comparative law are equally evolving due to the availability of statistical and empirical data which enable the assessment of the law in action, as opposed to the law in the books. Besides, it is still an open issue whether the methodological approach of traditional comparative law (i.e., distinguishing different legal families) corresponds to the evolution of procedural law, and whether and to what extent it can be applied to comparative procedural law. In light of this, it is particularly important for young researchers to reflect on the methods to be adopted in order to guarantee that research in the field of procedural law maintains its comprehensive explanatory power. Looking at the current landscape of research in the field of procedural law, a wide array of methods can potentially be used: comparison, inter-disciplinary approaches and quantitative and qualitative empirical analysis are only some of the lenses through which young scholars can scrutinize the reality of the process. The 2016 MPI-IAPL Summer School aimed at providing its participants with an enhanced awareness as to the methods to be chosen and applied when undertaking a research project in the field of procedural law. It is crucial to have a clear vision not only of the "what", but also and above all, of the "how" of legal research.

After the announcement of the school, forty four applications were filed to the Max Planck Institute; only fifteen of them could be admitted. The participants of the school came from different legal and academic backgrounds like Argentina, Belarus, Brazil, Germany, France, Greece, Italy, Lithuania, Norway, Spain, Switzerland and the United States of America. This book collects most of the papers which were presented at the conference. Reviewed and reworked in the light of the discussions of last summer, they address many different areas of procedural law; domestic, European, international and comparative. Its content ranges from the role of State systems challenged by the tendency of privatization of justice and process, to the impact of EU financial crisis on national procedural law, passing by the regionalization of courts, the various forms and norms of access to justice and especially, in this regard, the issues of collective redress and of the status of precedents in the development of the law.

Using again a proven method, the second edition of this summer school brought together different generations of researchers, allowing a fruitful dialogue between professors in the best age of their research careers and many young proceduralists. This dialogue was framed by two key speeches provided by Margaret Woo and Fernando Gascon Inchausti. Different continents, different perspectives, different experiences and approaches form the ingredients of this successful second post-doctoral summer school in procedural law.

To conclude, we wish to express our utmost gratitude to the collaborators of the MPI whose help was crucial in the success of the meeting. Never two without three. The challenge is now to prepare a third IAPL/MPI Summer School in Procedural Law which shall take place in summer 2018. A call for applications will be launched in fall of this year.

Luxembourg and Paris May 2017

Loic Cadiet / Burkhard Hess / Marta Requejo Isidro

Inaugural Lecture

I. Comparative Perspectives in Procedural Law: Some Remarks and Proposals

*Fernando Gascón Inchausti**

(I) Introduction

This contribution was conceived as the opening lecture of the 2nd IAPL-MPI Post-Doctoral Summer S*chool on European and Comparative Procedural Law, on the topic of *Approaches to Procedural Law. The Pluralism of Methods*. Its main purpose therefore, was setting the scene for the subsequent sessions of intensive and fruitful academic discussion and, more specifically, sharing some thoughts and reflections on one of the possible methods to approach the study of procedural law, the comparative one. Obviously, only some topics were addressed and not as exhaustively as they might have deserved.

These pages start from a premise: I am in favour of applying a comparative methodology to the study of procedural law.[1] Nowadays this view seems to be commonly shared, at least officially, but it has not always

---

* Prof. Dr. Fernando Gascón Inchausti is Professor of Law at the Complutense University of Madrid. His main fields of interest are civil and criminal procedure, both from national, European and comparative perspective. fgascon@ucm.es

1 See, for instance, M. Cappelletti (ed.), *International Encyclopedia of Comparative Law, Vol. XVI, Civil Procedure* (Mohr Siebeck – Martinus Nijhoff, Tübingen- Leiden- Boston, 1987); Id., *The Judicial Process in Comparative Perspective* (Claredon Press, Oxford, 1989); A.A.S. Zuckerman, *Civil Justice in Crisis. Comparative Perspectives of Civil Procedure* (OUP, 1999); F. Carpi, M.A. Lupoi (eds.), *Essays on Transnational and Comparative Civil Procedure* (Giappichelli, Turin, 2001); N. Trocker, V. Varano (eds.), *The Reforms of Civil Procedure in Comparative Perspective* (Giappichelli, Turin, 2005); C.H. van Rhee (ed.), *European Traditions in Civil Procedure* (Antwerp, Intersentia, 2005); O.G. Chase, H. Hershkoff (eds.), *Civil Litigation in Comparative Context* (Thomson West, 2007); C.H. van Rhee, A. Uzelac (eds.), *Civil Justice between Efficiency and Quality: From Ius Commune to the CEPEJ* (Intersentia, Antwerp-Oxford-Portland, 2008); J. Walker, O.G. Chase (eds.), *Common Law, Civil Law and the Future of Categories* (Lexis Nexis, Canada, 2010); A. Dondi, V. Ansanelli, P. Comoglio, *Processi civili in evoluzione. Una prospettiva comparata* (Giuffré, Milan, 2015); C.B. Picker, G.I. Seidman (eds.),

been so obvious in the past and, unfortunately, a serious comparative approach to (procedural) law is still missing in many jurisdictions and at many levels.[2]

There are quite a few reasons to justify recourse to a comparative methodology for the study of procedural law. In general terms, comparing is something natural, almost inborn, belonging to human nature from the very beginning of life. Children tend to instinctively compare themselves to others, and so do many adults. Comparisons help make us aware of what is better and also of what is worse. Comparisons can, of course, be morbid and destructive; but, if they are correctly administered, they tend to foster personal or collective improvements and achievements. At a scientific and academic level, comparison appears, almost automatically, as a sign of curiosity and open-mindedness towards what happens around oneself, which also lies at the core of the ideas of research and of *universitas*. And when it comes to legal studies *lato sensu*, a comparative approach shows an awareness that legal systems –like the social life and economic activity they tend to regulate– cannot live and evolve isolated from each other.[3] Departing from this positive and virtuous value of comparative enquiries, this paper will address three main topics and some issues regarding each of them: firstly, the scope of comparison when we deal with procedural law; secondly, the aims and purposes of applying comparative methodology in procedural law; finally, how comparison shall be performed.

The Dynamism of Civil Procedure – Global Trends and Developments (Springer, Dordrecht-Heidelberg-New York-London, 2016).

2 Although for the more restricted field of conflict of laws, this is also the assertion of G. Rühl, "Rechtsvergleichung und europäisches Kollisionsrecht: Die vergessene Dimension", in R. Zimmermann (ed.), *Zukunftsperspektiven der Rechtsvergleichung* (Mohr Siebeck, Tübingen, 2016) 103-138.

3 See, among many others, K. Zweigert, H. Kötz, *Introduction to Comparative Law* (3rd ed., Clarendon, Oxford, 1998); R. Schlesinger, H. Baade, P. Herzog, E. Wise, *Comparative Law. Cases – Texts – Materials* (6th ed., Foundation Press, New York, 1998); R. David, C. Jauffret-Spinosi, *Les grands systèmes de droit contemporains* (11th ed., Dalloz, Paris, 2002); H.P. Glenn, *Legal Traditions of the World – Sustainable Diversity in Law* (5th ed., OUP, 2014); V. Varano, V. Barsotti, *La tradizione giuiridica occidentale. Volume I. Testo e materiali per un confronto civil law common law* (4th ed., Giappichelli, Turin, 2010).

(II) The Scope of Comparison in Procedural Law

Dealing with the scope of comparison in procedural law requires answering a simple question: what should be compared? Of course, when the discussion is focused on comparative procedural law the immediate reaction is thinking of comparing different procedural legal systems as such and, more commonly, civil proceedings. Within this "common ground", nevertheless, some challenges should be put under the focus that might lead to considering the possibility of enlarging the field.

(a) Comparing the Regulation of Civil Proceedings

Firstly, it is a current trend not to concentrate the comparison on the legal regulation of civil proceedings ("the law in the books"), but rather trying to analyse how the legal provisions operate in practice. *Macrocomparisons*[4] should focus on the performance of the courts, at the general level of efficiency of the procedural systems; and *microcomparisons* should also share this functional approach, which is basic in comparative law:[5] we are interested in determining the solutions offered by different legal systems to common problems or to problems that are new for the jurisdiction interested in the comparative analysis.

When dealing, for instance, with the issue of collective redress, it is possible to analyse how several legal systems have regulated this institution in regard to many possible items or elements such as the "classical" ones: Have they chosen an opt-in or an opt-out approach? In the case of opt-out systems, are there sufficient safeguards for absent class-members?[6] But, beyond this, the really interesting point will be determining if the legal regulation has been followed or not by successful practice; and, if not –which is the case in many jurisdictions–, then research should focus

4 On the distinction between *macrocomparisons* and *microcomparisons*, see Zweigert/Kötz, *supra* n. 3, at. 4-5.

5 Zweigert/Kötz, *supra* n. 3, at 34 et seq.; insisting in the paramount relevance of this approach, see recently C. Wendehorst, "Rechtssystemvergleichung", in R. Zimmermann (ed.), *Zukunftsperspektiven der Rechtsvergleichung* (Mohr Siebeck, Tübingen, 2016), 1-37, at 30-31.

6 See, for instance, the widespread comparative study in V. Harsági, C.H. van Rhee (eds.), *Multi-Party Redress Mechanisms in Europe: Squeaking Mice?* (Cambridge – Antwerp – Portland, Intersentia, 2014).

on the grounds for the failure and on the other means –if any– used in practice to cope with collective harm or similar situations, like joinder of claims or public enforcement tools. Comparison, therefore, should involve not only legal texts, as enacted, but legal practice and the real level of protection reached by the rights and interests whose redress is able to be envisaged in collective proceedings.

Secondly, it is important to assume that the notion of civil justice and civil proceedings shall, in many cases and for many purposes, include ADR mechanisms. These "many rooms of justice" and this "multi-door approach" are not at all new, but it is still necessary to insist on it: for the sake of macro-comparisons the impact of the use of arbitration, mediation, conciliation or similar devices is needed if the comparative research wants to be built on a real picture of the way disputes are resolved within a jurisdiction.[7]

As many Scandinavian lawyers indicate, commercial litigation in the Nordic jurisdictions, especially if there is a cross-border element, is usually solved in arbitration.[8] And we should also bear in mind that in the Far-East tradition mediation and conciliation schemes are preferred to court litigation.[9] Describing the performance of dispute resolution in some geographical areas, therefore, requires a more global vision –a holistic one.

In a similar vein, no serious comparative study on procedural protection of consumers' rights can be accomplished without taking account of the existence of alternatives to court proceedings: the situation in the United Kingdom, for instance, would be misrepresented if only court decisions

---

7 This idea was first –at least clearly– suggested by M. Cappelletti, "Alternative Dispute Resolution Processes within the Framework of the World-Wide Acces-to-Justice Movement", 56 *The Modern Law Review* 282 (1993-3). Much more recently, see also C. Hodges, I. Benöhr, N. Creutzfeldt-Banda, *Consumer ADR in Europe* (Hart Publishing, Oxford, 2012); R. Caponi, F. Gascón Inchausti, M. Stürner (eds.), *The Role of Consumer ADR in the Administration of Justice. New Trends in Access to Justice under EU Directive 2013/11* (Sellier, Munich, 2015); F. Steffek, H. Unberath (eds.), *Regulating Dispute Resolution - ADR and Access to Justice at the Crossroads* (Hart Publishing, Oxford, 2013); T. Sourdin, "The Role of the Courts in the New Justice System" (January 11, 2016). Available at SSRN: http://ssrn.com/abstract=2713576 or http://dx.doi.org/10.2139/ssrn.2713576 (Last visited 22 December 2016); P. Cortés (ed.), *The New Regulatory Framework for Consumer Dispute Resolution* (OUP, 2016).

8 Varano/Barsotti, *supra* n. 3, at 487-488.

9 David/Jauffret-Spinosi, *supra* n. 3, at 403 et seq.; Varano/Barsotti, *supra* n. 3, at 531-532.

were analysed, leaving aside, among others, the prominent role of the Financial Ombudsman Service. And, using again an example taken from the English experience, one should not neglect the so-called pre-action protocols that have emerged in many fields of law[10] and their practical implementation.[11]

(b) Comparing Court Proceedings and ADR Mechanisms

In close relation with this need to include ADR mechanisms within the picture of a country's system of civil justice, we should also add another view to the comparison. Apart from comparing different legal systems, in the sense that has just been mentioned, we could also consider a comparison between "traditional procedural law" and the methods for alternative dispute resolution. It is something that is already frequently done, for instance when addressing the question of the advantages and disadvantages of arbitration compared to court adjudication, and not only from an academic point of view, but rather with a very important consequence when it comes to deciding if a contract will include, or not, an arbitration agreement. This comparison can be seen, indeed, as a two-way road.

On the one hand, there are many lessons that court proceedings could learn from arbitration, especially in the field of cross-border litigation: arbitration has proved to bring great flexibility to issues that would amount

10 Construction and engineering disputes, defamation, personal injury claims, clinical disputes, professional negligence, disease and illness claims, housing disrepair cases, possession claims based on mortgage or claims for damages in relation to the physical state of commercial property at termination of a tenancy are some of the fields covered by pre-action protocols.

11 See the Practice Direction – Pre-Action Conduct and Protocols (https://www.justice.gov.uk/courts/procedure-rules/civil/rules/pd_pre-action_conduct, ast visited 4 January 2017), according to which pre-action protocols explain the conduct and set out the steps a court would normally expect parties to take before commencing proceedings for particular types of civil claims, including trying to settle the issues without proceedings and considering a form of Alternative Dispute Resolution (ADR) to assist with settlement. Compliance with them is not a pre-requisite to engage court proceedings, but not doing so may have very important consequences in the field of costs (which might turn out to be very high) –especially, the court could reduce significantly the amount of the order to reimburse costs to the winning claimant.

to real hurdles in court cases, such as with the language of proceedings or with more flexible management of the case.

On the other hand, it is important to realize that we are experiencing times of intensive "dejudicialization",[12] which could have very dangerous side-effects. Some decades ago it was important to leave room for ADR mechanisms and to promote them as real alternatives to court proceedings, especially for litigants willing to find a different way to litigate. In recent years, however, in a scenario of economic downturn,[13] it looks as if ADR schemes, described as efficient, might be intended to replace the old-fashioned and non-efficient court systems, which are silently being dismantled by some governments. Apart from the prominent issue of costs,[14] more thorough studies should be carried out on that issue, including comparative research regarding court and ADR performance when it comes to the solutions given to some relevant factors, such as independence of the adjudicator or strict compliance with the rule of law when deciding a case. Litigants preferring recourse to judicial proceedings should not be deterred from seeking it –and somehow "forced" to (international commercial) arbitration– and, of course, national lawmakers should also make efforts to render judicial proceedings more attractive, especially in cross-border litigation contexts.[15]

---

12 See S. Amrani-Mekki, "L'économie procédurale", 6 *International Journal of Procedural Law* 7, 25-28 (2016-1).

13 See R. Marcus, "Procedure in a Time of Austerity", 3 *International Journal of Procedural Law* 133 (2013-1).

14 J. Nieva-Fenoll speaks of *an elitist certainty*, "Mediation and Arbitration: a Disappointing Hope", 6 *International Journal of Procedural Law* 350, 357-362 (2016-2).

15 A good example is the language issue, very flexible in the world of arbitration, where some interesting experiences start to appear. The most challenging is the Netherlands Commercial Court, very recently established in Amsterdam (1 January 2017), specialized in international trade disputes and where proceedings will be conducted in English (although by Dutch judges and according to Dutch procedural law). In France, the Tribunal de Commerce de Paris launched already in 2011 an international division (3ème chambre), with judges speaking and able to read documents written in foreign languages. Apart from overcoming language barriers, these experiences may foster the choice of those courts as appropriate fora for solving cross-border disputes and, at the same time, they may contribute to the development of those jurisdictions as appropriate places for international trade and financial activities.

(c) Comparing Civil Procedure and Criminal Procedure

Additionally, internal comparison should also be considered between civil and criminal proceedings. In many legal systems, sometimes due to academic reasons, civil procedure and criminal procedure "live" totally apart from each other. This is a regrettable situation, from many points of view, since civil and criminal procedures have much to learn from each other, and it is worth comparing their approaches and solutions to common issues. One cannot ignore the different principles and policies underlying to both procedures and it is important to be aware of them, in order to overcome the associated hurdles to comparison. Carnelutti clearly illustrated this risk with the powerful image of criminal proceedings being *Cenerentola,* or Cinderella, that civil proceduralists wanted to dress with the unfitting clothes of her step-sisters, that is, the categories of civil procedure (and of substantive criminal law).[16] The old ambition to build a common procedural model, encompassing all possible matters and objects (civil and criminal)[17] has proved to be both impossible and inconvenient. But it is again important to remember one of Zweigert and Kötz's basic statements on the functional approach of comparative law: we shall compare the pieces that serve the same purpose, that fulfil the same function.[18] And civil and criminal proceedings very frequently need to face similar problems, because they are linked to the function of procedure as the tool that allows a court to render the best decision to a dispute at the end of a fair chain of activities.[19]

The law of evidence is one of the fields where the comparison between civil and criminal proceedings could be more obviously fruitful. We should recall, for instance, that the US Federal Rules on Evidence are gen-

---

16 F. Carnelutti, "Cenerentola", 1 *Rivista di diritto processuale* 73 (1946).

17 For an overview (in Spanish), see V. Fairén-Guillén, "Perfiles en las relaciones entre proceso civil y penal: La teoría general del proceso", *Anuario de Derecho Civil* 51(1995-1) (available at: at http://www.boe.es/publicaciones/anuarios_derecho/anuario.php?id=C_2016_ANUARIO_DE_DERECHO_CIVIL).

18 Zweigert/Kötz, *supra* n. 3, at 10: "[...] only rules which perform the same function and address the same real problem or conflict of interests can profitably be compared"; and again at 34: "[...] in law the only things which are comparable are those which fulfil the same function".

19 In a similar vein, Christiane Wendehorst emphasizes the convenience of taking into account the civil procedure solution when facing the problem of forum shopping in criminal proceedings (*supra* n. 5, at 17).

erally applicable to all sorts of subject-matter. On the contrary, in continental systems there is a different regulation of evidence in the respective codes of civil and criminal procedure. Is this divide suitable or would some sort of harmonization or rapprochement be desirable or useful? It goes without saying that the topic appears recurrently in many jurisdictions where the borders are being progressively blurred, due to the trend to render criminal proceedings more "adversarial" (and thus depriving the courts of the power to order the taking of evidence on their own motion), on the one hand, and, on the other hand, the need to empower civil courts with *ex officio* evidentiary powers, as a procedural tool to foster the application of mandatory rules –such as those aimed at the protection of consumers, as the European Court of Justice recurrently reminds us lately. Comparative studies might be useful to cope with some of the involved questions, like the following:

- The problem of illegally obtained evidence in civil cases, where there is a struggle between the importation of the –criminal– strict exclusionary rule/fruit of the poisonous tree doctrine and the preference for more flexible solutions, involving a balance of all present interests. Would a common rule be desirable on both sides of the fence –and, if so, strongly exclusionary or more flexible?[20] Or, on the contrary, are the different rules on the burden of proof in civil and criminal matters an unsurmountable obstacle to deal with this issue in a uniform manner?[21]
- There are many empirical studies on witnesses' reliability, on memory, etc., which have displayed their main utility in the field of criminal proceedings, but that could also be valid for any evidentiary purpose, including civil cases. In fact, the admissibility of affidavits and written testimony which are more flexible in the civil proceedings of some ju-

20 Let us think, for instance, of a letter addressed to an ex-spouse sent by the bank to the old family domicile, where the other ex-spouse now lives and unduly opens the letter; let us think, further, that the bank information concerns an extraordinary income of money, which could serve as evidentiary basis for a civil claim to increase the amount of alimony granted to the children, but also for a criminal prosecution for money laundering. Should we really apply different standards?

21 See the suggesting contribution, from an Italian law perspective, of D. Dalfino, "Illegally Obtained Evidence and the Myth of Judicial Truth in the Italian System", in I. Díez-Picazo Giménez, J. Vegas Torres (eds.), *Derecho, Justicia, Universidad. Liber amicorum de Andrés de la Oliva Santos* (Ed. Universitaria Ramón Areces, Madrid, 2016) I, 897-913.

risdictions, tends to be banned from criminal ones. Is this a reasonable and justified division or should the practice change?

- What should be the case for privileges? Should the heads of privilege be the same in civil as in criminal procedural settings? Comparing legal provisions and practice in civil and criminal cases, and also in different jurisdictions, could lead to very interesting results as to the different techniques to define what should be confidential and what not, and as to the different ways to achieve this goal. The recent EU Directive on protection of commercial trade[22] is a very good proof of the raising importance of this topic.

Another area where comparative research between civil and criminal spheres could be pertinent is mediation, which has become the rising star of alternative dispute resolution. In the European Union, the 2008 Directive on Mediation dealt with civil and commercial cases;[23] at the same time, in the "parallel world" of criminal procedure, the 2001 Framework Decision[24] and the subsequent 2012 Directive on victims' rights[25] foster mediation as a tool of the so-called restorative justice, which could under certain conditions replace the development of a classical criminal procedure. Are we talking about the same thing when we address "mediation" in civil cases and "mediation" in criminal cases?[26] Are the same skills needed to be a mediator in both fields? It would be interesting to carry out some comparative research in this field, especially when the fear exists that national legislators in the European Union, under the pressure to im-

22 Directive (EU) 2016/943 of the European Parliament and of the Council of 8 June 2016 on the protection of undisclosed know-how and business information (trade secrets) against their unlawful acquisition, use and disclosure (OJ L 157, 15.6.2016, p. 1–18).

23 Directive 2008/52/EC of the European Parliament and of the Council of 21 May 2008 on certain aspects of mediation in civil and commercial matters (OJ L 136, 24.5.2008, p. 3-8).

24 Framework Decision 2001/220/JHA of 15 March 2001 on the standing of victims in criminal proceedings (OJ L 82, 22.3.2001, p. 1-4) [see recital 7 and Article 10].

25 Directive 2012/29/EU of the European Parliament and of the Council of 25 October 2012 establishing minimum standards on the rights, support and protection of victims of crime, and replacing Council Framework Decision 2001/220/JHA [see recital 46 and Articles 4.1(j) and 12].

26 The Council of Europe addresses now both issues separately: on the one hand, Recommendation No. R (99) 19 concerning mediation in penal matters (adopted on 15 September 1999); on the other, Recommendation (2002)10 on mediation in civil matters (adopted on 18 September 2002).

plement the provisions on mediation of the 2012 Directive on victim's rights, could fall into the temptation of simply expanding –maybe with a few amendments– the existing rules on civil mediation to the field of criminal prosecution.

(III) The Aims and Purposes of Applying Comparative Methodology in Procedural Law

Comparing legal systems is not an aim in itself, but rather a tool –a methodological tool– to achieve some goals. Scholarship on comparative law has attempted to define them, in connected but also different manners. David and Jauffret-Spinosi, for instance, highlight the importance of comparative law to build a good general theory of law, to know one's own legal system better, to improve one's own legal system, to better comprehend the international dimension of law, both from a public and a private perspective and, finally, to better harmonize legal systems.[27] Zweigert and Kötz, on their side, include some variations. According to them, the functions and aims of comparative law, apart from enlarging knowledge, cover four objectives: to serve as an aid for the legislator; to help when interpreting legal rules, especially those arising from uniform laws; to improve legal education; and to be a starting point for legal unification (especially in regional homogeneous contexts, like the European Union).[28] More recently, Varano and Barsotti indicate how comparison, and comparativists, seek relevant functions, like knowledge, the universality of legal science, understanding, communication, legal policy, interpretation of national law, globalization and harmonization of law.[29] Last, but not least, Basedow has brilliantly illustrated how comparative law has many possible "customers" (such as academics, legal professionals, national lawmakers, unification agencies): depending on the customer, the purpose, the approach and the methodology itself may differ, since those "clients" are the ones defining the objectives that the comparative research should serve.[30]

---

27 David/Jauffret-Spinosi, *supra* n. 3, at 3-8.

28 Zweigert/Kötz, *supra* n. 3, at 15-31.

29 Varano/Barsotti, *supra* n. 3, at 10-29.

30 J. Basedow, "Comparative Law and its Clients", 62 *American Journal of Comparative Law* 821 (2014).

In the limited context of these pages the focus will be on three of them: the improvement of national legislation, the harmonization of legislation and the action in a globalized world.

(a) Comparing to Improve National Legislation

One will not reinvent the wheel by saying that for a long time comparative approaches to procedural law were quickly neglected –or, at least, they were not given real practical utility– due to the strong liaison of proceedings to the legal culture of each nation: comparative approaches –it was argued– do not have much interest in the end, because it is impossible to "transplant" foreign procedural institutions;[31] it must be assumed, of course, that according to this restrictive view "transplants" were indeed the only possible useful outcome of comparative studies.

Scholarship –especially after Mauro Cappelletti– and law-making experience show that this vision was completely wrong and that comparative research can be a good basis when facing the endeavour to improve national legislation[32] –either considering a foreign solution as a model or as a contrast or a means for gaining perspective.[33] And, also, it is not just a question of "transplants" as a whole, but of identifying pieces and ideas that could help improve national legislations in a more diffuse way, taking always into account the legal culture.[34] In fact, really big procedural

---

31 On the notion of "legal transplant" see, of course, A. Watson, *Legal Transplants: An Approach to Comparative Law* (Scottish Academic Press, Edinburgh, 1974). On the evolution of this notion, see E. Grande, "Legal Transplants and the Inoculation Effect: How American Criminal Procedure Has Affected Continental Europe", 64 *The American Journal of Comparative Law* 583, 585-586 (2016).

32 On the relevance of comparative studies from the perspective of the reforms, see A. Dondi, "L'esperienza di un comparatista processuale", in V. Bertorello (ed.), *Io comparo, tu compari, egli compara: che cosa, come, perché?* (Giuffré, Milan, 2003) 89-94, at 91.

33 This two-sided focus is emphasized by Schlesinger et al., *supra* n. 3, at 6-21 and 26-29.

34 As clearly expressed by Peter Gottwald: "[…] comparative law may help to develop new ideas for your own national law, but [that] even excellent ideas are not adopted if they are not in line with national legal culture, with respect to the ideas of the majority of judges, lawyers and so on of a particular country" (in his comment to Rolf Stürner's work on the parties' duty to disclose information in civil proceedings)", in L. Cadiet, B. Hess, M. Requejo Isidro (eds.), *Procedural Science*

changes have been achieved within many countries, and those changes, in turn, have entailed effects on legal –including procedural– culture whose acceptance and feasibility were not easy to predict. Although it is not at all the rule, sometimes experience shows that the attachment of societies to legal culture and tradition –or, at least, to some aspects thereof– is not as strong as affirmed. Anyway, it goes without saying that "context" and "culture" are basic parameters to accurate legal comparative research; and this, in turn, renders the task complicated, due to the intrinsic difficulties of identifying the very notion of legal culture and, more precisely, of procedural legal culture.[35]

The hallmark of comparative research and of the influence of foreign legislation can be traced in many recent procedural reforms. This, of course, requires a certain starting point: it is necessary to feel not only the need to improve the current status of the justice system, but also to adopt the open mind approach to look outside in search of solutions. And "looking outside" might include –as previously mentioned– not just analysing other legal systems, but, for some purposes, also ADR schemes and criminal proceedings.

Posner and Sunstein hypothesize that "young states are more likely to rely on foreign law than old states are",[36] and also that as states build up their own jurisprudences [or their own legal systems] there is a reduced need for comparative analysis.[37] Apart from "young states", the need for comparison is also felt strongly in jurisdictions where there is an awareness that the legal or practical situation is not satisfactory. And comparison becomes also a trend, in general terms, when states are facing global legal changes or codification phenomena.

Spain is a good example of a country that has never been on the very "top of the ranking" (nor at the bottom) and where very big efforts have been carried out in the last decades to improve the performance of civil and criminal justice. The reform of the Spanish civil procedure was

---

at the Crossroads of Different Generations (Nomos, Baden-Baden, 2015) 379-383, at 379.

35 See the classic work of O.G. Chase, *Law, Culture, and Ritual: Disputing Systems in Cross-cultural Context* (NYU Press, 2005); more recently, the impressive work of P. Mankowski, *Rechtskultur* (Mohr Siebeck, Tübingen, 2016) –see, for instance, the issue of the more or less active role of judges in proceedings at 320 et seq.

36 E. A. Posner and C. R. Sunstein, "The Law of Other States", 59 *Stanford Law Review* 131, 173 (2006).

37 Posner/Sunstein, *supra* n. 36, at 174.

achieved in 2000 and comparative experiences where taken into account at several points: this is the case of the order for payment, that did not exist previously and that has very quickly absorbed half of civil litigation; comparative research was done, in particular, to opt between the German model (non-documentary) and the Roman version (based on documents showing *prima facie* the existence of the debt), to finally choose the latter. There was also a serious attempt to introduce in the new Code something very similar to the *ordonnance de référé*, *"à la française"*, although unsuccessfully: it was argued that such an institution would have been too strange to function within the Spanish legal system. The reform of criminal proceedings is still pending, and comparative research has been the background of the opposing proposals as to the crucial point of keeping the figure of the examining magistrate (the Spanish version of the classical institution of the *juge d'instruction*) or of attributing the direction of the investigation phase to the public prosecutors.

The same comparative way to improve and to change, to an even greater extent, can be traced in most procedural reforms –both civil and criminal– that have been carried out or that are still ongoing in Central and South America. The struggle between importing categories belonging to the common law tradition and keeping loyal or remaining faithful to the historical legal tradition has been strong. In the field of criminal proceedings the leitmotiv of most reforms (one might think now, as clear examples, of Argentina, Chile, Mexico, Peru and Nicaragua) has been linked with transition to democracy and with compliance with human rights defence requirements set out in the Inter-American Convention of San José. Thus, the discourse has always been moving from the old inquisitorial systems (allegedly inherited from the old continental –namely Spanish– schemes) to adversarial proceedings: in this context, the notions of "orality" and of "oral proceedings" have been the flags under which the US model has prevailed, although adequately tailored –thanks, especially, to the work of the Iberoamerican Institute of Procedural Law and its 1989 Model Code of Criminal Procedure for Iberoamerica.[38]

38 The text of which can be found at the official webpage of the Institute http://iibdp.org/images/C%C3%B3digos%20Modelo/IIDP_C%C3%B3digo_Procesal_Penal_Modelo_Iberoam%C3%A9rica.pdf

Some jurisdictions might not feel the need to improve their national legislation by means of comparison.[39] In fact, in some countries a negative approach to comparative research prevails, which is independent from any assessment of the degree of satisfaction experienced with the functioning of their system. It would be probably unfair to put such a simple label to the United States; nevertheless, the so-called "American exceptionalism"[40] and the consequences of "originalism"[41] are clear symptoms of reluctance towards a comparative approach.[42]

There are also countries, like Germany, Switzerland or the Scandinavian, whose civil justice systems, according to most studies[43] and rankings and to common general perception, are to be counted amongst the very best performing ones:[44] they enjoy reasonable duration of proceedings, adequate numbers of judges and court officers, sufficient resources, good quality of judicial decisions. Of course, also those "wonderlands" need, from time to time, to reform legislation, in order to adapt to new necessities and social, legal and economic challenges. One might wonder, at least from the position of countries with a lower level of performance, what could comparative law provide to those "top" systems: and it is not a mat-

39 This reluctance can also be traced at a different level: how open or closed are judges to have recourse to comparative law and foreign experience when they face new or difficult issues: see Varano/Barsotti, *supra* n. 3, at 19-21.

40 See O.G. Chase, "American 'exceptionalism' and comparative procedure", 50 *American Journal of Comparative Law* 277 (2002-2) . Also S. Dodson, "The Challenge of Comparative Civil Procedure", 60 *Alabama Law Review* 133, 134, 140-142 (2008-1).

41 "On one understanding of originalism, for example, the practices of other nations are generally irrelevant, because the interpretive goal is to recover the original understanding of the relevant provision, and on the original understanding, the constitutional issue must be resolved without reference to those practices" (Posner/Sunstein, *supra* n. 36, at 150).

42 See also Varano/Barsotti, *supra* n. 3, at 21-23.

43 See the classical essay of J.H. Langbein, "The German Advantage in Civil Procedure", 52 *University of Chicago Law Review* 823 (1985-4).

44 See, for instance, the reports of the European Commission for the Efficiency of Justice (CEPEJ), within the Council of Europe (last edition of 2016, with the data of 2014, at http://www.coe.int/T/dghl/cooperation/cepej/default_en.asp) or the 2016 EU Justice Scoreboard, sponsored by the European Commission (http://ec.europa.eu/justice/effective-justice/files/justice_scoreboard_2016_en.pdf).

ter of inferiority or superiority complex,[45] but of mere pragmatism. But, in fact, comparative studies are still the basis of the research underpinning many proposals for reform.[46] Why? Probably, because comparing is always a clever thing to do and "top" systems are "clever", in the sense that they never underestimate the possibility of learning good practices and good solutions from the experience of apparently "lower performing" systems. In fact, sometimes and in some fields certain jurisdictions are more *creative* or more *audacious* than others. Even if some ideas and/or regulations do not function properly in the system that has introduced and/or enacted them, they might be useful elsewhere, precisely because the peripheral conditions required for those ideas to be successful are met in the *borrower* jurisdiction, but were not present in the original one.[47]

The field of e-Justice is also a context in which many systems compete on an equal footing and where lessons can be learned and interesting ideas may be gathered from unexpected jurisdictions,[48] that have dared to establish efficient platforms for electronic communication and/or, for instance, the possibility of performing first service of the claim via electronic means, combined with the duty of legal persons of having a valid e-mail address available for such "official" purposes.

---

45 Obviously, measuring effectiveness and efficiency of legal systems is in itself a very controversial task, as clearly explained by N. Garoupa and C. Gómez Ligüerre, "The Syndrome of the Efficiency of the Common Law", 29 *Boston University International Law Journal* 287 (2011) (debunking the methodology of studies according to which common law based legal systems are economically more efficient than those based on French civil law).

46 See Basedow, *supra* n. 30, at. 844-846. As good proof, see the impressive study carried out by Profs. Micklitz and Stadler on collective redress on behalf of the German Federal Ministry for Consumer Protection in 2005: H.W. Micklitz, A. Stadler, *Das Verbandsklagerecht in der Informations- und Dienstleistungsgesellschaft* (Landwirtschaftsverlag, Münster, 2005).

47 Posner and Sunstein use a very clear phrase: "(…) relying on foreign legal materials is not meant to express approval of all aspects of the foreign country. Rather, it is simply a way of taking advantage of unexploited mines of information" (Posner/Sunstein, *supra* n. 36, at 159).

48 See M. Kengyel, Z. Nemessányi (eds.), *Electronic Technology and Civil Procedure. New Paths to Justice from Around the World* (Springer, Dordrecht-Heidelberg-New York-London, 2012).

(b) Comparing to Harmonize Legislation

The comparative method is a necessary element of any task of legal harmonization or approximation of legislation, in any legal field. Harmonization and/or approximation can be performed in different ways: hard law tools, like European Directives and Regulations, could appear as opposed to soft law tools, like Recommendations, used by the EU itself or the Council of Europe, and Model Laws. But, even within the EU experience of hard law harmonization, we are well aware that acceptance thereof is largely conditioned by the fact that the proposed regulation reflects some sort of consensus, and this can only be detected and analysed on the basis of previous comparative research.

The harmonization of procedural law is no longer a myth. The approval of the Federal Rules of Civil Procedure in the United States provides an excellent example of this, although at the peculiar level of a (complex) national playground. At an international level the way was opened in the field of arbitration by the 1985 UNCITRAL Model Law on International Commercial Arbitration, currently followed in 73 states.[49] The 2002 UNCITRAL Model Law on International Commercial Conciliation has been thus far a little less successful, with only 16 followers.[50]

But, in many ways, harmonizing arbitration and conciliation may be a much easier task than harmonizing the rules governing court proceedings: again, the argument of legal tradition and culture has been raised as an obstacle. In Europe it can be affirmed that the turning point was the presentation in the early 1990's of the so-called "Storme Project" on the approximation of judiciary law in the European Union, including the skeleton of a possible directive harmonizing crucial elements of civil procedural rules in order to facilitate legal understanding among jurisdictions and to foster the internal circulation of judicial decisions. This project was backed on thor-

49 According to the information provided by the institution itself at http://www.uncitral.org/uncitral/en/uncitral_texts/arbitration/1985Model_arbitration_status.html (Last visited 23 December 2016).

50 Again, according to http://www.uncitral.org/uncitral/en/uncitral_texts/arbitration/2002Model_conciliation_status.html (Last visited 23 December 2016).

ough comparative research carried out by a transnational team led by Professor Marcel Storme.[51]

However, the credit for laying one of the first stones in this path of harmonization is due to the Iberoamerican Institute of Procedural Law, which was able to approve in 1988-1989 two Model Codes, one for Civil Proceedings[52] and another one, already mentioned, for Criminal Proceedings. The Institute has always been a forum for comparison, highly committed to the improvement of the judicial systems of Iberoamerica, and no prejudices have impeded the Institute to retrieve ideas and possible solutions to problems from anywhere they were to be found. This open-minded approach is also very visible when one analyses the Model Code of Collective Proceedings for Iberoamerica, approved in 2004, combining pre-existing elements of local regulations (like the ones of Brazil and Colombia) with the US experience of class actions.[53]

A very significant step forward was the adoption in 2004 of the ALI/ UNIDROIT Principles of Transnational Civil Procedure,[54] a sort of model rules offered to national lawmakers as a primary pattern to shape specific national proceedings to deal with cross-border cases. The Principles represent a very difficult and valuable "meeting point" between different procedural cultures (mainly, but not exclusively, those of the United States, on the one hand, and of continental Europe, on the other), a compromise of different views and approaches on very sensitive matters, like the roles of judges, parties and lawyers, the management of a case, or access to information (especially, information controlled by an opponent or by non-par-

---

51 M. Storme (ed.), *Approximation of judiciary law in the European Union* (Kluwer, 1994).

52 The text of the *Código Procesal Civil Modelo para Iberoamérica* was approved in 1988 and can be acceded in the official website of the Institute, at http://iibdp.org/images/C%C3%B3digos%20Modelo/IIDP_Codigo_Procesal_Civil_Modelo_Iberoamerica.pdf

53 The text of the *Código Modelo de Procesos Colectivos para Iberoamérica* can also be found in the website of the Institute: http://iibdp.org/images/C%C3%B3digos%20Modelo/IIDP_C%C3%B3digo%20Modelo%20de%20Procesos%20Colectivos%20Para%20Iberoamerica.pdf

54 ALI/UNIDROIT, *Principles of Transnational Civil Procedure*, As Adopted and Promulgated by the American Law Institute (May 2004) and by the International Institute for the Unification of Private Law (April 2004) (Cambridge University Press, 2006). For a recent overview, see M. Taruffo, "Harmonization in a Global Context: The ALI/UNIDROIT Principles", in X.E. Kramer, C H. van Rhee (eds). *Civil Litigation in a Globalizing World* (Asser Press, The Hague, 2012) 207-219.

ties). And this commitment could only be reached after years of intensive comparison and serious analysis of the most suitable solutions.

At the present time, the ball is back in the court of the European Union, which has turned out to be the venue where harmonization and approximation of procedural legislation is being both practised and discussed.[55] For the purposes of the development of judicial cooperation in civil matters having cross-border implications, Article 81.2 (f) of the Treaty on the Functioning of the European Union enables the EU Institutions to adopt measures, particularly when necessary for the proper functioning of the internal market, aimed at ensuring, among other goals, the elimination of obstacles to the proper functioning of civil proceedings, if necessary by promoting the compatibility of the rules on civil procedure applicable in the Member States.

Having the legal basis to do it, the topic of harmonizing national civil proceedings is being discussed within the European Parliament[56] and within the Directorate General of Justice and Consumer Affairs in the European Commission. The paths to the future will probably be set by a major study which is currently being carried out by a Consortium under the leadership of the Max Planck Institute Luxembourg and Professor Burkhard Hess,[57] the outcome of which will be appearing soon. The ground on which the study has been constructed is, again, comparative research, aimed at determining the hurdles that national procedural legisla-

---

55 The literature on this topic is very broad; among many others, see E. Storskrubb, *Civil Procedure and EU Law. A Policy Area Uncovered* (OUP, 2008); M. Tulibacka, "Europeanization of Civil Procedure: In Search of a Coherent Approach", 46 *Common Market Law Review* 1527 (2009-5); E. Silvestri, "Towards A European Code of Civil Procedure? Recent Initiatives for the Drafting of European Rules of Civil Procedure", available on academia.edu (last accessed 22 December 2016); B. Hess, "Procedural Harmonisation in the European Context", in Kramer/Van Rhee (eds.), *supra* n. 54, 159-173, and more recently, "Ein einheitliches Prozessrecht?", 6 *International Journal of Procedural Law* 55 (2016-1) .

56 See European Parliamentary Research Service, In-Depth Analysis (R. Mańko), *Europeanisation of civil procedure. Towards common minimum standards?* PE 559.499 (June 2015); European Parliamentary Research Service, Study (M. Tulibacka, M. Sanz, R. Blomeyer), *Common minimum standards of civil procedure (European Added Value. Assessment. Annex I)*, PE 581.385 (June 2016).

57 *An evaluation study of national procedural laws and practices in terms of their impact on the free circulation of judgments and on the equivalence and effectiveness of the procedural protection of consumers under EU consumer law* (JUST/2014/RCON/PR/CIVI/0082; 2015/S 104-188196).

tion entails to effective cross-border litigation and to the swift circulation of judicial decisions among the Member States. The same comparative approach applies to a parallel initiative established jointly by the European Law Institute and UNIDROIT, called "From Transnational Principles to European Rules of Civil Procedure".[58] This initiative is rather spontaneous and independent from the EU Institutions, although it is intended also to impact on the legislative agenda of the EU Institutions and, from that point of view, it might be linked with the results of the mentioned study. Whatever the future may bring, the goal of the ELI/UNIDROIT project is to present a set of model laws and best rules, covering different parts of civil procedure, whose adoption or acceptance by the Member States (or by the EU Institutions) should help in harmonizing national systems of civil justice. The best common rules that are going to be proposed under the umbrella of this latter project shall emerge from comparative study and from comparative discussion on the practical performance of competing possible solutions.[59]

For instance, a choice needs to be made on the wider or narrower scope of the powers of a court to order on its own motion the taking of evidence that has not been suggested by the parties, but that might be relevant for the adjudication of a case. Comparative solutions to this issue are different in each jurisdiction and a neutral answer is not easy to find, due to divergences in the way the principles of disposition and party autonomy are understood.

Another example is deciding on the costs and benefits of a rule, such as the one established in 1843 by the English Court of Chancery in the *Henderson v. Henderson* case,[60] according to which a party may not in subsequent litigation raise any claim which it ought to have raised in a previous action. Is it better to have a limited or a broad scope for *res judicata* and preclusion? Once again, comparative solutions differ, but only by having all of them in mind will it be possible to offer –and to explain why– the

58 Relevant information can be retrieved from the ELI webpage (at http://www.europeanlawinstitute.eu/projects/current-projects/, last visited 10 January 2017) as well as from the UNIDROIT's one (Available at http://www.unidroit.org/work-in-progress-studies/current-studies/transnational-civil-procedure, last visited10 January 2017).

59 On the way such unification projects deal with comparative law, see Basedow, *supra* n. 30, at 850-851.

60 *Henderson v Henderson* (1843) 3 Hare 100, 67 ER 313 (Available on-line at http://www.uniset.ca/other/cs3/67ER313.pdf, last visited 3 January 2017).

solution adopted should be considered as preferable for a harmonized context.

Apart from harmonizing legislations, comparative methodology plays also a prominent role in a more subtle type of harmonization, the one concerning the interpretation of supranational instruments, especially those aimed at the protection of human rights. A good example can be found in relation to the European Convention on Human Rights, where the theory of "European consensus" or "emerging consensus" is used by the Strasbourg court as a criterion to adapt its case law to changes in different areas of law and to determine whether a contracting state has gone beyond the limits of the margin of appreciation left to it. In the case of *Glor v. Switerland*,[61] for instance, the following was stated: *"Since the Convention is first and foremost a system for the protection of human rights, the Court must, however, have regard to the changing conditions in Contracting States and respond, for example, to any emerging consensus as to the standards to be achieved. One of the relevant factors in determining the scope of the margin of appreciation left to the authorities may be the existence or non-existence of common ground between the laws of the Contracting States"*.

These notions of "European consensus" or of "emerging consensus" are the results of comparative study of the law and of the practice of contracting states on issues where the provisions of the ECHR are needed for interpretation. It has been used so far mostly for substantive issues, such as medically-assisted reproduction, showing of religious symbols, abortion, legal effects of gender reassignment, matters related to the right to life (beginning of life, euthanasia) or adoption (retraction of consent), where no consensus had been found, or the right to a name, the equality of children born outside marriage, conscientious objections, or the elements defining the crime of rape, where the existing consensus lead the Court to consider that the state had infringed the Convention.[62]

This comparative way to determine common standards could also apply to procedural issues connected to Article 6 of the European Convention, like the way to proceed to first service of a claim where the domicile of the defendant is unknown or does not seem to be valid anymore, a question recently addressed in the cases of *Dilipak and Kirikaya v.*

61 Application no. 3444/04, 30 April 2009, § 75.

62 See the résumé offered by the ECtHR itself at http://www.coe.int/en/web/help/article-echr-case-law (Last visited 3 January 2017).

Turkey[63] in 2014 and of *Aždajić v. Slovenia*[64] in 2015. In fact, the ECtHR for that purpose transplanted its pre-existing doctrine regarding default judgments rendered in criminal proceedings to the scope of civil procedure.

Such an approach, referring to international consensus and based on compared solutions, can also be observed sometimes in the way national constitutional and supreme courts face the new problems they are confronted with. This is the context, in fact, where Posner and Sunstein launched the idea to apply the so-called *Condorcet Jury Theorem* to the use of the law of other states: if a problem is resolved in a certain way in different jurisdictions, that have arrived at similar solutions on a well informed and independent basis, then it is very likely that the common solution would be the best possible one.[65]

The comparison of procedural legislation and practice, finally, can also serve as a very effective tool to detect international customs and, when possible, to foster the crystallization of international customary law into treaties. An example thereof can be found in the 2004 United Nations Convention on Jurisdictional Immunities of States and Their Property, which was approved after very long and comprehensive research into the rules and practices of jurisdictions all over the world, dealing not only with the substantive definition of the acts covered by immunity, but also with the procedural mechanisms to implement them (included in Article 6 on the *ex officio* appreciation of the existence of the immunity), or ancillary procedural matters, like service of the process on a defendant state, default judgments and privileges and immunities of foreign states during court proceedings (finally enacted in Articles 22 to 24).

63 ECHR *Dilipak y Karakaya v. Turkey* (7942/05 y 24838/05), judgment of 4 March 2014 (§§ 80 et seq.).

64 ECHR *Aždajić v. Slovenia* (71872/12), judgment of 8 October 2015 (§§ 50 et seq.).

65 Posner/Sunstein, *supra* n. 36, *passim*; see also the echoes of Posner and Sunstein's ideas, and its combination with the ECHR doctrine on emerging consensus in S. Dothan, "The Optimal Use of Comparative Law", 43 *Denver Journal of International Law and Policy* 21 (2014).

(c) Comparing to Act in a Globalized World

The last utility of comparative methodology that will now be addressed could be synthesized under the sentence of "comparing to act in a globalized world". Comparisons are not only useful for lawmakers or for courts (especially, for supranational and domestic constitutional courts), but also for lawyers practicing the law in many different fields. As just mentioned, any litigant that needs to rely upon an international custom or, more frequently, on the usages of international trade or commerce will need to know how things are done in other jurisdictions. A comparative knowledge on the functioning of different systems of civil justice could be more than desirable for lawyers engaged in international contracts, when it comes to take procedural decisions, such as subscribing to a choice of court agreement. And, in general terms, comparative studies on civil procedure are useful for more efficient conduct of cross-border litigation.

It is crucial, for instance, in order to determine when a procedure has begun, to correctly apply the rules on international *lis pendens*,[66] and it may be equally crucial if a party, against which the existence of related actions is claimed, wants to contest that the proceedings in the court of a third state are unlikely to be concluded within a reasonable time.[67]

The public policy clause, on which courts can rely to refuse mutual legal assistance to foreign authorities or to deny recognition and enforcement of foreign decisions, is also based on a comparative analysis; in fact, a functional comparative analysis underpins the new provision of Article 54 of the Brussels I bis Regulation, pursuant to which measures or orders unknown to the enforcing state shall be adapted to measures or orders known to it, which have equivalent effects and which pursue similar aims and interests.

It is true that, in many cases, even more than real comparative study, what practitioners will apparently need is the knowledge of one or several foreign regulations. But, on the one hand, comparison with another term of reference will always be required at the end of the day (for instance, to decide whether it is better to choose the French or the German courts); and, on the other hand, on many occasions it will be pre-existing compara-

66 See Article 32 of the Brussels I bis Regulation, establishing the way to determine the moment a court is deemed to be seized, depending on the different possible systems.

67 See Article 34 (2)(c) of the Brussels I bis Regulation.

tive research that will be used, since deadlines and work overload will not permit any practitioner to carry out a deep study by him/herself.

(IV) How Should Procedural Comparison Be Carried out?

In this last part of the paper some methodological issues and challenges will be addressed, that affect procedural comparison, although they might not be exclusive to the specific field of procedural law. The starting point, of course, is the general validity of the classical steps of comparative research, requiring a first gathering of information from the systems that are going to be compared, which will be followed by an analysis that will lead to conclusions on the detected similarities and differences, conclusions that in turn will be used for the purpose that guided the comparison: proposing a legal reform or deciding to submit disputes arising from a contract to the jurisdiction of the seller's or the purchaser's state, for instance. Although, as just said, this general methodological skeleton is valid, it might be of interest now to stress three possible challenges that are appearing more clearly in recent times: choosing the terms of comparison; the sort of information needed and the way to gather it; and the language issue.

(a) Choosing the Terms of Comparison

Comparative research cannot start without having previously decided the terms of comparison. On some occasions, of course, the choice is limited due to the purposes of the comparative analysis to be carried out. But, in general terms, when a comparative study is broad, the choice might not be simple.

Traditionally, the starting point was the division of the world's legal systems into a small number of legal families; and, within each family, it was considered as advisable to opt for the leading parents (for instance, England or the US for the Common Law family, or Germany and France as clear representatives for the Civil Law family).[68]

68 Zweigert/Kötz, *supra* n. 3, at 40-42.

In my view, there have been very significant changes in recent years, concerning the composition of the legal families. In fact, there has never been a real consensus to determine how many families there were and which were the main elements to set them apart.[69] Traditionally, the divides and the family memberships were built on the basis of the categories of private law, and this criterion is not always adequate for procedural law. In his worldwide known work *The Faces of Justice*,[70] Mirjan Damaška explained the divide between civil law and common law systems of civil justice on the basis of how procedural authority was conceived. His descriptions are still very helpful to understand the great overriding principles lying beneath the national regulations.[71] Nevertheless, each side of the fence is not homogeneous at all –or, at least, not as homogeneous as depicted; and, of course, there are more legal families than the alleged civil and common law ones. Globalization, in fact, has entailed a greater level of interaction not only among legal systems belonging to the "traditional" civil law and common law families, but also with other legal systems –such as the Chinese– that, until recent times, had stayed outside the boundaries of international trade.

Many procedural systems, indeed, have experienced very significant reforms. When reforming their procedural systems national lawmakers that have "looked outside" have not confined comparative studies to their parents, siblings or cousins within a legal family. The *motto* of most reforms is the "struggle for efficiency" and, therefore, something like "loyalty to the family" has not been a relevant element: ideas and solutions are picked from anywhere they can be found, regardless of their origins. Obviously, it is relevant to take account of these origins when it comes to deciding if a foreign idea, considered as better, could also have positive effects in one's own legal system, given the case after some necessary tailoring; and this,

69 It is a recurrent caveat in most general works on comparative law. See the concerns already expressed by J.H. Merryman, *The Civil Law Tradition* (2nd ed, Stanford University Press, 1985) at 5; M. Pargendler, "The Rise and Decline of Legal Families", 60 *American Journal of Comparative Law* 1043 (2012); in this volume, V. Rétornaz, "Beware of Legal Families: the Example of the Effects of Res Judicata towards Third Parties".

70 M.R. Damaška, *The Faces of Justice and State Authority. A Comparative Approach to the Legal Process* (Yale University Press, 1986).

71 Although they have not been exempt from criticism; see, for instance J. Zekoll, "Comparative Civil Procedure", in M. Reimann and R. Zimmermann (eds.), *The Oxford Handbook of Comparative Law* (OUP, 2006) 1327-1362, at 1331-1334.

because differences in the legal base may lead to different practical consequences. Historical background and awareness of the legal cultural framework, needless to say, are of the essence for good comparative research.

The result of this trend towards big procedural reforms is a progressive hybridization[72] of many procedural systems that can no longer be considered as completely belonging to a certain legal family. In fact, hybridization is fostered as a result of the harmonization of national procedural rules, which in turn are the result of previous comparative analysis: within the European Union, for instance, access to information and sources of evidence in IP rights or in anti-trust damages claims are harmonized by Directives[73] that, in turn, reflect an attempt to reach a compromise between the continental and the common law approach to discovery.

This procedural mixture renders comparison more difficult, but also more challenging and attractive. Of course, the idea of legal families and leading parents will continue to be useful when it comes to macro-comparisons and for academic, education and teaching purposes. But, when it comes to micro-comparisons, recourse to the leading parent of a family may not be appropriate, if the interesting idea is to be found in a different system. The Dutch regulation on class settlements, for instance, is almost unique; and the Argentinian class actions system, in turn, is also a very interesting exercise in the way that US-style class actions can operate in a legal surrounding which is deemed to belong to the Civil Law family.[74]

For these reasons, sometimes, finding the legal system that really provides the interesting approach and solutions that one is looking for, might be an issue of serendipity, a "fortunate happenstance" or "pleasant surprise", as acutely expressed by Ferrarese.[75]

---

72 M. Delmas-Marty, "The Contribution of Comparative Law to a Pluralist Conception of International Criminal Law", 1 *Journal of International Criminal Justice* 13, 16-21 (2003); Id., *Ordering Pluralism: A Conceptual Framework for Understanding the Transnational Legal World* (Hart Publishing, Oxford, 2009).

73 Directive 2004/48/EC of 29 April 2004 on the enforcement of intellectual property rights (OJ L 157, 30.4.2004) and Directive 2014/104/EU of 26 November 2014 on certain rules governing actions for damages under national law for infringements of the competition law provisions of the Member States and of the European Union (OJ L 349, 5.12.2014).

74 For a first approach, see F. Verbic, *Procesos colectivos* (Astrea, Buenos Aires, 2007).

75 M.R. Ferrarese, "La comparazione nel mondo globale: un'avventura della serendipity", in V. Bertorello (ed.), *supra* n. 32, 101-113.

(b) The Information Needed and the Way to Gather It

We can only compare two or more procedural systems if we have gathered enough information, of sufficient quality, as to the way they perform their function, in general terms or concerning a specific issue or problem.

The usual way to gather this information is through National Reports or similar works, with a homogeneous structure enabling comparison among the information appearing in them. These tools have been built traditionally upon the explanation of the legal regulation in each jurisdiction and of case law developments.

Thanks to IT technologies it has become easy to access online legislation and official databases containing relevant case law of other countries, especially if one masters the language in which they are expressed. Some governments provide online translation into other languages of some of the more relevant rules (like the civil code or the code of civil procedure). Those and similar devices, like the European Judicial Atlas, are really helpful to get a preliminary overview, and also when one knows exactly what one is looking for (a specific provision on a specific issue that one had already read about).

Anyway, attention shall be put on the fact that we are experiencing times of quick legal changes and of unpredictable case law revolutions. The confluence of different legal sources, at different levels, determines that national codes of civil (or criminal) procedure are no longer the only reliable element to get access to the state of the law in a country. Additionally, case law changes very quickly, especially in contexts like the European Union, where a decision of the ECJ can have almost immediate effects in many jurisdictions.

A very good example can be found in the *ex officio* application of consumer protective statutes, fostered by the ECJ in the last years, which has entailed a very big shift in the way the powers and duties of judges, parties and lawyers are understood.

This high volatility of written law and of case law amounts to a progressive shorter date of expiry of national reports on determined procedural issues. Just like dairy products, comparative studies are getting hard to be "reused" or to be "reliably" used for a long period.

From a different point of view, the harmonization of civil and criminal procedural rules that is being carried out in some regional integrated areas has a beneficial impact for comparison, because it enables the construction of a *praesumptio similitudinis* in many aspects. The rights of suspects and accused persons within the European Union, for instance, have been so strongly harmonized[76] that comparative research may be of interest only when it is focused on the different degrees of implementation and development, but not on the minimum standards –the differences seem to be what matters, rather than the similarities.

Anyway, beyond legal regulation and case law developments, comparative studies require today an additional empirical approach, essential to grasp an accurate idea of how things are functioning within different legal systems. And retrieving sufficient, homogeneous and reliable empirical data is proving to be a very, very difficult task.

On the one hand, legal scholars do not always have the background or the training to deal with empirical research in fields where traditionally dogmatic methodology is used –and should never be abandoned.[77] This is a gap in legal education, especially at the highest degrees: we should have the methodological tools to feel more comfortable –or, at least, not so uncomfortable– when we are expected to deliver national reports that reflect the reality of what is happening in our courts or within our ADR schemes.

On the other hand, empirical data in justice and procedural matters are not easy to retrieve, especially in large jurisdictions. The basic information should be provided by judicial statistics, but they are a one-way road: the information one can get is the information provided by the system and there is no room to build data on matters or following criteria that do not match those used by the system to collect and to process the information

---

76 Directive 2010/64/EU of 20 October 2010 on the right to interpretation and translation in criminal proceedings (OJ L 280, 26.10.2010, p. 1); Directive 2012/13/EU of 22 May 2012 on the right to information in criminal proceedings (OJ L 142, 1.6.2012, p. 1); Directive 2013/48/EU of 22 October 2013 on the right of access to a lawyer in criminal proceedings and in European arrest warrant proceedings, and on the right to have a third party informed upon deprivation of liberty and to communicate with third persons and with consular authorities while deprived of liberty (OJ L 294, 6.11.2013, p. 1); Directive (EU) 2016/343 of 9 March 2016 on the strengthening of certain aspects of the presumption of innocence and of the right to be present at the trial in criminal proceedings (OJ L 65, 11.3.2016, p. 1); Directive (EU) 2016/800 of 11 May 2016 on procedural safeguards for children who are suspects or accused persons in criminal proceedings (OJ L 132, 21.5.2016, p. 1); Directive (EU) 2016/1919 of 26 October 2016 on legal aid for suspects and accused persons in criminal proceedings and for requested persons in European arrest warrant proceedings (OJ L 297, 4.11.2016, p.1).

77 See R. Stürner, "Die Rolle des dogmatischen Denkens im Zivilprozessrecht", *Zeitschrift für Zivilprozess* 127 (2014), 271.

furnished by the courts. In short, research is conditioned by the way that the respective ministry of justice or the judiciary council have decided to inform themselves about what happens under them. And, of course, there is no uniformity in this either.

In short, making comparative empirical research turns out to be complicated, since the terms of comparison are quite often incomparable.

In recent years, access to empirical data and to comparisons of empirical data has improved thanks to some global or regional reports on the performance of the justice systems. The *Doing Business* reports of the World Bank, for instance, analyse "good practices in the judiciary" under the tag of "Enforcing Contracts"[78]. In a much more direct way, the European Commission for the Efficiency of Justice (CEPEJ) makes a yearly Evaluation of Judicial Systems, based on statistical information.[79] And, more recently, the European Commission has launched a new tool, the EU Justice Scoreboard, used –among others– as a basis for recommendations to Member States.[80]

These studies cannot be overlooked by any sensible scholar doing comparative research in the field of civil procedure. They furnish a remarkable amount of information and data that one could not have gathered on his/her own. And they also offer a comparison among jurisdictions, sometimes by means of graphics. But, nevertheless, some perspective and caution would be advisable, since, as has been pointed out, the reliability of the data can be questioned, and also their neutrality. Such reports have the legitimate aim to help national systems detect their weaknesses and to

---

78 See, on that topic, C. A. Kern, *Justice between simplification and formalism: a discussion and critique of the World Bank sponsored Lex Mundi Project on efficiency of civil procedure* (Mohr Siebeck, Tübingen, 2007); R. Michaels, "Comparative Law by Numbers? Legal Origins Thesis, Doing Business Reports, and the Silence of Traditional Comparative Law", 57 *American Journal of Comparative Law* 765 (2009-4); R. Caponi, "Doing Business" come scopo della giustizia civile?", *Foro Italiano* (2015, V, 3) (also available at https://papers.ssrn.com/sol3/papers.cfm?abstract_id=2568447).

79 See A. Uzelac, "Efficiency of European Justice Systems. The Strength and Weaknesses of the CEPEJ Evaluations", 1 *International Journal of Procedural Law* 106 (2011-1).

80 A. Dori, "The EU Justice Scoreboard – Judicial Evaluation as a New Governance Tool", *MPILux Working Paper* 2 (2015), available at http://www.mpi.lu/research/working-paper-series/2015/wp-2015-2/; C. Baldus et al., "Das „EU Justice Scoreboard" der Europäischen Kommission", *GPR-Gemeinschaftsprivatrecht* 108 (2016-3).

show where good examples can be found: and this is a real comparative law approach. But sometimes naming is also shaming: the current trend of building rankings of everything –also of judicial and procedural systems– has some dark sides[81] into which at least academics should not fall.

In fact, apart from the utility of the notion of legal families that has been addressed earlier, and again insisting on the functional approach, it is common to take as a basis of comparison the law of the so-called "Good States",[82] illustrated by the example of what happened in Japan during the Meiji era, where authorities adopted the legal institutions of the systems they considered to be the best. In a similar way, it is frequent to read that "veteran law" is considered as more suitable as a term of comparison.[83] But it is not always easy to decide which states are to be considered "Good States" and, on the contrary, states where "systemic deficiencies" are detected have the risk of giving rise to public policy precautions more easily than others.[84]

(c) The Language Issues

Finally, a few words on the language issue might be advisable. For many years, comparative studies were a kingdom of multilingualism, the place where different languages gathered in documents, reports, conferences and books.

81 See, for instance, K. Davis, A. Fisher, B. Kingsbury, S. Engle Merry (eds.) *Governance by Indicators. Global Power through Quantification and Rankings* (OUP, 2012); C. Arndt, C. Oman, *Uses and Abuses of Governance Indicators* (OECD-Development Centre Studies, 2006).

82 Again, Posner/Sunstein, *supra* n. 36, at 174-176.

83 Dothan, *supra* n. 65, at 29.

84 A good example is the Judgment of the ECJ (Grand Chamber) of 21 December 2011, joint cases C-411/10 (N.S. v. Secretary of State for the Home Department) and C-493/10 (M.E. and others v. Refugee Applications Commissioner and Minister for Justice, Equality and Law Reform), concerning Dublin II Regulation on asylum policy and the possibility of a Member State not to return to Greece, asylum applicants on the grounds that the systemic deficiencies of the Greek judicial and administrative system would entail a risk to their fundamental rights.

The language barrier has always been a hurdle to comparative studies,[85] especially for legal systems of jurisdictions with official languages that are not usually mastered by others outside the state's borders.[86]

Legal glossaries could be a very useful tool to overcome the language barrier and specific glossaries for the specific field of procedural law should be developed progressively, as a basis for common understanding.[87]

The rise of English as *lingua franca* in the legal field is also a relevant element. For a long time, probably due to strong feelings about the divide between civil law and common law, academic works in German, French and Italian were the rule in the European comparative context and contest. Nowadays, English clearly prevails. And English legal language is not adapted to the continental dogmatic subtleties and nuances that are sometimes necessary to make a clear depiction of a procedural institution or regulation. There is no criticism or complex of superiority of any sort in this remark; on the contrary, English legal language has its own subtleties and nuances that a continental scholar will only master –if ever– after intensive immersion. But it is necessary to be aware of the fact that one of the main tools –language– can be misleading due to the lack of existence of equivalent terms in the different languages that might be involved in comparative research.[88]

---

85 See, for instance, Schlesinger et al., *supra* n. 3, at 974-979. More recently, Marcel Storme wrote the following: "Je reste persuadé du fait qu'en procédure civile, les institutions, les procédures et leur terminologie sont tellement spécifiques qu'il est impossible de les transférer dans une autre langue" ("Civil Procedure in a Global World", 1 *International Journal of Procedural Law* 3 (2011-1)). One of the key factors explaining the success of the Iberoamerican Institute of Procedural Law as a venue for intensive and fruitful academic comparative work is the fact that all members share the same language, with the exception of the Brazilian scholars, who, nevertheless, do not find much trouble in Spanish speaking contexts, nor the other way round.

86 Posner and Sunstein, for instance, when dealing with the requirements that should be met in order to consider that courts can carry out inquiries on foreign laws, include this: "Judges should consult nations whose legal materials are translated into English and adequately understood in the English-speaking world" (Posner/ Sunstein, *supra* n. 36, at 170).

87 There is in fact a project aiming at this goal, promoted by the International Association of Procedural Law, whose first phase is almost finished.

88 See E. Jeuland, S. Lalani (eds.), *Recherche lexicographique sur la procédure civile – Research for the Development of a Civil Procedure Lexicon*, IRJS Éditions, Paris, 2017.

The need to overcome these obstacles is leading to the construction of a very peculiar "legal procedural English", typical of the EU directives and regulations: grammar and common vocabulary are fully English, but terminology is frequently strange to the categories of common law, because it is adapted to the expressive needs of all the other languages. This peculiar language is, in fact, a proof of the relevance of comparative methodology and of the need to use a common language as a prerequisite in order to be sure, when comparing, that "we are all talking about the same thing".

II. Comparative Law: A Plurality of Methods

*Margaret Woo**

(I) Introduction

At the 50th anniversary of the American Journal of Comparative Law, Mathias Reiman famously lamented that comparative law has not developed "into a coherent and intellectually convincing discipline."[1] What was Reiman referring to and has the discipline of comparative law not changed since his observation in 2002? This challenge to be a "convincing discipline" is even more critical today for the field of comparative law as nation states are increasingly turning inward, a perspective contrary to comparative studies.

Indeed, pressures of globalization have strained population movements, restructured markets have led to widening economic instability, and terrorism has been allowed to redefine national borders and identity. All of these pressures have led to an anti-globalization movement resulting in national responses such as Brexit (Britain's exit from the European Union), America First (U.S. President Trump's foreign policy platform),[2] and the Chinese Dream (a set of national ideals set forth by Chinese President Xi Jinping). These policy positions represent retrenchments that are notably distinct from the early 2000's when there were optimistic predictions of inter-

---

* Professor of Law at Northeastern University School of Law. Co-editor for the Journal of Legal Education. Associate of the East Asian Legal Studies Program at Harvard University. Elected member of the prestigious American Law Institute and the International Association of Procedural Law, and fellow of the American Bar Foundation. She previously served on the Board of Directors for the Law and Society Association and chaired the civil procedure section of the Association of American Law Schools.

1 M. Reimann, "The Progress and Failure of Comparative Law in the Second Half of the Twentieth Century," 50 *American Journal of Comparative Law* 671, 673 (2002).

2 S. Dunn, "Trump's 'America First' Has Ugly Echoes from U.S. history," *CNN Opinion*, 27 April, 2016, <http://www.cnn.com/2016/04/27/opinions/trump-america-first-ugly-echoes-dunn/>.Except otherwise stated all websites have been last visited 30 April 2017.

national integration, the interchange of world views and ideas, and even of a transnational legal system and globalized judiciary.[3]

This anti-globalization trend presents a challenge to those of us who work in and champion the cause of comparative law. Comparative law is said not only to promote better international understanding by looking outward. It also informs national law making, aids judges in difficult decisions, and provides a basis for legal unification or harmonization by seeking answers from other nations and states.[4] But how should comparative law respond to recent challenges to our tasks? In part, answering this question requires a better understanding of the trajectory of comparative law, its present-day critiques as well as some consideration of how next to proceed.

(II) What is Comparative Law?

Comparative Law describes the comparison of various laws; it is not itself a distinct body of law. Comparative law may be macro- comparisons - that is concerned with entire legal systems or general questions, or micro-comparisons - that deals with specific institutions or specific problems.[5] It is as Pierre Lepaulle once wrote, "to see things in their true light, we must see them from a distance, as strangers, which is impossible when we study any phenomena of our own country."[6] Hence, the comparatists, precisely because of their outsider perspective, can illuminate features of the law that internal observers would not realize.

But the comparatist cannot simply skim on the surface. Adequate knowledge of foreign law is an indispensable prerequisite of every legal comparison. Furthermore, comparative law goes beyond the mere study and understanding of a foreign legal system. In assessing and understanding the differences/similarities that exist between divergent laws and legal systems and discovering the attendant benefits of these differences/simi-

---

3 See K.I Kersch, "The New Legal Transnationalism, the Globalized Judiciary, and the Rule of Law," 4 *Washington University Global Studies Law Review* 345, 345-387 (2005).

4 H.E. Chodosh, *Global Justice Reform: A Comparative Methodology* 28 (2005).

5 K. Zweigert and H. Kotz, *An Introduction to Comparative Law* 4-5 (trans. Tony Weir, 3rd ed, 1998).

6 P. Lepreud, "The Function of Comparative Law with a Critique of Sociological Jurisprudence, 35 *Harvard Law Review* 838, 858 (1922).

larities,[7] comparative law can deepen one's understanding of inherent features of legal systems, as well as one's own home rules and legal system.[8] Comparative law is therefore said not only to promote better international understanding, but it also informs national law making, aids judges in difficult decisions, and provides a basis for legal unification or harmonization. In sum, the purposes of comparative law are understanding, reform and unification.[9]

While it was not until the end of the 19th century that the term "comparative law" was introduced, reformers and scholars have long used the technique of comparison. In the 4th century, Aristotle was said to have collected the constitutions of no fewer than 158 city-states in his effort to devise a model constitution. But it was not until the year 1900 that the first International Congress of Comparative Law was held in Paris, and chairs in comparative law established in universities with projects in foreign law undertaken all over the continent of Europe.[10]

The late 19th century was also a time of nation states and so it was to national laws that comparatists turned as the cornerstone of this new science of comparative law. Influenced by developments in the physical sciences, a comparatist's task in this era was to find a legal system's true and distinct identity and assign each system to a particular classification. Legal systems were primarily classified either as a common law or civil law system. The focus was on comparing legislation and codification because (with the exception of one English jurist) the first congress had attracted only jurists from continental European countries, all of which had coded law, in contrast to English common law. The focus was on the diversity of laws but the search was for a universal jurisprudence and the preparation of a "common law for the civilized world."[11]

---

7 R. Sacco, "Centennial World Congress on Comparative Law: One Hundred of Comparative Law," 75 *Tulane Law Review* 1159 (2000-2002).

8 R. Michaels, "The Functional Method of Comparative Law," in *Oxford Handbook of Comparative Law* (M.Reimann & R.Zimmermann, eds., 2006), https://papers.ssrn.com/sol3/papers.cfm?abstract_id=839826.

9 Chodosh, *supra* n.4, at 10.

10 Sacco, *supra*, n.7, at 1164.

11 Hence, the *Societé de legislation comparée* de Paris adopted Jus Unum (the correct one) as its motto. Sacco, *supra*, n.7, at 1166.

The interwar period of 1918 -1939 saw the rise of such anti-formalist as Eduordo Lambert, Rosco Pound, Ernst Rabel, Max Rheinstein.[12] These comparatists placed their emphasis on ideals, social facts, practical effects, rather than simply on comparing black letter laws. The upheavals resulting from World War I (1914–18) also broadened the comparative gaze from European interests to common-law countries, and then further still to socialist legal systems, until finally, after 1945, to the laws of the newly independent states of Asia and Africa. With such varied legal systems, a new focus was thus opened up to comparative law. Rather than limited to comparing legislation and codes, comparative law now also include examinations of legal institutions, practices as well as legal doctrine. "The comparative approach searches for all of the factors that, by nature, influence the creative process of law and shape the rule and life of the law." [13]

After the two world wars, the classification project remained strong, but with "legal families" expanding beyond the common law/civil law distinctions in an attempt to straddle cultural and technical divide. René David's legal families of "Romano-Germanic, Common Law, Socialists systems, Muslim-Hindu-Jewish and Far East" were proposed as a middle way between cultural particularism and universalism.[14] More recently, the classification project has evolved into classifications of legal traditions. Where legal families are seen as static and isolated entities, legal traditions suggest not only a historical contingency but also an ongoing and more dynamic process.[15]

In the classification project, comparatists varied in the typologies they reached. Some argue that typologies of legal systems should be based on "differences in social-economic system," [16] while others argue for categorizations based on the "philosophical underpinnings of broad principles of

---

12 Ernst Rabel was particularly influential in arguing that any element capable of influencing the law as a source and moving comparative law from being simply an invoice of different official sources of divergent laws.

13 Sacco, *supra*, n.7, at 1170.

14 R. David, "The International Unification of Private Law," in *International Encyclopedia of Comparative Law*, Vol. II, *Legal Systems of the World: Their Comparison and Unification* (1975).

15 See e.g. H. Patrick Glenn, L*egal Traditions of the World: Sustainable Diversity in Law* (5th ed., 2014).

16 See e.g. J. Quigley, "Socialist Law and the Civil Law Tradition", 37 *The American Journal of Comparative Law* 781-808 (1989).

law."[17] Using such variables as the historical background, the characteristic way of thought, the different institutions, the recognized sources of law, and the dominant ideology, Konrad Zweigert and Hein Kotz classified systems as Roman, German, Common Law, Nordic, and family of the Far East, Religious family (Jewish, Muslim and Hindu Law). Uno Mattei focused on three main sources of social norm "politics, law, and philosophical or religious tradition," to divide legal systems accordingly[18] Maine, Durkheim and Gluckman differentiated between technologically simple and technologically complex societies; while Diamond and Hoebel viewed legal systems according to different stages of historical development.[19]

Comparative law received a revival of sorts in recent years with the double process of economic globalization and Europeanization of law. Hence, comparative law is critical to the work of European Union (EU) institutions. From the basic question of whether the EU should and is permitted to act to whether legal differences create obstacles to the internal market, comparative law is called upon as the EU decides on new areas of regulation and assesses how it interacts with national law in complex ways. And where EU law does not merely replace national laws, a good comparative understanding of member state laws is a prerequisite for the successful implementation of EU laws.

(III) What Are the Methods of Comparative Law?

Rosco Pound aptly wrote nearly 70 years ago, "[M]uch if not all depends on what is compared and how it is compared."[20] But how to determine what is to be compared is hotly contested in comparative law. Beyond mere doctrinal comparison, there are fundamentally two different methods, functional and cultural legal comparison.

---

17 K. Zweigert and H. Kötz, *An Introduction to Comparative Law*, translation from the German original: *Einführung in die Rechtsvergleichung auf dem Gebiete des Privatrechts* (Tony Weir trans., 3rd ed., 1998).

18 Uno Mattei, "Three Patterns of Law: Taxonomy and Change in the World's Legal Systems," 45 *American Journal of Comparative Law* 5, 36 (1997).

19 See Chodosh, *supra* n.4, at 41.

20 R. Pound, "What May We Expect from Comparative Law?" 22 *American Bar Association Journal* 58-59 (1936).Pound reiterated this question nearly two decades later in another article. R. Pound, "Comparative Law in Space and Time," *American Journal of Comparative Law* 4 (1955).

First advocated by Ernst Rabel, functional comparison was later popularized by Konrad Zweigert and Hein Kötz in 1971, who declared that 'The basic methodological principle of all comparative law is that of functionality."[21] Functionalism starts from the premise that the function of law lies in responding to social problems and that all societies face essentially the same problems. But the focus is not on rules but the effects of rules. This makes it possible to compare legal institutions, even if they display different doctrinal structures, as long as they fulfill the same function, because in this case they are functionally equivalent.

If law is seen functionally as a regulator of social facts, then the legal problems of all countries are similar and every legal system in the world is open to the same questions and subject to the same standards, even countries of different social structure and different stages of development.[22] Functionalism inevitably leads to a search for similarities, turning the entire comparison into an exercise of more of comparing similarities than differences.

Understanding legal norms as responses to problems supposedly also makes it possible to designate which law is better.[23] And so, functionality often is called upon to serve an "evaluative" function and on this basis, is used to reform domestic law, or to create an international uniform law, or to urge law reform in a particular foreign system. Functionality remains highly influential and has in recent times received a further boost through various projects such as those that aim to harmonize or unify European private law.

---

21 Zweigert and Kotz, *supra* n.17, at 34.

22 Zweigert and Kotz, *supra* n.17, at 40.

23 According to Ralf Michaels, functionalist comparative law is characterized by four elements. First, functionalism focuses not on rules but on their effects, not on doctrinal structures and arguments, but on events. Second, functionalism combines its factual approach with the theory that its objects must be understood in the light of their functional relation to society. Third, function itself serves as *tertium comparationis*. Institutions, both legal and non-legal, even doctrinally different ones, are comparable if they are functionally equivalent, if they fulfill similar functions in different legal systems. Fourth, not shared by all variants of functional method, is that functionality can serve as an evaluative criterion .Functionalist comparative law then becomes a 'better-law comparison'- the better of several laws is that which fulfills its function better than the others. See Michaels, *supra* n.8; Michele Graziadei, "The Functional Heritage," in *Comparative Legal Studies: Traditions and Transitions* (Pierre Legrand & Roderick Munday, eds., 2003).

By contrast, cultural comparisons (sometimes called comparative legal studies or comparative legal cultures) reject the reduction of law to its function and instead seek to understand national law as an expression and development of its general culture.[24] The focus here lies on the mentality expressed in a legal system. Cultural comparisons tend to focus more on differences. Because cultural differences (particularly those between civil and common law) are sometimes seen as unbridgeable and because different legal cultures are deemed worthy of protection, cultural comparison usually opposes comparative evaluations and rejects legal unification as both impossible and undesirable. Instead, it promotes tolerance for foreign law and for differences in general.

The discrepancies between these two approaches may be smaller than the fierce debate suggests. Both approaches reject limiting comparative law to an analysis simply of black letter law; instead, both search for the role of law in society. Both approaches value and recognize the differences between legal systems. Properly understood, functional comparison does not, as is often claimed, fail to recognize or accept the identity of different legal systems and cultural comparisons does not necessarily reject a frame of analysis that can bridge differences. A comparison can grasp simultaneously the similarities in the solutions and the differences in the ways of reaching these solutions and vice versa. Recently, this insight has been used in the attempt to bring legal culture and functional equivalence together under the concept of legal paradigms. Paradigm describes the manner in which legal systems address problems in specific (cultural) ways to attain (functionally equivalent) solutions. Systems are classified as under the same "paradigm" if they share a hard core set of basic theories and concepts, e.g., a "common legal culture."[25]

There are other more recent approaches to comparative law. These include studies of legal history[26] law and economics[27] legal transplantation (that is, the study of relationships between legal systems and the migration

24 R. Cotterrel, "The Concept of Legal Culture," in D. Nelken, ed., *Comparing Legal Cultures*, 13-33 (1997).

25 M. Van Hoecke and M. Warrington, "Legal Cultures, Legal Paradigms and Legal Doctrine: Towards a New Model for Comparative Law," 47 *The International and Comparative Law Quarterly* 495, 510 (1998).

26 See for example, H. Berman, *Law and Revolution: The Formation of the Western Legal Tradition* (1983).

27 See e.g. U. Matttei, *Comparative Law and Economics* (1997).

of legal rules),[28] and as Professor Christoph Kern noted in this volume, the use of statistical methods. Nevertheless, each approach must still grapple with the tension between similarities and differences in defining the basis of comparison. Just as one needs to recognize similarities during the description and analysis of legal as well as non-legal context, one also needs to search for differences in order to find gaps within legal systems. Comparative law requires the right mixture of differences and similarities. Indeed, similar results may be most interesting if produced by different legal rules, institutions or systems, and different results may be most interesting if produced by similar rules, institutions or systems.[29]

(IV) The Critique of Comparative Law

In recent years, comparative legal studies have gained prominence as a tool for the Europeanization of private law. It also serves as the tool for the many "rule of law" projects underway in many countries and funded by multi-national organizations such as the International Monetary Fund. But several critiques continue to plague the field drawing from the methodological debates above.

As noted earlier, Mathias Reiman was less than sanguine about the progress of the field and accused its failure to develop a sound theoretical framework. Comparative law, Reiman argued, "has made little progress as a coherent enterprise generating broader insight of general interest. Most of its scholarship remains random, unconnected, and thus inconsequential." Supporters of this critique point to the body of existing scholarship that are mostly descriptive of foreign law, with or without explicit comparison. At its strongest, this body of scholarship contributes to the categorization and world mapping of legal families, traditions, or cultures but

---

28 See for example, A. Watson, *Legal Transplants: An Approach to Comparative Law*, at xi (2nd ed.1993).

29 Different scholars also have focused on different "things." Thus, Edouardo Lambert – attention to social and economic needs and desires; Rosco Pound – attention to legal ideals; Ernst Rabel – attention to practical outcomes; Arthur Schlesinger – "factual problems"; Rudolfo Saco – legal informants, see R.Sacco, "Legal Informants: A Dynamic Approach to Comparative Law," 39 *American Journal of Comparative Law* 1-34, Installment I of II (1991); also at <http://www.uni-heidelberg.de/institute/fak2/mussgnug/historyoftaxdocuments/schrifttum/aufsaetze/AUFS00030.pdf>.

has yet to develop any overarching theoretical basis or framework towards a better understanding of legal systems. Situating more along the similarities end of the similarities/difference approach, this critique would like to see the development of broader theories to explain certain functional legal phenomenon underlying different legal systems.

On the other extreme, there are those comparatists who cautioned against the pronouncement of such "grand theories."[30] Particularly those who studied non-western legal systems, these critics point to the danger of speculating broadly across cultures and across times, and the danger that "efforts at engaging in broad theoretical work may unwittingly lead us to believe that we are considering foreign legal cultures in universal or value-free terms when, in fact, we are examining them through conceptual frameworks that are products of our own values and traditions, and that are often applied merely to see what foreign societies have to tell us about ourselves."[31]

These comparatists emphasize our responsibilities to appreciate more fully the importance of "descriptions" and in particular, the type of textured, reflective examination that anthropologist Clifford Geertz termed "thick description."[32] Not wishing to run the risk of cultural relativism, these critics recognize that the effort to understand a different legal system necessarily entails the formation of judgments. But these critics argue for more thoughtful and careful comparisons and particular and modest, rather than grand, guidelines for our endeavor and conclusions.

Still other critics argue for incommensurability and question whether comparative law is even possible since law is so rooted in national traditions. Theorists, such as those in the "legal origins" school, would point to the force of legal traditions (placing primacy on the common law and civil law traditions) as the root of national economic development and of such indelible and irreconcilable distinctions.[33] The "legal origin" school traces common and civil law to different ideas about law and its purpose that England and France developed centuries ago and argues that the funda-

---

30 W. Alford, "On The Limits of 'Grand Theory' in Comparative Law," 61 *Washington Law Review* 945 (1986).

31 *Ibid* at 945-6.

32 C. Geertz, "Thick Descriptions: Towards an Interpretive Theory of Culture," in *The Interpretation of Cultures: Selected Essays* 3 (1973).

33 R. La Porta, F. Lopez-de-Silanes, and A. Schleifer, "Economic Consequences of Legal Origins," XLVI *Journal of Economic Literature* 286-288 (June 2008).

mental assumptions of each legal system survive today and have continued to exert substantial influence on economic outcomes. These theorists reject projects of unification because "minds of continental and common lawyers follow incommensurable patterns of thought." Such comparatists in particular point to the inherent power disparity in any legal reforms efforts and opined that the failure to recognize the power imbalances leads to hegemonic impositions of supposedly objective values by more economically developed countries on to less developed countries.[34]

Then, there are those who bemoan the self-professed apolitical stance of comparatists. Critics, such as David Kennedy, accuse comparatist of "talking about distributional effects like accidental tourists." [35] Pointing to comparative law giants such as Arthur Schlesinger and Rudolfo Sacco, critics such as Kennedy suggest that such post-war comparatists avoided ideological positions, and are less easily linked with particular social interests (labor, commerce) than their prewar predecessors. It is a decision by the comparatist, these critics assert, to downplay distributional consequences in assessing similarities and differences among legal regimes, and instead, to investigate and highlight technical similarities or cultural differences.[36]

For example, Kennedy argues that these scholars are methodologically eclectic and in being careful to remain "objectively" neutral, become disengaged from ideological debates and participated less readily in public life or government work.[37] Yet, not only is this "objectivity" intellectually impossible, this "objective" perspective also limits the impact and contributions that comparative law can make. The "objectively" neutral position would limit comparative law to societies that are comparatively similar,

---

34 See for example, P.G. Monateri, "Methods in Comparative Law: An Intellectual Overview," in *Methods of Comparative Law* 7-24 (P.G. Monateri, ed., 2012).

35 D. Kennedy, "Law and the Political Economy of the World" in *Critical Legal Perspectives on Global Governance* (G.D. Burca, C. Kilpatrick & J. Scott, eds., 2014), also in 26 *Leiden Journal of International Law* 7 (2013).

36 See O. Kahn-Freund, "On Uses and Misuses of Comparative Law," 37 *Modern Law Review* 1, 29 (1974)

37 The distance from practical engagement with government was explicitly promoted by Rodolfo Sacco, the Italian comparatist who provides the link between Schlesinger's Cornell project and the effort led by Sacco's students to mobilize researchers for a description of the common core of European private law in Trento project. As Sacco stated, "with regard to the unification of the law, comparative science is neutral." Sacco *supra* n.7, at 1162.

and hence, to areas of law that are decidedly "apolitical" such as private and commercial law. This emphasis only on private law is in contradiction to the change understanding of private law in the 20th century which reorients private law as a political tool of regulation, and constitutions and administrative law emerging and superseding private law as dominant areas of a country's legal structure.

(V) The Next Iteration of Comparative Law?

There is certainly no single answer to resolve this debate, but rather, there are a number of cautionary guidelines to keep in mind in our comparative work. First, we must keep in mind Rosco Pound's admonishment that "a fruitful comparative law… has to do much more than set side by side sections of codes or general legislation."[38] In order to understand law, one must not simply know the rules, nor how they operate in practice. One must also understand from where they derive, the choices they represent, and the imagination they encompass.

And so, our comparative task must very simply be to shed "cognitive lock-in" and engage in "cultural immersion," as Vivian Curren advocates. This requires "immersion into the political, historical, economic and linguistic contexts that molded the legal system and in which the legal system operates," the subterrainian.[39] Because law is recursive - that is, it is both reflective as well as constructive of social life - law cannot be studied in isolation, but must be analyzed within the context of the whole historical and cultural structure.[40]

Immersion could require an understanding of the interaction between multiple laws in producing "legal formants," as urged by Rudolfo Sacco. Understanding the historical and social context of a particular rule, institution or practice and in focusing on how law is "formed" will also assist in understanding the transferability of these rules, institutions or practice. In

38 R. Pound, "Comparative Law in Space and Time" 4 *American Journal of Comparative Law* 70, 75 (1955).

39 V. Grosswald Curran, "Cultural Immersion, Difference and Categories in U.S.Comparative Law," 46 *American Journal of Comparative Law* 43 (1998).

40 C. Geertz, *Local Knowledge: Fact and Law in Comparative Perspective*, in *Local Knowledge: Further Essays in Interpretive Culture* 167, 215 (1983); J.E. Ainsworth, "Categories and Culture: On the 'Rectification of Names' in Comparative Law", 82 *Cornell Law Review* 19, 28 (1996).

fact, as noted by Kahn Freund, when a law is more closely tied to its local habitat, a foreign rule is less transplantable. If we understand more closely law as a social activity and the contexts of a particular rule, we would be less likely to impose imperialistically our version of an "ideal" rule unthinkingly, since choices made are often only reflective of particular time and place.[41]

At minimum, then, a comparative study cannot simply be the juxtaposition of blackletter rules nor a search for presumed similarities which are then taken to elucidate shared principles. We must discard the three elements associated with what Jaakko Husa calls hardcore functionalism: namely the presumption of similarity, the search for causal explanations for similarity, and the notion of a neutral framework in comparative law. This will mean greater increase in serious interdisciplinary work and a long-term commitment to collaborations with our partners in sociology, political science, and history.[42] A deeper level comparative law could mean the pairing of comparative cognitive approach of law as reflecting jurisprudential concepts (that is, the 'cognitive structure of the legal system from the inside) and a comparative study of external socio-legal aspects of how law works. Towards these goals, partnerships with other methodologies, such as those utilized in law and society or law and economics, through the collection of quantitative or qualitative data, would enrich the study of comparative law.

Second, we should recognize the limitations of harmonization and convergence as the sole goal. The goal of harmonization has driven mainstream comparative legal studies in Europe harmonization since the Paris Congress of 1900, was envisaged by Ernst Rabel around the middle of the century. Unquestionably, comparative law has played an important role in the various harmonization projects of the European Union, including that of the Common Core Project.[43] This project is compiling the similarities and differences between European legal systems using detailed compara-

---

41 As Karl Llewlyn warned long ago, "Nowhere more than in law do you need armor against that type of ethnocentric and chronocentric snobbery – the smugness of your own tribe and your own time: We are the Greeks; all others are barbarians." K. Llewellyn, *The Bramble Bush: On Our Law and Its Study* 44 (1930).

42 Reiman, *supra* n.1 at 673.

43 See M.Bussani and U.Mattei, *The Common Core Project*, delivered at the first general meeting on 6 July 1995, < http://www.jus.unitn.it/dsg/common-core/meeting_10_project.html>; M. Bussani and U. Mattei, *The Trento Common Core Project* July 2004 <http://www.jus.unitn.it/dsg/common-core/meeting_10_html.>

tive law case studies, largely without evaluation of these solutions. Other groups connect comparative law surveys with normative searches for the best solution (Restatements). This is the case for the Lando Commission on European Contract Law (Principles of European Contract Law) and the Study Group on a European Civil Code, which emerged from it, as well as the European Group on Tort Law (Principles of European Tort Law).

But an undue focus on harmonization or convergence can limit one to an undue focus on looking for single answers and to the perennial common law/civil law divide.[44] Harmonization and convergence must be in the context of accommodating overlapping normative orders of national legal systems, the European Union and the European Convention on Human Rights. More problematically, harmonization/convergence can funnel one into a view that only the state can make law, and neglect other sources of legal norms. Theorists such as those of the legal pluralism school, recognize that legal orders may be rooted in differences sources of legitimacy, such as tradition, religion, or will of the people, with often the co-existence of such legal forms in the same field as state promulgated norms.[45] And the reality of pluralism between state and non-state legal orders inevitably take the comparative focus away from western legal systems to in the customary law of developing countries, and in the laws of groups and communities such as the Quakers, Romani, Native Americans and religious organizations.

Third, we must caution against the development of grand theories of law. Here, comparative law functions as the discipline that attempts to understand the various legal systems in their totality (similarities and differences) and in their relationship to each other. Without the ambition of promoting a generalized theory of the law, one can nevertheless examine one aspect of a legal norm in the context of "thick descriptions," and develop an understanding of how each is related to each other. Without leading to a politics of apology for totalitarian departures nor underestimate the positive force of the universality and rights, I am simply proposing a compara-

---

44 Rodolfo Sacco warned of this danger of looking for single answers as far back as the centennial celebration of the Society of Comparative Law. Sacco, *supra* n.7, at 1165.

45 F. von Benda-Beckmann, K. von Benda-Beckman, and A. Griffiths, "Introduction," in *The Power of Law in a Transnational World. Anthropology Enquiries*, pp.1-29 (F. von Benda-Beckmann, K. von Benda-Beckmann and A. Griffiths, eds., 2009).

tive law methodology that is more attuned to history culture, context and difference with more particular and specific understandings rather than grand theories.

Indeed, such a comparative method can provide a check on the claim of jurists within a legal system that their method rests purely on logic and deduction. Proponents of looking at "legal formants" make it possible to keep the ambivalence and multiplicity of legal rules in each system at play in the comparison. Living law contains any different elements such as statutory rules, formulation of scholars, decision of judges, and the multiplicity can give rise to several interpretations with no single one being correct and the other one false. "Within a given legal system with multiple 'legal formants' there is no guarantee that they will be in harmony rather than in conflict."[46]

Finally, we comparatists may want to be explicitly political. The call to recognize the political nature of our work may ring particularly true for those comparatists involved in legal reform projects. We cannot ignore the reality of power disparity between whichever legal system we study and the distributional effects of whatever solution we suggests. Indeed, the most important factor in the ability of transplanting foreign models is the congruence between the comparative power structure of the sending and receiver countries. If law reform is to be achieved, the political context and the recognition of distributional effects cannot be ignored. Otherwise, law will serve as a centrifugal rather than a centripetal force for nation states.

It is also an acceptance that no analytical frame is completely neutral. Law is "social engineering," and legal science is social science. Rather than largely concentrating on private law, which was viewed as apolitical and therefore appeared to be the only area of law fit for strict, scientific legal comparisons, comparative law could focus on legal practices, institutions and methods rather than simply on legislative text, and on constitutional, administrative, and procedural law. Indeed, comparative civil procedure law may be ideal for a study of comparative law in this regard.

46 Sacco, *supra* n. 24, at 23.

(VI) Development of Comparative Procedural Law

For a number of reasons, procedure law is fruitful for comparative studies. Specifically, rules of procedure uniquely combine the universal with the cultural. Procedural rules are simultaneously cultural messages about how we fight. Yet, procedural rules receive legitimacy precisely from their universal claim of "rule of law" and procedural justice.

Furthermore, civil procedure reforms have been unusually active in national systems of civil procedure. These trends and developments may serve as good starting points for comparative studies.

Indeed, while encompassing the participants' notions of rights and entitlement, the process of disputing and dispute resolution unveil "the meaning participants attach to going to court, [as well as] social practices that indicate when and how to escalate disputes to a public forum." [47] The administration of justice are less judgments based on objective reality and more, judgments made on legal facts that are "socially constructed by everything from evidence rules, courtroom etiquette, and law reporting traditions, to advocacy techniques, the rhetoric of judges and scholasticism of law school education."[48]

Yet, rules on how to dispute (what we call civil procedure) are also driven by universal norms of efficiency, predictability and consistency. Procedural law, or procedural justice, gets its legitimacy precisely from perceptions of its neutrality, rationality, and ability to curb individual and political discretion. This "neutrality" and "rationality" are said to rise above local particularities of time and place. Legal procedure rules are then not simply the practical way of ensuring the enforcement of substantive rights; they are also seen as an important aspect in securing the rule of law. Closely related and in tension are the comparative efforts to harmonize national procedural systems with attention to the relationship between domestic systems and international norms.

In regulating how a case is brought in court, how it is investigated, how it is argued, and how it is decided, civil procedure rules also distribute power amongst the parties, the judges, the lawyers, and the political authorities that house the courts. In turning disputes over to a neutral third party for resolution, disputing parties give up their powers in exchange for

---

47 S.E. Merry, "Disputing Without Culture," 100 *Harvard Law Review* 2057, 2063 (1987).

48 C. Geertz, *supra* n.40, at 173.

peace and resolution. In determining who gets to do what in a litigation, procedure rules distribute power among the players and in some instances, restore power disparities but in others, preserve existing power hierarchies. Thus, civil procedure situates the comparatist to be explicitly political and examine power distribution and how different societies allocate this power.

Finally, civil procedure is uniquely interrelated to the legal actors and institutions in which it rests. As Langbein pointed out, "legal procedure bears the most intimate relation to the institutions that operate the procedures."[49] Procedural rules are "insider" rules that regulated how lawsuits and actors operate with the legal system. Thus, one can argue that while substantive law can be easily changed by legislation, legal process as institutionalized may require more coordinated and sustained efforts in order for change to occur, precisely because of its embeddedness and interconnectedness.[50] This unique positionality of procedural law renders comparative study of it inevitable and informative.

And in many countries, civil procedure reforms have drawn attention. For one, the concern with high costs and undue delay, and increase in litigation rates in the last few decades, has occupied many civil justice systems. Some of the strategies employed include new rules of civil procedure; reorganization of courts and additional funding; and changing procedural culture. Specifically, this included considerations of the changing role of judges in different national systems resulting in judges having more power and authority to manage and steer litigation. This was true in Austria as a result of the 1895 Code of Civil Procedure, French law from 1935 onward, recent changes in English law and in U.S., managerial judging.[51] Yet, other systems are experimenting with different ways of diffusing authority by including the layperson in the judicial decision making

49 J.H. Langbein, "The Influence of Comparative Procedure in the United States" (1995). Faculty Scholarship Series. Paper 505. http://digitalcommons.law.yale.edu/fss_papers/505 9.

50 K. Pistor & P.A. Wellons, *The Role of Law and Legal Institutions in Asian Economic Development* 238 (1999); T. Ginsburg, "Does Law Matter for Economic Development? Evidence from East Asia," 34 *Law and Society Review* 829, 841-842 (2000).

51 G. Hazard, Jr. and A. Dondi, "Responsibilities of Judges and Advocates in Civil and Common Law: Some Lingering Misconceptions Concerning Civil Lawsuits" (2006). Faculty Scholarship Series. Paper 2329.http://digitalcommons.law.yale.edu/fss_papers/2329.

process. Where countries such as Korea and Japan[52] have introduced the jury system; in the U.S., this has meant the disappearance of the jury trial.[53]

Many systems have also instituted multi-track litigation with a small claims or simplified procedure solution as well as adoption of different alternative dispute resolution methods. In Austria, legislation on mediation accepted by the Nationalrat; in Belgium, there is in legislation in this field.[54] Within the framework of Council of Europe, the Committee on Experts on the Efficiency of Justice examines questions connected with mediation as an alternative to court proceedings in civil cases. Certainly, countries like China and Japan have long turned to mediation as a preferred alternative to litigation.

In this era of transnational conflicts, the pressure for harmonization of domestic civil procedure rules is particularly strong to prevent parties from forum shopping in transnational disputes. As international economic transactions aided by technology increasingly lead to complex legal problems without borders, efforts were being made to draft transnational rules. In the regime of globalized legal practice,[55] there were even optimistic predictions that judges will cooperate in "equal but distinct legal spheres, to the presumption of an integrated global legal system."[56]

And so, we see the trend of influential international regulations and conventions playing an important harmonization role, such as article 6 of the European Convention of Human Rights. Within Europe, the 1968 Brussels Convention on Jurisdiction and Enforcement of Judgments in civil and commercial matters, now converted into a European Regulation, applicable to all member states except Denmark. In the European Union, Article 65 of the Treaty Establishing the European Community (Articles

52 "Trial by Jury Returns to Japan," *The Guardian*, 3 August 2009; Jae-Hyup Lee, "Korean J Jury Trial: Has the New System Brought About Changes?" 12 *Asian Pacific Law and Policy Journal* (2010)

53 See S. Thomas, *The Missing American Jury: Restoring the Fundamental Constitutional Role of Criminal, Civil and Grand Juries* (2016).

54 See generally, *Global Trends in Mediation* (N. Alexander, ed., 2006); *Global Perspectives on ADR* (C. Esplugues Mota & S. Barona Vilar, eds., 2014)

55 For example, Anne-Marie Slaughter calls it "judicial globalization," a process of judicial interaction across, above and below borders, exchanging ideas and cooperating in cases involving national as much as international courts. A.M. Slaughter, 'Judicial Convergence,' 40 *Virginia Journal of International Law* 1103-04 (2000).

56 *Ibid* at 1115.

III-158, and III-170 of the proposed European Convention) provides a legal basis for the harmonization of civil procedural law, at least as regards civil matters having cross border implications and in so far as necessary for the proper functioning of the internal market. More globally, under the sponsorship of the American Law Institute and UNIDROFT, The Principles of Transnational Civil Procedure were drafted under the sponsorship of the American Law Institute and UNIDROIT aimed at providing a framework that a country might adopt for the adjudication of disputes arising from international transactions that find their way into the ordinary courts of justice.[57]

In sum, also in the field of comparative civil procedure, harmonization efforts are strong. Yet, law is national identity and in no stronger area than in civil procedure. For example, rules delineating a court's organizational structure and powers such as jurisdictional and civil procedure rules are actually delineating the political power of any given state.[58] A court's organizational structure defines where it sits in the political division of governance. Similarly, jurisdictional rules define a state's right to exercise coercive power over an individual or dispute. Thus, the growth of a court's jurisdiction often coincides with state expansion. A comparative look at jurisdictional rules then not only adds insight to how each society approaches the protection of individual basic rights and powers, but also the project of state building. As enactments of the state, procedural requirements are symbolic and physical messages as to the power of the state. Tensions between states often morph into more technical disputes over jurisdiction of the courts.

And so, the historic tensions of comparative law methodology – similarities and differences -functionalism and cultural studies - are all too clearly reflected in the study of comparative civil procedure. The interaction of the two trends - that is, global legal convergence and assertion of local cultural practices - also continue to shape the conversation and debate. Both local culture and a universal rule of law are features in contemporary social development and their interplay is the critical foundation for new and more adaptive values and institutions to emerge.

---

57 See Unidroit/ALI, Principles of Transnational Civil Procedure < http://www.unidroit.org/english/principles/civilprocedure/ali-unidroitprinciples-e.pdf>

58 M. Woo, "Manning the Courthouse Gates: Pleadings, Jurisdiction, and the Nation State," 15 *Nevada Law Review* 1261 (2015).

Procedural Law and Methodology

I. Mauro Cappelletti's Methodology in Comparative Civil Justice and the Coercive Powers of Courts as a Case Study

Carlo Vittorio Giabardo[*]

> «*Peter* [...] *n'est pas une traduction de Pierre pas plus que Londres n'est pas une traduction de London*»
> J. DERRIDA, *Psyche*, Paris, 1985, 209.

(I) Comparative Law in Theory – on Comparative Methodology

(a) Introduction. On The "Constitutive Tension" Between Similarities and Differences in Comparative Legal Studies. Comparative Law in Theory – on Comparative Methodology

If we look at the comparative law scholarship, and at comparative legal studies considered in its entirety, we will observe a curious and distinctive feature. Quite provocatively, it seems to me that comparative scholars are somehow *obsessed* with methodological issues. Much of their academic effort is spent in analysing different methodological frameworks rather than the outcomes of their research, and too often their focus seems to be more on the conditions of possibility and validity of comparative enquiry, or on its theoretical foundations, rather than on its actual results.[1] Admittedly in a very reductive way, comparative law itself, at least at a certain

---

* PhD in Law, Turin University.

1 For a thorough discussion of different methods existing in the comparative law domain, see P.G. Monateri (eds), *Methods of Comparative Law* (Edward Elgar Publishing, Cheltenham – Northampton, 2012); M. Van Hooke (eds), *Epistemology and Methodology of Comparative Law* (Hart Publishing, Oxford, 2004). On the emergence of new trends, J. Husa, "Methodology of Comparative Law: From Paradoxes to Flexibility?" 58 *Revue International de Droit Comparé* 1095 (2006). See also D. Kennedy, "The Methods and Politics of Comparative Law", in: M. Bussani and U. Mattei, *The Common Core of European Private Law: Essays on the Project* 131 (Kluwer Law International, The Hague, 2003) (but originally published in P. Legrand and R. Munday, *Comparative Legal Studies: Traditions and Transitions* 345, Cambridge, Cambridge University Press, 2003). A concise but detailed sum-

stage of its academic life, was said to be not an independent legal science, but just a method (or a set of methods) and its legitimate realm of inquiry was believed, by many authors, to be only that of constructing and assessing different methodological paradigms.[2] No surprise, then, that Gustav Radbruch, the great last-century German comparatist, wrote that "*Wissenschaften, die sich mit ihrer eigenen Methodenlehre zu beschäftigen Anlaß haben, sind kranke Wissenschaften*"[3] ("sciences which have to busy themselves with their own methodology are sick sciences"). Although this statement certainly contains some truth, I only partially agree with it. If methodological questions are so crucial for comparative research in general (not only in our field, but also in the social sciences, economics, literature, and so on), it is largely because, in embarking on it, we always have to handle differences and similarities at once: we always have to keep them, in some ways, simultaneously together.

In this first part I want to reflect precisely on this duality. I think, indeed, that comparative research harbours an immanent contradiction, a perennial tension that is *constitutive* of comparative research (I will clarify later in what sense I use this word here). This contradiction is between the search for disparities and the need for a convergence, which is between the necessity for differences and the quest for similarities. In a nutshell, as I see it, all the methodological debate in comparative studies can be entirely reduced to a major attempt to reconcile the uniqueness and singularity of legal traditions with their comparability.[4]

This point merits further explanation.

---

mary is provided by B. Jaluzot, "Méthodologie du droit comparé: bilan et prospectives", 57 *Revue Internationale de Droit comparé* 29 (2005).

2 This problem is discussed, for example, by J. Gordley, "Is Comparative Law a Distinct Discipline?", 46 *American Journal of Comparative Law* 607 (1998). See also J. Hage, "Comparative Law as Method and the Method of Comparative Law", in: M. Adams and D. Heirbaut (eds), *The Method and Cultures of Comparative Law: Essays in Honour of M. V. Hooke* 37 (Hart Publishing, Oxford, 2014). See also B. Markesinis, "Comparative Law – A Subject in Search of an Audience", 53 *Modern Law Review* 1 (1990).

3 G. Radbruch, *Einführung in die Rechtswissenschaft* 242 (Koehler, Stuttgart, 1958).

4 The deepest analysis of this duality is, in my opinion, that of P. Legrand, "The Same and the Different", in Id. and R. Munday (eds), *Comparative Legal Studies. Traditions and Transitions* 240 (Cambridge, Cambridge University Press, 2003). But see also G. Danneman, "Comparative Law: Study of Similarities or Differences?", in: M. Reinmann and R. Zimmermann (eds), *The Oxford Handbook of Comparative Law* 383 (Oxford, 2006). On a more general, as well as philosophical, scale, see P.

On the one hand, it is obvious that in doing comparative law, it is necessary to respect differences existing between legal systems. To put it bluntly: "There is only one thing in this word which cannot be compared, and that is "one thing".[5] Without alterity - i.e. without experiencing genuinely the "Other" as a real, *irreducible* "Other" being an entity original and independent from the observer - comparative endeavour itself makes no sense. Diversity is the very condition of possibility of comparative studies. "*Comment, d'ailleurs*" - wonders Pierre Legrand –" *le comparatiste lui-même pourrait-il exister sans l'autre?*".[6]

On the other hand, we unavoidably need a "contact point" – or, to borrow once again Pierre Legrand's evocative phrase, an "*interface semantique*",[7] a "semantic commonality" or "dialogical interface", as he wrote elsewhere-[8] for legal cultures to communicate with each other. Alterity, although essential, cannot be *absolutely absolute.* If the "Other" is conceived as a completely impenetrable entity, this would ultimately undermine the possibility of genuine comparative commitment. "*L'absolument autre ne pourrait être qu'indechiffrable, c'est-à-dire muet*".[9] In other words, to make a dialogue, we must speak the same language.

This dichotomy has been recently clarified by Catherine Valcke, and it is worth recalling here an as brief as meaningful passage from her article about the comparability of legal systems, where she used as an example the well-known comparative law "*topos*" according to which one cannot compare apples with oranges.

Richard, *Le jeu de la différence: réflexions sur l'épistémologie du droit comparé* (Les presses de l'Université de Laval, Québec, 2007).

5 F.J.M. Feldbrugge, "Sociological Research Methods and Comparative Law", in: M. Rotondi (eds), *Inchieste di diritto comparato*, vol. II, *Buts et méthods du droit comparé* 213 (Padova, 1973) (quoted by Legrand, *supra* n. 4, at 278, footnote 136).

6 P. Legrand, *Le droit comparé* 96 (Presse Universitaire de France, Paris, 2011). This author also convincingly argues for the "ethical" mission and moral responsibility of comparative lawyers. "I argue that comparative legal studies must assume the duty to acknowledge, appreciate and respect alterity. Without such recognizance, no ethics is possible. In other words, the *raison d'être* of the comparative project lies in the refusal of national pride, in the rejection of cultural taboos, in the awareness and valorization of differences and *in the emphatic articulation of the voices of alterity to the point where the self is actually prepared to accept being "othered" by otherness*" (Legrand, *supra* n. 4, at 284, emphasis added).

7 Legrand, *ibidem,* at 77.

8 Legrand, *supra* n. 4, at 282.

9 Legrand, *supra* n. 6, at 73.

> *"Comparison is possible only among objects that are, simultaneously but without contradiction, unified and plural. (...) By this reasoning, it is not possible to compare apples (or oranges) with themselves, or apples (or oranges) with, say, airplanes. Apples are not comparable with themselves because of the absence of plurality. They are not comparable with airplanes because of the absence of unity: apples have nothing in common whatsoever with airplanes. There is little sense in saying of apples and airplanes that they have different textures, sweetness, or propulsion mechanisms (although they clearly do). As a result, there simply is nothing to compare".*[10]

In a nutshell, as the author explicitly points out, comparability requires both unity and plurality. It is precisely in this sense that I believe the outlined dynamic between the uniqueness and similarities is constitutive of our discipline, for it is from the incredibly complex interplays between these two elements that we come to understand how legal phenomena are conceived and even differently adopted, adapted and translated into different cultural environments. This represents, I believe, the immense difficulty of our research. How it is possible, though, to combine respect for alterity and the need for communication? How it is possible to reconcile both those fundamental, and, to a certain extent, inconsistent, requirements? How can we fruitfully manage this sort of contradiction? These are the questions a good methodology has to provide answers to.

(b) Mauro Cappelletti's Comparative Law

In an attempt to respond to these challenges, I want to critically reflect on, but also go beyond, the comparative law methodology elaborated by Mauro Cappelletti (1927 - 2004), Full Professor of Civil Procedure at the University of Florence, former Director of the Law Department of the European University Institute and the Lewis Talbot and Nadine Hearn Shelton Emeritus Professor of International Legal Studies, at Stanford Law

10 C. Valcke, "Comparative Law as Comparative Jurisprudence – The Comparability of Legal Systems", 52 *American Journal of Comparative Law* 713, 720 (2004). These considerations are also emphasised again in "Reflections on Comparative Law Methodology – Getting Inside Contract Law", in: M. Adams and J. Bomhoff (eds), *Practice and Theory in Comparative Law* 22 (CUP, Cambridge, 2012). For broader insights, see E. Örucu, *Comparability: Theories and Presumptions*, in *The Enigma of Comparative Law. Variations on a Theme for the Twenty – First Century* 19 (Brill, Leiden – Boston, 2004).

School.[11] Mauro Cappelletti was one of the most prominent and internationally-renowned voices of the last century in the fields of both comparative law and civil procedure. A thinker of extraordinary intellectual vitality, he was one of the first to support the use of comparative law in civil procedure. Indeed, his comparative approach truly helped to overcome that "dogmatic" and merely "systematic" study of civil procedural institutions that characterised (but admittedly with great results for those times) much of the last-century Italian scholarship, which was more interested in building abstract concepts and categories, rather than in finding solutions for the present and actual needs of society.[12] Cappelletti was an enormously prolific author. His books have become central texts in comparative civil justice at international level, both because of their engagement with a non (entirely) positivistic approach to legal problems and high attention to the role social and political dimensions can play in forming our legal institutions. His works – and especially the edition, together with Bryan Garth, of the path-breaking, four volumes "Access to Justice" (1978/9), his best known book that gained international reputation – are philosophical in the broader sense, in that they attempted to excavate the "non-juridical" underpinnings that lie beneath procedural institutions, as well as the sentiment for justice in society. The problems of legal aid and access to justice for the poor (included the role alternative dispute resolution mechanisms

11 For a recent *hommage* to Mauro Cappelletti and to his legacy on legal studies in general, as well as on public law in particular, see the proceedings of the Symposium jointly organised by the Faculty of Law, University of Florence and the Law Department of the European University Institute, to mark the 10th anniversary of his death, published in 14, *International Journal of Constitutional Law* 439 (2016) (and in particular J.H.H. Weiler, "The Legacy of Mauro Cappelletti: a Preface", *ibidem* 439).

12 This (past) attitude of the Italian doctrine, with its pros and drawbacks, has been analysed by V. Denti, "Sistematica e post-sistematica nell'evoluzione delle dottrine del processo", *Rivista Critica di Diritto Privato*, 469 (1986), now in the collection of essays of the same author, *Sistemi e riforme. Studi sulla giustizia civile* 13 (Il Mulino, Bologna, 1999).

play in this context),[13] the constitutional checks on the judiciary[14], the role of courts and the troubled relationship between judges and law-makers,[15] European legal integration,[16] and much besides, are just some of the recurring themes of his life-long research.

What is more relevant to the purpose of this article is the study of the methodological framework he deployed to pursue his comparative law research. Cappelletti explicitly outlined his method as a part of a short, Italian-written book collecting some of his essays, entitled *Dimensioni della giustizia nelle società contemporanee*, 1994 (litt. trans., *Dimensions of Justice in Contemporary Societies*). [17] In the very first chapter, titled *Metodo e finalità degli studi comparativi sulla giustizia* (litt. trans., *Methods and Purposes of Comparative Studies About Justice),* he aimed to put into words for the first time his personal methodological scheme within which he had always conducted his research. I think that it represents one of the most rigorous, and arguably less known, attempts to handle at one and the same time the needs for unity and plurality in comparative law. Although he claimed his proposal to be totally original,[18] it is not controversial to say that it owes a heavy debt to *functionalism*, of which Cappelletti was

13 See, e.g., *Towards Equal Justice. A Comparative Study of Legal Aid in Modern Societies* (with J. Gordley and E. Johnson jr., eds.), (Guiffrè, Milano/New York, 1975). See also M. Cappelletti and J. Gordley, "Legal Aid: Modern Themes and Variations Part One: The Emergence of a Modern Theme", 24 *Stanford Law Review* 347(1972), and Id., "Legal Aid: Modern Themes and Variations Part Two: Variations on a Modern Theme", *ibidem* at 387.

14 *Il controllo giudiziario di costituzionalità delle leggi nel diritto comparato* (Giuffrè, Milano, 1968).

15 *Giudici legislatori?* (Giuffrè, Milano, 1984).

16 *Integration through Law. Europe and the American Federal Experience* (with J.H.H. Weiler and M. Seccombe, eds) (De Gruyter, Berlin, 1986); with M. Kohnstamm, *New Perspectives for a Common Law of Europe/Nouvelles perspectives d'un droit commun de l'Europe* (Bruylant, Leyden, London, Sijthoff, Bruxelles, 1978).

17 M. Cappelletti, *Dimensioni della giustizia nelle società contemporanee* (Il Mulino, Bologna, 1994).

18 "*Si tratta* – Cappelletti writes, *ibid.,* at 11 - *di una proposta del tutto personale, un tentativo metodologico mai prima d'ora messo da me per iscritto, anche se esso riflette lo schema dentro il quale sempre ho condotto le mie ricerche comparative*".

widely-recognised to be "an adept"[19] (I shall briefly return on this point later).

Through his methodology, he made it clear that law institutions (and procedural ones in particular) have never been formed in isolation. They are always forged in their historical, political, social, economic and religious (in one words: cultural) context and shaped differently by people's finalities and aspirations, and vice versa.[20] So, there is a lesson here. We, as legal scholars, must acknowledge entirely that law has to be conceived of as something which is deeply dependent on the broader social practices and cultural life in which it is situated. Law, indeed, is to be understood as a "*relational*" notion, in the sense that its meaning can be grasped only in relation to, and against the background of, other branches of reality.[21] Accordingly, in order to do seriously comparative law, we must focus not only upon the different normative details of an enacted set of rules and judicial practices, but we have, so to say, to look at the whole picture, that is to bring into our analysis those cultural elements that inform our judicial institutions – a point that seems to have been forgotten, or perhaps not always taken into proper consideration, by the vast majority of traditional civil procedural scholars, that is by the "typical proceduralist" (a figure as wittily as accurately depicted by Professor Michele Taruffo in his article about this too common attitude).[22]

---

19 For this definition, see, e.g., Graziadei, "The Functionalist Heritage", in: P. Legrand and R. Munday (eds), *supra* n. 4, at 109.

20 On these relations, see M. Taruffo, "Processo e cultura", *Rivista Trimestrale di Diritto e Procedura Civile* 63 (2009); in English language, id., "Transcultural Dimensions of Civil Justice", 23 *Comparative Law Review* 1 (2000). It must be stressed, however, that not only procedural institutions mirror societal structures, but also that society is in turn shaped and influenced by the ways in which legal disputes are solved. In his view, law and cultural practices/lived experiences are two mutually constructing notions. See O. Chase, *Law, Culture and Ritual: Disputing Systems in Cross-Cultural Context* (New York University Press, New York, London, 2005).

21 This topic has been tackled from a plethora of perspectives. Just to name two of the most significant ones, see R. Cotterrell, *Law, Culture and Society. Legal Ideas in the Mirror of Social Theory* (Ashgate, London, 2006); L. Rosen, *Law as Culture: An Invitation* (Princeton University Press, Princeton – Oxford, 2006), especially for fascinating anthropological insights.

22 M. Taruffo, *L'insegnamento accademico del diritto processuale civile, Rivista Trimestrale di Diritto e Procedura Civile* 551 (1990).

To sum up, I am convinced that the task of comparative law research is therefore to "unveil" and to critically decode those various hidden elements (or "invisible powers")[23] that lurk beneath our legal world and that unconsciously influence our modes of reasoning and shape, consciously or not, our ways of thinking about law and legality.

(c) A Closer Look: The Stages of the Comparative Law Research

Cappelletti organises his method around three key steps:

I) The search for the common problem or social need;
II) The analysis of the different legal answers to that problem or need;
III) The investigation of the extra-juridical and cultural reasons for the different legal responses.

Each of these elements deserve closer scrutiny.

Firstly, in his attempt to build a bridge between the legal traditions considered in the comparative research – in his attempt, in other words, to construct that element of "unity" necessary to connect the various legal experiences between them - Cappelletti writes that two or more legal institutions can be said to be comparable not when the final legal solutions adopted by each country are similar (quite the opposite, he thinks that the similarity of outcomes renders indeed the comparative research less fascinating), but rather when the problem or social need the normative intervention intended to address is similar. In Cappelletti's own words, this point represents the *tertium comparationis* of the research, considered as the element that serves as a term for comparison, as a "common ground" between legal solutions that renders their comparison possible. As I briefly mentioned above, the reference to the functional method is evident here. By and large, the basic purpose of functionalism is to discern universal, or at least *functionally equivalent*, problems and see how differently the systems taken into consideration (be they legal, social, political) react to them. In law, the main assumption of functionalism – as Zweigert and Kotz famously wrote - is that "the only things which are comparable are

23 B. Grossfeld and E.J. Eberle, "Patterns of Order in Comparative Law: Discovering and Decoding Invisible Powers", 38 *Texas International Law Journal* 292 (2003).

those which fulfil the same function".[24] What is worth stressing, here, is the fact that this social problem or need comes, at least from a logical viewpoint, *before* the law, i.e. before lawmakers had legally addressed the issues. As such, the problem to be discovered has not a "juridical" nature, but rather an economic, social and political one. The starting point of comparative law enquiry is, then, to be found outside the legal domain strictly considered.

Secondly, Cappelletti, in his desire to insist on differences - in his attempt to focus on diversity - argues that comparatists must examine from a technical viewpoint the legal norms, rules and/or practices by which the countries decided to solve the shared problem. These rules may also differ markedly from country to country – and the more they differ, the better for our research, the more our understanding of law is enriched and our horizons broaden. What I want to highlight here is that Cappelletti is particularly keen on stressing that the merely technical description of a legal state of affairs between two or more foreign countries does not mean doing comparative law, but simply "foreign" law research – and, as it is now widely acknowledged, there is a huge difference between doing comparative law and merely studying foreign laws.[25] Stated differently, comparative law scholars must not be "*simples répétiteurs d"un droit étranger*",[26] plain observers of alien legal experiences, motivated not by a sincere desire to advance reciprocal knowledge and mutual comprehension between legal cultures, but only by those reasons ("*dévitalisantes et dessiccatives*",

---

24 K. Zweigert and H. Kötz, *An Introduction to Comparative Law* 34 (Oxford University Press, Oxford, 1998). This methodology has attracted some criticism. See R. Michaels, "The Functional Method of Comparative Law", in: *The Oxford Handbook of Comparative Law*, *supra* n. 4, at 339; Graziadei, *supra* n. 19; G. Samuel, "Dépasser le fonctionnalisme", in: P. Legrand (eds), *Comparer le droits. Résolument* 405 (Presse Universitaire de France, Paris, 2009); *adde* J. Husa, "Functional Method in Comparative Law: Much Ado About Nothing?", 2 *European Property Law Journal* 4 (2013).

25 The difference between "comparative law" and "foreign law" is widely acknowledged. R. Sacco *Introduzione al diritto comparato* 17 (Utet Giuridica, Torino, 1992) at footnote 34, says that this distinction is the same as that between a person able to speak more languages (a "polyglot") and a linguistic, in the sense that the former "knows many languages, but he does not know how to measure and qualify the differences between them" (my translation). On the fact that the mere description of foreign laws is not comparative law, see also L.J. Constantinesco, *La méthode comparative* 9 (L.G.D.J., Paris, 1972) (quoting Erich Rothacker).

26 Legrand, *supra* n. 6, 33.

as P. Legrand described them)[27] that are in the main of interest for attorneys and practitioners. As the third thesis of the Trento group clearly reads "*Non si fa comparazione finché ci si limita [...] all"esposizione parallela delle soluzioni esplicitate nelle diverse aeree*" ("One does not do comparative law as long as he limits himself [...] to the parallel exposition of legal solutions enacted in the different areas").[28]

In Cappelletti's view, therefore, comparative law in its most authentic and genuine sense always entails a "fascinating research of the reasons that can explain the analogies and, most importantly, differences adopted as a response to the same problem: historical, sociological, ethical reasons, and the like" (my translation). He is aware that comparative law scholars "need to move outside the legal domain strictly conceived, recognising once again that law, in fact, is a fundamental element, not divisible from the others, of our complex social system" (my translation).[29] The third stage of the comparative law enquiry consists precisely of this: in seeking the non-legal reasons capable of accounting for the actual legal state of affairs. It consists of answering the foundational questions about law and legal institutions: why is it so, and not differently? What are the cultural factors, mediated through history, that have led to the current divergence?

From a broader perspective, what is at stake here is the very *object* of comparative law. Comparative law does not just mean to compare legal rules with each other, but rather, and more profoundly, "structures of thought", or "mentalities". Let's remember once again the words of Catherine Valcke, for whom, as law essentially represents *"une «mentalité», une constellation d'idées sous-jacentes à ces regles et textes mêmes",* doing comparative law means nothing but studying the plurality of those

27 Legrand, *ibidem.*

28 The five "Trento Thesis of Comparative Law", written in Italy under the mentorship of Rodolfo Sacco in 1987, are reported by E. Grande, "Development of Comparative Law in Italy", in: *The Oxford Handbook of Comparative Law*, *supra* n. 4, at 32.

29 "*Il terzo momento dell'analisi comparativa* – writes Cappelletti, *Metodo e finalità*, *supra* n. 17, at 18 – *è un'affascinante ricerca delle ragioni che possono spiegare le analogie, ma soprattutto le differenze adottate in risposta ad un medesimo problema: ragioni storiche, sociologiche, etiche, ecc. Ovviamente, qui di nuovo il comparatista deve muoversi al di fuori del campo del diritto inteso in senso ristretto, nuovo riconoscimento del fatto che il diritto è in realtà un elemento fondamentale, ma indivisibile dagli altri elementi, del complesso sistema sociale*".

"*structures de pensée, de ces mentalités, de ces idées sous-jacentes*"[30] (which is called, in her words, "comparative jurisprudence").[31]

As the Italian last-century procedural law scholar Vittorio Denti reminded us: "it is impossible to do seriously comparative law without a proper knowledge of political, economic, social, religious factors that lie behind the evolution of foreign legal systems" (my translation).[32]

By considering the extra juridical reasons underpinning our legal solutions, Cappelletti's method comes to an ideal end, through a movement that could be defined as "circular". Starting from the social problem (pre-juridical), we enter in the legal domain strictly considered, as to finally get out of it again, analysing how social reality in its wider meaning has contributed to build different legal responses.

(d) An Epistemic Critique

According to Cappelletti's method, these three stages - that is, the search for the common problem (I), the study of foreign technical solutions (II), the examination of underlying cultural reasons, (III) - should be followed by those respectively dedicated to the outline of trends and tenden-

30 C. Valcke, "Droit: réflexions sur une définition aux fins de comparaison", in : P. Legrand (ed), *Comparer les droits. Résolument*, 100 (Presse Universitaire de France, Paris, 2009). On the role of mentality in comparative law, see C. Amodio, "Mentalità giuridica e comparazione", *Pòlemos* 173 (2010).

31 Valcke, *Comparative Law as Comparative Jurisprudence*, supra, n. 10. For an early and different use of this notion, see W. Ewald, "Comparative Jurisprudence (I): What Was It Like to Try a Rat?" 143 *University of Pennsylvania Law Rev.* 1889 (1995).

32 V. Denti, "Diritto comparato e scienza del processo", *Rivista Diritto Processuale* 335 (1979) ("*è impossibile fare seriamente della comparazione senza una conoscenza adeguata dei fattori politici, economici, sociali, religiosi che stanno dietro all'evoluzione degli altri ordinamenti*"). See also A. Dondi, "L'esperienza di un comparatista processuale", in: V. Bertorello (eds), *Io comparo, tu compari, egli compara: che cosa, come, perché?* 92 (Giuffrè, Milano, 2003), according to whom it is not conceivable, especially in the area of dispute resolution, doing comparative law without taking into account the "anthropological-cultural aspects", as well as "elements such as religious cultures, wide social perceptions, the global structure of society" ("*è impensabile fare della comparazione, soprattutto nell'area del diritto processuale, senza tener conto degli aspetti antropologico-culturali circostanti e degli elementi come le culture religiose, le percezioni sociali diffuse, la strutturazione delle società*").

cies of evolution of laws (IV), to the assessment of each adopted model in terms of efficiency, in relation to the social problem identified at first (V), and lastly to the prediction of likely future developments (VI). To my mind, neither the fourth nor the sixth stages pose crucial problems or particular difficulties (and their overall importance in the methodological scheme is frankly limited); the same cannot be said regarding the fifth one, concerning the rating of legal systems according to the efficiency of their rules. Rather, this stage is expected to play a significant role within Cappelletti's frame. In his view, it should represent ambitiously the "dialectical overtaking" of the contrast between practice and abstraction, the reconciliation between the juridical element with its pre-juridical part, and the connection of the concrete legal solutions with the problems initially individuated.

Albeit the great importance accorded to this last stage, I believe it represents the weaker part of his approach. Simply put, the most common criticism, here, lies with the fact that it is not possible to establish with a sufficient degree of scientific correctness which is the best solution, or, more crucially, even to state in a neutral way what a "best solution" exactly means – and this not even in a relative way, i.e. in relation to the problem initially individuated, as Cappelletti claims. To better articulate this critique, Hans George Gadamer's and Hilary Putnam's epistemic views can prove helpful. On the one hand, following Gadamer's hermeneutics, comparative lawyers must acknowledge that all understanding is situated (historically, geographically, culturally and the like), and then no knowledge can be completely free of bias due to preconceptions. Prejudice – he famously taught – "can be only managed, not eliminated".[33] On the other hand, according to the well-known Hilary Putnam's epistemic view, there is not a "God's eye view" of reality, as reality is always mediated through one's own conceptual beliefs and schemes.[34] Accordingly, we must con-

---

33 "Understanding is, essentially, a historically effected event", H.G. Gadamer, *Truth and Method* 300 (2004) (translation by J. Weinheimer and D.G. Marshall).

34 "There is no God's eye point of view that we can know or usefully imagine; there are only the various points of view of actual persons reflecting various interests and purposes that their theories and descriptions subserves" (H. Putnam, *Reason, Truth and History* 50 (Cambridge, Cambridge University Press, 1981). For an application of these ideas to the legal domain, J. Husa, "Kaleidoscopic Cultural Views and Legal Theory – Dethroning the Objectivity?" in J. Husa, M. Van Hoecke, *Objectivity in Law and Legal Reasoning* 210 (Hart Publishing, Oxford, 2013).

clude that comparative lawyers, too, cannot have a God's eye view in comprehending legal cultures. There cannot be such a thing as an objective and value-free reading of a normative (and thus cultural) outcome. That is because, as has been pointed out, legal cultures are inherently *incommensurable*,[35] which neither means nor implies incomparability, but simply that there is not a "neutral" or "unbiased" way of making judgments about legal traditions. I am aware that the debate on this point is quite lively and that international institutions are increasingly committed to rating legal systems according to their standards of economic performance, and putting them into hierarchies which are questionable at best (I am referring here to the Doing Business reports annually drafted by the World Bank).[36] Nonetheless, I am deeply convinced that every judgment is inevitably formulated in one's own "normative language", reflecting various interests, considerations, identities, styles of thought and, ultimately, visions of the world. As philosophers would say; no one can "escape" the boundaries of his own language, in this case the language being his own legal-ideological discourse (the famous Ludwig Wittgenstein's quote, "*Die Grenzen meiner Sprache bedeuten die Grenzen meiner Welt*" ("the limits of my language mean the limit of my world"), can, then, prove useful for comparative law theory, too).[37] This is not to suggest that legal comparativists should not take positions on different legal solutions (this is indeed the very essence of critical thinking), but rather that this act of judgment will always be partial by definition.

---

35 H.P. Glenn, "Are Legal Traditions Incommensurable?" 49 *The American Journal of Comparative Law* 133 (2001).

36 This topic is too vast to be adequately tackled here; see, however, A. Gambaro, "Misurare il diritto?" in: L. Antoniolli, G.A. Benacchio, R. Toniatti (eds), *Le nuove frontiere della comparazione, Atti del Primo Convegno Nazionale della Società Italiana per la Ricerca nel Diritto Comparato 3, Milano, 5-7 Maggio 2011* (Trento, 2012). In English, R. Michaels, "Comparative Law by Numbers? Legal Origins Thesis, Doing Business Reports, and the Silence of Traditional Comparative Law", 57 *American Journal of Comparative Law* 765 (2009).

37 L. Wittgenstein, *Logisch-Philosophische Abhandlung*, (Austria, 1921) *Satz* 5.6. On the wider influence of Wittgenstein's thought on comparative law, and especially of its "linguistic turn", see the illuminating article of P. Richard, "Les apports de Wittgenstein à la réflexion comparatiste", 57 *Revue internationale de droit comparé* 899 (2005).

(II) *Comparative law in practice – on the coercive powers of courts in comparative perspective*

(a) *Introduction*

In this part, I would like to provide a concrete case of how this methodology can operate in practice. This example will be drawn from my PhD thesis, which dealt with the comparative study of the different coercive techniques employed by civil and common legal systems in order to enforce binding legal judgments - a topic that has received little attention by comparative law scholars, especially at international level.[38]

This subject may superficially and at first sight appear merely technical and, thus, not suitable for a comparative, cultural-based research focus in the sense here endorsed. But the desire to explore this subject below the surface has led me to investigate the plausible reasons for the differences (to be found, as I will argue later, in the divergent legal genealogy of the procedural institutions at stake here, rooted in the two different historical trajectories of legal families). In doing so, I have tried to move beyond a purely descriptive perspective of the problems tackled.

My initial interest in this subject originated in the quite recent introduction, in 2009, in the Italian code of civil procedure, of the possibility for a

38 See, however, the extremely important collection of essays titled *Trends in the Enforcement of Non-Money Judgments and Orders, The First International Colloquium of the International Association of Procedural Law*, Lund, June 1985, U. Jacobson and J. Jacob, eds. (Kluwer, Deventer, 1988). See, also, K.D. Kerameus, "Enforcement of Non-Money Judgments and Orders in a Comparative Perspective", in: J.A.R. Nafziger and S.C. Symeonides (eds), *Law and Justice in a Multistate World, Essays in Honor of Arthur T. von Mehren* 107 (Brill, New York, 2002); id., *Enforcement Proceedings*, Vol. XVI, in M. Cappelletti, *Civil Procedure* 19, in *International Encyclopedia of Comparative Law* (Tubingen, 2002). For a comparative perspective, M. Chesterman, "Contempt: in the Common Law, But Not in the Civil Law", 46 *International and Comparative Law Quarterly* 521 (1997); C. Cremonini, "An Italian Lawyer Looks at Civil Contempt: From Rome to Glastonbury", 3 *Civil Justice Quarterly* 133 (1984). Less recently, but still important, A. Pekelis, "Legal Techniques and Political Ideologies: A Comparative Study", 41 *Michigan Law Review* 665 (1943). In the Italian legal scholarship, see, especially for historical insights, S. Chiarloni, *Misure coercitive e tutela dei diritti* (Giuffré, Milano, 1980) and M. Taruffo "L'attuazione esecutiva dei diritti: profili comparatistici", in *Rivista Trimestrale di Diritto e Procedura Civile* 142 (1988). In German language, O. Remien, *Rechtsverwirklichung durch Zwangsgelsd: Vergleich – Vereinheitlichung – Kollisionsrecht* (Tubingen: Mohr, 1992).

judge to issue an order requiring a losing party to pay an increasing sum of money in case of non-compliance with a (non-monetary) judgment, a provision directly derived from the French model of the *astreintes* - making it, by the way, one of the best examples of a "legal transplant" in the field of civil justice.[39] What struck me is that common and civil law jurisdictions - despite their undeniable "gradual convergence" in many fields of law (as Basil Markesinis authoritatively dubbed this trend)[40] - still greatly differ in the ways in which they react to non-compliance with court judgments. In the Anglo-American systems to disobey a courts' orders constitutes "civil contempt of court", for which the losing party might even face prison if he fails to comply with legal judgments, especially the ones requiring him to do, or to abstain from doing, a specific act (such as orders of specific performance or negative injunctions).[41] On the contrary, in civil law countries the notion of civil contempt of court is, strictly speaking, totally unknown, and *it could not be but so*. Undoubtedly, civil law systems also have some forms of sanction or "threat" used to compel compliance with judges' orders - the *astreintes* in France,[42] the *Geldstrafen* in Ger-

39 This phrase is notoriously due to A. Watson's seminal book *Legal Transplant: An Approach to Comparative Law* (Scottish Academic Press, Edinburgh, 1974).

40 B. Markesinis (eds), *The Gradual Convergence. Foreign Ideas, Foreign Influences and English Law on the Eve of the 21st Century* (Oxford, Oxford University Press, 1994). For early discussion of this topic, see J. Merryman, "On the Convergence (and Divergence) of the Civil Law and the Common Law", in: M. Cappelletti (eds), *New Perspectives for a Common Law of Europe* 195 (Sijthoff, Leyden, 1978). But for a highly critical view, and for the highlight of an enduring "epistemological difference" between civil and common law, see P. Legrand, "European Legal Systems Are Not Converging", 45 *International and Comparative Law Quarterly* 52 (1996).

41 The (civil) contempt of court is a cornerstone of all common law civil justice systems around the world. For monographic accounts of this fundamental legal institution in the English context, see Arlidge, Eady and Smith, *On Contempt* 892 (Sweet and Maxwell, London, 2011); C.J. Miller, *Contempt of Court* (Oxford University Press, Oxford, 2000); Borrie and Lowe, *The Law of Contempt* (Butterworths, London, 1996); M. Zander, "Contempt of Court", in *Halsbury's Law of England* (LexisNexis, London, 2012), vol. XXII. In the American legal scholarship, see M. Livingston, "Disobedience and Contempt", 75 *Washington Law Review* 345 (2000); L.N. Gray, "Criminal and Civil Contempt: Some Sense of a Hodgepodge", 72 *St. John's Law Review* 337 (1998).

42 *Astreintes* are court orders for the payment of a fine for each day the debtor delays compliance with the judgment. They are for the benefit of the creditor. See S.

many,[43] and, indeed, the so called "coercive measure" introduced for the first time in 2009 in article 614-*bis* of the Italian code of civil procedure,[44] and so forth - but these are never regarded as ways to "vindicate" the court's authority or dignity. While in the common law world wilful disobedience of court orders represents a sort of profound offence (as the word "contempt" literally indicates) against the court itself or the State and has to be, as such, punished in a quasi-criminal manner, in the civil law legal family, non-compliance is a matter of significance for the enforcing party only. Breach of civil orders is never considered a question of "public policy".

As has been pointed out:

> "*[T]o the non-common lawyer the contempt power is a legal technique which is not only unnecessary to a working legal system, but also violates basic philosophical approaches to the relations between government bodies and people*".[45]

Or, as Alexander Pekelis (a sadly forgotten Italo–American civil procedural scholar of the last century) remarked convincingly:

> "*this very concept of contempt simply does not belong to the world of ideas of a Latin lawyer. It just does not occur to him that the refusal of the defendant to deliver to the plaintiff a painting sold to the latter (...) may, as soon as judicial order is issued, become a matter to a certain extent personal to the court, and that the court may feel hurt, insulted, "contemned", because its order has been neglected or wilfully disobeyed*".[46]

Guinchard and T. Moussa (ed.), *Droit et pratique des voies d'exécution* (Dalloz, Paris, 2014) sect. 400.05. This model has been transplanted – to remain in the European continent - also in Luxembourg, Belgium, and the Netherlands. See J. Van Compernolle, G. De Leval, *L'astreinte* (Larcier, Luxembourg, 2007).

43 § 888 and 890 of the *Zivilprozessordung*. The sum of money, unlike in the French and Italian model, is to be paid to the State (and not to the plaintiff). See, for a domestic as well comparative account, O. Remien, *Rechtsverwirklichung durch Zwangsgelsd: Vergleich – Vereinheitlichung – Kollisionsrecht* (Tübingen: Mohr, 1992).

44 For an overview in English, see E. Silvestri, "The Devil is in Details. Remarks on Italian Enforcement Procedures", in: R. van Rhee, A. Uzelac, *Enforcement and Enforceability. Tradition and Reform* 207 (Intersentia, Antwerp, 2010). In Italian, see the collection of essays edited by S. Chiarloni, "L'esecuzione indiretta ai sensi dell"art. 614 *bis* c.p.c.: confini e problemi", *Giurisprudenza Italiana* 731 (2014).

45 R. Goldfarb, "The History of the Contempt Power", 1961 *Washington University Law Quarterly* 1, 2.

46 Pekelis, *supra*, n. 38, at 668; Chesterman, *supra,* n. 38, at 541.

On the side of technical solutions, neither in France, nor Italy nor Spain is it possible to commit the unwilling debtor to prison. In Germany, this is theoretically possible, but only in very few cases, and even when it is possible, however, imprisonment as a way of enforcement is in fact almost never used. Conversely, in common law countries, the imprisonment of a person found guilty of civil contempt is a rather common practice, especially in the United States. According to their doctrine, as the saying goes, those in jail for civil contempt are ironically said to hold the keys to their cells, as all they need to be set free is to obey the court orders. The famous legal case *Chadwick v. Janecka* – just to name the most impressive one - is, to this extent, emblematic. Here, H. Betty Chadwick, a Pennsylvania lawyer, has been in prison for fourteen years only because he refused to disclose to the court his assets in a matrimonial proceeding. Needless to say that he would have spent less time in prison if he had "simply" stolen the money.[47]

My key questions are: how can we compare such different legal techniques to each other? And, most importantly, what results can be reached (i.e. how can this diversity in approaches be explained?) in order to advance our legal knowledge and mutual understanding, which is one of the purposes of comparative law analysis?

(b) In Search of the Common Need

According to the methodology initially proposed, the first step is to show that all coercive tools - no matter how differently they function in practice - are comparable with each other since they clearly respond to the same (and essentially political) *social need* of enforcing the principle of effect-

47 *Chadwick v. Janecka*, 312 F.3 d 597 (3 d Cir. 2002). This case is discussed in M.J. Frank, "Modern Odysseus of Classic Fraud – Fourteen Years in Prison for Civil Contempt Without a Jury Trial, Judicial Power Without Limitations, and an Examination of the Failure of Due Process", 66 *University of Miami Law Review* 599 (2012). On the implication of the obstinate disobedience on civil contempt of court, D. Rendleman, "Disobedience and Coercive Contempt Confinement: The Terminally Stubborn Contemnor", 48 *Washington and Lee Law Review* 185 (1991). To overcome this serious problem, in the English legal system, now, the contemnor can be condemned to up to two years of imprisonment, if the contempt conduct has occurred before a Superior Court. See the *Contempt of Court Act*, 1981, s14 (4).

ive judicial protection. Basically, their function is to turn judges' words into facts (when materially possible, ethically opportune or reasonable to do so[48]), to prevent that court decisions will not be followed by actions, to enhance, on a more general scale, the "rule of law", i.e. the supremacy of the law as embodied in a binding legal judgment over the personal will of people.[49]

More precisely, the task of all coercive tools is to foster the so-called principle of "Effective Judicial Protection", a principle that is provided, in Europe, now by Article 6(i) of the European Convention on Human Rights (which generally protects the right to a fair trial), but that is also a general rule which is part of the very foundation of any system ruled by law.[50]

---

48 It is neither opportune nor materially feasible to force the party to comply with judgments requiring to do something considered highly personal, or involving personal characteristics or abilities (for example in the case of contract for personal servicces). In such cases, in order to safeguard the personal freedom of the debtor, common law courts are very reluctant to grant specific remedies. For the common law development on this point, see the landmark decisions *Clark v. Price* [1819] 2 Wils Ch 157 and *De Francesco v. Barnun*, [1890] 45 Ch D 430; also, C.D. Ashley, "Specific Performance by Injunction", 6 *Columbia Law Review* 82 (1906). The same rule is applied in the field of labour law, in order to prevent what is called the "involuntary servitude" of the employee (see for example, in England, the *Trade Union and Labour Relations Act*, 1992, s.236). No statutory limitation exists in the French code, but a similar result is reached by judicial application (see, for a critical analysis, A. Lebois, "Les obligations de faire à caractère personnel", in *Juris Classeur Per.* (2008) I, 210). In Italy the text of the article 614 *bis* of the Civil Procedure Code expressly forbids the pronouncement of monetary penalties in such cases. Now, the same principle is applied by the Principles of European Contract Law (P.E.C.L.), art. 9:102, by the Unidroit Principles, art. 7.2.2., and by the Draft Common Frame of Reference (D.C.F.R.) of European Contract Law, art. 3:302, 3 and 4.

49 This link is especially stressed in common law systems. See, e.g., *Sherry v. Gunning* [2014] IEHC 411, *High Court of Ireland*: "The jurisdiction of the courts to enforce their own orders is an essential aspect of the rule of law". Cfr. also *United Nurses of Alberta vs. Alberta (Attorney General)* [1992] 1 S.C.R., 901 at 931 (Supreme Court of Canada): "The rule of law is at the heart of our society; without it, there can be neither pace, nor order, nor good government. The rule of law is directly dependent on the ability of the courts to enforce their process and maintain their dignity and respect. To maintain their process and respect, courts since the 12th century, have exercised the power to punish for contempt of court".

50 See A. Arnull, "The Principle of Effective Judicial Protection in EU Law, An Unruly Horse?" 36 *European Law Review* 51 (2011).

In the narrow sense used here - and for my current purposes - this principle means, amid many other things, that every national judicial institution *must* provide effective means to enforce judgments (especially non-pecuniary ones, such as injunctions) and that the remedies that courts deliver must be *effective*. All this has been clearly stated by the European Court of Human Rights for the first time in its path-breaking decision *Hornsby vs. Greece*.[51] In this case, Greek authorities refused to give permission to a British couple to open up an English language school, because they did not have Greek nationality. Although the Greek Supreme Administrative Court held that this refusal was contrary to the European Law that prevents nationality-based discriminations, and ordered the granting of a "specific remedy" (i.e., the permission to open up the school), Greek administrative officials did not comply with this order, and the couple was then only awarded damages, i.e. a sum of money for their actual loss. The European Court of Human Rights then condemned Greece, on the basis that Article 6 of the Convention requires final judgments to be *exactly* enforced, when possible. The Court persuasively argued (§ 40) that the right of access to court "would be illusory if a Contracting State's domestic legal system allowed a final, binding judicial decision to remain inoperative to the detriment of one party" and - more importantly - that (§ 37) the "action for damages" provided by Greek statutory legislation "cannot be deemed sufficient to remedy the applicants' complaints" as "compensation for non-pecuniary damage (…) would not have been an alternative solution". Here the mere monetary compensation was found to be a qualitatively *inadequate* remedy, compared to the specific relief.

This decision has led legal scholars to talk about the rising of a real and true right to an effective enforcement of binding legal judgments.[52] I think, therefore, it is quite clear that all coercive procedural devices, whatever their nature may be, are expected to play a crucial and unique role in

51 *Hornsby vs. Greece* ECHR (1997). For a discussion of this case, see G. Lautenbach, *The Concept of the Rule of Law and the European Court of Human Rights* 146 (Oxford University Press, Oxford, 2013).

52 On the emergence of this new phenomenon in the European legal context see, in French, J. Normand, "L'émergence d'un droit européen de l'exécution", *Mélanges en l'honneur de Jacques van Compernolle* 445 (Bruylant, Bruxelles, 2004); J. Van Compernolle, "Le droit à l'exécution: une nouvelle garantie du procès équitable" in : G. De Leval and M. Storme (eds), *Le droit processuel et judiciaire européen* 475 (Bruxelles, La Charte, 2003).

every contemporary legal system. They are, in some ways, *necessary*. Without them – as Guido Calabresi and Douglas Melamed stressed in their influential study – if the defendant can only be forced to pay a substituted sum of money for having failed to comply with his primary duty, "property rules" granted by law would be converted into mere "liability rules".[53] If things were really so, we could say that the right to disobey a judgment is obtainable by the mere payment of a monetary penalty, and this cannot be deemed acceptable.[54] It is worth noting, incidentally, that this is what always happened in Italy, before the introduction in the code of civil procedure of the general coercive power in 2009, especially in the case of judgements ordering to do or to abstain from doing an activity that could be done only by the debtor in person, i.e. *infongible*).

(c) Explaining the Differences: a Cultural Approach

Let us turn to the main question: how can the technical differences be explained? Why is civil contempt of court so essential in English-based legal proceedings, and even unthinkable in civil law ones? Here it comes down to the "explanatory" power of cultural elements. My argument is that contempt power to punish disobedience with courts' orders can be fully understood only if we look at the different "image" or "cultural representation" of the figure of the judge in each legal tradition.

Crucially, I think that there is a sort of correspondence, or a connection, between the, so to say, "zero tolerance" for disobedience with judicial orders in the Anglo-American tradition (well expressed, indeed, by the civil contempt of court doctrine) and the image and generalised social perception of common law judges. To put it simply, while in common law jurisdictions judges are characterised by high social prestige,[55] and the judicia-

53 G. Calabresi and A.D. Melamed, "Property Rules, Liability Rules and Inalienability: One View of the Cathedral", 85 *Harvard Law Review* 1089, 1124 (1972) ("we impose criminal sanctions as a means of deterring future attempts to convert property rules into liability rules").

54 "The right to disobey the law is not obtainable by the payment of a penalty (…)", *Francome v. Mirror Group Newspaper Ltd.* [1984] 2 All ER 408, at 412.

55 In this sense, also J. Cuniberti, *Grands Systèmes de droit contemporains* 124 (L.G.D.J., Paris, 2011): "[l]*a stature du juge anglais n'est peut-être pas étrangère au développement d'une institution propre aux droits de Common law sanctionnant la désobéissance aux ordres judiciaires"*.

ry function is strongly "personalised", on the contrary, in continental legal culture, judges are essentially seen as bureaucratic figures that completely lack that paternal authority that characterises their common law counterparts.

In relation to this, I think there are (at least) two justifications in play.

The first one I propose to call "institutional", and it deals with the fact that, in England, the authority of the judiciary was initially derived from the Sovereign's powers. I am aware that all this is, in some ways, true, also in relation to the civil law jurisdictions and moreover, some scholars have rightly stressed how the contempt of court doctrine to punish disobedience, strictly speaking, was firstly conceived in the context of continental, Roman-canonical proceedings, as opposed to the English trials.[56] But while the evolution of the continental legal culture is marked by a complete rupture with the previous legal order due especially to the French Revolution and its marked anti-judicial ideology, so that judges were no longer seen as patriarchal figures, in England the division between the Middle Ages and modern times is much hazier. As is commonly acknowledged, the development of common law is better described by the idea of "continuity" than that of "separation".[57] The following example might clarify this argument. In late Anglo–Saxon times, the King was described as the *fountain of all justice.* According to the famous Blackstone's metaphor, jurisdiction is lake water, springing from the Monarch:

> "*[t]he course of justice flows from the King in large streams. As those streams run through his courts, justice is subdivided into smaller channels (...) till the whole and every part of the kingdom were plentifully watered and refreshed*".[58]

Accordingly, Sovereigns themselves could, and in fact used to, take part personally in their own courts. In this picture, the King delegated his power to carry out justice to the judges, in that they were nothing but the "impersonification" of the Sovereign in the realm. All this can be seen still to-

56 C. Besso, "La discovery anglo-americana: un insospettato trapianto dal processo romano-canonico", *Aequitas sive Deus. Studi in onore di Rinaldo Bertolino* 1193 (Giappichelli, Torino, vol. II, 2011).

57 N. Picardi, *La giurisdizione all"alba del terzo millennio* 53, 61 (Milano, Giuffrè, 2007).

58 These words are quoted by P. D. Halliday, "Blackston's King" in: W. Prest, *Reinterpreting Blackstone's Commentaries. A Seminal Text on National and International Contexts* 175 (Hart Publishing, Oxford, 2014).

day - although only in a symbolic way. The courts are The Queen's Courts. Judges are Her Majesty's judges.[59] In the United Kingdom, all jurisdiction still formally derives from the Crown. In such a legal context, it was quite clear that disregard towards judges meant disregard toward the King himself, and to disobey to the equity orders issued by the Lord Chancellor (who was dubbed as the "keeper of the King's conscience") meant nothing but an indirect disobedience to the Monarch.[60]

On the contrary, in civil law countries, courts' coercive powers, after the French Revolution, have developed mainly as a means of guaranteeing the specific performance of every obligation[61] – a principle that descends from the natural law and moral maxim "*pacta sunt servanda*" (literally translated: promises must be kept) and that traditionally does not belong to the common law legal tradition (at least in the field of contract law).

The second observation - in terms of political theology, I would say - has to do with the religious derivation of all legal professions and of the community of jurists as an *élite* in the common law world. Indeed, at least until the late Middle Ages, the King of England was commonly named as the "earthly living image of Christ" or "Vicar of God".[62] It is no surprisc, therefore, that those features were transferred from the Sovereign to judges, who still remain today, in the mode of thought of the common law lawyer, the "priests" of justice (common law scholars often think of judges

59 J. Jacob, *The Fabric of English Civil Justice* (London, Sweet & Maxwell, 1987) at 205.

60 Goldfarb, *supra*, n. 45, at 8 ("[t]he courts of early England acted for the king through the realm. And their exercise of contempt powers derived from a presumed contempt of king's authority"). This point is highlighted also by J.H. Beale, "Contempt of Court, Criminal and Civil", 21 *Harvard Law Review* 161, 162 (1908) remembering that, during the case of the committal of Prince Henry for contempt, the Chief Justice Gascoyn said, "I keep here the place of the king, your sovereign lord and father, to whom ye owe double obedience".

61 For the historical development in France (after the French Revolution) and in Germany of a system of coercive powers not directed to the body of wrongdoer (as imprisonment for contempt), but only affecting his wealth, see the informed historical analysis of Chiarloni, *supra,* n. 38, at 68, 72 (quoting J. Kohler, *Ungehorsam und Vollstreckung im Zivilprozess*, in *Arch. Civ. Pr.*, 80 (1893), 141 ff).

62 In the Italian legal scholarship, this topic has been recently explored and analysed by C. Costantini, *La legge e il tempio. Storia comparata della giustizia inglese* (Roma, Carocci, 2007). The appellation of *Vicar of God* of early Norman kings, as well its influence of the discipline of contempt are underlined by Goldfarb, *supra,* n. 45, at 7.

in theological terms).[63] The implied syllogism was this: if the Monarch represents the image of God on earth, and judges represent the King, then people have to obey judges as they indirectly represent God.[64]

Moreover, until the 16th century, the Lord Chancellor, who exercised jurisdiction in civil matters, had always been a high ecclesiastic dignitary, and his procedural devices and techniques were those used in ecclesiastical courts. On the contrary, in civil law jurisdictions, again after the French Revolutions, judges are no more seen as "cultural heroes or parental figures", as "their image is that of a civil servant who performs important but essentially uncreative functions".[65] In relation to the civil contempt of court, all that has been said can be still perceived today from the highly revelatory point of view of the language. Words such as "disobedience", "purging" (i.e., that sort of confession of guiltiness, where the contemnor must admit before the court his misconduct, acknowledge the breach of the order, express his regret and show a "suitable remorse"),[66] "debarment" (i.e., the formal exclusion of the contemnor from the legal proceeding), all evoke concepts such as "sin" and "redemption", that seem more strongly to belong to the religious sphere (or to that of the "father-son" relationship), than to the field of the administration of justice.[67]

---

63 See, for instance, P. Soper, "Metaphor and Models of Law: The Judge as a Priest", 75 *Michigan Law Review* 1196 (1977). The judicial function is often dubbed "secular priesthood" (P. Raffield, *Images and Cultures of Law in Early Modern England. Justice and Political Power, 1558 – 1660* (Cambridge University Press, Cambridge, 2004, at 7), or "secular papacy" (R. Dworkin, "The Secular Papacy", in R. Badinter and S. Breyer, *Judges in Contemporary Democracy. An International Conversation* 67 (New York University Press, New York, 2004).

64 For this kind of reasoning, D. Marrani, "Confronting the Symbolic Position of the Judge in Western European Legal Traditions: a Comparative Essay", *European Journal of Legal Studies* 45 (2010).

65 J. H. Merryman, *The Civil Law Tradition* 37 (Stanford, Stanford University Press, 1969).

66 C. O'Regan, "Contempt of Court and the Enforcement of the Labor Injunctions", 54 *The Modern Law Review* 385 (1991). For the need of a "suitable remorse" of the contemnor, see *Enfield London Borough Council vs. Mahoney* [1983] 1 WLR 749.

67 Pekelis, *supra*, n. 38, at 669, wittily describing the common law "judicial thinking": "he just disobeyed – a term that for a Latin lawyer's ear is likely to suggest a parent-child relation, rather than a court-party relation – he has disobeyed the court, he has been a bad boy, and he has to stand in the corner until he changes his mind. Nothing mysterious about it!".

To this extent, John Merryman – one of the foremost American comparative law scholars, and learned expert on civil law systems – by specifically assessing the absence of civil contempt of court in the continental systems, lucidly wrote that the parties, in common law legal proceedings, play out their role before the "father–judge", and that the whole procedure is "permeated by a moralistic flavour" - and of course the Anglo-Saxon ethic of Protestantism may have played a great role in this.[68] On the contrary, in the civil law legal tradition, given that the judge is merely "an important public servant, but he lacks anything like measure of authority and paternal character possessed by the common law judge", parties and witnesses "can disobey his orders with less fear of serious reprisal". Even if this description is surely simplistic, it encapsulates well the difference of attitudes towards judicial disobedience, rooted in the fact that the civil law legal culture is "thoroughly secularized, less moralistic, and more immune to the ethic of the time and place".[69]

(III) Conclusion – Is Jacques Derrida right?

This short article did not aspire to provide a comprehensive explanation of the differences and similarities between the legal techniques employed by civil and common law jurisdictions to enforce courts' order. More generally, my contribution aimed at showing that the task of comparative law scholars is "*valoriser la singularité juridique* (…), *travailler avec acharnement à l'entendement du singulier*".[70] In a period in which the dominant and conventional comparative legal discourse is seemingly concerned with "constructing" similarities, often to the detriment of cultural diversity, the mission of comparative lawyers is emphasising and giving value to the enriching differences existing between legal system. The problem, here, is a deeply philosophical one, and involves the translatability of cultural products, the role of one's own system of beliefs in shaping our world and how, and whether, it could be communicated. I chose as an opening line of this article a puzzling phrase of Jacques Derrida, that reads

68 As Denti, *supra*, n. 32, at 335 rightly points out, the Anglo-Saxon system has a"*derivazione religiosa e morale* (religious and moral origin) and it has been deeply influenced by the *etica del protestantesimo* (ethics of Protestantism).

69 Merryman, *supra*, n. 65, at 60, and at 122.

70 Legrand, *Le droit comparé,* supra, n. 6, at 125.

as "Peter" (in English) is not a translation of *Pierre* (in French), nor is "*Londres*" (in French) the translation of London.[71] What does this statement exactly mean, *per se*? Among possible interpretations, I think that this claim means that, even if at first blush two terms are *translatable*, they are not the same – i.e., in the speaker's mind they will always evoke different meanings, different images, different "social representations". The diversity of cultural baggage (i.e. values, ideas, metaphors, and the like) and collective consciousness between speakers entails that the word "London", in English, transmits further meanings that the word *Londres*, in French, does not (and vice versa). In the same way, a legal institution, even though comparable to another one, may carry legal meanings which may be absent in other cultural environments. So, I think that the civil/common law divide, although in many ways overstated and misleading to a certain extent, should not be totally abandoned, especially in the field of civil procedure. The existence of coercive powers to enforce judges' words in common law jurisdictions is certainly just a tiny example of a wider picture, but it shows quite clearly that the ways in which the judicial function and the figure of the judge is conceived remain fundamentally different between these two legal cultures forming the Western Legal Tradition.

The job of comparative lawyers is, indeed, to unravel these diversities and to attempt to explain them by giving attention to the intimate relationship between legal solutions and their cultural roots. In other words, we always have to bear in mind that "*la comparaison des droits sera culturelle ou sera pas*".[72]

71 For an analysis of Jacques Derrida's thought in comparative law, see P. Legrand, "Siting Foreign Law: How Derrida Can Help", 21 *Duke Journal of Comparative and International Law* 595 (2011).

72 These words belong, once again, to Legrand, *Le droit comparé,* supra, n. 6, at 125.

II. Beware of Legal Families: The Example of the Effects of Res Judicata Toward Third Parties

Valentin Rétornaz[*]

(I) Introduction

It is now a common place that the various legal orders of the world can be classified into different legal families. Many important books on comparative law, written by leading scholars, contain such a classification.[1] Even if this taxonomic approach is sometimes challenged for being too oriented towards the Western World,[2] it is still considered a useful epistemological tool.[3] Coming to Europe, the most important distinction generally made is that between the *common law* family and the *continental European* legal family.[4] It has even been put forward that these families were "*the two greatest juridical systems of the world*".[5]

---

* Assistant Professor for Civil and Comparative Law at Galatasaray University (Istanbul); PhD in Law (Neuchâtel and Dijon Universities, 2013).

1 See for instance: R. David and C. Jauffret-Spinozi, *Les grands systèmes de droit contemporains*, (11th ed., Dalloz, Paris, 2002) ; H. P. Glenn, *Legal Traditions of the World – Sustainable Diversity in Law*, (5th ed., Oxford University Press, 2014) ; M. G. Losano, *I grandi sistemi giuridici: introduzione ai diritti europei ed extraeuropei*, (Laterza, Rome, 2000); K. Zweigert and H. Kötz, *Einführung in die Rechtsvergleichung: auf dem Gebiete des Privatrechts*, (3rd edition, J.C.B. Mohr (Paul Siebeck), Tübingen, 1996).

2 For a restatement to the critics directed to the approach followed by the above-mentioned authors: U. Mattei, "Three Patterns of Law: Taxonomy and Change in the World Legal Systems", 45 *The American Journal of Comparative Law* 5, 8-9 (1997).

3 H. P. Glenn, "Comparative Legal Families and Comparative Legal Traditions", in: M. Reimann and R. Zimmermann (eds), *The Oxford Handbook of Comparative Law* 422 (Oxford University Press, Oxford, 2006).

4 For instance, Glenn, *supra* n. 1, at 132 ss and at 236 ss; Zweigert and Kötz *supra* n. 1, at 73 ss and at 177 ss.

5 M. Sarfatti, "Roman Law and Common Law: Forerunners of a General Unification of Law", 3 *The International and Comparative Law Quarterly* 102, 102 (1954).

Even if nowadays a certain tendency to mutual approximation,[6] especially in Europe,[7] has been identified,[8] this way of classifying legal orders is certainly still justified as far as *macro comparison* is concerned, especially when "*structural divergences*"[9] or "*mentalités*"[10] are investigated. But is it still the case when the investigation occurs at a lower level (*micro comparison*) in civil procedure? The question is not an easy one to answer. It implies going beyond all appearances, a situation which is far from easy in comparative studies.[11]

At first glance, the existence of substantial differences between continental and common law civil procedure still continues to be the orthodox view concerning the general features of occidental legal orders.[12] It is currently mentioned when some particular issues are dealt with.[13]At the same

6 On the harmonization of civil procedure, see J. Zekoll, "Comparative Civil Procedure", in: M. Reimann and R. Zimmermann (eds), *The Oxford Handbook of Comparative Law* 1337 ss (Oxford University Press, Oxford, 2006).

7 Through, for instance, the identification of a "Common Core" of European private law: www.common-core.org (last visited 3 June 2016). Some authors have already identified a "European Federal Common Law": K. Laenarts and K. Gutman, "Federal Common Law in the European Union: A Comparative Perspective from the United States", 54 *The American Journal of Comparative Law* 1, 1 (2006).

8 This trend is not a total novelty, see for a historical perspective: J. N. Frank, "Civil Law Influences on the Common Law – Some Reflections on *Comparative* and *Contrastive* Law", 104 *University of Pennsylvania Law Review* 887-962 (1956), at 887; R. H. Helmholz, "*Continental Law and Common Law: Historical Strangers or Companions* ?", 1990 *Duke Law Journal* 1207, 1207 (1990).

9 See on this idea: R. B. Schlesinger, "The Past and Future of Comparative Law", 43 *The American Journal of Comparative Law* 477, 481 (1995).

10 P. Legrand, "European Systems Are Not Converging", 45 *The International and Comparative Law Quarterly* 52, 62 ss (1996).

11 See concerning copyright and the "infamous moral right", which was for a long time considered as being a common feature of civil law countries: C. P. Rigamonti, "Deconstructing Moral Rights", 47 *Harvard International Law Journal* 353-412 (2006).

12 Zekoll, *supra* n. 6, at 1329-1330.

13 See the very general statement concerning the opening of a case: T. Schuster, *Writ – Claim form – Klage - Eine rechtsvergleichende Untersuchung zur Klageeinleitung im englischen und deutschen Zivilprozess sowie in aktuellen Konzepten für internationale Zivilprozessordnungen*, PhD Thesis, Göttingen, 2006, p. 3: "*Das englische Recht, insbesondere das Zivilverfahrensrecht, das mit dem materiellen Recht bis vor gut 100 Jahren untrennbar verwoben war, ist historisch einzigartig gewachsen*" (available at https://ediss.uni-goettingen.de/bitstream/handle/11858/00-1735-0000-0006-B351-7/schuster.pdf?sequence=1; last visited 3 June 2016).

time, the existence of some convergence areas has been frequently noted.[14] Finally, the drafting of the ALI/UNIDROIT Principles of Transnational Civil Procedure has also revealed that a common position on some disputed issues could be envisaged.[15] So the situation is far from being as straightforward as some authoritative statements may suggest.[16]

In order to test the suitability of any classification into legal families, it is important to deal with a subject that has been less investigated from a comparative perspective than others. Evergreen topics are more likely to confirm what has already been said. Moreover, the topic should also have been dealt with adequately in different legal orders. This is the reason why we have chosen the effects of *res judicata* toward third parties. The topic has been discussed in depth in various legal orders. Even if it has already been investigated from a comparative perspective,[17] it has not been the subject of numerous studies from that perspective.

Our purpose is more methodological than purely comparative. We will not go into all the details of the topic. Even if it seems to be a strictly delineated one, it still encompasses many legal controversies which should be dealt within the framework of a book, since it exceeds what can reasonably be done in a research paper. The main reason for such a difficulty is the fact that a general theory of the effects of judgments is difficult to achieve since it concerns a great variety of legal relationships. What is indicated in one context may prove to be wrong in another.

---

14 K. D. Kerameus, "A Civilian Lawyer Looks at Common Law Procedure", 47 *Louisiana Law Review* 493-510 (1986-1987), especially the conclusion at 508; S. Dodson, "The Challenge of Comparative Civil Procedure (Review Essay)", 60 *Alabama Law Review* 133, 143 ss (2008).

15 See concerning the standard of evidence: M. Brinkmann, "The Synthesis of Common and Civil Law Standard of Proof Formulae in the ALI/UNIDROIT Principles of Transnational Civil Procedure", 9 *Uniform Law Review* 875-892 (2009), at 875 : "*The [...] Principles must be praised not only for dealing with this sensitive matte rat all, but for developing a formula that accurately addresses the core element of fact-finding at trial while reflecting influences from both legal traditions.*" For a general restatement on this question: G. I. Seidman, "The New Comparative Civil Procedure", in: C. B. Picker and G. I. Seidman (eds), *The Dynamism of Civil Procedure – Global Trends and Developments* 23 ss (Springer, Cham/Heidelberg/New-York/Dordrecht/London, 2016).

16 See also Zekoll, *supra* n. 6, at 1336-1337.

17 See for comparison of religious Jewish law with common law: Y. Sinai, "Reconsidering Res Judicata: A Comparative Perspective", 21 *Duke Journal of Comparative & International Law* 353 (2011).

This is even truer when considering the potential impact of material law on procedural issues. Since legal concepts concerning contracts, tort, property or family law are different from one country to the other, they are also likely to have an impact on the way the effect of judgment is considered in these countries. If we want to understand the purely procedural aspect of the question, it is necessary to examine the situation when the material background is closely connected in all the countries considered.

For this reason, we will focus on two specific issues. The first one deals with patent legislation. The concept of patent is similar among the different occidental countries. Even if differences exist, they are not as fundamental as those among the various laws on contracts or property. For this reason, we will more specifically address the issue of the effects toward third parties of a judgment declaring void, or revoking, a patent. The second main topic is the effect of a judgment declaring an individual liable in tort. Shall this also bind a court in a subsequent suit involving a different injured party? It is true that tort law may be very different from one place to another. But the most important features of the institution are shared by many countries. So it seems interesting to see how the procedural aspect of civil liability is dealt with by the courts.

Since our investigation is essentially about the validity of the classification into legal families, we will firstly examine the question of the effect toward third parties in general in two different legal families: continental and common law. Then, we will assess whether this classification is still accurate, in a general way and when dealing with the issue of the effect of judgment toward third parties when dealing with the invalidity or revocation of a patent and the impact of a judgment holding an individual liable in tort, before reaching an overall conclusion.

(II) The "Continental Paradox"

(a) Common Roots: Roman Ambiguities

As is frequently the case with the continental European legal order, a look at Roman law can give good clues as to the core of the problem. Concerning the effect of a judgment on third parties, it is even the best way to understand why the question may sometimes look so difficult to deal with. Specifically, there are some discrepancies between various statements made at different places within the Digest.

(i) The Definition of the Exceptio Rei Judicatae

The first section[18] explains that, as a matter of principle, a judgment does not have any adverse consequences on those who were not parties to the proceeding (*res inter alios judicata aliis non prejudicare*). The rather long list of exceptions accepted in this section does not affect the validity of these rules which can be found in other parts of the Digest.[19] This first principle seems to be clear and to leave no room for any comment.

(ii) The Locus Standi of Third Parties to Appeal

Besides the definition of *res judicata*, another section of the Digest deals implicitly with the effects of a judgment by admitting the *locus standi* of third parties to lodge an appeal against a judgment of first instance if they can show a good cause.[20] If a judgment does not affect individuals other than the parties to it, why should those individuals have the possibility to contest it? Unfortunately, this question is not directly answered by the Roman sources. To make the situation more confusing, the same section also gives a list of persons who can legitimately appeal a judgment to which they are not parties, a list that does not overlap with the one concerning third parties bound by the judgment.

Scholars have made an attempt to bring into harmony the broad recognition of the *locus standi* with the lack of effect *extra partes* of the judgment by considering that a third party is bound by a judgment when the proceeding may have an impact on him and he is aware of it.[21] By making a distinction between a third party whose rights are not at all influenced by a judgment and a third party whose rights may be at stake, but who is not a party to the procedural relationship, it is possible to adopt a coherent interpretation of the various sections of the Digest.[22] If a third party is not participating in the proceeding, this does not mean that a judgment will be a

18 D. 42.1.63 (Macer libro secundo de appellationibus).

19 See D. 44.2.1 (Ulpianus libro secundo ad edictum); D. 44.1.10 (Modestinus libro duo decimo responsorum); D. 33.2.31 (Labeo libro secundo posteriorum a Iavoleno epitomatorum); D. 20.4.16 (Paulus libro tertio quaestionum).

20 D. 49. 1. 5 (Marcianus libro primo de appellationibus).

21 R. Orestano, *L'appello civile in diritto romano* 325 ss (Giappichelli Editore, Torino, 1953).

22 Orestano, *supra* n. 21, at 329.

sententia inter alios acta.[23] If the third party is the holder of the subject right at stake,[24] if his right depends on the rights of those who are litigating[25] or if he may be affected by the outcome of the trial,[26] he should be considered as potentially concerned by the *res judicata* and allowed to lodge an appeal.

(b) *Modern Hesitations*

(i) A Uniform Definition of Res Judicata

Modern continental legal orders follow generally the same pattern concerning the definition of *res judicata,* a pattern which is still greatly influenced by Roman law. When a legal definition exists, it always claims as a matter of principle that third parties are not concerned by *res judicata.*[27] Countries without a legal definition of *res judicata*, like Switzerland, generally follow a similar model: as a matter of principle the judgment is only binding on the parties.[28]

An extension of *res judicata* is exceptionally admitted in some precise situations, like inheritance or assignment of a right subject to a judgment.[29] Some legal orders go slightly further and consider that a judgment delivered against the administrator of an estate is also binding on the

---

23 Orestano, *supra* n. 21, at 330.

24 Orestano *supra* n. 21, at 331-333.

25 Orestano, *supra* n. 21, at 334-336.

26 Orestano, *supra* n. 21, at 337-339.

27 See art. 1351 of the Belgian and Luxembourgish Civil Codes; art. 1355 of the French Civil Code; § 325 of the German Code of Civil Procedure; art. 324 of the Greek Code of Civil Procedure; art. 303(1) of the Turkish Code of Civil Procedure.

28 F. Bohnet, in F. Bohnet *et al.* (ed.), *Commentaire du Code de Procédure Civile* (Helbing & Lichtenhahn, Bâle, 2011), art. 59 n. 129.

29 Art. 325 of the Greek Code of Civil Procedure; § 325 of the German Code of Civil Procedure; art. 303(3) and (4) of the Turkish Code of Civil Procedure. *Swiss Federal Court, 3 November 1998*, ATF 125 III 8. Under French law, this results implicitly from the case law according to which, the heirs are represented by their predecessor and cannot therefore object to the judgment: *Court of Cassation, First Civil Division, 29 January 1975*, Bull. civ. I, nr. 41.

heirs.[30] An enlarged admission of *res judicata* is rather rare, but not totally inconceivable. For instance, under German, Greek and Swiss law a judgment declaring that a debt does not exist can be invoked by the guarantor[31] and a judgment against a juridical person is also binding on its partners, at least as far as their liability for debts is concerned.[32] On this last point, French law is not totally clear.[33] Some other differences may exist between countries belonging to the continental tradition, but they are only related to secondary points. For instance, under French law a judgment given against one joint-debtor is binding upon the other,[34] but Turkish, German and Swiss law refuses this expressly.[35]

---

30 § 326 of the German Code of Civil Procedure; art. 327 of the Greek Code of Civil Procedure.

31 Art. 328 of the Greek Code of Civil Procedure; § 767(1) of the German Civil Code is interpreted by the case law as enabling the guarantor to invoke the existence of the judgment in favour of the debtor, see for instance: *Federal Court of Justice, Twelfth Civil Senate, 28 June 2006,* casefile nr. XII ZB 9/04, NJW-RR 2006, at 1628-1630. A similar approach has been developed in Switzerland by academics about art. 502(2) of the Swiss Code of Obligations: S. Zingg, in: *Berner Kommentar – Zivilprozessordnung* (Stämpfli, Berne, 2012), art. 59 n. 147.

32 Art. 329 of the Greek Code of Civil Procedure. Under German law this is seen as a mere consequence of § 129(1) of the Commercial Code which allows objections raised by the partner liable for debts of the company only as long as the company itself can rely on it (M. Roth, in K. J. Haupt *et al.*(eds), *Beck'sche Kurz-Kommentar : Handelsgesetzbuch* (36th edition, Verlag C.H. Beck, Munich, 2014), § 128 n. 43). In Switzerland, a similar interpretation of the corresponding provision (art. 569 of the Swiss Code of Obligations) exists also: *Federal Court, 10 February 1945*, ATF 71 II 39, at § 1.

33 In May 2006 a case was decided in the same direction as under Greek, German and Swiss law, considering that the managing partner of the company is implicitly representing the other partners in the suit concerning the debts of the company (*Court of Cassation, Commercial Division, 23 May 2006*, Bull. civ. IV, nr. 129). However, a subsequent case decided in December of the same year admits a challenge by the partner to the judgment opening the bankruptcy proceeding upon the company, if the partner is liable for the debts of the company: *Court of Cassation, Commercial Division, 19 December 2006*, Bull. civ. IV, nr. 254. So the extent of the power of implicit representation may depend on the peculiar nature of the case.

34 *Court of Cassation, Social Division, 7 October 1981*, Bull. civ. V, nr. 764.

35 Art. 303(5) of the Turkish Code of Civil Procedure; § 425(2) of the German Civil Code; *Swiss Federal Court, 26 September 1967*, ATF 93 II 329, § 3.

(ii) Different Approaches Concerning the Impact on Third Parties

1. Countries Where Third Party Remedy Against the Judgment Exists

In some countries,[36] the Code of Civil Procedure allows third parties to contest a judgment to which they are not party, even if they are not subject to *res judicata.* This special avenue can be considered as the modern version of the third party appeal known in Roman law. A direct connection between the Digest and modern law can be established for France.[37] Other countries took the French model, with some modifications.

Since a remedy open to third parties exists, it should have a conceptual justification. Otherwise, it is difficult to understand why a judgment may be contested by someone who is not at all affected by it. In other words, these legal orders need to find a way to cope with the paradox created by Roman law. *Res judicata* cannot be used, since it is limited to the parties to the proceeding. So a different legal institution should be created that describes the effects of a judgment towards third parties without being the same as *res judicata*. This is called "*opposability*" in France[38], "*reflected effect*" in Italy[39] or, simply, "*effect toward third parties*" in Greece.[40]

However, the distinction between this special effect *erga omnes* and *res judicata* is not always easy to make. As a matter of principle, French scholars widely agree that every court decision is "opposable" to third parties, without binding them in the same way as if it was a *res judicata.*[41]

---

36 Art. 582 to 292 of the French Code of Civil Procedure (*tierce opposition*); art. 1122 to 1131 of the Belgian Judicial Code (*tierce opposition*); art. 404 to 408 of the Italian Code of Civil Procedure (*opposizione di terzo*); art. 586 to 590 of the Greek Code of Civil Procedure (*Τριτανακοπή*).

37 H. Roland, *Chose jugée et tierce opposition* 14 ss (LGDJ, Paris, 1958).

38 Opposabilité: N. Fricero, "Autorité du Jugement", in: S. Guinchard (ed), *Droit et pratique de la procédure civile – Droits interne et de l'Union européenne* 1085-1086 (7th edition, Dalloz, Paris, 2012).

39 Efficacia Riflessa: F. Roselli, "Libro VI : Della Tutella Dei Diritti", in: C. Ruperto (ed.), *La giurisprudenza sul Codice civile coordinata con la dottrina* 52 (Giuffrè, Milano, 2011).

40 Τριτενέργεια: On this concept, see S. N. Kousoulis, *Η δεσμεύσις τρίτων απο το δεδικασμένο* 63 ss (Sakkoulas, Athens, 2007).

41 For a short restatement, see M. Douchy-Oudot, *Autorité de la chose jugée – autorité de la chose jugée au civil sur le civil*, Juris Classeur Procédure civile, Fascicule nr. 554, at § 150 and 151 and A. Lecourt, *Tierce opposition – Nature – Conditions de recevabilité*, Juris Classeur Procédure civile, Fascicule nr. 738, at § 4.

But the extent of this opposability is far from clear and case law seems to consider it as a sort of binding effect *sui generis*. Thus, the French Court of Cassation considered that "*opposability*" only had the consequence that a third party may be bound by a judgment but could not claim rights based on it.[42]

Nevertheless, case law may not be so clear in this respect. A subsequent decision of the French Court of Cassation illustrates this ambiguity. The case concerned the opposability of an arbitral award. A third party relied on it to substantiate a claim in damages for unfair competition and the French Court of Cassation admitted that the award was also binding in this respect.[43] In Italy, the question has also been the topic of intense discussions among scholars.[44] The case law of the Italian Court of Cassation makes the distinction between a third party whose rights depend on those of the original parties and a third party whose rights are considered as being autonomous. In this last case, a judgment can only be considered as a "*precedent*" and any decision[45] on the factual issues is to be considered as a mere "*clue*" in a subsequent proceeding.[46] If the right asserted by a third party depends on those of the parties in the first trial, the effects of a judgment may be extended to the third party.[47]

A possible way to explain the distinction would be that "*opposability*" or "*reflected effect*" are applicable as long as the third party is not contesting the judgment. If the third party remedy is used, then a subsequent court decision will change it to *res judicata* after having heard both the parties to the first proceeding and the contesting individual. In any event, even with this interpretation of case law, it is difficult to say that contem-

---

42 *Court of Cassation, First Civil Division, 25 May 1992*, Bulletin civil I, nr. 108. A recent case concerning the effect of a judgment declaring the owner of one plot of land is entitled to an easement is also mentioning the fact that this judgment is "*opposable*" to the owners of neighboring plots not involved in the decision of the case: *Court of Cassation, Second Civil Division, 25 September 2014*, Bull. civ. II, nr. 200.

43 *Court of Cassation, Commercial Division, 23 January 2007, Revue de l'arbitrage* 135 (2007).

44 For a restatement of the debate, see A. Proto Pisani, *Lezioni di diritto processuale civile* 367 ss (Jovene, Napoli, 2012)ss. Many thanks to my friend Francesco De Santis, *ricercatore confermato* at the University of Napoli for his very useful explanations on this issue.

45 Italy being a civil law country, precedents are not binding.

46 See the many cases reported by Roselli, *supra* n. 39, at 53 ss.

47 Roselli, *supra* n. 39, at 52.

porary continental legal orders have found a way to overcome the paradox created by Roman law. The distinction between *res judicata* and "*opposability*", "*reflected consequence*" or "*effect toward third parties*" is a mere way to go on with the same configuration, only using other words to describe the same things.

2. Countries Without a Third Party Remedy Against the Judgment

Some countries have attempted to solve the Roman paradox in a radical way; that is by suppressing totally any third party remedy. This is the case in Switzerland, Germany and Austria. In those countries, third parties cannot contest a judgment delivered in a suit in which they did not take part. The only possibility to complain is to contest the execution of the judgment,[48] a very limited avenue. Outside of this, there is no possibility to contest and thus no effect of the judgment on third parties. Conversely, the effects of judgments are limited to *res judicata* and affect only the parties to the proceeding with the above-mentioned exceptions.[49] Courts do not accept the "*opposability*" or "*reflected consequence*" of judgments on third parties.

There are always certain types of judgment which shall bind third parties even if the judgments do not constitute *res judicata*. A strict application of the general principles in this case is not possible, at least for reasons of expediency. Consequently, the legislator may intervene in order to extend the binding force of a judgment upon third parties. For instance, German law explicitly provides that judgments in parenthood matters have an effect *erga omnes*.[50] When a specific provision does not exist, courts and scholars may however follow a similar pattern without giving too much explanation. For instance, under Swiss law, even if no specific pro-

48 See art. 346 of the Swiss Code of Civil Procedure and art. 106 to 109 of the Swiss Debt Enforcement and Bankruptcy Act; §§ 770 to 774 of the German Code of Civil Procedure; § 37 of the Austrian Code of Execution.

49 For a clear statement: P. Gottwald, in *Münchner Kommentar zur Zivilprozessordnung*, ZPO § 325 n 8. See also, *Federal Court of Justice, Second Civil Senate, 8 November 2004*, casefile nr. II ZR 362/02, NJW-RR 2005, at 338-339; *Federal Court of Justice, Fifth Civil Senate, 20 October 1995*, casefile nr. V ZR 263/94, NJW 1996, at 395-397.

50 See § 184(2) of the Law on the Procedure followed in Family Litigation (*Familienverfahrensgesetz*).

vision regulates the effect of judgments in parenthood matters, a similar position as under German law has been defended both by scholars[51] and courts,[52] without giving any reasons behind this point of view. Conversely, in a Swiss case concerning the effects of an interim injunction in antitrust matters, the Federal Court decided that third parties could rely on it to raise a claim against one of its addressees.[53] In this case, the Federal Court merely relied on the necessity to "*ensure the effective application of the antitrust legislation*" as a justification for the extension of the effects of the interim measure decision.[54]

The mere fact that in different countries the strict limitation of the effects of a judgment to its parties themselves is leading to unsatisfactory solutions is regularly considered as an incitement to re-examine the question in the light of new ideas. In a certain sense, the Roman paradox created by the conflicting sections in the Digest should still be overcome, and not only with the suppression of any appeal by a third party.

A recent work published in Germany suggests a different approach, based, as in those countries where it is already accepted, on the difference between *res judicata* and "*reflected effect*".[55]

Another interesting attempt to solve the issue can be found in Turkish law. Albeit third parties can theoretically contest a judgment to which they are not parties, the Turkish Code of Civil Procedure is so restrictive that the limited avenue given to them cannot be considered as a genuine third party remedy,[56] like the one existing under French, Greek and Italian law. However, under Turkish law, judgments are considered as "*strong evi-*

51 For instance, see E. Roth-Grosser, *Das Wesen der materiellen Rechtskraft und ihre subjektive Grenzen unter der besonderer Berücksichtigung der Wechselbeziehung Zivilprozessrrecht-Bundesprivatrecht* 133-135 (Juris Druck + Verlag, Zürich, 1981) with a reference to German law.

52 *Federal Court, 17 February 1955*, ATF 81 II 33, § 3.

53 *Federal Court, 6 March 2001,* case-file nr. 5C.253/2000 (unreported).

54 See judgment of 6 March 2001, at § 4) d).

55 M. Markoulakis, *Die Betroffenheit Dritter von der Rechtskraft* 238-241 (Carl Heymanns Verlag, Köln, 2013).

56 See M. Yavaş, "Hükme Karşı Üçüncü Kişilerin Müracaat Imkânı", *Medenî Usûl ve İcra İflâs Hukuku Dergisi* 605, 636-637 (2008), where Turkish and French law are compared.

dence" against third parties.[57] This means that the finding of facts and decisions on legal issues in a judgment could also be invoked against third parties, unless they can rely on fresh evidence or demonstrate that the motivation is inaccurate.[58] This approach may present some similarities to the one developed in Italian law, but the reasoning leading to the result is different[59] since it is based on the evidentiary nature of a judgment rather than on its legal authority or binding force.

(III) The ''Common Law Diversity''

(a) The Common Roots: "Res Judicata", "Estoppel by Record" and the Lack of Effect Toward Third Parties

(i) The Basic Concepts

In the common law world, the binding effect of a judgment was for a long time plagued with many uncertainties. This can be explained by the concurrent application of two different approaches. The first one, generally called "*res judicata*" was manifestly inspired by the Roman principles also applied in continental Europe.[60] Briefly, English courts historically consider that a same "cause of action" could not be disputed twice between the same parties. This implies the demands and legal grounds in the two proceedings are identical.[61] Since civil actions were for a long time corseted in different writs, identification of the "cause of action" was a rather easy

---

57 A. C. Iyilikli, *Hukuk Yargılamasında Kesin Hüküm* 247, 291-292 (Yetkin Yayınları, Ankara, 2016). The same author suggests besides (at 354-355), that when a judgment has been delivered after a trial mainly based on the same contract as in the second case but between different parties, it should have a full authority amounting to res judicata. Among recent court decisions, see *Court of Cassation, Twenty-First Civil Chamber, 4 February 2016*, case-file nr. 2015/22431, judgment nr. 2016/1045 (unreported).

58 There are still some disputes about the real nature of this "*strong evidence*", see for instance: R. Akcan, "Yargıtay Kararlarındaki 'Güçlü Delil' Kavramının Hukuki Niteliği", *Selçuk Üniversitesi Hukuk Fakültesi Dergisi* 7-25 (2004).

59 At least for continental Europe, since some parallel can be made with the concept of estoppel by records used in common law countries, see *infra*.

60 R. W. Millar, "The premises of the judgment as res judicata in continental and anglo-american law", 39 *Michigan Law Review* 238, 238-239 (1940).

61 *Ibid.*

task. Alongside with the Roman *res judicata*, English courts gradually developed the concept of "estoppel by record", which has been claimed to be of Germanic origin,[62] an assertion we will not discuss here.[63] This second approach to the effects of a judgment is not based on the prohibition of a second litigation of the same issue, but rather is a consequence of the evidential nature of the records of the proceeding. According to this approach, all the "*determinations made in a prior suit [are] conclusive in a subsequent suit*", even if it is "*based on a wholly different cause of action*".[64] In this case, what the parties postulated before the court is no longer essential to the determination of the preclusive effects of the judgment; only the findings of the courts are paramount. This makes it possible to bar any re-litigation of factual issues, or legal questions, without making a reference to the specific claims they are related to.

For a long time, both approaches coexisted without a clear line drawn between them. So we can find examples where the words *res judicata* are used in a judgment even if the legal reasoning is closer to that of estoppels by record. For instance, in *Brandling v Ord*[65] of 1738, the Court of Chancery held that the mere dismissal of a bill on the implied assumption that the plaintiff did not have a valid title was not *res judicata* in a subsequent proceeding on the existence of the title. It is clear that the issue then at stake was not the preclusion of a claim, but rather the re-litigation of the title in itself. So the debate was more on estoppel by records than *res judicata*. Clarification occurred in England in 1803 in *Outram v Morewood*[66] concerning the unlawful exploitation of a coal mine on a land estate belonging to a third person. In a first set of proceedings, the defendants were held to be in trespass; they were also prevented from contesting this in a subsequent suit aimed at recovering the illegitimate benefits of their operation. The second judgment distinguished between the "bar" on a re-trial through *res judicata* which may only occur on the same cause of action, and the broader effect of estoppel by record concerning all potential

62 R. W. Millar, "The historical relation of estoppel by record to res judicata", 35 *Illinois Law Review* 4142 (1940-1941).

63 This assumption is merely based on the existing similarities between the concept of "estoppel by record" and the effect of judgment in Frankish Law (see Millar *supra* n. 62, at 44).

64 Z. Steakley and W. U. Howell, "Ruminations on res judicata", 28 *Southwestern Law Journal* 355, 355 (1974).

65 *Brandling v. Ord*, [1738] 26 E.R. 359, 1 Atk. 571.

66 [1803] 102 E. R. 630.

claims where the same issue is discussed as in the first proceeding.[67] A similar clarification occurred, at the federal level, in the United States with *Cromwell v. County of Sac*[68] which quoted, *inter alia*, the English case of *Outram v Morewood.*[69]

(ii) Parties Bound by the Judgment

Until the end the nineteenth century, both English and American law excluded the application of *res judicata* and estoppel by records when the parties were not the same, or privies, in both proceedings. An English judgment dating back to 1776 confirms this implicitly: *The Duchess of Kingston's* case.[70] The Duchess was accused of bigamy, in spite of the fact that her first marriage had been subjected to a sentence of *jactitation* by a Consistory Court. The House of Lords, sitting as a House of Peers, declared "*that a sentence of the Spiritual Court against a marriage in a suit for jactitation of marriage is not conclusive evidence, so as to stop the Counsel for the Crown proving the said marriage in an indictment for polygamy*".

Even if the judgment does not contain a reference to *res judicata* or estoppel by record, it has always been interpreted in the same way. The fact that the parties were not the same in both proceedings, the Crown being the prosecutor in the second case, and the Duchess of Kingston assuming there the position of the accused person, after having been the plaintiff in the matrimonial case, was considered as the reason why the House of Lords refused to give any precluding effect of the first judgment in the second case.

Mutuality of parties was considered as a requisite to any effect of a judgment. The only exception was made for individuals considered as being *privies* of the parties. *Privies* are those whose claims are deriving from a claim made by an original party or who are in mutuality of interest.[71]

---

67 Millar, *supra* n. 60, at 239-240.

68 94 U.S. 351 (1876).

69 See the above-mentioned judgment at 353.

70 [1776] 168 E.R. 175, 1 Leach 146.

71 See P. Barnett, *Res judicata, estoppel, and foreign judgments* 68 ss (Oxford University Publication, Oxford, 2001).

Even if the concept of *privity* frequently gave rise to debate,[72] the strong limitation put thereby on the effect toward third parties of any judgments was conceptually not different from the one followed in some parts of continental Europe. It allowed the extension of *res judicata* and estoppel by record to limited situations where a third party had sufficient links to one of the parties. Basically, this was deemed to be the case where a third party was the successor of one of the parties to the judgment, if he had been represented, expressly or implicitly, at the trial by one party or if he was actually controlling the way one of the parties was behaving during the trial.[73] Concerning the first two situations, continental European law says the same.[74] So it is not a surprise to find in an English judgment the expression "*res inter alios acta*"[75].

(b) *Subsequent Developments: Increasing Divergence Between American and English Law*

(i) American Law: Admission of Non-Mutual Collateral Estoppel

The requirement of mutuality in estoppel by records, also called "collateral estoppels" in the United States, was gradually considered by American courts and scholars as making its application unnecessarily difficult. The reasons for such dissatisfaction are not always clearly voiced and it is also difficult to assess the turning point when American law began to sever itself from mainstream case law. A frequent reason put forward is the necessity to avoid a multiplication of proceedings and to spare the resources allocated to justice.[76] So the relinquishment of the mutuality requirement

---

72 For a presentation of the old American case law : A. Engelmann-Pilger, *Die Grenzen der Rechtskraft des Zivilurteils im Recht der Vereinigten Staaten – Eine Darstellung mit rechtsvergleichenden Anmerkungen* 103 ss (Dunker & Humblot, Berlin, 1973).

73 Engelmann-Pilger, *supra* n. 72, at 104-107 (control), at 107-112 (representation) and at 112-115 (succession).

74 See as a remembrance, § 325 of the German Code of Civil Procedure.

75 See for example: *Meddowcroft v Huguenin* [1844] 163 E.R. 771, IV Moore 386. It is true that the case being one about the nullity of a marriage, it concerned a part of English law that was traditionally more influenced by Roman law.

76 See for instance: G. R. Cunningham, "Collateral estoppel: the changing role of the rule of mutuality", 41 *Missouri Law Review* 521, 528 (1976); J. S. Ellis, "Non-

was a consequence of the same trend that encouraged widespread recourse to coordination of litigation in cases involving complex litigation in order to ensure a coherent adjudication of the whole case. In fact, the relinquishment of the mutuality requirement is sometimes considered as a practical substitute for a class action,[77] even by those who oppose the change.[78] This point of view, however, should be nuanced.[79]

In *Bernhard v. Bank of America,*[80] the Supreme Court of California had to decide whether a judgement delivered in a suit between the heirs of a deceased person could be invoked by the bank where the assets were deposed in a subsequent proceeding introduced by some heirs against it. The Court decided then to lift the requirement of mutuality. This first case was gradually followed by other State courts[81] before being endorsed at a federal level in 1971 in a case concerning the invalidity of a patent where a company wanted to retry the issue in a subsequent proceeding brought against a different defendant.[82] In both cases, non-mutual collateral estoppel was used in a defensive way -that is, by the defendant in the second case invoking a judgment against the claim in a previous proceeding with a third party. This change in the case law was masterfully confirmed some years later in a case where non-mutual collateral estoppel was invoked by the claimants in a class action for security fraud against a defendant whose behaviour had already been subject to a declaratory judgment after a trial at the initiative of the Security Exchange Commission.[83] Well conscious of the possible adverse effects of allowing non-mutual offensive collateral

mutuality: Taking the Fairness out of Collateral Estoppel" 13 *Indiana Law Review* 563, 572-575 (1980).

77 D. J. Gunn, "The offensive use of collateral estoppel in mass tort cases", 52 *Mississipi Law Journal* 765-802 (1982). See also, concerning work place discrimination: J. A. Seiner, "Weathering Wal-Mart", 89 *Notre Dame Law Review* 1343, 1357 ss (2013-2014).

78 The first page of the following paper is particularly enlightening in this respect: E. E. Overton, The restatement of judgments, collateral estoppel and conflict of law, 44 *Tennessee Law Review* 927 (1977).

79 For a more balanced approach, see J. Ratliff, "Offensive Collateral Estoppel and the Option Effect", 67 *Texas Law Review* 63 (1988-1989).

80 19 Cal. 2 d 807 (1942).

81 Mississipi is one of the few States which still applies the mutuality requirement: *Bell v. Texaco*, 2010 WL 5330729 (S.D.Miss).

82 *Blonder-Tongue Laboratories Inc. v. University of Illinois Foundation et al.*, 402 U.S. 313 (1971).

83 *Parklane Hosiery Co. Inc. et al. v. Shore*, 439 U.S. 322 (1979).

estoppel, the Supreme Court considered that courts have a broad discretion in deciding whether they should admit it or not.[84] There is however a positive approach toward non-mutual collateral estoppel. For instance, the Restatement (Second) of Judgments states that the preclusive effect of non-mutual collateral estoppel should not apply only when the party against whom it is invoked "*lacked a full and fair opportunity to litigate the issue in the first action or [in presence of] other circumstances justify[ing] affording him an opportunity to relitigate the issue*".[85] Subsequent case law tends to admit broadly the use of non-mutual offensive collateral estoppel,[86] in line with the solution proposed by the Restatement.[87]

(b) English Law: The Rise of "Abuse of Process"

The evolution of English law followed a different pattern from American Law. For a while, courts refused to relinquish the mutuality requirement.[88]The first trace of an evolution goes back to 1889, in an ecclesiastical case.[89] A clergyman brought a claim against the bishop and the patron of a benefice, claiming that his resignation was null and void. After having lost this first suit, he was sued by his successor who was seeking an injunction restraining him from occupying the parsonage-house[90]. The defendant put forward again that his resignation was not valid, relying vaguely on the *Duchess of Kingston's* case.[91] The House of Lords held that "*it would be a scandal to the administration of justice if, the same*

84 Above-mentioned judgment, at 331. As far as the different ground for refusing it are concerned, see C.R. Callen and D. D. Kadue, "To Bury Mutuality, Not to Praise It: An Analysis of Collateral Estoppel After Parklane Hosiery Co. v. Shore", 31 *Hastings Law Journal* 755, 760-761 (1979-1980).

85 See § 29(1) of the Restatement (Second) of Judgments (1982).

86 See for a restatement of the case law: A. Conley, "Promoting Finality: Using Offensive, Nonmutual Collateral Estoppel in Employment Arbitration", 5 *UC Irvine Law Review* 651, 658-662 (2015).

87 Conley, *supra* n. 86, at 659.

88 *Carl Zeiss Stiftung v Rayner & Keeler Ltd. (No. 2)* [1967] A.C. 853.

89 *Reichel v Magrath* [1889] 14 App. Cas. 665.

90 Above-mentioned judgment, at 666.

91 Above-mentioned judgment, at 667. The citation of the case is preceded by a lapidary mention of "*fraud avoids everything*", a statement which is a manifest translation of the medieval dictum "*fraus omnia corrumpit*". In the case of the Duchess of Kingston, it is well known that the judgment of jactitation was obtained by

question having been disposed of by one case, the litigant were to be permitted by changing the form of the proceedings to set up the same case again" and "*there must be an inherent jurisdiction in every Court of Justice to prevent such an abuse of its procedure*"[92]. No reference is made, in the opinion of the court, either to the precedent quoted by the appellant, or to the concept of *res judicata* or "issue preclusion". The court only relied on the fact that the defence in the second suit was abusive and should not be accepted. The issue was thus examined from a different point of view without introducing any modification to the fundamental concepts. This is highlights a fundamental difference between English and American law.

Even if the doctrine of "abuse of process" was clearly formulated in *Reichel v Magrath,* it took considerable time before this new approach led to a substantial change as far as the effect of a judgment toward third parties were concerned. For instance, in *Gleeson v J. Wippel& Co. Ltd,*[93] the Chancery Division of the High Court considered that a first judgment declaring that the copyright of the plaintiff had not been violated could not be invoked by a different defendant in a subsequent claim based on the same setof facts. After having insisted on thc nccessity to maintain the requirement of mutuality,[94] Vice-Chancellor Megarry reminded that "*the jurisdiction to strike out an endorsement or pleading, whether under the rules or under the inherent jurisdiction, should be exercised with great caution, and only in plain and obvious cases that are clear beyond doubt*"[95] considering that he could not "*say that it is in the least plain, obvious or clear beyond doubt that the action cannot succeed, or is an abuse of the process of the court*".[96] It is interesting to note that the issue the court had to deal with was similar to the one at stake in the American case of *Blonder-Tongue Laboratories Inc. v. University of Illinois Foundation et al.* In this case the courts had to decide whether a judgment about the

---

fraud, the relevant part of the marriage register being deleted before the trial in order to be sure that the conclusion of the marriage was almost impossible to demonstrate. This may explain the strange reference to the case. However, it is difficult to understand how the reasoning is accurate in the context of the litigation about the ecclesiastical benefice. This may be explained by the fact that the clergyman was representing himself before the House of Lords...

92 Above-mentioned judgment, at 668, per Lord Halsbury.

93 [1977] 1 W.L.R 510.

94 Above-mentioned judgment, at 514-516.

95 Above-mentioned judgment, at 518.

96 *Ibid.*

validity of a patent could be invoked in a subsequent infringement proceeding against a different defendant. The only difference between *Gleeson* and *Blonder-Tongue Laboratories* was that in the first one the invalidity of the intellectual property right was not at stake, but rather its infringement by the commercialization of a shirt.

The first case in which the loosening of the requirement of mutuality in English law through the doctrine of the abuse of process was confirmed concerned civil liability for torture. After having been convicted for the bombing of a pub in Birmingham, the defendants claimed that their confession had been extorted under duress by police officers. The Court of Appeal considered that the question of the behaviour of the police officers had already been discussed during the *voir dire* of the criminal trial and the reopening of the issue in a subsequent civil case amounted to "abuse of process" leading thus to the striking of the case.[97] On a further appeal by one of the co-plaintiffs, the House of Lords[98] confirmed the judgment of the Court of Appeal excluding any "collateral attack" of criminal convictions through a civil case for police misconduct, at least unless the plaintiff could rely on "*new evidence [that] must be such as entirely changes the aspect of the case*."[99]

At first sight, after *Hunter v Chief Constable of the West Middlands Police* it seems that there should no longer be any difference between English and American law. Instead of directly abandoning the requirement of mutuality, English courts merely considered that its invocation amounted to abuse of process, a statement that sounds then like a mere rhetoric precaution. However, subsequent development of the case law shows that English law is still more reluctant to consider that estoppel may be invoked in the absence of mutuality of parties. For instance, in *Bragg v Oceanus Mutual Underwriting Association*[100] the Court of Appeal considered that a retrial did not amount to abuse of process, since the retrial of the issue was not "*frivolous but substantial*". In the same way, in *Bradford & Bingley Building Society v Seddon Hancock and others,*[101] the Court of

97 *McIlkenny v Chief Constable of the West Middlands Police and another* [1980] 1 Q.B. 283.

98 *Hunter v Chief Constable of the West Middlands Police and another* [1982] A.C. 529.

99 See the above-mentioned judgment at 545, per Lord Diplock.

100 [1982] 2 Lloyd's Rep. 132.

101 [1999] 1 W.L.R. 1482.

Appeal considered that "*since the pleading and the judgment were equivocal*" no abuse of process occurred if the issue was raised a second time. English courts do not follow a clear pattern as those in the United States.

The qualification as an abuse of process of any subsequent claim involving one of the parties to a previous proceeding is far from being systematical under English law.[102] Instead of imposing a blanket ban on retrial under specific conditions, like American courts tend to do, English courts "*will examine each case contextually and look beyond the mere concern of relitigation to determine whether there are additional elements that might justify relitigation*".[103] As explained by Lord Bingham in *Arthur JS Hall & Co v Simons,*[104] the House of Lords "*did not decide in the Hunter case that the initiation of later proceedings collaterally challenging an earlier judgment is necessarily an abuse of process but that it may be*".[105] For this reason it is always necessary to "*consider with care (1) the nature and effect of the earlier judgment, (2) the nature and basis of the claim made in the later proceedings, and (3) any grounds relied on to justify the collateral challenge*".[106] This allows some flexibility when dealing with particular cases. For instance, the Court of Appeal[107] did "*see no reason why it should be manifestly unfair to the Secretary of State [for Trade and Industry] that he should be required to prove the serious allegations he makes with regard to the conduct*"[108] of the defendant in a case of company director's disqualification, instead of merely relying on a previous judgment stating that the dismissal of the defendant had been justified by his misconduct. In the same way, when a party is claiming that he is a victim of fraud or dishonesty, the court may refuse to strike a defence raised by the defendant against the allegation, even if the contested behavior has already been discussed before an arbitral tribunal in a case con-

102 For a restatement of the whole case law : *Michael Wilson & Partners Ltd v Sinclair* [2012] EWHC 2560 (Comm) and *OMV Petrom SA v Glencore International AG* [2014] EWHC 242 (Comm) both concerning the collateral attack on an arbitral award.

103 E.R. Hoaken and R. Huang, "Abuse of Process by Relitigation", 35 *The Advocates' Quarterly* 403, 404 (2009).

104 [2002] 1 A.C. 615.

105 Above-mentioned judgment at 643.

106 *Ibid.*

107 *Secretary of State for Trade and Industry v Bairstow* [2003] EWCA 321.

108 See per Vice-Chancellor Morritt, at § 39.

cerning a third party.[109] The effects of the judgment toward third parties may also depend on the particular nature of the litigation. When serious allegations are made, like those concerning fraudulent behaviour, any previous decision on the issue may not bindthe interested person during a subsequent case.[110] For this reason, in our view, it is not possible to say that English and American case law had a similar evolution. As we have already seen, under American law, there is a positive approach as far as non-mutual collateral estoppel is concerned, leading to its wide application by the courts. Because of the lack of the same attitude on this issue, it is difficult to reach the same conclusion for English law.

(IV) An Attempt at Synthesis

(a) A first Conclusion: the Necessity of Going beyond the Legal Families

When considering the ways different legal traditions deal with the question of the effect toward third parties in a judgment, the first idea that comes to mind is that the problem transcends the classification into legal families. Both common law and continental legal orders face the same question: what should be done when the issue at stake between two individuals has also some importance for those who are not participating in the proceedings? It is interesting to see that the same trend can be found in both legal traditions. There is a tendency to accept that judgments have some impact on third parties. This is clearly accepted in common law jurisdictions and in continental jurisdictions where third parties have access to a remedy against the judgment. Even in those legal orders which limit the effects of judgments to *res judicata inter partes*, there is still a debate on the necessity to admit exceptions, or to radically change the approach.

If we go into detail, we can see that huge differences may exist between various countries generally deemed to be part of the same legal tradition. This is especially noticeable within the continental legal tradition where some countries openly accept the effect of judgments toward third parties,

109 *OMV Petrom SA v Glencore International AG* [2014] EWHC 242 (Comm).

110 For a very detailed analysis of the situation of a solicitor who was struck off the roll for dishonesty in a transaction and then contested the allegations of dishonesty in suit with his former partners: *Conlon and another v Simms* [2006] EWCA Civ 1749, [2008] 1 W.LR. 484.

and others deny it, at least *de lege lata*. Even within the common law legal tradition, frequently seen as being more monolithic than continental Europe, discrepancies exist between the American and the English way of addressing the issue. In some specific cases, legal orders belonging to different traditions have a similar approach to the same issue. This is the case, for instance, as far as the effect toward third parties of an arbitral award is concerned. The solution adopted by the French Court of Cassation is not much different from the result reached by a common law court through "*non-mutual collateral estoppels*" or "*abuse of process*". By the way, the parallel has already been drawn.[111]

A good way to overcome the classification into legal families is to 'look back' at the historical evolution. Sometimes it may bring different legal traditions closer by highlighting their common roots. This is also a factor that, in our view, tends to diminish the appropriateness of the classification into legal families. As far as the effects of judgments toward third parties are concerned, we have seen that until the 19th century, English law denied any impact of the judgment on third parties and followed generally the Roman approach of *res judicata*. The change camc gradually through the growing importance of estoppels by records. Nowadays, if the collateral estoppel or preclusion issue may be considered as something peculiar to the common law, especially when it is applied to third parties, it should not be forgotten that those differences are not any older than many continental codifications of civil law and civil procedure.

(b) Discussion of Two Specific Issues

(i) Judgment about the Validity of a Patent

As far as the validity of a patent is concerned, the solutions generally accepted in the various continental and common law countries are the same, so it is difficult to see any difference. It is accepted that a third party can successfully invoke against the owner of a patent the existence of a previous judgment declaring the patent invalid or revoking it. In some countries, this extension of the *res judicata* is a consequence of specific provi-

111 See S. L. Brekoulakis, *Third Parties in International Commercial Arbitration* 248-252 (Oxford University Press, Oxford, 2010); S. Bollée, "Les effets de la sentence à l'égard des tiers", *Revue de l'arbitrage* 695, 709 (2015).

sions. This is the case in France,[112] Italy,[113] and Turkey.[114] The existence of a clear legal text makes those countries less interesting from a comparative point of view, since the solution is dictated by the legislator without room for further discussion. It is also true that the effect of judgments toward third parties are sometimes considered, at least among scholars belonging to the continental legal tradition, as mere consequences created by material law itself and not by procedural law.[115] In our patent case, it could be argued that the extension of *res judicata* in the above-mentioned countries belongs to this type of situation and is only indirectly related to the procedural institution of *res judicata*.

However, when the legislator has not addressed the issue, case law tends to adopt the same approach as in those countries where special provisions have been adopted. Moreover, the effect *erga omnes* of nullity or revocation decisions are justified in the same way in some countries, even if they do not belong to the same legal family. Be it in Germany[116] or England,[117] the effect *erga omnes* is justified by the fact that decisions declaring patents void or revoking them are taken with retroactive effect and shall have the same effect as the patents themselves. However, in Switzerland and the United States, the reasoning leading to the same conclusion is different. The Swiss Federal Court considers that the effect *erga omnes* is a consequence of the registration of the nullity judgment with the competent public authority,[118] whereas the American Supreme Court relies more on economical arguments to justify the relinquishment of the mutuality requirement in patent matters.[119]

Even if our examination of the topic is a limited one, as there are obviously so many other points to discuss, it is interesting to note that in spite of the differences of approach, there is a common view according to which

---

112 Art. L. 613-27 of the Intellectual Property Code.

113 Art. 123 of Industrial Property Code.

114 Art. 131(3) of the Legislative-Decree on Patents.

115 On this type of approach, see Markoulakis, *supra* n. 55, at 151 ss. Unfortunately the author does not address the issue of the judgment declaring a patent void.

116 S. C. Micsunescu, *Der Amtsermittlungsgrundsatz im Patentprozessrecht* 14 (Mohr Siebeck, Tübingen, 2010).

117 *Virgin Atlantic Airways Limited v Zodiac Seats UK Limited*, [2013] UKSC 46, at 58, per Lord Neuberger.

118 *Federal Court, 9 October 1951*, ATF 77 II 283.

119 *Blonder Tongue Laboratories Inc. v. University of Illinois Foundation et al.*, 402 U.S. 913 (1971).

the declaration of nullity of a patent has an effect *erga omnes*. Since our enquiry is limited to the validity of the classification of the various legal orders into families, the reasons invoked to justify this extension of *res judicata* are of a subordinated nature. Be it because of the admission of non-mutual collateral estoppels, or because of the consequences of the judgment under the point of view of the material law, the interesting point is that all legal orders converge as far as this question is concerned.

(ii) Judgment on the Liability of a Tortfeasor Who Inflicted Harm to Many Victims

In this part, we will examine if a third party can rely on a judgment delivered on the issue of the liability, the factual aspect of the dispute being essentially the same. This type of situation may be encountered when a single tortfeasor is inflicting damages ona great number of individuals through his behaviour. If one of the victims has successfully recovered his loss, can thc othcrs rcly on the judgment in order to bolster their position during a subsequent trial ?[120] Even if the answers given by the various legal orders are far from being as clear and unanimous as with the patent case, many interesting results can still be discussed.

Within the common law family, the position is quite clear: a third party can rely on the judgment in order to avoid that the tortfeasor attempts to evade his liability by contesting a second time factual and legal issues that have already been discussed during the first trial. This is particularly clear under American law where "offensive non-mutual collateral estoppel" was first allowed in a case concerning a high scale security fraud.[121] Even if the English "doctrine of abuse of process" leaves some door open, at least theoretically,[122] for a "collateral attack" on a judgment, this is only possible when the interested party can rely on serious ground. Otherwise, any further litigation on the issue would amount to bringing the administration of justice into disrepute. In a case concerning the tort of negligence, engi-

120 In some legal orders, the question can be answered with a class action. We will not discuss this particular issue.

121 *Parklane Hosiery Co. Inc. et al. v. Shore*, 439 U.S. 322 (1979).

122 See for a discussion of some apparent incoherencies within the case law: L. Haller, "Abuse of Process, collateral attack and claims against lawyers", 34 *Civil Justice Quaterly* 377, 386-387 (2015).

neers were held liable for the damages sustained by an individual during an explosion in a tunnel they had designed. The defendants then attempted to have the issue reopened when they were sued by the public body which commissioned the work. This was considered as being an abuse of process.[123] In spite of the peculiarities of the English case law, it seems that the tortfeasor would not be allowed to re-litigate his liability when he is sued by different victims.

Coming to the continental legal family, the situation is far from being so clear. As a matter of principle, there would not be any binding effect of the first judgment in a second trial as far as German law is concerned, even if a clear case cannot be found in this respect. It seems that the point is considered as being so obvious that it does not need clear case law. The situation is far from being so evident under Swiss law. As already explained, Switzerland does not recognize any effect of a judgment toward third parties as a matter of principle. But in an isolated case, an exception was made by the Federal Court without giving much explanation.[124] The case concerned antitrust legislation. An insurance company was sued by a private hospital claiming that the refusal to admit it as health service provider amounted to restrictive practice.[125] Within the course of the trial, an interim injunction was issued, according to which the insurance company had to provisionally admit the hospital as a health service provider. One of the insured persons underwent surgery in this hospital, but the insurance company still refused to pay the bill. The case was brought before the courts and the defending company claimed that its client could not rely on the interim injunction since she was not a party to it. The Federal Court considered that the necessity to "*ensure the effective application of the antitrust legislation*" implied that the insured person could benefit from the interim injunction even if it had never been a party to the suit during which it had been issued.[126] Should we consider that the smooth enforcement of tort legislation may, conversely, command the extension of the *res judicata* of a previous judgment holding the torfeasor liable? In the absence of subsequent cases litigating the issue, it is almost impossible to give a conclusive answer. Furthermore, academics generally do not discuss the issue. At the limit, indications are that an extension of the *res ju-*

123 *North West Water Authority v Binnie* [1990] 3 All E.R. 547.

124 *Federal Court, 6 March 2001*, casefile nr. 5C.253/2000 (unreported).

125 Above-mentioned judgment, at § D and F.

126 Above-mentioned judgment, at § 4) d).

dicata could be envisaged when its advantages override the potential risk of misadministration of justice[127] or when there is no risk of violation of the right to be heard.[128] Both approaches seem to very close to the justifications that can be encountered in common law jurisdictions in favour of an extension of the effect of a judgment toward third parties.

Even if the case law is more settled in France than in Switzerland, some difficulties remain when it comes to dealing with the issue of the consequence of a judgment declaring the liability of the tortfeasor in a subsequent suit based on the same damaging event. Some of the case law of the Court of Cassation tends to admit that a previous judgment on the liability for breach of a contract of an individual may be invoked in a subsequent trial, either by himself[129] or against him.[130] It is not difficult to figure out that the same point of view could be defended, even more easily[131], if the first trial was asserting the liability in tort. However, all the judgments have been rendered by the same division of the Court of Cassation, the Commercial Division, in cases concerning the effects toward third parties of an arbitral award. Considering the peculiarities of the issue at stake, it is difficult to determine whether the same principle would apply in the whole field of torts. Moreover, this case law has been strongly criticized by French scholars themselves and it does not seem to be followed by all the French courts.[132] For instance, the Court of Appeal of Colmar held that a judgment, delivered in a suit between the buyer and the seller of a flat affected by a design fault, could not be invoked by the administration of the condominium in a suit against the buyer concerning his liability in the aggravation of the situation.[133] Even if no mention is made of the case law on arbitration, it is implicitly repudiating it. But the issue will remain open until the Court of Cassation itself brings a conclusion to the debate.

---

127 Zingg, *supra* n. 31, art. 59 n. 132.

128 L. Marti-Schreier, *Vertragliche Drittschadensliquidation – Geltungsbereich und Durchführung* 175 (Bern, Stämpfli, 2015).

129 *Court of Cassation, Commercial Division, 7 January 2004*, Bull. civ. IV, nr. 4; *Court of Cassation, Commercial Division, 7 October 2014*, casefile nr. 13-22623 (unreported).

130 *Court of Cassation, Commercial Division, 23 January 2007*, *Revue de l'arbitrage* 135 (2007); *Court of Cassation, Commercial Division, 26 May 2009*, casefile nr. 08-11588 (unreported).

131 Since the liability in tort is based on the violation of general duties.

132 See for a restatement: Bollée, *supra* n. 111, at 709-712.

133 *Court of Appeal of Colmar, 3 April 2008*, casefile nr. 06/00607 (unreported).

In conclusion, we can see that the discussion of a very common issue, namely the effects toward third parties of a judgment on the liability in tort, may give rise to very interesting discussions in all the legal orders. Firstly, it brings closer the United States and England, two countries which do not usually always follow the same pattern in this field. Secondly, it highlights interesting debates within legal orders belonging to the continental tradition. Both in France and in Switzerland, there are some judgments which tend to follow the same approach as in the common law systems. Even if they do not constitute a well-established case law in this respect, they still show us that thesame type of argument may be encountered in different legal families. This is also reduces the importance of the taxonomy of legal orders.

(V) Conclusion

Our purpose with this paper was not limited to a presentation of the different approaches concerning the effects toward third parties of judgments. What we intended was to examine whether the classification into legal families is still accurate when doing '*micro comparison*'. Can we reach a conclusion on this point?

As already indicated, the differences between legal traditions tend to vanish from this perspective. Differences among the members sometimes look bigger than their similarities and, conversely, unpredictable reconciliation between members of different legal traditions may be noticed. So the classification into families may not be very important. This is especially striking when considering that historical research may also help in overcoming any bias linked to this way of thinking.[134]As well, the discussion of specific issues also shows that intellectual connections can be identified between the various legal orders, even if they do not belong to the same legal family. For instance, an interesting unity exists as far as the consequences of a declaration of the nullity of a patent are concerned, even if the reasoning may not be the same everywhere. Conversely, the effects of a previous judgment holding an individual liable may show that even if

134 See also Zekoll, *supra* n. 6, at 1329 : " *the historical perspective no longer support the idea that procedural systems can be neatly divided into the legal families of Romanic, Germanic, and Anglo-American procedure*".

the legal orders do not arrive at the same solution, the arguments on the topic may be widely shared.

This being said, we are well conscious of the fact that our conclusion may not be absolute. Our purpose is not to deny any pertinence to the classification of legal orders into the common law or continental legal families. There are areas where the differences are sharp and clearly noticeable. But sometimes it should not be forgotten that classification, like every rational product of the mind, may suffer exceptions.

III. Statistical Methods in Comparative Civil Procedure – Chances and Risks Christoph A. Kern

*Christoph A. Kern**

(I) Introduction

Comparative civil procedure can still be considered a relatively young field of study. Of course, some legal scholars have been interested in the procedural law of foreign countries at all times. However, it was only in the second half of the last century that comparative civil procedure developed into a field of study of its own. Thus, the modern comparative law movement, which had started around the transition from the 19th to the 20th century, reached civil procedure with a delay of half a century.

Despite this late beginning, comparative civil procedure today shares many of the trends and developments in other areas of comparative law. One of the latest trends is the use of statistical methods. This is not to say that using statistics was completely new for legal scholars. Traditional statistical data like the number of court filings have been collected for centuries, and they also were used by legal academics from time to time. What has not been done in the past, though, was to collect large, cross-country samples of empirical data and to combine these data using statistical methods to determine correlations. This, in turn, cannot come as a surprise: As far as collecting large cross-country samples of empirical data is concerned, international cooperation and communication was much more burdensome in less globalized times, in particular, before the internet had spread its web over the whole world and facilitated all forms of cooperation and communication. As regards combining large datasets using statistical methods, progress in the information technology played a role as

* Professor for Private Law and Civil Procedure, Heidelberg University, Institute for Comparative Law, Conflict of Laws and International Business Law, and professeur remplaçant, droit privé allemand, Université de Lausanne. Dr. iur. (Freiburg University); LL.M. (Harvard).

well: Only since a few decades, computers have been powerful enough to do the necessary calculations in reasonable time.

Still, even the best theoretical possibilities do not become relevant if nobody discovers how these possibilities can be used. This is where economists come into play – to be precise, a certain approach in economic research, namely Comparative Economics.[1] Historically, the main interest of this discipline was a comparison between capitalism and socialism.[2] It obviously lost much of its appeal with the collapse of socialism in Eastern Europe and the Soviet Union.[3] But, in its struggle to survive, this discipline has discovered that there exist considerable differences among those economic systems which are generally regarded as capitalist economies. Consequently, Comparative Economics scholars have started to focus on comparing capitalist economies. Using all means of international cooperation and communication as well as up-to-date hard- and software, these new comparisons have become more and more elaborated. Typically, they are based on large, cross-country samples of empirical data and make extensive use of statistical methods. Most of these studies aim at finding out which institutional and, in particular, legal environment "works best" in the sense that it has the highest correlations with other data which are considered to be positive. These other data are, for a large part, traditional economic data like a high market capitalization, but they can also be more specific like a short duration of court proceedings. Not surprisingly, many of these studies conclude by proposing reforms for those countries whose legal system is not in conformity with the "optimal" environment as discovered in the preceding analysis of the respective study.

---

1 S. Djankov, E. L. Glaeser, R. La Porta, F. Lopez-de-Silanes & A. Shleifer, "The New Comparative Economics", 31 *Journal of Comparative Economics* 595 (2003), first published as NBER Working Paper 9608 (2003), p. II, <http://papers.nber.org/papers/w9608.pdf> (last visited 5 May 2017).

2 See, e.g., A. Zimbalist, "The State of the Art of Comparative Economics", 31 *Comparative Economic Studies* 6 (1989); J. C. Brada, "What Is Comparative Economics, and What Ought It Be?", 31 *Comparative Economic Studies* 16, 18 (1989).

3 Djankov *et al.*, supra n. 1, at 596.

To date, such comparisons cover various aspects of our legal systems, as, for example, private credit,[4] the regulation of labor[5] and the regulation and supervision of banks,[6] media ownership,[7] and the regulation of entry of start-up firms.[8] Two of the studies deal prominently with civil procedure, one of them with procedural formalism,[9] another with judicial independence[10].

The purpose of this article is to briefly analyze some aspects of the approach in general, and to add some observations on the uses which have been made of this approach concerning civil procedure. A more thorough,

---

4 S.Djankov, C. McLiesh & A. Shleifer, "Private Credit in 129 Countries", NBER Working Paper 11078 (2005), <http://papers.nber.org/papers/w11078.pdf> (last visited 5 May 2017).

5 J. Botero, S. Djankov, R. La Porta, Florencio Lopez-de-Silanes & A. Shleifer, "The Regulation of Labor", 119 *The Quarterly Journal of Economics* 1339–1382 (2004), first published as NBER Working Paper 9756 (2003), <http://papers.nber.org/papers/w9756.pdf> (last visited 5 May 2017).

6 J. R. Barth, G. Caprio Jr. & R. Levine, "Bank Regulation and Supervision: 'What Works Best?", 13 *Journal of Financial Intermediation* 205 (2004).

7 S. Djankov, C. McLiesh, T. Nenova & A. Shleifer, "Who Owns the Media", 46 *Journal of Law and Economics* 341 (2003), first published as NBER Working Paper 8288 (2001), <http://papers.nber.org/papers/w8288.pdf> (last visited 5 May 2017).

8 S. Djankov, R. La Porta, F. Lopez-de-Silanes & A. Shleifer, "The Regulation of Entry", 117 *Quarterly Journal of Economics* 1-37 (2002), first published as NBER Working Paper 7892 (2001), <http://papers.nber.org/papers/w7892.pdf> (last visited 5 May 2017).

9 S. Djankov, R. La Porta, F. Lopez-de-Silanes & A. Shleifer, "Courts", 118 *Quarterly Journal of Economics* 453 (2003). Hereinafter, I will reference to this study as the "Lex Mundi Study" or simply the "Study". Unfortunately, the complete data used in the Study are not included in the Study's publication in the Quarterly Journal of Economics. Moreover, they are no longer available at the URL indicated in this publication's first footnote. However, the complete data were available in Excel format for download on the co-author A. Shleifer's website at the Harvard University Department of Economics at <http://www.andrei-shleifer.com/data.html> and on the co-author R. La Porta's website at the Tuck School of Business at Dartmouth, <http://mba.tuck.dartmouth.edu/pages/faculty/rafael.laporta/publications/LaPorta%20PDF%20Papers-ALL/Courts-LexMundiProject-All/Courts-LuxMundi.xls> (last visited 17 July 2006; these links are no longer good); there is no indication that these data are not the data actually used.

10 R. La Porta, F. Lopez-de-Silanes, C. Pop-Eleches & A. Shleifer, "Judicial Checks and Balances", 112 *J. of Political Economy* 445 (2004).

although still not exhaustive, discussion can be found elsewhere.[11] Whether the use of statistical methods in comparative law in general and civil procedure in particular will have a bright future or silently disappear, remains to be seen.

(II) Terminology

New fields of research typically bring about a new terminology. Indeed, it can fairly be said that the body of studies which compare the efficiency of legal systems in the world, with the help of extensive empirical data, analyzed with modern statistical tools, has not only developed into a new field of law and economics, but also added a new methodology and approach to comparative law. However, there is still no generally accepted label for this surging "new wave"[12] of quantitative studies. Sometimes, it is referred to as the "legal origins literature" or the LLSV papers, deriving this acronym four-letter code from the first letters of the last names of those four economists who pioneered this kind of research[13]. We prefer a less well-known, but more precise labeling, coined by a scholar active in the field, who calls this body of studies "numerical comparative law"[14] in place of "new comparative economics."[15]

For good reasons, this label contains as a signal the words "comparative law." Not only do these studies compare different legal systems, most of them also use the distinction of "legal families" or "legal origins", which

---

11 C. A. Kern, *Justice between Simplification and Formalism – A Discussion and Critique of the World Bank Sponsored Lex Mundi Project on Efficiency of Civil Procedure* (2007); C. A. Kern, "Perception, Performance and Politics: Recent Approaches to the Qualitative Comparison of Civil Justice Systems", 14 *Zeitschrift für Zivilprozess International* [ZZPInt] 445 (2009) = Percepção, Performance e Política: recentes formas de abordagem da comparação qualitative dos sistemas de justiça civil, 198 Revista de Processo [RePro] 321 (A. Will und T. Arruda Alvim Wambier, transl., 2011).

12 D. Vagts, "Comparative Company Law – The New Wave", in *Festschrift für Jean Nicolas Druey* 595 (R. J. Schweizer, Herbert Burkert & Urs Grasser, eds., 2002).

13 Cf. R. La Porta, F. Lopez-de-Silanes & A. Shleifer, "The Economic Consequences of Legal Origins", 46:2 *J. Econ. Lit.* 285 (2008).

14 M. M. Siems, 'Numerical Comparative Law: Do We Need Statistical Evidence in Law in Order to Reduce Complexity?', 13 *Cardozo J. Int'l & Comp. L.* 521 (2005).

15 Djankov *et al.*, supra n. 1.

is common in comparative law,[16] in their statistical analysis. Actually, these studies include a "legal origins" variable when determining correlations and running regressions; and the overwhelming number of studies find that most of their results are consistent with the distinction of legal families. This means that the "quality" of a legal system, the desirability of the solution which it has chosen in a particular context, appears to be dependent on this system's "legal origin".

The adjective "numerical" in turn, illustrates that this approach is not just a new trend in comparative law, not just a new way of describing and interpreting differences among the legal systems, but that it involves the use and analysis of information about the institutional environment, and in particular legal rules and concepts, expressed not in literary form but in numbers, thereby allowing the application of mathematical, more precisely, statistical tools. Herewith, it introduces a new methodology to comparative law.

Finally, our preference for this terminology has another, more pedagogical reason. By calling this body of studies "numerical comparative law" instead of using a more pale, and (for lawyers) frightening label (as new comparative economics with its reference to economics probably is), we hope to attract the attention of a greater number of legal scholars to this field. To date, the overwhelming number of researchers applying and discussing the new method has been economists. However, we are convinced that legal scholars could and should contribute to the debate.

(III) Quantitative Methods in Comparative Law

(a) Empirical Research on Legal Systems in General

This being said, let us now discuss some general questions of empirical research on legal issues.

Empirical research combined with statistical analysis is more or less widely accepted not only in natural sciences, but also in psychology, sociology, political science and, last but not least, economics. This fact of

16 Cf., e.g., R. David, *Les grands systèmes de droit contemporain*, passim (1st ed. 1964, today with Camille Jauffret-Spinosi in 11th ed., 2002); K. Zweigert & H. Kötz, *Einführung in die Rechtsvergleichung auf dem Gebiete des Privatrechts* 62 et seq. (3rd ed., 1996).

course suggests that it should also work in law. And indeed the collection and interpretation of statistical information on legal issues is by no means a sensational novelty. Rather, the use of statistical material before and after a law reform, has become increasingly popular with national and supranational lawmakers.[17] By the same token, courts and counsel have since long relied on statistical information provided by party or court-appointed experts – suffice it to mention the famous Brandeis brief.[18]

But there *is* an important difference between natural sciences, psychology, sociology, political science and economics on one hand and law on the other: Law can neither be understood merely by observing what happens in the real world, nor merely by looking into the codes, statutes and books. It is neither a mere description of social reality, nor does it limit itself to explaining how human beings interact. To the contrary, it is a theoretical framework, and a uniquely sophisticated at that, aimed at *influencing* the reality. Unlike other social sciences like economics, it cannot shy away from dealing with complex situations by limiting itself to simplifying models.

It is this combination of complex social reality and a uniquely sophisticated theoretical framework that makes the law – and, in particular, comparative law – so challenging, and grasping this difficulty with the tools of statistics is even more difficult. To our mind, it is crucial that researchers as well as their audience be aware of this extra level of complexity. This implies that researchers should ask themselves whether what they want to measure can reasonably be expressed in numbers. It further requires them to take into account functional equivalents as well as the respective social,

---

17 See, e.g., Lord Woolf, *Access to Justice*, Final Report, in particular Annex III, p. 349 et seq. (London 1996)(exhibiting statistical data on litigation costs); C. Hommerich, H. Prütting, T. Ebers, S. Lang & L. Traut, *Rechtstatsächliche Untersuchung zu den Auswirkungen der Reform des Zivilprozessrechts auf die gerichtliche Praxis – Evaluation ZPO-Reform* (Bundesministerium der Justiz, ed., Cologne 2006)(evaluating the 2001/2002 reform of German civil procedure).

18 L. D. Brandeis, Brief for the State of Oregon, Defendant in error (1907), in *Muller v. Oregon* (208 U.S. 412 [1908])(quoting, inter alia, from reports of the Massachusetts Bureau of Statistics of Labor, the California Bureau of Labor Statistics, the New Jersey Bureau of Labor and Industries, the New York Bureau of Labor Statistics, the Maine Bureau of Labor Statistics, the Maryland Bureau of Industrial Statistics, the Wisconsin Bureau of Labor Statistics, the Connecticut Bureau of Labor Statistics, and the Washington Bureau of Labor Statistics [p. 39-41, 47-48, 51-53, 57-63, 66-72, 74, 95, 97-98, 100-102, 104]).

cultural and economic environment. And it strongly suggests that they disclose to the reader the exact methods applied and that they openly discuss the strengths and weaknesses of their research.

(b) Particularities of the "Numerical Comparative Law" Studies

After these general remarks, let us now turn to the "numerical comparative law" studies in particular. As already mentioned, neither the use of quantitative methods nor the use of cross-country comparisons is something completely new.[19] However, there is something which is special about the new wave of "numerical comparative law" studies.

First, they use more sophisticated statistical methods to interpret the collected data. While in traditional studies, researchers often limited themselves to determining the mere numbers and, sometimes, the mean or median, researchers active in the field of numerical comparative law employ, *inter alia*, tests of means [t-stats], correlations and regressions.

Second, these studies typically claim to provide answers which hold true for the whole world, not only a country or a region with a relatively similar economic and cultural environment. This raises difficult questions about the collection and comparability of the data.

Third, many of these studies are authored not by unknown experts or private institutes hired by the state, a governmental agency or an international organization, but by famous academics from some of the most highly esteemed academic institutions in the world,[20] experts who appear to be neutral and therefore have a high credibility.

And fourth, these studies receive strong financial support not only by the institutions and countries where the researchers are based, but also by international development organizations like the World Bank. It is this important budget which allows them to conduct their extensive studies on an international scale. At the same time, the necessity of considerable sums of money and an institutional backing prevent others who lack such financial means and cooperation from engaging in the same type of research and thereby verifying the results.

---

19 Cf., e.g., Zweigert & Kötz, supra n. 16, at 14-16.

20 For other researchers, it is mostly impossible to receive or have access to research funds of the necessary scale; see infra.

These particular features give the "numerical comparative law" studies a particular weight in the national and international discussion not only among scholars, but also among policy makers. Therefore, such studies – that is, studies that can be expected, by their sophistication, comprehensiveness, and apparent neutrality, to find wide attention – should meet the highest standards. This is even more true if these studies aim at giving a recommendation: Due to the international institutions' (and, in particular, the World Bank's) attention to such recommendations, these studies have much more practical influence than open-ended, purely academic research.[21]

(c) The Siems Guidelines

Thus far, probably the most fundamental analysis and evaluation of this new method has been provided by Mathias M. Siems in an article published in 2005.[22] Unlike previous comments, this article does not focus on specific points of critique concerning particular studies and the data for particular countries, but asks whether the methodology as such, "numerical comparative law", "can be (or has to be) criticized or supported."[23] He assembles several "arguments against numerical comparative law" and confronts them with counter-arguments: Is it feasible to reduce complex legal phenomena to numbers? Is law extraordinary and therefore not a proper object of statistics? Is "numerical comparative law" too much focused on legal rules? And finally, is statistical analysis an acceptable method in the field of comparative law? He concludes that "[his] results are mixed" and proposes "guidelines"[24] which cover the following six topics: "necessity", "methodical awareness", "transparency", "comparability", "functional equivalents", and "reflections".

According to these guidelines, statistical methods may be "necessary" if a large sample of countries is to be compared.[25] Under the headline

21 Cf., e.g., J.-P., J. & H. Pauliat, "An Evaluation of the Quality of Justice in Europe and its Developments in France", 2 *Utrecht L. Rev.* 44, 45-46 (December 2006) (pointing to the "strategic importance" of the relevant World Bank documents and emphasizing that it is important "to avoid that quality becomes a political tool").

22 Siems, supra n. 14.

23 *Ibid.*, at 522, 528.

24 *Ibid.*, at 538.

25 *Ibid.*, at 539.

"methodological awareness", the guidelines contain a general appeal to scholars to be aware of methodological problems of numerical comparative law.[26] "Transparency" as used by the guidelines means information about the collection process and the meaning of the data;[27] one might add information about the way of aggregating the collected data the researchers have chosen.[28] "Comparability" as used by the guidelines refers to the question of whether information can reasonably be caught in data;[29] we would add the aspect of comparability in particular as to variables which decide on the "quality" or "desirability" of one or the other solution. To give an example, market capitalization can hardly be regarded as the perfect variable measuring the quality of certain aspects of corporate law, for countries differ as to the culture of corporate financing – while issuing new stock may be the preferred way in one country, in another country, corporations may have a traditional preference for bank loans, etc. The guidelines cover the latter aspect in part under the headline "functional equivalents", where they require that such functional equivalents should be included from the beginning.[30] Finally, under "reflection" the guidelines enlarge the field of research. Statistical data should not be seen as an aim of itself, but rather as the starting point of further research, which includes the "social, cultural and economic circumstances that underlie specific legal rules."[31]

(IV) The Importance of Transparency and Caution

In our view, the Siems article and the guidelines proposed therein do indeed address the most important problems faced by the use of statistical methods in comparative law. Despite the various lines of criticism, it seems unjustified from a conceptual point of view to categorically reject any statistical analysis in this field. However, it is extremely intricate to design a viable study. Therefore, any such study should disclose its weaknesses and make clear on which points it enters the area of subjective eval-

26 *Ibid.*, at 539.
27 *Ibid.*, at 539.
28 See Kern (2007), supra n. 11, at 64 et seq.
29 Siems, supra n. 14, at 540.
30 *Ibid.*, at 540.
31 *Ibid.*, at 540.

uations or even speculation. This is not only a matter of scientific candor and fairness. It also helps the authors themselves to fully and thoroughly contemplate their methods and conclusions. Last not least, the persuasiveness of a study is increased if its authors enter in an open dialogue with the readers, allowing them to better understand why, in the frequent case of alternatives, the authors preferred one over another.

In brief: We need *transparency* on the side of the study's authors, and we need *caution* on the side of both researchers and readers against a generalization of the results of statistical research. These two aspects, transparency and caution, will become even more important in the future. Recently, software developers have invented a system which is able to automatically generate the text of a story based on an input of statistical data.[32] Although this system to date only works for data about baseball games, it is out of question that an expansion of its uses is only a matter of time. It is perfectly conceivable that one day, computers automatically write papers in the field of "numerical comparative law", based on statistical data from various sources. However, computers generating texts based on statistical data are, at present, not able to verify or discuss the quality and reliability of the input and the adequacy of the process, and whether this will become true in the future as well is hard to predict. An automated production of studies based on data of questionable quality and reliability would be a serious threat to reliable comparative legal research. Therefore, read-

32 Northwestern University, Intelligent Information Laboratory, Project Stats Monkey, <http://infolab.northwestern.edu/projects/stats-monkey.html>; for first descriptions, see, e.g., D. Carr, "The Robots Are Coming! Oh, They're Here", *New York Times*, 19 October 2009, available at <http://mediadecoder.blogs.nytimes.com/2009/10/19/the-robots-are-coming-oh-theyre-here/> (both last visited 5 May 2017).

ers should acquaint themselves even today to require a maximum of transparency and to be cautious towards statistical research.

(V) "Numerical Comparative Law" and Civil Procedure

(a) The Special Case of Procedural Law

Having dealt with "numerical comparative law" in general, we can now focus on "numerical comparative law" studies dealing with civil procedure.

"Numerical comparative law" studies are based on the idea that the application of statistical methods to data from a large number of countries reveals interdependencies between certain characteristics of the legal system, its legal origin and the real world. Civil procedure is a difficult object for such an approach. The problem lies not so much in defining and comparing certain characteristics of procedural law, although this is not as easy as it may seem, but firstly rather, in determining the legal origins and, second and above all, in isolating meaningful real world aspects. The difficulty of determining the legal origin of a procedural system will be dealt with later. Let us first make a few remarks on the difficulty of isolating meaningful real world aspects.

As a general matter, procedural law only provides the regulatory framework for the process within which courts or other state officials deal with disputes from the filing of the complaint to the authoritative decision and, as the case may be, the enforcement of this decision. This regulatory framework is more or less the same for all types of cases. Needless to say, it would be erroneous to assume that the organization of the procedure has no effects whatsoever on the merits of the decision. However, the merits of the decision depend on this regulatory framework only to a rather small degree. Therefore, the merits of the decision cannot be seen as an immediate outcome of certain characteristics of the procedural framework. This, in turn, means that general data about the situation in a country which are relatively easy to gather, like success rates of certain types of cases or, even more general, market capitalization of listed corporations in a country, are ill-suited to be used as relevant "real world" aspects for a general "numerical comparative law" study on procedural law. Researchers therefore have to look for "real world" aspects which are closer connected to the proceedings. Obviously, the most interesting aspect of this type is the quality of civil justice.

(b) The Intricacies of Measuring the Quality of Civil Justice

Not only is procedural law special in that it requires researchers to select "real world" aspects which are closer connected to court proceedings, but also the most interesting aspect of this type, the quality of civil justice, does not lend itself perfectly to a quantitative assessment.

The quality of civil justice can be determined with regard to the actual performance of a civil justice system, that is, objectively, or with regard to how the performance of a civil justice system is perceived, that is, subjectively. Objective determinations rely on the wording of statutes and other first-hand data. Subjective determinations are based on inquiries among people or a group of people selected for the purpose at issue.

Both approaches present considerable difficulties. Even aspects as to which a quantitative assessment appears to be simple at first glance, like the duration of proceedings or costs, are fraught with considerable theoretical and practical problems. The problems become even more acute regarding more general aspects like fairness or impartiality. The present article cannot but hint at these problems.[33] In our eyes, it is improbable that these problems can be overcome in the near future. Nevertheless, as already mentioned in the beginning, civil procedure has not been spared by

---

33 For a comprehensive analysis, see Kern (2009), supra n. 11, at 446-480 = Kern (2011), supra n. 11, at 323-369. For a thorough discussion of such problems in the study P. Arida, E. Lisboa Bacha & A. Lara-Resende, "Credit, Interest, and Jurisdictional Uncertainty: Conjectures on the Case of Brazil", in *Inflation Targeting, Debt, and the Brazilian Experience, 1999-2003* 265 et seq. (F. Giavazzi, I. Goldfajn & S. Herrera, eds., 2005), see J. C. Barbosa Moreira, "Dois Cientistas Políticos, Três Economistas e a Justiça Brasileira", 91 *Rev. Bras. de Estudos Políticos* 29, 33 et seq. (Jan.-Jun. 2005). The author is grateful to Eduardo Talamini for having provided him a copy of this work.

researchers of the "numerical comparative law" school. Therefore, let us now have a closer look at the most prominent of these studies.

(c) The Lex Mundi Study "Courts" and its Follow-Up Paper

Without any doubt, the most prominent "numerical comparative law" study which deals with civil procedure is the so called Lex Mundi Study, which has ultimately been published under the title "Courts".[34] More recently, three of the four co-authors of the Lex Mundi Study have published, together with another fourth researcher, a new study entitled "The Divergence of Legal Procedures".[35] This new study is based on – and therefore can be understood as a follow-up paper to – the Lex Mundi Study. In the following lines, we provide a brief overview on these studies. This shall serve as a basis for a few evaluating remarks.

1. The Lex Mundi Study

The Lex Mundi Study aims at proving a relationship between the level of procedural formalism and the quality of the judicial system. To say it in the words of the four researchers, their study aims at clarifying the "crucial question" whether formalism secures justice.[36] For this purpose, they collect data on what they call "procedural formalism" and data on various "judicial quality measures" including duration, costs, fairness and corruption. They supplement these data by "other variables", covering, *inter alia*, income, legal origin, and education. On the resulting dataset, the researchers apply statistical methods.

Regarding procedural formalism and duration, the Lex Mundi Study is based on data collected by means of a questionnaire which was sent to cooperating attorneys in 109 countries, all working in law firms which be-

---

34 Djankov *et al.*, supra n. 9.

35 A. Balas, R. La Porta, F. López-de-Silanes & A. Shleifer, "The Divergence of Legal Procedures", original manuscript dated 1 February 2008, available at <papers.ssrn.com/sol3/papers.cfm?abstract_id=1091232> (last visited 5 May 2017); now published in 1 *American Economic Journal: Economic Policy* 138-162 (2009).

36 Djankov *et al.*, supra n. 9, at 477 and 506.

longed to the Lex Mundi network. The questionnaire asked the attorneys to describe the exact procedures used by litigants and courts in two hypothetical settings: the eviction of a residential tenant for non-payment of rent and the collection of a bounced check. Aspects of the procedure covered by the questionnaire were (1) step-by-step description of the procedure, (2) estimates of the actual duration at each stage, (3) indication of whether written submissions were required at each stage, (4) indication of specific laws applicable at each stage, (5) indication of mandatory time limits at each stage, (6) indication of the form of the appeal, and (7) the existence of alternative administrative procedures.[37]

The data on judicial quality, except for duration, and the input for the "other variables" stem from various external sources, among them, indices provided by Business Environmental Risk Intelligence and PRS Group, which are private enterprises, and by the World Bank's World Business Environment Survey.

The Lex Mundi Study's conclusion, put in a few words, is that procedural formalism is highest in countries with socialist and French legal origin and lowest in countries with English legal origin, that a higher level of formalism is accompanied by a lower quality of adjudication, and that therefore formalism should be reduced.

2. The Follow-Up Paper

The Follow-Up Paper is based on the approach of the Lex Mundi Study and adds a temporal perspective, in that it computes the formalism index every year for half a century, starting in 1950. For obvious reasons, the researchers did not try to gather data from practicing attorneys. Instead, they relied on legislation as well as manuals and other written material, and according to their own testimony, it took them "2-3 weeks to process the initial data for each country". They find that between 1950 and 2000, procedural formalism "did not converge, and possibly diverged, between common law and French civil law countries".

37 *Ibid.*, at 459-461.

The Follow-Up Paper does not address judicial quality directly. However, it must be seen as an expansion of the 'Lex Mundi Study' according to which higher formalism is associated with lower-quality justice.

(d) Some Evaluating Remarks on these Studies

It is not possible within this short article to provide an in-depth evaluation of these two studies. Therefore, we limit ourselves to some brief evaluating remarks.[38] Even so, we believe that the impartial reader will subscribe to our position that these studies do not meet the standards which should govern serious research.

1. The Lex Mundi Study

Regarding the Lex Mundi Study, it should first be noted that the baseline of the variables collected by the researchers, the "neighbor model", is not very convincing.[39] The Study defines procedural formalism as any deviation from the way disputes would be resolved among neighbors in an archaic world without courts. However, this model is too general to provide clear and non-ambiguous answers on how the dispute resolution process would look like in detail. It therefore leaves much room for the researchers to manipulate the results by defining the baseline themselves. In addition, today's world is obviously too complex to live without courts and a preestablished procedural framework. Moreover, the principle of equal and impartial justice under the law commands that courts deal with similar cases in a similar way. The interesting question is not whether there is formalism at all, but which formal elements provided for in the law governing court proceedings are necessary or desirable and which are not. Obvi-

38 For a comprehensive analysis of the Lex Mundi Study from the perspective of a procedural law scholar, see Kern (2007), supra n. 11, passim; for criticism from "within the approach", see H. Spamann, 'Legal Origin, Civil Procedure, and the Quality of Contract Enforcement', 166 *Journal of Institutional and Theoretical Economics* [JITE] 149 with comments by J. Klick 166-170 and G. Wagner 171-177.

39 See Kern (2007), supra n. 11, at 44 et seq.

ously, this question cannot be answered by a mere comparison of "degrees" of formalism regardless of the contents of the rules at issue.

Second, the Study is based on only two model cases, cheque collection and eviction of a residential tenant, which cannot be considered representative.[40] In many countries, cheques have been out of use for some twenty years. Landlord and tenant cases, in turn, involve very special questions and depend a lot on the conditions of the housing market in the country at issue. It is, e.g., no surprise that landlord and tenant law puts much more emphasis on the protection of the tenant in small and highly populated countries where apartments are scarce than in countries in which it is easy to find a new home. It is, then, no surprise that the duration of an eviction case is longer in the former and shorter in the latter countries. These circumstances have not been taken into account by the study at all.

Third, the variables chosen to determine procedural formalism are sometimes not very meaningful, are often poorly defined[41] and are aggregated in a way that is all but self-explanatory.[42] For example,[43] it is logically inconsistent to define and code the variable "filing" in the following way: "Equals one if the complaint is *normally* submitted in written form to the court, and zero if it *can be* presented orally."[44] Obviously, the two answers do not exclude each other: It is all but unusual that complaints are *normally* submitted in writing, even though an oral presentation would be possible.[45] As to countries where this is the case, it is unclear whether one should fill in "one" or "zero" – both solutions would be wrong. Apart from the poor definition of the variable "filing", it is also an example for a variable whose importance is questionable. In countries with a high rate of illiteracy, the option of filing complaints orally is much more important than in countries where almost everybody has the capability and means to write and read. A requirement that the complaint be filed in written form is much more burdensome for potential parties in the former countries, while it may not even be recognized in the latter countries. Finally, the

40 *Ibid.*, at 10 et seq.

41 *Ibid.*, at 49 et seq.

42 *Ibid.*, at 64 et seq.

43 For a similar example from the study "Credit, Interest, and Judicial Uncertainty" (supra n. 33), see Barbosa Moreira, supra n. 33, at 38 et seq.

44 Djankov *et al.*, supra n. 9, at 464 (emphasis added).

45 Cf., e.g., §§ 496, 253 German Civil Procedure Code (Zivilprozessordnung, ZPO) for cases in the local courts.

"filing" variable can also serve as an example for the questionable aggregation of the data: Does it really make sense to add up the binary answers on the "filing" variable with other binary answers on issues like the question of whether the judge can introduce evidence,[46] and if so, should all these answers have the same weight? To us, all this appears more than doubtful.

Fourth, the data from other sources on which the Study draws is disputable as well, and the selection of the other sources appears to be arbitrary – a detailed analysis has been provided elsewhere.[47]

Nevertheless, the authors of the study do not mention these problems and possible alternatives to their approach at all. Rather, they present it as if it were an eternal truth. All this fails the standards outlined above by far. All in all, the study can hardly be seen as reliable and is a quite disappointing application of the "numerical comparative law" approach.

2. The Follow-Up Paper

Turning now to the Follow-Up Paper, some additional criticism is in order. It is at the very least ridiculous to believe that one could determine for each country in "2–3 weeks" all the relevant data on procedural formalism for a period of half a century even if one limits itself to the "law in the books" – which is doubtful enough. Serious researchers would refrain from such form of speculative research. In addition, the quality of the written sources on which these data are based cannot be verified by the reader at all, as the researchers do not provide a list of the books and statutes consulted. The approach leaves enormous room for the researchers to intentionally or unintentionally influence the results; and even if all the data were correct, it appears questionable whether statistically significant results are more than a coincidence.

---

46 Cf. Djankov *et al.*, supra n. 9, at 465.

47 Kern (2007), supra n. 11, at 78 et seq.; cf. also C. A. Kern, "Licht und Schatten – einige Bemerkungen zum EU Justice Scoreboard" 2015, *GPR* 2016, 109, 110.

Before this background, it is hard to understand the self-confidence of the researchers and their ignorance towards all criticism that has been put forward.

(VI) The Studies' Use and Understanding of Comparative Law

Before concluding, we would like to address with a few words the Studies' use and understanding of comparative law.

(a) Comparative Law Literature and Quantitative Studies

It has already been mentioned that the studies we are talking about typically have resorted to the classification of legal origins developed by comparative law scholars. As a matter of principle, there is nothing wrong with that. Admittedly, some important criticism has been put forward lately against classifications of legal families, legal origins or the like.[48] It is even more interesting, from an academic point of view, to analyze whether data supports classifications or the critique. Taking into account the discrepancies in the definition and delimitation of legal families, it would be desirable that researchers use more than one classification.

However, we have other concerns with the studies' use of legal origins. Traditional comparative law literature often intends to draw a broad picture and to communicate fundamentals about the development, the style, and the particularities of legal systems.[49] It therefore does not always focus on one limited area of the law or legal question. Moreover, it often selects rather eclectically among the features of the covered legal systems, trying to catch the characteristics and significant highlights. Suffice it to mention that the traditional distinction between common law and civil law is, as regards the structure of the proceedings, no more correct.[50] After all,

48 See, inter alia, M. Reimann, "The Progress and Failure of Comparative Law in the Second Half of the Twentieth Century", 50 *Am. J. Comp. L.* 671, 685 et seq. (2002).

49 Cf., e.g., Zweigert & Kötz, supra n. 16, at 62 et seq.

50 See, e.g., R. Stürner & C. A. Kern, "Comparative Civil Procedure – Fundamentals and Recent Trends", in H. Konuralp Anısına Armağan/*Gedächtnisschrift für Halûk Konuralp*, Vol. 1, 997, 1001-1012 (Osman B. Gürzumar *et al.*, eds., 2009) =

the distinction of legal origins used by the general comparative law literature is not necessarily meaningful for all areas and details of a legal system.

Numerical comparative law studies, on the contrary, concentrate on a relatively limited question and claim to be comprehensive and precise, as far as their quantitative data is concerned. This does not necessarily match with the classification of legal origins developed by comparative law scholars for other purposes and presented not as precise data, but in a literary form. Problems are compounded if the study does not care as much about the correctness of its understanding of comparative law and legal history as it cares about its statistical calculations.

(b) Illustration: The Lex Mundi Study "Courts"

The Lex Mundi study shall serve as an example of these problems. In this study, the four authors follow a rather simplistic understanding of "legal origins" similar to one that three of them with another co-author have also published elsewhere.[51] According to this understanding, civil law countries' procedural codes are a product of the French "revolutionaries and

---

Processo civil comparado – Tendências recentes e fundamentais, 200 *RePro* 203, 207-217 (T. Arruda Alvim Wambier, transl., 2011).

51 See, e.g., R. La Porta, F. Lopez-de-Silanes, A. Shleifer & R. Vishny, "Law and Finance", 106 *Journal of Political Economy* 1113, 1115 et seq. (1998), first published as NBER Working Paper No. 5661 (1996), p. 4 et seq., <http://papers.nber.org/papers/w5661.pdf> (last visited 5 May 2017). See also Djankov *et al.*, supra n. 1, at 609 (suggesting that the French system was "exported" by Napoleon to Spain and Portugal and transplanted from there to Latin America by their colonial conquests); similarly T. Beck, A. Demirgüç-Kunt & R. Levine, 'Law, Endowments, and Finance', 70 *J. Econ. Fin.* 137, 138 (2003). This sounds a bit surprising, given that Spain's and Portugal's conquests occurred long before Napoleon was born. The prevailing view is that the influence of the Code Napoléon on 19th century codifications in the newly independent Latin American countries was due to its reputation as a "modern" – and probably also its flavor of a "liberal" or even "revolutionary" – code. See, e.g., P. Fernández de Córdova, *Estudios de Derecho Comparado* 100 (1997); J. Ayasta Gonzalez, *El Derecho Comparado y los Jurídicos Contemporáneos* 186 (1991); K. Zweigert & H. Kötz, *Introduction to comparative law* 113–115 (T. Weir, trans., 3rd ed., 1998). In the field of civil procedure, some countries have been influenced by French procedural law via French-speaking cantons of Switzerland; see R. Stürner, "Das deutsche Zivilprozeßrecht und seine Ausstrahlung auf andere Rechtsordnungen – von

Napoleon [who] did not trust the judges, and codified judicial procedures in order to control judicial discretion", whereas the English and the U.S. judiciary could preserve "a great deal more judicial independence" because "lawyers and judges were on the 'right' side of the revolutions." They argue that for this reason, and because of the supplemental nature of codes in the common law tradition, "less formalism is required in the judicial procedure."[52]

The history of codification in continental Europe and in those states for which continental European codes served as a model is, however, much more complicated. Although the French Revolution and Napoleon played an important role, the Study's restriction on this part of the story must raise some criticism.[53] Suffice it to say that codification did not start with Napoleon.[54] But more important for our purposes is the question of whether the codification of procedural law in continental Europe actually

Deutschland aus gesehen", in *Das deutsche Zivilprozessrecht und seine Ausstrahlung auf andere Rechtsordnungen* 3, 24 (W. J. Habscheid, ed., 1991). Today, it is rather Italian than French law and legal literature that still play an important role in Latin American countries; cf. R. Stürner, "Gegenstand und Formen der Rezeption im neueren Prozeßrecht", in *Law in East and West* 287, 290 (Institute of Comparative Law, Waseda University, ed., 1988). For an overview on the studies' understanding of legal history, see M. M. Siems, "Legal Origins – Reconciling Law & Finance and Comparative Law", Heinrich-Heine-University Düsseldorf Center for Business and Corporate Law Research Center Paper Series no. 0023 (01/2006), p. 4-6, available at <http://papers.ssrn.com/sol3/papers.cfm?abstract_id=879720> (last visited 5 May 2017).

52 Djankov *et al.*, supra n. 9, at 458.

53 Note that the revolutionaries' concerns were only in part identical with those of the rather restaurationist emperor Napoleon. See also M. R. Damaška, *The faces of justice and state authority: a comparative approach to the legal process* 208 (1986) (noting that "old forms of civil procedure survived the upheavals of the French Revolution with fewer changes than the administration of criminal justice") and generally R. David, *French Law* 12 (M. Kindred, trans., 1972) (explaining, for the French Code civil, that the draftsmen were lawyers and judges of the pre-Revolutionary era who "could not be expected to forget their education, experience, and preconceptions.").

54 Talking of France, a prior, although somewhat incomplete codification was the 1667 ordinance by Louis XIV (Ordonnance de Saint-Germain-en-Laye), called "Code Louis" (Ordonnance civile touchant la réformation de la justice), prepared by J.-B. Colbert; see S. Guinchard & F. Ferrand, *Procédure civile* 69, at 37 (28th ed., 2006). On earlier codifications in Germany, see L. Rosenberg, *Lehrbuch des Deutschen Zivilprozessrechts* 9-11 (2nd ed., 1929).

is linked to the alleged higher level of formalism in civil law countries.[55] On one hand, codified rules facilitate the postulating and controlling of formal requirements. On the other hand, though, these codifications not only clarified the formal requirements, but also unified them throughout most types of claims. Thanks to the codifications, pre-existing procedural rules which may have differed for different causes of action and provided for different courts were harmonized or aligned.[56] As a consequence, the total number of rules presumably was reduced.[57] The common law, in turn, has always contained some extremely formalistic procedural rules, mainly as regards the law of evidence, a field which was not covered by the variables of the Lex Mundi Study at all – more than a coincidence? These formalistic rules of the common law procedure have developed even in – or because of? – the absence of any codification. Therefore, the evidence from the codification story is at least mixed. Moreover, it somewhat contradicts the Study's argument that "procedural differences be-

55 Note that New York – apparently the place chosen by the Study to represent U.S. law – had a Code of Civil Procedure as early as the mid 19th century; see S. N. Subrin, "David Dudley Field and the Field Code: A Historical Analysis of an Earlier Procedural Vision", 6 *Law & Hist. Rev.* 311 (1988); D. S. Clark, "The Civil Law Influence on David Dudley Field's Code of Civil Procedure", in *The Reception of Continental Ideas in the Common Law World* 1820-1920 63 (M. Reimann, ed., 1993). Although what this code codified was not common law procedure (R. G. Bone, "Mapping the Boundaries of the Dispute: Conceptions of Ideal Lawsuit Structure from the Field Code to the Federal Rules", 89 *Colum. L. Rev.* 1, 5-78 (1989)), and although the perhaps most influential event for the creation of a – compared to what existed – modern and less formalistic civil procedural law in the U.S. and its States was the promulgation in 1938 of the Federal Rules of Civil Procedure (cf. P. D. Carrington, "Teaching Civil Procedure: A Retrospective View", 49 *J. Legal Educ.* 311, 323-325 (1999)), one might argue that these "codifications" stood in the tradition of the English legal origin. Yet this argument is ambiguous: If so, codification as such has no influence on the level of formalism.

56 See, e.g., the quotation in Bone, supra n. 55, at 3, of the New York Commissioners on Practice and Pleadings, 1849, Report to the New York Legislature of 1850, at v (Albany 1850): "The purpose of the constitutional provision and of the statute under which [the New York Field Code of Procedure] is prepared, was to make legal proceedings more intelligible, more certain, more speedy, and less expensive."

57 One can also hypothesize that due to the continental understanding of codes in the hierarchy of norms and the reluctance to accept judgments as a source of law, codification limited the power of judges to introduce new formal requirements. See also J. Leubsdorf, "The Myth of Civil Procedure Reform", in *Civil Justice in Crisis* 53, 63-65 (A. A.S. Zuckerman, ed., 1999) (doubting that codification results in any significant changes).

tween common and civil law actually go back to the twelfth and thirteenth centuries"[58] – that is, long before the French Revolution and Napoleon, and even long before most other great and influential codifications we know today, apart of course from Justinian's *Corpus Iuris Civilis*.[59]

The argument which explains higher formalism in French law with the less peaceful situation in France as compared to England continues by proposing that the differences in the law and order requirements entailed different approaches to legal procedure that were transplanted to most other countries "through conquest and colonization." Actually, the idea of legal transplants is widely accepted and can draw on important writings in the field. Yet in spite of legal scholar's centuries-old familiarity with the concept of legal transplants, there is still no distinct definition or uniform use of this term. Furthermore, what is required as evidence of a legal transplant is quite unclear, even more so if one concentrates on the field of civil procedure.[60] A look in the general literature on comparative law is a good starting point, but not the finish. It has already been explained that blind reliance on what "macro-comparison" tells us can lead astray in an analysis pertaining to civil procedure.[61] Admittedly, the Study cannot be

58 Djankov *et al.*, supra n. 9, at 458.

59 It is another question whether this second historical argument put forward by the Study is a complete explanation. Common law scholars often emphasize with much pride that their legal system is the result of a completely independent and autochthonous development. This thesis has been challenged, though; for an overview on these relatively new insights, see R. Stürner, "Procedural Law and Legal Cultures", in *Prozessrecht und Rechtskulturen/Procedural Law and Legal Cultures* 9, 15-17 (P. Gilles & T. Pfeiffer, eds., 2004) (Inaugural speech to the XIIth World Congress on Procedural Law 2003 in Mexico City, organized by the International Association of Procedural Law).

60 For an instructive discussion of both problems (with further references), see, e.g., M. Kohler, *Die Entwicklung des Schwedischen Zivilprozessrechts* 9-22 (2002).

61 See Kern (2007), supra n. 11, at 87 et seq. Note in addition that by focusing, on one hand, on the 12th and 13th century, and on codification on the other, the Study's historical sketch leaves uncovered crucial periods for the development of French and German procedural law, for example the "positive" influence of French civil procedure's principle of orality on the pre-20th century German procedural law, where a complex and cumbersome procedure based on writing prevailed (see P. L. Murray & R. Stürner, *German Civil Justice* 26-29 (2004)). Today, of course, mandatory oral hearings may be seen as formalistic, and legal systems which expressly follow a principle of orality typically provide for exceptions (e.g., Germany: §§ 128(2)–(4), 495 a ZPO). Yet at the time orality was clearly beneficial.

expected to make a substantial theoretical contribution on these issues. Nevertheless, the ease with which it keeps quiet about all these fundamental questions is remarkable. Finally, it should be mentioned that the Study's focus on involuntary forms of legal transplant is arguable even with regard to French law, and much more so for Italian law which owes its influence in Brazil not to "conquest and colonization" but to the linguistic ease of Brazilians to read Italian, the admiration for Italian legal theory and the personal and literary presence of Italian scholars in Brazil during the last century.

(VII) Conclusion

Comparative law has been enriched by a new methodology: the statistical analysis of various countries' legal solutions to specific social and economic problems. However, this approach is fraught with difficulties. What we need, is more transparency on the part of the authors of such studies, and extreme caution on the part of both the authors and the readers. The present state of this surging field of research is in its infancy. This is particularly true for the two important studies concerning civil procedure. Whether the publication of a convincing study in the field of civil procedure is just a matter of time or whether we will wait for such a study eternally, is still an open question. "Numerical comparative law" may develop into a serious scholarly approach, but may also burst like a bubble when the euphoria of these years (and the generosity of the institutions financing these studies) is over.

On the Role of the Courts

The Changing Role of Courts between the Privatization of Adjudication and the Privatization of Procedure

Juliana Pondé Fonseca[*]

(I) Introduction: Privatizing Adjudication and Privatizing Procedure

Perhaps as a consequence of legal realism, courts have been analysed in legal scholarship increasingly as institutions and not as theoretical constructs of political or legal theory. This methodological approach is oftentimes influenced by sociology, economics and legal history, drawing conclusions from primary sources and empirical research. It has been used all over the world, allowing the perception of gaps between the courts' declared and effectively performed functions in different traditions, and also revealing that these functions have not always remained the same. Change seems to be inevitable and is not always coherent.

Studies that follow this methodology have popularized the idea that, in civil litigation, adjudication is increasingly less public and more private. This process has generally been called "privatization of adjudication". The phenomenon takes on different characteristics in different legal traditions: in some cases, it describes the flight from courts, the migration of cases to other dispute resolution mechanisms, an overall reduction in the number of trials and an increase in the number of settlements. In all of these cases, judiciary adjudication has ceased to be the main paradigm for dispute resolution, and mechanisms previously referred to as "alternative" now share with the courts the general label of "dispute resolution".[1]

In other cases, the flight from courts is not so evident, for they remain the main reference for dispute resolution. There is still, however, migration to other dispute resolution mechanisms, usually combined with a push to make courts more affable to private purposes: faster, more efficient, more predictable. In both cases, however, there is still a shift in the locus

---

* PhD Universidade Federal do Paraná.

1 J. Resnik, "Diffusing Disputes: The Public in the Private of Arbitration, the Private in Courts, and the Erasure of Rights", 124 *Yale Law Journal* 2804, 2806-2807(2015).

of adjudication, accompanied by a transfer in law-making power.[2] Regulatory powers are transferred to other institutions along with the cases.[3]

I believe this phenomenon is somehow related to another one that I will call "privatization of procedure", referring to the *contractualization* of procedure and its adaptation to the interests of the parties within the courts. According to this idea, parties can change procedural rules through contracts, making them more adaptable to particular disputes, and bind courts to these new rules. If adjudication serves mainly to solve private issues, private parties should be able to opt for the rules they deem more appropriate.

So far, the correlation between the two phenomena is merely speculative. It has been suggested that courts should become more attractive to private actors in order to avoid the flight of cases.[4] In this sense, for courts to retain their law making functions they should allow the parties to design proceedings, accepting tailored dispute resolution in courts. This position implies not only correlation, but also causality. This paper will follow a more modest path and simply try to point to correlation, that is, to show that the two phenomena are usually related to the same topics in legal scholarship, such as freedom of contract and managerial judging; which

2 See generally J. M. Glover, "Disappearing Claims and the Erosion of Substantive Law", 124 *Yale Law Journal* (2015) 3052-92; S. A. Talesh, "The Privatization of Public Legal Rights: How Manufacturers Construct the Meaning of Consumer Law", 43 *Law & Society Review* 527 (2009).

3 Adjudication is certainly related to regulation. In private enforcement or collective adjudication (i.e. class actions) the relationship between both seems clearer. In private enforcement, the social goal that determines the creation of a statute or public policy depends entirely on adjudication, for monitoring compliance is extremely difficult. In the U.S., consumer rights and job discrimination statutes have been privately enforced for some time. See generally S. Farhang, "Public Regulation and Private Lawsuits in the American Separation of Powers System", 52 *American Journal of Political Science* 821(2008). Class actions have been directly compared to regulation, given the impact of litigation not only in terms of number of people affected, but also in terms of influencing the future behavior of potential defendants. R. G. Bone, "The Puzzling Idea of Adjudicative Representation: Lessons for Aggregate Litigation and Class Actions", 79 *George Washington Law Review* 577, 595 (2011).

4 See generally H. S. Noyes, "If You (Re) Build It, They Will Come: Contracts to Remake the Rules of Litigation in Arbitration's Image", 30 *Harvard Journal of Law and Public Policy* 579 (2007); C. W. Tyler, "Lawmaking in the Shadow of the Bargain: Contract Procedure as a Second-Best Alternative to Mandatory Arbitration", 122 *Yale Law Journal* 1560 (2013).

indicates that the scholarly rhetoric around both of them is practically the same. This seems odd, given the fact that, if you put courts at the centre of your inquiry, they point to opposite directions: privatizing adjudication takes cases away from courts, while privatizing procedure is supposed to bring them in.

The interaction of these two phenomena, regardless of correlation or causality, makes the discussion regarding the role of courts more complicated, and not only because they are supposed to attract and repel cases if examined together. Privatization of adjudication hinders the development of law, since the disputes that would be taken to court are resolved somewhere else – either in other institutions or settled in some way. The courts themselves dismiss cases or decide them summarily for various reasons. In all these examples, the problem is that the cases are not tried. Privatization of procedure, on the contrary, and if it manages to bring cases to court, will allow them to be tried in completely different ways. Here the problem is that there is no way to guarantee that the courts will be able to decide the cases according to the procedural rules that are supposed to secure the development of law.

Understanding the relationship between the two types of privatization is, however, problematic, for not a lot of research has been done on procedural contracts. While there is a lot of empirical research on the privatization of adjudication,[5] there is no data on the privatization of procedure. There is no way to know whether these contracts are frequently used or not, how detailed and creative they are, how stringent the changes made to procedural rules are or in which types of cases they are used. It is impossible, therefore, to understand how this phenomenon interacts with the privatization of adjudication.

---

5 The first volume of the Journal of Empirical Legal Studies was basically dedicated to the topic. M. Galanter, "The Vanishing Trial: An Examination of Trials and Related Matters in Federal and State Courts", 1 *Journal of Empirical Legal Studies*, 459 (2004); S. S. Diamond and J. Bina, "Puzzles about Supply-Side Explanations for Vanishing Trials: A New Look at Fundamentals", 1 *Journal of Empirical Legal Studies* 637 (2004); J. Resnik, "Migrating, Morphing, and Vanishing: The Empirical and Normative Puzzles of Declining Trial Rates in Courts", 1 *Journal of Empirical Legal Studies* 783 (2004); S. B. Burbank, "Keeping Our Ambition Under Control: The Limits of Data and Inference in Searching for the Causes and Consequences of Vanishing Trials in Federal Court", 1 *Journal of Empirical Legal Studies* 571 (2004).

The change in the role of courts is also evidenced by empirical research focused on other phenomena, some quite different from the ones discussed in this paper. There is research on the transformation of criminal procedure's purpose regarding misdemeanour justice, going from perpetrating punishment to social control;[6] and on the fact that, in general, courts have long ceased to effect sanctions through regular procedure, for most cases are "solved" through plea bargaining.[7] Other studies point to more positive developments, such as the unorthodox practices of drug treatment courts that seem to be more sensitive to addicts' needs and tend to be more efficient than "regular" courts.[8]

Courts are constantly changing and these modifications certainly affect the way they function as institutions in society. Between the two phenomena mentioned in this paper, not only their role towards the solution of private conflicts is under transformation, but also their function in regulation and on the development of the law. This reinforces the need for more research on procedural contracts and their actual impact on courts and their practices.

This paper will begin to address the problem by first describing procedural contracts in general terms. Then, a short comparative analysis will show the different approaches in Germany, France, Italy, Brazil and the United States. Finally, I will outline some preliminary conclusions and propose future empirical research focused on the privatization of procedure.

(II) Procedural Contracts

The discussion on procedural agreements started in Germany at the end of the 19th century with the writings of Josef Kohler and Oskar von Bülow.[9] The topic later regained attention in the 1980s after being introduced in

6 I. Kohler-Hausmann, "Managerial Justice and Mass Misdemeanors", 66 *Stanford Law Review* 611 (2014).

7 B. P. Smith, "Plea Bargaining and the Eclipse of the Jury", 1 *Annual Review of Law and Social Science* 131 (2005).

8 D. C. Gottfredson et al., "How Drug Treatment Courts Work: An Analysis of Mediators", 44 *Journal of Research in Crime and Delinquency* 3 (2007).

9 Bülow affirmed that procedural contracts were inadmissible due to the public nature of civil procedure. On the German discussions on the matter in the 1880s, see A.P. Cabral, *Convenções processuais* 97-102 (Salvador, JusPodivm, 2016).

the new French Civil Procedure Code in 1975, and in the Woolf Reforms in the United Kingdom.[10] At first, the idea did not have a big impact, but in recent years, many books and articles have been written about it. In 2008, one of the most traditional journals in civil procedure, the *Rivista Trimestrale di Diritto e Procedura Civile*, dedicated an entire special issue to the topic.[11] Most recently, the new Brazilian Civil Procedure Code included an article on procedural contracts and did not set any specific limits to them.[12] In fact, scholars have been pushing to extend the application of such contracts, not only to affect more people, but mostly to expand the number of procedural rules that can be modified by the parties.

In contractualized procedure, adjudication is still performed by public courts, but through tailor-made, private interest focused procedure rules. The number of legal systems that have embraced this possibility is rapidly increasing. In some, privatization of both adjudication and procedure coexist, with the adoption of rules in civil procedure codes that reinforce the adjudicative character of arbitration (limiting the possibilities for the review of awards, for example) and also rules that allow for the creation of specific proceedings to be followed by judges. In these cases (such as in France and Brazil), the two movements are present in the same statute, regardless of their opposite goals (once again, placing courts at the centre of the inquiry).

The privatization of procedure, however, may take place independently of the privatization of adjudication. One of the two phenomena might be much stronger than the other in a particular legal system. They are also independent in the sense that adjudication remains somewhat public in procedural agreements, because it still is performed by courts – regardless of the private origins and goals of the created procedural rules.

The *contractualization* of process has been embraced by scholarship and statutes with a promise of allowing the creation of more efficient methods of dispute resolution within the courts. In some systems these agreements exist despite the lack of legal provisions establishing and regu-

---

10 A. Fabbi, "*Privatizing* Civil Justice through Procedural Agreements: A Comparative Law Analysis", 6-7, text available electronically at <http://www.law.nyu.edu/sites/default/files/upload_documents/AlessandroFabbi2.pdf.>, last visited 7 April 2016.

11 Volume 62, entitled *Accordi di parte e processo* (agreements among parties and procedure).

12 See *infra* III (b) (iv).

lating them. Regardless of inclusion in any code, France, Germany, Italy and Brazil are some of the countries in which scholarship has devoted special attention to procedural contracts. They are also possible, to some extent, in the U.S., but it seems they do not receive the same attention.

Some of the scholarship devoted to procedural agreements regards them as consequences of the cooperative model of civil procedure that has replaced the well-known dichotomy between the adversarial and inquisitorial models. According to this model, parties and judge must cooperate for the best and most efficient conduct of proceedings, following a more complex pattern of behaviour.[13]

The ideal-type definitions of the actors' roles in both traditional models are seen as inadequate: in theory, in the adversarial system the parties do all the work, and in the inquisitorial model the judge has a very active role in the procedure, directing the behaviour of both parties and requiring the production of evidence. In the cooperative model, neither the judge nor the parties are solely in charge of moving a case forward, for they are supposed to do it together, regardless of the conflict that took them to court in the first place. Procedural contracts, according to this theoretical framework, are a feature of the cooperative model, since they allow a more balanced relationship between parties and judge.

The agreements assume different features in each legal system, but the main characteristics and possible problems in implementation remain similar, becoming more or less serious according to the efficiency and organization of the judiciary.

(III) A Short Comparative Approach

(a) Comparative Law Methodology

Fundamental questions regarding many fields of comparative law remain unanswered. Going beyond the study of foreign cases only for the sake of self-reflection or in search of authority in doctoral research (for some, a

13 L. Cadiet, "The Emergence of a Model of Cooperative Justice in Europe: Horizontal Dimensions", 14-15, text available electronically at <http://cadmus.eui.eu/handle/1814/32632.>, last visited 7 April 2016. See generally D. Mitidiero, *Colaboração no processo civil: pressupostos sociais, lógicos e éticos* (São Paulo, Revista dos Tribunais, 2015).

comparative chapter is seen as a necessary step in any research endeavour), it is difficult to trace links among pertinent variables or to rigorously test hypotheses. In fact, actual problem-driven comparative research – one that elaborates such hypotheses – is still not common.[14]

A first important step is therefore, to establish the main problem to be elucidated through comparative research, which should simultaneously drive and define the investigation. In this paper, the research is supposed to test the hypothesis of correlation between the two types of privatization, particularly the idea that they share the same scholarly rhetoric and then enable the analysis of how this rhetoric is used.

After delimiting the problem that is supposed to guide the investigation, further methodological issues should be considered. The selection of cases (i.e. legal systems to be compared) is rarely systematic and its importance is underestimated. In search of correlational connections between phenomena, social sciences generally depart from experimental research, from statistical analysis or from systematic examination of a small number of cases.[15] Comparative law predominantly deals with a small number of cases, not aiming for broad statistical analysis, and a careful selection is extremely important.

The selection can be guided by different principles, such as the most similar cases (comparing cases that have similar characteristics but differ in the dependent or independent variables that are relevant to the study) or, following the opposite logic, the most different cases principle (analysing cases that are different on variables that are irrelevant to the study but are consistent on the key independent variable).[16]

The research in this paper was guided by a different principle: the prototypical cases logic. The researcher should select prototypical cases that exhibit similar pertinent characteristics, but differ in others; and that may be used to extend the analysis to other cases (not analysed) through analogy.[17] All selected cases share the mentioned scholarly rhetoric, but differ in others, regarding the acceptance of procedural contracts in decisions

14 R. Hirschl, "The Question of Case Selection in Comparative Constitutional Law", 53 *The American Journal of Comparative Law* 125, 125 (2005). Hirschl writes on comparative constitutional law methodology, but his reflections are incredibly useful for civil procedure.

15 Hirschl, *supra* n. 14, at 132.

16 *Ibid.* at 133–142.

17 *Ibid.* at 142.

and scholarship, establishment in positive law and focus of the discussion. Since the paper does not aim to establish a causal reaction, the selected cases provide different contexts in which the rhetoric is used, allowing the analysis of how the same vocabulary is employed in describing the two phenomena in diverse backgrounds.

(b) Prototypical Cases

(i) Germany

In Germany, procedural contracts have been discussed by scholars since the 19th century, when judges accepted and enforced agreements that excluded the first instance of trial, taking the case directly to appeal courts.[18] The German Civil Procedure Code does not mention such agreements, even though it has undergone important reforms rather recently in 1975 and 2001; and yet the scholarly discussions on the matter continue.

Legal literature distinguishes between two different types of procedural contracts: a) procedural contracts in the strict sense ("*prozessuale Verfügungsverträge*"); and b) contracts that create an obligation between the parties regarding proceedings ("*prozessuale Verpflichtungsverträge*").[19] The differences between these contracts, however, are not so clear.

Procedural contracts in the strict sense are those that can be related to the *contractualization* of procedure, because they modify, create or exclude rules that govern the courts, binding them to the parties' agreement.[20]

Theoretically, the possibility of concluding such contracts is, however, debatable mainly due to the nature of the rules which are being modified. Procedural law is considered, in general, public law. *Freedom of contract* and other principles of private law, therefore, are not applied as fundamental principles in civil procedure.[21]

18 C. A. Kern, "Procedural Contracts in Germany", in: F. Didier Jr., A. P. Cabral, and P. H. P. Nogueira (eds), *Negócios Processuais* 183–184 (Salvador, Juspodivm, 2015).

19 Kern, *supra* n. 18, at 181 and 184.

20 *Ibid.* at 180–81.

21 *Ibid.* at 182.

In practice, these contracts are possible despite not being established by positive law, finding legal foundations in the dispositive rules from the Civil Procedure Code. These rules are non-mandatory and therefore parties can determine non-compliance through a procedural agreement. The possibility of such agreements (in the strict sense) is, thus, a matter of interpretation, implicitly established in the law.

The main examples of agreements are contracts which include choice of forum (§ 38 of the Code) and arbitration (§§ 1032 et seq.) clauses. In a sense, these clauses fit the definition of procedural contracts in the strict sense perfectly, for they modify a court's conduct by determining jurisdiction where there would be none (in the case of choice of forum). These clauses also bind a court that would otherwise have jurisdiction and demand the dismissal of a case, which is the same as happens when a court faces an arbitration clause.[22]

The agreements are limited by the mandatory rules, which cannot be altered through the exercise of freedom of contract. The 19th century provisions that used to be accepted by courts, excluding the first instance of trial, are not possible today, though it is possible to exclude appeals through contract.[23]

The second type of procedural contracts, which create obligations with respect to proceedings, are not as controversial. These contracts only bind the parties and, according to scholars, do not alter procedural rules: they establish an obligation not to use certain means of proof, or to withdraw an appeal, for example. A court, in the first example, can still demand evidence that was not presented by the parties (as long as it refers to the facts pleaded by them), even if they had excluded it in the agreement.[24]

The second example (obligation to withdraw an appeal), however, is not so easy and reveals that the differences between the two types of procedural contracts are not so clear. If this type of contract neither alters procedural rules nor binds judges, then if one party fails to withdraw an appeal, violating the agreement, a court can still hear it and the party can only be sanctioned by being ordered to pay damages. This interpretation is, however, considered too strict; and courts have already held that in these cases an appeal should be dismissed on the basis of the procedural obliga-

22 *Ibid.* at 183.
23 *Ibid.* at 183.
24 *Ibid.* at 184.

tion. If this is so, the contract is clearly binding on the courts, which cannot choose to admit the appeal.[25]

The disparity between the two types of procedural contracts, thus, is not very sharp. It is difficult to enforce a contract that "only binds the parties" without binding the courts. The obligation to forego all appeals (first type) and the obligation to withdraw an appeal in the light of certain circumstances (second type) have to be enforced in the same way if one believes that procedural contracts can be enforced through specific performance.[26] In this case, both types of obligations would end up binding the courts.

Supporters of the agreements see everything as a procedural contract. The tacit behaviour of a litigant who does not dispute the facts presented by an opposing party is considered a procedural agreement,[27] even though it could be seen through public law lenses: courts have limited resources and cannot waste them in examining facts that are not being disputed. This type of argument, though not convincing, opens a link to the past and allows the supporters to sustain that procedural contracts are not new creations.

I have focused so far only on the contractual aspects of the phenomenon, but case management and cooperation are also important in contemporary German civil procedure. Following the cooperative model, parties should never be surprised by the results of the dispute, therefore a judge should focus on the decisive questions of a case and give directions to the parties regarding pleadings; while the parties have the duty to provide clarifying explanations. This is supposed to improve a court's control of the merits of a dispute, providing a judge with managerial powers and assuring mutual cooperation.[28]

---

25 *Ibid.* at 185–186.

26 *Ibid.* at 186–187.

27 Fabbi, *supra* n. 10, at 10.

28 G. Walter, "The German Civil Procedure Reform Act of 2002: Much Ado about Nothing?", in: Nicolò Trocker et al. (eds), *The Reforms of Civil Procedure in Comparative Perspective* 74–75 (Torino, G. Giappichelli, 2005).

(ii) France

France is considered the most amenable legal system for procedural contract, also producing rich scholarship on the matter.[29] The New Code of Civil Procedure, from 1975, established the possibility of procedural contracts and also dedicated an entire part to international and national arbitration.[30]

The biggest indicator of the friendly posture towards procedural agreements can be found, nevertheless, in the first thirteen articles of the Code. They define and organize the principle of cooperation, which is the main principle of the "new paradigm" of cooperative procedure, and is meant to "reconcile the liberal principles of French tradition, which make the trial the business of the parties, with an affirmation of the powers of the judge [...]".[31] The principle is supposed to establish a balance between the parties and the judge, stimulating cooperation towards a fair and efficient resolution of a dispute.[32]

From the French experience also comes the "*calendrier de la procédure*", which authorizes the parties and the judge to establish, through agreement, an agenda for the *mise en état*. The Procedure Code determines that a *conseiller* (before the court of appeal) or *juge* (before the *tribunal de grande instance*) *de la mise en état* has to get a case ready for the courts. These judges manage the cases and organize everything in order to reach the stage in which the cases are ready to be decided. In these courts, the procedure is written, and the judges establish an agenda and deadlines so that the parties can present everything in time. In other courts, the procedure is mainly oral and the cases are managed during the

29 Fabbi, *supra* n. 10, at 6.

30 L. Cadiet, "Introduction to French Civil Justice System and Civil Procedural Law", 28 *Ritsumeikan University Law Review* 331, 343 (2011). This does not mean there were no arbitrations in France before the new code.

31 Cadiet, *supra* n. 30, at 349.

32 L. Cadiet, "Les Conventions Relatives au Procès en Droit Français: Sur la Contractualisation du Règlement des Litiges", 62 *Rivista Trimestrale di Diritto e Procedura Civile* 7, 15 (2008).

hearings.[33] Lawyers, however, should have discipline because they have to keep track of the proceedings without the help of a judge or notices.[34]

In the French notion, therefore, *case management* is supposed to symbolize effective cooperation between the litigants and the judge. The idea is that litigation is mainly a matter of private interests and the courts should promote social peace. The public aspects of the judiciary are mainly explained in terms of public budget and usage of finite resources, which seem to be the only limit to private initiative and control. Resources must be divided between all cases in the Judiciary, and this cannot be done by the parties.[35] *Case management* is also a synonym for deformalizing procedures, since a judge can adapt the proceedings to fit the cases – a single formalist sequence of acts is not necessary.[36]

This cooperative model is supposed to be deployed through procedural agreements drafted and signed not only by private parties, but also between parties and judges. Some agreements can also be defined in general protocols determined between the courts and their "habitual interlocutors, especially the bar".[37] The agreements, therefore, can assume multiple formats.

Procedural contracts are also related to the tendency of "dejudiciarization of cases"[38]– in other words, privatization of adjudication. A "plural system of justice" demands that dispute resolution is not only handled by courts, and in this system the judge is never the first (and preferably the last) resource.[39] The more concrete aspects of this relationship between the two phenomena, however, remain uncertain.

33 Cadiet, *supra* n. 30, at 356.

34 F. Ferrand, "The Respective Role of the Judge and the Parties in the Preparation of Case in France", in Nicolò Trocker et al. (eds), *The Reforms of Civil Procedure in Comparative Perspective* 21 (Torino, G. Giappichelli, 2005).

35 Cadiet, *supra* n. 32, at 15; Cadiet, *supra* n. 13, at 17.

36 See generally L. Cadiet, "Case management judiciaire et déformalisation de la procédure", 125 *Revue française d'administration publique* 133 (2008).

37 Cadiet, *supra* n. 32, at 16.

38 Cadiet, *supra* n. 30, at 368.

39 Cadiet, *supra* n. 32, at 17.

(iii) Italy

In the Italian Civil Procedure Code of 1942, jurisdictional activity was defined in terms of the application of the law to concrete cases and not in terms of dispute resolution. The statute, therefore, was (and is) more focused on reinforcing the authority of the judge[40] and not on the autonomy of the parties. Procedural agreements are at odds with this perspective, which highlights the public aspects of procedure, and with the idea that there is a complete separation between the procedure that happens in the courts and the freedom of contract that allows the parties to opt for arbitration. The concept of procedural contracts, as discussed by authors in the 1930 s and 1940 s, represented a step backwards and the rejection of the modern aspects of procedure, which emphasized its public nature.[41]

The cooperation principle has been added to the Code in more recent reforms, such that which changed article 101, in 2009, giving a new definition to the adversarial principle. The new article renders "surprise decisions" invalid: before deciding matters that are considered of "public order" and that can be examined *sua sponte* (such as the application of the statute of limitations), a judge has to hear the parties. The new provision is connected to a cooperative conception of the adversarial principle that demands that the parties and judge maintain constant dialogue and that there should be no surprises during a procedure – not even for matters of public order that can be decided *ex officio.*[42]

Cooperation, here, is still quite far from the French notion, centred in procedural contracts. There is no provision in the Civil Procedure Code that allows such agreements, which makes the matter highly controversial among scholars, as some believe the agreements are possible on the basis of the general principle of freedom of contract, defined in article 1322 of the Civil Code.[43] The matter, however, remains highly controversial.

---

40 R. Caponi, "Autonomia Privata E Processo Civile: Gli Accordi Processuali", 62 *Rivista Trimestrale di Diritto e Procedura Civile* 99, 107 (2008).

41 S. Satta, *Contributo Alla Dottrina Dell'arbitrato* 50 (Milano, Vita e Pensieto, 1931).

42 M. Gradi, "Il Principio Del Contraddittorio E La Nullità Della Sentenza Della *Terza via*", 4 *Rivista di Diritto Processuale* 826 (2010).

43 Caponi, *supra* n. 40, at 109.

Some procedural matters, however, are always seen as negotiable by the parties, such as opting for arbitration and choice of forum.[44] Waivers are usually possible, but courts are a bit sceptical in some cases, such as waivers of appeals.[45] Parties can also determine a different allocation for the burden of proof,[46] and, by failing to argue against the facts presented by an opposing party, limit the facts that will be decided by the judge.[47] These examples, however, seem rather modest in comparison to the ambitions of the *contractualization* of procedure, since they have been seen as negotiable for many years in the Italian tradition – and in many others (such as France and Germany).

In 2009, the Civil Procedure Code was also amended to include a provision on procedural calendars. The provision, however, is very different from the French version that is considered a model of cooperative procedure, as it is mainly directed at the judge. The court can set a calendar for a procedure, but not the parties, which means there are no negotiations regarding the time frame of the dispute.[48]

The general context does not seem to favour the acceptance of procedural agreements, since the statutory reforms do not appear to have departed from the public focus established in the first version of the Code. Yet those who argue in favour of the agreements point to the fact that a procedural system should adapt to its surroundings despite the lack of explicit legal authorization, giving way to individual autonomy. For them, the system should open itself to these private creations in order to achieve the richness and complexity that can cope with the ever-growing sophistication of juridical relations.[49] For now, it seems these are still only ambitious suggestions: the Italian system appears to be very attached to its public character.

---

44 Fabbi, *supra* n. 10, at 8.

45 *Ibid.* at 9.

46 *Ibid.*

47 For an opposing view, see M. Taruffo, "Verità Negoziata?", 62 *Rivista Trimestrale di Diritto e Procedura Civile* 69 (2008).

48 Fabbi, *supra* n. 10, at 6.

49 Caponi, *supra* n. 40, at 118–119.

(iv) Brazil

In 2015, a new Civil Procedure Code was passed into law. The previous Code dated from 1975 and had been amended several times, but had already authorized some form of procedural agreements in its original text. Article 158 allowed parties to create, modify or extinguish procedural rights through agreements or through unilateral acts (such as when a party withdraws an appeal or accepts a part of the claims of an opposing party).

Despite the text of the Code, there were no procedural agreements in terms of what I have been calling privatization of procedure in this paper. In fact, the term was not even used by scholars or practitioners. Parties were allowed to opt for arbitration, to draft a choice of forum clause, to agree to stay the proceedings (for up to six months), to postpone a hearing, to settle and to shift the burdens of proof. Yet none of those possibilities was called a procedural agreement.

The new Code establishes cooperation as a procedural principle (article 6) and expressly allows procedural contracts in article 190. It is also possible to create a procedural calendar (article 191), as long as it is defined in agreement between both parties and the judge. The calendar will set dates for all procedural acts and parties will not receive any notice of them.[50]

The limits to agreements were established in general terms (article 190, single section): a judge should not enforce them if they were part of adhesion contracts or if any of the parties is in a vulnerable situation. Since there are no specific limits regarding what the parties can and cannot agree to, scholars have been attempting to forge guidelines for interpreting article 190.

There has been a scholarly frenzy around procedural agreements, with many books and articles being published in 2015. The interpretive guidelines developed by procedure scholars and researchers are amenable to cooperation in general, allowing the parties to reduce or expand deadlines, determine oral arguments when a court does not allow them, make longer oral arguments than allowed, "negotiate on evidence matters", allow third

---

50 See generally E. J. F. Costa, "Calendarização Processual", in: F. Didier Jr., A. P. Cabral, and P. H. P. Nogueira (eds), *Negócios Processuais* 353 (Salvador, Juspodivm, 2015).

parties other than the ones authorized by law to join the litigation, establish sanctions for violations of the agreements and much more.[51]

Regarding the limits, authors also mention that the agreements cannot violate due process and that inequalities between the parties should be considered by a judge. Some authors, however, attempt to relativize the few clear limitations defined by the Code, asserting that agreements in adhesion contracts should generally be enforced, with the exception of cases of extreme vulnerability.[52]

Some procedural rules, nevertheless, seem to be considered out of bounds even to the friendliest authors, who say the agreements are not allowed to create new appeals or to modify rules of "absolute" jurisdiction (which are considered inflexible and can nullify an entire case if disrespected).[53] There are not, however, any coherent explanations for such rules being placed out of bounds. It is not clear why the parties cannot create an appeal but can create the possibility of oral arguments when they are not allowed, or to expand the deadlines for an existing appeal.

Brazilian scholars who oppose such extended possibilities for procedural agreements focus on thc public nature of procedure, on the equitable distribution of public resources (which should not allow parties to extend the duration of the proceedings, for example) and reject the idea that courts only exist to solve private disputes.[54]

(v) United States

Professor Judith Resnik has noted that the dominating values in U.S. procedure have shifted from process to contract. Since the 1980 s, due process procedure has been increasingly being transformed into contract procedure, referring both to the encouragement of dispute resolution through contract (choosing alternative dispute resolution mechanisms, judicial set-

---

51 L. C. Cunha, "Negócios Jurídicos Processuais No Processo Civil Brasileiro", in: F. Didier Jr., A. P. Cabral, and P. H. P. Nogueira (eds), *Negócios Processuais* 67–68 (Salvador, Juspodivm, 2015).

52 Cunha, *supra* n. 51, at 67.

53 *Ibid.* at 69.

54 See generally S. C. Arenhart and G. Osna, "Os *Acordos Processuais* No Novo CPC: Aproximações Preliminares", 4 *Revista Eletrônica Do Tribunal Regional Do Trabalho Da 9 a Região* 103 (2015) 103.

tlements) and to the enforcement of the parties' agreements that exclude conflicts from court litigation.[55]

This movement is usually connected to the idea of managerial judging, rather than with the creation of procedure contracts (or contracting for procedure) in the moulds mentioned in the previous sections. In fact, Professor Resnik examined the evolution of Rule 16 of the Federal Rules of Civil Procedure to demonstrate how the new procedural ratio was recently implemented.[56] The rule was changed in 1983 to give more control to judges, who can now use pre-trial proceedings to facilitate settlement or direct the litigants to extrajudicial dispute resolution. Managerial judges, therefore, move from adjudicating to negotiating disputes.[57]

Rule 16 actually allows a judge to do much more. It enables her to establish a schedule, modify the extent of discovery, order the amendment of pleadings, avoid unnecessary proofs, adopt special procedures to manage complex issues, and more. The rule gives judges more control than the adversarial system typically attributes to them, giving them more power.

This newly acquired power is, however, used mainly for the purpose of promoting settlement or streamlining trials.[58] In that sense, managerial judging is a synonym for informality (lack of public records), lack of formal rules, no reviewability and a certain deviation from the public purposes of trial.[59]

Apart from managerial judging and incentivizing settlements, the signs of application of contract law principles are related to more traditional examples of negotiable procedural rules, such as arbitration clauses, confidentiality of settlements, jury waivers and limitation of discovery.[60] Authors use the terms "designer trials"[61] and "consensual adjudicatory proce-

---

55 J. Resnik, "Procedure as Contract", 80 *Notre Dame Law Review* 593, 597-598 (2004).

56 *Ibid.* at 611–612.

57 *Ibid.* at 613–614.

58 *Ibid.* at 613.

59 See generally J. Resnik, "Managerial Judges", 96 *Harvard Law Review* 374 (1982).

60 E. G. Thornburg, "Designer Trials", *Journal of Dispute Resolution*, 109-204, text available eletronically at <http://papers.ssrn.com/sol3/papers.cfm?abstract_id=895001.>, last visited 7 April 2016.

61 Thornburg, *supra* n. 60, at 181.

dure"[62] to refer to these examples or to forum selection clauses and choice of law clauses.

The possibility of waiving statutory or contractual provisions was established in old precedent,[63] and the Supreme Court held in the 1970 s that forum selection clauses should be enforced unless a compelling reason made enforcing unreasonable.[64] In theory, parties could make procedural agreements regarding many other aspects, such as establishing different standards of pleadings, different timing and conditions for raising defences, limitations on joinder of third parties, timing and scope of review in appeals, and so on. The case law, however, shows that there is not so much creativity,[65] and procedural contracts, as seen in the other four systems examined (particularly the new Brazilian idea of negotiated procedure), do not seem to be common.

(IV) Preliminary Points of Analysis

(a) Why Have Procedural Agreements at All?

At a first glance, contractualizing procedure seems an ineffective way of trying to make courts more appealing to private actors, even if it succeeds in its attempts to adapt the courts to new demands or make them more efficient – and there is no particular evidence that it will. After all, it is not always the inflexibility of procedural rules that makes the judiciary unattractive; and even when that is the case, other aspects are equally discouraging, such as longer litigation and lack of technical knowledge. For the same reasons, parties might as well resort to arbitration. Having tailor-made proceedings, therefore, might not be enough to bring more cases to courts.

Scholars have tried to determine other factors that justify the adoption of procedural contracts. For some, it is a way of bringing the flexibility of

---

62 L. S. Mullenix, "Another Choice of Forum, another Choice of Law: Consensual Adjudicatory Procedure in Federal Court", 57 *Fordham Law Review* 291, 296 (1988).

63 *Shutte v. Thompson*, 82 U.S. 151 (1873).

64 *The Brennen v. Zapata Off-Shore Company*, 407 U.S. 1 (1972).

65 R. G. Bone, "Party Rulemaking: Making Procedural Rules through Party Choice", 90 *Texas Law Review* 1329, 1343–1351 (2012).

arbitration to those who cannot afford it. This assumption, however, is at odds with the costs of creating tailor-made procedural rules, which require a certain level of sophistication and considerable knowledge and experience from the lawyers who draft them. It is very unlikely that those who cannot afford arbitration will be able to hire such professionals.

In fact, designing your own proceedings might not be a benefit at all. Even if a party can afford an expensive lawyer, creating a particular procedural framework demands considerable time and effort. The extra costs of this legal service might be too high for its potential benefits. International arbitration agreements, for example, usually adopt one set of pre-established procedural rules, such as those created by the ICC (International Chamber of Commerce), UNCITRAL (United Nations Commission on International Trade Law) and other international chambers. The same is true for domestic arbitration agreements. Even in a setting that allows for total flexibility and tailored proceedings, many parties choose a standardized option, which indicates this "freedom" might not be so attractive after all.

Procedural agreements also seem to be at odds with crowded dockets (particularly in some of the legal systems) and with the extremely limited amount of time a judge is able to devote to each case. Setting schedules and using a different set of rules seems time consuming, while the relevance of such agreements remains obscure.

Commonly, the agreements are related to efficiency and to intelligent use of public resources, but there is no clear indication that they will make courts more efficient in general. If parties can decide on the applicable procedural rules, and judges must follow their determination, there is little chance for courts to correct excessive allocation of resources into a set of particular cases. The parties are free, in theory, to design the rules as they wish, even if that makes the proceedings less efficient or if they demand more time and resources than an average case.

Even if a judge is also drafting the agreement, as happens in the cases with a schedule or calendar, she may not be able to foresee the most appropriate timeframe to secure efficiency. There is no real connection between procedural agreements and more efficient dispute resolution.

Both private and public justifications for the adoption of procedural contracts, therefore, seem unconvincing. There is no evidence that their use will bring benefits to the parties or to the Judiciary, and some scepticism regarding their popularity is consequently plausible. The lack of empirical research on the matter, however, leaves the question unanswered.

(b) Managerial Judging and Procedural Agreements

The efficiency argument is also related to managerial judging. Different scholars emphasize different aspects of procedural management, to the point that it becomes hard to understand if they are discussing a singular phenomenon. In the U.S. context, it is related to promoting settlements, alternative dispute resolution and getting cases out of court. A completely different idea is behind case management in France, where a judge's managing capabilities are supposed to make the proceedings more adapted to each case. In the Brazilian case, a managerial judge should use her powers to cooperate with the parties; and if there is a procedural contract, she should steer away from ordinary procedural rules and follow the parties' determinations.

Managerial judging seems to be related both to cooperation and to the modification or adaptation of procedural rules. These two aspects seem to be directed to the judge and the parties, but the emphasis on one or the other varies according to the system examined. Cooperation refers mainly to the relationship between all the actors in litigation, and its implications are not foreseeable in the abstract – it may point to the enforcement of procedural contracts or only to avoiding surprises for the parties, as in the Italian tradition. As for the possibility of modifying procedural rules, it can be directed towards the judge, which allows for more stringent case management and the adaptation of the procedure to specific cases; or it can be directed towards the parties, allowing them to draft procedural contracts.

The possible link between the two phenomena through the use of similar rhetoric might be in this ambivalent aspect of the modification of procedural rules. In the privatization of adjudication, a judge has to be able to modify or adapt the rules to manage cases and direct them to other forms of dispute resolution and to encourage settlements. This power is particularly important for systems previously classified as adversarial, where a judge assumes a more passive role.

The adaptation, however, can be decisive in traditions previously regarded as inquisitorial (such as the Italian one), where a judge is considered to be bound to the public rules of procedure, if procedural agreements are to be made possible: they allow her the necessary flexibility to avoid the application of the rules and guarantee the enforcement of the contracts. For the privatization of procedure, the possibility of adapting procedural rules is not only directed at the parties, but also at the judge.

In any case, management broadens judicial power, which can be used towards many different goals. Managerial judging can promote the public aspects of procedure and can also attempt to make courts more efficient (and may not succeed); but if the newly acquired powers are only used to promote settlement, they confirm the contractual logic of procedure.

It seems that the concept of case management is yet a bit obscure, and its relationship to procedural agreements is unclear – despite both concepts being mentioned together in scholarship. Giving more power to a judge could actually be seen as contradictory to the idea that she should enforce all agreements. If she can decide which is the most efficient path to solve a dispute, what is to be done when that path is contrary to the wishes of the parties?

(c) Historical Background and the Uniqueness of Procedural Agreements

Scholars hesitate over the novelty of procedural agreements: they seem to believe that such contracts are new and inspiring, while affirming they follow a traditional idea. Some authors make an effort to forge a link to the past and point to older practices. The connected traditional practices are, however, not the same as the current *contractualization*.

Practices such as failing to argue against all of an opposing party's claims, or accepting part of them, or choosing a particular forum derive mainly from the substantive rights that are involved in a conflict and their alienability. I believe the conduct of the parties during the proceedings in these cases is an act of conscious discarding of that right, which is not exactly the case with procedural contracts – contrary to the efforts to use these examples as evidence of a long tradition of contracting procedural rules.

The attempts to forge this link to the past obscures that there is something different in the current proposals for viable procedural agreements (particularly in the Brazilian case). They demand (or may demand, depending on the case) a different attitude from the courts, which become subordinate to the will of the parties in matters that may cause an unreasonable expense of public resources in particular cases, generating disparate treatment. And this disparate treatment is not caused necessarily by the complexity of a case, but only by the will of the parties. It is not a case of standardized rules that interpret certain procedural actions (or inactions) as disposing of an alienable right – such as in choice of forum or arbitration clauses – it is a case of particular, tailor-made rules that bind courts and public servants. These agreements, in their most radical form, are nothing like rules of standard procedure.

(V) Empirical Research and the Two Privatizations

(a) The Importance of Empirical Analysis of the Privatization of Adjudication

Much of the implications of these agreements are obscure and further research is necessary. The lack of sufficient empirical research on the matter hinders any hypothesizing as to how desirable and useful procedural agreements actually are. There is no evidence that these agreements are actually being drafted and used by those who already favoured arbitration or for those who cannot pay for arbitration. Both hypotheses seem highly unlikely. There is also no data on how often they are used in the countries where they have been adopted for more than ten years.

The lack of any empirical research on these contracts hinders their analysis as a legal institute and as a phenomenon in themselves. Assessing theoretical correlation with other institutes is possible but attempting to establish causality between phenomena is basically impossible. Most of the scholarship on procedural contracts makes empirical claims when addressing the importance and the need for them, but these claims are not backed up by any research. Without some minimum understanding of how the institute functions, all the statements on the correlation of the privatizations of procedure and adjudication are only hypotheses.

The same is not true regarding the privatization of adjudication. Particularly in the United States, the phenomenon has been analysed through empirical data and important conclusions have been drawn, most of them counter-intuitive.

The number of cases that went to trial in the US has always been small – in 1962, only 11.5 percent of cases were trialled.[66] The small number reflects the architecture of the American court system, which can only give full treatment to a small minority of the matters which should be able

66 M. Galanter, "The Vanishing Trial: An Examination of Trials and Related Matters in Federal and State Courts", 1 *Journal of Empirical Legal Studies* 459, 461 (2004).

to use it and relies on costs barriers to keep cases away[67] – litigation is extremely expensive in many aspects, such as counselling, court fees and expert analysis.

The system has shifted the costs of dispute resolution from the state to private parties, allowing for a high level of litigation and extensive investigation of facts (through discovery) with low public investment in courts.[68] As a result, the number of trials has always been low, even if one considers that the costs and the high level of expert participation (evidenced, for example, by the use of jury analysts) have increased in recent decades.

Following this logic, one could expect that it would be natural for the number of claims to rise more rapidly than the capacity of the system to handle them, and the number of trials to be proportionally reduced. Instead, the absolute number of trials has decreased, and federal courts conducted more than twice the number of civil trials per year two decades ago than they do today.[69] In 2002, only 1.8 percent of cases filed went to trial.[70]

The decrease was not caused by a reduction in the number of filings: in federal courts, filings have increased fivefold since 1962.[71] In some state courts, filings went down, but trials were reduced by a bigger proportion.[72]

Regarding the migration to other dispute resolution mechanisms, the data also shows important conclusions. Many of the migrating cases were first filed in federal courts and went to ADR within the courts. In 2001, that happened to 24,000 cases, one seventh of those filed in that year.[73] According to the American Arbitration Association, their docket grew from 1,000 in 1960 to 17,000 in 2002.[74] However, these other mechanisms have flourished in particular areas, while the decline in trials is general.[75]

---

67 Galanter, *supra* n. 66, at 516.

68 S. C. Yeazell, "Getting What We Asked For, Getting What We Paid For, and Not Liking What We Got: The Vanishing Civil Trial", 1 *Journal of Empirical Legal Studies* 943, 964–965 (2004).

69 Galanter, *supra* n. 66, at 516 and 519.

70 *Ibid.* at 461.

71 *Ibid.* at 435.

72 *Ibid.* at 516.

73 *Ibid.* at 514.

74 *Ibid.* at 515.

75 *Ibid.* at 517.

There is not one single explanation for the phenomenon of privatization of adjudication, with many factors seemingly intertwined. The reforms in procedural law are also important, since they reflect the main principle that guided them: pre-trial settlement is cheaper, better and faster than trial.[76] Managerial judging is related to the "vanishing trials" in the sense that nontrial adjudication, mainly through summary judgments, has also increased. In 1975, 3.7 percent of trials were summary trials, while in 2000 it was 7.7 percent.[77]

The data reveals that the privatization of adjudication is not simply a flight from courts. The number of filings may have been reduced in state courts, but they have increased in the federal judiciary. And it is also not merely a choice towards other dispute resolution mechanisms, since many cases were first filed in court before being directed to ADR. The judges' actions, therefore, can direct parties to other mechanisms, to settlement or to various forms of non-trial adjudication. Many of these paths do not share the attributes of public courts, mainly the publicity aspect, and the consequences of the loss of these attributes are yet unclear.

The complexity of the phenomenon, in any case, is highlighted by its empirical analysis, even if firm conclusions cannot be drawn: the simple rejection of common sense conclusions already represents an increase in understanding. The same cannot be said of the privatization of procedure, where empirical research is yet to be done.

(b) Future Research Proposal

Looking at the short comparative analysis, two systems seem to be the most interesting for future research. France, having expressly included contracts in the procedural code more than 30 years ago, is the most obvious candidate. In the French courts, these contracts have been a clear possibility for a long time, and it is the perfect system to address their relevance and their usage.

Any attempt to find data on procedural contracts in France is, however, very frustrating. There is no scholarship on the topic and researches on *Juris Classeur* (the French equivalent of computer-assisted legal research

76 Yeazell, *supra* n. 68, at 948.

77 Galanter, *supra* n. 66, at 483.

providers) show less than 400 decisions mentioning the contracts from 1975 until 2016.

The research results are clearly not relevant for a serious analysis. The French system does not include all decisions in their internet database and there is no way of knowing, through the website, the number of procedural contracts that appeared before the courts. It serves to illustrate how further research is needed.

Another interesting system would be the Brazilian one. In Brazil, procedural contracts are a new institute, since the new Civil Procedure Code came into force in 2016, and Brazilian scholarship is pushing for a more liberal interpretation of the rules that limit these contracts and for a broader scope of application. It would be interesting to assess lawyers' and judges' views on the matter, as it is quite new – whether they are familiar with the institute and their views on its possible uses, its efficiency and the courts' reception of it.

In both systems, ethnographic research seems to provide the most adequate approach, since it allows the researcher to work with few cases and in great detail, and also permits her to work with primarily unconstructed data, that has never been coded before. In France, the data that is available is most probably incomplete. Since no empirical research has been done, this may be the most appropriate methodology, for it can provide a first overview of the cultural aspects of procedural contracts in practice.

In the Brazilian case, there is no data available, since the institute is too new and the official online database of judicial decisions is incomplete: like in France, it does not include all cases. Ethnography provides an approach that is both feasible and flexible to capture first impressions on a new institute. This is a unique moment (it is the only time such a research can be conducted – first impressions on a brand new institute) and the topic is very interesting.

For both countries, I would start with surveys sent to practicing lawyers and to judges, in a second phase.[78] The respondents would be asked to rank statements as true or false on a scale of 1-5, which would be grouped by topic: general perception/familiarity, perceptions on possible uses, efficiency, utility to clients and the courts' reception of the institute. I plan to

78 In Brazil, easy access can be provided by the national bar association (the Brazilian Order of Lawyers) and by the National Council of Justice (an agency in charge of the Judiciary's transparency and accountability.

approach the qualitative data through thematic coding, drawn inductively from the data.[79]

The surveys will provide some data on the phenomenon, which can guide future projects, such as a second ethnographic approach focused on interviews and observation, and provide support for more ambitious projects with big data and qualitative analysis in countries that have no reliable available databases.

79 On thematic coding and the analysis and interpretation of qualitative data, see C. Robson, *Real world research* 465-495 (West Sussex, John Wiley & Sons, 2011).

National Procedural Law

I. The Italian Assisted Negotiation for Legal Separation and Divorce

*Luisa Enna**

(I) Methodology and Introduction to the Theme

"Disputing will reflect the culture's values", with this sentence Professor C. Menkel-Meadow suggests prudence in copying dispute resolution methods from one judicial system to another,[1] since the result obtained in a specific frame of reference could be different in another.

This warning could in turn suggest a research method to study dispute resolution, especially alternative dispute resolution methods (ADRs) considering that they are better suited to be 'exported' in another system. In fact, if it is true that disputes will reflect a culture's values within a specific judicial system, it is also valid that the cultural context of a definite judicial system will affect the legislative choice in a particular historical moment. Indeed, when the lawmaker decides to create a particular framework for a determinate situation, it takes into consideration the needs and input coming from the societal context.[2]

For this reason, reversing the starting sentence, one could also argue that *"*the culture's values will be reflected in disputing*"*. Consequently, there is a reciprocal influence between the ways people dispute and their cultural context.[3]

---

* PhD in arbitration. Practising lawyer and teaching assistant in Private and Civil Law, Università degli Studi di Cagliari.

1 C. Menkel-Meadow, "Mothers and fathers of inventions: the intellectual founders of ADR", 16 *Ohio journal on Dispute Resolution*, I-30, 11 (2000).

2 In this regard see O. Chase, *Law, Culture and Ritual. Disputing systems in cross-cultural context* 2 (New York University Press, New York and London, 2005): "Dispute processes are in large part a reflection of the culture in which they are embedded … More, they are institutions through which social and cultural life is maintained, challenged, and altered, or as the same idea has been expressed, constituted or constructed".

3 The interrelationship between the dispute resolution process and culture is masterfully analysed by Chase, *supra* n. 2, at 48:"Any proposal to borrow procedures

On the basis of this preliminary consideration, the proposed method derives from the idea that knowledge of each specific legal disposition can be reached only after a historical and cultural analysis of the background in which it was drawn up.

In other words, knowledge of a specific norm and in-depth understanding of it could be reached only by starting with a research method that highlights the social context wherein the normative pattern is embedded.

This method will therefore be articulated in three steps: 1) an evaluation of the historical evolution of the legal framework concerning a particular juridical field; 2) an analytical overview of the rules set forth for a specific subject-matter; 3) an evaluation of the analysed rules in the light of the context in which they are embedded - highlighting the historical evolution and the specific framework that evinces from the precedent analysis; so as to emphasize the interaction between substantive and procedural law.

In the first phase of this study, an analysis of the historical evolution of a specific subject-matter, in a determined juridical system, is presented. In this phase, the objective of the method is to identify the interrelation between a socicty's needs and its lawmaker's choice of legal framework. By doing this, we realize our aim of highlighting the connection between the cultural context and the content of legislation. Hence, this method will encompass the whole spirit of a specific discourse, rather than merely outline the rationale for a single disposition. In this phase the analysis is done through a general approach, as an entire juridical niche is analysed, rather than singular dispositions.

In the second phase, the study proceeds detailing the pattern of a given procedure. More precisely, the study of a procedural scheme is chosen because dispute resolution methods are good visual angles from which to gain insight into values inherent in a specific social context. Furthermore, the procedure will be analysed by highlighting the most relevant aspects in the light of an interdisciplinary approach. In other words: singular proce-

---

from another society should prompt a cultural inquiry. One reason for this instrumental: Will the borrowed approach work in a new social setting? … A more important issue is raised by the reflexivity of culture and disputing: How will the new procedures impact on the society that adopts them? … Underlying these concerns are the subsidiarity claims that the formal procedures of dispute resolution found in any culture reflect and express its metaphysics and its values … and dispute procedures are in turn one of the processes (rituals if you will) by which social values and understandings are communicated and are therefore critical to the ongoing job of transmitting and maintaining culture".

dural aspects will be not evaluated with the mere purpose of acquiring knowledge of the procedure itself, but with the scope to highlight that procedural law may affect other fields of study and vice versa. For this reason, the method departs from an interdisciplinary perspective that will manifest itself in the final conclusion of the third and last step of the study.

In summary, the methodology proposes a circular movement: starting from social aspects and returning to them, aiming for an analysis of procedural patterns that can be observed in the light of the substantive effects on the subject.

At the end of the study one could argue that not only "Disputing will reflect the culture's values", but also that "the way people dispute will (be) affect(ed) the culture's values". Procedures influence the values of a judicial system rather than being unilaterally conditioned by them.[4]

For the application of this method, family law has been selected because of its potential to be evaluated with an interdisciplinary approach, involving different sciences - both social and legal, procedural and substantive.[5]

More specifically, the analysis of a recent Italian norm concerning dispute resolution in family matters is proposed as a case study to 'improve' the proposed method.

Thus, the order of the exposition also aims to reflect an interdisciplinary method, starting from a general presentation of the theme by a historical perspective, and passing through an analytical illustration of procedural legislation, to conclude with some final considerations on the impact of procedures in the national, Italian juridical system, and on the possibilities to apply this pattern from a European perspective.[6]

---

4 To understand the suggested visual angle it is also crucial to consider the basic idea that Professor Chase outlines at the end of his work Chase, *supra* n. 2, at 141: "systems of dispute resolution do not exist in nature – they are created by human beings and are culture specific; moreover, disputing procedures are one of the important institutions through which the construction of social life is in turn and accomplished".

5 For a most in-depth analysis of the relation between family law and society see W. Gephart, "Family law as a culture, in Family law and culture in Europe", in *European Law Series* 347 (K. Boele-Woelki, N. Dethloff, W. Gephart, Antwerp, Intersentia, 2014).

6 The choice of the theme could be considered as a paradox considering K. Boele-Woelki, *The Principles of European Family Law: Its Aims and Prospects*, 1 *Utrecht Law Review* 160, 162 (2005): "Due to so-called cultural constraints family law has,

(II) Family Law in the Italian System

In the Italian Civil Code, introduced in 1942, the entire legislative section addressing family relationships was based on a hierarchical model, in which the husband was the chief of that significant and acknowledged social group that we call family.[7] This authoritarian model reflected the historical period - characterized by a totalitarian regime - during which the (current) Italian Civil Code has been drawn up. In that historical context the family was, therefore, conceived as a projection of individuals in society, and so family relations acquired juridical relevance only to the extent that they had a position of utility and relevance in, and for, it.[8]

Later, when the Italian Constitution was drawn up, the cultural context had changed so much that the conception of the family within society had also been modified. The family was, indeed, considered as a socially and juridically recognized organization, in which the individual realizes his/herself and his/her personality; moreover, within the family group each in-

---

until recently, remained almost completely outside the comparative research-based process. In the last few years, however, family law has increasingly become the subject of comparative law as well as of harmonization and even - in the case of international relationships - of the unification of law".

7 "[La famiglia] Volta per volta essa fu concepita come aggregazione collettiva a base dello Stato (a sua volta inteso non come insieme di individui ma di famiglie), un'istituzione attraverso la quale garantire il buon funzionamento della società (buone famiglie sono alla base di un buono Stato) o come libera espressione di volontà e di autonomie individuali, in cui far prevalere i diritti e gli interessi dei singoli sul supremo bene dell'ordine sociale": L. Garlati, "Analisi storica e sociologica della riforma del diritto di famiglia", in *La riforma del diritto di famiglia: maggio 1975 - maggio 2011 cambiamenti e prospettive*, 27-37, 28 (Centro per la riforma del diritto di familia, Milano, 2011). For a complete analysis of the relevant values in the original Italian system of family law see L. Balestra, "L'evoluzione del diritto di famiglia", 2 *Riv. trim dir. proc. civ.*, 1105 (2010); G. Bonilini, *Manuale di diritto di famiglia* (5th ed., Utet, Torino, 2010); P. Schlesinger, "Il diritto di famiglia dal 1975 a oggi. Trasformazioni intervenute e prospettive odierne", in *La riforma del diritto di famiglia: maggio 1975 - maggio 2011 cambiamenti e prospettive*, 39 (Centro per la riforma del diritto di famiglia, Milano, 2011).

8 This model was coherent with the concept of the contract as an instrument to realize the interest of the community rather than a technical tool to satisfy the private interests of individuals. This concept of the contract was clear from the dogma of the "causa" of the contract proposed by Emilio Betti who affirmed a private contract was the instrument that the State conceded to individuals to realize their interests, on the condition they are consistent with the interests of the entire community.

dividual has the same role and bears a duty of solidarity and of mutual support. More specifically, it could be said that those duties were both related with the principles in Article 2 of the Italian Constitution. In addition, through Article 3 of the Italian Constitution, the idea of equality between individuals was also set forth, and this brought about equality between spouses in the family relationship.[9] Moreover, those fundamental principles were specifically set forth in Articles 29, 30 and 31 for the family based on marriage. Because of these principles, from that moment onwards the traditional differences between husband and wife, outlined in the civil code within the family relationship, were no longer coherent with the Italian legal context.[10]

Despite the crucial role that jurisprudence had in enhancing this change of context, it was only in 1975 that a real reform of the normative familial pattern was enacted.[11] Particularly, the more significant amendments concerned: economic equality between spouses - thus each should contribute to the needs of the family by his/her work, and even household tasks were recognized as an economic contribution, at least in terms of 'saving' (cf. frugality) (Article 143 c. III c.c.); spouses were considered equal with regard to deciding how to direct family life and on their children's education (Articles 144 and 147 c.c.); equality between man and woman, from a juridical perspective, was reached by lowering the marriageable age, which before was considered an adequate measure to protect women who were considered unable to understand the meaning of marriage and, therefore, in need of protection.[12] In addition, from a proprietary perspective, spous-

---

9 About the application of the Article 3 in family law notice that "L'uguaglianza dei coniugi … non è un doppione inutile dell'uguaglianza prevista quale principio generale dall'art. 3 cost. né è un'uguaglianza da concepire in senso materialista sullo stampo del rapporto di scambio: è appunto l'uguaglianza di persone unite dal rapporto di coniugio, non di individui uti singuli": A. Nicolussi, "La famiglia: una concezione neo-istituzionale?", 1 *Europa e dir. priv.* 169, 169 (2012).

10 For a general overview on the topic see F. Parente, "La libertà matrimoniale", 1 *Rass. dir. civ.* 129 (2010).

11 For a general overview of the essential point of the reform see G. Servetti, "Il diritto di famiglia dal 1975 a oggi. Trasformazioni intervenute e prospettive odierne", in *La riforma del diritto di famiglia: maggio 1975 - maggio 2011 cambiamenti e prospettive*, 65-73 (Centro per la riforma del diritto di famiglia, Milano, 2011).

12 In this sense see P. Mantini, in *La riforma del diritto di famiglia, maggio 1975 - maggio 2011 cambiamenti e prospettive*, 7, 7 (Centro per la reforma del diritto di familia, Milano, 2011).

es have the same property rights to goods acquired during the marriage – unless they decided to opt for a separation of means, instead of for community property.[13]

In this general context of renovation affecting the relationships between spouses, the reformation of legal separation and divorce also had a particular significance. In fact, the right to file for legal separation was conceded when "to lead a life together" had become "intolerable". This provision reveals that the family bond is conceived as a project for life, undertaken by individuals to shape their personal rather than public existence. Consequentially, when (and if) the project to achieve that desired happiness has shown itself to be impossible there is no longer any reason to persist in that project.[14]

At this point, the family relationship bond, created by marriage, has evidently more points in common with contractual agreements than with participation in public social existence. The only difference within the peculiar content of this undertaking, compared to a typical contract, was the achievement of joint happiness (i.e. to achieve happiness *together*).[15]

---

13 See on this topic M. Paladini, "Commento agli artt. 177-199. Della famiglia", 1-152 in *Commentario del codice civile* (E. Gabrielli, L. Balestra, Utet, Torino, 2010).

14 In fact "le relazioni familiari, prima intese … in senso pubblicistico secondo il modello gerarchico fatto proprio dalla concezione fascista della famiglia, si resero private … Il matrimonio stesso, giungendo a capo di un lungo processo di trasformazione, andava mutando di significato, non più inteso dalla collettività come un'istituzione deputata a svolgere certe funzioni sociali e a garantire l'ordine sociale stesso, ma percepito dalla coppia come uno spazio di costruzione della privata felicità tramite la realizzazione di un progetto condiviso da individui liberi ed eguali. Il mutamento di significato del matrimonio … fece anche impallidire l'idea che il conflitto familiare rappresentasse una patologia. Al di là del peso di sofferenza che la rottura di un rapporto affettivo sempre comporta, infatti, l'incremento numerico dei fallimenti matrimoniali … rappresenta piuttosto la naturale conseguenza del mutamento delle aspettative dei partner e delle funzioni stesse del matrimonio": V. Pocar, "Analisi storica e sociologica della riforma del diritto di famiglia", in *La riforma del diritto di famiglia: maggio 1975 - maggio 2011 cambiamenti e prospettive* 18, 22 (Centro per la riforma del diritto di familia, Milano, 2011).

15 Pocar, *supra* n. 14, at 23: "Se il senso del vincolo matrimoniale come fondamento della relazione di coppia è mutato, e alla base di questa relazione stanno gli affetti volti a un progetto di vita comune, è ben chiaro che tale scopo può essere perseguito e realizzato in forme e in modi diversi da quelli offerti e stabiliti dall'istituto del matrimonio. Se la relazione di coppia si fonda sulla negozialità e sulla condivi-

In light of these considerations, it is clear that within the family relationship there is a combination of both proprietary and personal interests, in which the emotional aspects of the relationship between individuals also manifest themselves, and are to be taken into consideration by the lawmaker.

As a consequence, the judicial system has gradually recognized the values of those emotional aspects, even if a legal marital bond is (was not previously) not existent. This recognition has occurred because the family was considered an expression of the personality of an individual – who expresses him/herself also through the union that we call family – and because of this expression of identity, constitutionally granted as a fundamental right of the individual (as indicated by Article 2 of the Italian Constitution), and also because the same situation cannot be ruled upon in various manners (Article 3 of the Italian Constitution). Indeed, by attributing significance to the content of the familial relationship, regardless of the existence of a formal union between individuals, some of the provisions set forth for the bond of marriage have been extended, by analogy, to unmarried couples.[16]

For all of these reasons, when we look at family law it is hard not to appreciate the interaction between social context and the choices of the judicial system, and how they influence each other.[17] It is evident that the same fundamental rights that released marriage legislation from its original order have also served as the basis for accepting a conception of the family that is not exclusively dependent on a formal bond.[18]

Therefore, on the one hand, there is the concept of family relationship as a mixture of emotional and personal expressions between two individuals, which has gained juridical relevance out of the necessity to fit in with

sione di un progetto, ogni coppia e ogni individuo può ricercare, e anzi deve essere messo nella condizione di ricercare, la forma e i modi specifici più adatti a realizzare quel suo proprio progetto".

16 Nicolussi, *supra* n. 9, at 175.

17 On this theme and for the consequences in terms of European harmonization see in particular M.G. Cubeddu, D. Henrich, "Due modelli europei di regime patrimoniale della famiglia", 1 *Riv. dir. civ.* 563, 563 (2010).

18 S. Piraino, "Famiglia, società e diritto", 2 *Dir. fam. per.*, 779, 779 (2014),: "La famiglia è un rapporto, come un rapporto è la società civile, entrambe rispettivamente costituite di uno status familiae e di uno status civitatis, nel senso che le due realtà, essendo sempre di là dalle singole inquadrature individuali, implicano il rapporto tra di esse, ovvero il vincolo che le tiene insieme".

the fundamental rights of the individuals. On the other hand, the marital relation is still connected to a formal act, by which the parties (i.e. the spouses) choose, on a voluntary basis, to be tied by a more complex set of rules. In other words: we have a substantive concept of family relationship and a formal concept of the marital relation. In the latter case, the aspects related to consent, and the application of specific legislation accentuate the contractual aspect of the relation, whereas the family relationship – which is acknowledged regardless of the, more or less, formal character of the act of union, and is subject to some but not all of the regulations set forth in the civil code – is a concept related to fundamental rights, and to interests in the public sphere.

Hence, in this context, not only the substantive regime, but also the procedural scheme to regulate the relation should have relevance to the interests involved in the private sphere.[19] And this seems to be well understood by the Italian lawmaker, when, at the end of 2014, a new legal framework for legal separation and divorce was introduced in view of a 'de-jurisdiction' of procedures in family matters.

(III) Law 10th November 2014 N. 162: A General Overview

In late 2014, with the main purpose of reducing the case backlogs in the civil courts, the Italian legislator took a significant legislative measure that was the starting point for a comprehensive modernization of dispute resolution procedures in civil cases. The scope of this reform, introduced by L.

---

19 About the connection between the substantive law and the effect in the process see the words of F. Tommaseo, "Riflessioni sull'evoluzione del diritto processuale familiare", in *La riforma del diritto di famiglia: maggio 1975 - maggio 2011 cambiamenti e prospettive*, 75, 76 (Centro per la riforma del diritto di famiglia, Milano, 2011): "Un tempo si poteva dire che "*nella materia delle relazioni familiari e dei rapporti con i minori, l'interesse pubblico predominava e affievoliva le posizioni dei privati" 1 e che, in tale contesto, il legislatore ben poteva anche affievolire le garanzie processuali delle parti e predisporre processi intensamente deformalizzati, aperti alle iniziative ufficiose del giudice... essendo mutato il quadro di riferimento, è anche mutato l'oggetto della tutela giurisdizionale che essendo ora, in materia familiare, sempre più spesso tutela di diritti soggettivi, reclama forme processuali idonee a dare un tutela effettiva con le garanzie del giusto processo*".

162/2014,[20] is evident from its title "Measures for the de-jurisdiction (alization) and other interventions for the decrease of backlogs in the Civil Process" that announces the objective of the Italian lawmaker to encourage the use of ADRs, rather than referral to Court to solve conflicts.[21]

More specifically, the new law has introduced four innovative ADR methods, in addition to those already existing in the Italian legislative system.[22]

Article 1 sets forth a form of 'incidental' arbitration that can be started when a dispute is already under way, is pending before court, and the parties agree to request the judge to transfer the dispute to arbitration. The particularity of this ADR is the possibility to maintain the substantive effects of the claim after the 'relocation' of the dispute to arbitration. Thus, in this respect, the 'incidental arbitration' cannot be defined as a pure form of 'de-jurisdiction' even if it could contribute to realizing the goal of reducing the court's workload.[23]

In Article 2 an 'assisted negotiation' is outlined, which is an ADR of French origin which consists of the option to reach an agreement to solve the dispute in an amicable way with the mandatory assistance of (at least one) lawyer.[24] The role of the lawyer is, therefore, central, and the final agreement derives its validity from the presence of the lawyer(s) during

---

20 It must be specified that Law 164/2014 is that by which the Italian Parliament converted into law the Decree Law 132/2014 enacted by the Italian Government on September 12th.

21 This new law can be regarded as a 'zero budget' attempt of the Italian legislator to tackle the problem of judiciary slowness, drawing up a procedural provision rather than taking structural measures in the Italian judicial system. For a general overview of the grave problem of trial duration in Italy, see the OECD's report on "What makes civil justice more effective?" presented in 2013, wherein an average length of 564 days for civil proceedings in their first term was noted.

22 For a general overview see P. Biavati, "Note sullo schema di disegno di legge delega di riforma del processo civile", 1 *Riv. Trim. Dir. Proc, Civ.* 209 (2015); R. Bolognesi, "Il "contratto" sulla procedura di negoziazione assistita da uno o più avvocati", in www. *judicium.it,* latest visited 18th February 2017 – latest update 13th February 2017; S. Chiarloni, "Minime riflessioni critiche su trasferimento in arbitrato e negoziazione assistita", 1 *Riv. Trim. Dir. Proc. Civ.* 221 (2015).

23 The term "de-jurisdiction" roughly means to withdraw the dispute from the State courts and to solve the controversy without the intervention of the jurisdictional authority.

24 For a more detailed analysis of the French origin see P. Farina, "La negoziazione assistita dagli avvocati: da praeambolum ad litem ad outsourcing della decisione del giudice", *2 Riv. dir. proc.* 514, 514 (2015), and Bolognesi, *supra* n. 22. The

the negotiation. Even if this procedure doesn't involve any intervention by the court – as in the case of the incidental arbitration cited earlier – this method cannot be considered an actual example of 'de-jurisdiction' of procedures.[25] In fact, the assisted negotiation does not substitute the claim to court, but defers it to a second phase after eventual failure of the procedure.[26]

Indeed, the only ADRs, in the context of L. 162/2014, which have an actual 'de-jurisdiction' impact, are the "assisted negotiation for legal separation and divorce" *(Article 6), and the* "joint request to the Mayor" (Article 12).[27] So in the field of family matters the objective has been reached of extricating from a juridical context a type of conflict that tradition has exclusively attributed to public procedures, and to mandatory intervention by a judge.[28] Therefore, with the introduction of two new alternative methods in the field of family matters, for the first time, the idea has been

---

second author, in particular, criticizes the way the Italian lawmaker has chosen to import the French model into the Italian system.

25 The opportunity to enhance the involvement of the legal professionals is highlighted by Chiarloni, *supra* n. 22, at 221.

26 Article 3 specifies that this procedure is mandatory for conflicts concerning vehicle liability and contracts with a value equal or lower than 50,000 euros. Consequently, before submitting a claim to the court it is compulsory to engage in the assisted negotiation. Even if the choice to make this procedure compulsory probably will increase its popularity, and maybe it is the better way to encourage the parties to use an ADR method, this won't guarantee a retreat from the State judicial which could in any case be asked for after a failure of the ADR procedure, thus it is merely postponed. On the theme see also Farina, *supra* n. 24, at 514.

27 Indeed, as will be evident hereinafter, it is to be noted that there is a significant difference, in terms of procedure, between the assisted negotiation and the 'joint request to the Mayor'. In fact, the joint request to the Mayor can *never* be considered a pre-trial phase because there is no element of jurisdiction – not eventual, nor postponed, nor simplified – and the only element of public relevance is the presence of the Mayor (or a delegate).

28 A renovation of the process in marital matters in the Italian judicial system has been in the air for a long time, considering the substantive law concerning family has been consistently modified over the last century and during the last ten years. Despite this no relevant changes have been adopted for the process until now. In this sense Tommaseo, *supra* n. 19, at 77: "La riforma del diritto di famiglia del 1975, pur così incisiva e articolata, ha investito quasi esclusivamente la disciplina sostanziale dei rapporti familiari. Infatti, ad eccezione di alcune modifiche alle disposizioni di attuazione del codice civile che hanno ampliato le competenze del tribunale per i minorenni, il legislatore da un lato ha preferito evitare altri interventi sui profili processuali del diritto di famiglia (oltre a quelli in precedenza compiuti,

challenged that family conflicts must be solved exclusively in a juridical context.

Nevertheless, even if the main spirit of the law is to relocate legal separation and divorce in a more contractual sphere, it does not clarify the nature of the final provision that defines the *status* of legal separation or divorce of spouses. In addition, the law demonstrates a lack of consideration for procedural aspects which appear, on several points, not very well ordered, as will be discussed in the remainder of this review. The cause of these problems can be associated with the application of an executive decree for the introduction of the reform, and the consequent haste in a context of urgency, which could account for the lack of coordination resulting from this approach.[29]

To anticipate some of the considerations that will be further analysed later, a lack of accuracy is signalled by the contradiction between the title and the content of Article 6 of L. 162/2014, which regulates negotiations assisted by lawyers for legal separation and divorce. If, in an initial phase, and in accordance with the framework for the assisted negotiation for contracts (set in Article 2), the provision was to let the spouses take care of their legal separation or divorce with the assistance of one lawyer only, the final provision stipulates the imposition of the assistance of a lawyer for both parties (i.e. for each spouse). Hence, even if the title of Article 6 is still "negotiation assisted by lawyer" in the singular, the content of the Article obliges, beyond any doubt, the presence of two lawyers – one for each party.[30] This contradiction emerges also at the third comma of Article 6, wherein, again, the word lawyer is used in the singular, even if it is not

prima con la legge sull'adozione speciale del 1967 e poi con quella del 1970 sullo scioglimento del matrimonio), dall'altro lato ha confermato la scelta di distribuire l'esercizio della giurisdizione in materia familiare fra il tribunale ordinario e il tribunale per i minorenni". See also the positive comment on the new procedure for family matters in Chiarloni, supra n. 22, at 222, even if the author is sceptical about the real impact in decreasing the backlog, confirming the opportunity of the new legislation only in a dogmatic sense rather than to solve the crisis of the Italian judicial system.

29 M. A. Lupoi, "Separazione e divorzio", 1 *Riv. Trim. Dir. Proc. Civ.* 283 (2015), and M. Vaccari, "Profili di incostituzionalita' della negoziazione assistita obbligatoria", in www.*judicium.it.*, latest visited 18th February – latest update 13th February 2017.

30 Vaccari, *supra* n. 29, criticizes the provision of Article 2 as it prescribes only one lawyer.

appropriate. Other signs of the consequences derived from the haste in implementing the new framework can be found in the (dis)coordination of communication between the *Pubblico Ministero* ('public prosecutor')[31] and the lawyers and within the framework addressing the effects of the refusal of the "nulla òsta" (i.e. an act of clearance) by the public prosecutor, when the procedure is applied in the absence of children; and, moreover, in the lack of a legal framework for procedures in case of an intervention by the President of the Tribunal for procedures including children. All of these problems will be, in any case, taken into consideration in the analytical overview of the procedure.

However, it is important to highlight that the revolutionary choice to push family matters outside of the public sphere, traditionally prescribed for them, has been made by the provision of two new procedures for obtaining legal separation and divorce.

In particular, this review will analyse the framework set up in Article 6, that regulates the already-mentioned assisted negotiation by lawyers, but it must be noted, that this amendment has also introduced the possibility of a "joint request to the Mayor", available for couples without children that don't have the need to reach an agreement on property rights after their separation (or divorce) either. This procedure, which should be considered as a very important step to place family matters in a more contractual perspective, along with the procedure outlined in Article 6, will be examined only for the purpose of identifying the differences regarding the main procedure of the assisted negotiation. Finally, another important characteristic of these procedures is their optional rather than mandatory nature. In fact, Law 162/2014 has introduced assisted negotiation for legal separation and divorce and joint request to the Mayor, in addition to those procedures already existing in Italian Law. Consequently, spouses can now choose the procedure that better fits their needs.[32]

---

31 In the Italian judicial system the duty to represent the public interests in the process (i.e. during a trial) is on the office of the public prosecutor. As a matter of fact, the public prosecutor has a crucial role in criminal procedure and a minor place in the civil process, thus, in the civil process public interests rarely must be safeguarded. For this reason, it is not entirely correct to refer to the public prosecutor in the context of the assisted negotiation and the definition of public party is then preferred.

32 Chiarloni, *supra* n. 22, at 221.

(IV) The Assisted Negotiations for Legal Separation and Divorce

After the general presentation of L. 162/2014, attention must be focused on the procedure stipulated by Article 6. As outlined above, one could say that the lawmaker extends the application of the use of negotiation assisted by lawyers to family matters. In this sense the law has realized its goal of 'de-jurisdiction'; in fact, matters related to marriage have always been identified as subject to mandatory intervention by the authority of a judge, and now are moved toward the contractual system of dispute resolution.

To be more precise, it must be clear that access to the procedure is possible only if the spouses are actually legally bonded in marriage, and they have access to this procedure mainly for the purpose of proceeding with their legal separation or divorce. By doing this, the Italian legislator demonstrates consideration of the differences that exist between the concept of family on the one hand, and that of a relationship based on marriage on the other. This choice appears to be coherent with the opinion of the European Court of Human Rights which proposes a definition of "family relationship" not necessarily linked to a formal act of marriage.[33] This also means that the concept of family (and thus the interests linked to this concept) is different from the concept of spouses.

Even if this choice is criticized,[34] actually, it is the natural consequence of the fact that the Italian legislator has had in view a reform of the procedure for the change of status, and this appears also coherent with the choice of the European Legislator, that, in the Regulation 'Rome III', refers only to the change of status and implies the presence of the bond of legal marriage between the parties.[35]

---

33 *Z.H. and R.H. v. Switzerland,* (ECHR), 8 December 2015 "The Court reiterates that the notion of 'family life' in Article 8 is not confined solely to families based on marriage and may encompass other de facto relationships ... When deciding whether a relationship can be said to amount to 'family life', a number of factors may be relevant, including whether the couple live together, the length of their relationship and whether they have demonstrated their commitment to each other by having children together or by any other means".

34 Some criticism of this exclusion is expressed by R. Masoni, "Negoziazione assistita in ambito familiare e problemi procedurali connessi", 4 *Dir. Fam. Pers.* (2015), 1385 – 1402, at 1390 and F. Danovi, "Il processo di separazione e divorzio", in *Trattato di diritto civile e commerciale*, Vol. 4, 2489, 2540 (Cicu, Messineo, Mengoni, Schlessinger, Giuffrè, Milano, 2015).

35 The same exclusion was obviously present in EU Reg. 2201/2003 on Matrimonial and parental judgments: jurisdiction, recognition and enforcement, for the Italian

Hence, the relationship linked to marriage gains relevance, not for the value attributed to familial affection, but due to the consequences of being part of a legally recognized couple, and for the obligations related to legal custody, duties, and responsibilities that are inherent to that status.[36]

As a consequence, the reference to "marriage" excludes the possibility to extend the procedure to those types of "unions" which are legally binding, but that are not contained within the framework of marriage. In this

---

references on those themes see A. Anceschi, *La famiglia nel diritto internazionale privato. Aggiornato con la legge 15 luglio 2009, n. 94 (Disposizioni in materia di sicurezza pubblica)*, (Giappichelli, Torino, 2010); M. C. Baruffi, "Il regolamento sulla legge applicabile ai 'divorzi europei'", 4 *Dir. Un. Eur.* 867 (2011); C. Campiglio, "Prime applicazioni delle norme europee sui divorzi «internazionali»", 4 *Nuova Giur. Civ.*, 173(2015); B. Nascimbene, *Divorzio, diritto internazionale privato e dell'Unione europea*, (Giuffrè, Milano, 2011); I. Ottaviano, "La prima cooperazione rafforzata dell'unione europea: una disciplina comune in materia di legge applicabile a separazioni e divorzi transnazionali", 1 *Dir. Un. Eur.* 113 (2011); N. Trocker, "Il diritto processuale europeo e le «tecniche» della sua formazione:l'opera della corte di giustizia", 2 *Europa e dir. priv* 412. (2010); F. C. Villata, "Obblighi alimentari e rapporti di famiglia secondo il regolamento n. 4/2009", 3 *Riv. dir. internaz.* 693 (2011).

36 About the theme of marriage, the ECHR has declared that it is up to the State's discretion to decide who can be bound in a marriage. Thus, the differences between the legal status – which has a formal evidence – and the individual right to be recognized as a part of a sentimental relationship – also relevant for the law but in a different way – is confirmed. In this regard see *Schalk And Kopf vs. Austria*, (ECHR) June 2010: "the question whether or not to allow same-sex marriage is left to regulation by the national law of the Contracting State ... In that connection, the Court observes that marriage has deep-rooted social and cultural connotations which may differ largely from one society to another. The Court reiterates that it must not rush to substitute its own judgment in place of that of the national authorities, who are best placed to assess and respond to the needs of society. In conclusion, the Court finds that Article 12 of the Convention does not impose an obligation on the respondent Government to grant a same-sex couple such as the applicants' access to marriage". The Court also suggests that the right of the State to decide the rule of the marriage must not turn into a form of discrimination: "According to the Court's established case-law, Article 12 secures the fundamental right of a man and woman to marry and to found a family. The exercise of this right gives rise to personal, social and legal consequences. It is 'subject to the national laws of the Contracting States', but the limitations thereby introduced must not restrict or reduce the right in such a way or to such an extent that the very essence of the right is impaired". Particularly, the respect of the principals of non-discrimination is highlighted in the sentence of the Grand Chambre in *Vallianatos and Others vs. Greece*, (ECHR) 7 November 2013 n. 29381.

regard, it must be said that the Italian legislator has recently introduced a new form of civil union, titled "Regulation of civil unions between same sex couples and cohabitation", similar to marriage in many aspects, and for this reason the new procedure of assisted negotiation is also applicable.[37] Of interest here, this civil union creates the same property regime between the two individuals as if they were married. Consequently, for these cases the choice to extend the framework of legal separation and divorce, as well as that of assisted negotiation, is understandable. In fact, even in the latter case there is a bond which has legal value, and the bonded individuals modify, in certain ways, their status, especially in matters of property regimes.[38]

That said, by looking at international private law addressing couples with an international element, the possibility to use assisted negotiation also depends on whether the status of legal marriage can be ascertained, taking into consideration the law under which they entered into matrimony, and access to this procedure can only be guaranteed if their relationship can be considered a marriage according to the law of the State where they married.[39]

Indeed, the scope of the new legislative pattern is to allow parties the choice of procedures, exactly as the provision of the Reg. Rome III for the

---

37 See in particular L. May 20th 2016 n. 76 at its 25th comma, that specifies: "si applicano in quanto compatibili … le disposizioni di cui … agli articoli 6 e 12 del decreto legge 12 settembre 2014, n. 132 convertito, con modificazioni dalla legge 10 novembre 2014, n. 162". This disposition confirms the idea that it is crucial in the legislator's sight to emphasize the relevance of the legal bond linked with the status to access the new procedure.

38 On the contrary, even after the adoption of the abovementioned L. 20th May 2016 n. 76, the discipline of the assisted negotiation for legal separation and divorce is not applicable in case of *"de facto couples"* even if they have signed a patrimonial agreement. More specifically, the new normative at the 36th comma of the L. 76/2016 designates "de facto couple" as two adults that have no kinship and live a permanent sentimental relationship who decide to sign a patrimonial agreement.

39 A positive outlook in the application of the Italian assisted negotiation for legal separation and divorce for transnational couples is predicted by Lupoi, *supra* n. 29, at 283. This conclusion also suggests, on the one hand, that the urgency to achieve a harmonization of the concept of marriage within the European realm is more immediate; on the other hand, it seems that the goal of a uniform solution for family matters may be reached only by (re-)drafting the concept of marriage from scratch, rather than by creating new forms of legally binding unions of various natures.

applicable law stipulates. Despite the differences between the procedures now available in the Italian normative context, it must be noted that the choice of the Italian legislator has been to leave spouses free to choose the procedure they think is more compatible with their needs and, at this point, this choice appears indeed to conform to the indication of the European Legislator.

At the end of this general presentation of the operational area of this new framework, it is important to understand what the applicable rules will be for the assisted negotiation for legal separation and divorce. In truth, apparently, the only applicable framework seems to be Article 6; nonetheless, this new procedure has been adopted in a wider context of reforms of ADR measures; for this reason, an analytical hypothesis of the applicable law must be reconstructed.

Considering the whole framework of L. 162/2014, the applicable rules can be divided into two types: the rules of the assisted negotiation in general that are extendible to assisted negotiation for legal separation and divorce; and the legislation that can't be applied for embedding the framework of assisted negotiation in legal separation and divorce.

Starting from the first group of rules, even if there isn't any express cross-reference to Article 6, the first comma of Article 2 should be considered applicable to assisted negotiation in marital matters. In fact, at the first comma of Article 2 the core of assisted negotiation itself is presented, which implies agreement to activate a collaborative procedure, based on "good faith and integrity", with the mandatory assistance of a lawyer. Considering the importance of the values involved in a fair dispute resolution system, the application of good practice rules must be considered applicable also to the procedure for legal separation and divorce.[40]

Another applicable provision is the one in the sixth comma of Article 2, which provides that the authenticity of the parties' signatures, in the final agreement, must be certified by the lawyers. This provision assigns to the

---

40 Bolognesi, *supra* n. 22, defines this act of consent as a new form of contract in the Italian system and particularly "procedural contract" or better "contract on procedural". The author also specifies this type of contract must be written and is an effective bonding between parties. Also see Lupoi, *supra* n. 29, at 283, the author specifies that Article 2 and Article 6 cover two different contracts even though they are linked: "Ritengo, dunque, che si tratti, dal punto di vista concettuale, di due istituti autonomi, per quanto complementari, dal momento che la disciplina della negoziazione matrimoniale presuppone l'applicazione delle norme sulla negoziazione assistita, in quanto compatibili".

lawyers a fundamental role for the formal validation of the final agreement; for this reason, considering the central function of the lawyers in the procedure described in Article 6, the provision must be applied also in this context.[41]

The procedure for legal separation and divorce, at the second comma of Article 5, must be viewed in the same light, in which it is prescribed that lawyers, after the authentication of signatures, must certify the compliance of the agreement with "public policy" and "mandatory rules". This is, maybe, one of the most relevant and significant stipulations of the entire legal framework, inasmuch as it conditions the possibility to apply the procedure in cases involving international couples, provided that Italian jurisdiction is existent, but that the spouses had entered into the agreement under the law of a different State – applicable in accordance with international private law. This particular situation, in fact, shows how the new Italian procedure reflects the concept of public policy in marital matters, and how, at the same time, it is liable to influence this concept.[42]

The connection between the validity of the agreement and the intervention of lawyers is emphasized in the ninth comma of Article 5. This article specifies that lawyers who take part in an assisted negotiation cannot afterwards challenge the agreement that was reached in their presence. In this case, we must specify, appeal is not inadmissible, but a lawyer who disregards this restraint, will be accused of illegal conduct as defined by their ethical code.[43] This provision is evidently linked to the key role of the lawyer in the context of the assisted negotiation and, for this reason, should also be extended to the procedure outlined by Article 6.

Another provision applicable to the procedure of assisted negotiation for legal separation and divorce is Article 9. This article contains a framework for lawyers that imposes the observance of confidentiality regarding information obtained during their assistance to the parties. In addition, the article imposes a prohibition on lawyers testifying in civil or criminal proceedings, concerning facts relevant to that procedure. Despite the possibility of the situation described in the article actually occurring, this provision should be extended to lawyers participating in procedures for legal

41 Farina, *supra* n. 24, at 514.

42 For the problem related to the public policy and the international private law see C. Tuo, "La nozione di ordine pubblico processuale tra Bruxelles I e CEDU", 4 *Dir. Un. Eur*. 923 (2010).

43 Lupoi, *supra* n. 29, at 295.

separation and divorce along with the other dispositions concerning lawyers already cited.

If the mentioned legislation describes a common core of assisted negotiation, for disputes over both contracts and marital matters, there are some provisions which will not be applicable to procedures for legal separation and divorce. These rules are those indicated in Articles 3 and 4, because they are established for the specific procedure for assisted negotiation of disputes concerning contracts or non-contractual liability; in the same perspective, also the second comma of Article 2, which prescribes a period of validity for the invitation to collaborative negotiation, is not compatible with a procedure chosen by spouses to dissolve or change their marital relationship.

In this regard, silence about the problem of admissibility of legal aid for access to the ADR procedure for legal separation and divorce should be criticized. In fact, Article 3 (sixth comma) excludes the possibility to give legal aid for assisted negotiation if the procedure is mandatory for parties, in conflicts concerning contracts indicated in the first comma of Article 3. This means that the lawyer(s) should give their assistance without any compensation if the client cannot bear the costs of their legal assistance. This choice is aligned with the framework of mandatory mediation, as described in Legislative-Decree n. 128/2010. The rationale of this provision is probably that, in case contenders find an amicable solution they will find an agreement to cover the legal expenses too; if so, if they do not find a solution for their case, they have access to legal aid for the subsequent claim to the Court.

Conversely, the same rationale cannot be applied to any assisted negotiation provided to legal separation and divorce, implying the exclusion of legal aid. Indeed, the exclusion of legal aid will affect the success of the new procedure and the use of it would be discouraged, because of its optional nature.

Nevertheless, in Italy, legal aid is usually associated with trial before court, so the possibility to admit legal aid for such alternative procedure would not be implied. Anyway, it could be said that spouses who want to be sure to have access to legal aid might choose an in-court procedure for their legal separation or divorce. As already suggested, this conclusion will discourage the use of the new ADR and would be in contrast with Directive 2002/8/EC, which extends legal aid also to the pre-litigation phase. Thus, an interpretative solution to admit legal aid should be investigated.

Indeed, by taking into account the compulsory presence of lawyers, it should be possible to concede to spouses access to legal aid, given that to take advantage of the ADR they need to be assisted by lawyers, and remarking that the rationale of the legal aid system is to guarantee a proper level of legal advice wherein the presence of lawyers is mandatory by law, regardless of the financial conditions of an individual, exactly as in the procedure outlined by Article 6 of the L. 164/2014.[44]

In conclusion, the advisability of granting legal aid complies more closely with the purpose of promoting and favouring the use of alternative dispute resolution and, thus, decreases the backlogs in Italian courts.

Before continuing the analysis of this analysing procedure, a brief overview about the parties involved in the procedure of assisted negotiation for legal separation and divorce must be taken.

As highlighted already, the core of the new procedure provided by Article 6 of L. 162/2014 consists of the involvement of an attorney, one for each part. The choice to assign to lawyers a specific role in the execution of this procedure is common in the Italian legislative framework, especially for legal separation.[45]

The role of the legal attorney varies according to the type of procedure – legal separation or divorce for instance – and also depends on whether the procedure is consensual or contentious.[46]

Regardless of the fundamental differences between procedures, it is important to consider those that issue a compulsory hearing wherein the spouses are asked to appear in person to attempt to reconcile in front of the President of the Tribunal. Within this context, the presence of the lawyers is not mandatory, even if the spouses may be 'assisted' by their attorney, optionally.

---

44 For an in-depth analysis of the discipline of the legal aid in the Italian process see Vaccari, *supra* n. 29.

45 About the opportunity to assign to the legal attorney this "function" see C. Consolo, "Un d.l. processuale in bianco e nerofumo sull'equivoco della 'degiurisdizionalizzazione'", 10 *Corriere giuridico* 1173 (2014).

46 Particularly, in Italy there are two kinds of procedures for legal separation: judicial separation (Art. 706 Civil Procedure Code) and separation by mutual consent (Art. 711 Civil Procedure Code). In the mutual separation the spouses ask commonly to proceed to their legal separation, while in judicial separation there is no agreement between them on the need for legal separation. The same division is established for the definitive dissolution of the marriage (i.e. divorce) which can be filed for jointly, in a consensual manner, or can be confrontational.

It must be noted that, in practice, it is usual that, in this phase, both parties are assisted by only one (common) lawyer, who can be, e.g., the family lawyer or a legal advisor they both trust. This is frequent, especially for non-contentious separation – which is the pattern with more points of commonality with the new model featured in Article 6 of L. 162/2014 in terms of procedure. For this reason, the choice to impose the presence of two lawyers (one for each spouse) for this new procedure is not coherent with the Italian tradition in these matters, and it might influence success in using this new model. Certainly, the lawyers have a very important propulsive role to encourage their clients to use the new procedure and the attorney will be (again!) discouraged to suggest the new procedure if they won't be able to assist both parties; hence, they will rather recommend the traditional procedure for separation by mutual consent.[47]

In fact, the legislator has assigned to the legal advisors a crucial role regarding the parties' awareness of the opportunity to accede to ADR procedures.[48] The legal attorney has a general duty to inform of the possibility to solve the conflict by using assisted negotiation. But, more importantly, the lawyers have a very active role within the procedure and they are, in a certain manner, the substitute of the President of the Tribunal in the attempt to reconcile.[49]

In particular, in the third comma of Article 6, the legislator prescribes that the final agreement must contain the advice to the spouses that they have been informed about the possibility to benefit from family mediation, and that "the lawyers have tried to reconcile the couple". In reality, the attempt at reconciliation has lost its original function even in the legal separation in front of the court, because the value attributed to marriage in Italian legislation has decreased and the purpose of keeping couples in wedlock no longer is a primary scope of the system. Consequently, the intervention of the lawyers in advising spouses during their conflict must be considered within the context of the substantial element of the validity of the final agreement, rather than as a part of the (formal) discouragement of

---

47 Criticizes the choice to impose the mandatory presence of two attorneys, one for each part, Danovi, *supra* n. 34, at 2531. The author argues that the rationale of this provision could have an ethical basis, thus the question whether the two attorneys could work for the same firm must be investigated.

48 About the consequences of the violation of this duty, see Lupoi, *supra* n. 29, at 295.

49 Danovi, *supra* n. 34, at 2532-2533.

the separation as such. Moreover, it seems that consent to the agreement is to be considered valid only if the legal advice flows from the content of the agreement, as the consent of the spouses by themselves is, by itself, not sufficient to conclude a lawful agreement.[50]

The presence of one or two lawyers, conversely, is not mandatory in the procedure established by Article 12. In that procedure the role of the legal attorney is, again, of mere assistance, and is non-influential on the validity of the agreement. Nevertheless, the procedure that starts with the "joint request" to the Mayor can be applied only if the couple has no children and on condition that there is no need to establish any agreement on property rights between the spouses. For this reason, it could be said that the absence of the legal attorney could affect the success of this procedure – which is probably already conceived as a residual option within the framework of the procedures for legal separation and divorce.

In conclusion, it seems that the lawmaker is more concerned with delineating in depth a procedure where property rights or children are involved, rather than rendering it public and regulating the change of status between the spouses. Otherwise, in the light of the 'de-jurisdiction' of procedures concerning legal separation and divorce, it is understandable why involvement of a judge is no longer mandatory.[51] More specifically, the only circumstance in which the President of the Tribunal will be involved in the

50 The role of the legal attorneys is similar but not identical to the collaborative practice of common law. In this regard see C. Healy, "Collaborative practice. An interdisciplinary approach to the resolution of conflict in family matters, in Family law and culture in Europe", *European law series* 119, 123 (K. Boele-Woelki, N. Dethloff, W. Gephart, Antwerp, Intersentia, 2014).

51 The system outlined by the new legislative pattern represents a revolution in the Italian system, see in this sense R. Lombardi, "Si abbrevia la distanza tra separazione e divorzio: la l. 6 maggio 2015 n. 55", 1 *Dir. e Fam.* 325, 325(2016): "In tal modo si è determinata una netta rottura rispetto al passato, allorché la modificazione dello status di coniuge rientrava nell'ambito della giurisdizione costitutiva necessaria, anche se tra i coniugi sussisteva pieno accordo e a prescindere dalla presenza o meno della prole". Also, the new discipline has several points of critically considering the Italian system for the transcription of the patrimonial agreement concerning real estate property. More specifically, considering the intervention of the President of the Tribunal is merely optional (*recte*: potential), this will prevent to enable the agreement to be transcribed in the public registry without the intervention of a notary. In fact, the authorization of the public prosecutor cannot be considered as a decision. Those problems are investigated in depth by G. Frezza, "'Degiurisdizionalizzazione', negoziazione assistita e trascrizione", 1 *Nuove Leggi Civ. Comm.* 18, 18 (2015).

procedure occurs when the public prosecutor denies the authorization to an agreement involving children. Regardless of the consequences in terms of procedure – which will be addressed in the following section – the marginal (and eventual) role of this jurisdictional function is significant in terms of the comprehensive framework that suggests a definition of "disposable rights" in Italian legislation. The main question around "disposable rights" has always proved to be controversial, and the new legislation could provide a precious contribution to studies in this field.[52]

In addition, and as mentioned earlier, the involvement of children has consequences/impact on the procedural pattern. If there are no children, the assisted negotiation will be handled by the lawyers, then the final agreement will be presented to the public prosecutor for their act of clearance; otherwise, when children are involved, the public prosecutor will conduct an in-depth examination of the agreement before giving the final authorization. For this reason, it is evident that the children's interests cannot be a private concern, but remain of public relevance, and intervention by the authorities is therefore mandatory to safeguard certain interests.[53]

More specifically, the law distinguishes under-aged children from adult children that have some form of invalidity, or haven't yet acquired their economic independence and so still depend on their parents on

52 More specifically, the new legislative pattern could have a deep impact in the field of prenuptial and postnuptial agreements. In fact, the validity of those contracts is much discussed in the Italian system. On this topic see in particular M. Giliberti, "Gli accordi della crisi coniugale in bilico tra le istanze di conservazione e la tutela dell'autonomia dei coniugi", 1 *Dir. Fam. Pers.* 476, 476 (2014); V. Pani, "Osservazioni a margine di talune problematiche applicative in tema di accordi sulla crisi coniugale", 2 *Dir. Fam. Per.*, 582, 590 (2014); C. Rimini, "I patti in vista del divorzio: spunti di riflessione e una proposta dopo l'introduzione della negoziazione assistita per la soluzione delle controversie familiari", 1 *Dir. Fam. Per.* 209, 209 (2015).

53 In the frame of the assisted negotiation "L'interesse pubblico, sotteso alla tutela della famiglia, è salvaguardato (ai sensi del comma 2° dell'art. 6) dall'intervento del Pubblico Ministero che, nel caso in cui l'accordo sia adottato da coniugi senza figli ovvero con figli maggiorenni economicamente autosufficienti, non portatori di handicap né altrimenti incapaci, concede il nulla osta; mentre, nel caso in cui sia adottato da coniugi con figli minori o comunque considerati 'deboli' e, quindi, bisognosi di protezione, emette un provvedimento autorizzativo": D. D'Adamo, "La mediazione familiare come metodo integrativo di risoluzione delle controversia", 2 *Riv. dir. proc.*, 377, 381 (2015).

the one hand, from all other children on the other.[54] The first commentators have found some critical points in the choice to exclude any participation by children in the procedure.[55] By way of explanation, even if the involvement of children is of central importance to the pattern of the procedure, they do not have the possibility to participate in the agreement, nor to make a contribution, because there are no provisions which allow the children to take part in the negotiation, to have their position represented, for instance with the assistance of their own lawyer. This amounts to a critical point in the procedure of assisted negotiation, inasmuch as it precludes directly hearing from the children, which, in contrast, has taken a quite central role, even in the international framework, for the safeguarding of children.

Finally, another figure whose presence is mandatory in the procedure is the (already cited) public prosecutor who represents the public interests in the case. More specifically, in this respect, it must be said that the role of the public prosecutor in a civil procedure is traditionally related to the protection of the 'non-disposable' rights and to safeguarding the weakest party.[56] Therefore, the key role played by the 'public party' in the procedure must be considered as a clue to the public interest being inherent in safeguarding certain interests in procedures for legal separation and divorce.

---

54 About the children without economic independence a recent decision of the Italian Supreme Court (February 1st 2016 nr. 1858) has specified that the obligation to provide support to adult children is not unconditional. Thus, if the parents have provided the children with all the necessary financial support to let them obtain autonomy but they haven't, the parents are no longer obliged to support them.

55 Danovi, *supra* n. 34, at 2534; Masoni, *supra* n. 34, at 1390.

56 The function of the public prosecutor in civil cases is rather different from that in the criminal justice. The role of the public prosecutor in the civil process is detailed in the Civil Procedure Code in Articles 69-74. It must be noted that they have a different function depending on whether or not they are allowed to begin a procedure. The range of their power is related to the relevance of the rights in the case, hence they can only intervene in the case or have a propulsive role to the extent of the rights involved in the dispute.

(V) *The Procedure of Assisted Negotiation for Legal Separation and Divorce: An Analytical Illustration.*

Looking at the procedure outlined in Article 6 of Law 162/2014, the first thing to be noted is that there is no indication as to the jurisdiction of tribunals. In other words, the legislator has not indicated 'where' the spouses and their lawyers must register their agreement on the act of validation by the public party. In Article 6, comma 2, a generic reference to the "competent Tribunal" is made but there is no specific indication about *how* to designate it. For this reason, it must be said that the "competent Tribunal" should be identified with reference to the rules of the Civil Procedure Code, which specifies jurisdictional procedures.[57] This is a bizarre solution, considering the fact that the new law has been formulated with the aim of 'de-jurisdiction'.

In any case, according to the Civil Procedure Code, the competent tribunal is located where the spouses have their joint residence or, if there is no such location, where the residence of the defendant is, or, in case these whereabouts are also unclear, where the claimant has his/her residence. It is worth stressing that the provisions contained in the Code do not perfectly fit the requirements of assisted negotiation, since they are designed for a confrontational process, and are not suitable for a non-controversial procedure. Instead, it would have been better to allow the couple the right to jointly designate a competent court.

In addition, the autonomy of the parties is further limited during the procedure. In fact, there is no applicable rule to coordinate the assisted negotiation with court procedures, in case the spouses decide to change their mind and to convert a negotiated procedure into a juridical procedure, or *vice-versa*.[58]

Apart from these remarks about the competent tribunal, procedures vary considerably depending on whether the married couple does or does not have children. More specifically, if there are no children involved, the pro-

57 Danovi, *supra* n. 34, at 2548; Lupoi, *supra* n. 29, at 287.

58 In this regard, it could be noted that the reform enacted by L. 162/2014 has an eclectic content. Indeed, it must be noted that the provision on arbitration in Article 1 of the new law is, on the contrary, mainly dedicated to regulate the coordination between the process and the ADR procedure. This confirms that, despite the fact that those procedures have been instituted all together, they have very little in common.

cedure ends with a mere act of 'clearance' of the public prosecutor. However, by contrast, if there are children involved, then a positive 'approval' by the public party is required to end the procedure.[59]

The presence or absence of children is crucial and shapes the role played by the public prosecutor in the assisted negotiation within the procedure. This distinctive trait is not only relevant from a procedural perspective but also with an eye on substance. In fact, the differences that are manifest in procedures, whether conducted with or without the involvement of children, might be significant to highlight the fact that public relevance of these matters is strictly linked to the interests of the children, rather than revolving around the choice of free individuals to maintain their nuptial binding.

As already outlined, when spouses decide to end their relationship temporarily (legal separation) or want to dissolve their marriage after a period of legal separation, they can enter the process of assisted negotiation and stipulate an agreement with the help of their lawyers (one for each party).[60] The contents of these agreements seem to vary because there is no prohibition on the regulation of proprietary aspects. Hence, they might decide to dispose of their proprietary rights altogether, including those concerning real estate. This conclusion is confirmed by comparing the provisions of Article 6 with the establishment of Article 12, in which there is an explicit prohibition on the elimination of proprietary transfers. Also, regarding real estate, Article 5 is to be applied, and the presence of a notary is mandatory for validation of the decision, and so the possibility to dispose of these rights is confirmed.[61]

Once a final agreement is reached it must be sent to the public prosecutor. From this point on, the procedures rather vary, because the supervision differs based on whether or not there are children involved in the agreement.

---

59 The law uses the term "nulla òsta" to identify the act of clearance of the public attorney in the procedure without children, whereas it uses the term authorization in presence of children.

60 About the Italian legislative on divorce, it must be noted that with Law 6th May 2015 n. 55 the Italian Legislator has drastically reduced the term to file for divorce. After a period of legal separation from a minimum of three years the term is now changed to six months, if the previous legal separation was consensual, and twelve months if the procedure for separation was controversial.

61 See in particular Frezza, *supra* n. 51, at 22.

First of all, in the absence of children no term of validity for the agreement is required, as there is no indication of the terms within which the agreement is to be sent to the public prosecutor for validation. Secondly, the procedure does not specify the function of the "nulla òsta" (act of clearance) to be granted by the public party. Moreover, the lawyers have already certified the conformity of the agreement with public policy and the prohibitive rules, so it seems that the public prosecutor is merely asked to verify the accuracy of the lawyers' declaration.[62]

Thirdly, the consequences if the public prosecutor denies the certification are not specified.

By way of explanation, the last part of the second period of the second comma of Article 6 prescribes "the Public Prosecutor communicates to the lawyer the act of clearance if there isn't any irregularity". Indeed, the use of the word "irregularity" poses some interpretation issues. First of all, the meaning of "irregularity" is quite different if we refer to a procedural provision, or to substantive law. At this point the solution is questionable. On the one hand, the irregularity concerns an agreement drawn up by private parties in a contractual context while, on the other hand, the irregularity is ascribed to the procedural phase of the validation of the agreement, with the purpose to give the agreement the effect of changing the *status* of the couple. It seems that the lawmaker has conceived a particular procedure, in which the procedural and substantive aspects are strictly connected, and so the irregularity will affect the agreement in its substantive validation, even if the flaw concerns a procedural aspect. For this reason, it could be said that the legal framework of family matters has been safeguarded by the imposition of very severe procedural burdens to ensure the accuracy of the final results, and to guarantee the protection of the most relevant interests involved in family matters.

Besides this questionable interpretation, the law also does not specify the consequences if the act of clearance is denied. One could argue that the agreement wouldn't permit the spouses to change their *status*, because modification of the *status* necessarily implies an act by the public prosecutor. Nor does the law say whether the parties (or better, their attorneys) may contest (appeal, maybe) the refusal of the public prosecutor; or whether they may appeal to the public attorney, in order to present a new

62 This provision may be cause of potential 'overlaps' between the function of the public party and the spouses' legal attorneys, Danovi, *supra* n. 34, at 2539.

agreement suitable for their approval. Furthermore, the term within which the public prosecutor should communicate the refusal is not indicated, nor is the formal act of communicating it regulated. The only possible solution seems, thus, that the lawyers will be charged to physically visit the court's clerk to check whether the public prosecutor has or has not yet expressed a conclusion on the agreement.

As mentioned earlier, this omission in the procedure could be ascribed to the context of urgency in which the law has been introduced. In conclusion, too many questions follow this pattern, and they are likely to determine the success of this procedure.

As already highlighted, some procedural differences in procedures arise in cases involving children. Despite the relevance, in terms of public interest, that the attention on safeguarding children's interests enshrines, the procedure appears only a little more consistent.[63]

In the first place, the law defines the public prosecutor's act as an "authorization" which implies a positive verification of the contents of the agreement, rather than a mere scrutiny of its validity (i.e. the establishment of the absence of irregularities). Hence, in this case the role of the public prosecutor is not the same as that of the lawyers, and it is not limited to the certification of the compliance of the agreement with public policy, or to prohibitive rules.[64]

Nevertheless there is no positive element to say the final agreement converts its nature if it is subject to the authorization rather than a mere act of clearance. In fact, in case of a positive response by the public prosecutor, the legal value of the agreement will be the same. For this reason, it

63 M. Sesta, "Negoziazione assistita e obblighi di mantenimento nella crisi della coppia", 3 *Fam. e Dir.* 295 (2015).

64 The choice to assign to the public prosecutor the function to safeguard the children's interests has not found many supporters. Indeed, the office of the public prosecutor is not a well-qualified figure to protect children's interests, not because of their role in the Italian system, but because of the set-up of his office, which is not properly organized to fulfil this function. In this regard see Lupoi, *supra* n. 29, at 300 and Chiarloni, *supra* n. 22, at 221 who suggests to create a specialized Family Law Court: "è legittimo il sospetto che i relativi uffici, in tutt'altre faccende affaccendati, non siano in grado, soprattutto i più piccoli, di dotarsi rapidamente delle competenze indispensabili per valutare se gli accordi presi dai coniugi siano nell'interesse dei figli medesimi. Forse, sarebbe stato meglio lasciare questo controllo ai giudici, soprattutto ora, in vista dell'istituzione del tribunale della famiglia".

seems that the modification of the *status* is, in both cases, linked to an act of the judicial authorities and has to be contextualized within the framework of voluntary jurisdiction.

Consequentially, the involvement of the public prosecutor in the final act of separation and divorce might reflect the nature of the agreement, which surely must not be considered of pure contractual nature. In fact, even if the agreement is reached by a contractual procedure – in which the assistance of lawyers is compulsory – the agreement could be still considered of a public nature (perhaps jurisdictional), due to the mandatory final confirmation by the public authority. For this reason, if the final agreement is considered of a jurisdictional nature, because of the presence of the public prosecutor, the framework of recognition of the judgments in the European area should be applicable to the agreement.[65]

Regardless, the most relevant differences in terms of procedure become manifest when the authorization by the public authority is denied when the procedure is filed in the absence of children, as there is no indication regarding the terms within which the agreement must be sent to the public prosecutor, nor is it clear what will become of such an irregular agreement. Conversely, when matters of children's interests come forward, both situations are taken into consideration by the lawmaker.

In order to specify, the agreement must be transmitted to the public prosecutor's department within ten days. Regrettably, there is no explicit sanction for violation of this rule, so this term of validity has no real, appreciable utility.

More importantly, what happens if the agreement is actually sent after ten days is not made explicit: does the public prosecutor carry the burden of verification, or does the agreement lose its validity automatically?

Considering this procedure within the context of voluntary jurisdiction, two interpretative hypotheses could be suggested: once the public prosecutor has been notified of the agreement, they are obligated to express their opinion on the agreement, because of their role as supervisor of the non-

65 This will create a disparity compared to the other procedure featured in Article 12 and designed for the joint request to the Mayor, because that procedure won't be assimilated into a juridical sentence and won't be able to be recognized in the light of international private law.

individual (i.e. general) interests;[66] or the private nature of the matter implies that the over-due notification does not have to be taken into consideration by the public prosecutor.

This second solution is more coherent with the general spirit of the law. In fact, the spouses are still in time to re-send the agreement to the public prosecutor and, if applicable, to sue their lawyers for professional liability, in case they are liable for the delay in communication. This is also coherent with the central role of the legal attorney and does not compromise the parties' rights.

Yet, a third interpretation could be also proposed. Indeed, the late communication of the agreement could be considered as an *irregular* agreement, and hence the public prosecutor could refuse the authorization without comprehensively analysing the contents of the agreement. In other words, the public prosecutor won't investigate the conformity of the agreement to the interests of the weakest parties, but will communicate the irregularity to the lawyers who will be charged to re-send a corrected agreement. This solution seems to be the more suitable to balance the role of the public prosecutor against the private interests involved. Also, it seems more appropriate considering it does not deprive the parties of the power to stay in control of their proper position.[67]

Whether or not the solution proposed may be found suitable for the problem, the question of how communications between the public prosecutor and the parties are coordinated still remains, and probably only practical experience will give an answer to these queries.[68]

In conclusion, it seems there is no real justification to the established term of ten days, except for the fact that the lawmaker probably intended

66 This solution is in conformity with the essence of the voluntary jurisdiction in which the rules on the extinguishment of the process are not applicable (i.e. the Art. 309 of Civil Procedure Code.). Also, this solution is suitable for the propulsive role of the public party stated in Art. 72 of Civil Procedure Code and it finds confirmation in several hypotheses of voluntary jurisdiction, e.g. in the scheme of Article 413 of the Code in which the procedure for who has custody over the incompetent is outlined.

67 For this reason, a fourth solution must be ruled out, according to which, if the agreement is not sent "in time", the public party should invoke the President of the Tribunal and the procedure will follow the pattern prescribed for negotiation in presence of children.

68 For this reason some offices have already indicated guidelines, see the comment in Masoni, *supra* n. 34, at 1390.

to highlight the convenience that the decision to proceed was close to the act of consent expressed by the parties, in order to bridge the distance between the parties and the Court.

As already mentioned, in case the public prosecutor finds the agreement not to be adequate for the safeguarding of the weakest parties, the President of the Tribunal will be involved in the procedure.

As a matter of fact, the law does not clarify if this participation modifies the nature of the procedure, transforming the process in a juridical one. The expression "the president convokes the parties" (Article 6) is similar but not identical to the provision set forth in the Civil Procedure Code, wherein the spouses have to present themselves in front of the court for the re-conciliation attempt. In fact, in using the word "parties" instead of "spouses" the law does not impose the presence of the couple in person. This could mean that the spouses (the parties) may be substituted by their lawyers who will participate in the hearing as their attorneys. In other words, the President won't convoke "the parties" to try a last attempt at conciliation, but the scope of their intervention is exclusively linked to the contents of the agreement, and it does not include the purpose to verify the actual intentions of the spouses to terminate (or change) their relationship. For this reason, the possibility that the involvement of the President changes the nature of the procedure – and transforms it into a jurisdictional one – should be discarded.

Nevertheless, in this case, the interests of children are involved and for this reason the power to impose urgent and provisional measures for the protection of children should be attributed to the President.

These considerations confirm that the regulation of the marital relationship and the management of higher-level interests revolving around kinship receive different degrees of attention from the lawmaker. And this will necessarily involve the concept of "private" and "public" relevance regarding the family context.

In summary, at the end of this presentation of the procedure one could say that the key role played by the public prosecutor is to understand what relevance the Italian legislator has now attributed to the rights (and interests) involved in the procedure, and it shows that modifications to the *status* itself are no longer the most relevant aspects of a family relationship from an institutional standpoint. Strictly speaking, the different procedural patterns to be adopted in the absence or presence of children could be considered an expression of a new concept of rights, one of which the parties may freely avail themselves. Indeed, if the public prosecutor has a mere formal role in the procedure, in which there is no obligation to protect the children's interests, one could say that change of *status* has lost relevance to public purposes. And the choice to be bound in marriage or not is now nothing but a private matter, which does not entail a role for public parties in the process.

This implication finds its confirmation in Article 12 of L. 162/2014, according to which a change of *status* can be decided by spouses without any form of intervention by the public party. In this case, the public authority's (i.e. the Mayor's) duty is purely to render public modifications to people's *status,* with an eye on the consequences, from a proprietary perspective, of the loosening of the marital binding.[69]

Otherwise, when the agreement has received the act of clearance, or when it has been authorized by the public prosecutor, the procedure can reach its conclusion. In those cases, a very onerous duty is imposed on the lawyers for the validation procedure. With the aim to render public modifications to the status of the (ex-)spouses, the lawmaker invests the parties' lawyers with an important function, and prescribes some severe pecuniary penalties in case of negligence.[70]

The lawyer(s) have the obligation to communicate the agreement to the office of marital status in order to guarantee public availability to the new *status* of the parties, and the modifications in their proprietary situation. The provision I refer to is in the third comma of Article 6 which prescribes a very short term for the lawyer(s) to discharge their duties, because the agreement must be notified "within ten days". Again, this term is not connected to any starting time, so an interpretative solution must be found.

Probably, these ten days should be considered to start from the moment of communication of the validation by the public prosecutor. For this reason, the already mentioned omissions in the coordination of communication between the public prosecutor and the parties' lawyers are quite pernicious for the parties' attorneys. In fact, failure to comply with the obligation to communicate is severely punished, and the lawyer(s) will be charged with a pecuniary penalty of 2,000 to 5,000 euros.

The intention of the lawmaker is actually to ensure the agreement will be made public, so it will have "the same legal value of the sentences in

69 At this point, the function of lawyers in attempting a re-conciliation before concluding the agreement is also confirmed as a guarantee of fully conscious consent to the agreement, rather than as a last attempt to save the nuptial bond.

70 Lupoi, *supra* n. 29, at 293.

the judicial process for family matters", and to guarantee notification to third parties, considering the impact of the agreement on the proprietary regime of the parties. This conclusion is confirmed if we look at Article 12, in which the agreement is reached without the assistance of lawyers – the legal attorney could, for instance, advise the parties, but they don't have any compulsory duty in this procedure – and publication is ordered directly by the public authority that files the agreement.

Taking into consideration the gaps in coordination, the communication between the public prosecutor and the lawyers, this provision could actually affect the success of its practice, but this is not the only critical point in the disposition.[71]

As already outlined, the word 'lawyer' in the singular appears again in the above mentioned Article 6. Considering that, beyond any doubt, each party will be assisted by her/his own lawyer, meaning that at least two lawyers will be involved, which one, exactly, would be charged for non-compliance with the communication duty is rather unclear. As already seen, the amount of the penalty fee is not merely symbolic, and whether or not both legal advisors would be charged for disregarding the obligation to communicate in time should be specified more clearly.[72]

(VI) Personal remarks

After a general overview of the principles underlying family law and a subsequent analytical illustration of the procedure created as a negotiated method to dissolve the marital *status*, some conclusive remarks can be made in order to highlight in which areas the new procedural pattern will affect family law, in both a substantive and a procedural perspective. Some conjecture as to what degree of success could be obtained applying this procedure in practice is also in order.

First of all, the new law confirms the tendency to affirm that the existence (or the absence) of a legal bond makes a relevant legal distinction for the couple, at least in terms of applicable law. In fact, the nuptial bond

---

71 Rimini, *supra* n. 52, at 212.

72 On the other hand, it seems to be clear that the sanction has public relevance, because the burden of communication has an administrative nature. For this reason, it must follow from the rationale of the administrative penalty rather than from the extra-contractual framework of what is illegal.

has an impact on the proprietary regime, so external relevance (and consequentially making it public) must be assured.

Nevertheless, this does not mean that the private – and mere contractual – nature of the familial relationship must be reserved only for the unmarried couple. On the contrary, both types of familial relationships are, nowadays, to be considered as private matters, but with some points of distinction. On the one hand, to be an unmarried couple guarantees the protection of family rights in a wide sense; on the other hand, to be married means to establish a particular proprietary regime that the world outside is to be made aware of. But to give publicity to something is not identical to say that it has a public nature. The assisted negotiation for legal separation and divorce confirms this distinction and balances the private nature of the relationship with the need to make aspects of it public.

After identifying the peculiarity of the marital relationship in its proprietary regime, the transposition of the procedure beyond the Italian borders also becomes a possibility. In this regard, it must be noted, in view of international private law, that, in case a couple has an international aspect, Italian jurisdiction will be prevalent if the 'defendant' has his/her residence or domicile in Italy, or if one of the spouses is an Italian citizen, or if the marriage was officiated in Italy. Thus, if Italian jurisdiction exists, the parties could use assisted negotiation. In this case, the choice of applicable law will determine the contents of the agreement, providing a convenient solution for issues relative to the application of a certain foreign law by an Italian judge. In fact, the public institutions will only concern themselves with the question of conformity to public policy and fundamental rights, without being bothered with in-depth knowledge of foreign legislation.[73]

Thus, Italian legislation takes a big step towards attributing to spouses personally the role of effectively managing their relationship. In this respect, it must be considered that, even if EU Regulation 1259/2010 has established, for the first time, the possibility for couples to choose the applicable law instead of the automatic application of international private law concerning conflict of legal provisions, the new Italian framework for assisted negotiation allows parties (the spouses) to be more aware of their

73 In this case the lawyers will be in charge of applying a specific legal framework, chosen by the spouses, and so it is more likely that an issue regarding the recognition of their professional qualifications in the European realm could emerge.

legal separation or divorce procedure and, thus, enables them to fully understand the content of the eventual agreement.

As we have seen, the relevance of higher level – and not individual – interests and rights is anyway granted with the stipulation of a more complex procedure, which is presented as an extreme measure to be used only in case of lack of protection of certain interests. But it must be noted that those interests – that are taken into consideration to modify the procedure – are no longer linked to the nuptial binding. Consequently, it is not the 'legal family' itself – as the family based on marriage was a distinct entity involving the individuals forming it – that is considered to be of public relevance and, so, in need of public preservation, but the singular individuals in the lawful family: the children and the weakest spouse.[74]

The aim to protect the weakest parties is indeed confirmed through the role of the lawyers, drawn up like a form of negotiation under legal protection, because of the importance of the lawyers in the legal validity of the final agreement.[75]

For this reason, we could say that the gaps in procedure that make the role of the lawyers more important and not identified with precision will affect the practical application of assisted negotiation for legal separation and divorce. Hence, it is in these critical areas that lawmakers should direct their attention, preparing an amendment in the future, so as to avoid practical difficulties that could discourage the application of this new legal framework.[76]

---

74 In fact, the function of public intervention seems related to the protection of the contractual autonomy of one party in the agreement.

75 Not so different – according to the procedural scheme – from a contract concluded with assistance from the legal guardian (i.e. the person who assists the incompetent under custody).

76 Considering the existence of a specific framework, it doesn't seem incorrect to say that the agreement reached after assisted negotiation for legal separation is a typical contract in the Italian legal framework which finds its function in regulating the nuptial crisis. Thus, the admissibility, in the Italian legal framework, of the contract in case of nuptial crisis can no longer be considered irrelevant. That contract could be considered valid, if not typical, because of its conformity to the disposition of Article 1322 of the Civil Code, confirmed by the stipulation of a specific contract with this function that amounts to agreement to legal separation and divorce, settled under assisted negotiation by lawyers. On this theme see in particular Giliberti, *supra* n. 52, at 476; E. Tagliasacchi, "Accordi in vista della crisi coniugale: from status to contract?", 2 *Nuova giur. civ.* 96, 96 (2014).

(VII) Conclusion

From the analysis of the new Italian framework for legal separation and divorce, a symmetry emerges between the substantive and the procedural rulings on family matters. To be more precise, the aspects related to general interests (e.g. the children's rights) are still to be safeguarded by public institutions, whereas the private aspects of the nuptial bond, or the interests arising from the marital relation which only have contractual relevance, are no longer to be dominated by public authority, which means there is no need for the jurisdictional power to decide on the interests of the couple at the end of their relationship. For this reason, one could say that the procedural rules for family matters are also part of the renewed concept of the family.

Moreover, the procedural rules also confirm the differences between a family relationship and a marital relation, underlining that the choice to adopt (or dispose of) the marital status is a matter of consent. By way of explanation, the marital agreement is gaining more contractual significance, as opposed to public relevance, because safeguarding the fundamental rights connected to the family relationship is no longer dependent on a formal union.

For this reason, consent is also the organizing principle for sorting out the interests at the end of a nuptial relation, and public intervention is no longer needed when there is harmony between spouses. Thus, the use of a form of negotiation to terminate the relation after marriage, and, contrarily, the need of public interference when an agreement is not possible (e.g. in a contentious separation or divorce), or when the regulation of fundamental rights is not well settled by the (ex-)spouses is established. Consequentially, the subsidiarity of jurisdictional intervention is also confirmed in order to encourage negotiation and other private instruments that reduce the public role.

To reach this conclusion, an interdisciplinary method of research has been suggested, in order to enforce the connection between the substantive rulings on family matters and the possibility of an equivalent procedural pattern.[77]

---

77 The basic idea is that the process is not the mere application of substantive rules. On the contrary, the procedural regime will have a deep impact in shaping and affecting substantive rules. This conclusion meets the concept of procedure, as a non-neutral instrument for the application (and creation) of substantive law. In

Also, the idea that the procedural pattern is able to affect the cultural context enhances the role of the comparison as long as the comparative method is a necessary tool for investigating the cultural context too.[78] In conclusion, one could note that an interdisciplinary research should aim to connect methods and to combine methods results. Thus, the empiric method will also be part of the research method, as long as the empiric results allow to 'test' the success of a specific solution.

Because one should expect the procedural pattern also to be able to influence the cultural model for modifications of the marital status, the Italian model might also exert a relevant impact on the harmonization of the legal framework in the European Union for the establishment of jurisdiction, and law applicable to matrimonial regimes, and to facilitate the mobility of legal tools among the Member States, too. In fact, by studying procedures, a new angle from which to investigate the entire legal nature of relationships within the family, in a national and in a European prospective, has been presented.

---

fact, the substantive rule of the case must be considered as an output of the process, hence the choice in terms of procedure will affected the resulting rule of the case. Moreover, the acceptance that people disputing make about the rule of the case is related to the acceptance of the procedural rules that have produced those rules. This consideration concludes the circular movement of the law, because the more the society context is consistent with the output of the process, as above delineated, the more the process will be effective in solving disputes. See in this sense S. Bruner, Foreword to Chase, *supra* n. 2 at IX "Justice must satisfy the appearance of justice … to resolve disputes in this even-handed way requires not just a spirit of justice but also agreed-upon procedures for judging the claims of contending parties".

78 In fact, it must be considered that "The task of contextualization is dependent on comparison and contrast; we see what is particular to a society by placing it next to those that differ": Chase, *supra* n. 2, at 3.

II. The Impact of the EU Financial Crisis in the Europeanization of the Greek Civil Procedural Law: A Multi-Methodological Insight to the New Greek Civil Procedure Code (2015), its Scope and Innovative Provisions

Anastasia L. Papadopoulou[*]

(I) Introduction

The radical reform of the Greek Civil Procedure Code (CPC) in 2015 is closely connected to the terms "EU financial crisis" and "Europeanization of civil procedural law". These two concepts may seem rather incompatible at first sight. From one point of view the term "EU financial crisis" describes the phenomenon under which several European countries, due to the external shock of the precedent global financial crisis and because of other macroeconomic imbalances, experienced severe financial turmoil including the collapse of their banking system, the disruption of external financing, a substantial capital and liquidity shortage, significant changes in their credit volume and asset prices, large scale balance sheet problems, a considerable increase of bond yield spreads in government securities and eventually very high government debt.[1] *Au contraire,* the term "Europeanization of civil procedural law" here implies the concept of approximation or harmonization between the various civil procedural systems of the EU member states through the adaptation or reform of the correspond-

* Aristoteles University of Thessaloniki Greece, Law Faculty, Department of Civil, Civil Procedural & Labour Law; PhD in Procedural Law, LLM in Civil, Civil Procedural & Labour Law, Aristoteles University of Thessaloniki Greece; MBA Finance & Banking, Hellenic Open University Greece. This paper includes selected references to publications until the end of August 2016; regarding specifically the main amendments of the Greek CPC (IV) and their correspondent categorization (a), relevant material published in Greece after that date and before the final submission of the paper in November 2016 shall be duly mentioned with the indication 'further reading' in the first note of each subsection (i-iv).

1 See St. Claessens and M.A. Kose, "Financial crises: explanations, types and implications", *Interna-tional Monetary Fund Working Paper* 1, 4-5 (2013).

ing legislation prompted either on purpose or by external influences.[2] In this context the question that logically arises is how the adoption of the new Greek CPC 2015 relates to these two seemingly incompatible ideas.

It is not difficult to ascertain that this reform of the Greek CPC emerged during the years of the EU financial crisis as a precondition for another Greek bailout. Since the EU financial crisis affected mostly those European countries with relatively small economies, it was inevitable that Greece would be influenced too. The need for the acceleration of civil trial proceedings became more than evident during the years of the crisis because of the increase in citizens' recourse to justice and the consequent overloading of courts' dockets; thus the modification of the relevant provisions of the Greek CPC was thought of as a one-way solution for the improvement of the country's judicial system. Yet, this is not the first time that Greece has faced a financial impasse and accepted such vital preconditions to be saved from an official bankruptcy. The agenda reform through the adoption of multiple austerity measures on financial, fiscal, administrative, judicial and social matters started in respect of the economic crisis around 2010, when Greece first sought direct financial assistance from the Eurozone countries and the International Monetary Fund (IMF). But the roots of this problem go back many years before, since even before its accession to the Economic and Monetary Union (EMU) the country already carried the inheritance of an excessive amount of sovereign debt,[3] which was simply exposed through the EU financial crisis contagion and then just continued to grow larger because of the gradual transformation of the Greek banks' debt into additional sovereign debt.

The judicial reform that eventually took place in Greece during 2015 tried to accelerate civil proceedings serving the scope of the administration of civil justice within reasonable time limits in combination with the adoption of sound and fair courts' decisions. In that way it launched the modification, completely or partially, of several provisions in basic regula-

---

2 See B. Hess, "Procedural harmonization in a European context", in: X. E. Kramer and C. H. van Rhee (eds.), *Civil Litigation in a Globalizing World* 160 (T.M.C. Asser Press, The Hague and Springer, Berlin-Heidelberg, 2012).

3 J. Gordon and G. Ringe, "Greece and the missing banking union", *VOX CEPR's Policy Portal* (2015), text available at: <http://voxeu.org/article/greece-and-missing-banking-union>, last visited 11 May 2016; V. Acharya, I. Drechsler and P. Schnabl, "A Pyrrhic Victory? Bank bailouts and sovereign credit risk", 29 *The Journal of Finance* 2689, 2689 (2014).

tory categories of the previous Greek CPC. The result was quite ambiguous since on the one hand the Greek legal community totally averted this new legislation, but on the other hand it was effective too, since many innovative provisions that were missing from the Greek civil procedural system were at last introduced. From this aspect it is worth reflecting on whether the reform of the Greek CPC contributed to the harmonization or approximation of Greek civil procedural law with equivalent procedural legislations of other EU member countries and therefore whether this reform added another piece to the broader puzzle -or challenge?- of the "Europeanization" of Greek civil procedural law.

The present research paper focuses on the impact of the EU Financial Crisis on Greek Civil Procedural Law and specifically examines the establishment of the new Greek CPC 2015, its aim and legislative scope as well as its main amendments and innovative provisions. Due to the complexity and ampleness of its subject matter, the analysis of the scope and content of the Greek CPC 2015 is carried out from a multi-methodological perspective. Thus, a different methodological approach is deliberately chosen for every section of this paper to demonstrate how the pluralism of methods in legal research can illustrate the causal link of an external asymmetric event -such as the EU financial crisis- towards the reformation of the Greek CPC; to present why and how the most important new provisions have been established; and mainly to show how this fundamental legislative reform eventually contributes to the "Europeanization" of Greek Civil Procedural Law. For that purpose the selected methodological approach for each sub-theme is clearly defined at the beginning of every section along with the outline of the main examined points.

(II) The Historical Context of the Civil Judicial Reform in Greece and the Establishment of the New Greek Civil Procedure Code (2015)

Taking into consideration that the new Greek CPC 2015 was established by the Greek Parliament in a response to the EU financial crisis and as a prerequisite for the granting of financial assistance by the involved European and international parties in an effort to save Greece from official bankruptcy, the way to the enactment of this legislation is mainly examined from a financial and economic perspective with the use of an interdisciplinary approach. The latter can be defined as a methodological approach that combines information, data, concepts and theories from two or more distinctive disciplines in order to obtain a deeper understanding or to find solutions to problems usually ranging beyond the standard scope of a single discipline or field of research.[4] Therefore in this section the historical and financial context in which the need for a fundamental civil judicial reform was detected and also the series of political events that led to the establishment of the new Greek CPC are briefly described. For reasons of objectivity, the political dimensions of this judicial reform as well as its link with transnational governance shall not be further analyzed. The research is here descriptive-explanatory with the use of literature review and secondary sources.

(a) Greece in the Storm of the EU Financial Crisis

The breakdown of the housing market in 2007 and the collapse of Lehman Brothers in 2008 marked the great economic recession in the United States during the years 2007-2009.[5] Its origins can be mainly detected in the severe exposure of banks to subprime mortgages[6] via a large diffusion of financial products such as Mortgage Backed Securities (MBS) among multiple investors globally, as well as in the creation of other interdependent but also precarious investing products such as Collateralized Debt Obligations (CDOs) and Credit Default Swaps (CDS), that further extended the derivatives markets causing unsafe investing conditions for the overall banking and financial community.[7] Since the impact of this shakeout was unprecedented for the overall financial sector, one can easily understand

4 Committee on Facilitating Interdisciplinary Research, Committee on Science, Engineering, and Public Policy, *Facilitating Interdisciplinary Research* 2 (The National Academies Press, Washington D.C., 2005).

5 See R. Wiggins, Th. Piontek and A. Metrick, "The Lehman Brothers Bankruptcy A", *Yale Program on Financial Stability* 1, 1-2 et seq. (2014),text available at: <http://som.yale.edu/sites/default/files/ files/001-2014-3A-V1-LehmanBrothers-A-REVA.pdf>, last visited 12 May 2016; J. Holt, "A Summary of the Primary Causes of the Housing Bubble and the Resulting Credit Crisis: A Non-Technical Paper", 8 *The Journal of Business Inquiry* 120 (2009).

6 See A. Chirita, "The impact of the European Union Current Crisis on Law, Policy and Society", 16 *Cambridge Yearbook of European Legal Studies* 255 (2014).

7 R. Jarrow, "The Role of ABSs, CDSs, and CDOs in the Credit Crisis and the Economy", in: A. S. Blinder, A. W. Lo and R. M. Solow (eds.), *Rethinking the Financial Crisis* 210 (Russell Sage Foundation, New York, 2012); J. Priewe, "What went wrong? Alternative interpretations of the global financial crisis", in: S. Dullien *et*

how the negative effects of the American credit crisis quickly spread worldwide and provoked a serious contagious threat to the global banking and financial system.

European countries could not stay unaffected by this universally generated financial downturn.[8] In 2008 the crumbling of Iceland's banking system signified the beginning of another financial turmoil that involved the majority of the EU member countries, especially those belonging to Eurozone, whose economies were more interconnected because of the common currency, as well as countries of the Euro area with relatively small economies and no considerable industry or exporting activity to withstand such an asymmetric shock. As a result the monetary and financial stability of the Eurozone was losing ground day by day and the future of the common currency was under question.[9] The EU financial crisis quickly escalated at the end of 2009, when many of the affected EU member states chose to bail-out their collapsing credit and financial institutions with government money aiming at avoiding official insolvency and thus it unfolded into a general sovereign debt crisis, when countries like Greece,[10] Ireland, Portugal, Spain and Cyprus were effectively unable to offset their increasing sovereign debts without the contribution of third parties.

Greece was among those European countries that were most affected by the EU financial crisis. In 2010 the country's fiscal deficit was remarkably high, investors feared that Greece would not meet its debt obligations and international credit rating agencies steadily downgraded the financial position of the Greek economy and government bonds;[11] hence the Greek government could no longer provide reliable collateral to borrow from the financial markets at a reasonable interest rate and so it was unable to cover its current needs.[12] In order to avoid a general suspension of payments in the public sector, which would mean a worse financial disaster for the

---

al. (eds.), *The Financial and Economic Crisis of 2008-2009 and Developing Countries* 17-50 (United Nations, New York-Geneva, 2010).

8 See N. Baltas, "The Greek Financial Crisis and the Outlook of the Greek Economy", 10 *The Journal of Economic Asymmetries* 32 (2013).

9 See Baltas, *ibid.*

10 See Chirita, *supra* n. 6.

11 See in terms of numbers Baltas, *supra* n. 8; M. Panezi, "A Description of the Structure of the Hellenic Republic, the Greek Legal System, and Legal Research", *GlobaLex* (2013), text available at: <http://www.nyulawglobal.org/globalex/Greece1.html>, last visited 12 May 2016.

12 See Chirita, *supra* n. 6.

country's economy and after the quite unsuccessful adoption of several cost-cutting measures, Greece was forced to seek immediate financial assistance from the Eurozone countries and other international parties and specifically applied for a bail-out loan from the European Commission, the European Central Bank and the IMF, all together forming a mechanism under the nickname "Troika".

The first bail-out package, under the formal name "First Economic Adjustment Program for Greece" and commonly known as "First Memorandum of Understanding (MoU)",[13] was signed by all involved parties on 3 May 2010 and enacted by the Greek Parliament under the Law 3845/2010.[14] It aimed to save Greece from an official sovereign default and tried to cover its financial needs via a 110 Billion Euros loan for the following three years[15] provided that the country would adopt and successfully implement another series of austerity measures on fiscal, structural and other reforms.[16] In simpler words, the approved loans were only to be granted upon specific conditions and requirements which included strict restructuring measures both in the public and private sectors. The enactment of the First MoU provoked severe social disorder and countless demonstrations throughout the country, since the majority of citizens were protesting against the agreed austerity measures. In the meantime, the unemployment and inflation rates reached a peak, while many Small-Medium Enterprises (SMEs) closed and the Greek banking sector gradually experienced a capital and liquidity shortfall.[17] Within this context the Greek government proved quite unable to implement successfully the demanded austerity measures and hence it was off target regarding the agreed conditions for the disbursement of the total amount of bailout loans. As a result, Greece applied in February 2012 for further financial assistance from the "Troika" parties in order to combat the continuously worsening economic situation.

---

13 European Commission, "The Economic Adjustment Program for Greece", *European Economy Occasional Papers* (2010) (61), *passim*, esp. at 3 et seq.

14 Greek Law 3845/2010 (FEK A' 65/06-05-2010).

15 See about this loan also E. Chiti and P.G. Teixera, "The Constitutional Implications of the European Responses to the financial and public debt crisis", 50 *Common Market Law Review* 683, 683, 686 (2013).

16 See European Commission, *supra* n. 13.

17 See Baltas, *supra* n. 8.

The second bail-out package, under the full name "Second Economic Adjustment Program for Greece" and commonly known as "Second MoU",[18] was initiated by the new Greek government, which had taken on duties some months before, intensifying the country's fiscal uncertainty. Its adoption was approved by the Greek Parliament on 13 February 2012 under the Law 4046/2012[19] and the main agreement was eventually signed by all involved parties on 1 March 2012. It included an extended financial assistance program, namely the non-disbursed loan amount that was left from the first program and an additional loan of 130 billion Euros, that was considered enough to cover the country's debt obligations-needs for the following two years; this financial support was provided under the condition of successfully implementing further austerity measures on fiscal, administrative, social, judicial and growth-enhancing structural reforms[20] as well as effectuating a voluntary government bond exchange with its private investors ("Private Sector Involvement -or PSI exchange offer"),[21] so as to boost the country's external financing along with its overall financial situation. After another round of Greek Parliamentary elections in May 2012, multiple protests against the austerity measures and joint efforts to comply with the conditions of the Second MoU, the country showed a slightly improved economic picture by the end of 2014.

The country's improved financial outlook did not last long, since the conduct of the next Greek Parliamentary elections in January 2015 changed the political scenery in Greece and triggered a series of discussions at national, European and international level regarding the previous bail-out packages and the valuation of the proper implementation of the previously agreed austerity measures. During the negotiations of the following months Greece fell into a deeper economic recession, while Greek banks began to face substantial capital and liquidity shortfalls stemming from panicked citizens, who rushed to withdraw their money from banks -and many of them to transfer it abroad- being afraid of a possible depositors' bail-in, like that of Cyprus in 2013, as a measure to avoid the overall collapse of the banking system.

18 European Commission, "The Second Economic Adjustment Program for Greece", 94 *European Economy Occasional Papers* (2012), *passim*, esp. at 5 et seq.

19 Greek Law 4046/2012 (FEK A' 28/14-02-2012).

20 European Commission, *supra* n. 18, at 21 et seq.; see also Baltas, *supra* n. 8.

21 European Commission, *ibid.*, at 7, 17 et seq.; Panezi, *supra* n. 11.

After a sequence of political events, one more round of Greek Parliamentary elections, an unprecedented default on the country's debt obligations towards the IMF, a referendum for the acceptance of another loan agreement from the "Troika", the closure of Greek banks and the Stock Exchange, the imposition of strict capital controls on depositors' withdrawals as well as the creation of multiple scenarios talking about the country's possible exit from the Eurozone and return to the "Drachma" national currency, the Greek government on 8 July 2015 made an official request for further financial support to the European Stability Mechanism (ESM) in order to meet its current debt and financial obligations and restore stability in the banking sector.[22] Greece finally came to an agreement with its creditors on 12 July 2015 for a new bail-out package under the *sine qua non* condition that before the signature of the new MoU another set of cost-cutting restructuring measures should be adopted and enacted, most of which were supposed to have already been implemented in the respect of valuating the previous bail-out programs.[23] The preconditioned measures may have implicated a top-down policy on behalf of the creditors, since Greece was already at a financial standstill, but they were eventually approved by the Greek Parliament. Their official approval took place in two phases, firstly on 15 July 2015 and secondly on 22 July 2015 and the following day a separate request for financial support was addressed to the IMF.[24] The adoption of the third bail-out package, which amounted to 86 billion Euros and is known as "Third MoU",[25] was approved by the Greek Parliament on 14 August 2015 along with other prior actions under the Law 4336/2015[26] and the final agreement was signed by

22 European Commission, "Commission signs three-year ESM stability support program for Greece", Press Release 20th August 2015, text available at: <http://europa .eu/rapid/press-release_IP-15-5512_en. htm>, last visited 13 May 2016.

23 See in detail about the prior-agreement measures Euro Summit Statement of the 12th July 2015, text available at: <http://www.consilium.europa.eu/en/meetings/eur opean-council/2015/ 07/12/>, last visited 13 May 2016.

24 European Commission, *supra* n. 22.

25 Memorandum of Understanding between the European Commission acting on behalf of the European Stability Mechanism and the Hellenic of the 19th August 2015, text available at: <http://ec.europa.eu/ economy_finance/assistance_eu_ms/g reek_loan_facility/pdf/01_mou_20150811_en.pdf>, last visited 13 May 2016.

26 Greek Law 4336/2015 (FEK A' 94/14-08-2015).

the European Commission, the Hellenic Republic and the Bank of Greece on 19 August 2015.[27]

(b) The Way to the Establishment of the New Greek Civil Procedure Code

From the adoption of the First MoU the restructuring of the Greek judicial system became a vital topic of discussions regarding the country's reform agenda. The enactment of the Second MoU brought up the same issues. Until then it had become more than evident that Greece should come up with a total reform of the judicial system in order to support its economic and financial activity.[28] As it has been observed, the effort to modernize the country's judicial system entailed aspects such as reviewing the existing legal framework, revising the basic regulatory codes, promoting alternative dispute resolution methods as well as implementing "a modern e-justice action plan" in Greek courts.[29] According to the same point of view, civil justice together with the enforcement of judgments procedure belong to the most significant aspects of such a radical judicial reform in terms of "economic security", "contractual trust" and "good faith" in the internal market.[30] In that respect it can be acknowledged that an improvement of civil justice could act as an additional driver for restoring overall financial stability of the country, and since the existing procedural framework could no longer meet the needs of contemporary society and its worsening economy,[31] the amendment of the Greek CPC had to be at the front of the country's reforms.

The first attempt at improving the civil procedural system in Greece on the occasion of the EU financial crisis was the adoption of Law 4055/2012 "on fair trials and their reasonable duration", which was published on 12 March 2012 only some days after the official signature of the Second

27 Memorandum, *supra* n. 25, at 3 et seq.

28 European Commission, "The Second Economic Adjustment Program for Greece – Fourth Review", 192 *European Economy Occasional Papers* (2014), *passim*, esp. at 59.

29 N. Kanellopoulos, "Civil Procedure reform in Greece", *eKathimerini* (2014), text available at: <http://www.ekathimerini.com/158631/article/ekathimerini/comment/civil-procedure-reform-in-greece>, last visited 12 May 2016.

30 Kanellopoulos, *supra* n. 29.

31 *Ibid.*

MoU and which became effective from 2 April 2012.[32] Law 4055/2012 amended several provisions of the Greek CPC aiming to accelerate civil trial proceedings, promote the delivery of fair courts' decisions and ameliorate the granting of civil justice.[33] Among the new settings many judicial deadlines were shortened, the reasons for postponing hearing procedures were restricted, the mediation process was introduced along with the pretrial conciliation process as Alternative Dispute Resolution (ADR) methods, significant elements of technological innovation and e-justice were adopted, and the Greek court network was then partially reshaped;[34] the results that emerged during the following months were actually pretty encouraging for the modernization of civil trial proceedings.[35]

However, as already described, since the Greek financial crisis deteriorated during the following years, the civil procedural system appeared unable to deal with the new economic situation; on the one hand there were many structural problems, especially in the district courts and, on the other hand, even the central courts could not cope with the remarkably high number of registered cases or bring sufficient closure of those pending.[36] Thus a fundamental reform of the Greek CPC was considered to be a necessary action for addressing "structural balance" in Greece, and for handling the majority of pending civil cases[37] as well as for the general desirable improvement of civil justice. The proposed legislation for the new Greek CPC was submitted for public consultation in March 2014 and was supposed to be enacted by the Greek Parliament before May 2014. Yet, due to multiple protests held by the Greek legal community during the following period against the submitted legislation draft and its intended amendments to the Greek CPC, the enactment of this legislative reform was postponed until November 2014. After the series of political and financial events that led to the agreement on the third bail-out package, the new CPC was eventually adopted by the Greek Parliament on 22 July 2015 under the Law 4335/2015[38] (Article 1), along with the adoption of

32 Greek Law 4055/2012 (FEK A' 51/12-03-2012).

33 Explanatory Report of Law 4055/2012, at 1-2; cf. A. Papadopoulou, *The concentration of opposition grounds in the civil enforcement procedure* 90 et seq. (Sakkoulas, Athens-Thessaloniki, 2016).

34 Explanatory Report, *supra* n. 33.

35 Kanellopoulos, *supra* n. 29.

36 European Commission, *supra* n. 28.

37 *Ibid.*

38 Greek Law 4335/2015 (FEK A' 87/23-07-2015).

the European Bank Recovery and Resolution Directive (BRRD)[39] (Article 2), both as a prerequisite and obligatory prior actions for the legal validation of the Third MoU by all involved parties[40] in an effort to prevent Greece from becoming officially insolvent. The new Greek CPC 2015, which belongs to the "modern state and public administration" policy chapter of the Third MoU[41] came into official effect according to its transitional provisions on 1 January 2016.[42]

(III) The Scope of the New Greek Civil Procedure Code (2015)

In this section the scope of the Greek CPC 2015 is thoroughly analyzed beginning with the detection of the dysfunctional parts of the previous civil procedural system, such as delays in delivering and enforcing civil judgments, under which the general need for acceleration of civil trial proceedings emerged. The latter problematic issues of civil trials are chosen to be approached mainly via the use of quantitative empirical analysis, exploiting statistical outcomes of the 2016 EU Justice Scoreboard, so as to be better understood and to show how this specific research method can deepen the considerations related to the establishment of such a procedural legislative reform. Quantitative analysis in terms of the legal research can thus be described as a research method that uses data collection and data analysis to perform inferences about a legal issue;[43] in the case of this paper the inference is causal,[44] since statistical data are used here to detect and define the real causes that imposed a fundamental reform in the civil procedural system in Greece. The paper then continues with a critical-explanatory analysis of the three basic pillars of the scope of the Greek CPC 2015 with the use of literature review and secondary sources.

---

39 Directive 2014/59/EU of the European Parliament and of the Council of 15 May 2014 establishing a framework for the recovery and resolution of credit institutions and investment firms, *OJ L 173* (12.6.2014) 190–348.

40 See Euro Summit Statement, *supra* n. 23.

41 Memorandum, *supra* n. 25, at. 5, 31.

42 See Greek Law 4335/2015, *supra* n. 38, Art. 1 (ninth article), at 832.

43 See L. Epstein and A.D. Martin, "Quantitative Approaches to Empirical Legal Research", in P. Cane and H. M. Kritzer (eds.), *The Oxford Handbook of Empirical Legal Research* 901 et seq. (Oxford University Press, New York, 2010).

44 See in detail J. Pearl, "Causla interference in statistics: An overview", *Statistics Surveys* 96 (2009).

(a) The Need for the Acceleration of Civil Trial Proceedings

The need for the acceleration of civil trial proceedings signifies the main idea for the fundamental reform of the Greek CPC 2015, which took place under the conditions of the Third MoU.[45] Greece could neither enhance its economic activity nor restore its overall financial stability, unless the civil judicial system was improved in terms of regaining the trust of individuals and businesses;[46] an important step towards this achievement could be taken by completing both the civil trial and the enforcement of judgments procedures within reasonable time and thereby speeding up the applicable civil proceedings. The acceleration of civil justice could obviously contribute to the cost-cutting policy of the country, since citizens and the Hellenic Republic would benefit to a significant degree by having their legal disputes solved quickly through simpler processes. In this respect it has been clearly explained that before the signature of the new financial agreement with the European parties and the disbursement of the first bail-out loan installment under the Third MoU, Greece had to complete "the adoption of the Code of Civil Procedure, which is a major overhaul of procedures and arrangements for the civil justice system and can significantly accelerate the judicial process and reduce costs".[47]

The excessive delays in delivering and enforcing civil judgments constitute a common problem of Greek civil courts. In pure numbers this problem is depicted in the statistical outcomes of the 2016 EU Justice Scoreboard;[48] the latter constitutes an information tool that uses quantitative data and statistical analysis to draw conclusions about the efficiency, independence, quality and overall functioning of justice systems in all EU member states and thus helps evaluate the impact of judicial reforms.[49] The data analyzed here come from 2010-2014, when the EU financial crisis reached a peak in many EU countries and are mainly provided by the Council of Europe Commission for the Evaluation of the Efficiency of

45 See Memorandum, *supra* n. 25, at 31; Euro Summit Statement, *supra* n. 23.

46 Kanellopoulos, *supra* n. 29.

47 Euro Summit Statement, *supra* n. 23.

48 COM (2016) 199 final, *The 2016 EU Justice Scoreboard* (European Union, 2016).

49 COM (2016) 199, *supra* n. 48, at 1; cf. A. Dori, "The EU Justice Scoreboard – Judicial Evaluation as a new governance tool", 2 *Max Planck Institute Luxembourg Working Paper* (2015), *passim*, esp. at 9 et seq.

Justice (CEPEJ) as well as from other sources.[50] The need for the acceleration of granting civil justice comes from indicators such as the length of proceedings, clearance rate and number of pending cases and determines the efficiency of the tested justice systems.

More specifically, in case of Greece the survey on the number of incoming civil, commercial, administrative and other cases in courts of first instance per one hundred inhabitants showed that the country was in the 16th highest position on average among European countries and that the number of these incoming cases had increased from 2010 to 2012 by 40%;[51] in a similar survey on the number of incoming civil and commercial litigious cases in the first instance per one hundred inhabitants, Greece occupied the 14th position on average and the number of these incoming cases had increased from 2010 to 2013 by 53%, while from 2013 to 2014 it had remarkably decreased by 66%,[52] since the legal community went on strike for several weeks against the reform of the Greek CPC. Regarding the length of proceedings for the same cases' categories, namely the time in days courts need to resolve civil and commercial litigious cases and reach a decision at first instance, Greece was in the 8th highest position on average among European countries and from 2010 to 2012 there was a significant increase of 153%, while from 2012 to 2014 the resolution time decreased by 33%.[53] Moreover, having in mind that the clearance rate is a percentage, which measures whether the judicial system of a country can carry through the incoming caseload,[54] the relevant survey on the rate of resolving litigious civil and commercial cases at first instance showed that Greece in 2010 had a clearance rate of 78%, in 2012 a rate of 58%, in 2013 a rate of 80% and in 2014 a rate of 115%;[55] translating these data it is adduced that during the period 2010-2013 the country had a clearance rate below 100% and hence Greek courts resolved fewer cases than the number of incoming ones, while in 2014, when the incoming cases were much fewer compared to the previous years, the percentage goes above 100% and hence Greek courts managed to tackle efficiently the incoming

50 COM (2016) 199, *supra* n. 48.
51 *Ibid.* at 5 Figure 2.
52 *Ibid.* at 5 Figure 3.
53 *Ibid.* at 7 Figure 5.
54 *Ibid.* at 8.
55 *Ibid.* at 8 Figure 8.

caseload.[56] Last but not least, as far as the number of litigious civil and commercial pending cases is concerned, the corresponding survey presented that Greece was in the 9th highest position among European countries and from 2010 to 2012 there was an increase of 147%, from 2012 to 2013 an additional increase of 31%, while from 2013 to 2014 there was a decrease of 60%;[57] the same numbers, if seen differently, show that from 2010 to 2013, when Greece was in the greatest financial recession, the total of pending litigious civil and commercial cases increased by an inconceivable percentage of 224%!

Considering the above quantitative data and the conducted statistical analysis, one can easily understand the extent of the deceleration of civil justice in Greece and how this issue worsened during the years of the EU and Greek financial crisis. Firstly, incoming civil cases increased since individuals and businesses experienced low or no income/low or no profits and hence severe liquidity shortages and overdue debts, so that every small dispute came before Greek civil courts. Secondly, the fact that the length of proceedings was increasing until 2012, while the clearance rate remained low enough until 2013, reveals that the civil judicial system already had some significant deficiencies that needed to be fixed, since even the central courts of the country could not sufficiently close incoming cases.[58] The slight improvement in the situation around 2014 may be explained initially by the introduction of the first step towards the reform of the Greek CPC under the Law 4055/2012,[59] which amended many procedural provisions in an effort to accelerate civil proceedings up to a certain degree; and also by the fact that Greek lawyers went on strike for several weeks in 2014 against the reform of the Greek CPC and the adoption of austerity measures that affected them, which led to a decrease in incoming cases in that year and hence to an increase in their clearance rate. Thirdly, the remarkable increase of pending civil cases between 2010-2013 can be explained by combining all these observations, and adding that the protests of the Greek legal community triggered the postponement of hearing dates of already pending civil cases and hence their accumulation for closure at a later stage. Apparently these phenomena in combination with already existing deficiencies in many provisions of the Greek CPC, was

56 COM (2016) 199, *supra* n. 48.
57 *Ibid.* at 10 Figure 11.
58 European Commission, *supra* n. 28.
59 Greek Law 4055/2012, *supra* n. 32.

the *coup de grâce* for further deceleration of civil trial proceedings, since the backlog of pending cases was increased beyond every expectation and beyond the capacity of the civil courts, and so the determination of civil cases' hearing dates reached an unthinkable time-frame ranging from 2-15 years!

Apart from the indicators related to the EU- and the Greek financial crisis, the unjustifiable delays in delivering and enforcing civil judgments, and the consequent need for the acceleration of civil justice in Greece can also be found in other factors. As it has been observed, the particular characteristics of Greek civil courts such as their complicated bureaucracy, procedural routines that could no longer conform with the recent socio-economic environment of the country, constant postponements of the necessary modernization of the judicial mechanism as well as a severe lack in using various ADR methods[60] are only some of the reasons why civil judgments take so long to be delivered, and hence why the Greek civil procedural system has fallen into a "deadlock".[61] It is true that the civil judicial system in Greece depends on an obsolete bureaucratic mechanism which suffers from significant structural problems, especially in regional courts[62] and which does not deploy the advancements of technological innovation to the degree other European countries do. The Greek CPC also entails proceedings created decades ago, during another era and under different circumstances and despite their multiple modifications they seem unable to deal effectively with today's high volume of more complex cases. In addition to these reasons, the majority of civil judgments in Greece go to the second instance, meaning that appeal rates are remarkably high compared to the country's population and the number of incoming civil cases. It has been rightly advocated that the high rates of appeal in Greece may be explained by the multiple function of appealing a civil judgment:[63] firstly, it provides correction to the judgments of courts of first instance, hence it ameliorates the quality of civil justice; secondly, it offers the possibility to improve the "bargaining position" of the defeated party as well

60 See also European Commission, *supra* n. 28.

61 Kanellopoulos, *supra* n. 29.

62 European Commission, *supra* n. 28.

63 M. Barendrecht, "Why is Angela Merkel needed to reform Greek civil procedure?", *Hiil Innovating Justice* (2015), text available at: <http://www.hiil.org/insight/why-is-angela-merkel-needed-change-greek-civil-procedure-rules>, last visited 13 May 2016.

as to provoke a deliberate delay in enforcement of the first instance judgment; and thirdly, it helps lawyers make more money from the handling of cases, especially when the procedural legality of the bill ends up being judged again by the Supreme Court, *Areios Pagos* in Greece. For all these reasons and in the respect of the financial crisis, the need for the acceleration of civil justice was set as a priority in Greece and thus a fundamental reform of the Greek CPC was considered as mandatory for restoring structural and procedural balance in Greek courts,[64] as well as for making them deal promptly with the high volume of pending civil cases.

(b) The Three Pillars of the Scope of the New Greek Civil Procedure Code

The new Greek CPC 2015 was enacted as a whole new code by Law 4335/2015, but it constitutes a product that also combines the numerous amendments in civil trial proceedings, which were introduced by the previous Law 4055/2012. Both these legislative initiatives emerged during the EU- and Greek financial crisis in the way described in the first section of this paper, and thus they both contributed to the fundamental reform of the existing civil procedural framework in Greece serving the same broader scope: the acceleration of granting civil justice. As explained in the Explanatory Report of Law 4055/2012, the right to judicial protection, which is guaranteed under the Greek Constitution *Syntagma* as well as under the European Convention of Human Rights (ECHR), can achieve its purpose only when the provided legal protection is complete and effective and is awarded within reasonable time; hence the aim of this law is to tackle the denial of justice due to delayed proceedings.[65] Within the same rationale, the Explanatory Report of Law 4335/2015 states that a basic requirement for the accomplishment of a civil trial's purpose is to issue correct and fair judgments together with the need for administration of justice within a reasonable time under the principle of procedural economy, therefore the primary aim of this law is to introduce reforms in the existing Greek CPC that will result in faster administration of justice without sacrificing the need for issuing correct and fair courts' decisions.[66]

---

64 European Commission, *supra* n. 28.

65 Explanatory Report of the Law 4055/2012, *supra* n. 33, at 1-2.

66 Explanatory Report of the Law 4335/2015, at 1.

In this respect it can be adduced that the perception of acceleration of civil trial proceedings, which gave birth to the radical reform of the existing Greek CPC is closely interrelated with concepts such as the issuance of sound, fair and quick civil judgments, adoption of judicial economy in the civil trial as well as fulfillment of the right to judicial protection. These concepts constitute the three basic pillars of the scope of the new Greek CPC 2015 and can be summarized as follows:

(i) The Issuance of Sound, Fair and Quick Civil Judgments

It is considered that the main purpose of a civil trial is to realize the protection of rights established under substantive law;[67] yet, the realization of this purpose requires not only the correct determination of the actual legal status by a right civil judgment, which shall develop commitment and enforceability, but it also demands the issuance of the relevant civil decision within a reasonable time.[68] Excessive delays in the judicial diagnosis of a civil case and in the articulation of the judicial judgment upon this case are indeed assimilated regarding their results to the refusal of issuing a decision[69] or to *non liquet*, both unacceptable for civil courts. If the legally binding decision that resolves a case is issued after a long time, it will

67 Mainly G. Mitsopoulos, *Civil Procedure A'* § 5 at 34 (Sakkoulas, Athens, 1972) [in Greek]; cf. N. Nikas, *Civil Procedure I* § 1.26 at 16 (Sakkoulas, Athens-Thessaloniki, 2003) [In Greek]; D. Kondylis, *Res Judicata according to the Civil Procedure Code* (2nd ed., Sakkoulas, Athens-Komotini, 2007), at 12 [in Greek]; C. Calavros, "Res judicata acquired with dolus as a ground for compensation", *Diki* 198, 200 note 12 with further ref. (1973) [in Greek].

68 Nikas, *supra* n. 67, at § 44.1 at 500; W. Habscheid, "Regarding the trends on the concentration of the civil trial in western Europe", *Armenopoulos* 88, 88 et seq., 93 (1974) [transl. in Greek by P. Ladas].

69 See K. Kerameus, "Intervention in the 10th Conference of the Greek Civil Procedural Law Experts Association, May 1982 in Nayplion", *Diki* 616, 616 (1982) [in Greek]; Nikas, *supra* n. 67, § 2.17 at 28; Ch. Apalagaki, *The Right of the Litigants to be Heard in the Civil Trial* 8 (Sakkoulas, Thessaloniki, 1989) [in Greek]; S. Chiarloni, "A comparative perspective on the crisis of civil justice and its possible remedies", in: W. H. Rechberger and T. Klicka (eds.), *Procedural Law on the Threshold of a New Millennium, XI. World Congress on Procedural Law* 149, 150 (Manz, Center of Legal Competence, International Association of Procedural Law, Vienna, 2002); A. A. S. Zuckerman, "Assessment of cost and delay, A multi-national perspective", *ibid* 167, 168-169.

have no practical value for the winning party and in fact it will be equal to the denial of justice.[70] Since civil trial proceedings serve the public interest in terms of maintaining the overall security of legal and commercial transactions, it is essential the clarification of judicial disputes to be completed without any delays and the differences between the interested parties, which also constitute the greatest cause for legal insecurity, to be resolved as quickly as possible.[71] Thus, an indispensable element for the achievement of these objectives is the formation of the structure, process and pattern of conducting a civil trial in such a way as to ensure the sound, fair and quick adjudication of affected substantive rights.

(ii) The Adoption of Judicial Economy in Civil Trial

In a broad sense judicial economy may be defined as the objective of saving time, procedural steps and costs in the conduct of civil proceedings, while in a narrow sense as the application of a rational process, which seeks to achieve the maximum possible result with the least possible procedural means and leads to the rapid completion of civil proceedings.[72] Judicial economy is linked with the purpose of a civil trial.[73] Since a civil trial aims at realizing the protection of substantive rights, judicial economy contributes to the quick, simple and inexpensive achievement of this objective;[74] therefore it aims to restrict the overall process through reducing the number of hearings and avoiding unnecessary procedural acts,

70 See Kerameus, *supra* n. 69; P. Dagtoglou, *Constitutional Law, Civil Rights* 1208 (4th ed., Sakkoulas, Athens-Thessaloniki, 2012) [in Greek]; D. Tsatsos, *Constitutional Law, Organization and Function of the State* 464-466 (2nd ed., Sakkoulas, Athens-Komotini, 1992) [in Greek]; Apalagaki, *supra* n. 69; St. Stamatopoulos, *The Principle of Judicial Economy in the Civil Trial* 35, 192 (Sakkoulas, Athens-Komotini, 2003) [in Greek]; Chiarloni, *supra* n. 69; Zuckerman, *supra* n. 69.

71 Papadopoulou, *supra* n. 33, p. 41.

72 Stamatopoulos, *supra* n. 70, at 33, 141 note 187 with further ref.

73 Stamatopoulos, *supra* n. 70, at 141 note 186 with further ref.; P. Hütten, *Die Prozeßökonomie als Rechtserheblicher Entscheidungsgesichtspunkt* 9-11, 19 (Diss. Würzburg, 1975).

74 Stamatopoulos, *supra* n. 70, at 141 note 187 with further Ref.; K. Makridou, "The delivery of the substantive judgment within a reasonable time in the civil trial", *Nomiko Vima* 1345, 1347 (2012) [in Greek]; Hütten,*supra* n. 73, at 19.

while ensuring the absolute fairness of judicial judgments.[75] More concretely, judicial economy in a civil trial points in two directions:[76] time-economy, namely reduction of the duration of civil trial proceedings and hence their acceleration; and costs-economy, namely simplification of the litigation process and hence reduction of its expenses.[77] Time-economy can be achieved though the joined hearing of actions and concentrated projection of claims on behalf of the litigant parties,[78] while costs-economy can be brought through a cost-effective structure of civil proceedings in terms of operating expenses. A rational and centralized process means greater economy of proceedings.[79] Considering that the current economic crisis has led to an overload of the judicial mechanism, one can easily perceive, on the one hand, the need for the fastest possible resolution of a dispute in the first and second instance and the fastest possible satisfaction of affected rights through the enforcement procedure; and, on the other hand, the emergence of the need for the highest possible reduction of overall judicial expenses.[80] Thus, judicial economy in the context of the civil trial and under these dimensions expresses the demand of contemporary society for a rapid and cost-effective judicial dispute resolution[81] through saving time, actions, resources and expenses for both civil courts and litigant parties.

(iii) The Fulfillment of the Right to Judicial Protection

The right to complete, effective and rapid judicial protection, which should be enjoyed by every individual from the start of the civil litigation process until the completion of the enforcement procedure is recognized in both Greek and European law and enshrined in Art. 20 § 1 of the Greek

---

75 Stamatopoulos, *supra* n. 70, at 138; Hütten, *supra* n. 73, at 6; E. Schumman, "Die Prozeßökonomie als rechtsethisches Prinzip", *Festschrift für K. Larenz* 271, 271, 278 (1973).

76 See Kerameus, "Contemporary speed problems in granting civil justice", *Armenopoulos* 89 (1984) [in Greek]; Stamatopoulos, *supra* n. 70, at 72-75, 122-123; cf. in detail Papadopoulou, *supra* n. 33, at 46 et seq.

77 Stamatopoulos, *supra* n. 70, at 40 notes 28-29 with further ref.

78 *Ibid.* at 39 note 24 with further ref., and at 242.

79 Schumman, *supra* n. 75, at 277-278.

80 See Makridou, *supra* n. 74, at 1345.

81 Makridou, *supra* n. 74.

Constitution *Syntagma,* and in Art. 6 § 1 ECHR. In particular, the first of these provisions guarantees the right of every individual to resort to courts and file an action and to receive judicial protection from them.[82] The protection provided by courts has as basic content the restoration of affected substantive rights and fulfills its purpose only when it is granted as complete and effective as possible.[83] The judicial protection is complete when there is no legal dispute for which recourse to courts would be excluded, and effective when it is provided at the appropriate time and in a way that really ensures the granting of justice.[84] Even though Art. 20 § 1 of the Greek Constitution does not explicitly refer to the right to rapid completion of a trial,[85] the requirement to resolve a dispute within a reasonable time should also constitute content of the right to judicial protection,[86] since the provided protection can be effective only when it is granted without excessive delays.[87] Furthermore, Art. 6 § 1 ECHR guarantees the right of every individual to free access to justice and for a fair trial within a reasonable time.[88] This established right has two interrelated aspects: the right to a fair trial and the right to a trial within a "reasonable deadline".[89] These aspects supplement the rule for judicial protection as enshrined in

---

82 N. Klamaris, *The Right to Judicial Protection according to the Art. 20 § 1 of the Greek Constitution 1975* (Sakkoulas, Athens-Komotini, 1989), *passim*, at 55, 64, 109, 115, 129, 297 et seq. [in Greek]; Dagtoglou, *supra* n. 70, at 11196 et seq.; K. Chrysogonos, *Civil and Social Rights* 423, 429, 433 et seq. (Nomiki Vivliothiki, 3rd ed. Athens, 2006) [in Greek].

83 Dagtoglou, *supra* n. 70, at 1201; Stamatopoulos, *supra* n. 70, at 191.

84 See among others Stamatopoulos, *supra* n. 70, at 74, 191-192.

85 Stamatopoulos, *supra* n. 70, at 191.

86 Chrysogonos, *supra* n. 82, at 442; Makridou, *supra* n. 74, at 1346; V. Schlette, *Der Anspruch auf gerichtliche Entscheidung in angemessener Frist, verfassungsrechtliche Grundlagen und praktische Durchsetzung*, (Duncker and Humblot, Berlin, 1999), *passim*, esp. at 24 et seq., 25-27.

87 Chrysogonos, *supra* n. 82, at 442 note 97; Stamatopoulos, *supra* n. 70, at 191.

88 See Chrysogonos, *The Incorporation of the European Convention on Human Rights to the National Legal Order* 393 (Sakkoulas, Athens-Komotini, 2001) [in Greek]; idem, *Civil and Social Rights*, *supra* n. 82, at 442-443; Nikas, *Civil Procedure I*, *supra* n. 57, § 2.17 at 28 note 47 with further ref.; Stamatopoulos, *supra* n. 70, at 199-200.

89 Chrysogonos, *supra* n. 88; idem, *Civil and Social Rights*, *supra* n. 82, at 442-443; Stamatopoulos, *supra* n. 70, at 201 et seq; cf. Naka v. Greece ECHR (10.1.2012), No 33585/09· Fergadioti-Rizaki v. Greece ECHR (10.1.2012), No 370/09, Glykantzi v. Greece ECHR (30.10.2012), No 40150/09.

Art. 20 § 1 of the Greek Constitution.[90] The requirement for judicial economy in terms of the civil trial's proceedings is closely related to the right for a fair trial within reasonable time, since the prompt settlement of a litigious legal dispute "can only be achieved through economical solutions".[91] Without the existence of economical proceedings, judicial protection cannot be provided rapidly. For that reason the concept of a fair trial under Art. 6 § 1 ECHR shall also cover its reasonable duration, so as to allow for the fastest completion of both the proceedings of first and second instance and the enforcement procedure and ultimately to ensure the effectiveness of the granted protection.[92] The meaning of these provisions is therefore that civil proceedings should be formed -or reformed- in such a way as to ensure that the right for a fair trial within a reasonable time is satisfied completely and effectively.

(IV) The Main Amendments of the New Greek Civil Procedure Code (2015)

The main amendments of the new Greek CPC 2015 are initially presented in this section by grouping them into four categories: the changes in ordinary proceedings before courts of first instance; in special proceedings and the payment order; in interim proceedings on precautionary measures; and those in the compulsory civil enforcement procedure. The paper then continues with a brief critical-explanatory analysis of the most innovative provisions of the new Greek CPC 2015 and their contribution to the acceleration of civil proceedings in a European context, while approaching each of them with a different methodology depending on its scope and function. Apart from the inter-disciplinary approach and quantitative empirical analysis, which have already been defined for the purposes of this research, the comparative method is also deployed in order to show how the newly-introduced provisions in Greek procedural law resemble those of other European countries. Additionally, qualitative empirical analysis is used, with the clarification that it takes here the meaning of a "case-based

---

90 Mitsopoulos, *supra* n. 67, at 39-40; P. Arvanitakis, "Verfassungsrechtliche Probleme der Zwangs-vollstreckung zur Befriedigung privatrechtlicher Ansprüche nach griechischem Recht", *ZZP* 463, 463 et seq., 465 (1998).

91 Stamatopoulos, *supra* n. 70, at 199.

92 See Chrysogonos, *supra* n. 82, at 442 et seq.; Papadopoulou, *supra* n. 33, at 53.

method" for the configuration of the existing procedural law, which uses "documents" -court decisions- as its main source material[93] and which aims to demonstrate how Greek and European case-law, via the relevant final judgments, has been simply incorporated into the new provisions of the Greek CPC 2015.

(a) *The Categorization of the Amendments of the New Greek Civil Procedure Code*

Analytically, the four basic categories of the recently introduced amendments in the new Greek CPC 2015 are presented as follows:

(i) The New Ordinary Proceedings before the Courts of First Instance

The main characteristic of the amendments that were introduced in the new Greek CPC 2015 is the abolishment of the until now partly-oral debate on the hearing date before courts of first instance and its replacement with a more flexible, simpler and quicker written procedure.[94] The new ordinary process is described in Arts. 237-238 and is based on the pleadings -along with the entailed claims- of the litigant parties.[95] The pleadings are submitted together with proving means and procedural documents within a deadline of one hundred or one hundred thirty days from the filing of the action depending on the case (237 § 1), the additional pleadings within the

93 See for this aspect L. Webley, "Qualitative approaches to empirical legal research", in: P. Cane and H. M. Kritzer (eds.), *The Oxford Handbook of Empirical Legal Research* 926 (Oxford University Press, New York, 2010).

94 Explanatory Report of the Law 4335/2015, *supra* n. 66, at 2. Further reading for the new ordinary proceedings before the courts of first instance: Nikas, *Manual of Civil Procedure* § 70.1 ff. at 453 et seq. (2nd ed., Sakkoulas, Athens-Thessaloniki 2016), [in Greek]; K. Makridou, Ch. Apalagaki and G. Diamantopoulos, *Civil Procedure* 1 (Sakkoulas, Athens-Thessaloniki 2016) [in Greek]; Sp. Georgouleas, "The trial before the courts of first instance according to ordinary proceedings: technical-legal issues, practical application problems and suggested solutions", *Elliniki Dikaiosyni* 41-58 (2016) [in Greek].

95 Explanatory Report, *supra* n. 94; cf. G. Orfanidis, "The ordinary proceedings before the courts of first instance", in the Scientific Symposium for Prof. Nikas *The Civil Trial at a Crucial Point* 27 et seq. (Sakkoulas, Athens-Thessaloniki 2016) [in Greek]; Papadopoulou, *supra* n. 33, at 24 et seq.

following fifteen days from the expiry of the aforementioned pleadings deadline, and then the file of the case is considered as completed (237 § 2).[96] The judge of a case or the court composition is appointed within the following fifteen days, and the hearing date is determined within thirty days from the appointment of a judge (237 § 4).[97] The hearing of a case is now typical,[98] no witnesses are examined and the case is discussed without the presence or participation of the litigant parties or their attorneys,[99] while the postponement of a hearing according to Art. 241 is not allowed[100] (237 § 4). If the court considers that a case has not been sufficiently clarified so as to enable the delivery of a substantial decision, a repetition of the hearing is ordered aiming to examine witnesses (237 § 6).[101] Within a deadline of eight days from the witnesses' examination, the litigants can assess the testimonies by adding a statement, but the introduction of new pleadings or evidence is excluded (237 § 7).[102] Interventions, third party summoning, notification of the trial as well as counterclaims are submitted and served to every involved party within a deadline of sixty or ninety days from the submission of an action, depending on the case, while their pleadings together with the means of proof and procedural documents are submitted within the general deadline of Art. 237 §§ 1,

---

96 See Calavros, *Civil Procedure, General Part* § 35. 42, 43, 46 at 356-357(4th ed., Sakkoulas, Athens-Thessaloniki 2016) [in Greek]; Papadopoulou, *supra* n. 33.

97 Explanatory Report, *supra* n. 94, at. 4, 12; cf. Calavros, *supra* n. 96, at§ 35. 49 at 359.

98 The "typical" hearing has been set in order to protect the fundamental principle of publicity according to Art. 93 of the Greek Constitution and also to enable the performance of specific procedural acts· Explanatory Report, *supra* n. 94, at 12; cf. Calavros, *supra* n. 96, at § 35.51 at 359-360; Papadopoulou, *supra* n. 33, at 24 note 80.

99 Explanatory Report, *supra* n. 94, at 2, 5, 12; cf. Calavros, *supra* n. 96, at § 35.54 ff. at 361 et seq.

100 The postponement of the hearing according to Art. 241 CPC is no more allowed in ordinary proceedings, but it still remains applicable in special proceedings· Explanatory Report, *supra* n. 94, at 12; cf. Papadopoulou, *supra* n. 33, at 25 note 82.

101 Explanatory Report, *supra* n. 94, at 2, 5, 12-13; cf. Makridou, "The suggested amendments of the Draft New CPC 2014 on the ordinary proceedings – the oral hearing", *EPolD* 187, 188, 190 (2014) [in Greek]; Calavros, *supra* n. 96, § 35.59, 65 ff. at 363, 365 et seq.; Papadopoulou, *supra* n. 33, at 25 note 84.

102 Explanatory Report, *supra* n. 94, at 5; Calavros, *supra* n. 96, at § 35.59, 73 at 363, 369-370; Papadopoulou, *supra* n. 33, at 25.

2, namely within one hundred or one hundred thirty days from the submission of the initial action (238 § 1).[103]

(ii) The Reformation of the Special Proceedings and the Changes in the Payment Order

Special proceedings are consolidated and systematically grouped into three broad categories:[104] a) disputes arising from family, marriage and civil partnerships (592-613), b) property disputes (614-622B), including *inter alia* the lease disputes, labor disputes, differences for losses from cars or from publications, as well as differences from debt securities, and c) orders (623-646), which include the payment order and the expelling order from leasehold use. The written procedure of Arts. 237-238 CPC does not apply to special proceedings, since the oral hearing and witnesses' examination are still maintained.[105] The applicable procedure for the adjudication of disputes falling within these categories is thoroughly de-

103 Explanatory Report, *supra* n. 94, at 5, 13; cf. Makridou, *supra* n. 101, at 187; Calavros, *supra* n. 96, § 35.83 ff. at 373 et seq.

104 Explanatory Report, *supra* n. 94, at 5-6, 16; cf. St. Pantazopoulos, "The amendments of the CPC on the legal remedies, on the special proceedings and on the general part of the civil enforcement procedure according to Law 4335/2015", *EPolD* 266, 270 et seq. (2015) [in Greek]; P. Yiannopoulos, "The special proceedings of CPC after the Law 4335/2015", *EPolD* 453, 455 et seq. (2015) [in Greek]; Papadopoulou, *supra* n. 33, at 27; P. Tsogias, "The special proceedings after the Law 4335/2015", in the Scientific Symposium for Prof. Nikas *The civil trial at a crucial point* 89 et seq. (Sakkoulas, Athens-Thessaloniki 2016) [in Greek]. Further reading for the reformation of special proceedings and the changes in the payment order: Makridou, Apalagaki and Diamantopoulos, *supra* n. 94, at 10 et seq.; Pantazopoulos, "The legislative amendments of the Law 4335/2015 on the payment order issuance procedure and on the trial of the opposition against it", *EfAD* 134 (2016) [in Greek]; ibidem, "The legislative amendments of the Law 4335/2015 on the trials of special procedures (articles 591 ff. CPC)", *Elliniki Dikaiosyni* 658 (2016) [in Greek]; K. Oikonomou, "The special proceedings according to CPC", *Elliniki Dikaiosyni* 34-(2016) [in Greek]; Chr. Sevastidis, "The special proceedings in the new CPC (Law 4335/2015)", *Elliniki Dikaiosyni* 73 (2016) [in Greek]; K. Rigas, "The orders and the non-contentious proceedings in the new Civil Procedure Code (after the Law 4335/2015)", *Elliniki Dikaiosyni* 109 (2016) [in Greek]; S. Mouzoura, "The general provisions of the special proceedings- The disputes arising from the family, marriage and civil partnership- Property disputes", *Elliniki Dikaiosyni* 78 (2016) [in Greek].

105 Explanatory Report, *supra* n. 94; cf. Papadopoulou, *supra* n. 33.

scribed in the amended Art. 591 CPC.[106] The deadline for summoning the litigant parties is thirty or sixty days before the hearing date (591 § 1 a'),[107] while the intervention, third party summoning and notification of the trial are submitted at least ten days before the hearing (591 § 1 b). The pleadings shall be submitted not later than during the oral hearing (591 § 1 c) and the additional pleadings for the evaluation of evidence by the third working day after the oral hearing date (591 § 1 f').[108]

Regarding the payment order (623-636) the introduced amendments aim either to remove obstacles for its issuance, especially those that were rather incompatible with the European Payment Order (Regulation 1896/2006)[109], to resolve disputes of jurisprudence regarding the issue of an order, or to reassure -for the sake of judicial economy- the common adjudication of the opposition against a payment order with the opposition against the compulsory civil enforcement procedure, when the latter is based on an enforceable order for payment.[110] Thus, it is explicitly defined that the issue of a payment order demands a monetary claim or a requirement of securities deriving from a private law dispute (623); likewise, in the case of persons with unknown residence, the impediment for issuing an order is also abolished, under the condition that they have legitimately appointed a procedural representative (624 § 2).[111] The deadline and the exertion of opposition to a payment order do not influence its enforceability, unless the order was issued against a person residing abroad or with unknown residence, so for the debtor's protection the enforceability of an order is suspended during the exercise period of an opposition under Art. 632 CPC (631).[112] Additionally, there is now the possibility of cumu-

106 See Gr. Timagenis, "Disputes from the family, marriage and civil partnership", *EPolD* 215, 217-218 (2014) [in Greek]; D. Babiniotis, "The special procedure of property disputes according to the new CPC", *EPolD* 222, 223-224 (2014) [in Greek].

107 Explanatory Report, *supra* n. 94, at 15-16; cf. Pantazopoulos, *supra* n. 104, at 270-271.

108 Explanatory Report, *supra* n. 94 at 16; cf. Pantazopoulos, *supra* n. 104, at 271; Yiannopoulos, *supra* n. 104, at 465 et seq.; Papadopoulou, *supra* n. 33, at 27.

109 Regulation (EC) No1896/2006 of the European Parliament and of the Council of 12 December 2006 creating a European order for payment procedure, *OJ L 399* (30.12.2006) 1–32.

110 Explanatory Report, *supra* n. 94, at 6.

111 *Ibid.* at 6-7, 17; cf. Pantazopoulos, *supra* n. 104, at 272.

112 *Ibid.* at 7, 17; cf. Pantazopoulos, *supra* n. 104, at 273.

lating an opposition against a payment order in the same application document with an opposition against the enforcement procedure, being curtailed by an enforceable order for payment, provided that all the other conditions for the objective joinder of remedies under Art. 218 CPC are also met (632 § 6).[113]

(iii) The Modifications in the Interim Proceedings Regarding Precautionary Measures

As far as the interim measures procedure is concerned, the basic provision on the granting of precautionary measures has been amended so that these measures, which can be arranged in urgent cases or to prevent imminent danger, require the existence of a substantive right, which may be subjected to a condition or a deadline or which may concern a future claim (682 § 1). The inclusion of substantive rights on a future claim was adopted so as to cover cases such as claims to participate in acquisitions after filling a divorce action or annulment of marriage or spouses' separation before the irrevocable judgment for termination of marriage, or before the completion of the two-year spouses' separation as a prerequisite for a divorce action.[114] Furthermore, to accelerate the granting of temporary judicial protection it is now sufficient for the delivery of a judgment on interim measures that the judge be persuaded only on the probable cause of claims (690 § 1). that is, the judge may decide freely on the case, without restrictions of rules on the proving power of the evidence.[115] Within the same concept, the relevant judgment shall contain concise reasoning and shall be recorded in a separate procedural document within a deadline of forty-eight hours or thirty days from the lapse of the deadline for submitting

113 *Ibid.*; cf. E. Podimata, "Comments on the new Articles 623 till 646 ("Orders") of the Draft CPC 2014", *EPolD* 230, 236-237 (2014) [in Greek]; Papadopoulou, *supra* n. 33, at 237-238.

114 Explanatory Report, *supra* n. 94, at 17; cf. D. Kranis, "Modern topics of interim measures", in the Scientific Symposium for Prof. Nikas *The civil trial at a crucial point* 99, at 99-100 (Sakkoulas, Athens-Thessaloniki 2016) [in Greek]. Further reading on the modifications of the interim proceedings regarding precautionary measures: A. Kagiouli, "The amendments of the Civil Procedure Code in the interim proceedings according to the Law 4335/2015", *Elliniki Dikaiosyni* 138(2016) [in Greek].

115 Explanatory Report, *supra* n. 94, at 18.

briefs in exceptional cases, if such a deadline has been prescribed (691 § 3).[116] If the interim measure has been ordered before the filling of the main action, there is no concrete deadline for submitting the main action, but the court may prescribe such a deadline, with a duration of no less than thirty days (693 § 1);[117] in case the latter deadline lapses with no filled main action, then the interim measure is automatically lifted, unless the applicant issues and serves a payment order within the same period (693 § 2). Only in the case of an interim payment shall the applicant submit the main action within the deadline of sixty days from the serving of the judgment: otherwise the interim payment ceases to apply (729).[118]

(iv) The Amendments in the Compulsory Civil Enforcement Procedure

Considering that the greatest delays appear mostly during compulsory enforcement procedure, the amendments here follow two main directions: firstly they try to limit the number of remedies that can be exercised against the execution-procedural acts, and secondly, to reduce the time that is required for the completion of the process and materialization of the enforceable title.[119] Thus, all complaints about defects of the enforcement procedure are exercised only in two stages:[120] the first stage is before the mandatory auction and comprises all the grounds for the invalidity of execution acts that have occurred until then, and these grounds shall be all collected and displayed with a single opposition against the enforcement procedure according to Art. 933 CPC, which will be adjudicated before the auction (934 § 1 a'); and the second stage is after the mandatory auc-

116 *Ibid.*

117 *Ibid.*

118 *Ibid.* at 19.

119 *Ibid.* at 8. Further reading on the amendments in the compulsory civil enforcement procedure: Makridou, Apalagaki and Diamantopoulos, *supra* n. 94, at 33 et seq.; P. Mazis, "Regarding the introduction in the CPC of the multiple seizures system according to the Law 4335/2015", *Elliniki Dikaiosyni* 144 (2016) [in Greek]; A. Plevri, "The amendments of the Law 4335/2015 on issues of the compulsory civil enforcement", *Elliniki Dikaiosyni* 152 (2016) 152 [in Greek]; Mouzoura, "The most important amendments in the compulsory civil enforcement according to the Law 4335/2015", *Elliniki Dikaiosyni* 982 (2016) [in Greek].

120 See Papadopoulou, *supra* n. 33, at 120 note 178.

tion and includes all the grounds for invalidity that occurred until the completion of the auction and the awarding, and these grounds shall be all collected and displayed in a second single opposition against the enforcement procedure of Art. 933 CPC, which will be judged after the auction (934 § 1 b').[121] If the enforceable title is a court decision or a payment order, the projection of complaints against the claim is allowed only up to the point that they are not already covered by res judicata of the final judgment on the previous main trial (933 § 4).[122] The possibility of an automatic suspension of the enforcement procedure is also abolished, and it now may be granted only upon the condition of a successful appeal against the judgment on the exercised opposition (937 § 1 b', c').[123] Moreover, introduced for the first time in contemporary Greek procedural law is the possibility of imposing multiple seizures of the same asset and in a parallel manner by several lenders of the same debtor, and every enforcement process is conducted separately and independently (958).[124] Concerning the satisfaction of monetary claims, the creditors' ranking in distribution tableau is also modified as to their general privileges; hence in the third ranking class one can find, along with the claims of employees and lawyers, also the state claims stemming from VAT and withholding taxes together with related surcharges and interest (975. 3), while in the fifth class the state and the municipalities are ranked for their claims for any cause (975. 5).[125] Last but not least, changes have been made regarding the creditors' ranking as to the distribution of the auction's proceeds, so that non-privileged creditors now have a chance to be satisfied and hence they are encouraged to attempt an enforcement procedure;[126] indeed claims equipped with a special privilege are highly favoured, particularly those of credit institutions, since they can be satisfied up to 65% of the auction's proceeds in case of concurrence with generally and specially preferential claims and up to 90% when they concur only with non-preferential claims (977 § 3).

---

121 Explanatory Report, *supra* n. 94, at 8, 22; cf. Pantazopoulos, *supra* n. 104, at 275; Papadopoulou, *supra* n. 33, at 120-121 note 179, and at 324.

122 Explanatory Report, *supra* n. 94, at 9; see in detail Papadopoulou, *supra* n. 33, at 262 et seq.

123 Explanatory Report, *supra* n. 94, at 21; cf. Pantazopoulos, *supra* n. 104, at 275-276; Papadopoulou, *supra* n. 33, at 146 note 60.

124 Explanatory Report, *supra* n. 94, at 22.

125 *Ibid.* at 23.

126 *Ibid.* n. 94.

(b) A "European" Approach to the Most Innovative Provisions of the New Greek Civil Procedure Code

The new Greek CPC 2015 entails many provisions that improve, modernize and accelerate civil trial proceedings. Among the most innovative adjustments, either in newly established or amended provisions of the CPC, are the following:

(i) The Establishment of Judicial Economy as a Fundamental Principle of the Civil Trial

Law 4335/2015 introduced Art. 116 § 2 CPC, which emphasizes the increased responsibility and hence the genuine procedural obligation[127] of litigant parties to contribute via their overall procedural behavior -and especially via the diligent conduct of the trial on their behalf, timely undertaking of all procedural acts, timely projection of claims and timely bringing of evidence- to the acceleration of civil trial proceedings and to the speedy resolution of the legal dispute.[128] This new provision, which is placed systematically within the fundamental procedural principles,[129] completes the general rule of Art. 116 § 1 CPC for the *bona fide* conduct of a civil trial, integrates to this rule the need for a speedy trial and quick resolution of a case and specifies the procedural steps that could enable its realization.[130] In this way judicial economy is incorporated into the Greek CPC -at least to a certain degree- as a fundamental principle of the civil trial and with the ambitious aim of reducing the excessive and unjustified delays, that were hitherto observed in the operation of Greek courts and for which Greece has been repeatedly convicted under the case law of the ECHR.[131]

---

127 *Ibid.* at 4, 10.

128 See Calavros, *supra* n. 96, § 35.45 at 356-357; Papadopoulou, *supra* n. 33, at 77-78.

129 Explanatory Report, *supra* n. 94, at 4, 10.

130 Papadopoulou, *supra* n. 33, at 78; yet, cf. Sp. Tsantinis, "The New CPC –General Part", *EPolD* 178, 182 (2014) [in Greek], who expresses concerns regarding the practical application of the provision because of its general wording.

131 See indicatively *Glykantzi v. Greece* ECHR (pilot judgment), *supra* n. 89; *Fergadioti-Rizaki v. Greece* ECHR, *supra* n. 89; *Naka v. Greece* ECHR, *supra* n. 89; *Anagnostopoulos and Others v. Greece* (07.11.2000), No 39374/98. In the Fact-

(ii) The Promotion of ADR Methods

Law 4055/2012 CPC introduced Art. 214B CPC establishing judicial mediation[132] and Law 4335/2015 added Arts. 214C, 116A CPC enabling recourse to intermediation process[133] and establishing the duty of the court to encourage litigant parties to choose ADR methods.[134] These innovative sections enhance significantly the acceleration of a civil trial, since they seek to largely discharge the courts' dockets. More specifically, Art. 214B § 1 CPC provides that private law disputes can also be resolved through judicial mediation, which is optional and can be activated either before filing an action or during the pendency of proceedings.[135] In a similar way, Art. 214C § 1 CPC foresees that if a case's circumstances are appropriate, the court may propose -or the litigant parties may decide- during the pendency of the civil trial to have recourse to the intermediation process and

---

sheet -Pilot Judgments, *ECHR Press Unit July 2015*, text available at: <http://www.echr.coe.int/Documents/FS_Pilot_judgments_ENG.pdf>, last visited 30 May 2016, it is reported that "from 1999 to 2009 the Court delivered about 300 judgments against Greece finding excessive the duration of judicial proceedings, including of a civil nature", a number which clearly depicts the "deficiencies in the Greek legal system at the root of excessive length of proceedings in the civil courts". See also the Greek Law 4239/2014 (FEK A' 43/20-02-2014) on the "fair satisfaction for exceeding the reasonable duration of the trial in civil and other courts".

132 See V. Thanou-Christophilou, "Judicial mediation (Art. 214B CPC)", *Elliniki Dikaiosyni* 937, 937 et seq. (2013) [in Greek].

133 See the Greek Law 3898/2010 (FEK A' 211/16-12-2010), which transferred into Greek law the Directive 2008/52/EC of the European Parliament and of the Council of 21 May 2008 on certain aspects of mediation in civil and commercial matters, *OJ L 136* (24.5.2008) 3–8; cf. in detail Klamaris, "The regulation of mediation in Greek draft laws", *EPolD* 473 (2010) [in Greek]; G. Diamantopoulos and V. Koumpli, "On mediation law in Greece", *RHDI* 361 (2014); ibidem, "The intermediation as a private dispute resolution means", *Nomiko Vima* 136 (2015) [in Greek]; G. Valmantonis, "Some thoughts on mediation and its relationship with the court proceedings", *Elliniki Dikaiosyni* 344 (2013) [in Greek].

134 Explanatory Report, *supra* n. 94, at 10-11.

135 It is rightly observed that this provision contrary to those of Arts. 213, 214A § 1 CPC and Art. 2 Law 3898/2010, does not demand fulfillment of the substantive conditions for a valid compromise as a prerequisite for the subjection of the disputes to judicial mediation· see Calavros, *supra* n. 96, § 31.62 at 31; cf. for the Art. 214B § 1 CPC Diamantopoulos and Koumpli, *RHDI* (2014), *supra* n. 133, at 368 et seq.; ibidem, *Nomiko Vima* (2015), *supra* n. 133, at 142 et seq. with further ref.

in such a choice the hearing of the case shall be postponed for three months or it shall be canceled, if it is adjudicated through the ordinary proceedings.[136] The difference between these two provisions is that the former refers to a process carried out exclusively by a judge mediator, although not the one that hears the case but a senior judge who is affiliated to the competent court as a mediator for a period up to three years in total, while the latter provision deals with the private intermediation process, which is conducted solely by a lawyer, who has already been trained and accredited as a mediator. Yet, in both cases if the litigant parties come to a mediation agreement, this agreement shall bring binding effects for them and indeed the judicial mediation agreement, which is also included in the courts' records, is considered as an enforceable title under the conditions of Arts. 214B § 5 and 904 § 2c' CPC. As far as Art. 116A CPC is concerned, it introduces for the first time in Greek procedural law the duty of the court to encourage in every procedural stage and in every type of proceedings the compromising resolution of the legal dispute and the choice of intermediation as a measure in its extrajudicial settlement,[137] and adds this duty -or better integrates it- to the fundamental principles of the civil trial.[138] The promotion of ADR methods through the aforementioned provisions takes place in accordance with corresponding settings in other European countries.[139] In this regard, according to the 2015 statistical findings EU member states such as Germany, Lithuania and Denmark are ranked first in promoting and giving incentives for ADR methods, while Greece finds itself among the last ten.[140]

---

136 See Calavros, *supra* n. 96, § 31.70 at 34; Orfanidis, *supra* n. 95, at 36-37; D. Theocharis, "The new provisions of CPC for intermediation and extrajudicial dispute settlement -Innovative settings or empty letter?", *Sinigoros* 46 (2015) [in Greek].

137 A similar provision is detected in Art. 3 Law 3898/2010, which has not been applied until today; see Theocharis, *supra* n. 136, at 46 et seq.

138 Explanatory Report, *supra* n. 94, at 10-11; Orfanidis, *supra* n. 95, at 36.

139 See Orfanidis, *supra* n. 95, at 44 with further ref.

140 COM (2016) 199 final, The 2016 EU Justice Scoreboard, *supra* n. 48, at 23 Figure 27.

(iii) The Establishment of a New System for the Concentration of the Litigants' Claims

In the new Greek CPC 2015 the accelerated process of the civil trial focuses on the changed temporal-procedural spots, at which all the claims of the litigant parties shall be concentrated and projected so as to be admissible. More concretely, in the new ordinary proceedings before courts of first instance the submission of pleadings and additional pleadings according to Arts. 237 §§ 1, 2 and 238 § 1 CPC, as amended by Law 4335/2015, consists the new central procedural point for the concentration of the litigants' defensive claims (objections), so that any claims displayed after that point are considered as inadmissible and are excluded from the rest of the process.[141] The exceptionally late submission that was recognized for certain categories of claims is now abolished,[142] and any possible belated claims, based on events after the completion of the case's file, can only be taken into account before courts of the second instance or via an opposition during the civil enforcement procedure.[143] Within the same concept, in special proceedings the new central procedural point for the concentration of the litigant's defensive claims is defined by the submission of pleadings according to the amended Art. 591 § 1 CPC,[144] and in proceedings before courts of second instance is demarcated by the likewise amended Art. 527 CPC;[145] in the latter rule the CPC has also set six limited exceptions under which the delayed projection of claims shall be admissible,[146] such as in case of belated claims (ex-ante), claims attested on the spot by document or by judicial admission of the opposite party, claims not promptly projected because of justified reason, etc. Regarding the compulsory civil enforcement procedure, the procedural point for the concentration of opposi-

---

141 Calavros, *supra* n. 96, § 35.47 at 357-358; Papadopoulou, *supra* n. 33, at 25-26.

142 Papadopoulou, *supra* n. 33, at 26.

143 Explanatory Report, *supra* n. 94, at 4; cf. Makridou, *supra* n. 101, at 189-190; Papadopoulou, *supra* n. 33, at 26 note 90; yet with cautious comments Calavros, *supra* n. 96, § 35.48 at 358-359.

144 Papadopoulou, *supra* n. 33, at 27.

145 Arvanitakis, "The contribution of Prof. Nikas in the law of legal remedies -Recent legislative and jurisprudential developments in the field of ius novorum, particularly with respect to preferential claims", in the Scientific Symposium for Prof. Nikas *The civil trial at a crucial point* 69 (Sakkoulas, Athens-Thessaloniki 2016) [in Greek]; similarly Papadopoulou, *supra* n. 33, at 33 et seq.

146 Papadopoulou, *supra* n. 33, at 34-35.

tion grounds is given by Art. 935 CPC, as amended by Law 4055/2012[147] and according to which all the grounds for invalidity of the execution acts of every enforcement stage shall be concentrated and projected via a single opposition of Art. 933 CPC for each stage, otherwise they are inadmissible.[148] Article 935 CPC under the new legislation contains almost word for word the content of the corresponding § 767 Abs. 3 ZPO in German civil procedural law, which transfers the principle of concentration ("Konzentrationsmaxime") into the enforcement procedure and hence functions within the frame of the opposition § 767 ZPO ("Vollstreckungsgegenklage") in a quite similar way with the opposition of Art. 933 CPC of Greek law.[149] The concentration of opposition grounds under Art. 935 CPC if combined with the amended Art. 934 CPC, which reduces the stages for annulment of the compulsory enforcement procedure to just two,[150] significantly restricts the possibility of challenging execution acts[151] via an opposition, and hence prevents the exercise of deliberately repeated or successive oppositions that would unnecessarily delay the enforcement process.[152]

---

147 *Ibid.* at 89 et seq.

148 *Ibid.* at 36 et seq., 315 et seq., 324-325.

149 See Papadopoulou, *supra* n. 33, at 91 et seq. with further ref. in German literature; cf. esp. for § 767 Abs. 3 ZPO L. Rosenberg/ H.-F.Gaul/ E. Schilken/ E. Becker-Eberhard, *Zwangsvollstreckungsrecht* § 40.112-118 at 760-763 (12th ed., C.H. Beck, München, 2010); F. Stein/ M. Jonas (-Münzberg), *Kommentar zur Zivilprozessordnung* § 767.52 ff. at 628-631 (22nd ed., Mohr Siebeck, Tübingen, 2002); R. Zöller (-Herget), *Zivilprozessordnung* § 767.22 at 1751-1752 (29th ed., Dr. Otto Schmidt, Köln, 2012); F. Baur/ R. Stürner/ A. Bruns, *Zwangsvollstreckungsrecht* § 45.23 at 544 (13th ed., C. F. Müller, Heidelberg-Berlin, 2006); H. Brox/ W.-D. Walker, *Zwangsvollstreckungsrecht* § 43.1352 ff. at 629-631 (9th ed., Vahlen, München 2011); H. Otto, *Die Präklusion, Ein Beitrag zum Prozeßrecht* 73 et seq. (Duncker and Humblot, Berlin, 1970); ibidem, "Die inner-und außerprozessuale Präklusion im Fall der Vollstreckungsgegenklage", *Festschrift für W. Henckel* 615, 619 et seq (1995); K. Schmidt, "Präklusion und Rechtskraft bei wiederholten Vollstreckungsgegenklagen, Zur Abgrenzung von § 767 Abs. 2 und Abs. 3 ZPO", *JR* 89 (1992).

150 Explanatory Report, *supra* n. 94, at 8; Papadopoulou, *supra* n. 33, at 324-325.

151 Calavros, "Introduction –The physiognomy of the new settings", *EPolD* 172, 176 (2014) [in Greek].

152 Explanatory Report, *supra* n. 94, at 8; cf. Explanatory Report, *supra* n. 33, at 17.

(iv) The Deployment of Technological Innovation

The new Greek CPC 2015 entails many elements of e-justice in an effort to deploy technological innovation to accelerate civil trial proceedings. Provisions exist regarding the proceedings before the courts of first instance that foresee the drawing of judicial reports electronically (117 § 2), the electronic submission of actions, pleadings and proving means -under the condition of bearing an advanced electronic signature[153]- as well as the obligation of including in legal documents the e-mail address of the litigant's attorneys (119 §§ 1, 4 and 215 § 1),[154] the serving of legal documents electronically (122 § 5), the keeping of electronic courts' dockets, the notification of the hearing date through electronic means[155] as well as the electronic submission of the pleadings, additional pleadings and proving means (237 §§ 4, 6, 9), the obligation of electronic delivery of the courts' judgments (304) and also the possibility of examining witnesses via teleconference (393 § 3). As far as the civil enforcement procedure is concerned, the new legislation establishes the notification of enforcement suspension in urgent cases via electronic means (939 § 1),[156] the electronic delivery of the judgment after the corrective opposition against the seizure report (954 § 4), the electronic publication of the seizure report abstract and other information on the mandatory auction as a prerequisite for its legitimate conduct (955 § 2, 995 § 4),[157] the electronic publication of the repeated sale auction (965 § 5), and that of the statement on the auction continuation (973 §§ 1, 3). In the latter cases, the publication takes place on a special internet site for the notification of auctions.[158] Despite rumors before the enactment of the new Greek CPC 2015, electronic conduct of the mandatory auction has eventually not been established as a rule, but it was only included in the transitional provisions as a future scheme, since the technological infrastructure of the Greek courts could not support such a possibility immediately. However, the above provisions and their newly

---

153 See Hellenic Presidential Order 150/2001 (FEK A' 125/25-05-2001).

154 See Hellenic Presidential Order 25/2012 (FEK A' 53/12-03-2012) and 150/2013 (FEK A" 234/01-11-2013).

155 The same also exists in the interim measures proceedings, see Art. 686 § 4 CPC.

156 See also Pantazopoulos, *supra* n. 104, at 276.

157 See Papadopoulou, *supra* n. 33, at 143 note 41.

158 For the procedure of the electronic publication in the special site for the notification of the auctions see Hellenic Presidential Order 67/2015 (FEK A' 110/17-09-2015).

introduced settings already constitute reliable evidence of the significant improvement, modernization, acceleration and increasing of transparency in civil trial proceedings, especially if one considers that statistical surveys' outcomes of recent years have shown how low until now the use of technological innovation in the country was in comparison with similar use in other European countries; indeed Greece is ranked last regarding electronic submission of claims and access to online published judgments[159] and only second from the end in electronic communication between courts and lawyers.[160]

(V) Conclusion: Towards the Europeanization of the Greek Civil Procedural Law? Problems, Challenges and Prospects

Instead of an epilogue one should reflect on the close connection between civil procedural law, the EU financial crisis and the concept of "Europeanization". The main idea of the research is that economic crises give the opportunity to implement judicial reforms, but the point of interest is the concrete identification and characterization of the effects of such reforms. After having analyzed the historical context, scope and innovative content of the new Greek CPC 2015, the question that consequently arises is whether the EU financial crisis eventually contributed to the "Europeanization" of the Greek civil procedural law, and if so, to what extent, as well as which problems, challenges and prospects have been detected from the application of this procedural legislation in Greece so far.

At the beginning of this paper the concept of "Europeanization of civil procedural law" was defined in terms of the approximation or harmonization of civil trial proceedings between EU member states and was linked to procedural reforms that can also be triggered by external events.[161] In the case of Greece, the external event that affected the civil procedural system and led to a radical reform of the Greek CPC was the EU financial crisis. The deteriorating economic condition of the country during recent years initially revealed significant existing problems in civil trial proceedings and then it lead to further deceleration of granting civil justice. It is true that the Greek civil procedural system endures some chronic deficien-

159 COM(2016) 199, *supra* n. 48, at 20 Figure 21 and at 22 Figure 25.
160 *Ibid.*at 21 Figure 23.
161 See Hess, *supra* n. 2, at 160.

cies.[162] These deficiencies can be attributed not only to unsuccessful previously-adopted legislative initiatives but also to several malfunctioning components of the public mechanism, such as the insufficient judicial infrastructure, organizational weaknesses and meritocracy deficit.[163] Other additional factors provoking excessive delays in the conduct of civil trial proceedings and in the closure of pending cases, such as the complicated bureaucracy, poor use of technological innovation and remaining 'old-fashioned' procedures, were already approached and hence complete the overall picture. The EU financial crisis and its impact on Greece added the cost-cutting policy of the country, which, on the one hand, made the aforementioned problems even worse but, on the other hand, pushed for radical reform in the Greek CPC.

In respect of procedural approximation or harmonization, it should be borne in mind that the existence of EU internal market and completion of economic and political European integration require the formulation of an effective and well-functioning civil judicial system that overcomes the particularities and specificities of the corresponding national ones.[164] Resultantly, the effectiveness of a civil trial becomes an indispensable element for further deepening integration between EU member states. As it has been observed,[165] European countries, whose civil procedural systems function effectively, have adopted characteristics in elements of civil trial such as the prompt determination of a hearing date, collection of evidence by litigant parties, avoidance of dilatory actions, completion of the civil procedure in one hearing, promotion of ADR methods, enhanced communication between litigant parties, direct rejection of inadmissible or groundless actions and appeals, direct enforceability of the first instance civil courts' decisions and other measures regarding judicial economy.

The fundamental reform of the Greek CPC, which took place in the context of the EU financial crisis as a prerequisite for the legal validation of the third financial assistance package to Greece from the involved

---

162 Makridou, 'Introductory speech: The civil trial at a crucial point', in the Scientific Symposium for Prof. Nikas *The civil trial at a crucial point* 7, 9 (Sakkoulas, Athens-Thessaloniki 2016) [in Greek].

163 *Ibid.*

164 Nikas, "The (long) way to a single European courts proceedings", in the Scientific Symposium for Prof. Nikas *The civil trial at a crucial point* 221, 223 (Sakkoulas, Athens-Thessaloniki 2016) [in Greek].

165 Makridou, *supra* n. 162, at 8.

European parties, entails enough of the above-mentioned traits so as to signify a major step towards the effectiveness of a civil trial and acceleration of its judicial proceedings. As it was thoroughly analyzed, the new Greek CPC 2015 includes amendments and introduces provisions which *inter alia* restrict deadlines for performance of procedural acts and delivery of civil judgments, reduce the time-frame for the abiding projection of claims in the procedure before courts of first and second instance and in the civil enforcement procedure, decrease the number of legal remedies that can be lodged against the compulsory enforcement of a civil judgment, group special proceedings into three main categories and hence they help improve the basic problem of the deceleration of civil trial proceedings along with the great accumulation of pending civil cases. Within the same rationale, parts of European law were transferred into the Greek procedural system because of this radical reform, such as the inclusion of judicial economy as a fundamental procedural principle as well as the legislation on meditation processes promoting the use of ADR methods to boost quick closure of cases which, despite its existence in foreign jurisprudences, was a missing element in the Greek CPC. Last but not least, there has been a genuine attempt to deploy technological advancements in favour of the civil trial; for that purpose, many elements of e-justice have been introduced -truly innovative by Greek standards-, which may possibly lead to the updating and modernization of the functioning of the Greek civil judicial system so that it would be able not only to match but also compete with other judicial systems at the European level.

All these substantial measures born in the storm of the EU financial crisis and incorporated in the new Greek CPC 2015 compose together a progressive legislative initiative towards the approximation of the Greek civil procedural system with those of other EU member states, and therefore they undoubtedly contribute –at least up to a certain degree- to the "Europeanization" of Greek civil procedural law both in the strict sense regarding the adjustments of proceedings, deadlines, procedural acts and legal remedies, and in the broader sense regarding the overall improvement of Greek civil courts' functioning and the acceleration of granting civil justice. It may not be the first time that Greece faces a crisis, but it is evidently the first time that such a crisis brings a 'European' effect on reformation of procedural law. Indeed, it is not an exaggeration to say that even the examination of this fundamental procedural reform from the EU financial perspective, via the use of an inter-disciplinary approach, opens itself the discussion on the "Europeanization" of Greek civil procedural law.

However, before ending this research paper, two more issues shall be taken into consideration: Firstly, the Greek legal community shall find a way to justify delays in the application of legal reforms that are hard to apply but which have proved successful in other countries,[166] and in case of the new Greek CPC 2015 this happened again after its adoption through another strike of the country's legal bars, lasting several months, in an effort to protest not against the judicial reform this time, but against the modification of their pension scheme as a fresh austerity measure, whose introduction coincided with the procedural reform. The strike resulted in the application of the new legislation for only ten days during the first semester of 2016 and to the postponement of thousands of pending civil cases especially in the central courts of Athens and Thessaloniki (!); the proper application of the new procedural framework eventually began in September 2016 and it now remains to be seen how courts and lawyers will put it into practice. Secondly, since a country's civil procedural system is directly connected to its financial and fiscal situation, it would be potentially recommendable to attempt initially deeper approximation of the fiscal policies between EU member states, and only then to enact such radical reforms in their civil procedural systems. In other words, the procedural reforms cannot alone fix all the deficiencies of a country's judicial system or smooth and unify its rough edges in accordance with other European jurisdictions. For those reasons it becomes clear that there is still a long way before one could actually talk about a forthright harmonization of civil court proceedings among European countries and hence an even longer way before the potential creation of a single European civil process becomes a reality.[167]

166 See Makridou, *supra* n. 162, at 10.
167 Nikas, *supra* n. 164, at 238.

III. Supreme Courts: "Filters" and the Case Selection. Argentina's Writ of Certiorari in a Comparative Perspective

Leandro J. Giannini[*]

(I) Presentation

This article deals with the experience of the so-called "writ of certiorari" in Argentina,[1] a case-selection device established by art. 280 of the *Código Procesal Civil y Comercial de la Nación* (CPCN)[2] that enables the Federal Supreme Court to admit or deny matters brought to its judgment on a flexible qualitative basis (mainly: the "importance" of the matter involved) explicitly allowing the use of discretional criteria.

Until 1990, the Argentine Federal Supreme Court had not been given by the Parliament explicit powers to *decide which cases to accept* without rigid parameters. Before 1990, the Court had developed a jurisprudential tradition of "easing" the limits of its own jurisdiction, combining a sort legislative rigidity ("rigid" requirements for mandatory appeal) with considerable jurisprudential flexibility to *allow* inadmissible appeals. But in 1990 Congress passed Act n° 23.774, which amended articles 280 and 285 of the CPCN. This reform gave the Federal Supreme Court the ability to reject, according to its "sound discretion" ("*sana discreción*") and with the single quote of article 280 CPCN, extraordinary appeals that carry *insufficient*, *unsubstantial* or *irrelevant* federal issues. This has been called the

* Chair Professor of Procedural Law, University of La Plata, Argentina, https://unlp.academia.edu/LeandroGiannini.

1 For deeper explanation on this topic both in national and comparative perspective, I should refer to: L. Giannini, *El certiorari. La jurisdicción discrecional de las Cortes Supremas* (Platense, 2016).

2 At a local or state level, the Supreme Court of Buenos Aires Province has a similar case selection device established in that state's Judiciary Act (art. 31 bis, ley 5827). The present article will only deal with the federal regime, to preserve obvious length requirements. For a detailed analysis of Buenos Aires Province's certiorari mechanism, see: Giannini, *supra* n. 1, t. 2, at 271-667.

"Argentine certiorari"[3] or -with a more ironic tone- the "certiorari criollo",[4] given the self-proclaimed (and seriously debatable) filiation of the aforementioned amendment, with the American traditional "writ of certiorari".[5]

The category of "relevance" (in Spanish, "*trascendencia*") of the questions presented before the Supreme Court, is the most important innovation of Act n° 23.774. It is also the deepest reform on the extent of Supreme Court jurisdiction in the 20th century. That is why I will refer especially to it as the main selection device. The other two grounds for denial (insufficiency and insubstantiality) were already known in the Supreme Court's case law, although the 1990's reform gave them explicit

---

3 N. Sagüés, "El 'writ of certiorari' argentino (las reformas de la ley 23.774, respecto al recurso extraordinario", *LL* 1990-C (sección doctrina), at 717; L.E. Palacio, "Experiencia del denominado 'certiorari argentino'", *LL* 1995-E (sección doctrina), at 1056.

4 Multiple authors have used this terminology to describe the institute referred to in Article 280 of the CPCN, such as: H.E. Sabell, "El rechazo 'sin motivación' del recurso extraordinario cuando la cuestión federal es intrascendente, ¿es constitucional? (sobre el *certiorari* criollo)", *JA* 2003-I, at 1343; J. Vanossi, "La extensión jurisprudencial del control de constitucionalidad por obra de la Corte de la Argentina (Balance de una década de 'certiorari' criollo)", *Anales de la Academia Nacional de Derecho y Ciencias Sociales de Buenos Aires*, Año XLV – Segunda Época – n° 38 – Diciembre 2000 (also in *Anuario Iberoamericano de Justicia Constitucional*, Madrid, Centro de Estudios Políticos y Constitucionales, 2001, n.° IV). Opposing the use of the term "Argentine certiorari" or "certiorari criollo": N. Lugones, *Recurso extraordinario* 399-400, (Lexis Nexis, Bs. As., 2° ed., 2002) (orig.: 1°ed., Depalma, 1992); R.O. Berizonce, "Las funciones de la Corte Suprema: en el tránsito hacia un nuevo modelo", in: *Cortes Supremas. Funciones y recursos extraordinarios* 123-124 (Rubinzal Culzoni, Santa Fe, 2011).

5 More recently, the legislature incorporated expressly in our positive law another one of the renowned exponents of the aforementioned "discretionary jurisdiction" of the Supreme Court, as it is the so-called *per saltum* (articles 257 bis and ter, CPCN, conf. Act n° 26.790 [2012]). This device, born in Argentina in a troubled precedent ("Dromi" case [1990]) and now explicitly enacted by Parliament, allows the CSN to review decisions of federal courts in cases that doesn't fulfill the requirement of coming from a court of final resort, provided that they involve matters of "notorious institutional gravity" and that the direct avocation of the Supreme Court is the only effective remedy for the protection of the pertinent federal law. It's an additional advance of the legislator in a subject (the extent of Supreme Court jurisdiction) that is always plagued by indetermination, grey areas and endless discussions about the way in which the highest court exercises its "positive" (institutional gravity, *per saltum*) or "negative" (art. 280, CPCN) power of selection, in the thousands of cases that are brought each year to its attention.

legal recognition and conferred wider powers to the Court to apply them without further explanation (regarding the topic of motivation, see *infra*, V.2).

(II) Overview of Argentina's Supreme Court and Federal Judiciary System. The Fusion of Two "Legal Traditions"

Like almost every constitutional institution in Argentina, the federal judiciary and Supreme Court were designed in 1853 (the date of the actual Constitution), based on the U.S. federal constitution. Article 116 of the Federal Constitution, for example, is a practical transcription of art. III of the U.S. Constitution (that defines the basic role of federal judiciary). Similarly with Act 48, that delineates –since 1863– the scope of federal questions that define the Argentine Supreme Court appellate jurisdiction. Its philosophy, form and text are practically replicas of section 25 of the U.S. *Judiciary Act* of 1789.

American constitutionalism had and has a deep influence on our original and actual institutional organization, as it was the main inspiration of our framers in the mid-19th century. It is fair to say that if constitutionalism only dealt with statutes and constitutional provisions, there wouldn't be anything interesting to say about the Argentine Federal Supreme Court and writ of certiorari, after knowing the American ones.

But, as is well known, that is not the case: constitutional law, civil justice and civil procedure are far more than statutory provisions. Although the American influence was deeply felt by our framers and by our Supreme Court practice and case law, those institutions were transplanted into a completely different society and legal tradition, in short: into a Spanish post-colonial socio-economic environment that was followed by a wave of immigration from central Europe (especially from Italy and Spain) during the late nineties and early 20th century.

The fusion of American constitutionalism at a federal level, with classic European continental civil law institutions, is a significant feature of the Argentine legal system.[6] Multiple aspects of our legal culture, procedures

6 Oteiza summarizes that phenomenon in clarifying terms (*translated by author*): "The measure of power granted by the Constitution to the Administration of Justice and its position in relation with the executive and legislative branches, come from two different political processes. On the one hand the Constitution was modeled af-

and judiciary organization derive from that fusion. For example, regarding the topic of this contribution, it explains our "American Style" Federal Supreme Court coexisting with 24 State Supreme Courts (one in each Province and one in the City of Buenos Aires), mainly role-modeled on the traditional French, Spanish and Italian "cassation" systems.

It also explains why it took so many years to implement qualitative or discretional filter devices like the so-called 'certiorari', uncommon in the continental regimes until recent years. But, when they were introduced, in 1990, we relied, again, on the American experience.

In Argentina, the Federal Supreme Court has 5 judges and concludes around 15,000 cases per year with inadmissibility decisions (around 73%) or decisions on the merit (around 27%). As can be seen, like other apex bodies, the Argentine Federal Supreme Court suffers from a significant overload.

At this point, an obvious question arises: if the Supreme Court has control over its own docket with a powerful case selection device … why is there an overload situation?

A main feature of this quantitative crisis actually depends of a "qualitative" dilemma: the definition of the institutional role that the Federal Supreme Court plays in our legal system.

There is sufficient consensus on the general institutional roles of the Argentine Federal Supreme Court: 1) it is a constitutional court (final guardian and interpreter of the Federal Constitution); 2) also, it is a sort of cassation court regarding federal law (final supervision of the interpretation and application of federal legislation,[7] that should lead to some consistency of precedents on these matters); 3) its performance as "head" of

---

ter the U.S. Constitution, and on the other it was influenced by the ideas coming from the French Revolution…": E. Oteiza, *La Corte Suprema. Entre la justicia sin política y la política sin justicia,* 8 (Platense, 1994).

7 Unlike the USA, in Argentina's federal system, civil, commercial, criminal and labor law, are unified legislation passed by the National Congress. But, as in the USA, the final interpretation and application of that legislation, together with local law (the general legislation that each state reserves as its own), corresponds to state courts, unless there are grounds for the exercise of federal jurisdiction (for example, if the Federal Government is a party or there are inter-jurisdictional issues of national public interest at stake). That is why it is stated in the text that the Federal Supreme Court only has a sort of cassation role over "federal" points of law. On the rest of the subjects (civil, criminal, labor, etc.), the final custody and interpretation of law resides on each of the State Supreme Courts.

the judiciary, that combines as well an heterogeneous mix of institutional, administrative and jurisdictional tasks oriented towards dialogue between the judiciary and other branches of government, the preservation of judicial independence and the improvement of justice service; and, finally 4) the exercise of a broad and diverse "axiological" mission (mainly exerted through the doctrine of "arbitrariness").

Regarding the "axiological role", it is fair to say that this does not imply that the Court will remedy any injustice, except those which, through their gravity and egregiousness, represent an unacceptable departure from the due process constitutional clause ("arbitrariness" doctrine). However the breadth and vagueness of the formulas used by the Court to define the scope of the "arbitrariness" doctrine, have transformed it into a versatile and ungraspable device on which any litigant (internalized in the extraordinary appeal's technique) can rely, to try to open the gates of the Supreme Court.

As it can be seen, the fundamental roles of the Argentine Federal Supreme Court are examples of "ambiguity at the apex", using Taruffo's happy expression.[8] Might an apex body be at the same time a constitutional court of last resort, and cassation court commissioned to develop a legal check on lower courts decisions and also accomplish a "uniformization role" to prevent inconsistencies in lower courts? Can it be also the final inspector of egregiousness to prevent flagrant errors or arbitrariness and, at the same time, the institution responsible for representing the judiciary in its dialogue with other departments of State? Can we also add the responsibilities of the administration and improvement of the judiciary? Is it possible to play so many roles at the same time without having a "personality crisis"? Argentina shows no exception in this field: it is not possible.

(III) The Two Dimensions of the Supreme Courts' Crisis

(a) "Quantitative" Dimension

Concern about the overload of courts of last resort is common in many jurisdictions. The most obvious reason for this concern derives from the position of these courts in the judicial structure. Being institutionally posi-

8 M. Taruffo, *Il vertice ambiguo: saggi sulla Cassazione civile* (Il Mulino, Bologna, 1991).

tioned on the apex of the justice system, supreme courts could potentially review the whole judicial production of a State. Without proper limits, these bodies could be forced to review each and every decision of each and every lower court, for any injustice alleged by parties in any case processed before a respective jurisdiction.

Such a position would be unacceptable, useless and materially impossible to assume. That is why historically all kinds of limits have been designed to try to avoid overexposure of the highest courts to an unbearable burden of work. These attempts were initially based on criteria that were meant to be safe and reasonably predictable. In this sense, there are limits widely used in comparative law, such as those related to the *types of decision subject to extraordinary appeals* (e.g., the restriction based on the concept of "final judgment", emanating from the "court of last resort" or similar formulas), *chapters of the judgment that can be reviewed* (e.g., the always controversial limitation of the appellate jurisdiction of supreme courts only to review "points of law" and the consequent lack of jurisdiction to review questions of fact, as the evaluation of evidence), or the *amount of damage* produced by the error of a judgment (as happens with the different systems of *suma gravaminis* intended to limit access to the highest courts) or other punitive-oriented mechanisms, aimed to deter the promotion of unfounded extraordinary appeals (such as the requirement to deposit a sum of money that will be only returned to an appellant if the decision is reversed).

However, all these limitations have been overcome in real life, and often by the same supreme courts whose overload was to be prevented by those traditional boundaries. In fact, most of these limitations find exceptions that, more than confirming the rules, threaten to destroy them. In Argentina, for example: i) there are different forms of "matching" to the final judgment rule (e.g, when an interlocutory decision causes an injury that is "very difficult" or "impossible" to repair in the future); (ii) the "Strada-Di Mascio" doctrine greatly reduces the effectiveness of *suma gravaminis* required in numerous local jurisdictions to limit access to their own supreme courts, by imposing on them a review of every case in which a federal question is involved;[9] (iii) the powerful doctrine of "arbitrariness" affects the distinction between questions of fact and of law; (iv) "institutional

9 CSN, Fallos: 308:490, "Strada" (1986); 311:2478 "Di Mascio" (1988). In those precedents the Argentine Federal Supreme Court stated that each case coming from local courts should necessarily pass through the State Supreme Court before arriv-

gravity" grants access to the court of appeals that suffer from all kinds of imperfections or that have grounds for inadmissibility. And so on.

Obviously, this is not the place to detail the way in which this phenomenon has taken place in ancient and recent history of the Federal Supreme Court in Argentina, or in local higher courts such as, for example, the Supreme Court of Buenos Aires. It is enough to say that, through these jurisprudential constructions, supposedly rigid barriers designed by the legislature to, among other reasons, prevent the collapse of the superior courts, are shown, in the best of cases, as perforated dams: they stop much of the litigious stream, but an ever larger flow rate which the "downstream" population cannot tolerate passes through its holes. Although this attitude allows a supreme court to speak virtually in any case that sparks its interest, it also can be transformed into a kind of self-immolation. In other words, in return for not closing its eyes to notorious injustices or for preserving a starring role in any discussion that it feels is of institutional interest, supreme courts ends up reaffirming the bases of their own collapse.

And so we return constantly to the initial dilemma: (a) the place reserved for supreme courts in the judicial structure, confronts them with the risk of carrying out an impracticable legal control; and (b) the traditional limits, in their alleged rigidity, have been insufficient to prevent this quantitative crisis.

By consequence, in many countries, the environment at the top of the judicature remains the same: one marked by the overexposure of the superior courts to the need to decide more cases that those that they can reasonably handle with their material and human resources.

(b) "Qualitative" Dimension

Apart (although related) from the sustained quantitative crisis which has been discussed, there is a phenomenon that is more difficult to verify, define and categorize, but which can also be seen in different places. We re-

---

ing at the last instance. And if that provincial apex court has any statutory or judge-made rule that prevents it from addressing the case, that limit should be declared unconstitutional. Therefore, when there's a federal question (for example, a federal constitutional issue), no case-value or material jurisdictional limitation can be used to mitigate a State Supreme Court's overload.

fer to what might be called the *qualitative* dimension of the supreme courts' crisis, derived from the deep dilemmas that occur within these judicial bodies, when it comes time to define and respect the institutional role that they are called upon to meet in a particular society.

In Argentina, for example, the same institutional roles that the superior courts have assumed as their own, shows a strong heterogeneity and risk of inconsistency. An example of that are the diverse aforementioned functions exercised by the Federal Supreme Court (see *supra*, II).

Sometimes the "qualitative" crisis has been considered a mere derivation of the "quantitative" one. Professor Nieva Fenoll, for example, has considered that the distinction previously held between the "qualitative" and "quantitative" dimensions is, indeed, a euphemism that conceals an indisputable fact: that the first is a product of the second[10]. In other words, that the debate on the institutional role of the supreme courts starts and finishes with the discussion about its overload. Without the overload, it is stated, no one would speak about the institutional role.

I do not fully share this point of view.

It is true that when a particular legal system decides to alleviate the quantitative crisis of its superior court with "overproduction" mechanisms, there is a demonstrable risk of inconsistency in its precedents with a consequent effect of one of the main missions of any Supreme Court, i.e., the guidance of the interpretation and development of law and management of precedents in a particular jurisdiction.

Although we will refer to this issue in greater detail in the following section, what has just been said is enough to express a substantial agreement with those who consider that there is a close relationship between the *quantitative* and *qualitative* crises of courts located at the apex of the judiciary. However, this agreement is not absolute, since this second manifestation of the dilemmas faced by the highest courts in the world (the quali-

---

10 J. Nieva Fenoll, "El modelo anglosajón en las cortes supremas: ¿solución o elusión del problema de la casación?", in: *Cortes Supremas. Funciones y recursos extraordinarios* 69-70 (Rubinzal Culzoni, 2011) stating that: "... all the past controversies about the *Cassation* seem to have been cornered in a single discussion: how to remove the overload of appeals? Usually this issue is disguised somewhat through another seemingly more technical one: what is the genuine function of Cassation? But what actually it is trying to address even in this euphemistic way, is the overload of affairs. In fact, I believe nobody would call into question currently the Cassation role if it were not for the existence, precisely, of the problem of the excessive workload of the Supreme Courts".

tative crisis), does not only appear in collapsed courts. Even in courts with an outcome of no more than 80 or 100 rulings per year (like the US Supreme Court), it is possible to find deep discrepancies and public debates about the role that they play (or should play) in their respective jurisdictions, and about the way they exercise that role. Those debates, which often takes the form of sharp criticism on case selection criteria, on the decision-making process (or the "no decision" techniques), on the ideological influence of its composition over the interpretation of law, etc., allow us to affirm the existence of a qualitative crisis that is not necessarily caused by an overload of the highest courts.

In short, it is true that, in general, the overproduction of decisions derived from an overload of supreme courts causes them serious inconveniences to adequately play their institutional roles. In this sense, there is a *close* relationship between the quantitative and qualitative crisis. However, we do not believe that there is a *necessary* relationship between the two, by which the qualitative crisis is just an elegant creation to complicate the analysis of the quantitative crisis. Qualitative crises (the dilemmas or conflicts over the definition and exercise of the institutional role of supreme courts) can also occur in a court with a numerically manageable agenda and, therefore, is a phenomenon that can be (and deserves to be) treated with relative independence from the quantitative crisis.

(IV) Mechanisms to Address the Crisis

This reality has been attacked from various angles both in Argentina and in comparative law. A very general -and deliberately simplified- systematization of the paths followed to alleviate the aforementioned *quantitative* crisis of Supreme Courts (the overexposure of such courts to a volume of cases that goes beyond their material ability to respond), distinguishes two categories of instruments: a) overproduction mechanisms, and b) case selection mechanisms.

(a) "Overproduction" Mechanisms

Overproduction mechanisms try to avoid collapse by assisting courts to solve more and more cases so as to be "up to date". Examples of this type can be: the decision to increase the number of judges and divide them into chambers, the allocation of decision powers to individual judges within the court, the decrease of the "burden" of motivation, the simplification of procedures (for example, limiting hearings), the enlargement of delegation in the decision making process (i.e., entrusting to different types of advisers, e.g., clerks, different aspects of the decision making process, typically: analysis of the record, legal research, opinion drafting, etc. Experience has shown that trying to remedy the collapse of the supreme courts in this way, apart from being something similar to "cutting the heads of a Hydra",[11] usually ends up affecting the strength and consistency of Supreme Courts' precedents and, thus, weakens their main institutional role.

In a comparative perspective, examples can easily be found of supreme courts with more than 100 judges (divided into chambers and sections), that reach more than 30,000 judgments per year (like the French *Cour de Cassation*). Or courts like the Brazilian *Supremo Tribunal Federal* (STF), with 11 members -and powers of each one of them to decide individually (widely exercised in practice)[12]- with an outcome of more than 100,000 cases a year. This reality increases dramatically the risk of inconsistencies and diminishes the ability to understand and manage its precedents. Thus, the 'omnipresent' court puts at risk its own authority and removes itself from its most important role, transforming its case-law –using CHIARLONI and TARUFFO's metaphor– in a sort of supermarket where everyone can find what he's looking for ... and the opposite too.[13]

---

11 I borrow R. G. Stevens' metaphor in his "Introduction" to F. Frankfurter, J. Landis, *The business of the Supreme Court. A Sudy in the Federal Judicial System* xxvii (Transaction Publishers, New Brunswick, New Jersey, 2007).

12 From 2011 to 2014, an average of 86% of the decisions of the Brazilian STF were taken individually by one of its judges, leaving 14% remaining as the collegiate court decisions (see full statistics in Giannini, *supra* n. 1, at 562-563).

13 S. Chiarloni, "Las tareas fundamentales de la corte suprema de casación, la heterogeneidad de los fines surgida de la garantía constitucional del derecho al recurso y las recientes reformas" [trad.: J.J. Monroy Palacio], in: *Los recursos ante los Tribunales Supremos en Europa. Appeals to Supreme Courts in Europe* 61 (Difusión, Madrid, 2008); *íd.* "Ruolo della giurisprudenza e attività creative di nuovo diritto", 56 *Rivista Trimestrale de Diritto e Procedura Civile* 11, 16 (2002/1) (metaphorically stressing that the jurisprudence of the Italian *Corte di Cassazione* resembles a "supermarket in which clients -litigants- are able to easily find the product they are looking for" and that "the defeated in the judgement on the merit can also find favourable precedents"; M. Taruffo , "Precedente y jurisprudencia" (trad.: C., Martínez Valdecilla, F. Gandini), in: *Precedente. Anuario Jurídico*, 90 (Cali,

(b) Case Selection Mechanisms

Given this scenario, multiple case selection mechanisms are gaining momentum in different legal traditions. They seek to deal with the aforementioned crises through a reverse strategy: reducing the agenda of the superior courts on a qualitative basis, trying to focus their material and human resources on deciding only the issues that enable them to satisfy or improve their institutional role.

Filters on appeals, as the "certiorari argentino" (article 280, CPCN at the Federal Supreme Court; art. 31 bis, Act 5827 at the Supreme Court of the Province of Buenos Aires), are examples of this kind of strategy.

It's a solution that, despite not being innovative, expands progressively in courts of different legal traditions, such as the US Supreme Court with its traditional *writ of certiorari*; in the Supreme Court of the United Kingdom by the "permission to appeal"; in the Spanish *Tribunal Supremo* and *Tribunal Constitucional*, with their case selection mechanisms respectively based on the "cassational interest" ("*interés casacional*") or the "special constitutional importance"; with the "fundamental significance" in the German Federal Supreme Court (*Bundesgerichtshof* -BGH-) or the requirement that the matter is "constitutionally significant" as a condition for the opening of the original jurisdiction of Federal Constitutional Court (*Bundesverfassungsgericht* -BverfGe); and with the "general impact" ("*repercussão geral*") as an admissibility requirement to stand before the Brazilian Constitutional Court (*Supremo Tribunal Federal* –STF–).

In addition to the ordinary filters, other instruments can be included in the category of mechanisms of agenda-rationalization of higher courts. For example, the resolution mechanisms of repetitive cases, such as the one prevailing in Brazil, which seeks to prevent the entry of a multiplicity of records that carry similar issues of law, holding them at lower levels and bringing before the Supreme Court just one or a few paradigmatic cases. The principle of law adopted in these "test cases" should be subsequently applied by courts *a quo*, to resolve every other case whose proceedings were suspended pending the ruling of the first.

I have elsewhere analyzed more carefully different instruments adopted in comparative law to selectively reduce the agenda of superior courts.[14]

Colombia, 2007); *íd.*, "Una reforma della cassazione civile?", 60 *Rivista trimestrale di diritto e procedura civile* 757 (2006).

14 Giannini, *supra* n. 1, t. I, at 211-578.

Another example of case reduction techniques is the restrictive interpretation that supreme courts develop over the extent of their own jurisdiction. In Argentina, for example, as well as the introduction of the 'certiorari' in 1990 as a tool for qualitative selection of cases, the Federal Supreme Court tackled overload from other angles also. Thus, in addition to using the mentioned filter to get rid of irrelevant issues, it has cut, through its own interpretation, most of its "mandatory" jurisdiction. Some paradigmatic cases of this restrictive trend, supported for reasons of "institutional significance" which, in the Supreme Court's opinion, forced it to reexamine the entryways and rationalize its agenda, which can be noted are: 1) the reduction of the original jurisdiction in cases in which a State is a party, attending the restrictive interpretation of article 116 and 117 of the Argentine Federal Constitution (*Constitución Nacional Argentina*) and article 24, inc. 1° of Act 1285/58;[15] b) the recent invalidation (unconstitutionality declared by the same Supreme Court), of the ordinary mandatory appeal established in cases in which the federal government is a party (art. 24, inc. 6), ap. a), Dec. Ley 1285/58 (CSN, Case "Anadon", 2015).[16]

Such jurisdictional strategies (restrictive interpretation of the conditions of access the Court or invalidation of rules that allow too wide mandatory jurisdiction), can also be considered as examples of case selection mechanisms diverse from filters themselves.

---

15 V. CSN, Fallos: 329:759, "Barreto" (2006).

16 CSN, Case "Anadon" (2015). In this precedent, the Court departed expressly from its historical jurisprudence that considered legitimate this formal path to its courtrooms. Attending a "dynamic" interpretation, it went on to consider that the subsistence of this mandatory appeal (only subjected to the classical case-value requirement -*suma gravaminis*-) constitutes an unreasonable exercise of the Parliament powers to legislate about the Supreme Court appellate jurisdiction (art. 117, Const. Nac.). The concepts used to question the reasonableness of *suma gravaminis* are quite eloquent: "... the Supreme Court must decide all matters in which some constitutional principle may be involved, issues that cannot be measured by the amount of money involved, because a case in which a large amount of money is at stake can be resolved on local or common legislation, and a few cents problem can affect the property clause as a whole and even the whole constitutional system. Thus, quantitative-based criteria can never be taken into account, as it should be the qualitative one".

(V) The Requirement of "relevance" (trascendencia) in an Extraordinary Appeal at the Federal Supreme Court (Argentina)

How does our filter work?

(a) Partial Discretion

Article 280 of the CPCN expressly provides for the authority at its discretion to reject appeals that carry insufficient, unsubstantial or irrelevant federal issues. The court, "according to its sound discretion", can apply this instrument *to deny* extraordinary appeals in such conditions.

If we assume the classical but debated distinction between proper judicial discretion and judicial interpretation of vague legal concepts, we could start by saying that the Argentine certiorari only gives *partial discretionary selection power* in its proper sense. The Argentine Supreme Court could not refuse by 'certiorari' *relevant* cases with self-proclaimed grounds of opportunity or convenience. Instead, it is only authorized to use its full discretion for the purpose of admitting or discarding *irrelevant* issues with the single quote of the aforementioned article.

Using another widely adopted terminology (Dworkin), the Argentine Supreme Court has a "weak" discretion to determine the presence of a relevant question, and a "strong" discretion to admit or deny irrelevant issues.

From a comparative perspective, this quality (partial discretion) distinguishes the Argentine certiorari from: 1) the American writ of certiorari (that could be considered as "fully" discretional – Rule 10's parameters are mere guidelines that do not control the Court's discretion)[17]; and 2) the Brazilian regime of *repercussao geral*, that only allows an appeal to pass the gates when the case has a kind of overall impact, but does not allow the Court to make discretional exceptions to that rule.

---

17 "The following, although neither controlling nor fully measuring the Court's discretion, indicate the character of the reasons the Court considers ..." (USSC, Rule 10, "Considerations Governing Review on Writ of Certiorari").

(b) No Motivation

The second important feature of the Argentine writ of certiorari is that the intellectual process of case selection remains hidden from the parties and from public scrutiny. There's no motivation whatsoever and no other device adopted to promote transparency (for example, there's no "Rule 10" stating the general parameters to be used, there's no public data base summarizing the general characteristics of each case with the result of case selection).

Simply quoting article 280 of the CPCN, any appeal may be dismissed:

> "Buenos Aires, ... (date) The extraordinary appeal is inadmissible (article 280, Code of Civil Procedure)".

With this repeated formula, signed by a majority of the Supreme Court (at least three of its five justices), the "certiorari" device is applied and passed on the record of the case.

(c) Parameters to select by "transcendence". Relevance, institutional roles and the Argentinian approach to the "ius litigatoris dilemma".

The third fundamental aspect of our case selection device is the complex definition of the main selection parameter: the "transcendence" of the questions involved in a given case. I will use the word "transcendence" as a synonym for relevance, significance or general public importance. There's no point, I think, in trying to compare the meaning of these expressions, used in different countries, just on a linguistic basis.

In Argentina we have no explicit regulation to allow the operators who act before (and within) the Court, to determine with some accuracy the parameters used to decide which cases to decide. In this kind of environment, it is extremely difficult to approximately predict (or even decide without the risk of inconsistencies or unfairness), which issues will trespass the Supreme Court's borders.

This complexity, coupled with the absence of motivation of admission decisions and the lack of commitment to improve transparency in the selection process, has been the primary source of criticism levelled at the Argentine filter. That disrepute explains the radical skepticism of many authors, who consider that the only criteria followed in this field is the mere "taste" of the gatekeepers. That's why this author openly proclaims the unconstitutionality of article 280 of the CPCN, for encouraging arbitrariness in this field. However, as to be expected, the Supreme Court repeatedly overruled this challenge to the validity of its main filtering mechanism.

In a recent research I've tried to build the basics guidelines to identify some suitable parameters to study the exercise of the Argentine Supreme Court's case selection process.[18] In very few words, there are two conditions that should necessarily coexist in assessing the significance of the issues raised in an extraordinary appeal.

The first condition is the correspondence between the matter involved and the institutional missions of an apex judicial body, so that a case can only fulfill this requirement if a ruling on the merits places the court in the exercise of one of those fundamental roles (I call this requirement: *institutional pertinence*).

The institutional missions of the Argentine Supreme Court have already been explained (final custody and interpretation of the Federal Constitution, "cassation" of federal law, axiological custody from arbitrariness, institutional leadership of the judiciary). I won't insist on them, but it is useful to recall their extent, to appreciate that this requirement (institutional pertinence) is necessary but not sufficient. In Argentina, a device that would only be based on the idea of coupling a case to the Court's institutional roles ends up transforming the so-called "filter" into a tautological mechanism: as every appeal with a proper technique could compromise the exercise of some of the Supreme Court's expanded roles, none of them could be considered "irrelevant". In this manner, filters like the Argentine 'certiorari' would lose all possible effectiveness.

That is why a *second condition* is necessary: the general impact of the topic discussed, understood as the ability to expand its effects, directly or indirectly, in a considerable portion of the community.

This last requirement would leave an important number of cases outside the appellate jurisdiction of the Court, in particular, those alleged constitutional violations that do not have that kind of overall impact. Gross mistakes that would leave an arbitrary decision as the last expression of the judiciary in the case would have no correction available at the last instance.

---

18 Giannini, *supra*, n.1, t. II, at 152-198.

However, as we have seen, article 280 of the CPCN empowers the Court to admit irrelevant issues, according to its sound discretion. Therefore, it is possible that even a question with no general impact would be ruled on its merits. In such situations, the Court does not set relevant criteria for the future. On the contrary, those kinds of matters are –in general– a repetitive application of traditional rules and principles, limiting the activity of the Court to examine its violation in a single case. So, if that flagrant-error-correction ability, although exceptional, is able to justify the admission of cases with no general impact: how is or should that positive case selection ability be exercised?

Two main parameters can be found in Supreme Court practice regarding the admission of irrelevant questions. Although further research may give rise to some other informal criteria, those two principal parameters are: "verisimilitude" and "necessity". The first one (*verisimilitude* of the appeal), is well known in comparative law. It consists of a *prima facie* examination of its merit. It's similar to a "real prospect of success" test. The second criterion is the possibility of treating *irrelevant questions* raised in *relevant cases*, when elucidating the first is essential to resolve the second. For example, when an important constitutional dilemma has not been addressed by an inferior court for reasons that arise on unimportant topics (e.g., formal requirements of motions, pleadings, etc.), the Supreme Court may "pick up" the case and control that decision regarding the irrelevant issue, to be able to set a precedent over the significant constitutional debate that was postponed by the first.

Those parameters are examples of criteria that are useful to prevent extreme solutions to a Supreme Court crisis. On one hand, they resist the traditional equal protection constitutional challenge, giving reasonable (although flexible) guidelines, independent from the mere whim or caprice of the gatekeepers.

On the other hand, they prevent "all or nothing" responses to the *ius litigatoris* dilemma. In Argentina, that dilemma does not seem to be solvable by simply "deleting" every form of error correction (for example, overturning the "arbitrariness doctrine"). After more than 25 years of 'certiorari', the Court insists on including within its core missions that kind of individual due process protection doctrine. In other words: the so-called "axiological role" and its "arbitrariness doctrine", although exceptional, will still be alive in its case law.

The price of that decision is simple to appreciate in Argentina:[19]

CSJN – 2013			
Type	New income	Pending cases	Decided
Ordinary	9.054	9.486	9.604
Pension	6.509	5.679	5.681
Original	121	3.337	91
Total	**15.563**	**15.165**	**15.376**

Focusing on the outcome, the results can graphically be expressed this way:

Not all of the inadmissibility decisions are taken by certiorari. Depending on the year, between 36% and 50% of the total outcome are rejections based on that filtering device:

Tasa de rechazo de recursos extraordinarios por aplicación del 'certiorari' (art. 280 CPCN) (CSJN: 2010-2011)			
Year		**Decisions**	**%**
2010	Total decisions (admission and merits) regarding extraordinary appeals	10.871	100%
	Total certiorari inadmissibility decisions (art. 280 CPCN)	4.096	37,68%
2011	Total decisions (admission and merits) regarding extraordinary appeals	12.975	100%
	Total certiorari inadmissibility decisions (art. 280 CPCN)	6.448	49,70%
2012	Total decisions (admission and merits) regarding extraordinary appeals	14.314	100%
	Total certiorari inadmissibility decisions (art. 280 CPCN)	5.233	36,56%

As the numbers show, although the certiorari filter mechanism has a strong impact on reducing the Argentine Supreme Court's docket, many cases pass through that filter every day. There are some legal explanations for that phenomenon. But, usually, the main reason for that relies on our cultural configuration and on our appreciation of the Supreme Court's institutional role.

19 For more detailed statistical information, see: Giannini, *supra* n. 1, at 235-253.

Regarding the first (legal explanation), it has already been explained that article 280 of the CPCN allows the Court to admit and decide irrelevant questions, based on its own discretion. The Court uses this possibility to preserve its "axiological" role, although critics still reject the lack of transparency of that positive selection of unimportant issues.

Regarding the second (cultural and institutional configuration), many factors may explain this phenomenon. One of them is the culture of the "right to appeal", a general perception that every litigant has a constitutional right ... not to have a day in Court, but to have a day in the Supreme Court. It's a progressively vanishing perception, not only because that constitutional right never existed in Argentina, but thanks to the certiorari mechanism itself and the significant in-admission rate.

The second cultural aspect is the discreet confidence that we have in our judges (50% according to the Trust Index of FORES & Universidad Torcuato Di Tella for 2010[20]). That perception obviously impacts on the distrust that citizens and lawyers have over first and second degree decisions.

A third institutional factor is the role that the Court itself continues to identify as its own: as we saw, the persistence of its flagrant error correction "arbitrariness" doctrine. This insistence has a lot to do with the aforementioned distrust on ordinary judges, that is not only a social evaluation but also a paternalist conception coming from the top.

20 See Universidad Torcuato Di Tella: "Índice de Confianza en la Justicia" (2005-2010), available in: http://www.utdt.edu/ver_contenido.php?id_contenido=521&id_item_menu=1601.

International Courts

I. The Court of the Eurasian Economic Union: Basic and Some Controversial Questions of Jurisdiction and Procedure

Yuliya Barel[*]

(I) Introduction

The Eurasian Economic Union (EAEU) was formed on 1 January 2015 by the Republic of Belarus, the Republic of Kazakhstan and the Russian Federation on the basis of an already existing Customs Union in the region and the Eurasian Economic Community (EurAsEC). While the Union has five Member States at the moment (the Republic of Armenia[1] and the Kyrgyz Republic[2] have also joined the Union), the population of the Members States is 182.7 million people and the territory is over 20 million sq. km. which is 14 % of the world's farm land.

The Treaty on the EAEU of 29 May 2014 (TEAEU) provides for free movement of goods, services, capital and labor, and pursues a coordinated, harmonized and single policy in various sectors such as common customs tariffs, antitrust regulation, trade remedies imposed on products originating in third countries and imported into the customs territory of the EAEU (such as safeguard, anti-dumping and countervailing measures). The Treaty also establishes the governance structure of the Union, which includes the Supreme Eurasian Economic Council, the Eurasian Intergovernmental Council, the Eurasian Economic Commission (permanent executive body), and the Court of the Eurasian Economic Union (Court of

---

* PhD in Law, Senior Lecturer at the Belarusian State University, Judicial Assistant to the Judge of the Court of the Eurasian Economic Union, former Research Fellow at the National Center of Legislation and Legal Research of the Republic of Belarus.

1 Art. 1, Agreement on Accession of the Republic of Armenia to the Treaty on the Eurasian Economic Union dated 29 May 2014 (adopted 10 October 2014, entered into force 2 January 2015), text (English version) available at <https://docs.eaeunion.org/docs/ru-ru/0057297/itia_11102014>, last visited 28 May 2016.

2 Art. 1, Agreement on Accession of the Kyrgyz Republic to the Treaty on the Eurasian Economic Union dated 29 May 2014 (adopted 23 December 2014, entered into force 12 August 2015), text (Russian version) available at <https://docs.eaeunion.org/docs/ru-ru/0147066/itia_26122014>, last visited 28 May 2016.

the EAEU).[3] The Court of the EAEU is a permanent judicial Body of the Union[4] and has its seat in Minsk, Belarus. The Court's status, composition, jurisdiction, functioning and formation procedures are determined by the Statute of the Court (Annex 2 to the TEAEU).

Thus, the administration of justice within the Union[5] is governed by the Statute of the Court of the EAEU and the Rules of Procedure of the Court of the EAEU.[6]

Bearing in mind that "so far most, if not all, scholarly literature about judicial bodies and dispute settlement mechanisms of regional economic organizations other than ECJ has been merely descriptive. It is difficult to find articulate assessments of the factors determining their success or failure. Legal scholars and political scientists have preferred focusing on the ECJ success story. However, the pathology of regional economic courts can be as illuminating as success stories to determine what are the factors under which international courts thrive and can be effective",[7] I consider it necessary to analyze profoundly some aspects of structure, jurisdiction and procedure of the new Court.

As this region of post-Soviet countries has experience in creating these so-called "regional courts" (for example, the predecessor of the Court of the EAEU was judiciary in the EurAsEC[8] and the still-functioning Economic Court of the Commonwealth of Independent States (Economic

3 Art. 8 (I), Treaty on the Eurasian Economic Union (TEAEU) (adopted 29 May 2014, entered into force 1 January 2015), text (English version) available at < https: //docs.eaeunion.org/docs/ru-ru/0057353/itia_05062014>, last visited 28 May 2016.

4 Art. 19 TEAEU.

5 Settlement of disputes between the Member States on observance their obligations under the TEAEU and other sources of the Union law, disputes between the Member States and the Commission or between individuals and the Commission on compliance of the actions and decision of the latter with the Union law etc.

6 Decision of the Supreme Eurasian Economic Council implementing Rules of Procedure of the Court of the Eurasian Economic Union (adopted 23 December 2014, nº 101, entered into force 1 January 2015), text (Russian version) available at <https:// docs.eaeunion.org/docs/ru-ru/0147026/scd_25122014_101>, last visited 28 May 2016.

7 R. Mackenzie et al., *The Manual on International Courts and Tribunals* 333 (2nd ed., Oxford University Press, New York, 2010).

8 The Court of EurAsEC was founded by Art. 8 of the Treaty establishing the Eurasian Economic Community (adopted 10 October 2000, entered into force 30 May 2001), English text available at < http://www.wipo.int/wipolex/en/regeco_treaties/text.jsp?file_id=234738> (last visited 28 May 2016), but factually started to operate from 1 January 2012 (till 31 December 2014) after adoption on 19 Decem-

Court of the CIS) was started in 1992)[9], the aim of this article will be to conduct an analysis using historical and comparative law methods. It will also be quite useful to compare jurisdictional, structural and some procedural aspects of the Court of the EAEU with the judicial body of one of the most successfully developing regional integration unions – the Court of Justice of the European Union (CJEU).[10]

(II) Structure and Composition of the Court, Questions and Independence

(a) Nomination of Judges and Terms of Tenure

The Court of the EAEU includes two judges from each Member State of the Union.[11] As such the Court of the EAEU is a so–called "full representation" (regional) court like the CJEU and the European Court of Human Rights (ECtHR).[12] Judges are appointed for a term of nine years by the Supreme Eurasian Economic Council (by the Heads of the Member

---

ber 2011 of the Decision of the Interstate Council nº 583. Official webpage: www.sudevrazes.org/en/main.aspx/.

9 Agreement on the Status of the Economic Court of the Commonwealth of Independent States (adopted and entered into force 6 July 1992). Official webpage: www.sudsng.org.

10 Though the Court of the EAEU has just been created and issued only several orders and decisions the Russian and Kazakh academia has already compared its jurisdiction and even drawn some analogy while analysing its decisions with those of the CJEU even from the material law perspective. See: T. N. Neshataeva, "Edinoobraznoe pravoprimenie – tsel Suda Evraziyskogo ekonomicheskogo soyuza [Uniform enforcement of law is a purpose of the Court of the Eurasian economic union]", 2 *Mezhdunarodnoe pravosudie* 243-248 (2014); A. Ispolinov, "Pervoe reshenie Suda EAES: revisiya nasledstva i ispitanie iskusheniem [First decision of the Court of the EAEU: revision of heritage and fight with temptation]" (available at Professor's personal blog < https://zakon.ru/blog/2016/01/22/pervoe_reshenie_suda_eaes_reviziya_nasledstva_i_ispytanie_iskusheniem>; Zh. Kembaev, "Sravnitelno-pravovoi analiz funktsionirovaniya Suda Evraziyskogo ekonomicheskogo soyuza [Comparative Law Analysis of the functioning of the Court of the Eurasian economic union]", 2 *Mezhdunarodnoe pravosudie* 30-45 (2016).

11 Art. 7 Statute of the Court of the Eurasian Economic Community (adopted by Decision of Interstate Council 5 July 2010 nº 502), hereinafter Statute.

12 A. Torres Perez, "Can Judicial Selection Secure Judicial Independence?: Constraining State Governments in Selecting International Judges", in M. Bobek et al., *Selecting Europe's Judges* 181, 189 (Oxford University Press, New York, 2015).

States) after being proposed by the Member States.[13] The length of term corresponds to recent developments in international law relating to judicial independence. Thus, while studying the judicial independence of the International Court of Justice, the International Criminal Court, the International Tribunal for the Law of the Sea, the ECtHR, and international *ad hoc* tribunals, Zimmerman has noted that both the term length of nine years and the omission of the possibility of re-election are in line with what applies to more recently established international courts, and in particular those which directly affect individuals.[14]

However, Zimmerman is not convinced about the influence of tenure term on judicial independence and points out that "judicial tenure, regardless the length, cannot secure judges' independence unless it is also protected against possibilities of facile removal from office. This makes the conditions under which removability is possible one of the main tests of judicial independence."[15] At the same time, while "the selection of judges is regarded as crucial from the perspective of judicial independence," as several scholars have pointed out, judicial independence might be conditioned by a much broader range of factors including: composition of the court; dissenting opinions; remuneration and financing.[16]

Turning to the selection process of the judges of the Court, I consider the nationality rule of selection (that is, the full representation rule) can commonly have a positive effect on the representativeness and legitimacy of a court of any regional international organization. The number of ten judges for a five Member States regional international organization is comfortable and affordable from both procedural and financial perspectives. The "nationality rule of selection" is less useful for international organizations with a higher number of Member States.

Historical comparison with the predecessor Court of the EurAsEC shows that the role of the Member States in the process of judicial selection has increased. The representative body Inter-Parliamentary Assembly was previously involved in the selection of the judges of the Court of the EurAsEC. The judges were appointed by the Inter-Parliamentary Assem-

13 Art. 8, 10 Statute.

14 D. Zimmerman, *The Independence of International Courts: The Adherence of the International Judiciary to a Fundamental Value of the Administration of Justice* 510 (Nomos, Baden-Baden, 2014).

15 *Ibid,* at 179.

16 A. Torres Perez, *supra* n. 12 at 182.

bly on the proposal of the Interstate Council of the EurAsEC.[17] The proposal of a national nominee was made by common accord of the Heads of State and Government of the Member States (in the supreme body of the EurAsEC). However, the final decision was made by the body of parliamentary cooperation in the framework of the EurAsEC – the agreed nominee was appointed by the Inter-Parliamentary Assembly. Thus, both the proposal of a national nominee and his final appointment as a judge of the Court of the EurAsEC was made under the general consensus of all Member States in different forms. The Member States did not even decide on the proposal of a national nominee independently. Certainly, the involvement of the Inter-Parliamentary Assembly can only be characterized as a positive, but presently, such a representative body does not exist. And so, the current process of EAEU judicial selection with a higher discretion given to individual Member States is heavily criticized by academia. The criticism concerns the fact that a Member State (Head of a Member State) independently decides on a national nominee and in the absence of a representative body like the Inter-Parlimentary Assembly (comprised of members elected by citizens) the Heads of the Member States jointly decide on the appointment of a nominee. [18]

Still, it is common international practice that it is the Member State who decides on a nominee to a judicial post in any so–called "court of full representation". For example, an analogous rule with an even higher discretion of the Member State is that for nomination of judges to the Economic Court of the CIS.[19] Here a Member State can directly appoint a judge and is entitled to use the same procedure as that for its own domestic economic courts under national legislation. However, for CJEU judicial appointments, the additional consent of the governments of all Member States is needed before the Member State's nominee is ratified.[20]

Some criticisms exist against the use of national procedures for the selection of judicial nominees for the CJEU (and ECtHR): "National author-

---

17 Art. 5(I) Statute of the Court of the Eurasian Economic Community (adopted by Decision of Interstate Council 5 July 2010 nº 502).

18 Kembaev, *supra* n. 9 at 31.

19 Art. 7, Provisions on the Economic Court of the Commonwealth of Independent States. Annex Agreement on the Status of the Economic Court of the Commonwealth of Independent States (adopted 6 July 1992).

20 Art. 253, Treaty on Functioning of the European Union (Consolidated Version) available at < http://eur-lex.europa.eu/legal-content/EN/TXT/?uri=celex%3A12012E%2FTXT>, last visited 28 May 2016.

ities have huge responsibility. Open calls for applications and transparent, reasoned selection could help find qualified candidates. The involvement of national parliaments could improve transparency and public visibility of the processes. Here much needs to improve in both systems. What differs, however is the lever employed: while the PACE has openly stated that it would reject lists if the national process does not conform with a number of basic principles, such a stance cannot be observed in the EU. It appears from the Panel's activity reports that it conceives the national and supranational elements of the selection process as two separate and detached spheres. In a 255 Panel's conception, a candidate who emerges from a deficient, if not corrupt, national pre-selection can proceed to the CJEU's bench under the sole condition that she confirms with the Panel's substantive criteria. This means the fact that deficient national pre-selection might have excluded a host of excellent candidates is, according to the Panel, none of its business. It even goes so far as to set the national pre-selection of judges outside the scope of EU law, an argument which is utterly unconvincing in light of the composite structure of European governance framed by common principles. The PACE on the other hand underlines the shared principles for selection. Only if these principles have been respected by all involved can the whole process claim to have been legitimate. The composite nature of the selection process has moreover implications for the number candidates proposed. In the EU, where only one candidate is presented, her rejection involves high reputational costs for all actors involved, including the candidate herself. A list of at least three candidates, as practiced in Council of Europe selection procedures, appears preferable. This can be easily achieved in the EU: nothing in the text of the relevant provisions, namely Articles 253 and 254 TFEU, regulates how many candidates national governments initially nominate."[21]

So the main criticisms are lack of uniformity, transparency and selection (only one national nominee). Certainly, transparency is an important issue. But the criticism of lack of uniformity gives rise to some questions. Apart from the qualification criteria, why should there be totally different procedures and techniques for election of a national nominee to the post of judge in an international court than for a national court? If the courts are

21 A. von Bogdandy, Ch. Krenn, "On the Democratic Legitimacy of Europe's Judges. A principles and Comparative Reconstruction of the Selection Procedures", in M. Bobek et al., *Selecting Europe's Judges* 162, 177-178 (Oxford University Press, New York, 2015).

fully representative and the main indispensable principles are presumed to be the principles of independence of the court and impartiality of the judge, why should the national particularities be eliminated and the nomination procedure of international judges be especially unified? And why are the Member States presumed to be corrupt simply because they follow their own procedure of nomination? Making no claims and speaking from the experience of the Eurasian region, I would argue that the national systems of nomination have the right to exist. Unfortunately, the process of nomination in the EAEU Member States still lacks transparency.

Finally, the main criteria for selection of a judge of the Court of the EAEU are high moral character, and high qualification in the field of international and domestic law. An EAEU judge also should usually meet the requirements applicable to judges of the highest judicial authorities of the Member States.[22]

(b) Removal from the Office

The powers of an EAEU judge may be terminated on the following grounds: termination of the Court; expiration of the term of office of the judge; a written statement of resignation tendered by the judge due to his/her transfer to another job or for other reasons; inability to exercise the powers of a judge due to poor health or other valid reasons; participation in activities incompatible with the office of a judge; termination of membership in the Union of the State represented by the judge; if the judge no longer has the status of a national of the Member State represented; in case of serious misconduct incompatible with the high status of a judge; in case of entry into force of a judgment of conviction against the judge or a court decision on the application of compulsory medical measures with regard to the judge; in case of entry into force of a court decision on the limited capacity or incapacity of the judge; in case of death of the judge or entry into force of a court decision declaring him/her dead or missing.[23] The list is exhaustive.

The initiative to terminate the powers of a EAEU judge on these grounds can be put forward by a Member State represented by the judge,

22 Art. 9 Statute.
23 Art. 12 Statute.

the Court or the judge concerned. Nevertheless an EAEU judge can only be dismissed by a vote of the Supreme Eurasian Economic Council (meaning by the Heads of the Member States only).[24]

The EAEU rules are partially similar to those governing the status of the Economic Court of the CIS.[25] Similar to the Economic Court of the CIS, only the Member States can recall their judges and the grounds are: poor health, commitment of a crime, or abuse of power or authority.[26] Since there are no provisions on the initiation of a termination *prima facie,* this lacuna may be interpreted as a potential problem for any judge who himself wishes to initiate the procedure of removal from office (in the case of poor health for instance).

This mechanism of judicial removal not by the collective organs of an international organization but by the individual home States has been criticized by scholars as potentially "undermining the neutrality of individual judges".[27] By contrast, the EAEU Court predecessor, the Court of the EurAsEC, had the same procedure both for nomination of judges and for their removal from the office: by the collective organization of Inter-Parliamentary Assembly after the initiation (recommendation) of the Interstate Council.[28]

Commentators on the present mechanism of removal from the office of judge of the Court of the EAEU highlight the more positive, to their mind, experience of the CJEU.[29] Indeed the Statute of the CJEU contains an absolutely different procedure for judicial removal from the procedures for EAEU judicial removals. A CJEU judge may be deprived of his office only if, in the unanimous opinion of the judges and Advocates-General of the Court, the judge no longer fulfills the requisite conditions or meets the obligations arising from his office. The judge concerned does not take

24 Art. 11, 13 Statute.

25 Art. 7 Provisions on the Economic Court of the Commonwealth of Independent States.

26 To my mind, extremely vague notion for a regulation on the status of a judge.

27 G.M. Danilenko, "The Economic Court of the Commonwealth of Independent States", 4 *New York University Journal of International Law and Politics* 893-918 (1999).

28 Art. 5(I) Statute of the Court of the Eurasian Economic Community (adopted by Decision of Interstate Council 5 July 2010 nº 502).

29 Kembaev, *supra* n. 10, at 32.

part in any such deliberations.[30] While discussing the system of peer review and judicial removal, some very interesting comparison by Zimmerman should be mentioned. In considering the voting mechanism (unanimous or qualified majority) in the ECtHR, Zimmerman stated "it is probably easier for a camel to go through a needle's eye than 44 judges to agree on a necessarily subjective assessment of a colleague's fulfillment of required conditions. [...] Since it is not so much the percentage of the whole bench that makes the hurdle too high, but rather the actual number of individuals who are required to agree on a particular issue that usually promises to be controversially assessed, it must be concluded that the bar has been raised rather high, and with it the level of protection of independence."[31] Furthermore, whether it is possible for such a great number of individuals to agree unanimously may depend on individual perception of each researcher.

By comparison, then, the EurAsEC method of judicial removal, by the Inter-Parliamentary Assembly after a recommendation by the Council is both more efficient and more realistic.

(c) Immunities

Judges of the Court of the EAEU enjoy privileges and immunities as provided for by the Vienna Convention on Diplomatic Relations of 18 April 1961 for a diplomatic agent.[32] However, according to Zimmerman, the reference to the immunities of a judge of an international court to the Vienna Convention "can [...] be provision's weakness". Paragraph 4 of the preamble to the Vienna Convention on Diplomatic Relations (VCDR) describes the purpose of diplomatic privileges and immunities as "not to benefit individual but to ensure the efficient performance of the functions of diplomatic missions as *representing States*. [...] The (ICJ) judge is not the representative of a (sending) State. Instead, he is a 'servant of international law'".[33] Considering the remarks of Zimmerman, I adhere to the

30 Art. 6 Statute of the Court of Justice of the European Union (Protocol 3 to Treaty on Functioning of the European Union).

31 Zimmerman, *supra* n. 14, at 500.

32 Art. 18, Regulation on Social Guarantees, Privileges and Immunities within the Eurasian Economic Union (Annex 32 to the TEAEU).

33 Zimmerman, *supra* n. 13 at 194-195.

point of view that the reference to the Vienna Convention rules on immunities which proved to be effective in practice is quite a normal practice, especially having in mind that the Annex 32 to the TEAEU refers to the specific rules on immunities of diplomatic agents and not to the full text of the Vienna Convention and the aforementioned paragraph 4.

The named immunities do not extend to the following cases: property claims relating to private immovable property located on the territory of the host State; claims relating to succession, when a judge or a family member acts as a testamentary executor, a trustee for the inherited property, an heir or a legatee as a private person and not on behalf of a Body of the EAEU; claims relating to professional activities extending beyond the powers provided for by the TEAEU.[34]

It is important to note, however, that the statutory documents differentiate the privileges and immunities of judges who are nationals of the host State (Belarus) from privileges and immunities of judges from other States.[35] The above-mentioned rules work only for judges who are not nationals of the host State. By contrast, judges of the Court who are nationals of the host State have only the following functional immunities: they are not subject to criminal, civil and administrative liability for words spoken or written by them and all actions performed by them in their official capacity.

Analysis shows that the TEAEU and its annexes create a complicated system of privileges and immunities for both judges of the Court and members of the Commission of the EAEU as well as for officials and employees. While this study is beyond the scope of the article, I would like to make some remarks concerning immunities.

A recent article on the Court of the EAEU contains an interesting comparison. Kembaev states that unlike CJEU judges who enjoy privileges and immunities in all Member States, judges of the EAEU are immune in a host State only.[36] Indeed, CJEU judges enjoy immunities in all Member States. For example, under art. 3 of the Statute of the CJEU, CJEU judges are immune from legal proceedings, and after they cease to hold judicial office they continue to enjoy immunity in respect of acts performed by them in their official capacity, including words spoken or written. Addi-

34 Art. 18, Regulation on Social Guarantees, Privileges and Immunities within the Eurasian Economic Union (Annex 32 to the TEAEU).

35 Art. 18, 19, *ibid.*

36 Zh. Kembaev, *supra* n. 10 at 32-33.

tionally, art. 3 of the Statute of the CJEU on immunities questions refers to arts. 11-14 and art. 17 of the Protocol on the Privileges and Immunities of the European Union.[37] Article 11 of the Protocol starts with "*In the territory of each Member State and whatever their nationality officials and other servants of the Union shall* [...] *be immune* from legal proceedings in respect of acts performed by them in their official capacity...", which means that CJEU judges enjoy immunities in all Member States.[38]

However, to my mind, the conclusion of Kembaev can be challenged. Omission of a precise provision stating that judges are immune in the territory *of all Member States* in the Regulation on Social Guarantees, Privileges and Immunities within the Eurasian Economic Union (Annex 32 to the TEAEU) does not undermine the effect of art. 107 of the TEAEU itself. Article 107 states: "*On the territory of each Member State of the Union*, all members of the Council of the Commission and Board, *judges of the Court of the Union*, officials and employees of the Commission and the Court of the Union *shall enjoy* all social guarantees, *privileges and immunities* required for the implementation of their powers and service duties. *The scope of these social guarantees, privileges and immunities shall be determined in accordance with Annex 32 to this Treaty*."[39] Thus, under art. 107 of the TEAEU judges enjoy privileges and immunities in all Member States and not only in a host State.

The judges of the previously existing Court of the EurAsEC also enjoyed immunities with distinction of nationality of a host State.[40] The main difference concerned remuneration taxes, customs duties and other kinds of duties.[41] The immunities were functional and concerned only words spoken or written in their official capacity. The law of the CIS regu-

37 Protocol on the Privileges and Immunities of the European Union (Protocol 7 to the Treaty on Functioning of the European Union) available at <http://eur-lex.europa.eu/legal-content/EN/TXT/?uri=CELEX%3A12012E%2FPRO%2F07>.

38 *Ibid.*, Art. 11.

39 Emphasis added.

40 Art. 7 Statute of the Court of the Eurasian Economic Community referred to the Convention on Privileges and Immunities of the Eurasian Economic Community (adopted 31 May 2001, entered into force 15 December 2002), text (Russian version) available at <https://evrazes.com/docs/view/9>, last visited 28 May 2016.

41 Art. 11 Convention on Privileges and Immunities of the Eurasian Economic Community.

lates the status of the Judges of the Economic Court of the CIS in a similar way.[42]

It is interesting to note that the international agreement between the EAEU and the host State (Republic of Belarus) on the conditions of residence of the Court of the EAEU contains more specific rules on privileges and immunities of judges' family members than the rules in Annex 32 to the TEAEU. The agreement between the EAEU and the Republic of Belarus provides for more exceptional cases to guarantee higher immunities for family members of judges with nationality of the host State (Belarusian nationality). In other words, the international agreement provides better protection.[43]

(d) Composition of Panels and Presidency

To begin, it should be noted that substantial difference between the rules of internal organization of the courts of the EU and the EAEU makes any analogy almost impossible.

In principle, the CJEU sits in Chambers consisting of five (most frequently) or three judges, or in the Grand Chamber when a Member State or an institution of the Union that is party to the proceedings so requests, or when the Court considers that a case before it has an important value as a precedent. For specific cases listed in the Statute or where the Court considers that the case before it is of exceptional importance, the Court may even sit as a Full Court. At present, the Court has five Chambers of five judges and five Chambers of three judges. The judges elect the Presidents of Chambers from among their number. The Presidents of the five judge chambers are elected for three years and may be re-elected once. The Pres-

---

42 Art. 3, 17, Agreement on the Status of Officials and Employees of the Commonwealth of Independent States Bodies (adopted 25 April 2003, entered into force 28 June 2005). The paradox is that the Republic of Belarus, on the territory of which the Economic Court of the CIS and the Executive Committee of the CIS have their seat, did not ratify the Agreement.

43 Art. 14 Agreement between the Eurasian Economic Union and the Republic of Belarus on the Conditions of Residency of the Court of the Eurasian Economic Union on the territory of the Republic of Belarus (adopted 29 April 2016, temporary application before the implementation procedure under the legislation of the Republic of Belarus is complete), text (Russian version) available at <https://docs.eaeunion.org/docs/ru-ru/01410263/itia_19052016>, last visited 28 May 2016.

idents of the three judge chambers are elected for a term of one year. The Grand Chamber consists of 15 judges and is presided over by the President of the Court. In order to avoid the important cases assigned to that chamber always being heard by the same judges, its composition varies. For each case, the Grand Chamber is composed of the President and the Vice-President of the Court, three Presidents of Chambers of five judges, the Judge-Rapporteur of the Court, and the number of judges necessary to reach 15. When the Court sits in Chambers, there is a quorum of three judges in the case of three-or five-Judge Chambers and of 11 judges in the case of the Grand Chamber. Decisions of the Full Court are valid if 17 judges are sitting.[44]

By contrast, the idea of representativeness gets its highest level of implementation in the rules of internal composition of the Court of the EAEU. The Court of the EAEU examines cases either by the Grand Panel of the Court, by the Panel of the Court or by the Appeals Chamber of the Court. The Court sits as the Grand Panel when it hears a case where one of the parties is a Member State or when it gives "clarifications" of the law of the EAEU. In cases when the claimant is an individual (or a legal person), the Court sits as a Panel of the Court.[45] The Grand Panel of the Court includes all judges of the Court. When the Court of the EAEU sits in the *Grand Chamber, there is a quorum of all the Judges of the Court.*[46] The Panel of the Court includes one judge from each Member State participating alternately by the names of the judges, beginning with the first letter of the Russian alphabet. A session of the Panels of the Court is deemed *valid in the presence of one judge from each Member State.*[47]

The Appeals Chamber of the Court includes judges of the Court from Member States who did not participate in the proceedings that resulted in the decision of the Panel of the Court in question. A session of the Appeals Chamber of the Court is deemed valid in the presence of one judge from each Member State.[48] In other words, the Appeal Chamber is com-

44 Issues are governed by the Statute and the Rules of Procedure of the CJEU (Consolidated version 25 September 2012), text available at <https://curia.europa.eu/jcms/upload/docs/application/pdf/2012-10/rp_en.pdf>, last visited 28 May 2016. Written under: K. Lenaerts *et al.*, *EU Procedural Law* 19-20 (Oxford University Press, New York, 2014).

45 Art. 70-71, 73, 76 Statute.

46 *Ibid.*, Art. 74-75.

47 *Ibid.,* Art. 77-78.

48 *Ibid.*, Art. 80-81.

posed of judges (from each Member State) who did not participate in the proceedings of first instance. If in one case the first Chamber (permanently created by alphabetical principle of judges from each Member State) considers the case in the first instance, in another case the same Chamber hears the case on appeal.

These same mechanisms of panel composition and quorum rules were used with only with minor differences by EAEU's predecessor Court of the EurAsEC.[49]

Academia has criticized the rules of composition of Appeals Panel that were utilized by the Court of the EurAsEC and now by the Court of the EAEU. Ispolinov draws attention to "the weakness and vulnerability to criticism of the appeal mechanism […] This approach looks like some kind of fiction ("today you hear complaint on my decision, tomorrow I will hear complaint on your decision") and turns into potential conflict of interest."[50] The author does not recommend means of solution.

I would like to add some comments on the quorum rules of the Court of the EAEU. The established rules demand the constant presence of all the judges in the Court and do not consider unexpected circumstances, or self-recusation. The rules are also too complex to apply when a new Member State accesses the Union. Long term procedure of the appointment of judges from a new Member State, the principle of full representation of all Member States and quorum rules may cause problems for administration of justice. In fact, such a situation lasted for almost a year at the EAEU from the accession of the Kyrgyz Republic to the Union (12 August 2015) until the final appointment of judges from this Member State (1 June 2016). Another spectacular example is the current activities of the Economic Court of the CIS. Under its statutory documents, the Economic Court of the CIS shall be composed of equal numbers of judges from each Member State of the CIS (11 at the present time), with the panels to be settled by the Full Court and composed *of three and five judges with a*

---

49 Art. 6, 15 of the Statute of the Court of EurAsEC, Art. 4-6 of the Rules of Procedure of the Court of EurAsEC (Decision 12 July 2012 nº 21), Art. 7-9 of the Rules of Procedure on Requests of Economic Entities (Decision 22 May 2012 nº 12).

50 A. Ispolinov, "Sud Evraziiskogo soobshchestva effektno ushel v istoriu. U nas teper Sud Souza [Court of the Eurasian Community effectively gone down in History. Now we have Court of the Union]" (available at Professor's personal blog < https://zakon.ru/blog/2015/03/10/sud_evrazijskogo_soobshhestva_effektno_ushel_v_istoriyu_u_nas_teper_sud_soyuza>.

quorum of three judges.[51] After recent resignations, however, new judges have not yet been appointed. And notwithstanding the rules of law at least four recent decisions of the Economic Court of the CIS were decided *by only two judges.* [52]

All activities of the Court are managed by the President of the Court. The President of the Court and the Deputy President are elected to their positions from among the judges of the Court by Court judges in accordance with the Rules of Procedure subject to approval by the Supreme Eurasian Economic Council. The President of the Court and the Deputy President may not be nationals of the same Member State. Upon termination of office, a new President and Deputy President are elected from among the judges representing other Member States, different from those represented by the former President or the Deputy President respectively. The term of office for the President of the Court and the Deputy President is three years. This term is consistent with the term of the President of the CJEU, elected by the judges of the CJEU.[53] The Statute of the Court of the EAEU, however, demands additional approval by the Heads of the Member States. The presidency of the Court of the EurAsEC was conducted under rotating rule using alphabetic order of the first letters of the names of the Member States in Russian. One of two judges from a Member State was elected by the judges. The term of presidency in the Court of the EurAsEC is two years.[54] By contrast, the President of the Economic Court of the CIS is elected by judges for the term of five years, and the elected nominee needs subsequent approval by the Council of Heads of the CIS Member States.[55]

The allocation of cases and appointment of a Judge-Rapporteur are considered to be among the most important tasks and responsibilities of a President of any court. Zimmerman notes that "The provisions pertaining

---

51 Art. 7 Provisions on the Economic Court of the Commonwealth of Independent States, Art. 9, 11, Rules of Procedure of the Economic Court of the Commonwealth of Independent States (adopted 10 July 1997 by the Decision of the Court n° 2).

52 Decisions of 17 June 2016, 23 December 2015, 26 November 2015, 30 October 2015, texts available (in Russian) at < http://sudsng.org/database/deed/>, last visited 30 July 2016.

53 K. Lenaerts *et al.*, *EU Procedural ...*, *supra* n. 44, at 18.

54 Art. 8-9 Statute of the Court of the Eurasian Economic Community.

55 Art. 7 Provisions on the Economic Court of the Commonwealth of Independent States.

to the distribution of cases between the sections of the Court are somewhat worrying from the perspective of ensuring assignment that is not susceptible to bias and e.g. politically motivated allocation of cases."[56] The clear provisions on appointment of a Judge-Rapporteur without any possibility of discretionary interpretation is especially important in actions against Member States. It seems to be more correct politically that the Judge-Rapporteur is not a national of the Member States involved in the dispute.

It is the job of the President of the Court to oversee the distribution, management and progress of CJEU cases. O'Leary comments on procedure of the CJEU: "There seem to be no rules on attribution of cases to Judge-Rapporteurs and those that have developed have never been made public. By examining the Court Reports one can see that long-serving Judges may, over the years, develop specialization in a particular field and this specialization may be inherited by the member nominated for appointment by that Judge's Member State government. However, the Court has never openly allowed particular Chambers to specialize in any one field."[57]

The President of the Court of the EAEU also allocates cases and appoints a Judge-Rapporteur to a case. But unlike other international courts here his opportunity for discretion is nullified by strict and transparent rules which do not permit any speculation. Alphabetic order is used in the Rules of Procedure of the Court of the EAEU.[58] It is noteworthy that this and all other norms of the Rules of Procedure of the Court were drafted without interference of the Court and adopted by a decision of the Heads of the Member States.

---

56 D. Zimmerman, *supra* n. 14 at 473.

57 S. O'Leary, *Employment Law at the European Court of Justice: Judicial Structures, Policies and Processes* 36 (Hart Publishing, Oregon, 2002).

58 Art. 14-16 Rules of Procedure of the Court of the EAEU.

(III) Jurisdiction of the Court

(a) Direct Actions

(i) On the Claim (request) of a Member State

At the request of a Member State the Court of the EAEU decides cases: 1) *on the compliance of an international treaty* within the Union or its certain provisions *with the TEAEU*; 2) *on observance by another Member State* (other Member States) of the TEAEU, international treaties within the Union and/or decisions of the Bodies of the Union, as well as certain provisions of these international treaties and/or decisions; 3) *on the compliance of a decision of the Eurasian Economic Commission* or its certain provisions with the TEAEU, international treaties within the Union and/or decisions of the Bodies of the Union; 4) *on* challenging *actions (failure to act) of the Commission.*[59] The Statute establishes a pre-trial dispute resolution procedure. [60]

Unlike its predecessor EurAsEC,[61] the Eurasian Economic Commission is not entitled to file a claim. Though the Commission has right to request "clarification" of the law of the EAEU.

It is the Eurasian Economic Commission who is entitled under the main statutory documents to monitor and control the implementation of the international treaties that form the Union law and this is one of its main functions. Being of crucial importance for the normal functioning of the Union, such monitoring is conducted by the Commission on a permanent basis. If a Member State does not observe its obligations and does not implement the international treaties within the Union, the Commission notifies the Member State.[62] It would be reasonable to entitle the Commission to file a claim against such a Member State who ignores notifications requiring implementation and observance of the treaties within the Union. Granting the right to apply to the Court of the EAEU to the Body that continually and impartially secures the implementation of the Union law is of great importance for the functioning of the EAEU.

59 Art. 39 Statute.

60 *Ibid.*, Art. 43-44.

61 Art. 14 Statute of the Court of the Eurasian Economic Community.

62 Art. 43, Annex nº 1 to the TEAEU.

Although according to Vandersanden "Judging is a craft with no place for improvisation"[63]; academia and the legal community have pointed out the alarming judicial activism of the Court of the EurAsEC.[64] And in analyzing the practice of the CJEU De Freitas stated that "There is of course a price to be paid for the achievements […] Costs may be felt also at the level of judicial authority, which may result weakened".[65]

Whether connecting these two facts or not, but after judicial activism by the Court of the EurAsEC, the Statute of the new Court of the EAEU implemented several noteworthy rules of law. Firstly, *the jurisdiction* of the Court of the EAEU *does not include extension of the competence of Bodies of the Union* in excess of that expressly provided for by the TEAEU and/or international treaties within the Union. Secondly, the Statute named *the sources of law* which are to be used by the Court of the EAEU. Thus, compared with its predecessor, the Statute of the new Court contains distinct and quite restrictive rules about judicial activism.

While adjudicating the Court shall apply: 1) the generally recognized principles and regulations of international law; 2) the TEAEU, international treaties within the Union and other international treaties to which the States that are parties to a dispute are participants; 3) decisions of the Bodies of the Union; 4) the international custom as evidence of the general practice accepted as a rule of law. Thirdly, the Statute implemented the following rules: *no decision* of the Court *may extend beyond the issues stated in the claim* (request), *no decision of the Court may alter and/or override the effective rules of the Union law and the legislation of the Member States, nor may it create new ones.*[66] This limitation on

63 G. Vandersanden, "The Real Test – How to Contribute to a Better Justice: The Experience of the Civil Service Tribunal", in M. Bobek et al., *Selecting Europe`s Judges* 86, 94 (Oxford University Press, New York, 2015).

64 N.A. Sokolova, "Evraziiskaya integratsiya: vosmozhnosti Souza [Eurasian Integration: Opportunities of the Union]", 11 *Lex Russica* 96-103 (2015); A.S. Ispolinov, "Evraziiskoe pravosudie ot Suda Soobshchestva k Sudu Souza [Eurasian Justice from the Court of the Community to the Court of the Union]", 1 *Gosudarstvo i pravo* 80-88 (2015).

65 V.L. de Freitas, "The Judicial Activism of the European Court of Justice", in L.P. Coutinho et al., *Judicial Activism: An Interdisciplinary Approach to the American and European Experience* 173, 179 (Springer International Publishing, Switzerland, 2015).

66 Art. 42, 50, 101-102 Statute.

EAEU jurisdiction and its choice of law means that judges of the EAEU are restricted in their activism.

Another important issue for research is competition of jurisdictions. The CJEU has a much longer history and has passed through a long process of interrelation with national constitutional courts. The CJEU come a long way in defending its own competence to interpret the community law without the intervention of the constitutional and supreme courts. The evolution of the CJEU and the constitutional courts of the Member States approaches and views happened through continuous interaction with each other.

Surprisingly, "the young EAEU Court" has already faced some opposition from the constitutional court. The Court of the EurAsEC and the new Court of the EAEU have both faced some competition of jurisdiction. Most of the questions have arisen in the context of the Rulings of the Constitutional Court of the Russian Federation.[67] The Constitutional Court of the Russian Federation analyzed the decision of the Court of the EurAsEC of 1 November 2013 in the case *SeverAutoProkat LLC* and in 2015 ordered its own point of view of interpretation and application of the community law, on dialogue with the Court of the EurAsEC and gave instructions to the national authorities not to follow the decision. All was done from the points of view of constitutionalism, human rights etc.

Still it seems that it is the task of Court of the Union to create uniform practice in the application of the law of the Union and not that of the national courts including the constitutional courts. The Member States of the EAEU have agreed that it is the Court of the Union that ensures uniform application by the Member States and Bodies of the Union of the Treaty within the Union, international treaties of the Union with a third party and decisions of the Bodies of the Union. Disregard of this inter-State arrangement by the constitutional courts of Member States can lead to multiple contradictory interpretations and goes against *the principles of primacy of international law* and *pacta sunt servanda.* Such a situation leaves no chance for uniformity of application of the Union law.

---

67 Ruling of the Constitutional Court of the Russian Federation 3 March 2015 n° 417-O at the request of the Arbitration Court of the Central District to review the constitutionality of paragraph 4 of the Regulation on Application of Exemption from Customs Duties on the Import of Certain Categories of Goods to the Common Customs Territory of the Customs Union, text (in Russian) available at <http://doc.ksrf.ru/decision/KSRFDecision190708.pdf>, last visited 28 May 2016.

(ii) On the Claim (request) of an Economic Entity

At the request of an economic entity, the Court of the EAEU can decide cases: 1) *on compliance of a decision of the Eurasian Economic Commission* or its certain provisions directly affecting the rights and legitimate interests of the economic entity in the sphere of business and other economic activities *with the TEAEU and/or international treaties within the Union*, if such a decision or its certain provisions entailed a violation of any rights and legitimate interests of the economic entity envisaged by the TEAEU and/or international treaties within the Union; 2) *on challenging actions (failure to act) of the Eurasian Economic Commission* directly affecting the rights and legitimate interests of the economic entity in the sphere of business and other economic activities, if such actions (omissions) entailed a violation of any rights and legitimate interests of the economic entity envisaged by the TEAEU and/or international treaties within the Union.[68]

The term "economic entity" means a juridical person registered under the legislation of a Member State or a third State or a natural person registered as an individual entrepreneur in accordance with the legislation of a Member State or a third State.

Thus under art. 39 of the Statute, individuals and legal persons (economic entities), even those of third countries, have a right to request the Court to annul such acts (decisions) of the Commission. To initiate the procedure, an economic entity should demonstrate that the decision (act) of the Commission or its certain provisions *are directly affecting its rights,* legitimate interests and afterwards that the contested decision or its certain provisions entailed a violation of the rights and legitimate interests of the economic entity as envisaged by the TEAEU and/or international treaties within the Union. It can be easily seen that the initiation takes some effort from the economic entity. It must show "direct concern".[69]

---

68 Art. 39 Statute.

69 The practice of the Court of the EAEU shows that its approach is more strict to the "direct concern" than that of the CJEU. Moreover the defendant in the cases – the Eurasian Economic Commission argues and stands on the point that the wording of the Treaty should be interpreted in the meaning of "individual concern" (cases *Sevlad LLC v Commission* 7 April 2016, *General Freit CJSE v Commission* 4 April 2016, and in the orders where the Court dismissed the claim or stopped the procedure (*Remdizel LLC v Commission* 8 April 2016, *Unitrade CJSE v Commis-*

A comparative analysis shows that the Statute has brought in a new mechanism of justice administration for some categories of disputes (antidumping measures, state support of agriculture etc.).[70] The mechanism implements a group of *ad hoc* experts from an agreed-upon list. The list is formed by the Member States. The novelty is that the opinion of the group of experts has compulsory character for the Court of the EAEU. But in all fairness, it has to be said that in not all questions does the opinion of *ad hoc* experts have mandatory character. Thus, these experts can be seen as neither the same as experts in national courts, nor do they fall under concept of *amicus curie.*[71] The nomination of experts for a case is obligatory. They are nominated from the list, and their conclusion is obligatory for the Court. Under the procedural principle in national legislation, it is the judge who determines and evaluates the permissibility, relevancy and acceptability of proof. The conclusion of an expert is one of such proofs. The judge of the Court of the EAEU does not have the opportunity to reappoint for a second investigation with another group of *ad hoc* experts but rather, has to decide on the basis of the first investigation even if he is not satisfied with the results. This seems to be in conflict with his freedom in the meaning of the mentioned principle of procedure. I consider it important for a judge to have the option not to take into account the results of an investigation he reasonably considers inapplicable. For instance, since the *ad hoc* experts in antidumping measures deal mostly with the rules of law (answering questions like whether the investigation before implementation of an antidumping measure was conducted in accordance with the rules of the Treaty etc.) and the field of their expertise is law (which is confirmed by their list with qualification), the judge being highly qualified in the field of international and domestic law should be given an opportunity to question the conclusions of such an expert or use the conclusions as a supplement.

The Economic Court of the CIS permanently uses the opportunity granted by its Rules of Procedure and employs the services of a "Council

sion 15 April 2015, *Unitrade CJSE v Commission* 1 April 2015, *Gamma LLC v Commission* 10 March 2015).

70 Art. 39 Statute; art. 57-59, Rules of Procedure of the Court of the EAEU.

71 G.G. Shinkaretskaya, "Institut "druzei suda" v mezhdunarodnom sudoproizvodstve [The Institute of *amicus curie* in the international judicial procedure]l', in V.L. Tolstikh et al., *Instituti mezhdunarodnogo pravosudiya [The Institutes of international justice]* 34, 34-38 (Mezhdunarodnie otnosheniya, Moscow, 2014).

General". A study of the Rules of Procedure of the named Court shows that a "Council General" usually is *an expert in international law, who gives his reasoned report on a question of law in the case and writes draft decision for the Court.*[72] There are no lists of such experts, and the Court has wide discretion for the nomination of such an expert. The Economic Court of the CIS is not obliged to follow the report and the draft of the decision. Apparently, the concept of *ad hoc* experts in the Court of the EAEU and the concept of "Council General" in the Economic Court of the CIS are completely different.

(b) Interpretation on the Union Law, Civil Service Issues

The most important change regarding competence was in the sphere of interpretation of international treaties. The previous Court of the EurAsEC had interpreted the international treaties which formed the Customs Union.[73] Now, only at the request of a Member State or a Body of the Union, can the Court of the EAEU provide *clarifications* to provisions of the TEAEU, international treaties within the Union and decisions of the Bodies of the Union. Here the Eurasian Economic Commission is entitled to apply to the Court. But regretfully, the statute says that "Providing clarifications by the Court shall mean providing *an advisory opinion* and shall not deprive the Member States of the right for *joint interpretation of international treaties*."[74]

The legal force of decisions of regional economic courts, such as the Economic Court of the CIS, interpreting international treaties was widely discussed in the doctrine. Some papers were even published by Members of the Court. F. Abdulloev being the President of the Economic Court of the CIS published a paper under the title "Justice cannot be recommendatory".[75]

---

72 Art. 40-1, Rules of Procedure of the Economic Court of the Commonwealth of Independent States.

73 Art. 13 (3) Statute of the Court of the Eurasian Economic Community.

74 Art. 46-47 Statute.

75 F. Abdulloev, "Pravosudie ne mozhet bit rekomendatelnim [Justice cannot be recommendatory]", 1 *Zhurnal mezhdunarodnogo prava i mezhdunarodnih otnoshenii* 3-9 (2011).

The questions of judicial protection of public servants of the EAEU are of crucial importance. Here, there has been some development of jurisdiction of the EAEU Court, though thus far insignificant. Under the Statute, the EAEU Court provides only advisory opinion on labor questions within the public service in the EAEU bodies. Under art. 46 of the Statute, the Court gives only advisory opinion regardless the existence of a concrete labor dispute and simply "provides clarifications to the provisions of the Treaty, international treaties within the Union and decisions of the Bodies of the Union [...] regarding labor relations". A comparative look at, for instance, the UN and the EU, shows that it will take a long time for the legislator to implement the rule that international servants of the EAEU are a separate category of employees and their disputes should be decided by a special tribunal for such categories of cases rather than by national courts. Today the Court of the EAEU is limited to clarifying provisions of international labor law and does it not pursuant to a national court, but only at the request of an international public servant.

(c) Waived Competence of Preliminary Rulings

As distinct from the CJEU, which was tasked with the additional duty of the preliminary reference procedure in order to guarantee uniformity of interpretation of EU law though the ultimate monopoly over it of the Court[76], the Court of the EAEU does not have such competence. While analyzing the competence one can notice the loss of any competence to give preliminary rulings as compared to the Court of the EurAsEC.

The Court of the EurAsEC interpreted the rules of international treaties within the Community, and the decisions of the institutions (bodies) of the Community at the request of the higher courts of the Member States;[77] meaning that in this sphere, the Court of the EurAsEC had analogous competence to that of the CJEU.[78]

It might be that the controversial past practice of the Court of the EurAsEC on a request for preliminary ruling gave rise to the elimination of such competence for the now existing Court of the EAEU. In the case

76 S. Sankari, *The European Court of Justice Legal Reasoning in Context* 23 (Europa Law Publishing, 2013).

77 Art. 13 (3) Statute of the Court of the Eurasian Economic Community.

78 Art. 267 Treaty on the Functioning of the European Union.

of 10 of July 2013[79] the Court of the EurAsEC issued a preliminary ruling albeit the national Supreme Economic Court withdrew the request for preliminary ruling. Such action could create a precedent. Indeed, a judge of the Court of the EurAsEC (also a judge at the Court of the EAEU), Neshataeva, states that the main role in the elimination of such competence was played by the national courts and such competence was waived on their demand.[80]

However, it seems that the loss of the competence can have negative effect and does not correspond to the needs of a unified application of the law of the EAEU. The law of the EAEU consists not just of international treaties but also of a great number of acts of the Eurasian Economic Commission[81] which are directly applicable and create rights and obligations for individuals and legal persons in the Member States. Still national judges from Member States with different cultures, mentalities, and legal traditions can have varying approaches to their interpretation of the rule of law. So there must be a mechanism to provide for uniform interpretation of the rules of the Union law, having in mind that in its absence, the same act or rule of the Union law may be applied differently to individuals and legal persons in the courts of the Member States. The request for the preliminary rulings is one of the most effective tools to ensure uniform interpretation.

Moreover, a study of the cases in the Court of the EAEU shows that individuals and legal persons while applying to the Court to annul an act of the Commission would in the process also try to argue that their activity or their imported or exported products did not fall under its action. In other words, these claimants wanted the Court of the EAEU to do the job of the national court and to decide the case. They neither wanted to prove that the act of the Commission did not comply with the TEAEU and/or international treaties within the Union nor believed in that. The only thing they

79 Decision of Grand Panel of the Court of the Eurasian Economic Community 10 July 2013 under request of the Supreme Economic Court of the Republic of Belarus on application of separate rules of Customs Union Commission Decision nº 130 27 November 2009, text (in Russian) available at <http://sudevrazes.org/main.aspxqueguideq20991.html#>, last visited 28 May 2016.

80 T. Neshataeva, "Edinoobraznoe pravoprimenenie – tsel Sude Evraziiskogo economicheskogo souza [Unified law enforcement is a target of the Court of the Eurasian Economic Union]", 2 *Mezhdunarodnoe pravosudie* (2015) 115-125.

81 The Commission consists of a Council and a Board, both issue obligatory acts (art. 18, TEAEU; art. 13, Annex 1 to the TEAEU).

wanted was proper interpretations. If the Court of the Union had the competence of preliminary rulings, the majority of this category of claimants would apply to the national courts. Thus, the Court wouldn't be overloaded with questionable claims of annulment of an act of the Commission (none of which has been sustained), but could issue preliminary rulings with proper interpretation of the Commission's acts, and in such a manner, form a uniform interpretation of the Union law on the territory of the Member States and place in equal conditions all the individuals and legal persons originating from different states.

The significance of the competence to give preliminary rulings was widely discussed and affirmed in the doctrine in the context of the CJEU competence.[82] Advocate General at the Court, Lenz, stated "because Community law, by reason of its supremacy and direct effect, impacts relationships between individuals, Member State courts are asking the Court to decide Community law questions more frequently. Although the law to be applied in these cases is the same in all Member States, *there is a potential danger to the functioning of the EC legal system as a whole if the law is not applied uniformly in the Member States*. The founding fathers of the Community averted this situation by conferring upon the Court of Justice *a monopoly of interpretation on questions of Community law. This transfer of competence would have been incomplete if Member State courts were not permitted to refer disputes arising under Community law to the Court of Justice.*[83] [...] Abolishing the right of lower courts to make references to the Court of Justice, however, would not only limit the options open to the courts of the Member States, but would also severely curtail the opportunities for the Court of Justice to ensure that Community law is observed. The opportunities for litigants and their lawyers would also be diminished. The road to the European Court of Justice would then be open only to those parties able and willing to exhaust all legal remedies."[84]

---

82 A. Norberg, *Preliminary rulings and the cooperation between national and European Courts* (Master Thesis, University of Lund), at 99; C. Arnold et al., *Explaining the Use of Preliminary References by Domestic Courts in EU Member States: A Mixed-Method Comparative Analysis* (11th Biennial Conference of the European Union Studies Association, 2009).

83 Emphasis added.

84 C.O. Lenz, "The Role and Mechanism of the Preliminary Ruling Procedure", 18 (Issue 2) *Fordham International Law Journal* 387-409 (1994).

(IV) Conclusion

The rules of the EAEU law on nomination, term of tenure, removal from office, immunities and privileges of the judges, as well as rules on the structure and composition of the Court of the EAEU ensure the enforcement of judicial independence. However the comparative study unequivocally shows that the Court of the EAEU has lost much of the competence its predecessor possessed. The significant digression of the competence of interpretation is a glaring example. There can hardly be found any reasons other than the judicial activism of the previously existing Court of the EurAsEC. The extension of the right of access to the public servants of the Union can be characterized as one of the positive developments, even though they are entitle to request only "clarifications" of the Union law on employment issues.

Trying to think positively, it should be mentioned that all the courts with which the competence of the Court of the EAEU was compared had a much longer history including a history of development of their jurisdiction. But the competence for preliminary rulings is of crucial importance at this primary stage of development of the law of the Union and its enforcement, and is sorely needed now.

II. The Court of Justice of the European Union as an Institutional Model for the African Court of Justice and Human Rights

Antal Berkes[*]

(I) Introduction

The never-established Court of Justice of the African Union, the already-functioning African Court on Human and Peoples' Rights [ACtHPR] and the future African Court of Justice and Human Rights [ACtJHR] are the products of an emulation of several international courts and procedural rules. Among regional courts, especially the Court of Justice of the European Union [CJEU] and the European Court of Human Rights [ECtHR] serve as models for the reform of the African Union's international judicial system.

Scholarly authors have abundantly analysed various connections between the current structure of the ACtHPR, the African Commission of Human and Peoples' Rights and the European model, especially the ECtHR, both at the level of procedural and substantial law.[1] It is well known that the merger of the European Commission on Human Rights with the

---

* Postdoctoral research fellow, University of Manchester, School of Law. The author holds a Master in Law from the Eötvös Loránd University (Budapest), and two postgraduate degrees from the Central European University (Human Rights LLM) and the Université Aix-Marseille III (Master in International Law). He completed his PhD at the Université Paris 1 (Panthéon-Sorbonne) in co-supervision with the Eötvös Loránd University (Budapest) in 2015. He has also conducted studies in contemporary history (Bachelor in history from the Eötvös Loránd University (Budapest); MA in history from Université Aix-Marseille I and Ma in contemporary history from Université Paris 4 Paris-Sorbonne) and in Latin-american studies (MA from Université Paris 4 Paris-Sorbonne).

1 E.g. E. de Wet, "The Present Control Machinery under the European Convention on Human Rights: its Future Reform and the Possible Implications for the African Court on Human Rights", 29(3) *Comparative and International Law Journal of Southern Africa* (1996) 338-359; R. Murray, "A Comparison between the African and European Courts of Human Rights", 2(2) *African Human Rights Law Journal* 195-222 (2002); F. Viljoen, A.K. Abebe, "Amicus Curiae Participation be-

ECtHR and the actual statute of the ECtHR served as a model for the future ACtJHR and that the case law of Strasbourg plays a vital role in the decisions of the ACtHPR and Commission on Human and Peoples' Rights. However, as for the CJEU, relatively few studies have demonstrated the influences of the European Union [EU], and its judicial body, the CJEU, in the judicial reform proposals of the African Union [AU].[2] At the level of the institutional structure and procedure of the future ACtHR, the role of the CJEU is visible especially in the draft protocols and debates concerning the reform. The Protocol of the Court of Justice of the African Union served as an amalgam of the procedure of the International Court of Justice and the CJEU, and several authors have argued as to which international organization more reflects the African unified court's structure as foreseen by the 2008 Protocol on the Statute of the African Court of Justice and Human Rights.

The paper applies comparative procedural law to identify the competences and procedural norms of the CJEU which could and should be adapted to the context of the AU. The paper argues, *de lege lata* and *de lege ferenda*, that the EU's efforts to serve as an institutional model for the African Court should be further strengthened, while the specificities and context of the African integration should be taken into account. In other words, the European model could not be applied to the ACtJHR in a copy-paste manner, but should be one of the institutional good practices before the eyes of the African Union's leaders.

The paper starts with a summary of the creation and ongoing reform of the AU's judicial system which forms part of a fragmented procedure of establishing judicial institutions in African (sub-)regional organizations, in general, and in the AU, in particular. The second part demonstrates how the CJEU could serve as a model specifically for the jurisdiction of the future ACtJHR, while the third part analyses selected procedural solutions of the CJEU which are of particular relevance in the proceedings of the ACtJHR. The paper concludes with several recommendations as to the application of the CJEU's model in setting up the future ACtJHR.

---

fore Regional Human Rights Bodies in Africa", 58(2) *Journal of African Law* 22 (2014).

2 As for the early exceptions, see C. Baudenbacher, "Judicialization: Can the European Model Be Exported to Other Parts of the World?", 39 *Texas International Law Journal* 381, 393 (2004) (emphasizing that the AU adopts both the ECtHR and the CJEU as a model).

(II) The Reform of the AU's Judicial System

The ACtHPR, a treaty body, and the African Court of Justice [ACJ] to be established, an organ of the AU, have been subject to various negotiations, draft conventions and adopted protocols. The finally adopted structure of the AU's judicial body is deemed to be a rationalized, merged court (a). In the elaboration of the AU's judicial body, the European Union has provided expertise, political and financial support (b).

(a) The Rationalization as a Goal

The envisaged court system of the AU is the result of the simultaneous development of two different regional courts. One is not an AU body, but a treaty body established by some member states of the Organisation of African Unity [OAU]: the ACtHPR was established under the Protocol to the Charter on Human and Peoples' Rights on the Establishment of an African Court on Human and Peoples' Rights [Protocol on the ACtHPR], adopted in June 1998 by the OAU Assembly.[3] The Protocol on the ACtHPR came into force on 25 January 2004, 30 days after it had been ratified by 15 states parties to the Charter. The first judges were elected in January 2006 and the court officially started operations in November 2006. As of 1 June 2016, the Protocol on the ACtHPR had been signed by 52 and ratified by 30 states parties to the Charter.[4]

The other major regional court is the judicial body of the AU: the African Economic Community Treaty[5] and later, replacing the former's judicial body, the AU Constitutive Act (2000) provided for an African Court of Justice to be established as one of the AU's principal organs.[6]

3 Protocol to the African Charter on Human And Peoples' Rights on the Establishment of an African Court on Human and Peoples' Rights, 10 June 1998, Ouagadougou, Burkina Faso [Protocol on the ACtHPR].

4 See Status list at OAU/AU Treaties, Conventions, Protocols & Charters, available at the website of the AU, http://www.au.int/en/treaties (last visited 1 June 2016).

5 Treaty establishing the African Economic Community Treaty, 3 June 1991, Abuja, Nigeria, Articles 7(e) and 18.

6 African Union Constitutive Act, Lome, Togo, 11th July 2000, Articles 5(1)(d) and 18.

The Protocol of the Court of Justice of the African Union[7] was adopted in July 2003 and it entered into force after the 15th state ratified it, on 11 February 2009.[8] However, the Court of Justice has never become operational because before the entry into force of the Protocol, the AU Assembly decided in July 2004,[9] and confirmed in July 2008, to merge the ACJ with the ACtPHR. The Executive Council in January 2005 nevertheless allowed the operationalization of the ACtHPR notwithstanding the continuing discussions on the merger.[10] Following the recommendation of the meeting of the Permanent Representatives' Committee and Legal Experts, the decision was taken to realize the merger by adopting a single legal instrument to establish a new integrated court in the form of a protocol, while bearing in mind that the procedure might be complex and time consuming.[11] Furthermore, this option entailed difficulties as to the mandate of the judges elected during the interim period as well as the Registry and seat of the court taking into account that different sets of countries had offered to host the two courts.[12] The result of the drafting process was the adoption of the Protocol on the Statute of the African Court of Justice and

---

7 Protocol of the Court of Justice of the African Union, Maputo, Mozambique, 11 July 2003.

8 As of 1 June 2016 AU member states have signed it and 16 member states have ratified it. See Status list at OAU/AU Treaties, Conventions, Protocols & Charters, available at the website of the AU, http://www.au.int/en/treaties (last visited 1 June 2016).

9 Assembly of the AU, Third Ordinary Session 6 – 8 July 2004 Addis Ababa, Ethiopia, Assembly/AU/Dec.45 (III) Rev. 1, Decision on the seats of the African Union.

10 EX.CL/Dec.165 (VI) Decision on the Draft Protocol on the Merger of the African Court on Human and Peoples" Rights and the Court of Justice of the African Union – Doc. EX.CL/162 (VI) 1, Sixth Ordinary Session 24 – 28 January 2005 Abuja, Nigeria.

11 Draft report of the meeting of the Permanent Representatives' Committee and Legal Experts on certain matters, 29 March – 1 April 2005, EX.CL/195 (VII), Annex I [Draft report of the meeting of the PRC and LE], para. 28; Executive Council, EX.CL/Dec.283 (IX), Decision on the Draft Single Legal Instrument on the Merger of the African Court on Human and Peoples' Rights and the Court of Justice of the African Union - Doc. EX.CL/253 (IX), Ninth Ordinary Session, 25-29 June 2006, Banjul, The Gambia; Assembly of the African Union Seventh Ordinary Session, Assembly/AU/Dec.118 (VII), Décision sur le Projet d'Instrument unique relatif à la fusion de la Cour africaine des droits de l'homme et des peuples et la Cour de Justice de l'Union africaine – Doc.EX.CL/253 (IX) Rev. 1.

12 Draft report of the meeting of the PRC and LE, *op. cit.*, para. 20.

Human Rights [ACtJHR Protocol I] on 1 July 2008. It will enter into force after the deposit of the instruments of ratification by 15 member states[13] – as to 1 June 2016, 30 member states have signed and only five of them ratified it.[14] The ACtJHR Protocol I replaces the 1998 and 2003 Protocols, providing for the establishment of the ACtHPR and the Court of Justice of the AU, respectively[15] and expressly recognizes that the integrated court will be the principal judicial organ of the AU.[16]

The merger of the ACtHPR and the ACJ was decided mainly for financial reasons, to lower the high costs of having two regional courts.[17] On the one hand, as the next part will demonstrate (III), the rationalization efforts might lead to a complicated structure with multiple simultaneous jurisdictions. On the other hand, the well-known model of regional integration, the EU, has consistently supported the AU's judicial reforms.

(b) The EU's Institutional Support

After the relatively loose intergovernmental framework of the OAU, the Heads of State and Government of the OAU expressed their will to establish the AU with a view to "effectively address the new social, political and economic realities in Africa and in the world", to fulfil their "peoples' aspirations for greater unity in conformity with the objectives of the OAU Charter and the Treaty establishing the African Economic Community" and to implement their "development and integration agenda".[18] In its regional cooperation policy, the EU has tried to encourage such "sub-regional" groupings and it has cooperated since 1994 with the OAU and the lat-

13 Protocol on the Statute of the African Court of Justice and Human Rights, Sharm El-Sheikh, Egypt, 1st July 2008 [ACtJHR Protocol I], Article 9(1).

14 Namely Benin, Burkina Faso, Congo, Libya and Mali. See Status list at OAU/AU Treaties, Conventions, Protocols & Charters, available at the website of the AU, http://www.au.int/en/treaties (last visited 13 May 2016).

15 ACtJHR Protocol I, Article 1.

16 ACtJHR Protocol I, Annex, Statute of the African Court of Justice and Human Rights, Article 2(1).

17 D. Juma, "Lost (or Found) in Transition? The Anatomy of the New African Court of Justice and Human Rights", 13 *Max Planck Yearbook of United Nations Law* 267, 276 (2009).

18 Sirte Declaration, 8-9 September 1999, Sirte, Libya, EAHG/Draft/Decl. (IV) Rev. 1, para. 6.

ter AU in the form of a political dialogue.[19] In April 2000, the EU held a summit with all of the African countries, which recognized "the important interrelation between political stability, peace and security on one hand and regional integration on the other".[20] In December 2005, the European Council adopted a "strategic partnership" with Africa,[21] engaging to provide "direct support to African Union"[22] and to help build the capacity of the AU in the matter of human rights and good governance programs.[23] In 2007, the "Africa-EU Strategic Partnership" explicitly stated that "the institutional architecture promoted by the Joint Strategy will, on the African side, be centred on the AU" since the latter is considered the "natural interlocutor for the EU on continental issues".[24] Finally, the EU (including its member states) is the African Union Commission's main financial contributor providing more than 80% of its budget.[25]

The ambitious project of the AU from 2012 foresees the consolidation of all Regional Economic Communities [RECs] in Africa to a Continental Free Trade Area [CFTA] by 2017 and to an Economic and Monetary Union (with a single currency) by 2023,[26] with an African-wide central

---

19 K.E. Smith, *European Union Foreign Policy in a Changing World* 73 (3rd ed., Cambridge, Polity Press, 2014).

20 "Cairo Declaration", Africa-Europe summit under the aegis of the OAU and the EU, Cairo, 3-4 April 2000, para. 2.

21 Council of the EU, "The EU and Africa: towards a strategic partnership", document no. 15961/05 (Presse 367), 18 December 2005.

22 *Ibid*, para. 4(b).

23 *Ibid*, para. 5(b).

24 Council of the EU, "The Africa-EU strategic partnership: a joint Africa-EU strategy", document no. 16344/07 (Press 291), 9 December 2007, para. 111.

25 European Commission - Press release, African Union Commission and European Commission meet to address shared EU-Africa challenges, Brussels, 5 April 2016, available at http://europa.eu/rapid/press-release_IP-16-1226_en.htm (last visited 9 June 2016).

26 See in detail in: African Union, Update on the Continental Free Trade Area (CFTA), 2014, available at http://www.au.int/en/sites/default/files/newsevents/workingdocuments/12582-wd-update_on_the_report_on_the_continental_free_trade_en.pdf (last visited 30 May 2016); The African Union Commission, AGENDA 2063. The Africa We Want. A Shared Strategic Framework for Inclusive Growth and Sustainable Development, First Ten-year implementation plan 2014-2023, September 2015, at 22-23, 44, available at http://agenda2063.au.int/en/sites/default/files/Agenda%202063%20Final%20revised%20First%20Ten%20Year%20Implementation%20Plan%2012%2010%2015.pdf (last visited 30 May 2016).

bank by 2028.[27] As the Constitutive Act of the African Union already expressly recognized, one of the objectives of the AU is, as in the EU,[28] to "accelerate the political and socio-economic integration of the continent".[29] However, unlike the EU's founding treaties, the Constitutive Act of the AU "is hardly the charter for the politically integrated Africa that some African political leaders or commentators have made it out to be", nor a program of action, but simply an organization framework to realize a future political integration.[30] At least one can say that the Constitutive Act emphasized the objective of an economic integration and the coordination of the socio-economic agenda of the member states which is, on the model of the EU, a long-term and gradual integration process.[31]

It is no wonder that the overall objectives and the institutional structure of the AU have not only been inspired by the EU, "but the processes and outcome of African integration must also follow the logic and trajectory of European integration".[32] Among the institutional inspirations provided by the EU,[33] one can mention the CJEU as an example for the institutionalization of the Court of Justice of the AU and the future ACtJHR.[34] The Court of Justice, as most organs of the AU, was already foreseen by the Treaty establishing the African Economic Community (AEC), the so-called Abuja Treaty adopted in June 1991 which came into force after the requisite numbers of ratification in May 1994. The Abuja Treaty provided

27 On the entire plan of six stages, see the Treaty Establishing the African Economic Community, Abuja, Nigeria, 3 June 1991, Article 6(2).

28 Treaty on the European Union, Preamble, paras. 9, 14.

29 Constitutive Act of the African Union, Lome, Togo; 11 July 2000, Article 3(c).

30 T. Maluwa, "The Transition from the Organization of African Unity to the African Union", in: A.A. Yusuf and F. Ouguergouz (eds.), *The African Union: Legal and Institutional Framework. A Manual on the Pan-African Organization* 25, 50-51 (Leiden/Boston, Martinus Nijhoff Publishers, 2012).

31 *Ibid.*, at 51.

32 *Ibid.*, at 38.

33 For other institutional parallels, see A. Adebajo, "Paradise Lost and Found. The African Union and the European Union", in: A. Adebajo and K.Whiteman (eds.), *The EU and Africa. From Eurafrique to Afro-Europa* 45, 60-72 (London, Hurst & Company, 2012); D. Bach, "The AU and the EU", in : J. Akokpari *et al.*, *The African Union and its Institutions* 355, 355-370 (South Africa, Fanele, Centre for Conflict Resolution, 2008); O. Barbarinde, "The EU as a Model for the African Union: The Limits of Imitations", 7(2) *Jean Monnet/Robert Schuman Paper Series* 1, 8-9 (2007), available at http://www6.miami.edu/eucenter/BabarindeEUasModel long07edi.pdf (last visited 31 May 2016).

34 Maluwa, *supra* n. 30, at 38-39, fn. 24.

for a regional court with jurisdiction to settle actions brought by a member state or the Assembly and to give advisory opinions.[35]

The EU has, on several occasions, tried to help resolve regional conflicts or potential disputes in Africa; EU "special representatives" (envoys) were sent to the AU,[36] with the policy objectives of providing support to the AU in matters of human rights, governance, "sustainable growth, regional integration and trade" and with the mandate to maintain close contact with AU organs.[37] As a further step, the EU has contributed to the establishment of judicial bodies for the AU: from the very beginning of the process of creating judicial institutions for the AU, the EU welcomed the initiative of creating a court for the AU. The European Parliament urged African states to ratify the protocol setting up an African Court on Human and Peoples' Rights[38] and the protocol on the establishment of the African Court of Justice.[39] Financially, the European Commission supported the AU governance agenda through a comprehensive program of 1.9 million euros (European Initiative for Democracy and Human Rights budget line)[40] and the European Parliament called for such as a support as well.[41] The EU and the AU have maintained a regular Human Rights Dia-

35 Treaty establishing the African Economic Community, Abuja, Nigeria, 3 June 1991, Articles 7(e), 8(3)(k)l-(l), 11(3)(f), 18, 19, 87.

36 Smith, *supra* n. 19, at 57.

37 Council Joint Action 2007/805/CFSP of 6 December 2007 appointing a European Union Special Representative to the African Union, *OJ* L 323/45, 8 December 2007, Articles 2(c) and 3(f).

38 Joint Parliamentary Assembly of the Partnership Agreement concluded between the members of the African, Caribbean and Pacific group of states, of the one part, and the European Community and its member states, of the other part - Resolution on the situation in West Africa (ACP-EU 3552/03/fin), *OJ* C 231, 26.9.2003, at 46–49, para. 4.

39 P6_TA(2007)0483, EU-Africa relations, European Parliament resolution of 25 October 2007 on the state of play of EU-Africa relations (2007/2002(INI)), *OJ* C 263E, 16.10.2008, at 633–648, para. 51.

40 Answer of the Commission to the written question E-0389/04: African Court on Human and Peoples" Rights, *OJ* C 84E, 3.4.2004, at 579–580.

41 Human Rights in the World 2007 and the EU's policy on the matter, European Parliament resolution of 8 May 2008 on the Annual Report on Human Rights in the World 2007 and the European Union's policy on the matter (2007/2274(INI)), *OJ* C 271E, 12.11.2009, at 7–31, para. 7.

logue since 2008 which takes place annually[42] and the Africa-EU Strategic Partnership declares the two regional organizations' cooperation in the promotion of human rights "through enhanced dialogue between relevant institutions from both continents such as the European Court of Human Rights of the Council of Europe, the African Court on Human and Peoples' Rights and the African Commission on Human and Peoples' Rights".[43]

(III) The CJEU'S Jurisdiction as a Model

The ACtJHR Protocol I and a new amending protocol of 2014 foresee a regional court with multiple types of material jurisdiction which would integrate in one institution several judicial organs for entirely different types of litigation. In that regard the example of the CJEU, in the progressive enlargement of its various jurisdictions, is comparable: as a judicial organ of the EU, it consists of two courts, namely the Court of Justice and the General Court (the latter incorporating also the former Civil Service Tribunal). However, among the various functions of the ACtJHR, the CJEU seems to have an influence only on one or two types of jurisdictions whereas the others are not included in the European model. This is the reason why the various jurisdictions of the ACtJHR should be briefly summarized (a) before showing in which particular functions the EU's judicial organ might be relevant (b).

(a) The Question of Multiple Jurisdictions of the ACtJHR.

The jurisdiction of the merged ACtJHR is extremely broad. It is composed of five types of different international judicial jurisdictions:[44] 1. Jurisdiction in the field of human rights, like the ECtHR; 2. Jurisdiction in consti-

42 See the website of the Africa-EU Partnership, http://www.africa-eu-partnership.org/en/priority-areas/democracy-good-governance-and-human-rights (last visited 1st June 2016).

43 The Africa-EU Strategic Partnership. A Joint Africa-EU Strategy, Lisbon, 9 December 2007, 16344/07 (Presse 291), para. 29.

44 See this classification in: F. Ouguergouz, "The African Court of Justice and Human Right", in: A.A. Yusuf and F. Ouguergouz (eds.), *The African Union: Legal and Institutional Framework. A Manual on the Pan-African Organization* 130-

tutional issues arising from the institutional structure of a regional organization, the AU, like the CJEU; 3. Jurisdiction to deal with any issues of international law, like the International Court of Justice [ICJ]; 4. Jurisdiction in the field of staff appeal, like the United Nations Dispute Tribunal within the UN Internal Justice System or the General Court's civil service jurisdiction within the CJEU; 5. Jurisdiction in international criminal law, like the International Criminal Court [ICC]. Each of the jurisdictions should be briefly explained below.

First of all, the jurisdiction in human rights matters succeeds the jurisdiction of the ACtHPR which will continue to function as one of the sections of the merged court, the so-called "Human Rights Section".[45] There are transitional provisions guaranteeing the continuing functioning of the ACtHPR until the newly elected judges of the ACtJHR are sworn in so that the risk of a gap in human rights litigation could be eliminated.[46] Furthermore, many other provisions show that the merged court will succeed the characteristics of the ACtHPR: for example the seat of the merged Court shall be the same as the seat of the ACtHPR in Arusha,[47] the ACtJHR will succeed the Registry of the ACtHPR etc.[48] Especially in the matter of jurisdiction *ratione materiae*, the two courts are similar: the Human Rights Section has jurisdiction to hear cases related to "the interpretation and the application of the African Charter, the Charter on the Rights and Welfare of the Child, the Protocol to the African Charter on Human and Peoples' Rights on the Rights of Women in Africa, or any other legal instrument relating to human rights, ratified by the States Parties concerned".[49] The Protocol on the ACtHPR provided for the same jurisdiction, although it failed to refer expressly to the African children's rights and the women's rights conventions.[50] Other competences related to the jurisdiction in human rights, to give advisory opinions in human rights matters and the interpretation and the revision of rulings are the same in

131 (Leiden/Boston, Martinus Nijhoff Publishers, 2012), although he did not include the fifth, international criminal jurisdiction.

45 ACtJHR Protocol I, Annex, Statute of the ACtJHR, Article 16.

46 ACtJHR Protocol I, Chapter II, Articles 4-7.

47 ACtJHR Protocol I, Annex, Statute of the ACtJHR, Article 25(1).

48 ACtJHR Protocol II, Article 7.

49 *Ibid*, Article 28(c).

50 Protocol on the ACtHPR, Article 3(1).

the two courts.[51] However, a major difference is that the new Human Rights Section, unlike the ACtHPR or the ECtHR,[52] does not have jurisdiction to refer a case to amicable settlement. This lack of competence is heavily criticized by human rights NGOs.[53]

The second type of jurisdiction, the jurisdiction in constitutional issues arising from the institutional structure of the AU, is common to most courts of regional organizations: they have the competence to interpret and apply the constitutive act and the secondary legislation (acts, decisions, regulations, directives etc.) of the organization. Among the jurisdictions of the merged Court listed in Article 28 of the ACtJHR Protocol I, this type covers "the interpretation and application of the Constitutive Act" and disputes related to "all acts, decisions, regulations and directives of the organs of the Union".[54] Furthermore, the decision on a breach of an obligation owed to the AU and on its consequences, namely the nature or extent of the reparation to be made for the breach of that obligation, may be competences which relate to constitutional issues arising from the institutional structure of the AU, especially to the control of the respect of the obligations arising from the Constitutive Act or from the AU's secondary legislation. These types of competences are also enlisted in Article 28 of the ACtJHR Protocol I[55] and will be detailed below.

The third type of jurisdiction, the jurisdiction to deal with any issues of international law, covers all types of competence with regard to the interpretation, application or validity of international instruments binding member states not by virtue of their membership in the AU as such. The ACtJHR provides for the jurisdiction to hear cases related to "the interpretation, application or validity of other Union Treaties and all subsidiary legal instruments adopted within the framework of the Union or the Organization of African Unity", to "such other matters or appeals as may be re-

---

51 Advisory opinions: Protocol on the ACtHPR, Article 4; ACtJHR Protocol I, Article 53; revision of rulings: Protocol on the ACtHPR, Article 28(3)-(4); ACtJHR Protocol I, Articles 47-48.

52 Protocol on the ACtHPR, Article 9; European Convention on Human Rights as amended by Protocols Nos. 11 and 14 supplemented by Protocols Nos. 1, 4, 6, 7, 12 and 13 [ECHR], Article 39.

53 FIDH / International Federation for Human Rights, *Practical Guide: The African Court on Human and Peoples' Rights towards the African Court of Justice and Human Rights* 153 (Paris, 2010).

54 ACtJHR Protocol I, Articles 28(a), (e).

55 *Ibid*, Articles 28(g)-(h).

ferred to it in any other agreements that the Member States or the Regional Economic Communities or other international organizations recognized by the African Union may conclude among themselves, or with the Union"[56] and to "any question of international law".[57] The latter function especially opens for the merged Court an unlimited jurisdiction in the matter of international law. It is not surprising that it is vehemently criticized by authors, claiming that the primary responsibility for determining crucial issues of international law should lie with the ICJ rather than with a regional court, further contributing to the risk of "fragmentation of international law".[58] Furthermore, the merged ACtJHR shall decide on "all matters specifically provided for in any other agreements that States Parties may conclude among themselves, or with the Union and which confer jurisdiction on the Court".[59]

As for the fourth type of jurisdiction, that of staff appeals, it is common to most courts of international organizations that the civil servants of the international organization can initiate disputes under the terms and conditions laid down in the staff rules and regulations of the organization.[60] The detailed rules of the merged court could thus be inspired from various international models such as the above-mentioned UN staff appeals system or the EU's model.[61]

Finally, the fifth type of material jurisdiction, the jurisdiction in international criminal law, is the most recent and most contested additional competence of the merged Court. It has been foreseen in the Protocol on Amendments to the Protocol on the Statute of the African Court of Justice and Human Rights [ACtJHR Protocol II],[62] adopted on 27 June 2014,

---

56 Protocol on Amendments to the Protocol on the Statute of the African Court of Justice and Human Rights, 27 June 2014, Malabo, Equatorial Guinea [ACtJHR Protocol II], Article 3(2).

57 *Ibid*, Articles 28(b), (d).

58 K.D. Magliveras, G.J. Naldi, "The African Court of Justice", 66 *Zeitschrift für ausländisches öffentliches Recht und Völkerrecht* 187, 199 (2006).

59 ACtJHR Protocol I, Article 28(f).

60 ACtJHR Protocol I, Article 29(1)(c).

61 See Staff Rules and Staff Regulations of the United Nations, Secretary-General's bulletin, UN Doc. ST/SGB/2014/1 (1 January 2014), Chapter XI (Appeals); Statute of the United Nations Dispute Tribunal; Statute of the United Nations Appeals Tribunal; on the European Union's reformed staff appeals system, see *infra* n. 103.

62 ACtJHR Protocol II.

quite contestably before the first Protocol entered into force.[63] The ACtJHR Protocol II calls the ACtJHR "the African Court of Justice and Human and Peoples' Rights" and extends its jurisdiction to crimes under international law and transnational crimes. It creates a third section, the International Criminal Law Section which tries individual criminal cases.[64] Although the Protocol sets up the first permanent, regional, and criminal international tribunal in Africa, it must be highlighted that the member states' primary intention with its adoption might have been to avoid the humiliation of seeing African political leaders being prosecuted before the ICC.[65] Furthermore, a heavily-attacked provision of the ACtJHR Protocol II, as opposed to the Statute of the ICC, grants jurisdictional immunity for serving heads of state or government, and senior officials.[66] The EU in particular, at the November 2015 African Judicial Dialogue, declared that "the EU is not in a position to support the Malabo Protocol creating the additional Criminal Chamber as it includes the provision of immunity for sitting Heads of State and Senior state officials and lacks complementary with the ICC".[67] Nevertheless, the criminal competence of the ACtJHR would help to eliminate an individual criminal responsibility gap and impunity emerging in case of a rupture with the ICC's jurisdiction.[68] Furthermore, the ACtJHR would try an impressive list of international crimes, many of them not included in the ICC Statute such as unconstitutional

63 The adoption of Protocol II has been criticized because under Article 58(2) of ACtJHR Protocol I, amendments can only be adopted by the Assembly "after the Court has given its opinion on it". Therefore, the 2008 Protocol's entry into force is a condition for any amendments. See especially G.J. Naldi, K.D. Magliveras, "African Union Establishes an International Criminal Court", 30(11) *International Enforcement Law Reporter* 430, 430 (2014).

64 ACtJHR Protocol II, Annex, Article 6.

65 R.-C. Liwanga, "From Commitment to Compliance: Enforceability of Remedial Orders of African Human Rights Bodies", 41 *Brooklyn Journal of International Law* 99, 123 (2015).

66 ACtJHR Protocol II, Annex, Article 46Abis of the modified Statute; on the criticisms see e.g. Naldi, Magliveras, *supra* n. 63, at 430 and ff., fn. 29; Amnesty International, Malabo Protocol. Legal and Institutional Implications of the Merged and Expanded African Court, Index: AFR 01/3063/2016, 2016 [Amnesty International, Malabo Protocol], at 35.

67 "EU statement at the African Judicial Dialogue, 6 November 2015, Arusha, Tanzania", available at http://eeas.europa.eu/delegations/african_union/documents/press_corner/eu-statement-judicial-dialogue-06-11-2015_en.pdf (last visited on 16 May 2016).

68 *Ibid.*

change of government, piracy, terrorism, mercenarism, corruption, money laundering, trafficking in persons, etc. Like Protocol I, the ACtJHR Protocol II enters into force after the deposit of instruments of ratification by 15 member states; however, as of 1 June 2016, only nine member states have signed and none of them have ratified it.[69] It is thus likely that a multi-speed ACtJHR will be operational in the sense that less states parties would accept the court's criminal jurisdiction than the other types of jurisdictions of the General Affairs Section and the Human Rights Section.

Each of the five main types of jurisdiction is modelled after another international tribunal: the human rights competence reflects the model of the ECtHR and the Inter-American Court of Human Rights; the jurisdiction in constitutional issues corresponds to the logic of the CJEU (see below); the broad competence in international law entirely follows the Statute of the ICJ; the civil servants' litigation is common to most courts of international organizations; whereas the criminal jurisdiction is closely modelled on the ICC. The principal criticism raised against the multiple jurisdictions of the ACtJHR is precisely its eclectic nature: as some commentators have argued, mixing them in one institution might be counterproductive. The ACommHPR warned that the ACtHPR and the ACJ two courts had "essentially different mandates and litigants" and that the decision could have "a negative impact on the establishment of an effective African Court on Human and Peoples' Rights".[70] To give a concrete example, considering that the judges of the Court will be appointed on the basis of their expertise in only one of the three thematic Sections covered in the jurisdiction of the Court, the judges might be required adjudicate over issues that they have little or no expertise in when they sit in the Full Court.[71] Furthermore, unlike the eight judges foreseen by Protocol I for each of the two Sections, Protocol II maintains the total of 16 judges for the merged court and provides for only five judges for the General Affairs Section and the Human Rights Section, with six judges for the International Criminal Law

69 See Status list at OAU/AU Treaties, Conventions, Protocols & Charters, available at the website of the AU, http://www.au.int/en/treaties (last visited 13th May 2016).

70 African Commission on Human and Peoples' Rights, Res. 76 (XXXVII) 05: Resolution on the Establishment of an Effective African Court on Human and Peoples" Rights, adopted in Banjul, the Gambia on 11 May 2005.

71 Under Article 18 of ACtJHR Protocol I (Referral of matters to the Full Court), as amended by Article 8 of ACtJHR Protocol II; see the same concern in: Amnesty International, Malabo Protocol, *op. cit.*, at 25.

Section.[72] It is likely that with such a broad and multiple jurisdiction *ratione materiae*, the members of the Sections will be overburdened. Notwithstanding the challenges and the negative effects that the merged Court's multiple jurisdictions may provoke, the CJEU could provide various good practices for the jurisdictions specifically of the future General Affairs Section.

(b) The Jurisdiction of the General Affairs Section and the European Model

Under the Statute of the merged Court, "[t]he Human and Peoples' Rights Section shall be competent to hear all cases relating to human and peoples' rights", "[t]he International Criminal Law Section shall be competent to hear all cases relating to the crimes specified in this Statute", while the "General Affairs Section shall be competent to hear all cases submitted under Article 28 of the Statute except those assigned to the Human and Peoples' Rights Section and the International Criminal Law Section as specified" in Article 17 of the Statute.[73] In consequence, the General Affairs Section has a complementary jurisdiction to hear all cases which do not fall within the competence of the two specialized Sections but which fall within the Court's jurisdiction *ratione materiae* under Article 28 of the ACtJHR Protocol I. Among the five above-mentioned main types of jurisdictions, the General Affairs Section is charged with jurisdiction in constitutional issues arising from the institutional structure of the AU, the jurisdiction to deal with any issues of international law including the interpretation, application or validity of AU or OAU Treaties or disputes related to such other matters or appeals as may be referred to the ACtJHR in any other agreements, and staff appeals. It is noteworthy to detail such analogies according to each of the above-mentioned jurisdictions. Before starting with the specific jurisdictions, it must be highlighted that the ACtJHR has contentious and advisory jurisdiction: in the latter case the Court could give a non-bind-

72 Article 6 of ACtJHR Protocol I, Annex, as amended by ACtJHR Protocol II, Annex, Article 4.

73 ACtJHR Protocol I, Article 17 as amended by ACtJHR Protocol II, Annex, Article 7.

ing interpretation of law.[74] This fourth and general jurisdiction will precede the analysis of all the above-mentioned special jurisdictions.

(i) Advisory Jurisdiction

Advisory jurisdiction is defined as a competence of a standing international tribunal to give an opinion on a legal question at the request of a defined class of international bodies, where the opinion constitutes an advice without any binding effect either on "the requesting entity or any other body or state to take any specific action pursuant to the opinion".[75] The ACtJHR's advisory competence, as opposed to all kinds of contentious competences, is general in the sense that it can be requested "on any legal question" by some AU bodies determined under Article 53 of ACtJHR Protocol I. As a comparison, one can note that in the so-called preliminary rulings procedure, the CJEU shall give a ruling on the interpretation of the Treaties or the validity or interpretation of EU acts referred to it by any court or tribunal of a member state.[76] Although some authors compare this procedure to an advisory jurisdiction,[77] the CJEU's preliminary ruling is binding on the referring national court and the courts of all other member states[78] whereas the CJEU lacks jurisdiction to give advisory opinion on general issues. Thus, the preliminary ruling does not fall within the above-mentioned definition. Nevertheless, given the success that the preliminary rulings played in the uniform application of EU law by domestic authorities and in the development of EU case law, the future ACtJHR should be ac-

---

74 See this definition of "advisory opinion" at Cornell Law School, Legal Information Institute, Wex, available at https://www.law.cornell.edu/wex/advisory_opinion (last visited on 2 June 2016).

75 H. Thirlway, "Advisory Opinions", in: I *Max Planck Encyclopedia of Public International Law* 97, 97 para. 1 (Oxford, Oxford University Press, 2012).

76 TFEU, Article 267.

77 E.g. D. Akande, "The Competence of International Organizations and the Advisory Jurisdiction of the International Court of Justice", 9 *EJIL* 437-467, at 458, fn. 89 (1998); Jacobs, White, and Ovey, *The European Convention on Human Rights* 51, fn. 223 (Sixth ed., Oxford, Oxford University Press, 2014), (recognizing the major difference).

78 This is the "factual *erga omnes*" effect of the Courts rulings. See e.g. C. Baudenbacher, "The Implementation of Decisions of the ECJ and of the EFTA Court in member states' Domestic Legal Orders", 40 *Texas International Law Journal* 383, 396-398 (2005).

corded the same competence. However, this supposes three simultaneous developments: beyond the institutions of the AU authorized to request advisory opinions, national courts and tribunals should be granted the same right of initiative under Article 53(1) of ACtJHR Protocol I. Furthermore, the AU should acquire a level of integration where its law has primacy over domestic law and, consequently, advisory opinions should have binding effect. Such developments are certainly desirable, but the present state of affairs of the AU's context does not yet allow such an analogy.[79]

Another, more appropriate European analogy which some authors consider a true advisory function[80] is the CJEU's competence to give opinion on the international agreements to be concluded by the EU. Under the Treaty on the Functioning of the European Union [TFEU], "[a] Member State, the European Parliament, the Council or the Commission may obtain the opinion of the Court of Justice as to whether an agreement envisaged is compatible with the Treaties". However, the ruling is binding in the sense that "[w]here the opinion of the Court is adverse, the agreement envisaged may not enter into force unless it is amended or the Treaties are revised".[81] The same competence could be applied by the ACtJHR, under Article 53 of ACtJHR Protocol I, if the AU were in the state of integration of concluding international agreements on its own, although the opinion would still be non-binding. In sum, unlike the CJEU's model, the advisory function of the merged African Court could not advance the treaty-conform application of domestic and international acts with a binding force, but it could certainly contribute to this goal of legal integration with a recommendatory effects.

79 In the same sense, in the domain of human rights: AP van der Mei, "The Advisory Jurisdiction of the African Court on Human and Peoples' Rights", 5(1) *African Human Rights Law Journal* 27, 44 (2005).

80 E.g. M. M. Aljaghoub, *The Advisory Function of the International Court of Justice 1946-2005* 13 (New York, Springer, 2006); G. Itzcovich, "The European Court of Justice as a Constitutional Court. Legal Reasoning in a Comparative Perspective", 4 *Sant' Anna Legal Studies. STALS Research Paper* 1, 10 (2014).

81 TFEU, Article 218(11).

(ii) Jurisdiction in Constitutional Issues Arising from the Institutional Structure of the Organization

Under this type of jurisdiction, the ACtJHR is expected to deal mainly with contentious matters of a political and economic nature,[82] similarly to the core original mission of the CJEU; and to advance, by its case law, the objectives of the AU as provided for in the Constitutive Act. Beyond the interpretation and the application of the Constitutive Act, it encompasses the settlement of disputes related to "all acts, decisions, regulations and directives of the organs of the Union".[83] This competence is an action for judicial review which resembles that of the CJEU which shall review the legality of legislative acts and of acts of the EU's institutions or the acts of bodies, offices or agencies of the Union intended to produce legal effects *vis-à-vis* third parties. In case of an incompatibility, the CJEU can annul those acts.[84] However, unlike the CJEU, the ACtJHR does not have the express power to annul an act incompatible with AU law and it is not clear whether its pronouncements will have such a binding or only declarative effect.[85] It is submitted that to advance economic and legal integration, the ACtJHR should interpret this jurisdiction as having the effect of annulment of acts which have been found to be incompatible with AU law.

(iii) Jurisdiction to Deal with Any Issues of International Law

As some authors note, the EU was the model for the binding powers of the ACtJHR on issues relating to disputes between member states[86]. However, in the EU, a member state can only initiate an action before the CJEU against another member state if it considers that another member state has

82 F. Viljoen, E. Baimu, "Courts for Africa: Considering the Co-Existence of the African Court on Human and Peoples' Rights and the African Court of Justice", 22(2) *Netherlands Quarterly of Human Rights* 241, 251 (2004).

83 ACtJHR Protocol I, Articles 28(a), (e).

84 TFEU, Articles 263-264.

85 Magliveras, Naldi, *supra* n. 58, at 200.

86 G. Finizio, "The EU and the Promotion of Democracy through Interregional Relations", in: M. Teló *et al.*, *Interregionalism and the European Union. A Post-Revisionist Approach to Europe's Place in a Changing World* 155-156 (Burlington, USA, Ashgate, 2015).

failed to fulfil an obligation under the Treaties,[87] i.e. the constitutive acts of the EU (the Treaty on European Union and the TFEU). Thus, unlike the ACtJHR, the CJEU does not have automatic jurisdiction to hear cases related to any international agreements concluded by its member states within the framework or under the auspices of the EU, e.g. the Agreement establishing the European Bank for Reconstruction and Development which provides for its own mechanism of arbitration.[88]

On the basis of its jurisdiction to hear cases related to "the interpretation, application or validity of other Union Treaties and all subsidiary legal instruments adopted within the framework of the Union or the Organization of African Unity", the ACtJHR might have a much broader competence than that of the CJEU. Among AU and OAU treaties, the future General Affairs Section could decide on cases related to such important treaties as the OAU Convention on the Prevention and Combating of Terrorism, ratified by 41 member states; the Convention of the African Energy Commission, ratified by 32 member states; the African Civil Aviation Commission Constitution, ratified by 44 member states or its Revised Constitution, ratified by six member states; the African Union Non-Aggression and Common Defence Pact, ratified by 20 member states.[89] In economic matters, the General Affairs Section would certainly be charged with disputes related to the African Nuclear-Weapon-Free Zone Treaty (Pelindaba Treaty), ratified by 40 member states or the African Convention on the Conservation of Nature and Natural Resources, ratified by 31 member states.[90] The General Affairs Section might furthermore decide on

87 TFEU, Article 259(1).

88 Agreement establishing the European Bank for Reconstruction and Development, *Official Journal of the European Communities*, 31.12.1990, No L 372/4, Article 58.

89 OAU Convention on the Prevention and Combating of Terrorism, 1 July 1999; Convention of the African Energy Commission, 11 July 2001; African Civil Aviation Commission Constitution, 17 January 1969; Revised Constitution of the African Civil Aviation Commission, 16 December 2009; The African Union Non-Aggression and Common Defence Pact, 1 January 2005. See Status list at OAU/AU Treaties, Conventions, Protocols & Charters, available at the website of the AU, http://www.au.int/en/treaties (last visited 13th May 2016).

90 The African Nuclear-Weapon-Free Zone Treaty (Pelindaba Treaty), 11 April 1996; African Convention on the Conservation of Nature and Natural Resources, 15 September 1968; See Status list at OAU/AU Treaties, Conventions, Protocols & Charters, available at the website of the AU, http://www.au.int/en/treaties (last visited 13th May 2016).

disputes related to treaties of economic cooperation not yet entered into force such as the African Maritime Transport Charter (adopted in 1994, ratified by 13 member states), the Protocol on the Establishment of the African Monetary Fund (adopted in 2014, not yet ratified by any state) or the African Union Convention on Cross-Border Cooperation (Niamey Convention) (adopted in 2014, ratified only by one state).

Depending on the interpretation of the notion "human and/or peoples' rights", the General Affairs Section might be charged with disputes arising from rights not protected by the core human rights treaties of the AU enlisted under Article 28(c) of the ACtJHR Protocol I ("African Charter, the Charter on the Rights and Welfare of the Child, the Protocol to the African Charter on Human and Peoples' Rights on the Rights of Women in Africa"). For example it is uncertain whether the OAU Convention Governing the Specific Aspects of Refugee Problems in Africa, ratified by 45 AU member states, or the African Union Convention for the Protection and Assistance of Internally Displaced Persons in Africa (Kampala Convention), ratified by 25 AU member states,[91] fall within the category of "any other legal instrument relating to human rights, ratified by the states Parties concerned" and thus relate to the jurisdiction of the Human Rights Section rather than to that of the General Affairs Chamber. However, other treaties such as the Cultural Charter for Africa, ratified by 34 member states, the African Union Convention on Preventing and Combating Corruption, ratified by 32 member states or the African Charter on Democracy, Elections and Governance, ratified by 25 member states and entered into force in 2012,[92] seem rather mixed in the sense that they provide both on human rights and institutional duties of member states and AU organs. They might fall within the jurisdiction of the General Affairs Section which will have certain difficulties in delimitating its cases from those of

91 OAU Convention Governing the Specific Aspects of Refugee Problems in Africa, 10 September 1969; African Union Convention for the Protection and Assistance of Internally Displaced Persons in Africa (Kampala Convention), 23 October 2009; See Status list at OAU/AU Treaties, Conventions, Protocols & Charters, available at the website of the AU, http://www.au.int/en/treaties (last visited 13th May 2016).

92 Cultural Charter for Africa, 5 July 1976; African Union Convention on Preventing and Combating Corruption, 1 July 2003; African Charter on Democracy, Elections and Governance, 30 January 2003; See Status list at OAU/AU Treaties, Conventions, Protocols & Charters, available at the website of the AU, http://www.au.int/en/treaties (last visited 13th May 2016).

the Human Rights Section. In this regard, the CJEU's model is certainly exemplary: it has developed, over several decades, from the 1970 s, case law which has progressively incorporated principles of human rights and democracy, until the recognition of the binding nature of human rights-related *jus cogens* norms ("fundamental rights forming an integral part of the general principles of Community law") as superior even to EU Acts.[93] Thus, a progressive and organic case law integrating AU economic, political and "constitutional" law and AU human rights law is highly recommended in the case law of the General Affairs Section so that the distribution of affairs among the two concerned sections could not lead to contradictory judgments.[94]

As mentioned above, beyond regional treaties, the ACtJHR has jurisdiction to decide "on all matters specifically provided for in any other agreements that states Parties may conclude among themselves, or with the Union and which confer jurisdiction on the Court".[95] The CJEU has a similar competence, but limited to matters falling within European Union law: it decides on disputes submitted to it under an arbitration clause "contained in a contract concluded by or on behalf of the Union" or by reason of the subject matter, "in any dispute between Member States which relates to the subject matter of the Treaties if the dispute is submitted to it under a special agreement between the parties".[96] Whereas the CJEU's jurisdiction under an arbitration clause or a special agreement shall include a subject matter falling within the EU's competences,[97] the Statute of the ACtJHR does not require such a special AU sphere and even broader private or public contracts could foresee the merged Court as a dispute settlement mechanism. What makes the EU particularly attractive to litigants is the fact that all claims, after being brought before the General Court at

93 Cases C-402/05 P and C-415/05 P, *Yassin Abdullah Kadi and Al Barakaat International Foundation v Council of the European Union and Commission of the European Communities*, [2008] ECR 6351, paras. 326-327.

94 In the same sense, claiming that even the General Affairs Section, charged with the interpretation of AU law other than human rights law, can elaborate a human rights based case law, see Juma, *supra* n. 17 at 280. For the expertise of the judges in human rights law, see below, part 3.

95 ACtJHR Protocol I, Article 28(f).

96 TFEU, Articles 272-273.

97 Janek Tomasz Nowak (ed.), *EU Procedural Law* 687 (Oxford, Oxford University Press, 2014).

first instance, can be appealed before the Court of Justice;[98] it is submitted that such an appeal should be foreseen through the amendment of the ACtJHR's Statute, beyond the revision of judgments as provided for under Article 48.

(iv) Staff Appeals

Any staff member of the AU is entitled to submit cases to the Court on appeal, in a dispute and within the limits and under the terms and conditions laid down in the Staff Rules and Regulations of the Union.[99] At first instance, the Administrative Tribunal is competent to hear appeals submitted by staff members, alleging violation of the terms of appointment, including all applicable provisions of the Staff Regulations and Rules, or appeals against administrative and disciplinary measures.[100] As a second instance, staff members can file an appeal to the future ACtJHR,[101] similarly to the division of work between the former Civil Service Tribunal and the General Court of the CJEU before 1 September 2016, date of the entry into force of the reform of the General Court and dissolution of the Civil service Tribunal,[102] and after the reform, between the General Court at first instance and the Court of Justice at second instance.[103] However, considering the limited number of judges and the numerous competences of

98 *Ibid*, at 689.

99 ACtJHR Protocol I, Articles 29(1)(c).

100 2010 AU Staff Regulations and Rules, Assembly of the Union, Fifteenth Ordinary Session, 25 - 27 July 2010, Kampala, Uganda, Assembly/AU/4(XV) [Staff Regulations and Rules], Rule 62.2.

101 *Ibid*, Rule 62.3.

102 TFEU, Annex on the European Union Civil Service Tribunal, Article 9.

103 On the reform, see Regulation (EU, Euratom) 2015/2422 of the European Parliament and of the Council of 16 December 2015 amending Protocol No 3 on the Statute of the Court of Justice of the European Union, *OJ* L 341/14, 24.12.2015, preamble para. 9; on the first instance jurisdiction of the General Court, see European Parliament legislative resolution of 9 June 2016 on the draft regulation of the European Parliament and of the Council on the transfer to the General Court of the European Union of jurisdiction at first instance in disputes between the Union and its servants (N8-0110/2015 – C8-0367/2015 – 2015/0906(COD)) (Ordinary legislative procedure: first reading).

the ACtJHR, it seems reasonable to limit the possibility of appeal to points of law, as is the case with the CJEU staff appeals.[104]

(v) Other Competences?

Finally, one might ask whether the ACtJHR might have other competences inspired by the jurisdiction of the European model. It must be added that the CJEU served as model not only for the ACtJHR, but for the sub-regional courts of the African continent, i.e. the Court of Justice of the West African Economic and Monetary Union (WAEMU), the Court of Justice of the Common Market for East African States (COMESA), the Court of Justice of the Central African Economic and Monetary Community (CEMAC), the East African Court of Justice (EACJ), the Community Court of Justice of the Court of Justice of the Economic Community of West African States (ECOWAS) and the Tribunal of the Southern African Development Community (SADC). Each of the six African sub-regional courts was granted at least three of the competences of the CJEU and three of them applies all the European court competences (see Table 1 – footnotes added to exemplify the effective use of those competences and the referrals to the CJEU case law), i.e. the compliance monitoring and compliance procedure against the respondent state by a supranational commission, a preliminary rulings procedure, a review procedure to challenge community acts, a staff appeals procedure, arbitral jurisdiction and advisory jurisdiction. Furthermore, four African sub-regional courts regularly refer to case law of the CJEU in their decisions. This shows that while establishing the competences of the sub-regional courts, member states of sub-regional organizations agreed to consider the CJEU as the major source of inspiration.

As for the ACtJHR, it even has a non-compliance procedure similar to the CJEU (see below, Part III).[105] Thus, the ACtJHR is granted all of the above-mentioned competences except for the preliminary rulings procedure. As mentioned above, even this competence could be foreseen, *de lege ferenda*, depending on the integration of the law of the AU. Furthermore, the more the AU can advance its legal integration, the more relevant

104 TFEU, Annex on the European Union Civil Service Tribunal, Article 11(1).

105 ACtJHR Protocol I, Articles 43(6) and 46(4).

are decisions of the CJEU as a source of inspiration for the case law of the ACtJHR. Finally, beyond the common competences, the CJEU inspires some procedural rules of the ACtJHR.

(IV) The CJEU's Procedural Rules as a Model

The procedural rules of the CJEU provide sufficient basis for the similar norms of the ACtJHR with respect to the number, eligibility and required expertise of judges (a) and the enforcement mechanism (b) – those two aspects appearing particularly important from the point of view of the Court's effectiveness.

(a) The Number, Eligibility and Required Expertise of Judges

The number and the composition of the ACtJHR judges have been subject to harsh debates and different treaty provisions. There have been various versions as to the number of judges, while the consecutive drafts and protocols have been similar with respect to the representativeness of judges as regards gender balance, major geographical regions and principal legal traditions of Africa.

As for the number of judges, the original ACJ was supposed to consist of 11 judges,[106] whereas the ACtJHR with two sections shall consist of 16, and in its new form with a third International Criminal Law Section also of 16 judges.[107] However, the increase of number of the sections results in a decreased number of judges sitting in each of the sections: instead of 11 judges as in the structure of the original African Court of Justice, only five judges shall sit in the General Affairs and the Human Rights Section and six in the International Criminal Law Section. The limited number of judges is explained by the limited resources available for the functioning of the Court,[108] and in this regard any comparison with the European mod-

---

106 Protocol of the Court of Justice of the African Union, Maputo, Mozambique, 11 July 2003, Article 3(1).

107 ACtHJHR, Protocol I, Annex, Article 3(1); ACtJHR Protocol II, Annex, Article 6(3) of the modified Statute.

108 Furthermore, in the debates the sixteen member-Court represented the more extended view, whereas some delegates argued for a Court with twelve judges. See

el would be unrealistic: in the EU, the Court of Justice consists of one judge from each member state, i.e. of 28 judges in 2016.[109] Furthermore, the CJEU decided to deal with the increase in the number of pending cases and its backlog of pending cases by increasing the number of the judges of the General Court to (a) 40 judges as from 25 December 2015; (b) 47 judges as from 1 September 2016; and finally (c) two judges per member state as from 1 September 2019.[110] It is clear that with an annual budget of 357 million euros,[111] the CJEU is not comparable to the AU where the entire organization's annual budget is 416 million USD[112] and where the functioning ACtHPR's annual costs amount to only 9-12 million USD.[113]

From the limited number of judges, a logical representativeness arises: the elected judges shall represent the principal legal traditions of Africa (Islamic law, Common law and Civil law, African customary law and South African Roman-Dutch law), while each geographical region (South, West, East, north and Central Africa) shall be represented by a predetermined number of judges.[114] Here the European model where a judge from each member state sits in the CJEU is obviously not comparable. They shall be appointed by common accord of the governments of the member

Summary report of the meeting of the Permanent Representatives' Committee and Legal Experts on legal matters, 16-19 May 2006, Addis Ababa, Ethiopia, PRC-Exp/Legal//Rpt, para. 14.

109 TEU, Article 19(2).

110 Consolidated version of the Statute of the Court of Justice of the European Union, Article 48.

111 Court of Justice of the European Union, Annual Report 2015. Management Report (annual activity report by the Authorising Officer by Delegation), April 2016, at 76-77. However, it should be highlighted that almost 3.5 % of this budget (12.16 million Euros) covers the costs of "external services in the linguistic field" (freelance interpreters and translators). See Draft general budget of the European Union for the financial year 2016, vol. 4, Section IV, COM(2015) 300, 24.6.2015, at IV/18.

112 African Union Handbook 2016, African Union Commission, at 170.

113 See e.g. Report on the activities of the African Court on Peoples' and Human Rights, Executive Council, Twenty-Second Ordinary Session, 21-25 January 2013, Addis Ababa, Ethiopia, EX.CL/783(XXII), paras. 32-33.

114 Protocol of the Court of Justice of the African Union, Maputo, Mozambique, 11 July 2003, Article 3(5)-(6) (each region by no less than two judges); ACtJHR Protocol I, Article 3(3) ("Each geographical region of the Continent, as determined by the Decisions of the Assembly shall, where possible, be represented by three (3) Judges except the Western Region which shall have four (4) Judges.").

states for six years,[115] whereas in Africa, a more competitive election is assured through a secret election by the Executive Council, and the elected judges are appointed by the Assembly similarly for six years.[116]

An African particularity is that in all protocols the list of African judges were supposed to reflect "an adequate gender representation" in the nomination process and the election of judges[117] – a culturally determined requirement which is absent in the nomination and election process of the CJEU's judges. Indeed, beyond the generally applicable non-discrimination requirement,[118] there is no requirement of affirmative action in gender issues in the selection of the members of the CJEU. However, the requirement does not necessarily lead to an "equality" of gender balance: whereas the Protocol of the Court of Justice of the African Union provided for an "equal gender representation" in the election of judges by the Assembly, ACtJHR Protocols I and II require only an "equitable gender representation", which is a less stringent wording.[119] As a matter of fact, there are only two female judges out of 11 at the ACtHPR, whereas in Europe, seven out of 28 members are women at the Court of Justice and eight out of 28 at the General Court.[120] Thus, finally, there is not much difference if the expressed affirmative action is not reflected in the concrete decision-making.

A further comparable standard is the required expertise: the judges of both the ACtJHR and the CJEU shall be elected from among persons of high moral character, whose independence is beyond doubt and who possess the qualifications required for appointment to the highest judicial offices in their respective countries or who are jurisconsults of recognised competence.[121] Beyond these general requirements of independence, im-

115 TEU, Article 19(2).

116 ACtJHR Protocol I, Article 7.

117 Protocol of the Court of Justice of the African Union, Maputo, Mozambique, 11 July 2003, Article 5(3) and 7(3); Protocol on the ACtHPR, Articles 12(2) and 14(3); ACtJHR Protocol I, Annex, Articles 5(2) and 7(5); ACtJHR Protocol II, Annex, Article 3(4) of the modified Statute.

118 TEU, Article 2; Charter of Fundamental Rights of the European Union, Article 28(1).

119 Magliveras, Naldi, *supra* n. 58, at 195.

120 As of 1st July 2016.

121 TEU, Article 19(2); TFEU, Article 253(1) (Court of Justice) and 254 (General Court); ACtJHR Protocol I, Annex, Article 4; ACtJHR Protocol II, Annex, Article 4 of the modified Statute.

partiality and recognized experience in the legal field, judges at the ACtJHR shall also possess recognized competence and experience in one of the fields corresponding to the concerned section. Whereas the judges of the Human Rights and Criminal Law Sections shall have recognized competence and experience in the respective field, the candidates elected to the General Affairs Section shall have "recognized competence and experience in International law".[122] This is a logical requirement given the fact that the main competence of the Section is the interpretation and application of the AU Constitutive Act and other issues of international law as detailed above. The competence of this section is not required from the candidates to the CJEU, but in general all appointed judges have a high profile expertise in EU law. However, since the AU Constitutive Act expresses a strong commitment towards the protection of human rights in its objectives and principles,[123] it is to be reiterated that judges at the General Affairs Section – like at the CJEU – should adopt a human rights-conform interpretation of international law, in accordance with the AU human rights instruments.[124]

Finally, the European model is relevant regarding the nomination process of the judges. For the nomination of the African judges, "[e]ach state Party may present up to two (2) candidates",[125] from whom "[t]he Judges shall be elected by the Executive Council, and appointed by the Assembly".[126] Some authors have criticized this procedure, claiming that it leads to "political appointees" who "may inject politics into the process and may compromise competence".[127] It is true that in the EU an independent filter body exists, with a panel set up in order to give an opinion on candidates' suitability to perform the duties of judges, composed of national high-level

122 ACtJHR Protocol I, Annex, Article 6(1); ACtJHR Protocol II, Annex, Article 6(1) of the modified Statute.

123 African Union Constitutive Act, Lome, Togo, 11th July 2000, Articles 3(g)-(h) and 4(h), (m), (n), (o).

124 In the same sense: K. Kindiki, "The Proposed Integration of the African Court of Justice and the African Court of Human and Peoples' Rights: Legal Difficulties and Merits", 15 *African Journal of International and Comparative Law* 138, 142 (2007).

125 ACtJHR Protocol I, Annex, Article 5(2).

126 ACtJHR Protocol I, Annex, Article 7(1).

127 J.M. Isanga, "The Constitutive Act of the African Union, African Courts and the Protection of Human Rights: New Dispensation?", 11 *Santa Clara Journal of International Law* 267, 296 (2013).

judges, lawyers and former judges of the CJEU.[128] Only judges found by the panel suitable for the post can be appointed by common accord of the governments of the member states – this filter mechanism ensures the criteria of independence and expertise of the nominees. However, even judges of the CJEU whose independence is rarely challenged, are finally nominated by the member states and the one judge-one member state rule makes political influence more likely than the African system where only 16 judges are elected from a potentially high number of candidates. A filter mechanism is nevertheless recommended in order to ensure that the states parties nominate only qualified persons, for example by granting the Commission the right to screen and/or audit nominees before establishing alphabetical lists of candidates.[129] Be that as it may, the present procedural norms on the judges of the ACtJHR might ensure the expected independence, expertise and representativeness of the Court, provided that states parties comply with those rules in good faith.

(b) Enforcement Mechanism

Among the procedural rules of the ACtJHR, commentators agree that the strongest development is the enforcement mechanism of the binding decisions compared to the weak supervision mechanism of the ACtHPR, consisting only of the Council of Ministers' monitoring of the judgments' execution on behalf of the Assembly[130] which in practice does not function. Under ACtJHR Protocol I, "[t]he Executive Council shall also be notified of the judgment and shall monitor its execution on behalf of the Assembly",[131] which is a monitoring by a political body consisting of the foreign ministers of member states, similarly to the current enforcement mechanism of the ACtHPR or the ECtHR. Furthermore, as a novelty, "[t]he Assembly may impose sanctions by virtue of paragraph 2 of Article 23 of the Constitutive Act".[132] Certain authors claim that this provision is "a *mutatis mutandis* extract of its equivalent in the European Convention on Human

128 TFEU, Article 255(1).
129 ACtJHR Protocol I, Article 6; ACtJHR Protocol II, Article 4.
130 Protocol on the ACtHPR, Article 29(2).
131 ACtJHR Protocol I, Annex, Article 43(6).
132 ACtJHR, Protocol I, Annex, Article 46(5).

Rights",[133] but it presents similarities with the enforcement mechanism of the CJEU as well. In both European enforcement mechanisms, a political body of the regional organization (the Committee of Ministers in the Council of Europe and the Commission of the EU) may decide to refer to the judicial body the question whether the state has failed to fulfill its obligation.[134] Contrary to the two European mechanisms where a sanction may be imposed after a new referral to the judicial body, non-compliance with the ACtJHR's decisions may give rise to sanctions directly imposed by the Assembly of the AU which seems at first glance more effective.[135] Nevertheless, it seems that the political character of the supervisory body hinders such decisions: since they are composed of the representatives of member states (deputies of the ministers of foreign affairs at the Committee of Ministers and heads of states and government at the Assembly of the AU) and they decide by a majority vote of two thirds (Committee of Ministers) or by consensus (Assembly of the AU),[136] it is no surprise that neither of the two bodies has ever referred a non-compliance case to the judicial body.[137] Contrary to the ACtJHR and the ECtHR, the enforcement mechanism of the CJEU is rather depoliticized in the sense that the Euro-

133 M.C. Ogwezzy, "Challenges and Prospects of the African Court of Justice and Human Rights", 6 *Jimma University Journal of Law* 1, 16 (2014); in the same sense: Liwanga, *supra* n. 65, at 139-140.

134 ECHR, Article 46(3)-(6); Rules of the Committee of Ministers for the supervision of the execution of judgments and of the terms of friendly settlements (Adopted by the Committee of Ministers on 10 May 2006 at the 964th meeting of the Ministers" Deputies) [Rules of the Committee of Ministers for the supervision of the execution of judgments], Rule 11; TFEU, Articles 258 and 260(3).

135 However, *de lege ferenda*, Naldi and Maglievas recommend that a new case will have to be brought before the ACtJHR whose subject matter "will be that it recognizes the fact that the respondent State has failed to observe and give effect to the obligations arising under the previous judgment". See G.J. Naldi, K.D. Magliveras, "The African Court of Justice and Human Rights: A Judicial Curate's Egg", 9(2) *International Organizations Law Review* 383, 433-434 (2012).

136 Rules of the Committee of Ministers for the supervision of the execution of judgments, *supra.* n. 134, Rule 11(1)-(2); In the case of the Assembly of the AU, failing the consensus, the decision shall be adopted also by a two-thirds majority. See Constitutive Ct of the African Union, Article 7(1) and Rules of procedure of the Assembly of the Union, Rule 18(1).

137 As for the Committee of Minister, see Committee on Legal Affairs and Human Rights, Implementation of judgments of the European Court of Human Rights: 8th report, Report, 2015, para. 34; as for the Assembly of the African Union in respect of the decisions of the ACtHPR, see Liwanga, *supra* n. 65, at 139.

pean Commission is a supranational body, mandated to "promote the general interest of the Union" as the "motor of the European integration", deciding by majority in case of a vote but in practice by consensus.[138] It is no accident that it has systematically recourse to the Court of Justice as a reaction to the non-compliance; for example in 2015 the Court gave 25 judgments under the non-compliance procedure, of which 18 (82 %) were in the Commission's favour.[139] While bearing in mind the intergovernmental and not supranational structure of the AU and the fact that AU law in general and judgments of the ACtJHR in particular do not have direct effect in states parties, the integration goals of the AU show in that direction. Consequently, one could recommend that the sanctions regime of the AU Assembly be depoliticized (e.g. by granting non-political bodies such as the Commission of the AU a greater role in the mechanism), strengthened (e.g. by creating a sub-committee within the Executive Council charged with the periodic evaluation of the states' enforcement) and, more importantly, that the compliance of states parties with the legally binding decisions go hand-in-hand with their political commitment, the increased role of domestic courts and national human rights institutions in monitoring the enforcement of the ACtJHR's judgments and the participatory role of civil society.[140] It is to be noted that the context is entirely different: unlike the decisions of Africa's international organizations, the CJEU's judgments have always been complied with by EU member states, even though sometimes with delays, given their overall interest in European integration.

(V) Conclusion

The study has demonstrated the influence of the EU, and its judicial body, the Court of Justice, in the judicial reform proposals of the African Union

138 Rules of Procedure of the Commission [C(2000) 3614], *OJ* L 308 , 08/12/2000, at 26-34, Article 8 ("Commission decisions shall be adopted if a majority of the number of members specified in the Treaty vote in favour.").

139 Report from the Commission, Monitoring the application of European Union law, 2015 Annual Report, Brussels, 15.7.2016, COM(2016) 463 final, at 25.

140 In the same sense, see: Ogwezzy, *supra* n. 133, at 17; on the crucial role of national judicial institutions and national human rights institutions in the enforcement of international judgments, see Liwanga, *supra* n. 65, at 140-146 and 148-151.

especially with regard to the rule on jurisdiction and the procedure. Since ACtJHR Protocol I has attracted a low number of ratifications so far and since the detailed Rules of Court shall be adopted by the future merged Court, international good practices and especially the most well-known model of regional integration, the EU's judicial system should be taken into account.

As regards the question of jurisdiction, the CJEU has an influence mainly on the competences of the ACtJHR's General Affairs Section which has a complementary jurisdiction to hear all cases which do not fall within the competence of the two specialized Sections but which fall within the Court's jurisdiction *ratione materiae*. Within those competences, it is recommended that the CJEU's advisory jurisdiction on the conclusion of international agreements should be taken into consideration. In disputes arising from constitutional matters of the AU, the ACtJHR should interpret its jurisdiction as having the effect of annulment of acts which have been found to be incompatible with AU law, similar to the CJEU's jurisdiction. In its case law, the ACtJHR should integrate the AU's primary and secondary law and AU human rights law so that the distribution of affairs among the concerned Sections could not lead to contradictory judgments, just like the CJEU has done. Since the ACtJHR has a very wide arbitral jurisdiction, it is recommended that its decisions could be appealed, just like the decisions of the CJEU rendered on the basis of an arbitration clause. In elaborating the detailed rules of staff appeals, the CJEU staff appeals system should equally be considered as a model. However, all such jurisdictions shall correspond to the actual state of integration of AU law: for example given the immaturity of legal integration at the AU level, it would be premature to apply the CJEU's competence to give preliminary rulings.

As regards procedural rules, the limited resources and restricted number of judges of the ACtJHR make any comparison with the EU's one member state-one judge rule difficult. However, some European good practices should be followed such as the equitable gender representation in the nomination and election of judges or the filter mechanism in the nomination procedure. In the enforcement mechanism, it is recommended that the sanctions regime of the AU Assembly be depoliticized and strengthened, similar to the European Union's system.

In sum, the influence of the European Union's Court of Justice as an institutional model for the merged African Court should be further strengthened, while the specificities and context of African integration should be taken into account.

III. When Titans Clash: Setting Standards for Child Abduction by the CJEU and the ECtHR

*Michele Angelo Lupoi**

(I) Introduction

For my presentation during this Summer School dedicated to "the pluralism of methods" I have chosen the topic of child abduction in the international setting.[1] This may appear an odd choice: however, in truth this area of the law is very interesting from a methodological standpoint, for a number of different reasons.

First, international child abduction necessarily involves at least two judicial systems, in a setting where culture and context are extremely important and the capacity of domestic courts to wholly cooperate with each other is put to the test more than in other legal areas. As a matter of fact, in matters of child abduction, sometimes the divergence between theory and practice is striking.

Dealing with child abduction, moreover, requires an interdisciplinary approach since substantial law and procedural law are strictly interconnected. Normative sources are stratified and superimposed, at the international, regional and domestic levels and an interplay between different courts takes place in different forms: national courts *vis à vis* national courts (see, e. g., Art. 11 of EU Regulation 2201\2003), domestic courts *vis à vis* international courts, international courts *vis à vis* international courts.

* Professor for Civil Procedural Law, Facoltà di Giurisprudenza dellà Università degli Studi di Bologna.

1 See, recently, J. Paton, "The correct approach to the examination of the best interests of the child in abduction convention proceedings following the decision of the Supreme Court in Re E (children) (Abduction: custody appeal)", 8 *Jour. Priv. Int. Law* 547 (2012). Abduction cases from one EU Member State to another appear to be growing in number: see K. Trimmings, *Child abduction within the European Union* 104 (Oxford, 2013).

This interplay fosters a comparative approach and, as the case law shows, multiple (and often parallel) proceedings which sometimes lead to conflicting decisions, both provisional and final.

Another interesting aspect of the topic examined here, from the methodological point of view, is that data are available to examine and compare: central authorities created under the Hague Convention of 25 October 1980 [2,3] compile statistics which help to understand how the rules work in real life.[4] From these data, the impact of culture on the application of the rules can be noted, and, possibly, actions may be taken to bring an eventual change in this "culture".

In this context, I would like to explore a recent "tension" in the relations between the Court of Justice of the European Union (CJEU) and the European Court of Human Rights (ECtHR) in this area of the law.

Both courts apply provisions on child abduction. The CJEU interprets the provisions on child abduction (Arts. 10-11) contained in EU Regu-

---

2 Among others, see A.E. Anton, "The Hague Convention on International Child Abduction", 30 *Int. Comp. Law Quar.* 537 (1981); A. Bucher, *L'enfant en droit international privé* (Geneve, 2003); G. Carella, "La convenzione dell'Aja del 1980 sugli aspetti civili della sottrazione internazionale dei minori", 30 *Riv. Dir. Int. Priv. Proc.* 777 (1994); A. Fiorini, "Habitual residence and the newborn – A French perspective", 61 *Int. Comp. Law Quar.* 530 (2012); T. Kruger, *International child abduction. The inadequacies of the law* (Oxford, 2011); B. Lena, "Affidamento e custody quali presupposti per il rimpatrio del minore, tra convenzione de l'Aja e diritto interno", *Fam. Dir.* 190 (2004); A. Salzano, *La sottrazione internazionale di minori. Accordi internazionali a tutela dell'affidamento e del diritto di visita* (Milan, 1995); L. Silberman, "Hague Convention on International Child Abduction: A Brief Overview and Case Law Analysis", 28 *Fam. L. Quar.* 9 (1994); S. Vigers, *Mediating International Child Abduction Cases. The Hague convention* (Oxford, 2011).

3 The duties and functions of central authorities are listed in Art. 7 of the Hague Convention. See, recently, C. Dereatti, "La tutela del provvedimento di affidamento nei rapporti internazionali", in *L'affidamento dei figli nella crisi della famiglia* 1088 (Sesta, Arceri eds., Turin, 2012); M. Distefano, *Interesse superiore del minore e sottrazione internazionale di minori* 79 ss (Padua, 2012). On the conciliation function of the central authorities see *Article 11 Working Group – Information on national proceedings*, which may be found *online* at https://e-justice.europa.eu/fileDownload.do?id=6c30ffe7-40e7-4d9a-96b0-7c9a14370c3 c, at 8.

4 E. g., reading the statistics, one finds that Italy has far more "outgoing" abduction cases than incoming and that, as a rule, in deciding incoming cases, Italian courts are ready to order the return of abducted children: see C. HONORATI, "La prassi italiana sul ritorno del minore sottratto ai sensi dell'art. 11 par. 8 del regolamento Bruxelles II-bis", 50 *Riv. Dir. Int. Priv. Proc.* 280 (2015).

lation 2201\2003 (the so-called Bruxelles II bis);[5,6] the ECtHR's role is to enforce the application of the European Convention on Human Rights (ECHR) and in particular Art. 8 on the right to the protection of family life.

(II) The Approach of the CJEU to the "Automatic Return" Principle

As is well-known, in relation to child abduction, EU Regulation 2201\2003 aims at implementing the provisions of the Hague Convention of 1980 in the relations between the Member States (see, in particular, Arts. 59, 60 and 62),[7] by way of integration of the two legal instruments.[8]

The Regulation makes the principle of automatic return of an abducted child, sanctioned by Art. 4 of the Hague Convention, even stricter among the Member States, giving the final word on such return to the courts of the State of origin, whose decisions are deemed to prevail over any potentially conflicting decisions granted in the State of abduction.

In other words, even though the Hague Convention allows the courts of the State where a minor has been abducted to deny the minor's return under some specific exceptions (see, in particular, Arts. 13 and 20), according to EU Regulation 2201, the application of such exceptions by the courts of the State where the minor has been brought fall to be reviewed by the courts of origin,[9] whose decisions may therefore prevail over a con-

5 In the words of Lord Wilson in U. K. Supreme Court, 15 January 2014, case *In the matter of LC (Children)*, in [2014] *UKSC* 1, "B2R has added a dramatic further dimension to proceedings under the Convention in which the application is for the child's return to a fellow EU state".

6 See, for further bibliographic and case law reference, M.A. Lupoi, "Il regolamento (CE) n. 2201/2003 del Consiglio, del 27 novembre 2003, relativo alla competenza, al riconoscimento e all'esecuzione delle decisioni in materia matrimoniale e in materia di responsabilità genitoriale", in *Manuale di diritto processuale europeo* 107 (Taruffo, Varano eds., Turin, 2011).

7 *Cass.*, 14 July 2010, n. 16549, *Nuova Giur. Civ. Comm.* 130 (2011, I).

8 *Cass.*, 14 luglio 2010, n. 16549, *cit.* n. 7.

9 On the "evolution" of Regulation 2201 in this context, see E. PATAUT, in *Brussels II bis Regulation* 120 (Magnus, Mankowski eds., Munich, 2012).

flicting "no return" order rendered in the State of abduction[10] (Art. 11, para. 6-8).[11]

One could wonder whether this review mechanism really implements the principles of mutual trust and equivalence of jurisdictions on which the European space of justice is built, as the CJEU claims.[12] To give the court of origin the power to review the "no return" decisions of the courts of another Member State appears to be a denial in principle of the very notion of mutual trust.

Arguably, the European lawmaker's policy was to curtail forum shopping more than fostering mutual trust.

Moreover, decisions granted by the State of origin ordering an abducted child to be returned in compliance with Art. 11, para. 8, following a "no return decision" under Art. 13 of the Hague Convention by the foreign court, are automatically enforceable with no need of an *exequatur* (Art. 42 Reg. 2201\2003).[13]

The courts of the State of enforcement of these decisions may only verify their enforcing authority, with no means to opposing their enforcement,[14] apart from the "incompatible decision" exception under Art. 47, with reference to a conflicting decision rendered in the State of origin.[15]

The CJEU, in *Povse v. Alpago*, clarified that such enforcement may not even be denied by alleging new circumstances in the relevant facts, since such changes must be raised before the courts of the rendering State.[16]

Moreover, in *Zarraga v. Pelz*,[17] the Court ruled that the enforcement court may not oppose a return decision by saying that the court of origin has violated Art. 42 of the Regulation through a severe infringement of

---

10 See. Pataut, *cit.*, n. 9, at 130; Paton, *cit.*, n. 1, at 550; CJEU, 22 December 2010, case 491/10 PPU, *Andoni Aguirre Zarraga c. Pelz.*, ECLI: EU:C:2010:828.

11 See Pataut, *cit.*, n. 9, at 145.

12 CJEU, 11 July 2008, case 195\08 PPU, *Inga Rinau*, ECLI: EU:C:2008:406; see also C. Honorati, *cit.*, n. 4, at 276 ss.

13 For critics to this provision, see Honorati, *cit.*, n. 4, at 278.

14 CJEU, case *Andoni Aguirre Zarraga c. Pelz*, *cit.*, n. 10.

15 CJEU, 1 July 2010, case 211/10 PPU, c. *Povse c. Alpago*, ECLI: EU:C:2010:400.

16 CJEU, case *Povse c. Alpago*, *cit.*, n. 15.

17 CJEU, case *Andoni Aguirre Zarraga c. Pelz*, *cit.*, n. 10: in that case, the mother, opposing the enforcement in Germany of a Spanish return order of her son to Spain, argued that the certificate release under Art. 42 falsely declared that the duty to hear the child before the relevant decision was granted had been fulfilled.

fundamental rights: such violation may be ascertained but only by the very same courts of the State of origin.

In the context of the European space of justice, the CJEU, in applying the regulation provisions on child abduction, is somehow compelled to stress that the *ad quem* courts should defer to the decisions of the first courts and enforce the automatic return policy underlying Arts. 11 and 42, without any possibility to oppose or deny such enforcement.

In CJEU case law, moreover, human rights do come into the picture, but reference to ECtHR case law appears to be scarce.

In relations between Member States, mutual trust is the cornerstone of the whole system: this leads to the inexorable conclusion that human rights should be dealt with and protected by the courts of origin only. In other words, CJEU case law appears to be mainly concerned with the implementation of the principles of mutual trust and equivalence of jurisdictions, which are the pillars of the European common space of justice.

It is also preoccupied with enforcing the automatic enforcement principle with no hesitation, as *Povse v. Alpago* clearly shows.[18]

This "functionalist" approach also influences the style of decisions, which is rather axiomatic and sometimes characterised by statements that at times appear to be self-affirming truths.

(III) The Position of the ECtHR

On the other hand, the ECtHR has a different "political" role, i.e., to safeguard human rights and make sure that contracting States' statutes and case law do not infringe on those rights and sanction them when they happen to do so.

From the stylistic point of view, ECtHR decisions tend to be longer than those of the CJEU. The relevant facts are reported and analysed in depth. CJEU decisions are quoted as well as domestic ones.

International conventions, EU regulations, and domestic laws are analysed and compared in order to define legal notions, such as that of "best interest of the child" which, indeed, is not in itself mentioned in the Convention but is regularly referred to in the interpretation of Art. 8.

---

18 CJEU, case *Povse v. Alpago*, *cit.*, n. 15.

The ECtHR case law on child abduction is concerned neither with mutual trust nor with the principle of equivalence of jurisdictions.

Its approach is therefore rather different to that of the CJEU.

In particular, as concerns us here, in recent times, ECtHR decisions have appeared to question the application by the Member States of the automatic return principle sanctioned by the Hague Convention and made even more imperative by Regulation 2201.

In some cases, Member States have been brought before the Court in Strasbourg for allegedly violating Art. 8 of the ECHR by applying the provisions on the automatic return of the child, which they indeed had the duty to apply under the provisions of Regulation 2201\2003, as interpreted by the CJEU.

The standing point of the ECtHR is that any return order is an infringement of the right to respect family life protected by Art. 8 of the parent against whom the order is granted. [19]

This infringement, however, may be justified under three standpoints: firstly, that such interference with a fundamental right is provided for by the law; [20] secondly, that it aims at fulfilling a legitimate result or aim, as is clearly the case in matters of child abduction.

Finally, and most importantly, such interference must be deemed to be necessary in a democratic society.[21]

It is under this third standard that, in recent times, the ECtHR has been called to evaluate whether fulfilling the obligations deriving from belonging to an international organization may lead to a violation of the ECHR in this area of the law.

(IV) A "Non Mechanical" Return? The Neulinger Case

With this background, the question that this paper is concerned with is whether the principle of automatic return of abducted minors implemented by the Hague Convention and made even more imperative by EU Regulation 2201\2003 (and CJEU case law interpreting the latter's provisions) has been somehow "weakened" by ECtHR case law.

---

19 See. e. g., ECtHR, 12 July 2011, case *Šneersone and Kampanella v. Italy.*

20 See, e. g., ECtHR, 25 June 2013, case *Anghel v. Italy.*

21 See, e. g., ECtHR, case *Anghel v. Italy* , *cit.*, n. 20.

The question arises in the light of *Neulinger v. Switzerland* in 2010,[22] where the Court ruled that a child's return under the Hague Convention of 1980 cannot be ordered automatically or mechanically.[23]

In that case, a mother and her son had filed an application against the Swiss Confederation under Art. 34 of the ECHR, alleging that, by ordering the return of the son to Israel, the Federal Court had breached their right to respect for their family life as guaranteed by Art. 8, taken separately and in conjunction with Arts. 3 and 9 of the Convention.

The Court started its decision with an analysis of the 1989 United Nations Convention on the Rights of the Child and put at the centre of its reasoning the best interests of the child. It went on to state that, in this area, the decisive issue is whether a fair balance between the competing interests at stake – those of the child, of the two parents, and of public order – has been struck, within the margin of appreciation afforded to States in such matters, bearing in mind, however, that the child's best interests must be the primary consideration, as is indeed apparent from the Preamble to the Hague Convention, which provides that "the interests of children are of paramount importance in matters relating to their custody". According to the Strasbourg judges, the child's best interests may, depending on their nature and seriousness, override those of the parents. The parents' interests, especially in having regular contact with their child, nevertheless remain a factor when balancing the various interests at stake.

The Court then observed that the Hague Convention in principle requires the prompt return of the abducted child unless there is a grave risk that the child's return would expose it to physical or psychological harm or otherwise place it in an intolerable situation (Art. 13, sub-para. b)): in this light, therefore, also in the Hague Convention, the concept of the child's best interests is an underlying principle.

The Strasbourg Court, therefore, took the view that Art. 13 of the Hague Convention should be interpreted in conformity with the ECHR and that, accordingly, under Art. 8 of the latter, a child's return cannot be ordered automatically or mechanically when the Hague Convention is applicable.

According to the Court, it is on the national court to ascertain, on a case by case basis, whether the child's best interests make it appropriate for

22 Case *Neulinger and Shuruk v. Switzerland*, 6 July 2010.

23 See also ECtHR, case *Anghel v. Italy*, *cit.*, n. 20.

him to be returned to the country of origin, taking into consideration a variety of individual circumstances, in particular his age and level of maturity, the presence or absence of his parents and his environment and experiences. In this analysis, the domestic courts enjoy a certain margin of appreciation, which remains subject, however, to a European supervision whereby the Court reviews under the Convention the decisions that those authorities have taken in the exercise of that power.

In other words, according to the Court in *Neulinger*, before ordering the return of the abducted child to the country of origin, the domestic court should conduct an in-depth examination of the entire family situation and a whole series of factors, in particular of a factual, emotional, psychological, material and medical nature, and make a balanced and reasonable assessment of the respective interests of each person, with a constant concern for determining what the best solution would be for the abducted child in the context of an application for his return to his country of origin.

In the case at hand, with these premises the Court found that the Swiss courts had not paid careful attention to the facts of the case, in the necessary balance between the significant disturbance that the second applicant's forced return was likely to cause in his mind and any benefit that he might gain from it. Moreover, the Court considered that the Swiss courts had not given enough weight to the father's personal history. Conclusively, the Court came to doubt that such circumstances, assuming they are established, would be conducive to the child's well-being and development. Moreover, the Court considered that the mother's return to Israel could expose her to a risk of criminal sanctions, possibly even a prison sentence: clearly, for the Court, such a scenario would not be in the best interests of the child, since the mother was probably the only person to whom he related. The Court was thus not convinced that it would have been in the child's best interests for him to return to Israel, while the mother would have sustained a disproportionate interference with her right to respect for her family life if she were forced to return with her son to Israel.

In the end, the Court ruled that there would have been a violation of Art. 8 of the ECHR in respect of both applicants if the decision ordering the second applicant's return to Israel were to be enforced.

The idea that a domestic court should consider in a discretionary way all the relevant factor of the individual case and not order the child's return in a mechanical way could appear to be in contrast with the mechanism provided by the Hague Convention and made more imperative between the Member States by EU Regulation 2201\2003. The *Neurlinger* decision, in particular, appears to be in contrast with the "no discretion" principle enucleated by the CJEU in the *Povse* case mentioned in paragraph two.

The principles expressed in *Neurlinger* were subsequently confirmed in *Šneersone and Kampanella v. Italy* of 12 July 2011. This case, unlinke *Neulinger*, was an intra-EU case: the Italian courts had ordered an abducted child's return from Latvia and this, according to the applicants, amounted to a violation of their right under Art. 8 of the ECHR.

The Court followed the same argumentative path of *Neulinger*, requiring the domestic court to perform an in-depth analysis of the circumstances of the case and came to the conclusion that the Italian courts had not paid enough consideration to the psychological implications of the child's forced return to Italy nor to the risks referred to in the Latvian courts' decisions and that such interference with the applicants' rights was not necessary in a democratic society: as a consequence, Italy was found to be in violation of Art. 8 of the ECHR.

Interestingly, the Court stressed that in applying the Hague Convention provisions, one should always keep in mind that this Convention is essentially a procedural instrument and not a treaty on human rights, protecting persons on an objective basis: this remark appears to reduce the relevance of the Hague Convention in relation to other instruments of international law protecting fundamental rights.

(V) A Procedural "Compromise": the Povse v. Austria Case and its Progeny

These decisions were met with critical remarks by academics and case law, arguing that the Court ruling conflicted with the founding principles of the system on child abduction created by both the Convention and the Regulation.[24]

The Strasbourg Court, however, soon had the opportunity to clarify its position in relation to the application of the "automatic return" policy within the EU Member States in *Povse v. Austria*.[25]

Here, an Austrian woman had left the family home in Italy with her daughter. Proceedings were also started in Austria, on the mother's mo-

24 See e. g. HONORATI, *cit.*, n. 4, at 300.

25 ECtHR, 18 June 2013, case *Sofia Povse e Doris Povse v. Austria.*

tion. Conflicting decisions were granted in the two States in relation to the return of the child to Italy: eventually, Austrian courts had to give way and accept the fact that the Italian concurring court (the Venice Youth Court), in the application of Art. 11, para. 8 of Regulation 2201\2003, had ordered the child to be returned to the Italian father, issuing a certificate of enforceability under Article 42 of the Brussels 2 Regulation, which the father then requested to be enforced. The father's request was finally granted by the Leoben Regional Court, noting that a certificate of enforceability under Article 42 of Regulation 2201\2003 had to be recognised and enforced by the Austrian courts, with no possibility for them to establish anew whether the first applicant's return would be against her best interests. This decision was appealed by the mother before the Austrian Supreme Court (*Oberster Gerichtshof*), which requested a preliminary ruling by the CJEU.

The Luxemburg Court, at that point, released the *Povse v. Alpago* decision basically saying that enforcement of a certified judgment ordering the child's return could not be refused by the Member State of enforcement because, as a result of a subsequent change of circumstances, it might be seriously detrimental to the best interests of the child, since such a change had to be pleaded before the court which had jurisdiction in the Member State of origin which also had to hear any application to suspend the enforcement of its judgment.

At that point, the Austrian Supreme Court dismissed the mother's appeal on points of law, noting that, according to the CJEU ruling, the Austrian courts' only task was to take the necessary steps for the enforcement of the return order, without proceeding to any review of the merits of the decision and that, if the second applicant asserted that the circumstances had changed since the Venice Youth Court had given its judgment, she had to apply to that court, which would also be competent to grant such an application suspensive effect.

The case however went on, with a series of Italian and Austrian decisions concerning the child and her return to Italy. At the time the ECtHR was involved in the case, the Wiener Neustadt District Court had ordered the mother to hand over the child to her father by 7 July 2013 and had stated that in case of failure to comply coercive measures would be applied. Such order, however, at the time the Strasbourg Court rendered its decision, had not yet been enforced.

The Court started its reasoning by observing that it was not in dispute that the Austrian courts' decisions ordering the enforcement of the Venice

Youth Court's return orders interfered with the applicants' right to respect for their family life within the meaning of Article 8 of the Convention. It then went on to analyse whether such interference could anyway be tolerated under the three-pronged test mentioned earlier in this paper.

Having concluded that, in the specific case, the interference with Art. 8 was "in accordance with the law"[26] and pursued one or more of the legitimate aims referred to in paragraph 2 of that Article,[27] the Court went on to decide whether such interference was necessary in a democratic society.

As to this, the Austrian Government had submitted that the Austrian courts had merely fulfilled the obligations flowing from Austria's membership in the European Union and that all they had done was to apply the relevant provisions of the Brussels II a Regulation, as interpreted by the CJEU in its preliminary ruling of 1 July 2010. Thus, relying on the Court's *Bosphorus Hava Yolları Turizm ve Ticaret Anonim Şirketi* judgment, they contended that Austria must be presumed to have complied with the requirements of the Convention, as the protection of fundamental rights by the EU was "equivalent" to the protection provided by the Convention.

The two applicants, on the other hand, contested that there had been "equivalent protection" in the case at hand, arguing that, in contrast to the *Bosphorus* case, the CJEU had not addressed the question of a possible violation of their rights guaranteed by the Convention.

The Court recalled that, according to the *Bosphorous* decision, the mere fact that a Contracting State complies with its obligations as member of an international organisation to which it had transferred a part of its sovereignty does not completely free it from its Convention responsibility, because this would be incompatible with the purpose and object of the Convention itself, since its guarantees could be limited or excluded at will, thereby depriving it of its peremptory character and undermining the practical and effective nature of its safeguards.

---

26 In the present case the decisions ordering the enforcement of the Venice Youth Court's return orders were based on Article 42 of the Brussels II a Regulation. Since this Regulation is directly applicable in Austrian law, the Court concluded that the interference was "in accordance with the law".

27 "[T]he Court considers that the interference, which was aimed at reuniting the first applicant with her father, pursued one of the legitimate aims set out in the second paragraph of Article 8, namely the protection of the rights of others. Furthermore, the Court reiterates that compliance with European Union law by a Contracting Party constitutes a legitimate general-interest objective."

However, the Court confirmed also that action taken in compliance with such obligations is justified where the relevant organisation protects fundamental rights, as regards both the substantive guarantees offered and the mechanisms controlling their observance, in a manner which can be considered at least equivalent – that is to say not identical but "comparable" – to that for which the Convention provides.

Any such presumption, however, would be rebutted if, in the circumstances of a particular case, it is considered that the protection of Convention rights was manifestly deficient: in such cases the interest of international cooperation would be outweighed by the Convention's role as a "constitutional instrument of European public order" in the field of human rights.

The Strasbourg Court then went on to say that, as it had already found, the protection of fundamental rights afforded by the European Union is in principle equivalent to that of the Convention system as regards both the substantive guarantees offered and the mechanisms controlling their observance, with particular regard paid to the role of the CJEU.

In the case at hand, the question was whether the Austrian courts did no more than implement the legal obligations flowing from Austria's membership of the EU, without exercising any discretion, when ordering the enforcement of the Venice Youth Court's return order of 23 November 2011.

As to this, the Court had to stress that, as we have already pointed out, when it comes to the enforcement of a return decision rendered under Art. 42 of the Brussels II a Regulation, the enforcement State courts enjoy no discretion at all. It is up to the court issuing the decision under Art. 42, in fact, to make an assessment of the question whether the return will entail a grave risk for the child: as the CJEU had ruled in its decision of 1 July 2010, the enforcement court has no possibility to review the merits of a return decision taken according to Art. 42.

In such a situation, therefore, the Court ended up accepting that the Austrian courts could not and did not exercise any discretion in ordering the enforcement of the return orders and that Austria has done no more than fulfil the strict obligations flowing from its membership of the European Union.

Turning to the applicants' arguments, the Court observed that the case at hand differed from the *Bosphorous* case in so much as the CJEU had here been called upon to interpret the Brussels II a Regulation and to clarify the scope of jurisdiction of the Italian courts on the one hand and the Austrian courts on the other, without being required to rule on the alleged violation of the applicants' fundamental rights.

However, the ECtHR stressed that the CJEU had made it clear that within the framework of the Brussels II a Regulation it was for the Italian courts to protect the fundamental rights of the parties involved and that, as a consequence, the applicants' rights have to be asserted before the Italian courts, which the applicants so far had failed to do.

On these grounds, the applicants' petition was doomed to fail.

That the Court intended to take a step back in respect of *Neulinger* was confirmed by *X v. Latvia*,[28] where the Court basically examined the theoretical and practical sustainability of its own very recent case law.

As a matter of fact, the Strasbourg Court overruled its previous approach based on the external control over the activities of the convention State and ruled that the protection of the best interests of the child have to be based on a constitutionally oriented interpretation of the Hague Convention of 1980.

According to the Court, the Hague convention is grounded on the cogent presumption that returning the child to the country of origin represents the best safeguard of the best interests of the child. This presumption, however, is rebuttable, in the light of certain exceptions provided for by the Convention itself.

In other words, it is an inherent characteristic of the system created by the Convention of 1980 that the return of an abducted child should never be considered as automatic but rather a consequence of an appreciation of the best interests in the given case.

In particular, the Court was prepared to point out that para. 139 of the *Neulinger* decision did not per se establish any principle for the application of the Hague Convention by the domestic court.

What Art. 8 of the ECHR requires of the domestic authorities involved in decisions over child abduction is to genuinely take into account in their reasoning the factors which, under the Hague Convention, exclude the return of the minor must and which must be evaluated in the light of Art. 8.

When such appreciation and balance of the rule (returning the child) against the exception (not returning the child) are not duly made by the courts then Art. 8 is violated in this context.

28 26 November 2013.

The *X v. Latvia* decision reaches some sort of compromise in coming to the conclusion that Art. 8 of the ECHR imposes on the domestic authorities a particular procedural obligation: i.e., to give specific reasons in the light of the circumstances of the case.

In other words, the Court affirmed that no new limits were introduced by its case law: on the contrary, it only ruled that in applying the criteria of the Convention, courts should consider Art. 8 and give sound reasons for their decision.[29]

(VI) Concluding Remarks

The evolution of the ECtHR shows that the Court has succeeded in avoiding a sharp conflict between the ECHR and the Hague Convention of 1980.

In particular, it has made clear that the "automatic" return duty imposed by EU Regulation 2201\2003 on the Member States where the child has been abducted to under Art. 11, para. 8 and 42 is not incompatible with a case-by-case approach to the best interests of the child.

The Court, in particular, has succeeded in balancing the "automatic return principle" sanctioned, as a general rule, by the Hague Convention, with the "flexibility" somehow required by the *Neulinger* decision.

In conclusion, what the Strasbourg Court said is that human rights considerations are not part of an "external" review performed by the ECtHR but rather an "intrinsic" part of the analysis which domestic courts are re-

29 These principles have been later confirmed in *G. S. v. Georgia* of 21 July 2015, where the Court stated that Article 8 of the Convention imposes on the domestic authorities a particular procedural obligation in this respect: when assessing an application for a child's return, the courts must not only consider arguable allegations of a "grave risk" for the child in the event of return, but must also make a ruling giving specific reasons in the light of the circumstances of the case. Both a refusal to take account of objections to the return capable of falling within the scope of Articles 12, 13 and 20 of the Hague Convention and insufficient reasoning in the ruling dismissing such objections would be contrary to the requirements of Article 8 of the Convention and also to the aim and purpose of the Hague Convention. Due consideration of such allegations, demonstrated by reasoning of the domestic courts that is not automatic and stereotyped, but sufficiently detailed in the light of the exceptions set out in the Hague Convention, which must be interpreted, is necessary. This will also enable the Court, whose task is not to take the place of the national courts, to carry out the European supervision entrusted to it.

quired to made under the provisions of the Hague Convention itself (in particular, under Art. 13).

In this context, the role of the ECtHR is not to impose on domestic courts a further "exception" to the automatic return principle but rather to review the reasoning of the return decision to check whether domestic courts took every relevant circumstance of the case in applying the no return exceptions provided for by the Hague Convention.

In other words, the ECtHR, with a diplomatic and practical approach, has adopted what we could call a "procedural" solution to the potential conflict which the *Neulinger* decision had somehow created.

With specific reference to the role of the ECtHR towards EU Member States, the most recent Strasbourg case law preserves the integrity of the system created by EU Regulation EU 2201\2003 (and by the CJEU in its "interpretative" – and sometimes "creative" – function).

The Courts of the State where the child has been abducted are deemed not to infringe on Art. 8 of the ECHR when they (as they are required to) enforce decisions certified under Art. 42 of Brussels II a by the courts of origin.

This doesn't mean, however, that, in the system created by Regulation II there is no room for a review by the ECtHR as to the safeguard of the right provided for by Art. 8 when the mechanism of Art. 11, para. 8 of the Regulation itself is applied. Such review (and the applicants' petitions…) must be referred to the decisions of the courts of the State from which the child was abducted: as a matter of fact, since they have the final word as to the return of the child under Art. 11, para. 8, it is up to them to give a sound application of Art. 13 of the Hague Convention in such a way as to take into consideration the remarks of the ECtHR as to the protection of the right to family life under Art. 8.

From this point of view, the CJEU and the ECtHR appear to follow the same approach.

Collective Redress

I. Collective Due Process of Law: Reconciling Representation and Participation

Edilson Vitorelli[*]

(I) The Matter

The purpose of this study is to provide a justification for the restriction of individual participation in collective actions, in an attempt to reconcile the need for procedures to be representative with the constitutional idea of participation. As a result, it becomes possible to establish the safest parameters for the use of collective procedural techniques that require the restriction of individual participation and, therefore, justify the existence of collective actions as something more than just pragmatic necessity.

After establishing these points, I present a model of collective litigation that can be applied to any jurisdiction that values individual participation in judicial processes, but is also concerned with the peculiar needs of collective disputes, which are the fair, economical and effective resolution of claims regarding thousands or even millions of persons. This model is developed from the characteristics of collective disputes. Instead of establishing participation based on rights analyzed "ex ante", I propose that the best way to define which cases deserve greater or lesser participation of individuals is by addressing the characteristics pertinent to the concrete case at hand. These features will be the basis of the definition of three classes of disputes, each containing their own requirements for participation.

* Associated Professor at Mackenzie Law School, Brazil. PhD in Law from Federal University of Paraná (Brazil); visiting scholar at Stanford Law School, sponsored by professor Deborah Hensler; visiting researcher at Harvard Law School, sponsored by professor David Rosenberg. Federal Prosecutor and former Federal Judge.

(II) Participation and Due Process of Law

Over the past century, the notion of procedural participation has evolved in the United States from several Supreme Court decisions into what Henry Friendly[1] described in the 1970 s as "due process explosion".[2] In *Goldberg v. Kelly,*[3] the Supreme Court held that one who is in danger of losing a social security benefit has the right to be notified and heard before security is discontinued. This opportunity is not exactly a trial, but rather a hearing before an impartial authority with competence to hear and question witnesses and to receive a written reasoned decision, based only on legal rules and the facts found in the audience. Thus, an informal hearing does not satisfy this need.

Another important decision in that period is *Wolff v. McDonnell*[4] (1974), in which the Supreme Court affirmed the right of prisoners to be heard before disciplinary measures were employed against them. This precedent is in the context of a number of other cases related to due process for the benefit of prisoners and convicts[5] and also cites other situa-

1 H. Friendly, "Some Kind of hearing", 123 *University of Pennsylvania Law Review* 1267 (1975). Friendly, who died in 1986, was a Judge in the 2nd Circuit Court of Appeals for nearly 20 years. He was the first student to graduate from Harvard Law School *summa cum laude* in 1927. This information is provided by the Harvard Crimson newspaper on June 23, 1927.

2 See in the Supreme Court *Board of Regents of State Colleges v. Roth*, 408 US. 564 (1972) and *Perry v. Sindermann*, 408 US. 593 (1972). See also D. Mixon, "Procedural Law Due Process and the Teacher", 29 *Arkansas Law Review* 87 (1975).

3 397 US. 254 (1970).

4 418 US. 539 (1974).

5 In *Morrissey v. Brewer*, 408 US. 471 (1972), the Supreme Court stipulated the following requirements for the revocation of parole: "(a) written notice of the claimed violations of parole; (b) disclosure to the parolee of evidence against him; (c) opportunity to be heard in person and to present witnesses and documentary evidence; (d) the right to confront and cross-examine adverse witnesses (unless the hearing officer specifically finds good cause for not allowing confrontation); (e) a 'neutral and detached' hearing body such as a traditional parole board, members of which need not be judicial officers or lawyers; and (f) a written statement by the factfinders as to the evidence relied on and reasons for revoking parole". In *Gagnon v. Scarpelli*, 411 U. S. 778 (1973), the same requirements were applied to non-compliance with probation rules. As regards this matter, please see. J.C. Rea, "Procedural Due Process in Parole Release Decisions", 18 *Arizona Law Review* 1023 (1976). In Brazil, the Superior Court of Justice has examined a number of similar cases also concerning criminal execution, and producing similar findings to those produced in

tions, in which the Supreme Court had affirmed the right of anyone to be heard before issuing decisions that affect them.[6] Therefore, this element of hearing interested parties has been regarded as an essential part of due process.[7] Finally, the *due process* clause was applied in this period to the most diverse contexts, such as rights as varied as those of car drivers, employees, students and many others referred to in the 798 footnotes of the thorough work penned by Doug Rendleman.[8]

---

the United States, in the sense that the convicted must be provided the right to be heard before the criminal offence committed during the execution is taken into effect. V. HC 196,126 / SC, Assigned Justice Marco Aurélio Bellizze, Fifth Panel, trial date: 22/05/2012.

6 "This analysis as to liberty parallels the accepted due process analysis as to property. The Court has consistently held that some kind of hearing is required at some time before a person is finally deprived of his property interests". *Anti-Fascist Committee v. McGrath*, 341 U. S. 123, 341 U. S. 168 (1951) (Frankfurter, J., concurring). The requirement for some kind of a hearing applies to the taking of private property, *Grannis v. Ordean*, 234 U. S. 385 (1914), the revocation of licenses, *In re Ruffalo*, 390 U. S. 544 (1968), the operation of state dispute settlement mechanisms, when one person seeks to take property from another, or to government-created jobs held, absent "cause" for termination, Board of *Regents v. Roth*, 408 U. S. 564 (1972); *Arnett v. Kennedy*, 416 U. S. 134, 416 U. S. 164 (1974) (J. Powell, concurring); id. at 416 U. S. 171 (WHITE, J., concurring in part and dissenting in part); id. at 416 U. S. 206 (Marshall, J., dissenting). Cf. *Stanley v. Illinois*, 405 U. S. 645, 405 U. S. 652-654 (1972); *Bell v. Burson*, 402 U. S. 535 (1971).

7 For example: *Joint Anti-Fascist Refugee Committee v. McGrath* 341 US. 123 (1951): "One of these principles is that no person shall be deprived of his liberty without opportunity, at some time to be heard". *The Japanese Immigrant Case*, 189 U. S. 86 (1903): "By 'due process' is meant one which, following the forms of law, is appropriate to the case, and just to the parties to be affected. It must be pursued in the ordinary mode prescribed by the law; it must be adapted to the end to be attained; and wherever it is necessary for the protection of the parties, it must give them an opportunity to be heard respecting the justice of the judgment sought". *Hagar v. Reclamation District*, 111 U. S. 701 (1884): "Before its property can be taken under the edict of an administrative officer, the appellant is entitled to a fair hearing upon the fundamental facts". *Southern Railway Co. v. Virginia*, 290 US. 190 (1933): "Whether acting through its judiciary or through its Legislature, a state may not deprive a person of all existing remedies for the enforcement of a right, which the state has no power to destroy, unless there is, or was, afforded to him some real opportunity to protect it". Brinkerhoff-Faris Trust & *Savings Co. v. Hill*, 281 U.S. 673 (1930): "the judgment violates due process of law, in its primary sense of an opportunity to be heard and to defend one's substantive right".

8 D. Rendleman, "The new due process: rights and remedies", 63 *Kentucky Law Journal* 531(1975).

Nevertheless, affirming the importance of participation in a process does not answer what role that participation plays. As the Supreme Court of the United States has stated for more than a century, the core of due process is clear: those whose rights will be affected have the right to be heard and, therefore, must be notified.[9] But why is that? Is the Supreme Court correct when it states that a substantially proper decision is improper if it disregards the right to participate in the process and, on the contrary, a substantially reprehensible rule can be considered adequate if it is applied in a procedurally appropriate way? It is true that the right to be heard has been culturally introjected in humanity long before the actual drafting of due process.[10] Nevertheless, that does not say much about its role in the process.

Stephen Subrin and Richard Dykstra[11] mention that although the courts are eloquent so as to guarantee this right, they hardly address the reasons for its importance. Reasons given for participation in the process are quite varied. On one side, Carnelutti and others consider participation as a means to obtain a good decision and not an end in itself.[12] In their view, participation is of an instrumental nature, allowing the parties and the judge to assist one another in order to achieve the best procedural result possible. On the other hand, others believe that participation in an adversary proceeding is its very essence, and they deem it inappropriate to even name something that does not provide for participation as procedure.[13]

9 Judge Stewart's opinion in *Fuentes v. Shevin*, 407 US. 67 (1972): "For more than a century, the central meaning of procedural due process has been clear: "Parties whose rights are to be affected are entitled to be heard; and in order that they may enjoy that right, they must first be notified". *Baldwin v. Hale*, 1 Wall. 223, 68 U. S. 233. See Windsor v. McVeigh, 93 U. S. 274; *Hovey v. Elliott*, 167 U. S. 409; *Grannis v. Ordean*, 234 U. S. 385. It is equally fundamental that the right to notice and an opportunity to be heard "must be granted at a meaningful time and in a meaningful manner": *Armstrong v. Manzo*, 380 U. S. 545, 380 U. S. 552.

10 H. W. R. Wade, C. F. Forsyth, *Administrative Law* 403 (10th Edition, Oxford: OUP, 2009).

11 S. Subrin, R. Dykstra, "Notice and the right to be heard: the significance of old friends", 9 *Harvard Civil Rights: Civil Liberties Law Review* 449 (1974).

12 F. Carnelutti, *Lezioni di diritto processuale civile* 168 (II vol, Padova, CEDAM, 1933). The writer believes that the adversary nature "is a means and not an end in itself (...) since the enforcement of the law through the means of a fair decision can be reached even in the absence of the parties".

13 I. W. Sarlet, L. G. Marinoni, D. Mitidiero, *Curso de direito constitucional* 647 (São Paulo, Editora Revista dos Tribunais, 2012).

Fazzalari, for instance, affirms that a process is the procedure that develops in an adversary manner.[14] It follows from this that the judicial activity necessarily involves participation.[15]

Regardless of what aspect of it is considered - and many writers, although they don't elaborate the distinction much, emphasize both the inner and the instrumental values of participation – these positions raise strong objections to justify the possibility of conducting any procedures of a merely representative nature. If participation is essential for a process to be legitimate, it is impossible to justify a collective process, in which the true holders of substantive rights do not participate, as they are merely represented by legal advisors. If participation is perceived as being instrumental, then the difficulty of justifying a procedure by representation is reduced but revising elements firmly established in the procedural doctrine is still necessary, including the possibility that the participation of the interested parties is dispensable for an adequate decision to be obtained. In order to do so, the current procedural theory must be seen from a different perspective.

(III) Outcome-based Approaches and Process-based Approaches

Finding a possible coexistence between participation and representation demands revising elements of both concepts. Those who write about participation (or the adversary system, for that matter), whether in Brazil or abroad, in the context of individual proceedings, insist that participation is essential for procedures in such a way that representation would either hinder or make it very difficult for procedures to be developed in the prop-

14 "If the procedure is regulated in such a way that those who shall be affected by the decision also take part in the proceedings (and, therefore, the plaintiff should be informed of their participation), and if such participation is provided in such a way that the other "interested" parties (those who aspire for a decision - i.e., "interested" in the strict sense of the word - and those who want to avoid such a decision - the defendants or "counterinterested") are in a situation of symmetric equality; then the procedure is adversarial, articulated and complex. In that case, from the genre "procedure", one can branch out the species "process". E. Fazzalari, *Istituzioni di diritto processuale* 60 (Padova, CEDAM, 1992).

15 A. Frassinetti, *La notificazione nel processo civile* 1 (Roma, Giuffrè, 2012), states the following: "The judicial activity is participative by nature, in any of its manifestations".

er manner. On the other hand, those who accept representation as an alternative for participation shall consider the possibility that the lawmaker may institute virtually any other species of representative litigation without crossing constitutional principles, thus excluding individuals from procedures in which their own rights are being debated.

Robert Bone divides the many conceptions regarding process and participation into two categories: *outcome based approaches* and *process based approaches.*[16] An outcome based approach is concerned with the instrumental value of participation; i.e., it holds that this is a value as long as it provides a boost in the quality of the procedural outcome. According to Laurence Tribe, due process in its instrumental aspect ensures that the rules of conduct set by society as well as the benefits of distribution rules are correctly and consistently applied. The process uses participation to implement the rule of law and will be valuable to ensure the application of the rules concerning substantive law to the situation brought into court.[17]

A process based approach assumes that participation is an important procedural value in itself, regardless of its contribution to the procedure's outcome. Lon Fuller[18] states that adjudication is distinguished from other forms of social organization in society, such as voting and contracts, because

> "the distinguishing characteristic of adjudication lies in the fact that it confers on the affected party a peculiar form of participation in the decision, that of presenting proofs and reasoned arguments for a decision in his favor. Whatever heightens the significance of this participation lifts adjudication toward its optimum expression. Whatever destroys the meaning of that participation destroys the integrity of adjudication itself".

The best decision or the best possible realization of the substantive right would still be worthy of criticism if it were obtained without proper safeguarding of the parties' participation rights. Robert Bone mentions that the reasons for that are variable, which was also addressed in the previous item. Some argue that participation is essential in order to defend the dig-

---

16 R. Bone, "Rethinking the "day in court" ideal and nonparty preclusion", 67 (2) *New York Law Review* 193 (1992). Laurence Tribe (see n. 17) shares Bone's view and uses the expressions "intrinsic and instrumental values of procedural due process".

17 L. Tribe, *American Constitutional Law* 666 (2nd ed., Mineola, The Foundation Press Inc, 1988).

18 L. L. Fuller, "The Forms and Limits of Adjudication", 92 *Harvard Law Review*, 353, 354 (1978).

nity of the parties against state action embodied in the court decision,[19] or that it is symbolic of individual equality, or that it tends to promote civic virtues, since the individual contributes to the construction of state action.[20] There are also those who conceive of participation as a realization of the very concept of rights adjudication, which can be done by any means, including court.[21] Laurence Tribe states that there is an intrinsic value in the right to be heard because it guarantees individuals against whom state decisions operate an opportunity to express their dignity as persons.[22] Whatever the outcome of the procedure, this type of hearing provides an opportunity which Tribe calls "a valuable human interaction", in which people who will be affected by the decision at least have the satisfaction of participating in its formation and eventually receive an explanation of its motives.[23]

(a) Would the Process Survive without Participation? Critique to the Notion of Essential Participation.

All the above arguments put the idea of procedural representation in check. When it is taken seriously, the postulate that participation is an absolute principle, and therefore there is no process without the right to participate, means very little remains to legitimize a process in which the holders of rights have no opportunity to participate and they are not bound either legally or de facto to each other or their representative. In such a context, one could derive that the representative's performance, for some reason, would be equivalent to that of the persons s/he is representing and who are not present.[24] However, contrary to this reasoning, none of the ar-

19 "Focus on results makes us forget that the procedure is what rules the many forms of power". A. P. Cabral, *Nulidades no proceso moderno* 171 (2nd ed., Rio de Janeiro, Forense, 2010).

20 Bone, *supra* n. 16, at 202.

21 This is the case of Fuller, *supra* n. 18.

22 Tribe, *supra* n. 17, at 666.

23 Tribe, *supra* n. 17 at 666.

24 Bone expresses this concern in the following manner: "the principle of litigative autonomy cannot limit autonomy claims where there is no relationship of any kind between the party and the absentee. This fact has serious implications for mass tort and mass accident cases. With a few possible exceptions, process-oriented theory should guarantee injured parties in such cases a chance to make their own strategic

guments supporting the right to participate, as mentioned in the previous item, is exempt from criticism. In the words of Cynthia Farina, "we seem unable to make peace with due process".[25]

When the reasons for demanding participation begin to be closely analyzed, their power of persuasion is reduced. The alleged connection between the process and the democratic state, for example, which seems to be one of the most compelling reasons to consider participation in the process as an essential characteristic of it, derives most of its appeal from motives of an emotional nature. After all, according to Lawrence Sager, concepts such as democracy and popular sovereignty are difficult and problematic, because they have an appeal which is elastic and deeply rooted in our values.[26] Assuming that certain procedural characteristics which have only recently been incorporated would be intrinsically linked to the concept of democracy is not historically accurate.

In connection with the argument of democracy, one commonly states that participation is essential because it prevents the judge's abuse of authority by submitting his/her conduct to the supervision of the parties. Although the problem presented here indeed occurs, it isn't intrinsically connected to participation in the process. Conceiving of a non-participatory process that nevertheless adopts containment mechanisms of authority is perfectly possible. That could be the case, for example, by use of correctional mechanisms and mandatory revisions, as well as the compulsory disclosure of decisions, which would expose them to social control. All of this does not depend on the participation of specific individuals, whether or not they are affected by the decision. Participation can be a form of authority control, but it is not the only one, nor is there convincing evidence that it is the most effective one.

Like Louis Kaplow, one may object that, in real life, the only persons who are going to complain about their participation (or lack thereof) in a process are those who didn't obtain the results they had longed for. If this

---

choices-unless, of course, there is some reason to doubt the coherence of process-oriented theory". Bone, *supra* n. 16 at 266.

25 C. Farina, "Conceiving due process", 3 (2) *Yale Journal of Law and Feminism* 189 (1991). Similarly, see T. Terrell, "Liberty and Responsibility in the Land of New Property: Exploring the Limits of Procedural Due Process". 39 (2) *University of Florida Law Review* 351 (1987), criticizing the Supreme Court for failing to give a coherent meaning to due process.

26 L. Sager, "The incorrigible constitution", 65 *New York University Law Review* 983 (1990).

is true, it is more likely that they complain because they believe that their participation could have led to a different result. In that case, their concern regarding their participation is of a instrumental and not of an essential nature.[27] Even Laurence Solum, who advocates for the establishment of purely procedural criteria, concedes that dignity is not an appropriate criterion to support the value of participation for two reasons: firstly, because all the participation in the world would not justify a fraudulent trial, and secondly, because participation is unlikely to overcome other elements such as the accuracy of the result.[28]

Another argument given is that participation would be essential for the process to be legitimate. Laurence Tribe defends a rather dynamic view of due process, which is centered in the development of policies over time, taking into account not only the results obtained but also the decision-making process itself.[29] The requirement for participation in the process is regarded as a value shared by the community, and therefore constitutes an element of its legitimacy. However, contrary to what Tribe defends, in practical terms, it is not so easy to define whether the impression of legitimacy one derives from one's right to participate is linked to the participation itself or the perception that participation provides better results. Both laymen and experts tend to say that the greatest defects of the civil process are its delay and ineffectiveness, not the lack of opportunities to participate. This suggests that the process is seen primarily from a perspective of the results one can achieve with it, which requires legitimation by its ends, and not by its means.

Nevertheless, even if one considered hypothetically that persons could be completely excluded from taking part in a process and that this should be enough to create the feeling that the process does not care about them, such a scenario would not prevent them from participating more or less in the process. Their level of participation would depend entirely on the peculiarities of each process. Participation may be important, but it should

27 L. Kaplow, "The Value of Accuracy in Adjudication: an economic analysis", 23 *The Journal of Legal Studies*, 307, 390 (1994). On page 390, the author states: "one does not often hear stories of individuals who win complaining that they did not get their day in court".

28 L. Solum, "Procedural justice", 78 *Southern California Law Review* 181, 264 (2004).

29 L. Tribe, "Structural Due process", 10 *Harvard Civil Rights-Civil Liberties Law Review* 269, 290 (1975).

also be evaluated within the system as a whole. Similarly, a restriction on participation may be assessed in relation to the reasons that motivate such a restriction.[30] After all, if one assumes that the public is perceptive enough to suffer from the restriction of participation, imagining it is also sensitive enough to understand the motivation for this restriction is also reasonable. Thus, restricting participation in an individual litigation with unique characteristics would be considered more serious than the same restriction in situations where a person takes up very similar positions to those of several others.[31] In order to consistently assume that people are sensitive to the point of minding the reduction of their participation opportunities in the process, one must accept that they are also sensitive to the difference between these two cases and the reasons that differentiate them. In addition to that, David Rosenberg mentions a crucial point: in everyday life, participation in the process is not exercised by the party but by his attorney, so it is doubtful whether it produces any evident psychological effects evident for ordinary citizens,[32] since their effective participation is only at the end of the process, when they get to know whether they have won or lost their case.

In spite of the fact that the analysis here is focused on American doctrine, there is no evidence that the European scenario would lead to a different conclusion. Although it has valued the adversary system as a means to demonstrate that the accused person is not an object but a subject of a judicial decision, the German Constitutional Court, for example, valued the adversary system as a right to influence the progress and the outcome of the process.[33] As a result, that Court holds the view that the adversary

30 Bone, *supra* n. 16 at 235.

31 Bone, *supra* n. 16 at 235.

32 "Collective processing is berated for its 'preemption of control over litigation'. The consequences of such preemption, are expressed in the dire but cloudy terms of 'important symbolic and psychological effects'. These critics do not claim that collective processing deprives individuals of actual control over litigation, nor could they. Realistically and quite sensibly, control over tort claims, whether prosecuted separately or in the aggregate, rests largely with the expert lawyer, who normally finances the claim in return for a contingent percentage of the proceeds from the settlement or verdict. The projected appearance of a system protecting claimant autonomy may help perpetuate the perception that it is doing individual justice, but in reality, individual victims do not control their actions". D. Rosenberg, "Of End Games and Openings in Mass Tort Cases: Lessons from a Special Master", 69 *Boston University Law Review* 695, 701 (1989).

33 See, for example, BVerfGE 7, 53.

system is strongly tied to instrumental purposes; i.e., it is not an absolute right and is subject to weighing pros and cons arising from other interests at stake.[34] If the law sets forth that pros and cons can be weighed in relation to participation, then it cannot be regarded as essential as a constitutional value, in the sense that the term is employed here.

(b) Would the Process Survive Without Participation? Critique to the Notion of Instrumental Participation

If participation is not essential to any kind of process in a democratic state, the only thing left for a proceduralist to do is to cling to the notion of instrumental participation. After all, as affirmed by the Supreme Court of the United States, there is no better mechanism to get to the truth than to give the person whose rights are in jeopardy notice of the case and an opportunity to meet it.[35] Of course this notion is not as comfortable as that of essential participation, as it is vulnerable to the idea that, in certain cases, the right that citizens have of participating in the process can be restricted on behalf of other purposes provided that, analyzed as a whole, the procedural instrument is suited to the adjudication of substantive rights.

However, even this more nuanced view of the value of participation as a tool for obtaining a proper decision is not without criticism. Its first challenge is that it only makes sense in the context of an adjudication theory. One needs to know what outcome of the process one wishes to achieve and what the appropriate way to measure it, which can be quite controver-

34 BVerfGE 9, 89. On its 1959 decision, the Constitutional Court stated that despite the fact that the right to defend oneself was now being regarded as a constitutional basic right, nothing had changed in relation to the legitimacy of interests that oppose it and in relation to the need for a compromise to be met between those interests and the interest of those affected by the hearing. Article 103, I, GG shan't be interpreted in a manner that would reject the weighing of pros and cons regarding interests to be assessed in each type of process, not to mention the limitations to the right to defend oneself associated with it. See J. Schwabe, *Fifty Years of the German Constitutional Federal Court* 916 (Translated by B. Hennig *et. al.* Montevideo, Fundación Konrad Adenauer, 2005).

35 "No better instrument has been devised for arriving at truth than to give a person in jeopardy of serious loss notice of the case against him and the opportunity to meet it. Nor has a better way been found for generating the feeling, so important to a popular government, that justice has been done": *Joint Anti-Fascist Refugee Committee v. McGrath*, 341 US. 123 (1951).

sial. According to Robert Bone, the first possibility here is an analysis of efficiency. The process is instrumentally appropriate when it adjudicates its substantive rights in an efficient manner.[36] Nevertheless, this general concept is used by Bone in order to criticize the idea that participation in the process must necessarily be individual as a means to obtain a more accurate decision (instrumental participation).[37] The writer states that a collective process will be as accurate as a multiplicity of individual processes if conducted properly. The increase in the number of processes does not increase the system's accuracy, because the same probability that the decision of the collective process is "wrong" may befall each of the individual processes.[38]

In addition, a substantial number of scholars agree that the concept of justice in decisions should be seen not only from the perspective of the case but also from that of the system.[39] The idea that justice in the process is evaluated only in the light of each party's rights in every lawsuit entails injustice to all current and potential litigants. The total social cost of the process needs to be evaluated, including its financial cost. In a study in the 1980 s, the Rand Institute showed that for every dollar paid to the victims of disease stemming from asbestos, USD 1.56 had been spent in legal costs.[40] It is unlikely that, in the context of a state which seeks to increase access to justice, but at the same time has many other duties to comply

36 See, for example, Bone, *supra* n. 16 at 238.

37 R. Bone. *The Economics of Civil Procedure* (New York, Foundation Press, 2003), and in general, R. A. Posner, *Economic analysis of law* (9th ed. Austin, Wolters Kluwer, 2014).

38 Bone, *supra* n. 16 at 240.

39 J. O. Newman, "Rethinking Fairness: Perspectives on the Litigation Process", 94 *Yale Law Journal* 1643, 1644 (1985). On page 1644, the writer states the following: "A broadened concept of fairness - one that includes fairness not only toward litigants in an individual case but also to all who use or wish to use the litigation system and to all who are affected by it - can lead to changes that directly confront the challenges of delay and expense. Rethinking the concept of fairness can produce a litigation system that broadly achieves fairness. (...) We must then determine whether that incremental benefit to the litigants in each case justifies the delays and consequent loss of fairness to all others affected by the litigation process (...) Fairness of system reflects the aggregate impact of the litigation process upon the lives of all actual and potential litigants".

40 J. S. Kalalik et. al. *Variation in asbestos litigation compensation and expenses* 89 (Santa Monica, Rand, the institute for civil justice, 1984).

with, one can sustain that the exercise of procedural rights is more important than any cost projections.

The final challenge of instrumental participation is to determine if it effectively ensures better substantial results. Jerry Mashaw opines that this is not the case, at least not in all contexts. Working with administrative processes in which social benefits were cut, Mashaw states that a participatory structure may, depending on the situation, have the side effect of generating opposition among those involved: each party becomes entrenched in their position, therefore becoming insignificant from the perspective of results obtained.[41] Thus, even in its weakest form, it is impossible to ascertain that participation contributes to better decisions in all cases.

(IV) A New Concept of Procedural Participation

In light of all the above, one can conclude that, contrary to doctrine and jurisprudence, participation in the process is not so important in the current legal system, either as an instrumental element of the process or, even less, as an essential element of it. Participation in the process is not a right that can be regarded as essential or inherent to the civil process structure, as it is not directly linked to guarantees of dignity, democracy or the individual's satisfaction with the process. Participation is an instrument for the materialization of substantive rights can and must be exercised within the limits in which it contributes to this purpose and in accordance with systemic considerations that go beyond individual litigation. Accidentally, the right to participate in the process can contribute to democracy, to dignity or the satisfaction of individuals, but it can also be disregarded whenever other values that the law deems as more important are being curbed by demands for participation. Therefore, participation is not the only means of obtaining representative processes.

However, the challenge here is balancing how to restrict participation effectively. The right to participate in the process is deeply inserted into the notions of justice in the Western world and there are moral reasons that support this notion. Being an instrumental value does not mean not to

41 J. L. Mashaw, "The management side of due process: some theoretical and litigation notes on the assurance of accuracy, fairness, and timeliness in the adjudication of social welfare claims" 59 *Cornell Law Review* 772 (1974).

have value, but the need to be seen in the context of a system that seeks to establish fair processes that must be regarded beyond the parties in litigation, taking into account all the millions of cases that are processed by courts every year.

What elements should be taken into consideration to restrict participation effectively? What should be the parameters used to create a system which restricts or at times suppresses participation for important reasons – i.e., to enable the use of class proceedings - and, at the same time, is able to materialize substantive rights involved in litigation?

One should notice, at the preliminary, two important points. First, even if participation is not an essential feature of every lawsuit, representation is also a quite problematic concept, both in political science and in civil procedure. As will be detailed in the next topic, it is not possible to assume that a process can have effects on people who were prevented from intervening, just because someone is supposed to talk on their behalf. Participation and representation are both complex concepts that have to be combined in order to forge a new idea of collective redress. It is pivotal to define, at least, on behalf of whom the representative is acting, how the represented group is going to control his/hers actions and how free the representative is to infer the will and the interests of the group.

Second, the right to participate in a lawsuit does not mean, necessarily, to have standing to bring the case. As French correctly pointed out, "it may be only an historical accident that most legal cases are cases in which 'the subject of right X' and 'the administrator of right X' are co-referential"..[42] In many occasions, such as in criminal offences, it is not the right-holder that can bring the lawsuit, and this does not imply that the rights that were violated are held by the state or by the prosecution office.[43] Therefore, it is possible to advocate the prerogative of the right-holders to participate in representative lawsuits, without having to propose changes in the standing rules. Standing, in collective disputes, has much more to

42 P. A. French, "The corporation as a moral person", 16 (3) *American Philosophical Quarterly* 207, 210 (1979).

43 This circumstance is also highlighted by M. A. Jovanovic. *Collective Rights: a legal theory* (Cambridge, CUP, 2012). Some countries, such as Spain, however, allow private prosecution ("acusador particular") in criminal cases, but this is highly unusual. The provision is article 102 of the Spanish Criminal Code (Ley de Enjuiciamiento Criminal).

do with the ability of the representative party to properly conduct the lawsuit, than with the identity of the right-holders.

(V) Who is Entitled to Collective Rights?

Defining what collective rights are and who is entitled to them is not an easy task. The environment, public safety, preservation of historical heritage, and consumer market integrity are rights that make no sense if thought of purely from an individual point of view. The explanatory memorandum of the Model Code of Collective Processes for Ibero-America deems clear "the social dimension of recognition and protection of trans-individual rights and interests, because they are common to a community of people, and only to these".[44] The reality of such legal theory couldn't be more far-fetched from this supposed clarity. There is no definition of what this "community" would be and how they would be entitled to such rights. Until the 1980 s, Brazilian law suggested that the environment was a property of the state, which was bound to protect it in the same manner it protected public property. The problem is that the state is often the cause of environmental damage. This poses an inconvenience to have this tortfeasor as an entity which is entitled to rights over the environment. This is debated in *Chevron v. Ecuador,* in which the defendant claims to have been discharged by the Ecuadorian government in relation to environmental damage caused. Should that be the case, such a discharge would make the collective action for environmental damages impossible. Damages in that collective action were as high as USD 9.5 billion. However, writers state that the discharge granted by Ecuador prevents only the filing of a lawsuit by the public entity, but not by the citizens, who are also entitled to the damaged environmental heritage.

To avoid assigning the entitlement of collective rights to the state, Brazilian writers usually consider them as belonging to "all" or to "society" or even to a "collectivity". The matter is that not all environmental damage concerns everyone equally. It is true, for example, that air pollution in a city matters much more to the inhabitants of that city than to peo-

---

44 R. Berizonce, A. P. Grinover, A. L. Sosa, "Explanatory memorandum of Collective Process Model Code for Iberoamerica". Available at http://www.pucsp.br/tutelacoletiva/download/codigomodelo_exposicaodemotivos_2_28_2_2005.pdf, last visited 16 March 2017.

ple living thousands of kilometers away. Environmental damage resulting from the installation of a hydroelectric power plant concerns the inhabitants of the region much more than it would concern people who do not reside there.[45]

Another difficult matter in the current debate on the entitlement of the trans-individual rights is whether the reference to all or to society is actually addressed to all the inhabitants (or to society) of a country, and to each state recognized by international law, or if there is a transnational entitlement to these assets. In other words, does the Brazilian environment belong to all Brazilians or instead to all the inhabitants of the planet? This information is usually hidden behind the mask of calling these groups or individuals who hold such rights as "undetermined and indeterminable".[46]

Nevertheless, this information is essential. To claim that a diffuse right belongs only to the population or to the Brazilian society sounds like one is laying the concept down on a nationalist view from the nineteenth century. Such a view is disconnected from the globalized world, which is mainly characterized by the trans-nationalization of the nation-state's regulation and by the progressive irrelevance of political boundaries.[47] The fact that trans-national collective disputes tend to repeat themselves over time only serves to demonstrate how dated such a nationalist concept is. Ricardo Luis Lorenzetti states that a number of new risks have been created which potentially affect individuals beyond national borders, due to the mass society system and the global economy we live in today.[48] Michele Taruffo also points to the problem, noting that "in today's globalized world, serving justice and protecting rights cannot be regarded - as it has

45 Remo Caponi also realized the inadequacy of the classification of trans-individual rights as indivisible, and sensed the need for a sub-classification, while adopting a different perspective from the one defended here. According to Caponi, it is necessary to differentiate the trans-individual rights which are also individual, such as the protection of the competition market, from trans-individual rights that are nothing but trans-individual, as in the case of false advertising. R. Caponi, "Tutela collettiva: interessi proteti e modelli processuale" in: *Dall'azione inibitoria all'azione risarcitoria collettiva* 129, 142 (Bellelli ed. Padova, CEDAM, 2009).

46 J. C. Barbosa Moreira, *Temas de direito processual civil*: *terceira série* 174 (São Paulo, Saraiva, 1984).

47 In this sense, please see B. S. Santos. *La Globalización del Derecho*: *los nuevos caminos de la regulación y la emancipación* 74 (Bogota, ILSA, 1998).

48 R. L. Lorenzetti, *Justicia colectiva* 13 (Santa Fe, Rubinzal-Culzoni, 2010).

been until now - as issues pertaining only to the post-Westphalian sovereignty of nation-states".[49]

Because of this theoretical obscurity, which allowed for collective rights to be entitled to a "society" whose outlines are not clearly defined, the legal defense of those rights was attributed, in Brazil, to public and private institutions that have no personal interest in the cause, mainly the Prosecution Service. The reasoning behind this is that as the members constituting Brazilian society are somewhat difficult to pinpoint, it suffices for them to be represented by a state agency, which is granted independence.[50] In order to avoid that individuals are harmed by the fact that proceedings might be poorly conducted by the entity with legitimacy to take part in the process, the rules were set forth in such a manner that *res judicata* shall not be definitive, which means that it is possible, under certain circumstances, to file a second lawsuit regarding the same matter which had been rejected by court.[51]

The Brazilian collective process disregards the actual situation of individuals to consider, instead, that their rights may be collectively protected, since they belong to a collectivity in broad terms. This is very different from the North-American system, in which the matter is resolved on the basis of how homogeneous the rights of class members are or not. In a *class action*, the representative must demonstrate the existence of factual or legal issues that the class members hold in common. The idea here is that a person acts on behalf of others due to their rights in common: this means that one's performance in the process is motivated by the need to

49 M. Taruffo, "Notes on the collective protection of rights", *I Conferencia Internacional y XXIII Jornadas Iberoamericanas de derecho procesal: procesos colectivos class actions* 23, at 27 (2012).

50 The Brazilian Prosecution Service's layout differs entirely from that of its North-American counterpart (the US Department of Justice). The Brazilian Prosecution Service is not organized hierarchically and its prosecutors are as autonomous as judges are in the carrying out of their official duties, which includes filing collective actions.

51 In fact, the aforementioned statement has been disputed by many respected writers, one of the most prominent being A. Gidi, *Coisa julgada e litispendência em ações coletivas* (Res judicata and lis pendens in collective actions) (São Paulo, Editora Saraiva, 1995). Data hasn't been found to demonstrate what the theory establishes, i.e., that a lawsuit which had originally been rejected by the court has indeed been filed a second time around. This means that these Brazilian legal provisions are, in fact, more theoretical than effective.

defend oneself in the best way possible. In doing so, one also represents all those who have the same right(s).

The underlying problem in both systems is the nature of representation in the collective process. Obviously the representative is not a mere spokesman for the group of plaintiffs. Nevertheless, s/he is also not someone who represents others if s/he says "yes" in all situations in which the plaintiffs would say "no".[52] As it is taken for granted that not all the holders of rights shall take part in the collective action, at least not at all times, one must create some kind of mechanism to ensure that the representative will perform in the best interests of his/her representees. The problem is that if this mechanism is very demanding, it will jeopardize representation, therefore jeopardizing the process. If it is too changeable, the bond between representative and representees shall be broken. As a consequence, the representative will perform as s/he sees fit, thus imposing undesirable results on his/her representees. To make matters worse, the latter wouldn't have had the opportunity to oppose such actions.

It follows from this that the main issue involved in collective actions is how to balance the relationship between the representatives in the process and those they represent, who are absent from the process. Participation and representation are essential elements in shaping collective actions, but the permanent tension between the two forces has yet to be further researched in both legal systems.

What I propose here is an attempt at creating a criterion for shaping this relationship. In my proposal, I assume that collective rights belong to a society. But what society is being addressed here? This concept seems to be deceptively simple but is rather one of the most complex concepts in sociology. This study adopts a classification regarding the concepts of society as created by Anthony Elliott and Bryan Turner. Because of that, I shall firstly explain this classification so that I can clarify how rights can be attributed to the groups.

(VI) The Concept of Society

The word "society", according to Elliott and Turner, does not denote any identifiable or definable quality throughout sociology. In fact, the concept

52 H. F. Pitkin, *The concept of representation* 146 (Berkeley, UCP, 1984).

has long represented (and still represents) a challenge to the work of sociology.[53] Society, for Elliott and Turner, is one of the most difficult and confusing terms, as perceived by classical sociology to the present day,[54] especially because the world is not the same as when the primary concepts which came to be sociology were formulated by Durkheim, Simmel, Weber and Marx. There are even those who propose that in a globalized world, where telecommunications are an ever present reality, there is no point in fixing a concept for society, since it will define a temporary cooperation, made up of arrangements and rearrangements.[55]

Defining society, therefore, is not an easy task, not even for the sociologist. This is a "zombie category", as Ulrich Beck phrased it.[56] In an attempt to reconstruct the concept, Anthony Elliott and Bryan Turner argue that the various conceptions of society, which can be found in the writings of several sociologists can be classified into three groups: a) society as structure; b) society as solidarity or communities of care and consensus; and c) society as a creative process or the imaginary dimensions of communication and sociability.[57]

Society as structure is the collectivity of concepts that classify society as a discourse of social order, rules and structure. In this view, the group has priority over the individual. It is a line of thought that originates with the classic sociology of Durkheim[58] and Marx. Society as structure is

---

53 A. Elliott, B. S. Turner, *On Society*, 1 (Cambridge, Polity Press, 2012).

54 Elliott, Turner, *supra* n. 53, at 2.

55 Elliott, Turner, *supra* n. 53, at 6. The writers emphasize the fact that this criticism about the uselessness or the impossibility of drawing a concept for society can be found in an article from 1912, as written by Albion W. Small, which comes to illustrate that the concept has been giving people pause for longer than it may initially seem.

56 "Zombie categories are 'living dead' categories which govern our thinking but are not really able to capture the contemporary milieu". D. Slater, G. Ritzer, "Interview with Ulrich Beck", 1 *Journal of Consumer Culture* 261, 261 (2001).

57 Slater, Ritzer, *supra* n. 56, at 20.

58 Slater, Ritzer, *supra* n. 56, at 35. This interpretation is not unanimous among sociologists. Pedro Bodê de Moraes, for example, states that "contrary to what is said about the absence of the individual or rather his alleged unimportance in Durkheim's theory, we believe that the notion of individual is just one of the major points of inflection and tension in the French sociologist's text (...). P. R. B. Moraes, "Émile Durkheim: para uma Sociologia do mundo contemporáneo" in: *Tecendo o presente - oito autores para pensar o século XX* (Codato ed., Curitiba, Sesc/PR, 2006).

deeply interwoven with the theory of the state, which is its most obvious manifestation. Durkheim describes society as an organic whole, and not as an aggregation of individuals, while the state is responsible for providing the overall direction of society.[59] Individual rights can only flourish under the protection of state authority. Consequently, the state inherently represents the interests of the governed individuals.[60]

The second classification of this analysis is called society as solidarity. Here one shall find the writers concerned with the concepts of community and social solidarity, as united by the discourse that seeks the realization of an ideal care, affection and empathy, which should be able to create a sense of community. Elliott and Turner classify Ferdinand Tönies, Hegel and Habermas[61] as belonging to this group, suggesting that this line of thought gained momentum shortly after the World War II when Keynesian policies introduced into Europe the idea that the state should pay for provisions that allow the welfare of citizens.

Society as solidarity is a "*sticky society*", as it is a society that values the loyalty of its members to the group. In this sense, becoming part of society is extremely hard, which implies, for instance, restrictions on migration, while also making it somewhat difficult to leave such society, as abandonment is characterized often as disloyalty or even treason.[62] The theories of society as solidarity assume that the natural affection and the existing dialogue in the communities are the basis for democracy. Moral codes are freely shared among different groups of individuals.

Finally, Elliot and Turner elaborate the concept of society as creation. The attempt here is to go beyond abstraction of society as a structure, a concept which ignores the uniqueness of the individual as well as the nostalgia and sentimentality of society as solidarity. The central point for these theories is social creativity and openness to innovation. There is an

59 Moraes, *supra* n. 58, at 50. See the general theory of E. Durkheim, *Da divisão do trabalho social* (2nd ed., Translation into Portuguese by Eduardo Brandão, São Paulo, Editora Martins Fontes, 1999). The characteristics described in the text allow for one to classify Durkheim in line with the so-called structural functionalism.

60 A. Giddens, *A contemporary critique of historical materialism: the Nation-State and violence* 18 (UPC, 1985), "But Durkheim goes on to suppose that the state thereby inevitably represents the interests of those it rules, save in certain exceptional and 'pathological' circumstances".

61 Elliott, Turner, *supra* n. 53, at 74.

62 Elliott, Turner, *supra* n. 53, at 74.

imaginative core in social relations. Society, as seen in these conceptions, is an "elastic" society in which people are only indirectly connected to the physical space. While traditional societies were linked by blood and land, much of contemporary social relations take place online, being “stretched” in time and space.[63]

Thus, one cannot understand society as if social relations existed only in the forms of classical sociology of the nineteenth century. In society as creation, social relationships are constantly changing, which makes it radically decentralized, indeterminate and fluid.[64] The best reference among the classical sociologists for this type of concept would be that of Georg Simmel. While other sociologists conceive of society as a whole, Simmel considers it as a secondary phenomenon. To his mind, the main point is what he calls “sociation”, which are interactions, from the most ephemeral to the most enduring, which at the same time bring people together and set them apart. Simmel describes society as a web of interactions among individuals, composed of invisible wires of sociability,[65] affirming its existence wherever several individuals interact with one another.[66] What characterizes society is not the existence of a cluster of people, but instead the various interactions between them, the mutual influence of each other's actions on one another's lives.[67]

As a result, if society is nothing but the relations between individuals, giving up the traditional metaphysical foundations seeking to substantiate it is necessary. After all, treating society as a static object is impossible. It is something that is constantly happening. There is no such a thing as a static, ready-made society. Instead, there is an ongoing process of making society as we go.[68]

(VII) The Species of Collective Disputes

Based on the sociological premise developed above, one can develop a sense of entitlement of collective rights. However, a premise must be es-

---

63 Elliott, Turner, *supra* n. 53, at 109.
64 Elliott, Turner, *supra* n. 53, at 113.
65 Elliott, Turner, *supra* n. 53, at 114.
66 G. Simmel, *Sociologia* 59 (São Paulo, Attica, 1983).
67 Simmel, *supra* n. 66, at 61.
68 E. Macedo, Preface to Simmel, *supra,* n. 66, at 21.

tablished: this entitlement cannot be developed from the notion of the complete right, but rather of the empirically verified dispute.

Thinkers in Civil Law countries tend to classify the entitlement to rights abstractly. This technique does not work for collective rights. It is impossible to determine who is entitled to an unpolluted environment, because it is, in fact, a continuum of rights and interests that cannot be defined. Even if it were feasible, this definition would be useless: there is no reason to know who is entitled to an unpolluted environment. The point is to define the entitlement to the violated right, since it is he that demands that the court intervenes. According to Bauman,[69] society is a performative concept that creates the entity it names. In a similar way, it is possible to define the entitlement of the trans-individual rights from their violation or from the threat of their violation, that is, from the collective dispute.[70] Violation creates entitlement. This is similar to Savigny's findings when he sought the concept of action from the violation of the right, which is able to change its status.[71]

Thus, collective rights, while intact, do not make up the patrimony of specific people, have no economic value, cannot be traded or seized individually or enjoyed in shares. But that does not mean that, once a tort is committed (or one threatens to commit it), all persons will be entitled to these rights in the same way. When analyzed from the empirically-verified

---

69 Z. Bauman, “Between us, the generations” in: *On generations: On the coexistence between generations* 365 (Larossa ed., Barcelona, Fundació Viure i Conviure, 2007).

70 For brevity’s sake, we shall no longer repeat the expression "or threat of their violation" from now on. Nevertheless, it shall be understood that, whenever we refer to violation, we are not addressing only violations that have already happened, but we also make reference to the threat of violations that could trigger a prohibitory injunction, or we might also be making reference to the practice of the forbidden act, which would entail a cease and desist order. See S. C. Arenhart. *Perfis da tutela inibitória coletiva* 184 (São Paulo, Editora Revista dos Tribunals, 2003), and also L. G. Marinoni. *Técnica processual e tutela dos direitos* 199 (4th ed., São Paulo, Editora Revista dos Tribunais, 2013).

71 “Whenever one examines a right under the special relation of its violation, this right is seen under a new light; i.e., its defense state: as a result, the violation itself, just like the regulations established to fight such violations, rework the contents and the very essence of the right itself”. M. F. C. Savigny, *Sistema del derecho romano actual* 8 (Tomo IV. Translated into Spanish by M. CH. Guenoux. Madrid, F. Góngora y Compañía, 1879). On Savigny and the concept of action, please see L. G. Marinoni, *Teoria Geral do Processo* 163 (2nd ed., São Paulo, Editora Revista dos Tribunais, 2007).

dispute perspective, one may see that an individual's or a social group's interest in a conflict involving collective rights is empirically variable.

This variation can be measured by two indicators: how intense the personal interest of those affected by the collective violation is (which might potentially make conflicts rise within the group), and in how many ways the problem can be solved; i.e., how many different judicial remedies are applicable to that case. These elements will be referred to herein as confliction and complexity, respectively.

Therefore, it is irrelevant to say who is entitled to the environment. Instead, it matters to determine who is entitled to the remedies designed to mitigate damages due to torts committed against the environment. The entitlement of the right comes into existence from the violation. Therefore, one must define who the relevantly affected group is, so that, if appropriate, this group may be called to participate in the collective process or serve as a reference for determining the adequacy of representation. The existing dilemma between participation and representation in collective lawsuits can only be solved if one can define who is entitled to participate and, likewise, who is entitled to be represented in the process.

(a) Global collective disputes

The first category of trans-individual (or collective) disputes regards situations in which the violation does not reach directly the interests of any given person. A relatively small amount of oil being spilled in deep drilling in the ocean, for instance, does not reach anyone directly. Apart from the interest shared by every human being in relation to the world environment, no one is particularly damaged by this kind of violation. In this situation, in which the violation to a trans-individual right does not affect any one particular person, its entitlement should be attributed to society as structure. This is the category that comes closest to the current formulations of the collective process, as society is seen therein as a supracollective, disidentified being that defends its interests by applying the law. In its turn, the law is interpreted by those who are authorized to do so.[72] The point here is not to protect legal interests because their violation concerns someone specifically, but because it generally concerns everyone.

---

72 Please see *above*, Item 2.1. See also Elliott, Turner, *supra* n. 53, at 41.

This global society as structure is entitled to global trans-individual rights, even though it is further divided into smaller groups, which correspond to the national societies within each state or nation. Not that the state is the holder of those rights,[73] but the lack of a transnational system of collective protection still requires that each state protect such rights in accordance with their domestic laws.[74] In this type of situation, as no person is injured in a specific way, no opinion matters especially. This does not mean to exclude society from holding the right to process, but only to limit individual participation of its members in the lawsuit.

Global disputes are also verifiable in situations of minor violations to consumer groups, since remedies awarded due to such violations are not especially relevant to any of the individuals involved. The focus of the process in this case is to prevent the violator from making a profit out of the violation. This objective is relevant and concerns society as a whole, and not only those individuals involved directly, whose patrimony was reduced in a negligible extent. Awarding remedies to those directly involved is a secondary objective of the process.

In this sense, the degree of confliction regarding the society entitled to the rights is very low in global disputes, for the individuals involved sense the violation in a uniform and almost imperceptible manner individually. As it is, there is virtually no personal interest in litigation in these cases. Everyone benefits equally from remedies awarded and are equally violated should the violators not be made to repair their wrongdoing, thus incorporating into their patrimony the costs that they would incur to avoid the wrongdoing from happening. Although there may be variations, the complexity of these cases tends to be small. Disputes like these may be simple, where the remedy involved consists of something obvious, which one can-

---

73 García de Enterría and Fernández have clearly affirmed that, as follows: "The public administration does not represent the community, but is instead an organization placed at their service, which is an essentially different notion. Their actions are not regarded as being done by the community (it is precisely this legal provision which gives the public administration its superior legal status and its provisions their characteristic of enforceability), but rather as actions made by a dependent organization, which must be justified in each case, as its actions are bound to be done in the public interest" (E. G. Enterría, T. R. Fernández, *Curso de direito administrativo* 50 (São Paulo, RT, 2014).

74 On the issue of state action in the global context, see D. Held, *La democracia y el orden global: del estado moderno al gobierno cosmopolita* (Barcelona, Paidós, 1997).

not imagine that any member of the group would disagree with. For example, when the remedy provided is restitution of the amounts originally paid. On the other hand, there may be cases of legitimate scientific disagreement about the best way to protect the legal interest of those affected, which entails greater complexity.

(b) Local Collective Disputes

The second category of disputes to be analyzed, and that requires a different concept of entitlement concerning trans-individual rights, are the violations that reach communities in a very specific and meaningful manner, in the sense that this expression has to Ferdinand Tönnies,[75] i.e., small groups which share strong social, emotional and territorial bonds resulting in a high degree of internal consensus. This is the case of communities such as indigenous ones, of "quilombolas" (descendants of freed slaves in Brazil), and other minority traditional groups, as referred to by Convention 169 of the International Labor Organization. These groups represent the very expression coined by Elliott and Turner: "sticky societies",[76] societies with a deep sense of self-identity whose loyalty to the group is essential.

Violations of trans-individual rights that reach these groups cause such serious effects on them, shaking their very foundations so deeply, it is justifiable to consider that, in this case, they are the holders of the violated trans-individual rights. Even if one can admit that other people have a connection with the damaged environment within an indigenous community, it is unthinkable that this indigenous society, which was directly affected by the violation, should be entitled to remedy rights in the same proportion as people who live thousands of kilometers away, simply because the Constitution provides that "everyone has the right to an ecologically balanced environment", as it does in Brazil.

As one can see, the difference between violations belonging to the previous category and this one is remarkable. Environmental damage occurring within traditional indigenous territory causes that community such deeply felt effects as opposed to the rest of the global society that the only

75 F. Tönnies, *Comunidad y Sociedad* 19 (Buenos Aires, Losada, 1947).

76 Elliott, Turner, *supra* n. 53, at 74.

solution compatible with this reality is attributing the entitlement of the violated rights to that community. The existing cultural bond between indigenous people and their territory, which goes far beyond the simple notion of property,[77] makes the relationship of the indigenous group with the damage so severe that one must consider its relevance to other individuals not belonging to the indigenous group as unimportant.

Confliction is average in local disputes. On the one hand, the community involved is highly cohesive, which gives them the same perspective on the dispute,[78] and certain homogeneity in relation to the outcome of the process. On the other hand, the stereotypical view that an indigenous community has a single opinion and the same interests simply because they all belong to the same ethnic group is wrong. These groups also have internal dissidence, from which majorities and minorities result. As the community's interest in this outcome is high, these internal differences tend to exacerbate, thus bringing about confliction. On the other hand, the community retains its power as a group which stems from the group's internal connections. This bond limits confliction in comparison to other situations in which such a group identity amongst rights holders doesn't exist, as we shall analyze in due time.

One may extend the category of local disputes to create a second circle, encompassing other minority groups whose members share with each other a social perspective, though having a weaker bond. As a result, it does not seem difficult to argue, for instance, that the trans-individual rights to gender equality belong to women. Although men are interested in living in a society where there is no such inequality, women's interest in the trans-individual disputes related to it is so much more significant that male representation in such disputes seems to be irrelevant. The same could be said of other minorities, such as racial or sexual orientation minorities, where the litigious trans-individual right relates to the social perspective that permeates and identifies the group itself, even if among its members there

77 On this issue, please see VITORELLI, Edilson. *Estatuto do Índio.* 2nd Edition Salvador: Juspodivm, 2013; and also E. Vitorelli, *Estatuto da Igualdade Racial e comunidades quilombolas* (Salvador: Juspodivm, 2012).

78 The word "perspective" is used here in the sense given by Iris Marion Young. I. M. Young. *Inclusion and democracy* (New York, OUP, 2000). In a nutshell, social perspective derives from the position of an individual in society, which influences their way of seeing the world, though not necessarily their interests or their opinions.

may be disagreements over how to deal with violations and what the best expected outcome may be.

This concept also applies to situations in which the individual violations resulting from collective disputes are very grave, resulting in substantial financial losses, illness or death of the individuals involved. Such is the case of *mass torts* in the United States.[79] Although these people do not have, as a rule of thumb, an identity bond that allows them to be identified into the so-called first degree of local trans-individual rights, the violation quite often causes them to create a solidarity bond, sharing common views about the event that affected them. In such situations, the concern of rights protection, when performed collectively, is not to avoid the enrichment of the tortfeasor, but rather to provide restitution of the affected group's patrimony, as best as possible. In this category, therefore, the interests of individuals absent from the process are substantially more important than the first one, and the focus of collective action is therefore quite different.

(c) *Irradiated Collective Disputes*

The last category proposed includes situations where the dispute arising from the violation directly affects the interests of several people or social groups, but these people do not make up a community, do not have the same social perspective, and will not be affected in the same way and with the same intensity by the dispute's outcome. This makes their views about a desirable outcome different from one another, if not completely oppo-

79 For some examples, such as contamination caused by inhalation of asbestos or by *agent orange,* see P. H. Schuck, *Agent Orange on Trial*: *Mass Toxic Disasters in the Courts*. Cambridge, HUP, 1987; J. B. Weinstein. *Individual justice in mass tort litigation.* Evanston, Northwestern University Press, 1995; D. Rosenberg, "Class Actions for Mass Torts: Doing Individual Justice by Collective Means", 62 *Indiana Law Journal*, 561(1987). One of the cases analyzed by Hensler et al., on the environmental contamination with significant patrimonial losses also exemplifies a case of *mass tort.* See D. Hensler et al., *Class Action Dilemmas*: *Pursuing Public Goals for Private Gain*. Santa Monica, RAND, 2000.

site.[80] These events give rise to changeable[81] and multipolar[82] disputes, which pit the rights-holding group against not only the defendant but also each other.

This category can be illustrated with the conflicts arising from the installation of a hydroelectric power plant, structural reform of a public institution and so on. Impacts of the lawsuit are multiple, multipolar and variable. These conflicts cannot be solved by simply prohibiting the construction of hydroelectric power plants, nor by naively attempting to develop such construction works without any environmental impacts. This is not the typical situation in which torts are opposed to rights, but rather of a conflict arising within the boundaries set forth by legal provisions. Constructing power plants is certainly useful to society. Nevertheless, social and environmental impacts shall still befall the local community inhabiting that location, regardless of all reasonable care having been taken previously. Situations like these also take place in other countries. India has been facing problems concerning remediation actions attempting to reverse the pollution of the Ganges river. The remediation works are opposed by the Hindus, whose religious beliefs hold the Ganges river as the representation of goddess Gaṅgā. According to believers, Gaṅgā's purity and holiness fight off the negative effects of pollution.[83]

Irradiated disputes are situations of high confliction and complexity, in which there are multiple possible outcomes for the dispute and where the

---

80 As mentioned by H. N. Mazzilli, *A defesa dos interesses difusos em juízo* 49 (20nd ed., São Paulo, Saraiva, 2007).

81 The ever changing quality of these conflicts is emphasized by R. C. Mancuso, *Direitos difusos*: *conceito e legitimação para* agir 110 (8th ed., São Paulo, RT, 2013).

82 The word "multipolar" is used herein to refer to the existence, at least potentially, of a large number of dissonant opinions concerning the conflict. It should be noted that there is an important aspect of dispute studies which denies the existence of multipolar conflicts, stating that they always will result in bipolarity. Cf. R. F. Entelman, *Teoría de conflictos*: *hacia un nuevo paradigma* 86. (Barcelona, Gedisa, 2005).

83 The reference to this interesting conflict was initially found in C. R. Barbosa Moreira, "Os direitos difusos nas grandes concentrações demográficas", 70 *Revista de Processo* 146 (1993). The writer, it seems, had no access to bibliographical sources on the subject, probably because of when the article was written. For further details on the matter, please see V. R. Nagarajan, "The Earth as goddess Bhu Devi: toward a theory of "embedded ecologies" in folk Hinduism" in: *Purifying the Earthly Body of God*: *religion and ecology in Hindu India,* 269, 276 (Nelson ed., New York, State of New York University Press, 1998.

rights-holding society has conflicting interests in the matter, which can at times be the very opposite of one another. As the above examples illustrate, these circumstances are different from those of the previous two categories. The dispute here is not global, because it is possible to identify the people who were more affected by the violation than others who are not as affected by it. Neither is it a local dispute, because the affected people don't share social bonds. Not even legal provisions stipulate what to do under such circumstances. It stems from this that such conflicts are always fraught with social, political and economic elements.[84]

The most appropriate concept of society to identify people who are entitled to these rights is that of society as creation. In this line of thought, society is elastic, decentralized and fluid. Using Simmel's term, what matters is *sociation*, which means society on the move, and not a static concept of society. Interwoven social interactions among individuals is society itself. Social structures are nothing but the crystallization of these social interactions.[85] However, as Simmel says, “one must still bear in mind that the human existence is only achieved by individuals without thereby disregarding the concept of society”.[86] For this reason, one must find ways to identify or at least to define the group of those who hold trans-individual rights that fall into this category.

A society holding trans-individual rights whose violation reaches certain individuals specifically, but in varied ways, when the affected individuals don't share the same social bond, is a group simply because all of them have been affected by the same violation. Nothing else constitutes this group as a society: not any laws, territory or frontiers. Instead, what brings them together as a group is only the violation of their rights, which affects each of them in different degrees. The members of this group aren't entitled to their trans-individual right in the same measure, but in proportion to how severe the violation they suffered is. One may use the image of a stone being thrown into a lake, making waves from the center to the extremities, or that of the explosion of a bomb, to picture the violation.

---

84 R. C. Mancuso, *Jurisdição coletiva e coisa julgada*: *teoria geral das ações coletivas* 205 (São Paulo, RT, 2006). For a similar view on the matter, please see C. Salomão Filho. *Direito concorrencial*: *as condutas* 73 (São Paulo, RT, 2003), on which the writer states the following: “[...] the protection of diffuse interests is very deeply political in nature”.

85 Simmel, *supra* n. 66, at 83.

86 Simmel, *supra* n. 66, at 82.

The more someone is affected by that violation, the closer that person is to the center. Naturally, this person is entitled to a more prominent position in the group of right-holders.

People who experience the violation to a lesser degree are located further from the center, which is not to say that they don't belong to the group. Finally, people who haven't been directly affected by the violation don't belong to the group and, therefore, are not holders of rights, regardless of having a hypothetical or abstract interest in the matter.

Confliction and complexity on irradiated trans-individual rights are high. Many factors contribute for confliction and complexity to bring about controversy and a diversity of interests within the group: i) the members within the group tend not to share any identity or social bonds; ii) they experience the consequences of the violation bringing them together at different levels; iii) some of them may have experienced such consequences so deeply that their lives may have been completely changed; iv) because the matter is so complex, there may be many different venues in which it can be adjudicated, or multiple legal solutions can be proposed, which can't be solved by the formula tort = remedy. Some members within the group are interested in ending the violation, as they want things to return to how they used to be: to their minds, what the violation cost them is worth more than any other kind of compensation. Others may feel that their interests are better served if they are compensated for their burdens in housing, jobs or other kinds of entitlements, allowing the enterprise to go on. Still others may believe that being paid damages is the best alternative. None of these is impossible or illegal in themselves, although some of them may exclude each other. For this reason, there is a conflict between the group and the tortfeasor, but there are also a number of conflicts within the group, which are more or less severe. As far as these internal conflicts are concerned, one cannot define which is more important or relevant in principle.

In conclusion, the third category regards collective disputes that reach certain people in varied ways and intensities. As a complicating factor, people within the group don't share the same point of view in relation to what a good outcome for the conflict would be. Irradiated disputes therefore involve an elastic group made up of the people who actually experienced the effects of the violation, and who are entitled to their rights in proportion to how much of the violation they have experienced.

Since the three concepts of society that serves as right-holders for global, local and irradiated disputes have been clearly defined, these shall be used to balance the procedural requirements applicable to collective litigation in each of these instances, especially regarding participation of the individuals that form each of these societies in the lawsuit and, on the other hand, the behaviour of their representative. The delicate equilibrium between participation and representation shall be differently established in each of these three types.

(VIII) A Procedural Model for Collective Disputes

The issue to be addressed in this topic relates to the numerous procedural techniques available to conduct collective actions. Many of them are regarded with suspicion in many countries, because they would have the potential to cause undue restriction of individual rights. This segment aims to demonstrate that such discomfort stems from the lack of adequate analysis regarding the matters proposed. Not all collective procedural techniques are suitable for all cases. The purpose of this part is to specify how the representative may act in each type of disputes described in Part II. The idea here is to prevent an undue restriction on participation in cases where it should be granted. Additionally, another important point is to facilitate the introduction of procedural mechanisms of representation. On many an occasion, these are essential to the matter at hand, as shall be demonstrated.

My proposal is that any legal practitioner who is involved in a class action should assess its complexity and its confliction so as to decide in which category the matter fits. Global disputes have little confliction, since personal interests of those involved in the case are reduced. Its complexity is variable and a solution for the matter may be either evident or complex, as these cases may involve reasonable scientific doubt concerning the best way in which to protect the affected society. Local disputes entail major impact on a group that share identity bonds. These people have a lot to lose with the dispute, which increases their degree of confliction. Nevertheless, the conflict is contained by their identity bond. The degree of complexity is hardly low, since such disputes tend to oppose the society and others surrounding it. Finally, irradiated disputes reach different people who share no bonds at different levels. Therefore, such disputes involve a high degree of complexity and confliction. These people have conflicting interests in the cause and, therefore, converging or opposing interests overlap, depending on how the case is handled.

The purpose of this topic is to establish the types of collective procedural techniques that are well adapted to each type of case and the degree of participation due to the rights-holders. These parameters shall outline the work of the group's representative.

(a) The Process in Global Disputes

If a dispute affects people so that each of them has very little personal interest in the cause and if the proposed line of action is not controversial, the resulting class action must attempt to prevent the tortfeasor from taking advantage of its outcome. In such instances, the process works as an additional regulation of the state. If the financial loss incurred by a large group of consumers is of only a few cents, it is unlikely that they will mind having those cents restituted. It is more likely that they prefer to live in a society where regulatory standards are met in order to prevent suppliers from making a spurious profit out of harming their consumers.

According to David Rosenberg, the procedural problem posed by these violations is that suppliers enjoy a "structural asymmetry" which unbalances the situation in their favour: they harm a large group of consumers, each of whom experience such harm individually. The traditional legal system in which each consumer files an individual lawsuit allows for suppliers to pulverize procedural costs into hundreds or millions of similar procedures.[87] As far as the tortfeasor is concerned, he is always involved in some "de facto" class action whenever he is being sued by a large number of consumers: all he needs to do is hire the legal services of the same law firm to represent him in every one of the cases, produce evidence which applies to all of them, hire the services of experts which shall be repeatedly used in all of them, and search favourable legal precedents that apply to all of them. All of these may be better and more easily handled by him than by the plaintiffs in each of these cases. In an extreme situation, the defendant may settle out of court with all plaintiffs who have sure cases, forcing them into non-disclosure clauses. This kind of outcome serves the tortfeasor in two senses: i) he is able to conceal the gravest individual

87 D. Rosenberg, "Mass Tort Class Actions: What Defendants Have and Plaintiffs Don't", 37 *Harvard Journal on Legislation*, 393 (2000). Rosenberg applies his own theory to the situation of *mass torts,* which are here treated as local disputes. Therefore, the technique described in this topic does not apply to those cases.

torts he committed; ii) he succeeds in making the courts analyze firstly those individual cases that are not so strong, which increases the odds that rulings provided will be in his favour. This means that the procedural system generally favours he who commits mass torts.[88]

Moreover, from the perspective of the plaintiffs, who do not earn nearly as much as the defendant, the procedure offers only an illusion of being in control. In reality, a rationale of economy will cause both lawyers and judges to bring these cases together informally by reproducing the same pleadings and rulings to as many cases as possible.[89] The notion of the individual as *dominus litis* in global disputes represents nothing but a nostalgic view of how procedures used to be in the past. However, that past is long gone.[90] This notion only deprives the affected people of their right to take part in a class action, and does not provide them with anything else in return.

Therefore, the collective procedural treatment of violations is not meant to unduly favour the plaintiffs to the detriment of the defendant, but is rather a means to rebalance a system which was previously unbalanced. In the words of Hay and Rosenberg, the most important reason to accept the

---

88 Lahav mentions that much of the anger aroused against *class actions* is precisely due to the fact that they rebalance the situation of the parties in the process, which was previously unequal in substantive terms. A. Lahav, "Symmetry and class action litigation", 60 *UCLA Law Review* 1494 (2013).

89 H. M. Erichson, "Informal aggregation: procedural and ethical implications of coordination among counsel in related lawsuits", 50 (2) *Duke Law Journal*, 381 (2000). The writer states that "true litigant autonomy may be unattainable in many situations involving multiple related claims". Similarly, please see D. R. Hensler, "As times goes by: asbestos litigation after Amchem and Ortiz", 80 *Texas Law Review* 1898 (2002) and S. Issacharoff, "Shocked: Mass Torts and Aggregate Asbestos Litigation after Amchem and Ortiz" 80 (7) *Texas Law Review* 1925 (2002).

90 Erichson states in the sense of the text: "As long as the economy features mass marketing, mass employment, mass entertainment, mass transportation, mass production of goods, and mass provision of services, disputes will arise in which a mass of claimants seek relief from a common defendant or set of defendants. Lawyers on both sides naturally handle such matters collectively rather than individually. With or without the judicial imprimatur of class certification, multi-claimant disputes routinely are litigated and resolved on a collective basis. The real question is not whether there will be mass litigation, but whether mass litigation will be subject to formal procedural safeguards or will instead proceed without clearly defined ethical duties or meaningful judicial supervision".
H. M. Erichson, "Mississippi class actions and the inevitability of mass aggregate litigation", 24 *Mississippi College Law Review* 285 (2005).

aggregation of demands in this type of case is levelling the rules so that the plaintiffs are put in an equal economic position to that enjoyed by the defendant.[91]

In sum, the objective of a collective procedural system whenever individual characteristics or preferences are not at stake shouldn't be to favour the individual nature of the violated rights, but instead the protection of society's interests as a whole through obtaining an optimum level of disincentive to committing torts (deterrence).[92] According to Rosenberg, the optimum level of disincentive to committing torts benefits everyone because it reduces costs stemming from accidents through reasonable prevention, which means an economy of resources that can then be returned to society.[93] Simple global collective litigation demands a collective procedural system in which the courts process the lawsuit in an exclusively collective manner without the opportunity for individuals to sue individually: such litigation consists of cases in which the individuals within a society have no reason to be personally interested in its outcome and where adjudication is necessary so that the substantive rights involved are duly protected. In such cases, there is no reason why individual lawsuits would be filed. They display situations to which the only possible solution for obtaining the desired social outcome is collective litigation.[94]

---

91 B. Hay, D. Rosenberg, "*Sweetheart* and *blackmail* settlements in class actions: reality and remedy", 75 *Notre Dame Law Review* 1377 (2000).

92 Even though he didn't endorse the economic analysis of law, Mauro Cappelletti addressed the matter in a similar way: "The consumer who has suffered a minor damage due to having acquired a defective product may not feel strongly motivated, or have enough information or enough financial resources to sue the almighty supplier, the "mass-wrongdoer". Even if he did, the outcome of his victory would be minimal and his representation certainly wouldn't impact the supplier and make him change his wrongdoing". M. Cappelletti, "Formações sociais e interesses coletivos diante da justiça civil", 61 *Revista de Processo* 144 (1991).

93 Rosenberg, *supra* n. 87 at 408.

94 Even though the European Economic and Social Committee has defended the adoption of collective procedural mechanisms within the Union, it has asserted that "The EESC welcomes the Commission's rejection of a US-style class action. This is precisely the form that collective redress within European law must not take. (…) The Commission also quite rightly points out that compensatory collective actions should be geared to compensating for harm demonstrably caused by an infringement of Union law. The punishment and deterrence functions should be exercised by the public authorities". See Opinion of the European Economic and Social Committee on the Communication from the Commission to the European Parliament, the Council, the European Economic and Social Committee and the

Consequently, the procedural representative's performance is more autonomous in relation to the group's will in order to decide how to conduct the case. It is highly recommended that this agent performs with transparency, publicizing information and justifications for the decisions s/he makes, especially when a public agency is involved, and carrying out public hearings from time to time to provide an opportunity for interested persons to question his/her performance. Even so, his/her degree of independence from the affected group is quite high. The representative's performance reflects the group's will, as s/he performs on their behalf. However, this performance favours the representative character of the process rather than its participative one.

A balance between participation and representation in global litigation leans towards representation because: a) individuals have very little to gain from participation; b) it is highly unlikely that participation helps the decision to be more accurate; c) eventual negative results are bound not to be meaningful; d) it is more likely that the representative manages to counterbalance the systemic advantages of a habitual litigator than the individual on his own; e) the optimum social outcome in this context is the reduction of procedural costs and the maximization of deterrence.

(b) The Process in Local Disputes

Local disputes are the antipodes of global disputes. Even though the interest in question may indirectly concern society as a whole, in local disputes the violation concerns a smaller group, who shares identity bonds. They have been impacted by the violation to such an extent that, by comparison, anyone else's situation become irrelevant. For this reason, it should be understood that the society entitled to the rights is the community of people suffering from the violation's direct effects. The degree of cohesion between the individuals that make up each of these communities varies and tends to be higher when there is a common territorial base, but "communities can be formed despite geographical aspects, particularly if its mem-

---

Committee of the Regions Towards a European Horizontal Framework for Collective Redress. Available at http://eur-lex.europa.eu/legal-content/EN/TXT/HTML/?uri=CELEX:52013AE5439&from=PT, last visited 16 March 2017.

bers share a significant experience in common, a social network or an emotional connection".[95]

While many situations can be perceived as having interest to society as a whole, the direct victims of the violation shall be favoured whenever their positions are comparatively more relevant for the case than anyone else's, because of the extension of their harm or the closer relationship with the violated right. Compensation, in these cases, should come before deterrence. Under these circumstances, it is unthinkable that their representative acts "on their behalf" by requesting some redress that this community does not explicitly want, without providing them some explanation as to why s/he is doing that. According to Hanna Pitkin, the individual is the best judge of his interests. In no sense is it possible to treat the interests of a person or group as being totally objective and independent from their ideas or desires. Each person has the right to define what's good for them. Should they reject something, no one has the right to insist that it is the best alternative for them.[96]

Thus, the main feature of a local dispute is that its representative acts in the interests of the group entitled to the rights. The group's interests are necessarily defined from their collective will. For this reason, every local dispute is complex and brings with it considerable confliction. This confliction is just limited because the group shares some bond for being in the same position opposing the tortfeasor. This happens even though the members of the group may have different opinions and interests regarding the conflict. As a rule of thumb, confliction will be inversely proportional to how deep the group bond is.[97]

Contrary to what occurs in global disputes, the balance between participation and representation in local disputes must favour the participation and control of the representative's acts by the representees because: a) the

---

95 E. C. Burch, "Litigating groups", 61 (1) *Alabama Law Review* 1, 22 (2009).

96 H. F. Pitkin, *The concept of representation* 159 (Berkeley, University of California Press, 1984).

97 Elizabeth Bruch offers a simple but efficient example of an internal conflict in a local dispute: two people inhabit a region that suffers from soil contamination. However, one of them plans to leave the area, preferring to receive monetary compensation, while the other wishes to stay, preferring that the defendant's resources are used to restore the natural environment. Burch, *supra* n. 95, at 27. As can be seen, if these individuals belonged to a more cohesive group, such as an indigenous community, it is likely that both would prefer to stay in that place, thus reducing confliction.

representees are highly interested in the outcome, which triggers them to want a meaningful participation in the process; b) the process can lead to a considerable change in the lives of representees. Therefore, it would be very difficult to explain democratically that the process could be carried out without their consent or participation; c) it is likely that individual participation is able to help the judge see the big picture, thus increasing the quality of the decision; d) an optimum social result in the context of local disputes is fair compensation of people especially damaged by the violation. Admittedly, this does not mean that the collective process should be changed into an individual process. Instead, the representative should be very concerned about learning of and protecting the real interest of his/her representees, allowing them to participate in the most important moments of the process. In many cases, the life of the class members can be dramatically altered by the outcome of the process. For this reason, the rights-holders must be given the opportunity to participate in the formulation of the claims and be a part of their development, whether in or out of court.

(c) The Process in Irradiated Disputes

Of all the types of collective disputes, certainly those that represent the greatest challenge to the development of a procedural model are irradiated disputes. In simple terms, the root of the problem resides in the fact that such disputes are not meant to be resolved by means of a process. They involve a wide group of people affected in different ways by a violation. These people hold different views on what the best outcome would be and, therefore, hold different interests to be represented in the process. These disputes are so ingrained in society that it is difficult to make a cut that will be demonstrative of reality and make it fit in a judicial process that will hopefully end one day. Because of these characteristics, irradiated disputes have the highest degree of complexity and confliction of all the types proposed.

The judge, in this type of process, will not be a neutral adjudicator, as is expected of him in an individual civil procedure. He is not called upon to decide whether the plaintiff or the defendant is entitled to their rights, but to establish and carry out substantive rights whose limits are unclear and whose factual limits of implementation are highlighted,[98] i.e., in the words of Martha Minow, it is his duty to resolve the situation as a whole.[99] The decision is only the starting point to consider venues of implementation by comparing costs and benefits.

Moreover, in a traditional process, the judge considers the past to determine how reality should be in the future. As far as irradiated disputes are concerned, the reality of the moment of compliance with the ruling will affect how its abstract goals, defined some time before, are going to be outlined.[100] The many ways in which rights can be awarded may influence the understanding of those very rights. The facts of these cases are not historical but rather social facts, which are under constant modification.[101]

---

98 A. Miller, "Of Frankenstein Monsters and Shining Knights: Myth, Reality and the Class Action Problem", 92 *Harvard Law Review* 664 (1979). On page 667, the writer states the following: "Some of these cases obligate federal judges to undertake supervisory tasks requiring enormous expenditures of time and effort, converting their role from one of passive adjudicator of a dispute staged by opposing counsel to that of active systems manager".

99 M. Minow, "Judge for the situation: Judge Jack Weinstein, creator of temporary administrative agencies", 97 *Columbia Law Review* 2010 (2010).

100 As pointed by Barry Friedman, the exact match between *right* and *remedy* is something that was resolved during the twentieth century: "If Marbury's fundamental tenet were correct, we would expect to find a tight congruence in constitutional law between right and remedy. What emerges from a study of the law of remedy and enforcement, however, is the picture of a system in which there is tremendous flexibility in the fit between right and remedy and therefore a system in which rights receive far less respect than the rhetoric would suggest. Indeed, close examination reveals a system in which failure to comply with, if not outright defiance of, judicial remedial orders is tolerated to a certain degree.
This divergence between the ideal and reality is not surprising; it reflects a similar divergence between our idealized view of the judicial function and the reality imposed by the milieu in which courts must operate". B. Friedman, "When rights encounter reality: enforcing federal remedies", 65 *South California Law Review* 735 (1992).

101 Similarly, Berizonce states the following: "The judicial decision does not provide an ending that will resolve the conflict in relation to the past. Instead, it usually looks forward into the future and tends to influence public policies of the sector involved, whether the goal is to propose new or different institutional practices or systemic changes that reach far beyond the case under scrutiny. In this sense, jurisdiction takes on a remedial function because the decision is more aligned with the search of remedies for the complex situation that involves strong interests in relation to the future than with finding a solution in the most traditional sense of

The process does not focus on what happened, but on what will happen after it changes reality.[102]

Thus, the judicial process must become, in the words of Yeazell, a *town meeting*. In this model, the judge takes direction of the process, defining the relevant issues and presiding over the production of evidence[103] to promote dialogue opportunities with the impacted society, similar to the performance of administrative or legislative bodies. Hearings and public events are carried out to foster the direct and informal participation of a broad range of interested people.[104] This helps to overcome the problem of large numbers of people who will be impacted by the process and the variety of factual situations in which they are, which "makes it desirable for the judge to hear at least some affected groups, even (or especially) those who are unhappy with the measure to be applied".[105] Such events can be used to hear people's complaints, to verify if the proposed solution is feasible, to indicate flaws in the proposals or to indicate alternatives. In addition, the model also provides a chance for the facts to be constantly reassessed, since the context of structural disputes are changeable by nature. "The judge uses his central position in the process to influence far beyond the immediate boundaries of the case that is before him, assessing the impact of the results within the court in the distribution of influence out of it".[106]

In summary, the process in an irradiated dispute needs to face three hard realities: the first is that judges issue more legislative decisions than

---

the term and using traditional criteria: it is more driven to pondering the principles and values under scrutiny than to subsumption": R. Berizonce, Los conflictos de interés público, *Revista Iberoamericana de Derecho Procesal* 161 (2015).

102 J. Rosenberg, W. R. F. Phillips, "The Institutionalization of Conflict in the Reform of Schools: A Case Study of Court Implementation of the PARC Decree", 57 *Indiana Law Journal* 427 (1982).

103 This model was described by Judith Resnik as *managerial judge*, a manager of the process. During discovery phase, this idea is not so new to a reader whose system is that of civil law rather than that of common law. During enforcement phase, however, the Brazilian judge is as far removed from the process as his North-American counterpart. See J. Resnick, "Managerial Judges", 96 *Harvard Law Review* 376 (1982).

104 S. Sturm, "The Normative Theory of Public Law Remedies" 79 (5) *Georgetown Law Journal* 1370 (1991).

105 Sturm, *supra* n. 104, at 1370.

106 C. S. Diver, "The Judge as Political Powerbroker: Superintending Structural Change in Public Institutions", 65 (1) *Virginia Law Review* 43 (1979).

they would like to admit, and than the theory of separation of powers would allow. The second is that all constitutional values are specifically subjected to limitations, and although they may be rhetorically reputed as important, the judges are willing to accept results that contradict their own views. Third, that however uncomfortable the first two findings seem to be, there is no other way to act when the circumstances so impose. Structural reform exemplifies irradiated disputes very well and shows that the certainties need to be "equipped with elastic limits"[107] or else they simply won't work.

The central problem of irradiated disputes is that they encompass non-aligned interests which may even be opposite among group members. It may be that the result desired by a group put others in the group in a worse situation than where they would be if the process did not exist. For this reason, it is unlikely that a representative can defend all those interests involved in the process equally. These interests will then shape up to become a *town meeting*. Thus, in an irradiated dispute, it is necessary to seriously consider the distribution of representation to more than one representative.

Each of these representatives should see clearly their assigned subgroup and try to meet their wishes in order to define their interests around which his/her performance must be oriented. Therefore, these representatives should organize meaningful participatory moments with their subgroup regardless of those generally promoted by the judge in the process. This participation should be increased in proportion to the complexity of the dispute, in order to explore, among the various possible solutions, the one that best serves the interests of the class. If there are conflicts within the subgroup, participation can also help solve them and avoid new dissents.

In addition, participatory events will be the contact of subgroups with society as a whole, allowing for a debate between the subgroups and the society to take place. In such opportunities, one may find out how much each group is willing to concede so that an acceptable solution can be drawn to the benefit of all. The amount of participation and representation will depend on the position of each sub-group, regarding how affected they had been by the violation. Groups which have been more affected by the violation will be granted more participation, meaning that the representative's performance will be greatly connected to their wishes. As far as

107 Diver, *supra* n. 106, at 43.

the least affected groups are concerned, the fact that their representative's performance is more autonomous will be acceptable. Similarly, when it comes to the most affected groups, dividing their representation into smaller groups is something that should be examined more closely so as to ensure consistency with the sub-group's interests. Nevertheless, if confliction exists within subgroups which haven't been severely affected, such confliction is acceptable, as it is preferable to the excessive division of the litigation, which could ultimately prevent the procedure from continuing.

Thus, the irradiated collective disputes require a procedural model that accounts for its inherent complexity and confliction. One does not make a structural reform with specific court orders which determine specific behaviour changes for institutions, nor shall one achieve social change through thousands of individual processes which require the state to provide services or hand assets to plaintiffs. The process, in such instances, may not be that traditional procedure where plaintiff, defendant and judge are the main characters. Facts change quite rapidly while a diversity of perspectives requires completely new and disassociated instruments from that traditional notion of process as an exercise in solving past problems through means of their subsumption to the legal system. The process in irradiated disputes must be a *town meeting* whose structure should favour that different affected social subgroups express their concerns, and where their interests are weighed. Irradiated disputes involve "a point of view of society", which no one is entitled to say that belongs to themselves. In this sense, Robert Ackerman's contribution is quite relevant:[108]

> "We should be careful, however, when we speak of the "interests of the community" with regard to disputes and disputing behavior. Repressive authoritarianism potentially lurks behind that phrase if it is employed as an abstraction without substance, or without inquiry as to the values being promoted".

William Fletcher describes this phenomenon from the concept of polycentrism, which is "the property of a complex problem with a number of subsidiary problem "centers", each of which is related to the others, such that the solution to each depends on the solution to all the others".[109] The writer uses the metaphor of a spider web, stating that the tension of its many

---

108 R. M. Ackerma, "Disputing together: conflict resolution and the search for community", 18 *Ohio State Journal on Dispute Resolution* 28, 44 (2002).

109 W. Fletcher, "The discretionary Constitution: institutional remedies and judicial legitimacy", 91 (4) *The Yale Law Journal* 635, 645 (1982).

threads is determined by the relationship between all parts of the web, so that touching one thread leads to the redistribution of tension throughout the structure, implying its full reconfiguration. These polycentric problems pervade the whole society and are not, as a rule, very prone to being solved exclusively by the government.[110] The legal polycentrism is characterized by the simultaneous presence of various interests which are legally protected in the same conflict. As highlighted by Lon Fuller, this problem cannot be adequately solved by traditional adjudication techniques.[111]

The polycentric character of irradiated disputes requires the pluralization of procedural dialogue as a condition for a solution that takes into account all the elements of the problem. The technique to achieve this goal can be built from the adaptation of the postulates of deliberative democracy, as developed by Joshua Cohen. The writer presents five major characteristics of this democratic model: a) it is a present and independent association whose members expect it to continue indefinitely in the future; b) the debates involve free and equal participants under rules decided by themselves and to which they are bound; c) these people are a pluralistic association, whose members have several preferences, beliefs and ideals that govern their lives. Although they share a commitment to solving their problems, they also have different objectives; d) individuals prefer institutions in which the connection between the debates and the results is evident; e) members of the debate recognize each other as being able to act reasonably and in accordance with the result of public reason.[112]

In irradiated disputes, the community divided into subgroups according to how affected they are by the decision also engages in dialogue that is expected to continue for a reasonable time, although it should seek partial solutions to the problems it faces as it advances. One must recognize that people have different interests and perspectives regarding the dispute and its possible outcomes. It might also be that some other legitimate interests are involved, which are opposed and mutually exclusionary, although these are defended by people who mutually recognize one another's delib-

---

110 Idem, at 646.

111 L. L. Fuller, "The Forms and Limits of Adjudication", 92 (2) *Harvard Law Review* 398 (1978).

112 J. Cohen, "Deliberation and democratic legitimacy" in: *The good polity: normative analysis of the state* 17, 21 (Hamlin/Pettit ed., New York, Basil Blackwell, 1989).

erative capacities.[113] All the people involved hope that the procedural dialogue will provide them with social outcomes. Consequently, they may be very motivated to take part in the procedure when they realize this connection clearly.

The only adaptation needed in order to use Cohen's theory in the context of irradiated disputes is that the participants in the dialogue must be fully equal. The main feature of this type of dispute is that different social subgroups are affected in different ways by the violation. For this reason, the more intense the consequences for a subgroup are (the more they have been affected by the violation) the more their views and interests should be considered and valued. On the contrary, the less affected by the violation a subgroup is, the less relevant their contribution will be. According to Laurence Tribe, the clearer the identity of those affected by the effects of the decision, the clearer the need for their participation in the process.[114] It is also true that, differently from Cohen`s theory, in class actions one is before a deliberative structure within a representation, since the dialogue, except in specific procedural events, will not occur primarily among individuals who are entitled to each interest, but rather between their representatives.

Pragmatically speaking, participation can be built with the help of public participation as conceived by the *International Association for Public Participation*, which demonstrates increasing stages of social participation, all adaptable to the collective process in irradiated disputes. The most basic level of participation is information, whose purpose is to help the public to understand the issue at hand, its alternatives, opportunities and solutions. At this stage, participation can be implemented through handing out folders, holding open meetings and making data available on websites. The second level of participation is consulting with the public, which means obtaining feedback regarding the information provided, by acknowledging their concerns and aspirations. The appropriate techniques

---

113 The possibility of conflicts between legitimate vs. legitimate rights was clarified by R. F. Entelman, *Teoría de conflictos*: *hacia un nuevo paradigma* 54 (Barcelona, Gedisa, 2005).

114 Tribe, *supra* n. 17 *at* 667: "On either view – the intrinsic or the instrumental – the case for due process protection grows stronger as the identity of the persons affected by a governmental choice becomes clearer; and the case becomes stronger still as the precise nature of the effect on each individual comes more determinately within the decision-maker's purview".

for this level are receiving public comments, conducting opinion polls and *foci groups* and promoting public meetings with specific segments of the community concerned. At the third level, the goal of participation is to involve those affected by the process, making them work together with the representative in research and formulation of the claim, which ensures that their concerns will be understood, considered and reflected in the final result. As this step involves a greater degree of detail, participatory events must have smaller dimensions, which enable a more qualified dialogue. Sanchez suggests conducting workshops with the participation of some leaders of the social group as well as deliberative consultations.[115] At the fourth level, involvement becomes collaboration. At this stage, one seeks to establish partnerships with the public for every aspect of the decisions to be adopted because of the process, including the proposal of alternatives and the identification of the group's preferred solution among the possibilities built in the previous levels. Setting up advisory committees composed of citizens, participatory decision-making and consensus building are appropriate at this level. Finally, the last degree of participation, which is the ultimate goal of public participation, is empowerment, in which the final decision is placed in the hands of the public and the course of action follows what they decide. The techniques here are the delegation of decisions to community members and voting.

Surely, civil procedure might not be the best environment to solve irradiated disputes and, in countries where administrative boards act effectively, it might be better to settle them out of court. However, considering everything that is at stake in irradiated disputes, it is likely that every country, at some point, is going to find itself wondering if regulatory agencies, subjected to political and economic constraints, can properly and fairly deal with all conflicting interests that are presented in these cases. Judicial autonomy, as problematic as it seems in some aspects,[116] may still overcome all the disadvantages that are posed by the limitations of the traditional procedural model. By reforming this model, we might be able to reconcile the best of these two words. In complex societies, conflicts tend

---

115 L. E. Sánchez, *Avaliação de impacto ambiental*: *conceitos e métodos* 16 (2nd ed., São Paulo, Oficina de Textos, 2013).

116 See, among others, A. Bickel, *The least dangerous bench.* (2nd ed., Binghamton, Bobbs-Merrill Company Inc., 1986); R. Gargarella (ed.), *Por una justicia dialógica. El poder Judicial como promotor de la deliberación democrática* (Buenos Aires, Siglo Veintiuno Editores, 2014).

to be more and more complex and we are going to need a complex procedural model to deal with them.

(IX) Conclusion

Participation is a fundamental value of contemporary civil procedure, that is rooted in its historical evolution and became a part of the procedure itself.[117] However, the reasons for such high regard are less than clear and, when closely examined, one may perceive that even though procedural participation is important, it is not essential to obtain a good decision nor for other systemically appreciated values to come to be, such as the dignity of those involved or democracy. The value procedure scholars usually attribute to participation seems to be higher than what it actually has.

Thus, procedural participation is reconcilable with the urgent need to establish representative processes, whose goal is protecting rights that belong to a society (which can be a community or a group). Because there are several ways to describe society, there are also many notions of societies engaging in collective disputes. This means that the process needs to be adapted to the characteristics of each society involved.

Global dispute processes are aimed at preventing society from suffering unlawful damages due to the absence of appropriate mechanisms for judicial protection. Thus, the role of representation is stronger here than that of participation, since the impact of the violation on the individuals that form the society is reduced. In contrast, when local disputes are concerned, the right to participation imposes more restrictions on the representative's performance, given that the dispute is more meaningful for the lives of those entitled to the scrutinized rights. Finally, in irradiated disputes, the process should function as a flexible instrument for participation of the subgroups involved, comprising varied degrees of intensity which will depend on how affected by the violation each group was.

Above all, the characteristics of representation; i.e., the relationship between the representative and his/her representees, are the central point for defining rules for a technically adequate collective process to provide legal protection for violated substantive rights. When the social objectives to be pursued by the plaintiffs are established, and to what extent they must

117 E. Fazzalari, *Istituzioni di diritto processuale* 60 (Padova, Cedam, 1992).

be conditioned by what the absent persons want, then outlining compatible rules with both the constitutional rights of those who do not participate in the process and with the efficiency one expects from one's procedure becomes possible.

The presented construction may also be used to overcome resistance to the implementation of collective actions, verified, for instance, in some European countries. Reservations regarding the implementation of "US-style class actions" could be alleviated if the procedural model was designed to be applied according to the characteristics of the empirically verified dispute.

Even for the US system, this proposal could be helpful in finding a balance that avoids the unnecessary imposition of certification requirements in cases where they are useless.[118] Notifications and *opt-outs* may be important in local disputes, but they certainly involve unnecessary expenditures of time and money in global disputes. Notably, this results in harm for those who were victims of the violation. On the other hand, when it comes to irradiated litigation, the adequate perception of the subgroup's relative position could allow people who have suffered the most serious impacts to have their positions favoured in relation to those who haven't been as affected.

Distinguishing such situations could mean a gain in efficiency for the system of collective protection of rights, reducing its costs on the one hand and increasing the quality of the result on the other. For a long time now it has been public knowledge that it's both convenient and necessary to have collective processes,[119] but it is also true that they turn all the traditional procedural concepts upside down.[120] The distinction of types of dispute, for which the collective procedural rules are applied differently, with appropriate adjustments to the features of each case, can reduce the discomfort of leaving behind traditional values and enhance the gain stemming from the existence of a collective procedural system.

---

118 As was the case in *Eisen v. Carlisle & Jacquelin*, 417 US. 156 (1974). For a critique of this decision due to the unnecessary imposition of procedural requirements, see R. G. Bone, D. S. Evans, "Class certification and substantive merits", 51 *Duke Law Journal* 1251 (2002). See also G. C. Hazard Jr., "Class certification based on merits of the claims", 69 *Tennessee* Law *Review* 1 (2001).

119 F. Calvert, *A Treatise upon the Law Respecting Parties to Suits in Equity* 19 (Philadelphia, John S. Littell, 1837).

120 Hensler et. al., *supra* n. 79, at 15.

II. Access to Justice of Disadvantaged Groups and Judicial Control of Public Policies through Class Actions in Argentina

Francisco Verbic[*]

(I) Research Project

The main objective of my PhD research project is to critically analyze the way judicial review and conventionality control of legislative and administrative decisions which regulate public policy issues operate in Argentina, particularly when put in motion through class action lawsuits filed by citizens, non-governmental organizations (NGOs) and public officers on behalf of disadvantaged groups.

My aim is to work on the strengths and weaknesses of traditional judicial review and control of conventionality doctrines to face this phenomenon, as well as on the political legitimacy of decision-making proceedings and judicial institutional structures, when it comes to dealing with relevant public policy issues affecting specific groups of people whose fundamental rights mostly depend on timely and effective judicial protection because of their lack of political power to influence other democratic and institutional channels, i.e. indigenous peoples, consumers, sexual minorities, poor people, religious minorities, prisoners, disabled people, among others.

In doing this, my thesis project scrutinizes the rules and standards developed by both the Inter-American System of Human Rights (Court and Commission) (IASHR) and the Supreme Court of Justice of Argentina (SCJA) regarding: (i) the features and distinctive profile of these kind of groups of people that make them subject to special protection under the law; (ii) their problems and challenges in accessing justice; (iii) the scope of class actions as a means of access to justice and enforcement of their fundamental rights; (iv) the scope and binding effect of the opinions deliv-

* LL.M. in International Legal Studies (New York University School of Law, USA). Adjunct Professor of Civil Procedure and Academic Secretary of the LL.M. in Procedural Law (Faculty of Law and Social Sciences, National University of La Plata, Argentina).

ered by those judicial (or quasi-judicial) bodies; (v) the new profile of judicial review and conventionality control over statutes and administrative decisions, in particular the redefinition of the "case or controversy" doctrine as a prerequisite of judicial intervention in a dispute.

I plan to complete these general analyses with a thorough description and critical analysis of what is happening (and has happened) with several class actions involving disadvantaged groups in Argentina. The objective is to show the deep evolution of the role of the Judiciary and the SCJA within the new institutional and separation of powers paradigms that were established by the federal constitutional reform of 1994. A reform that, among other things, has given constitutional status to several international human rights covenants, treaties and conventions, and also has explicitly recognized collective standing to sue of citizens, NGOs and the Ombudsman for acting in defense of "collective incidence rights".

With my research I want to demonstrate two fundamental hypotheses.

The first one is the profound inadequacy of current Argentine federal civil procedure (enacted in the National Code of Civil Procedure and several special statutes) to provide for an open, robust, transparent and informed discussion for the sort of socially, politically and economically complex collective conflicts that affect disadvantaged groups, and, because of that, its usual failure to deliver politically legitimate collective decisions before society. The second hypothesis is the urgent need for reform, not only of those procedural rules but also of the institutional structures in charge of processing cases raised by these kinds of social and political conflicts, in order to make judges accountable for the huge amount of political power they have gained due to the constitutional and conventional review of public policies. A power they are exercising very frequently, particularly since 2009 thanks to the interpretation the SCJA gave to the "case or controversy" doctrine in the leading case *Halabi*.[1]

(II) Introduction

Argentina is a federal country, whose central state coexists with 23 local states called provinces and with the City of Buenos Aires, which has a

1 *Halabi, Ernesto c/ P.E.N. – Ley 25.873 y dto. 1563/04 s/ amparo ley 16.986*, SCJA (24 February 2009), *Fallos* 332:111.

very peculiar constitutional status already recognized by the SCJA. Similar to what happens in the US (from where we have copied part of our constitution), federal government only has powers which have been delegated by the provinces. As a consequence, the political system assumes that everything not expressly delegated remains in hands of the provinces.[2]

As far as we are concerned for the analysis that follows, we should take into account that Art. 5 of the Argentine Federal Constitution (AFC) establishes as a condition for recognizing the autonomy of the provinces that they must organize their own justice administration system, a task that includes the enactment of procedural regulations. So, we have at least 25 different procedural systems in Argentina. This paper focuses on the federal one.

In *Section III* I present an overview of the constitutional, statutory and case law landscape in which class actions operate in Argentina, focusing particularly on the provisions of the General Environment Act N° 25.675 (GEA), the Consumers Protection Act N° 24.240 with the reform introduced by Act N° 26.316 (CPA), the *Halabi* case and several administrative regulations enacted by the SCJA in order to deal with mass conflicts. In *Section IV* I briefly assess the barriers preventing access to justice and the capacity of class actions to provide for a reasonable and efficient way to avoid them, while in *Section V* I explore that capacity in relation to situations where the people who need to vindicate their rights belong to a disadvantaged group.

Departing from these premises, *Section VI* analyses a parallel and intimately related issue: the scope of the "case or controversy" doctrine in Argentina, particularly since 2009, and its influence on judicial review of public policies through class actions. In this section I argue that the redefinition of that doctrine has been a game changer in the field of constitutional separation of powers and checks and balances mechanisms, affording the Judiciary –particularly the SCJA- a huge amount of political power.

---

2 See A. Molinario's explanation in J. F. Molloy "Miami Conference Summary of Presentations", 20 *Ariz. J. Int'l & Comp. L.* 47, 49 (2003) (stating that in Argentina "The founding fathers of our country took inspiration from the U.S. Constitution. Thus, our system evolved in the same way as the U.S. system in that states, which we call 'provinces', existed before the federal government. These provinces got together in a Congress and adopted a constitution").

Finally, in *Section VII* I present some preliminary conclusions and hypothesis for the discussion. I mainly support that, as Professor Chayes described 40 years ago concerning the US situation, nowadays in Argentina *"enforcement and application of law is necessarily implementation of regulatory policy. Litigation inevitably becomes an explicitly political forum and the court a visible arm of the political process"*.[3] Because of that, there is a need for an urgent and comprehensive reform of both proceedings and institutional structures.

(III) Class Actions in Argentina

(a) General Constitutional and Statutory Overview

It is not possible to find in Argentina, even at the local level,[4] a systematic and comprehensive procedural mechanism to deal with class actions. The lack of adequate procedural devices at the federal level is particularly problematic because, since the 1994 reform to the AFC, standing to sue to enforce collective rights has acquired constitutional pedigree, as well as some collective substantive rights labeled as "collective incidence rights".[5]

---

3 A. Chayes, "The Role of the Judge in Public Law Litigation", 89 *Harv. L. Rev.* 1281-1316 (1976).

4 There are several local statutes dealing with collective procedural devices in the Argentina's Provinces. However, none of them provide a coherent and comprehensive system to face mass conflicts. The reform to the "amparo" proceeding in Buenos Aires Province can be seen as an example of that (Act N° 14.912, introducing reforms to Act Nº 13.928). Although it still lacks a systemic structure, the current version of the statute can be considered as an improvement because -among other modifications- it contemplates therein the idea of adequacy of representation for the first time in the Province (Art. 7).

5 For an explanation of the problem, see E. D. Oteiza, "La constitucionalización de los derechos colectivos y la ausencia de un proceso que los *ampare*", in: E. D. Oteiza (coordinator), *Procesos Colectivos* 28 (Rubinzal Culzoni Ed., Santa Fe, 2006). For a survey of some of the most relevant precedents in the area of collective rights in Argentina and further discussion about the problems entailed in the absence of adequate procedural means, particularly after the 1994 reform to the AFC, see L. J. Giannini, *La Tutela Colectiva de Derechos Individuales Homogéneos* (Librería Editora Platense, La Plata, 2007); J. M. Salgado, "La corte y la construcción del caso colectivo", *L.L.* 2007-D, 787; F. Verbic, *Procesos Colectivos* (Astrea Ed., Buenos Aires, 2007).

Since 1994, Art. 43, 2nd paragraph of the AFC explicitly recognizes that different social actors (the "affected" person and certain kinds of NGOs) and a governmental institution (the ombudsman) have the right to bring "amparo colectivo" on behalf of groups and against "any kind of discrimination and with regard to the rights that protect the environment, the free competition, users and consumers, as well as rights of collective incidence in general". Art. 86 of the AFC, in turn, is even more explicit about the ombudsman (it plainly states that the figure "has standing to sue"). We can add the Public Ministry to the list of collective plaintiffs, because Art. 120 of the AFC states that it has *"functional autonomy"* and freedom to allocate its budget in order to fulfill its constitutional mission: protect the general interest of the population.

On top of that, Articles 41 and 42 of the AFC (also incorporated in the text by the 1994 reform) recognize several environmental and consumers and users' substantive rights, while Art. 75, section 17° vested Congress with power to enact protective legislation on indigenous peoples. These and other collective rights have been expressly recognized by the 1994 reform to the AFC. The scope of class action litigation becomes even wider if we take into account the constitutional status recognized by Art. 75, section 22° of the AFC to several international covenants subscribed to by Argentina (in which text we could easily find rights that belong to certain kinds of disadvantaged groups).[6]

Notwithstanding those constitutional provisions, the only federal regulations available to deal with collective conflicts involving groups of people in Argentina are the GEA and the CPA.[7] Both of them have been passed by Congress and can be characterized as "substantive" laws. However, in both of them we can find certain isolated procedural provisions applicable, in principle, to deal with collective conflicts involving those particular areas of substantive law.

The CPA was originally enacted in 1993 and underwent several minor reforms regarding its substantive content until 2008, [8] when Act N° 26.361 introduced relevant modifications that included several provisions on class

---

6 Among others, the American Convention on Human Rights.

7 R. Lorenzetti, *Justicia colectiva* 275-276 (Rubinzal Culzoni Ed., Santa Fe, 2010), arguing that the CPA establish an "acción colectiva", but in a "very insufficient way taking into account the abundant comparative law materials completely omitted by the legislator").

8 Acts N° 24.568, N° 24.787 and N° 24.999.

actions. It is important to clarify that even though it is for the Provinces to enact procedural provisions according to Art. 5 of the AFC (as already explained in the introduction), the SCJA has long since recognized the federal government's power to do that when such regulations are deemed absolutely indispensable to enforce substantive rights.[9] In fact, the new Civil and Commercial Code (2015) contained many procedural regulations.

The reform introduced to the CPA by Act N° 26.361 made the system regain the minimal coherence it had lost when the provision on *res judicata* included in the original text of Act N° 24.240 was vetoed by the President.[10] In its current version, the CPA states that a favorable judgment for the plaintiff will produce *res judicata* effects in respect of the defendant and also to all consumers similarly situated, except those who express their will to avoid being bound by the solution.[11] It is considered as a *secundum eventum litis* mechanism,[12] and that right to opt-out should be exercised before the opinion is delivered, and according to the *"the terms and conditions imposed by the judge"*.[13]

The GEA was enacted in 2002, and it also includes procedural regulations to enforce protection of the environment. These provisions concern tort proceedings as well as injunctions to cease polluting activities. In this respect the GEA includes provisions on standing to sue, evidence, provisional and interim measures, powers of the courts in these procedural contexts, *lis pendens*, scope of *res judicata* (a system based on the principle of

9 *Correa, Bernabé c/ Barros, Mario B.,* SCJA (22 June 1923), *Fallos* 138:154.

10 Presidential Decree N° 2089/93. The main reason invoked to sustain this veto was the governmental interest in avoiding the proliferation of cases. The Decree says that the eventual costs of those lawsuits would prejudice merchants and industries, and, through them, the consumers themselves by increasing the final costs of the products.

11 Some justifications for this recognition has been provided by Irigoyen, who was the Reporter of the Commission that worked on the new Art. 42 AFC during the meetings that preceded the constitutional reform of 1994. In a scholarly article published soon after the reform was passed, he said that "the scope of res judicata in *amparo* actions should be expansive because it is evident that the situation which trigger the application of that proceeding involves the interest of many people, and because it would be nonsense to recognize *res judicata* effects only in respect to the individual who filed the suit" (R. Irigoyen "Fundamentos de la cláusula constitucional sobre defensa del consumidor", *L.L.* 1994-E-1020).

12 Lorenzetti, *supra* n. 7, at 282-283.

13 Art. 54, 2nd para. of the CPA.

secundum eventum probationem), and jurisdiction.[14] This regulation is really incomplete and insufficient to deal with environmental collective conflicts.

(b) Case Law General Overview: The Halabi Case and its Progeny

The turning point in class actions development in Argentina was the opinion delivered by the SCJA at the beginning of 2009 in the *Halabi* case. Though striking, the opinion was not unexpected as the SCJA had already delivered some opinions regarding different aspects of class actions. Most of these opinions had been rendered in environmental and human rights cases. Moreover, the rationale of the majority opinion in *Halabi* had been insinuated, at least in its more relevant aspects, in some of the dissenting opinions in those earlier cases.[15]

Ernesto Halabi was a lawyer and user of mobile phones and internet services, who filed an "amparo" seeking a declaration of unconstitutionality of a federal statute that had allowed the interception of private phone and Internet communications without prior judicial order.[16] The case reached the SCJA with the substantive issue already solved: the Court of Appeal had already declared the Act unconstitutional and extended the binding effects of the solution to all users of the telecommunication system who were similarly situated. That is why the only issue to be discussed in the SCJA was the collective binding effects of the Court of Appeal's opinion.

When deciding the case, the majority of the SCJA asserted that it is possible to file in Argentina class actions (which it labeled "acción colectiva") with "analogous characteristics and effects to the US class actions". It also plainly held that Art. 43 AFC provisions are clearly operative and must be enforced by the courts, even in the absence of legislation. More-

---

14 Arts. 30 to 34 GEA.

15 *Mendoza I,* SCJA (20 June 2006), File n° M.1569.XL; *Asociación de Superficiarios de la Patagonia I,* SCJA (29 August 2006), case A.1274.XXXIX; *Defensoría del Pueblo*, SCJA (31 October 2006), File n° D. 859. XXXVI; *Mujeres por la Vida*, SCJA (31 October 2006), File n° M.970.XXXIX; *Mendoza II*, SCJA (8 July 2008), File n° M.1569.XL; *Asociación de Superficiarios de la Patagonia II*, SCJA (26 August 2008), case A.1274.XXXIX.

16 Act N° 25.873 and Executive Decree N° 1563/04 (the media referred to the Act as "the spy statute").

over, the SCJA enunciated constitutional requirements for obtaining a valid collective opinion under due process of law standards. After underscoring the lack of an adequate procedural regulation enacted by Congress on class actions, the Court made some remarks to provide guidance in order to protect the due process of law for absent class members in future uses of the "*acción colectiva*".[17]

The SCJA held that the *"formal admissibility"* of any "acción colectiva" must be subject to the fulfillment of the following requirements: (i) there has to be a precise identification of the group of people that is being represented in the case; (ii) the plaintiff must be an adequate representative of the class; (iii) the claim has to focus on questions of fact or law common and homogeneous to the whole class; (iv) there has to be a proceeding capable of providing adequate notice to all persons that might have an interest in the outcome of the case; (v) that notice of proceeding has to provide members of the class an opportunity to opt-out or to intervene; and (vi) there should be adequate publicity and advertising of the action in order to avoid two different but related problems: on the one hand, the multiplicity or superposition of collective proceedings with similar causes of action; and on the other, the risk of different or incompatible opinions on identical issues.

So far, so good. However, the issue of cases involving positive value claims may bring about some difficulties in the near future. As we have said, the SCJA asserted that Art. 43 of the AFC is operative and that it is an obligation for the courts to enforce it. But this holding was qualified in the same opinion: the Court continued by saying that the enforcement should proceed "when there is clear evidence about the harm to a fundamental right and to the access to justice of its holder".[18] According to this statement, those cases involving positive value claims would not qualify to be litigated on a representative basis (because, in the view of the Court, there is no harm to the access to justice right of its holder, who has sufficient interest at stake to file an individual lawsuit on his own).

Taking into account this holding, it can be said that -as a matter of principle- the SCJA forbids class actions for damages when individual interests at stake justify individual lawsuits. This is hard to justify because there are neither constitutional nor legal or principle foundations to sustain

17 Para. 20 of the majority opinion.
18 Para. 13 of the majority opinion.

such a narrow view of the scope of class action litigation. Art. 43 of the AFC does not contain any sort of limitation in this sense. The same could be said about the CPA and GEA. The problem with such an approach to the phenomenon of collective redress, which seems to be aligned with the European one, is that it deprives class actions of one of the main advantages they could advance in contemporary litigation landscapes: judicial efficiency.[19]

The SCJA case law (*Halabi* and its progeny) provides no explanation at all regarding why collective redress could only be performed in Argentina when access to justice is compromised. That is particularly striking if we take into account the fact that official statistics from the national and federal judiciary show a quite heavy caseload to deal with every single year (and, everybody knows even in the absence of official statistics, that many of those cases are repetitive and could be efficiently handled together).

In 2013 (latest available statistics) the National Commercial Appellate Court, with jurisdiction only in Buenos Aires City, delivered 13,453 opinions, while Commercial Courts of First Instance (district courts) had 210,898 pending cases. The Federal Civil and Commercial Appellate Court, in turn, at the end of 2013 had 4,594 pending cases, while Federal Civil and Commercial Courts of First Instance (district courts) had 50,449 pending cases. Other forums which present a huge number of repetitive litigation are those dealing with social security lawsuits: The Social Security Federal Appellate Court had, at the end of 2013, 59,446 pending cases; while the Social Security Courts of First Instance (district courts) had

19 European Commission Recommendation of 11 June 2013 (2013/396/RU), Art. 1 defines its purposes without mentioning judicial efficiency among its goals: "The purpose of this Recommendation is to facilitate access to justice, stop illegal practices and enable injured parties to obtain compensation in mass harm situations caused by violations of rights granted under Union law, while ensuring appropriate procedural safeguards to avoid abusive litigation". Efficiency value is only mentioned in that Recommendation in respect to ADR (para. 16 of the preamble: *"Alternative dispute resolution procedures can be an efficient way of obtaining redress in mass harm situations..."*) and the enforcement of injunctive orders (Art. 20: *"Efficient enforcement of injunctive orders"*). For recent developments on collective redress in Europe, see S. Voet, "European Collective Redress: A Status Quaestionis", 4 *Int'l Journal of Procedural Law* 97; E. Silvestri "Towards a Common Framework of Collective Redress in Europe? An Update on the Latest Initiatives of the European Commission", 1 *Russian Law Journal* 46 (2013).

138,266 pending cases.[20] Numbers at the SCJA are equally compelling: in 2012 the Court delivered 9,586 opinions in "no social security cases" and 6,452 in social security cases; in 2013 a total of 15,792 opinions; and in 2014 a total of 23,183 opinions.[21]

In this complex context, and perhaps in order to preserve its discretion in this delicate field of litigation, the SCJA established in *Halabi* an exception to this rule of "meritorious individual lawsuits" as a limit for class action litigation. A relevant exception in what matters the most for the purposes of this paper: class actions would also be admissible when the case involves a *"strong state interest"* in the protection of the rights involved in the dispute (not a *"public interest"* but a *"state"* one, whatever that may imply). The Court held that this "state interest" could arise either from *"the social significance"* of the rights in dispute (the SCJA mentioned environmental, consumers and health rights), or from the *"particular features of the affected class"* (the SCJA referred to *"traditionally disadvantaged or weakly protected groups"*).[22]

The exception is so broad that it affords the SCJA almost absolute discretion to deal with collective conflicts every time it wants to (even when individual actions are justified). I maintain that because consumer and environmental rights are the main fields of collective litigation in Argentina. And if we talk about disadvantaged or weakly protected sectors of the population, the spectrum could include several minority groups who are way beyond consumer and environmental fields. Last but not least, what sort of collective conflict would not demand a "strong state interest" in its peaceful, equal and just resolution? As was stated, this exception almost deprives the rule under analysis of any meaningful content.[23]

The SCJA has already begun to make use of the broad discretion provided by this exception. In a recent opinion, it voided a Federal Appellate Court opinion in order to allow a class action where an NGO was seeking declaratory and economic relief for a group of children, women, elders

---

20 All statistics available at http://www.pjn.gov.ar/07_estadisticas/ (Last visited 5 June 2016).

21 These SCJA opinions are not necessarily on the merits of cases, but they demonstrate the demanding caseload that must be faced every year by a Court which, nowadays, has only three Judges.

22 *Halabi*, para. 13 of the majority opinion; *PADEC*, para. 10 of the majority opinion.

23 F. Verbic, "Class actions in Argentina: the need for a wider scope to embrace judicial efficiency", 6 *Civil Procedure Review*, 95 (2015).

and disabled people.[24] In this precedent, the SCJA held that, even though individual actions were justified due to the economic stakes in dispute, collective redress was still admissible because it was "not possible to avoid the unquestionable social content of the rights involved in the dispute, which pertain to groups that must be subject to preferential protection by constitutional mandates due to their vulnerable condition".[25]

Besides *Halabi*, there is another relevant precedent to consider in this field: *PADEC c. Swiss Medical*.[26] This opinion was delivered four years and a half after *Halabi*. There, the SCJA corroborated the collective redress model currently operational in Argentina. A hybrid model, where the definition of certain kinds of substantive collective rights (following the Brazilian Consumers Protection Code system) is merged with procedural safeguards taken from the US Federal Rule of Civil Procedure 23 (FRCP 23).[27] Between *Halabi* and *PADEC v. Swiss Medical,* the SCJA delivered only a few opinions regarding specific aspects of class actions.

(c) SCJA Administrative Regulations

Due to the institutional relevance and the public interest involved in class actions, the SCJA put in motion its inherent powers and enacted different administrative regulations in order to amplify and strengthen citizenship involvement, improve publicity and increase transparency in those kinds of cases. These regulations include: (i) Acordada N° 36/2003, on the proceeding to provide priority treatment to cases of *"institutional transcendence"*; (ii) Acordada N° 28/2004 (amended by the Acordada N° 7/2013), on the *amicus curiae*; (iii) Acordada N° 30/2007, providing for public hearings; (iv) Acordada N° 36/2009, creating an Economic Analysis Unit to perform *"economic studies"* ordered by the Court to assess the eventual

---

24 *Asociación Civil para la Defensa en el Ámbito Federal e Internacional de Derechos c/ Instituto Nacional de Servicios Sociales para Jubilados y Pensionados s/ amparo*, SCJA (10 February 2015), file N° CSJ 000721/2007(43-A)/CS1.

25 Para. 9 of the Court opinion.

26 *PADEC c/ Swiss Medical s/ Nulidad de cláusulas contractuales*, SCJA (21 August 2013), file Nº P.361.XLIII.

27 F. Verbic, "La decisión de la SCJA en *PADEC c. Swiss Medical*. Ratificación de *Halabi* y confirmación de las bases para un modelo de tutela colectiva de derechos en Argentina", *Revista de Derecho Comercial, del Consumidor y de la Empresa,* 124 (2013).

impact of its decisions; (v) Acordada N° 1/2014, creating an Environmental Justice Office for better treatment of environmental cases; (vi) Acordada Nº 36/2015, creating the Judicial Secretary of Consumers Relationships; and (vii) Acordada Nº 42/2015, creating the Secretary of Communication and Open Government.

Notwithstanding the relevance of these decisions, their implementation has been far from satisfactory. For example, since 2004 only eight cases have been published by the SCJA to allow the intervention of *amicus curiae*.[28] Other *amicus* have been filed in other cases, for example in the leading case *Halabi*. But the number of official publications (which operate as a public invitation) may indicate that the SCJA is not comfortable with opening for discussion every public interest proceeding. Something alike happens concerning public hearings. From its enactment in 2008, only 25 of these hearings have been performed.[29] It is far from a significant number if we take into account the cases of institutional, social, political and economic relevance the SCJA has decided in that period.

Two other regulations must be particularly taken into account because they have translated the *Halabi* requirements and standards into positive law: (i) Acordada N° 32/2014, creating the Collective Proceedings Public Registry and establishing in its Art. 3 a sort of "certification stage" because it demands Federal Judges to deliver an opinion on admissibility requirements, notice and adequacy of representation before communicating the existence of a case to the Registry; and (ii) Acordada N° 12/2016, in effect since 1 October 2016, enacting a Regulation of Collective Proceedings which contains provisions on jurisdiction, appeals, registration and *lis pendens*, among others.

It is difficult to sustain the constitutionality of these last two regulations because they provide for procedural law that should be enacted by Congress. However, it is hard to believe that the SCJA would review its own administrative acts in such a way. Besides that, it is worth mentioning that these regulations came to occupy a statutory empty space which implies huge problems of legal certainty as well as severe difficulties of co-

28 See at http://www.csjn.gov.ar/causas-en-tramite/amigos-del-tribunal (last visited 6 May 2016).

29 See the SCJA special website here: http://www.cij.gov.ar/audiencias.html (Year - Number of public hearings: 2008 – 5 / 2009 – 4 / 2010 – 2 / 2011 – 2 / 2012 – 6 / 2013 – 2 / 2014 – 2 / 2015 – 2) (last visited 6 May 2016).

ordination between overlapping and parallel litigation (just to mention a couple of critical issues).

(IV) Barriers on Access to Justice

Many studies have shown that there are two predominant factors which block access of individuals to the civil justice system. The first is the lack of financial resources to afford the costs of litigation, while the second is lack of ability to understand and use the legal system.[30]

(a) Economic Barriers

The most relevant economic barriers to access to justice are those imposed by the high cost of lawyers, experts witnesses (when necessary for the correct adjudication of the dispute) and, at least in some jurisdictions, the high costs imposed by courts as a condition of filing lawsuits.[31] As Smith put it many years ago, it is not possible to identify a principle governing the issue of litigation costs: "they are too low to deter the rich, but high enough to prohibit the poor".[32] The features and names of the different kind of expenses and fees have certainly changed since then, as well as some of the rules governing the allocation of those costs. However, two relevant facts remain unaltered in the Argentine context: on the one hand, the fundamental difficulty for litigants posed by the high costs of counsel; and on the other, the relevance of counsel in order to have an adequate defense within the case.[33]

---

30 See Michael R. Anderson, "Access to Justice and Legal Process: Making Legal Institutions Responsive to Poor People in LDCs", at 18, available at http://siteresources.worldbank.org/INTPOVERTY/Resources/WDR/DfiD-Project-Papers/anderson.pdf (Last visited 6 May 2016).

31 J. E. Bonine, "Best Practices – Access to Justice (Agenda for Public Interest Law Reform)", at 2, available at http://www.accessinitiative.org/resources/best-practices-access-justice (last visited 6 May 2016).

32 R. Heber Smith, "Justice and the Poor", *The Carnegie Foundation for the Advancement of Teaching*, Bulletin nr. 13, 23 (1919).

33 Smith *supra* n. 32, at 31 (arguing that "The expense of counsel is a fundamental difficulty because the attorney is an integral part of the administration of justice").

(b) Cultural Barriers and the Complexity of Modern Law

A report produced by a state Access to Justice Commission in the US highlights the fact that the lives of poor people "are highly regulated and the intersection between statutes, regulations and decisional laws is not obvious to those without experience".[34] Indeed, the real problems faced every day by disadvantaged groups are intimately related to issues of legal language, access to information about rights and other cultural factors that converge to deny equal access to justice.[35] These difficulties are more severe with regard to some particular groups, such as immigrants.[36]

What are the sources of these problems? Perhaps the main cause is the extreme complexity of contemporary legal systems (not only for lay people, but also for lawyers themselves).[37] This phenomenon is not new, af-

34 "Rationing Justice: the Effect of the Recession on Access to Justice in the District of Columbia", *Joint Report of the District of Columbia Access to Justice Commission and the D.C. Consortium of Legal Services Providers*, (November 2009), at 4, available at http://www.dcaccesstojustice.org/files/Rationing_Justice_Report_final_PDF_.pdf (last visited 6 May 2016).

35 See the Amicus Brief in support of the University of Michigan presented before the Supreme Court in the case *Grutter v. Bollinger and Gratz v. Bollinger* by the Hispanic National Bar Association and the Hispanic Association of Colleges and Universities [14 *Berkeley La Raza L.J.* 69, 83 (2003)]; R. R. Kuehn, "Undermining Justice: The Legal Profession's Role in Restricting Access to Legal Representation", *Utah L. Rev.* 1039, 1040 (2006), arguing that "lower-income persons likely encounter greater geographical, literacy, cultural, and language barriers just to access the justice system, much less to use the system successfully".

36 See R. T. Y. Moon, "Access to Civil Justice: Is There a Solution?", 88 *Judicature* 155 (2004-2005) (noting that "for the increasing number of immigrants who have come to the U.S. in recent years, the problem of access to justice has been compounded by issues pertaining to language barriers, cultural differences, and difficulties associated with assimilating into the mainstream of American life"). The same kind of problems affect this group in other areas as well, see J. C. Dubin, "Clinical Design for Social Justice Imperatives", 51 *SMU L. Rev.* 1461, 1485 (1998) (arguing that language and cultural barriers also place obstacles to immigrants in their search of employment).

37 N. Black, "Lawyers Should not be Wary of Cloud Computing", 72 *Tex. B.J.* 746 (2009) (arguing that "The complexities of modern law practice are such that managing a law office in the absence of practice management software programs is nothing short of impossible"); K. Mazza, "Divorce Mediation. Perhaps not the Remedy it was Once Considered", 14 *SPG Fam. Advoc.* 40, 42 (1992) (arguing that "Given the complexities of modern law, both statutory and case law, and its continuing evolution, non-lawyers are ill-equipped to give advice on legal is-

fects almost every area of law and, of course, is not exclusive to Argentina or the US.[38] For the purpose of this paper, what matters the most is that, as Jennings stated in 1932, "so great is the complexity of modern law that the citizen is unable to determine his rights and duties in any situation which is even a little out of his normal course of life".[39]

Even though achieving the elimination of the complexities of substantive and procedural law is a kind of utopia,[40] it has been argued that the legal system *"may be amenable to simplification"*.[41] Different proposals have been presented to accomplish that objective (e.g. reduce legal technicalities and simplify legal language,[42] altering the lawyer's monopoly on the justice system and demystifying the law so that lay people can under-

---

sues"); J. M. Fischer, "External Control Over the American Bar", 19 *Geo. J. Legal Ethics* 59, 67 (2005) (arguing that this complexity has led to a trend among lawyers "toward specialization"); in the same line, S. K. Berenson, "A Family Law Residency Program?: A Modest Proposal in Response to the Burdens Created by Self-represented Litigants in Family Court", 33 *Rutgers L.J.* 105, 160 (2001) (arguing that "The economics and complexities of modern law practice have only served to increase the forces pushing in the direction of further specialization"); H. G. Pollack, "The Admissibility and Utility of Expert Legal Testimony in Patent Litigation", 32 *IDEA* 361 (1992) (noting the complexity of modern law as one of the factors which "may have changed the prevailing judicial attitude toward the utilization of legal experts").

38 T. Schmitz, "Matthias Ruffert (ed.). The Transformation of Administrative Law in Europe", Book Review, 19 Eur. *J. Int'l L.* 617, 625 (2008). She points to the high degree of complexity of modern administrative law, which has made it "unteachable".

39 See W. I. Jennings, "Declaratory Judgments against Public Authorities in England", 41 *Yale L.J.* 407 (1932). See also Smith, *supra* n. 32, at 31 (arguing that "With a vast body of ever changing law, which a man after a lifetime of devotion is only beginning to master, it is apparent that the layman, in order to understand his rights, what can and cannot do, must have the assistance of counsel").

40 History seems to show that the trend is going exactly in the opposite way. See M. Weber, *Economy and Society* (University of California Press, Berkeley and Los Angeles, 1978), at 895 (arguing that "Whatever form law and legal practice may come to assume … it will be inevitable that, as a result of technical and economic developments, the legal ignorance of the layman will increase").

41 D. R. Johnson, "The Legal Needs of the Poor as a Starting Point for Systemic Reform", 17 *Yale L. & Pol'y Rev.* 479, 486 (1998).

42 M. R. Anderson, "Access to Justice and Legal Process: Making Legal Institutions Responsive to Poor People in LDCs", at 25, available at http://siteresources.worldbank.org/INTPOVERTY/Resources/WDR/DfiD-Project-Papers/anderson.pdf (last visited 6 May 2016).

stand it,[43] etc.). However, an overview of any contemporary legal system shows that we are far away from that.

(c) A Dangerous Combination

Both economic and cultural barriers bring about severe obstacles to access the civil justice system. While this is true in general terms and can be proven in relation to any middle class citizen, the concern is even deeper when assessed in relation to disadvantaged groups of people. Undeniably, the combination of both barriers is almost always involved every time that a group of this kind needs access to justice to vindicate a fundamental right affected by the public policies of decision makers. As a report on access to justice explains "It is the experience of long-time legal services lawyers that many potential clients fail to seek services because they lack information about their rights, they cannot afford transportation or they are discouraged by prior experiences of not receiving services at an office that was too busy to help".[44]

The situation in Argentina is quite similar. A recent empirical study from Asociación Civil por la Igualdad y la Justicia (an NGO) concluded that: (i) lack of information regarding the extension of legal context and individual rights is a structural problem, at least in socioeconomic disadvantaged groups; (ii) data shows that there is a gap regarding access to information and widespread ignorance of available mechanisms to solve conflicts.[45]

---

43 Johnson, *supra* n. 41, at 484 (1998).

44 "Rationing Justice: the Effect of the Recession on Access to Justice in the District of Columbia", *Joint Report of the District of Columbia Access to Justice Commission and the D.C. Consortium of Legal Services Providers* (November 2009), at 2, available at http://www.dcaccesstojustice.org/files/Rationing_Justice_Report_final_PDF_.pdf (last visited 6 May 2016).

45 ACIJ, "Sectores populares, derechos y acceso a la justicia" (December 2013), available at http://acij.org.ar/wp-content/uploads/2014/06/Informe-Sectores-populares-derechos-y-acceso-a-la-justicia.pdf (last visited 6 May 2016).

(V) Access to Justice, Class Actions and Disadvantaged Groups

(a) Access to Justice as One of the Main Goals of Class Actions

Since the 1966 reform to the Federal Rule of Civil Procedure 23 in the US (the model for the Argentine class actions procedural system, as we have already seen), class actions have a potential *"broadly to affect access to court"*. In fact, that appears to have been one of the main goals of the reform.[46] According to Kaplan, that kind of procedure works plainly as *"something like the function of an administrative proceeding where scattered individual interests are represented by the Government*". This is especially true when the rights at stake are not relevant and/or the people entitled to them are more likely to neglect or abandon their claims due to different reasons (like ignorance, economic limitations, timidity or unfamiliarity with business or legal matters).[47]

How do class actions provide a plausible channel to access the civil justice system? The answer can be found in the fact that they eliminate (or at least drastically diminish) the power differential which exists between the group of affected people and the defendant. The clearest example of this can be seen in relation to "small claims", i.e. claims for which the costs of litigation do not justify the effort of bringing them before a court of justice because those costs have no reasonable relation with the best result that can be achieved by winning the case. The possibility of pooling those small claims in a class action suit increases the defendant's potential liability and ensures that they can enter the judicial system by attracting lawyers to litigate the case on a contingency fee basis.[48]

It is relevant for this study to underline that class actions do not only play a role in relation to claims that otherwise would not be litigated on grounds of economic reasons. From the same access to justice perspective,

46 S. B. Burbank, "Civil Procedure Reform in Comparative Context: The United States of America", 45 *Am. J. Comp. L.* 675, 684 (1997).

47 B. Kaplan, "Continuing Work of the Civil Committee: 1966 Reforms of the Federal Rules of Civil Procedure (I)", 81 *Harv. L. Rev*. 356, 398 (1967).

48 See K. Melnick "In Defense of the Class Action Lawsuit: An Examination of the Implicit Advantages and a Response to Common Criticisms", 22 *St. John's J. Legal Comment.* 755, 790 (2008). But see also C. Silver, "'We're Scared to Death: Class Certification and Blackmail", 78 *N.Y.U. L. Rev.* 1357, 1373 (2003) (arguing that defendants tend to settle the case for substantial amounts once the class action is certified because the suit creates remote risks of financial ruin).

class actions represent a particularly interesting device when it comes to deal with the other sort of barriers to the courts that we have pointed out in Section IV (b): the social, cultural and educational ones. In this sense, class actions can also enable litigation by bringing into the legal system claims which individuals are otherwise unaware of.[49]

(b) Access to Justice and Disadvantaged Groups of People

Several examples in Argentina can demonstrate how deep this access to justice goal of class actions can go when it comes to dealing with disadvantaged groups of people. As we have seen, in *Halabi,* the SCJA held that Art. 43 AFC provisions are clearly operational and must be enforced by courts, even in the absence of legislation.[50] In that precedent, the SCJA also stressed the importance of providing for collective means of access to justice for certain groups or social classes that it characterized as *"traditionally disadvantaged or weakly protected"*.[51] The same holding stands for cases involving rights of *"social significance"* like –according to the SCJA ruling- environmental, consumers and health rights.

Before expressing in such a clear way this essential principle of collective access to justice, the SCJA had already delivered several opinions in collective cases involving disadvantaged groups. For example, it provided for collective redress in cases involving prisoners' human rights,[52] poor people with health problems caused by environmental pollution,[53] prisoners' right to vote,[54] people with HIV who couldn't get their medicine even

49 See RAND Institute for Civil Justice "Class Actions Dilemmas: Pursuing Public Goals for Private Gain" (Santa Monica, Calif. 2000), at 49 (arguing that class actions require telling people that "they may have a claim of which they were previously unaware, but does not require them to take any initial action to join the litigation").

50 *Halabi,* para. 12 of the majority opinion.

51 *Halabi*, para. 13 of the majority opinion; *PADEC*, para. 10 of the majority opinion.

52 *Recurso de hecho deducido por el Centro de Estudios Legales y Sociales en la causa Verbitsky, Horacio s/ habeas corpus*, SCJA (5 March 2005), *Fallos* 328:1146.

53 *Mendoza, Beatriz Silvia y otros c/ Estado Nacional y otros s/ daños y perjuicios*, SCJA interlocutory opinion delivered in 20 June 2006, *Fallos* 329:2316, and opinion on the merits delivered in 8 July 2008, *Fallos* 331:1622.

54 *Mignone, Emilio Fermín s/ promueve acción de amparo*, SCJA (9 April 2002), *Fallos* 325:524.

though an Act of Congress recognized that right and ordered the Executive to implement it.[55] And this is without counting a relevant number of consumers' cases where the SCJA, even though not deciding on the merits, had vacated and remanded decisions rejecting different sorts of collective claims on formal grounds.[56]

(VI) The Scope of "Case or Controversy" Doctrine and its Influence on Judicial Review of Public Policies through Class Actions

In almost every case mentioned in this paper, the SCJA has reviewed Legislative Acts, Executive Decrees and even omissions of the Legislature and the Executive (both federal and local) regarding relevant public policy issues. Is it constitutionally plausible? Is it politically appropriate?

First of all, it is undeniable that the Judiciary has both a constitutional and conventional duty to intervene in the context of "cases or controversies". This scenario is a consequence of the organic and institutional model of checks and balances the AFC adopted in 1853, which is –as we have mentioned- a copy of the US Federal Constitution in this respect.[57]

It is undeniable as well that, in exercising this duty, it has to review the conventionality and constitutionality of omissions, acts and administrative decisions delivered by the other branches of government when they affect

55 *Asociación Benghalensis y otros c/ Ministerio de Salud y Acción Social - Estado Nacional s/ amparo ley 16.986*, SCJA (6 January 2000), *Fallos* 323:1339.

56 *PADEC c/ Swiss Medical s/ Nulidad de cláusulas contractuales*, SCJA (21 August 2013), file N° P.361.XLIII; *Unión de Usuarios y Consumidores c/ Telefónica Comunicaciones Personales S.A.*, SCJA (03 June 2014), file N° U.2.XLV; *Consumidores Financieros c/ Banco Itaú Buen Ayre Argentina S.A. s/ ordinario*, SCJA (24 June 2014), file N° C.1074.XLVI; *Consumidores Financieros c/ La Meridional Compañía Argentina de Seguros S.A. s/ ordinario*, SCJA (24 June 2014), file N° C.519.XLVIII; *Unión de Consumidores de Argentina c. CTI PCS S.A. s/ Sumarísimo*, SCJA (15 July 2014), file N° U.24.XLVI; *Asociación Civil para la Defensa en el Ámbito Federal e Internacional de Derechos c/ Instituto Nacional de Servicios Sociales para Jubilados y Pensionados s/ amparo*, SCJA (10 February 2015), file N° CSJ 000721/2007(43-A)/CS1.

57 For a historical analysis of the relationship between the SCJA and the other branches of government in Argentina before the 1994 reform, see E. D. Oteiza, *La Corte Suprema. Entre una justicia sin política y una política sin justicia* (Librería Editora Platense S.R.L., La Plata, 1994).

individual or collective fundamental rights.[58] Since the 1994 reform, that duty has been reinforced by the new profile acquired by the AFC. Particularly because of the constitutional status given to "collective incidence rights" and collective standing to sue to protect them, as well as the recognition of the constitutional status of several human, economic, social, cultural, political and civil rights in international covenants.

The power of judicial review, however, has traditionally raised well known complex and deep criticisms based, mostly, on the lack of democratic legitimacy of judges.[59] If we are talking about collective conflicts involving public interest issues and disadvantaged groups, we need to take a position in this respect.

First of all, Argentine Judiciary is a public power as democratic as the Executive and the Legislative powers are, even though its political legitimacy does not stem from a public vote (in Argentina federal judges are appointed by the Executive Power with the Senate agreement).[60] This idea takes as a premise that democracy is not only the rule of majority, but also a core of fundamental rights that must be respected.[61]

Secondly, I consider that the Judiciary's participation in solving collective and public interest conflicts involving judicial review of public poli-

---

58 On conventionality control see F. Verbic, "Control de convencionalidad en el sistema interamericano de protección de derechos humanos. principales características y algunos apuntes sobre su aplicación en el ordenamiento jurídico argentino", 14 *Revista Iberoamericana de Derecho Procesal* 283 (2012).

59 Among others, see J. H. Ely, *Democracia y Desconfianza* (Ed. Siglo del Hombre, Santa Fe de Bogotá, 1997); R. Gargarella, *La justicia frente al gobierno* (Ed. Ariel, España, 1996); R. Gargarella, "La dificultad de defender el control judicial de las leyes", *ISONOMÍA* N° 6 (Abril 1997) at 55-70; R. Gargarella, *Crítica de la Constitución. Sus zonas oscuras* (Ed. Capital Intelectual, Bs. As., 2004); O.M. Fiss, "The Supreme Court 1978 term", 93 *Harv. L. Rev.* 1 (1979); C.S. Nino, *Fundamentos de Derecho Constitucional* 657 (Ed. Astrea, Bs. As. 2000); C. Nino, *La Constitución en la democracia deliberativa* 258 (Ed. Gedisa, Barcelona, 1997); R. Dahl, "La toma de decisiones en una democracia: la Corte Suprema como una institución que crea políticas públicas", *Revista Jurídica de la Universidad de Palermo*, año 8, N° 1 (2008).

60 Verbic *supra* n. 5, at 278-288. But see also a different opinion from Brazil in J. M. R. Tesheiner, "Acoes coletivas e legitimidade democrática do poder judiciario", (27 December 2010) available at http://www.processoscoletivos.com.br/index.php/9-ponto-e-contraponto/729-acoes-coletivas-e-legitimidade-democratica-do-poder-judiciario (last visited 5 June 2016).

61 See, in general, R. Dworkin, *Talking Rights Seriously* (Cambridge: Harvard University Press, 1977).

cies does not necessarily imply an invasion of other State powers (as some sectors dogmatically argue). If the Judiciary acts within the scope of its powers, exercising an adequate self-restraint when necessary, it will be accomplishing its constitutional duty and nothing more.[62]

This position has been held by the SCJA in several precedents. Among them, we can mention two recent opinions. The first one was delivered in a case filed by the Ombudsman with the aim of controlling the conditions of the rail public transportation service.[63] Justice Fayt stated in this case that "the republican form of government [...] and the separation of powers principle, impose the necessity of harmonizing the exercise of that essential judicial role with the power of the other branches of government in order to ensure their equilibrium and coexistence" (para. 7). The other opinion was delivered in the context of an environmental case filed by an NGO to stop the construction of two major dams in the south of the country. The opinion of Chief Justice Lorenzetti and Justice Maqueda held that the AFC demands from the Judiciary "a control over the activities of the other branches of government".[64]

Third, we must underline that the AFC (from its origins, not only since the 1994 reform) vested the Judiciary with exclusive and inalienable powers and duties. What I intend to say in this obvious statement is that the discussion and adjudication of collective conflicts is a true obligation of the Judiciary when those conflicts are presented before it in the form of a "case or controversy" (Art. 116 AFC).[65]

In this regard it is essential to bear in mind that the SCJA has redefined in *Halabi* the notion of "case or controversy" by making crystal clear that there are both "individual cases and controversies" and "collective cases and controversies". Through this holding, in my view one of the most rele-

---

62 See M. S. Sagües, "Perfil de la Corte Suprema de Justicia de la Nación en el marco del pacto de Estado para la justicia. Ámbito institucional y revisor en la dinámica jurisdiccional y política actual", in: E.D. Oteiza, *Reforma Procesal Civil* 493 (Ed. Rubinzal Culzoni, Santa Fe, 2010).

63 *Defensor del Pueblo de la Nación c/ Trenes de Buenos Aires (TBA) y otro s/ Amparo Ley 16.986*, SCJA (24 June 2014), File n° D.275.XLVI.

64 *Asociación Argentina de Abogados Ambientalistas de la Patagonia c/ Santa Cruz, Provincia de y otro s/ amparo ambiental*, SCJA (26 April 2016), file N° CSJ 5258/2014 - ORIGINARIO.

65 Art. 116 of the AFC states that *"Is for the Supreme Court and for the national inferior courts"* to decide *"every cases* ("causas") *which involve aspects regulated by the Constitution and the Laws of the Nation".*

vant of the whole opinion, the SCJA has drastically amplified the possibilities for discussing before courts conflicts involving large groups of people.[66] And, by doing this, it has also drastically amplified its own political power and changed the way separation of powers work in Argentina.

Summing up, we maintain that –theoretically and as a matter of principle- it is not possible to argue that the Argentine Judiciary is invading other's privative public powers when it acts within the context of a "collective case or controversy". On the contrary, the invasion will effectively occur if the Judiciary exceeds that context, which operates as nothing more than a limit to its power.

However, this statement warrants at least two cautions.

The first one is that the doctrine of "case or controversy" is nothing more than a discursive instrument that has been traditionally used (and is being used) by the Judiciary in a clearly political way to avoid dealing with certain delicate social and economic issues or, instead, to start being part of those delicate discussions, as has been the case with the SCJA for the last 7 years (since *Halabi*). This implies that it is the Judiciary itself that delineates and determines the scope of its own powers and competences through the interpretation of the notion of "case or controversy". From this perspective, I think it is quite interesting to observe how this doctrine has taken the place in Argentine judicial opinions formerly occupied by the doctrine of "political questions"[67] and then by the doctrine of "standing to sue".[68]

The second caution has to do with knowing that Judiciary abuses can also arise in the remedy stage. That is: even when acting correctly within

66 See G. Maurino, E. Nino, M. Sigal, *Las acciones colectivas* 210 (Ed. LexisNexis, Bs. As., 2005); J. M. Salgado, "La corte y la construcción del caso colectivo", *L.L.Sup.Const.* 2007 (June), 1; Verbic, *supra* n. 5, at 294-296.

67 On the scope and use of this doctrine see R. Haro, "El control jurisdiccional y las 'cuestiones políticas': Nuevas perspectivas", *Academia Nacional de Derecho y Ciencias Sociales de Córdoba*, available at www.acaderc.org.ar/doctrina/articulos/artcontroljurisdiccional/at_download/file (last visited 5 June 2016).

68 On the political role of standing to sue doctrine in Argentina, see Verbic, *supra* n. 5, at 91-103. Precedents interpreting the scope of Art. 86 of the AFC, regarding the ombudsman standing to sue, in the first 10 years after the 1994 constitutional reform is quite demonstrative of that political use (see F. Verbic, "La (negada) legitimación activa del Defensor del Pueblo de la Nación para accionar en defensa de derechos de incidencia colectiva. Buscando razones a la doctrina de la Corte Suprema", *RDP* 2007-1 at 603-626.

the frame of a "collective case or controversy", judges can exceed their limits when defining the scope and characteristics of the solution given to the case, and even in the context of enforcement proceedings entertained to make those remedies effective.[69]

(VII) Provisional Conclusions

Social conflicts have changed in Argentina, but civil procedure and judiciary institutional structures have not.

The SCJA case law recognizes the existence of disadvantaged groups in Argentine society, characterized as "traditionally disadvantaged or weakly protected".[70] And these groups of people have found in the Judiciary a very interesting forum to discuss their structural conflicts, improving drastically their potential incidence in the way budget is allocated by the major branches of government. In many cases, class actions –similar to the US model- have been the means to make this happen because the FCA recognizes collective standing to sue and substantive collective rights of those (and others) groups of people.

In this sense, we have to underline that class actions in Argentina can become an important and effective procedural mechanism to enforce individual's rights of access to the civil justice system, because they provide for legal counsel and representation to huge number of individuals without demanding from them neither economic contribution nor active participation to achieve that goal. This is particularly relevant when it comes to dealing with disadvantaged groups.

It is also relevant to bear in mind that SCJA case law has strongly and repeatedly emphasized that constitutional provisions on collective standing to sue and collective redress are operative and, because of that, must be enforced by judges even in the absence of regulations enacted by Congress.

This phenomenon is provoking a deep change in the separation of powers and its checks and balances system in Argentina, because the discus-

69 Some alternatives to face the issue are presented in R. Gargarella, "Un papel renovado para la Corte Suprema. Democracia e interpretación judicial de la Constitución", *Gaceta Constitucional, Lima*, 573-590 (2008).

70 *Halabi*, para. 13 of the majority opinion; *PADEC*, para. 10 of the majority opinion.

sion of group conflicts before judges has strong implications that are not present in the administrative and legislative arenas.

In that context, the Judiciary -with the SCJA at its summit- is playing a key role in dealing with collective conflicts that traditionally have been discussed and solved within majoritarian branches of government. This new role has vested the Judiciary with a huge amount of political power, and demands similar huge changes both in proceedings and institutional structures that have been designed –a long time ago- to face individual and private conflicts.

III. Financial Consumer Redress by ADR and ODR. New European Approaches

Ana Isabel Blanco García[*]

(I) Introduction

The economic and social crisis, and, in general, the crisis of the banking system itself, has highlighted the necessity to correct its failures. On the one hand, through legislative reform, in order to increase of the transparency of banking products and services and to strengthen the long-term financial stability of banks. On the other hand, through a reinforcement of the protection and defence of banking customers and their rights and economic interests. Indeed, building and enhancing consumer confidence and trust in a well-functioning financial market promotes efficiency and stability in that market.

Furthermore, with globalization comes increased legal, regulatory and cultural complexity of the transactions executed. A higher number of international financial and commercial transactions results in a bigger number of complaints both domestic and cross-border, making ADR cooperation mechanisms essential to guarantee effective customer protection.

This paper aims to offer the keys for the knowledge of the regulation and the non-jurisdictional redress available for financial users, with especial regard to the figure of the Spanish Banking Ombudsman, in correlation with the structure and functioning of the original system, the English Ombudsman. The Ombudsman has assumed greater importance after the reform of the European dispute resolution framework and its new challenges, by developing cooperation mechanisms such as the European Consumer Centres Network (ECC-Net) and the Financial Dispute Resolution Network (Fin-Net) as a pan-European ADR / ODR body mediating between banking entities and customers, and being the binomial-solution of the financial banking conflicts with consumers.

* Ph.D in Law; Assistant Lecturer, Department of Administrative and Procedural Law, University of Valencia.

The paper's methodology is closely related to the field studied. It follows a legal methodology where the literature, legislation, regulation, jurisprudence and other practical information must be gathered and analysed all together, to broaden the perspective beyond the financial activity and dispute resolution aspects to include a unique and more realistic view of the current economic situation and the need for more effective redress.

This deductive method and data collection is followed by a comparative law analysis between the continental and common-law legal systems, which is also based on a data collection methodology. Indeed, this paper presents a theoretical and analytical approach to financial cross-border consumer redress not only by ADR mechanisms but also by ODR, and proposes pragmatic and useful reforms that guarantee effective protection for the user of financial services.

(II) Financial ADR Mechanisms

Since the outbreak of the crisis in 2007 customers have had to deal with some of the most important disputes arising from consumer banking contracts in recent times. Banking is not infallible. Indeed, quite the contrary, there are weaknesses whose negative consequences strongly affect customers´ economic status. In fact, financial services providers hold all the power, often abusing it to achieve higher profitability, especially considering that banking contracts are drawn up as standard-terms contracts.[1]

Most current disputes are a consequence of, among other reasons, the imbalance of power between the parties and an asymmetry of information. Conflicts are the consequence of the lack of information provided to consumers about product features and the rights and obligations arising from the contract, as well as the inclusion of unfair terms in the contracts.

An unfair term which causes major problems in Spain is the so called "floor clause" in mortgages. This clause has resulted in massive evictions within the mortgage crisis based on enforceable titles deriving from unfair terms. In this regard, the Court of Justice of the European Union, in a

1 E. Vázquez de Castro, "El consumidor ante el predisponente en la contratación seriada. Aproximación desde el Derecho europeo y español", in: J. Tomillo Urbina, (dir.), *El futuro de la protección jurídica de los consumidores* 658 *(Actas del I Congreso Euroamericano de Protección Jurídica de los Consumidores,* (Aranzadi, Cizur Menor, 2008).

judgment in response to a preliminary ruling,[2] held that the impossibility of citing unfair terms under the enforceable instrument as grounds to challenge foreclosures is incompatible with Council Directive 93/13/EEC of 5 April 1993 on unfair terms in consumer contracts. Therefore, the Spanish legislator introduced the Law on Measures to Strengthen the Protection of Mortgagors, Debt Restructuring and Social Renting (Law 1/2013 of 14 May 2013) to modify the Law 1/2000, of 7 January, on Civil Procedure by adding the existence of unfair contract terms as an opposition cause to the foreclosure process (§ 557.1.7º).

In fact, whether judicial proceedings are facing social problems is an issue to consider. The current financial crisis is not just an economic crisis, but also social and political. Even if traditional legal measures aim to balance the relationship between a bank and its customers, they fail to address social problems and enhance effective consumer protection mechanisms. In addition, the growing complexity of banking contracts and products has multiplied the number of cases before the courts, rendering them inadequate and ineffective for current customer needs and circumstances. Thus, means of settling disputes outside of the courtroom have grown in importance as they are based on rationality and sense of fairness. These out-of-court dispute resolution mechanisms fall within the "Alternative Dispute Resolution" concept, or ADR, born in the Anglo-Saxon legal systems throughout the 20th Century.[3]

Nowadays, there is a wide range of efficient mechanisms commonly employed to settle financial disputes out-of-court, which vary from the facilitative ADR such as mediation or conciliation, to adjudicative ADR such as arbitration. All of them offer greater advantages as compared to traditional justice. However, the specificity and complexity of current problems have led to the development, or even the creation of new ADR techniques. In this sense, the more recent response to the main banking disputes worldwide are the industry-based consumer dispute resolution schemes, the so-called Financial Ombudsman Service and, particularly for Spain, the new and still unregulated mortgage brokering mediation procedure.

---

2 Case 415/11, *Aziz v Caixa d"Estalvis de Catalunya,* [2013], ECLI:EU:C:2013:164.

3 See S. Barona Vilar, *Solución extrajurisdiccional de conflictos «alternative dispute resolution» (ADR) y Derecho Procesal* 40-41 (Tirant lo Blanch, Valencia, 1999).

(III) Financial Ombudsman Complaint-Handling Procedure

The starting point in the use of a private sector Ombudsman was the self-regulated Insurance Ombudsman Bureau in 1981 in the United Kingdom. Some years later, in 1986, the Complaints Service of the Bank of Spain,[4] "Servicio de Reclamaciones del Banco de España", became operational as an independent dispute resolution mechanism that worked as a mediator or conciliator between financial services providers and customers. Currently this Service is called the Market Conduct and Claims Department. Even if this Service was created within the Bank of Spain´s structure only one year later than the English Banking Ombudsman, they have experienced different development, especially in terms of effectiveness. Indeed, the Spanish Market Conduct and Claims Department is less known and used than the English Financial Ombudsman because the notion of customers is defined differently. This is the reason why it is possible to suggest how this out-of-court procedure can be improved in the Spanish legal system based on the experience of the English system.

This section aims not only to explain and expose the complaints-handling procedure but also to identify the weaknesses of this scheme in order to develop a model and strategies that could improve the effectiveness and usefulness of this ADR mechanism in solving consumer disputes with financial services providers, while keeping the confidentiality and independency of the third-party experts.

(a) Differences between the English System and the Spanish System

The full complaints-handling procedure is divided into two stages: An internal dispute resolution scheme (IDR) carried out through the development of a Customer Care Department or Service within the financial services provider organization, and an external one (hereinafter, EDR) which acts as a second instance body and is represented by the Financial Ombudsman.

---

4 D. Leibowitz, C. Lester, "Banking and finance disputes", in: R. Caller, *ADR and Commercial Disputes* 32-35 (Sweet&Maxwell, Londres, 2002); M.M. Andreu Martí, *La protección del cliente bancario* 174-181 & 187-197 (Tecnos, Madrid, 1998).

However, the Spanish system is quite peculiar because while it is divided into two stages, it has a tripartite structure. Indeed, as pointed out by Marimón, we have a "dual step system [...]: The Ombudsmen appointed by credit entities individually or collectively and a public defender enabled by the State and integrated within the organizational structure of the Bank of Spain".[5]

Therefore, there are two types of Ombudsmen. On the one hand, there are those instituted by financial institutions themselves (Customer Ombudsman, in Spanish *Defensor del Cliente*), that still have little presence in conflicting banking practices, and, on the other hand, the Market Conduct and Claims Department. The latter type might be called the real Financial Ombudsman given that its requirements and nature are along the lines of the English Financial Ombudsman, which due to its public nature, opens major policy areas and is also common to all financial institutions.

A distinction under Spanish law must be noted. *Defensor del Cliente* and Ombudsman are often used interchangeably, as the former is the Spanish translation of the latter. However, the figure of the *Defensor del Cliente* or Customer Ombudsman is an independent institution from the Market Conduct and Claims Department and even from the Customer Care Service, and exclusive to the Spanish legal system.

The requirements and duties of the Customer Care Departments and the *Defensor del Cliente* of financial entities are regulated by Spanish Order ECO/734/2004 of 11 March 2004.[6] It establishes the duty to provide a Customer Care Department but, in the discretion of the banking entity, it may provide with the *Defensor del Cliente*.

For both stages, we are going to analyse three main aspects: the organization and composition of the institution, the deadlines established to issue a resolution and the legal nature of the decisions issued.

5 R. Marimón Durá, "La nueva regulación de los órganos de defensa del cliente bancario. La experiencia del Servicio de Reclamaciones del Banco de España", in V. Cuñat Edo (dir.), *Protección de particulares frente a las malas prácticas bancarias* 219 (Consejo General del Poder Judicial, Madrid, 2005).

6 *Orden ECO/734/2004, sobre los Departamentos y Servicios de Atención al Cliente y el Defensor del Cliente en las Entidades Financieras*. BOE n. 72, 24 March 2004.

(b) Internal Dispute Resolution Scheme

A Customer Care Service acts autonomously and independently through its separation from the organization's commercial service while a *Defensor del Cliente* is an individual or legal entity acting independently from the financial services provider (as they are external to the organization thereof), and with total autonomy with regards to the criteria and guidelines applicable to the exercise of their functions. In addition, before resorting to the Financial Ombudsman is available, the regulation on transparency and the protection of banking service customers, requires evidence that the customer has already filed a complaint before the Customer Care Service or, whenever possible, the *Defensor del Cliente.*[7]

As an internal department of the financial services provider, it becomes more difficult to guarantee an environment which allows the complaint-handlers to decide on an autonomous basis even given its statutory separation from the rest of the services, because complaint-handlers are members of the service staff whose salaries are covered by the financial services provider itself.[8]

Another problem is that the internal regulations governing complaint-handlers are established by the banking entities themselves. Therefore, we cannot consider them as a neutral third party unrelated to customers, becoming also the main cause for the customer reluctance. Essentially, their independence with respect to the banking entity and, especially and above all, their impartiality is brought into question.

Regarding the deadlines to issue a resolution, the Customer Claim Department has 2 months/8 weeks to solve the complaint in Spain[9] and in the United Kingdom[10] while this term is shorter in other legal systems, e.g. in

---

7 Art. 4 Order ECO/734/2004.

8 See Santander Bank Customer Care Service regulation. Text available at: https://www.bancosantander.es/cssa/BlobServer?blobcol=urldata&blobheader=application%2Fpdf&blobheadername1=Content-Disposition&blobheadervalue1=inline%3Bfilename%3DReglamento.pdf&blobkey=id&blobtable=MungoBlobs&blobwhere=1305546675327, last visited 30 October 2016.

9 Art. 8 Order ECO/734/2004.

10 Financial Ombudsman UK Consumer Factsheet on How we deal with your complaint. Text available at: http://www.financial-ombudsman.org.uk/publications/factsheets/how-we-deal-with-your-complaint.pdf, last visited 2 September 2016.

Australia the deadline is reduced to up to 45 days.[11] Once this deadline has passed or if the customer is not satisfied with the decision, the complaint can then escalate to the next stage. But, in any case, customers still have the right to file the complaint before the Courts.

Apart from the variance in the deadline, being shorter in the Australian system, the binding effect of the decisions differs from system to system. In Spain, the entities decide the nature of their decisions because *prima facie* they are not legally binding but in the Anglo-Saxon systems – both the United Kingdom and Australia- the binding effects to the decision are established only by the acceptance of the customer.

(c) External Dispute Resolution Scheme

The Spanish figure of the *Defensor del Cliente* can be considered as an EDR scheme; the real Ombudsman is the Claim Services of the Supervisory Authorities in terms of configuration and jurisdiction established for them in the English system. Indeed, the Ombudsman is an expert and a person of recognized honourability and prestige in economic and financial fields.

(i) Defensor del Cliente (Customer Ombudsman)

A Customer Care Service acts autonomously and independently through its separation from the organization's commercial service,[12] while the *Defensor del Cliente* is an individual or legal entity acting independently from the financial services provider (as they are external to the organization thereof), and with total autonomy with regards to the criteria and guidelines applicable to the exercise of their functions.

Consequently, the *Defensor del Cliente* is not as problematic as the Customer Care Department, since it is a third party who solves the claim as an expert on the subject and with a recognised reputation in the legal, economic or financial sector. In addition, this third party does not have a

11 Financial Ombudsman Australia Quick Process Factsheet. Text available at: https://www.fos.org.au/resolving-disputes/our-dispute-resolution-process/, last visited 3 September 2016.

12 Art. 7 Order ECO/734/2004.

labour relationship with the entity which is a party to the claim. Indeed, the important aspect which makes this situation "well regarded" by consumers is that the decision-maker is a person external to the financial services provider, despite the appointment being made by the Board of Directors of the entity and, therefore, to a greater or lesser extent, being linked to that entity.

Regardless of the jurisdiction established, the *Defensor del Cliente* is an optional institution not provided for all financial entities because of the legal provision. This undermines legal certainty and, hence, is detrimental to customers´ confidence in the procedure.

(ii) Market Conduct and Claims Department (Financial Ombudsman)

The Market Conduct and Claims Department acts as a real Financial Ombudsman and fulfils dual functions: the adjudicative function and the informative function. On the one hand, the adjudicative function basically involves the reception, processing and settlement of all claims and complaints from customers of supervised credit entities concerning the adequacy of actions as good banking practices. On the other hand, regarding the informative function, the Ombudsman prepares a range of documents whose purpose is to ensure that consumers and users of banking services have adequate information on operational banking criteria, requirements and standards. These publications not only differ in their frequency, but also in their content. Quarterly reports, annual reports, statistics, factsheets, and so on are all published on the entity´s website. All these publications prove to be very useful, since they provide a range of data on the performance of this non-judicial redress mechanism within the banking sector.

From our point of view, one way of explaining all the contents and the practical impact of the functioning of the complaints-handling procedure in the guarantee of effective remedies before an independent and impartial assessor is by analysing the Annual Reviews.[13] These reports contain analytical and statistical data regarding the complaints submitted by the cus-

13 See, 2015 Market Conduct and Claims Department of the Bank of Spain Annual Review. Text available at: http://www.bde.es/f/webbde/Secciones/Publicaciones/PublicacionesAnuales/MemoriaServicioReclamaciones/15/MR2015_Documento_Completo.pdf, last visited10 August 2016.

tomers against the financial services providers and provide extensive background information about the Ombudsmen's fundamental purpose, the nature of their work and the services they provide. This information offers a realistic perspective on the substance of disputes and possible redress regarding the circumstances of a case. In this regard, one way of explaining the outcomes of these institutions is to represent the activity data by graphs, which enables us to better understand the procedure and functioning of these redress mechanisms.

For example, the 2015 Annual Review of the Market Conduct and Claim Department is divided into three chapters. The Review begins with a brief introduction or background of the service and the economic scenario. Secondly, the Report analyses the performance of the Department and describes the areas in which claims and complaints were lodged, as well as the affected entities. Finally, the third chapter indicates the transparency regulations and the best practice criteria applied in the resolutions issued during the corresponding year.

The procedure followed by the customer is relatively simple and comprehensible for an average user. Otherwise, it would lose its effectiveness in solving disputes without the intervention of any lawyer or prosecutor. Meanwhile, before going to the final stage headed by the Financial Ombudsman, the customer must meet a previous formality: the submission of the claim or complaint to the Customer Care Department of the financial services provider or, if provided, to the competent *Defensor del Cliente*.

The Market Conduct and Claim Department is competent to deal with complaints and claims submitted by users of financial services concerning the adequacy of the actions of the credit entities as regards good banking practices. The Department issued 13,354 reports (recommendations) during 2015 in response to the 20,262 files received, while in 2014 the Department issued 29,528 reports.[14] In the same period, the Investors Division of National Securities Market Commission (CNMV) issued 3,754[15]

14 Market Conduct and Claims Department Annual Review 2014, at 37. Text available at: http://www.bde.es/f/webbde/Secciones/Publicaciones/PublicacionesAnuales/MemoriaServicioReclamaciones/14/Resumen_de_la_actividad.pdf, last visited 25 October 2016.

15 CNMV Complaints Report 2014, at 15. Text available at: http://www.cnmv.es/DocPortal/Publicaciones/Informes/Memoria2014_web.pdf.pdf, last visited 25 October 2016.

reports and the Complaints Service of the Directorate-General of Insurance and Pension Funds (DGSFP) issued 9,321 decisions.[16]

The number of decisions issued by the Market Conduct and Claim Department in 2015 is lower than those issued in 2014 (15,370 decisions) due to the reduction of claims filed[17] concerning the inclusion of unfair terms such as the floor-clause in contracts although such claims still represent 46 % of the total complaints filed.[18] Of these reports, 74.2% ended in favour of the interests of the claimant and in the other 22.7% the Department did not consider that there was any infringement of the rules of transparency or good banking practices.

However, claims or complaints would not be admitted if:

- they related to issues within the jurisdiction of judicial, arbitral or administrative bodies, or when a previous judgment on the same issue by these bodies existed, or when a legal case also being heard by those bodies was involved (e.g. 1,067 files rejected in 2015).
- essential data for processing had been omitted and was not correctable (e.g. 1,503 files rejected in 2015).
- they related to private law issues strictly interpreted, such as matters concerning the interpretation and application of contract terms (e.g. 160 files rejected in 2015).
- they fell within the specialized competence of the other two financial complaint-handlers, the Investors Division of CNMV[19] and the Complaints Service of the DGSFP[20]. From our point of view, this is a practical problem for customers, who are confused about the competent institution to which they must address the complaint and, consequently, it could lead to a delay in settling the conflict.

---

16 DGSFP Complaints Service Annual Report 2014, at 10. Text available at: https://www.dgsfp.mineco.es/sector/documentos/Informe%20anual%20Servicio%20de%20Reclamaciones%202014.pdf, last visited 25 October 2016.

17 Market Conduct and Claims Department Annual Review 2015, at 33. Text available at: http://www.bde.es/f/webbde/Secciones/Publicaciones/PublicacionesAnuales/MemoriaServicioReclamaciones/15/MR2015_2_Resumen_Actividad_DCMR.pdf, last visited 25 October 2016.

18 Market Conduct and Claims Department Annual Review, *supra* n. 14, at 22.

19 See the official website at: http://www.cnmv.es/Portal/inversor/Como-Reclamar.aspx, last visited 28 October 2016.

20 See the official website at: http://www.dgsfp.mineco.es/reclamaciones/, last visited 28 October 2016.

In this regard, note that within the English legal system, the Financial Ombudsman Service institution comprises the banking, insurance and investments sector together while in Spain a different institution is set for each sector. The Market Conduct and Claims Department acts as the Ombudsman for banking contract disputes, the DGSFP Complaints Service resolves insurance disputes and, finally, the CNMV Investors Division deals with disputes about investments. This tripartite structure has created confusion in the customers in as to which Ombudsman to choose to address their complaints in the case of complex products or even regular contracts. However, even though there are three platforms, when a complaint is misfiled, it will be redirected internally to the corresponding competent body, applying the so-called the One-Window Principle. Indeed, 982 files originally submitted to the Market Conduct and Claim Department were transferred in 2015 to the other Supervisory Authorities.[21]

Once again, the main differences among the Ombudsmen lie in the deadlines and the binding effects of the decisions. Only the Spanish system establishes clear deadlines for solving complaints (4 months), claims (3 months) and enquiries (1 month).[22] In contrast, the English Financial Ombudsman scheme has no determined timelines to resolve disputes lodged by customers, taking in some cases more than one year to send a final response to the complainant or, in complex cases, up to two years as with Payment Protection Insurance complaints that represent 56% of new complaints.[23]

How long the English Financial Ombudsman takes to resolve a complaint is related to customer satisfaction with this type of ADR. Thus, when the Financial Ombudsman Service (FOS) takes too long to consider the complaint, the complaint handling procedure becomes inefficient and, in addition, this delay infringes the rights to defence as well as affecting legal certainty. Indeed, the English legislator should set a maximum time for issuing the final decision that may not exceed six months in any case, irrespective of the complexity of the subject-matter. Therefore, customers will be able to know the maximum length of this procedure to decide

---

21 Market Conduct and Claim Department, *supra* n. 14.

22 Order ECC/2502/2012, of 16 of November, BOE 281, 22 November 2012.

23 2015-2016 Financial Ombudsman Annual Review, at 46. Text available at: http://www.financial-ombudsman.org.uk/publications/annual-review-2016/ar16.pdf, last visited 15 October 2016.

whether they withdraw the complaint or submit the request before the Court.

Finally, the structure of the procedure relates to the decision´s binding nature. The Spanish Ombudsman´s decisions are always recommendations and, therefore, not binding nor enforceable in any case. However, under the English legal system, the Adjudicator´s view must be distinguished from the Financial Ombudsman's decision. The Adjudicator's view will be binding on both parties while the Financial Ombudsman's decision will be binding on the financial services provider only if the customer agrees with it.

The non-binding nature of the Spanish Ombudsman's decisions is the main reason why the out-of-court procedure is less effective than in the United Kingdom. Furthermore, even though this institution is administrative in nature, the report is not an administrative act, which means it cannot be appealed. In cases when the report was contrary to the claims of the customer or when, albeit being favourable, the bank has not fulfilled the recommendations contained therein, the customer will always be able to go before the Courts and provide the report as strong documentary evidence.

(iii) Funding Scheme

Unlike the Spanish system which is publicly funded and therefore free of charge, both for customers and for financial services providers, the English systems are privately funded, since they are financed by the credit entities through a financing model based on the imposition of levies and case fees. Consequently, the systems do not follow the same pattern since they differ in structure and functioning.

The private financing by one of the conflictual parties, the financial services provider (the strong party), is one of the most controversial aspects of the procedure. Indeed, it undermines the perception of customers that the service is independent and that the Ombudsman is an impartial institution. Thus, some consumers consider that the Ombudsman is, ultimately, an instrument at the service of the banking institutions, since they pay for the Ombudsman labour fees. In this sense, consumers may believe that, with the sole exception of visible errors or actions which have resulted in grievous harm, the Ombudsman will agree with the entity or, even in those cases where the decision is favourable to the client, the measures taken will not be relevant to the entity.

However, the other side of the coin is represented by banking entities which consider these levies and fees as sanctions. Indeed, this funding scheme implies that if a complaint is admitted, the institution must proceed to pay the stipulated rate, regardless of the favourable or unfavourable outcome of the decisions made by the Ombudsman. Hence the fact that the Ombudsman must issue an interim decision on its jurisdiction.

Once the Ombudsman's provisional decision stating its jurisdiction to hear the complaint is issued and forwarded, the banking entity has the right to plead to justify whether the claim falls outside the Ombudsman's jurisdiction. For example, the claim would be inadmissible if the financial services provider could prove the ignorance of any such claim, or the deadline for filing the complaint to the Financial Ombudsman has passed. If the lack of jurisdiction of the institution is confirmed, the Financial Ombudsman shall inform the customer of the impossibility of processing his/her claim, with no fees charged. Otherwise, when the jurisdiction of the institution is accepted, the company is compelled to pay the corresponding fee.[24]

Once the amount has been paid by the financial intermediary, even when the adequacy of the financial services provider´s performance with the regulations and good banking practices is confirmed, the amount paid for such claim as a fee is not returned. In our opinion, the imposition of levies and fees for filing claims should become an incentive for credit entities to comply with the laws and regulations and to respect good banking practices, which would in turn help raise the standards of consumer protection.

The funding structure established by the Financial Ombudsman consists of a fixed fee and an additional fee. However, the charges are applied after 25 claims. In other words, entities have a margin of 25 "free claims", so that, from claim number 26 on the costs will be applicable.

In the last few years we have seen two changes in the economic value of these fees and charges. Prior to April 2012 only a fixed rate of £500 was charged. However, from April 2012 to April 2014, the FOS introduced a supplementary fee of £350 for Payment Protection Insurance

24 Financial Ombudsman Service Quick Guide to funding and case fees. Text available at: http://www.financial-ombudsman.org.uk/publications/technical_notes/QG 1.pdf, last visited 3 September 2016.

(PPI) for mis-selling cases, which means that for these cases, the entities should pay a total fee of £850, while the remaining claims still cost £500. Finally, with the last reform introduced in April 2013, the fee of £500 was increased to £550, even though the additional rate remained at £350.

This means in practice that all claims -from the 26th on - carry a charge of £550, while PPI claims entail £900. These fees, which can become substantial particularly when considering the number of claims and the individual rate, should not be cancelled until the end of claim file is enacted. Therefore, banking entities should allocate a corresponding accrual sum to ensure the availability and reliability of the entity.

In summary, this line of private funding credit institutions support could become a deterrent measure to bad banking practices and, correspondingly, an incentive for financial services providers to adjust their policies to the principles of transparency and consumer protection. Nevertheless, we do not believe that the choice of this funding scheme violates the principles of independence and impartiality required for the figure of the Ombudsman and, by extension, the other members of the Financial Ombudsman.

(IV) The Importance of the Networking of ADR Financial Institutions: Fin-Net

Financial services have a very significant impact on the daily life and welfare of consumers. Their regulation is changing both at European and national level. High level consumer rights protection and consumer trust in the business sector can be achieved through cooperation between the European organizations and national competent financial authorities within the Single Market. This cooperation must aim to guarantee both the fair and transparent functioning of financial services as well as an effective protection provided by financial ADR mechanisms. Moreover, as stated in the previous section, financial ADR schemes also apply different procedures. For example, the decision-maker within the Financial Ombudsman scheme can issue a decision that can be binding on both the consumer and the financial service provider or binding only on the financial service provider (e.g. the English Financial Ombudsman Service), while the Spanish complaint-handler makes a recommendation to the parties.

(a) Development of ADR on Cross-Border Disputes Resolution

The importance of establishing effective consumer protection is a fact, especially for users of financial services. However, since there are significant differences in legal customer protection in the Member States, a collaborative network among the ADR financial mechanisms becomes essential. One of the strategies taken under Objective III (Rights and redress) within the Programme of Community action in the field of consumer policy and the Regulation (EU) 254/2014 of the European Parliament and of the Council of 26 February 2014 on a multiannual consumer programme for the years 2014-2020 and repealing Decision 1926/2006/EC is the accessibility to alternative dispute resolution mechanisms for consumers, including through a Union-wide online system and the networking of national alternative dispute resolution entities.

This new regulation pays specific attention to adequate measures to protect vulnerable consumers' needs and rights and to improve the control and supervision of domestic financial institutions and the coordination among them, with special emphasis on the development of Networks of ADR institutions in cross-border disputes, including also out-of-court general online resolution schemes (the European Consumer Centres Network, ECC-Net).[25]

Apart from these cooperation strategies, the EU has previously adopted other measures as part of the Commission's Digital Single Market initiative[26] by breaking down borders to cross-border commerce. To that end, Regulation (EC) 524/2013 of the European Parliament and of the Council of 21 May 2013 on online dispute resolution for consumer disputes and amending Regulation (EC) 2006/2004 and Directive 2009/22/EC has been approved. Regulation 524/2013 on consumer ODR introduces to the Member States the European Commission's online dispute resolution platform (the ODR Platform to encourage cross-border purchasing by con-

---

25 This action is derived from Objective IV (Enforcement) which consists in "financial contributions for joint actions with public or non-profit bodies constituting Union networks which provide information and assistance to consumers to help them exercise their rights and obtain access to appropriate dispute resolution, including out of court online resolution schemes (the European Consumer Centres Network)".

26 More information at: http://ec.europa.eu/priorities/digital-single-market_en, last visited 10 September 2016.

sumers across the EU). Also, Directive 2013/11/EU of the European Parliament and of the Council of 21 May 2013 on alternative dispute resolution for consumer disputes and amending Regulation (EC) 2006/2004 and Directive 2009/22/EC (the so-called ADR Directive) has been passed. Therefore, we can affirm the EU bets strongly for the ADR/ODR binomial to solve consumer disputes and to guarantee customer confidence in the economic system.

(b) Fin-Net

Within the framework of these legal bodies, different measures were taken to ensure an effective cross-border out-of-court complaints network for financial services through the Financial Dispute Resolution Network (Fin-Net).

Fin-Net complements the ECC-Net as a network of cooperation between European institutions for consumer protection, but now related to the financial sector.[27] Fin-Net meets three specific objectives:

First, ensuring and guaranteeing an effective exchange of information between European systems, so that financial cross-border consumer complaints can be handled with efficiency and expertise.

Second, regulating and establishing controls to ensure that systems of dispute resolution in the various countries of the European Economic Area (EEA) meet certain minimum guarantees to protect the right to effective protection of the financial services user.

And third, in case of cross-border conflict, it ensures that non-judicial redress mechanisms are advertised and accessible to the consumer. Indeed, credit entities have developed procedures which are free of charge for customers.

27 F. Petrauskas and A. Gasiūnaitė, "Alternative Dispute Resolution in the field of Consumer Financial Services", 19(1) *Jurisprudencija/Jurisprudence* (2012) 179–194; V. Andreeva Andreeva, "Resolución extrajudicial de conflictos relacionados con los contractos con consumidores celebrados en los mercados financieros internacionales", 4(3) *Arbitraje: revista de arbitraje comercial y de inversiones* 751, 751-754 (2011).

Fin-Net was formally created through the adhesion of various Member States to a Memorandum,[28] which consists of a declaration of intent on cross-border cooperation between the parties. While not all EEA member countries have been part of this network since its creation, in 2016 it had 58 members from 25 countries of the EEA (some EU Member States, plus Norway, Iceland and Liechtenstein), Spain being a founding State.

Cooperation is required due to the lack of harmonization of the regulations and procedures of the Member States. Besides, cooperation refers to complaints filed by consumers against financial services providers established in a Member State other than the one in which the consumer has the residence. Therefore, this Memorandum acts as a kind of Code of Good Practice, regulating the procedure of the Fin-Net, although its provisions are not legally binding for entities. Indeed, provisions do not create rights or obligations for the entities or even third parties. However, Member States adhered to it have tried to comply with the provisions therein.

Unlike in the United Kingdom, where there is full-sector coverage, in Spain three institutions are part of this network:[29] for the investment sector, the Investor Assistance Office – Investors Division of the CNMV; for the insurance sector, the Complaints Service of the DGSFP and; for the banking sector, the Market Conduct and Claims Department. Nevertheless, the general rule of organisation of Fin-Net is to be represented by the single institution of the Financial Ombudsman, covering the three subsectors (banking, insurance and investment), simplifying the procedure and the necessary cooperation to properly perform its functions.

Another aspect to analyse is how this network helps consumers in solving cross-border conflicts with banking entities, when the credit institution is situated in another EU country. Contrary to what one might think, it has not been designed as a complex procedure, as this would increase existing reservations and prejudices about its use and effectiveness by consumers. Thus, the procedure has been designed by thinking about the average customers´ understanding, especially considering that national financial ADR procedure differs between countries.

---

28 Memorandum of Understanding on a Cross-Border Out-of-Court Complaints Network for Financial Services, text available at: http://ec.europa.eu/finance/fin-net/docs/mou/mou_en.pdf, last visited 10 September 2016.

29 Information available at: http://ec.europa.eu/finance/fin-net/members_en.htm, last visited 31 August 2016.

Fin-Net provides consumers via its website[30] the possibility of identifying the appropriate out-of-court system of the country in which the financial services provider to whom the complaint is addressed is situated. However, the normal procedure is governed by the rule of "nearest procedure". Following this rule, it is enough if the consumer contacts the Ombudsman in their own country of residence to report the procedure for filing the claim. This Ombudsman contacts the competent authority of the corresponding country of the bank. Once the competent body has received the complaint, it handles the claim and gives its decision in accordance with its own rules, guaranteeing effective compliance with the basic principles set out in Commission Recommendation 98/257/EC and therefore, the defence and protection of rights and interests of users of financial services. The importance of this network is reflected in the quantity of cases solved. In 2015, FIN-NET members handled 4,195 cross-border cases, of which 1,300 were in the banking sector, 699 in the insurance sector, and 559 in the investment sector.[31]

We firmly believe that the creation and promotion of cooperation networks between national institutions for managing and processing claims will be positive. Indeed, legal certainty, confidence and functioning of the internal market are positively reinforced by networks such as the ECC-Net or Fin-Net. However, improvements are needed in the protection of bank customers, as well as further equality and harmonisation of criteria for the defence of the rights and economic interests.

(V) ADR/ODR as EU Binomial Solution for Consumer Conflicts: Controversial Aspects

ADR Directive and ODR EU Regulation of 2013 aim not only to promote ADR mechanisms, but also to improve cross-border and online trade. The ADR Directive establishes harmonised quality requirements for ADR entities and ADR procedures to ensure that consumers have access to high-quality, effective, transparent and fair out-of-court redress mechanisms throughout the European Union. In addition, ODR Regulation establishes

30 Fin-Net Consumer Factsheet, text available at: http://ec.europa.eu/finance/fin-net/docs/guide/consumer-guide_en.pdf, last visited 31 August 2016.

31 2015 Fin-Net Activity Report, at 5. Text available at: http://ec.europa.eu/finance/fin-net/docs/activity/2015_en.pdf, last visited 25 October 2016.

a platform in the form of an interactive website[32] that acts under the one-window principle for consumers' complaints against traders, including financial providers. The platform will provide information on out-of-court dispute resolution and will also send complaints to the competent national ADR entity (named RAL), which will then deal with the complaints. In this sense, the procedure of the platform is similar to that of Fin-Net.

Nevertheless, as these new legal rules do not provide the specific criteria for the procedure for the financial sector, some questions arise regarding its effectiveness in this complex trade sector.

The ADR Directive applies to out-of-court resolution of domestic and cross-border disputes concerning contractual obligations stemming from sales contracts or service contracts between a trader established in the European Union and a consumer resident in the European Union, and provides a minimum level of consumer protection.

In addition, Member States may maintain their existing rules or introduce new rules on alternative dispute resolution that ensure a higher level of protection. Member States had to transpose the ADR Directive into national law by designating the national competent authorities of all compliant ADR schemes. Many Fin-Net members are part of the ODR platform. However, the Directive has still not been transposed in Spain, where the Draft Bill exposed shortfalls regarding the regulation about the coexistence of these new institutions and the remaining ones.

(a) Nominal Fee for Consumers

Art. 8 of the Directive establishes that Member States must ensure that the ADR procedures are free of charge or available at a nominal fee for consumers. This enables Member States to establish a fee -generally up to €30- to submit the complaint even if it is rejected for legal cause.

Even though €30 is not a large sum, this could become a problem in terms of effectiveness and acceptance by customers, because we must consider that in most cases customers are applying for an apology or an explanation of what happened or they ask whether any simple solution for their issue exists.

32 See ODR website: https://webgate.ec.europa.eu/odr/main/?event=main.home.show&reload=false, last visited 20 October 2016.

Indeed, nowadays customers are provided with different and various free of charge proceedings, such as consumer arbitration or even the Ombudsman complaint handling procedure. Therefore, considering that the majority are small claims asking for the refund of reversals or any other charges, we believe that this amount could become a barrier of accessibility, leaving customers without an effective protection. This measure has effects on the number of complaints submitted to these entities and the choice of another ADR means.

(b) Pre-specified Monetary Thresholds

Art. 5.5 of the Directive establishes that "Member States shall ensure that, when ADR entities are permitted to establish pre-specified monetary thresholds to limit access to ADR procedures, those thresholds are not set at a level at which they significantly impair the consumers' access to complaint handling by ADR entities". For example, the Spanish Draft Bill establishes a monetary threshold between €50 and €3,000, consequently limiting access to this proceeding. Moreover, as small claims could be rejected because of the inferior limitation, customers could be induced to use other ADR redress mechanisms or even Court proceedings to solve their dispute. This, indeed, will affect not only the accessibility but also the effectiveness of this special proceeding.

(VI) Improvement Proposals

Concerning the failures of the Ombudsman complaint-handling procedure, we propose some measures to improve its functioning and effectiveness.

(a) The Removal of the Spanish Institution Defensor del Cliente

The main problem within the Spanish system arises from the existence of both the Customer Care Department and the *Defensor del Cliente* institution. In this case, the financial services provider has the regulatory power to define the jurisdiction of the *Defensor del Cliente*. Therefore, a conflict of authority and jurisdiction with the Customer Care Department could arise. Indeed, sometimes they have the same jurisdiction, thus becoming alternative stages, while at other times the *Defensor del Cliente* acts as a second instance body. However, even in the latter case, there is no obligation to submit the complaint to this body, enabling customers to go directly to the final stage, the Market Conduct and Claim Department, the Investors Division of the CNMV or the Complaints Service of the DGSFP.

Regardless of the jurisdiction established, the *Defensor del Cliente* is an optional Service not provided for all financial entities. This undermines legal certainty and, hence, is detrimental to customers´ confidence in the procedure. From our point of view, this "optional second instance" or, even, "optional alternative instance", only causes unnecessary delays in obtaining an effective final decision, as well as increases the costs in human resources. These are the reasons why the *Defensor del Cliente* is inefficient and expensive and, therefore, should be abolished.

(b) Single Financial ADR Body

We support the modification of the tripartite structure by the merger of the Market Conduct and Claims Department of the Bank of Spain, Complaint Service of the DGSFP and the Investors Division of the CNMV into the Financial Ombudsman as one single body which is separate and independent from the Supervisors Authorities.

The Financial Ombudsman Service in the English legal system comprises banking, insurance and investments while in Spain three different institutions are set for each sector. This complaint-handling procedure may seem easy, and it is in practice. However, the tripartite structure also multiplies both human and economic resources, and the time spent to decide on their jurisdiction from the first instance by determining the jurisdiction in each institution. Besides, as some complaints deal with complex contracts that involve products from more than one sector, at least two of these institutions are then competent to solve a part of the dispute, which therefore takes more time in issuing a final decision.

For these reasons, we consider that all these Ombudsmen should be joined into a single body, thereby minimizing costs and resources as well as establishing a uniform procedure. Furthermore, this institution should be separate from the Supervisory Authorities to guarantee the principle of independency and impartiality of this redress mechanism.

(c) Final Decisions with (Half)-Binding Effects

Unlike the English Financial Ombudsman, the Spanish Ombudsmen´s decisions are always recommendations and, therefore, not binding in any case. This is the main reason why the out-of-court procedure is ineffective when compared with the United Kingdom.

According to the Annual Review of 2015,[33] 40% of decisions in favour of the customer were accepted by the financial services providers, an important figure when compared to the 25.6% of the previous year.[34] Despite the substantial improvement of banking conduct in protection of customers, there is still an imbalance of power between financial entities and consumer rights in favour of the former. Thus, the advantages of this method are overshadowed by the lack of consumer confidence in their rights being defended through it.

Taking into consideration that effectiveness is directly related to the enforcement of the final decisions, we advocate for the convenience of giving legally half-binding effects to the recommendations when they favour claimants if they agree with its content. This could be the means to encourage financial entities to correct and amend their policies and to strictly adhere to the Codes of Good Banking Practices. Nevertheless, it should be noted that this binding obligation should not be an obstacle to full entitlement to protection before the Courts, to the right to appeal to other mechanisms for resolution of disputes, nor to administrative protection.

(VII) Conclusions

The discussion on the non-judicial redress mechanisms used to solve disputes which arise between financial services providers and their customers provides a forum within which we can reach some findings and conclusions.

33 *2015 Annual Review*, Market Conduct and Claims Department, at 37.

34 *2014 Annual Review*, Market Conduct and Claims Department, at 45.

(a) Financial Consumer Protection is essential to guarantee the Market Stability

This research is based on the understanding that financial consumer protection is essential to guarantee market stability. Indeed, there has always been a concern to protect and promote the rights of financial consumers. However, the global financial crisis highlighted the need for more effective consumer protection measures, especially for those consumers affected by the mortgage crisis and for those who bought derivative or complex products such as preferred stock. Thus, in developing the mortgage market, hybrid complex financial products were sold to customers, some of whom had financial difficulties aggravated by the securitization of household credit.

Research confirms the growing importance of financial consumer protection since there is an imbalance of power within the banker-customer relationship. By building and enhancing consumer confidence and by guaranteeing transparency within the relationships it is possible to make the financial system itself stronger and more efficient. This strength and stability could be achieved by providing suitable legal actions and useful out-of-court dispute resolution mechanisms to solve important financial disputes such as evictions and foreclosure proceedings.

Therefore, jurisdictions should provide consumers with adequate complaints handling and redress mechanisms that should be accessible, affordable, independent, fair, accountable, timely and efficient as set out in the G20 High-level Principles on Financial Consumer Protection. ADR mechanisms have experienced a significant growth due to the inadequacy and ineffectiveness of the traditional (judicial) Justice.

(b) The Customer Care Departments or IDR Schemes are not Out-of-Court Settlement of Consumer Disputes Procedures in the proper Sense

The Law requires financial services providers to have in place a dispute resolution redress that consists of internal dispute resolution (IDR) procedures meeting the standards or requirements made or approved by the Regulator Authority, Bank of Spain (Spain) and Financial Conduct Authority (United Kingdom), and to adhere to an external dispute resolution (EDR) scheme. Therefore, the full complaints-handling procedure is divided into two stages: An Internal Dispute Resolution scheme carried out through the development of a Customer Care Department, and an External and public one that acts as a second instance body represented by the Financial Ombudsman.

Both are intended to provide out-of-court settlement of consumer disputes and, in that sense, they must comply with the requirements and principles set out in Commission Recommendation 98/257/EC.[35] The decision-making body's impartiality and objectivity are essential for safeguarding the protection of consumer rights and for strengthening consumer confidence in this complaint-handling procedure.

However, IDR schemes are structured as a department within the financial services provider´s organization. Therefore, it becomes more difficult to guarantee an environment which allows the complaint-handlers to decide on an autonomous basis even if its separation from the rest of the services is statutory imposed, because complaint-handlers are members of the service staff whose salaries are covered by the financial services provider itself.

Nevertheless, these procedures ensure access to an easy, timely and cost-free financial dispute resolution. Besides, these Departments are not an Out-of-Court settlement of consumer disputes procedure in the proper sense because they are a sort of self-regulatory mechanism on the procedure´s weaknesses and failures that enables financial services providers to correct and amend their policies.

(c) The Financial Ombudsman is an ADR Category of its Own

The Financial Ombudsman Service -represented in Spain by the Market Conduct and Claim Department- is a mechanism for complaint handling and redress that meets the principles of independency and impartiality, as well as accessibility for any customer whose rights and legitimate interests have been infringed by a financial service provider´s policy. Besides, this institution has jurisdiction to hear complaints that are not efficiently re-

35 Commission Recommendation 98/257/EC of 30 March 1998, OJ 1998 L 115/31. This Recommendation establishes the adversarial principle and principles of independence, of transparency, of effectiveness, of liberty, of legality and of representation.

solved via the financial services providers and authorised agents' internal dispute resolution mechanisms.

Regarding conflict management, this private sector Ombudsman follows a different procedure to those in conciliation, mediation or arbitration. Indeed, contacts between the Ombudsman and the parties are limited to written communications and, additionally, final decisions are not binding –at least in the Spanish legal system– or, if they are, only on acceptance by the customer –in the English legal system– that makes this redress mechanism alternative yet not exclusive to other ADR techniques.

Technically speaking, the Financial Ombudsman institution is a sensible, efficacious, cost-effective and quick alternative dispute resolution compared to the courts. Nevertheless, even if this institution was first created as a pragmatic and suitable procedure for resolving consumer disputes with financial services providers, its practical design and implementation becomes crucial for its effectiveness. Thus, both the non-binding legal nature of final decisions and the absence of fixed deadlines for compliance with decisions result in a situation of legal uncertainty as to the rights of customers and the duties of credit entities. This undermines the confidence of consumers and promotes ineffective and inadequate functioning of this out-of-court redress procedure, which entails a barrier to access Justice and to obtain an effective resolution of the conflict with the financial service provider.

IV. Eduardo J. Couture. Footmarks that Help in Understanding the Present

Eduardo Oteiza[*]

The sixtieth anniversary of the death of Eduardo J. Couture was one of special significance; it aroused the collective memory of those who, from various perspectives, attach a special merit to his legacies. The use of the plural, *legacies,* to characterize what new generations of academics have received from Couture, is justified by the multiple repercussions of a well-remembered, multi-faceted track record. There are many reasons for looking back on his ideas, his deeds, his work and his uniqueness as the witness of an era already past, but which in many aspects remains alive in the present: particularly, in the doctrinal approach that connects procedural law with outstanding constitutional values and the protection of human rights in democratic societies with egalitarian aspirations.

These notes address only a few aspects of Couture's life and work. They do not seek to be descriptive. They only try to share a handful of reasons to understand why his teachings are still current today.

Couture passed away on May 11, 1956. A few months after, on September 27, Piero Calamandrei also died. The *Revista de la Facultad de Derecho de la Universidad Autónoma de México*[1], on the initiative of Niceto

---

* Professor for Procedural Law at the Universidad de la Plata, president of the Ibero-American Institute of Procedural Law (2014) and vice-president of the International Association of Procedural Law (2011). Former president of the Argentine Association of Procedural Law (2011-2013) and the Association for Civil Rights (2010-2011).

1 October – November 1956, Volume IV, issue 24, http://www.juridicas.unam.mx/publica/rev/indice.htm?r=facdermx&n=24 (last visited July 2016). A brief and interesting summary of Calamandrei's work may be found there: M. Cappelletti, "Piero Calamandrei (biographical data), at 9-11; N. Alcalá-Zamora and Castillo, "Bibliography of Piero Calamandrei", at 17-38; C. Furno "Piero Calamandrei", at 243-252. See also S. Sentís Melendo, "Ha muerto Piero Calamandrei", in *Teoría y Práctica del Proceso. Ensayos de Derecho Procesal,* Buenos Aires, 1959, vol. I, at 442-477; P. Grossi, "Lungo l´itinerario di Piero Calamandrei", *Rivista Trimestrale di Diritto e Procedura Civile,* 865et seq (2009); P. Andrés Ibañez, "Piero Calamandrei: pasión por la legalidad" in *Piero Calamandrei. Sin legalidad no hay libertad,* 24 (Madrid

Alcalá-Zamora y Castillo[2], decided to publish a special issue dedicated to both. In addition to the valuable contributions contained in this issue of the *Revista*, the immediate tribute shows the influence Couture and Calamandrei had on the academic community. The commemoration united them in farewell and showed that they were two unique players, whose careers showed clear points of contact, notwithstanding the different contexts in which each of them acted. They were qualified points of reference of an era. They metabolized, as few others did, the expectations and beliefs of the world in which they participated from the particular standpoint of their discipline. Their life, work, and the respect of their contemporaries had brought them close.

Couture and Calamandrei were particularly influential to a discipline in which a consolidated dogma replaced proceduralism, to then accept the importance of an approach related to constitutional law and to human rights. This step occurred in the turmoil of the first half of the 20th century. A time in which events such as World War I, the Russian Revolution, the Spanish Civil War and World War II suddenly occurred in Europe,

---

2016). Perhaps the deepest tribute are the few pages of M. Cappelletti, "Ricordo di Piero Calamandrei scritto dal suo ultimo discepolo", in *In memoria di Piero Calamandrei,* 92-94 (Padua 1957). For visions which also include criticism see, among others, G. Tarello, *Dottrine del proceso civile. Studi storici sulla formazione del Diritto procesuale civile,* 251-256 (Bolonia 1989).

2 The track record of Alcalá-Zamora y Castillo is also one of the keys to understanding a central issue of this essay, namely the relationship between American and European procedural law specialists, forged as a result both of the political climate prevailing in Europe in the thirties and the institutionalization of the spaces for scientific coexistence created in the second half of the 20th century. Couture and Alcalá-Zamora y Castillo had a clear impact with respect to both issues. Among the many references to Alcalá-Zamora y Castillo in the book *Ponencias generales del XII Congreso Mundial de Derecho Procesal,* México, September 22-26, 2003: V Fairén Guillén, "El profesor Alcalá-Zamora y Castillo (1906-1985), 3-10; R. Berizonce, "Niceto Alcalá-Zamora y Castillo: un puente entre dos mundos", 11-13; F. Carpi, "Niceto Alcalá-Zamora y Castillo e la dottrina italiana", 13-17; A. Said, "Breve semblanza del doctor Niceto Alcalá-Zamora y Castillo, y tres expresiones de sus afanes en México (1946-1976)". The following biographical notes are of interest as well: V. Denti, "Niceto Alcalá-Zamora y Castillo", *Rivista di Diritto Processsuale,* 326-329 (Anno XL (Seconda Serie) n. 2, 1985); F. Gascón Inchausti, "Niceto Alcalá-Zamora y Castillo (1906-1985)", in *Juristas Universales,* 731-732 (Madrid 2004), and V. Fairén Guillen, "In memoriam Niceto Alcalá-Zamora y Castillo", *Revista de Derecho Procesal. Dirigida a Iberoamérica,* 335-337 (1985, vol. 1).

with ramifications in a Latin America also affected by circumstances leading to radical transformations. The aforementioned social events had repercussions of different kinds on the development of procedural law. In particular, the links between Latin America and Europe became narrower as a result of the forced migration of European proceduralists and the hospitality of Latin American ones. Those links, forged in painful circumstances, had a wide-ranging human and scientific influence. Focusing on them may help unravel the evolution of some concepts that have survived until our times without losing any of their vitality.

Certain events leave traces to which we need to go back in order to understand the importance later acquired by those who were their protagonists. In this context I would like to present three letters addressed to Couture. They show, among other things, his closeness to Calamandrei.

The first letter was sent by Enrico Tullio Liebman in late 1938. Couture was thirty-four years old at the time[3], and Liebman thirty-five. In the letter he said: "*While I am Catholic by birth and the son of a Catholic mother, I must, forced by the most recent regulations, leave University teaching in Italy*", in view of which he asked him for help "*as soon as possible to secure for me any university or secondary position that will allow me to provide for the most basic needs of life, since I will only be able to leave the country if I have a small amount of money. Furthermore, in order to obtain a visa on my passport I need to show that I have a position in the country of destination. I therefore fervently entreat you to take an interest in this matter.*"[4] In this letter, Liebman mentions that Calamandrei had encouraged him to write to Couture.

---

3 He was born in Montevideo on May 24, 1904, and passed away in the same city on May 11, 1956. In the aforementioned issue of the *Revista de la Facultad de Derecho de la Universidad Autónoma de México* A. Gelsi Bidart and N. Alcalá Zamora y Castillo provide a curriculum entitled: "Eduardo J. Couture (Biographical Data)". See also in the same issue the article by N. Alcalá Zamora y Castillo, "Bibliografía de Eduardo J. Couture y de Calamandrei".

4 The extract of the paragraph of Libman's letter to Couture was taken from Couture de I. Landoni y A. Landoni Sosa, "Semblanza de Eduardo J. Couture", *Obras Eduardo J. Couture. Fundamentos de Derecho Procesal Civil,* XXIX – XXXV (Montevideo, La Ley Uruguay, 2016, vol. I). Liebman's letter to Couture, as the authors explains, was written in Milan and dated November 22, 1938. It may be retrieved here: http://164.73.178.207/html/index.php/carta-liebman-e-tullio-prof;isad (last visited July 2016). In the first paragraph of the letter, Liebman says that he is writing to Couture on Piero Calamandrei's advice.

The timely help of Couture allowed Liebman to leave Italy, settle in Uruguay and teach at the Universidad de la República. In 1940, Liebman decided to accept an invitation from Brazil, where he lived until 1946, when he returned to Italy without losing touch with his colleagues in Sao Paulo. The letter shows both the climate of intolerance prevailing in Europe and the timely solidarity of Couture, which had direct consequences on the development of the Brazilian school of procedural law, directly related to Liebman's contributions and those of his disciple, Alfredo Buzaid.[5]

The second letter was sent by James Goldshmidt.[6] In the lecture entitled *"James Goldschmidt, un judío muerto por la libertad de la cultura" (James Goldschmidt, a Jew who died for freedom of culture*),[7] Couture tells that in 1939 he received a letter from Goldschmidt, sent from Cardiff, in which he said: "*I know your books and I know you by reference. I am in England and my residence permit expires on December 31, 1939. I can't go back to Germany because I am a Jew; I cannot go to France either because I am German, and to Spain, even less. I must leave England and I do not have a consular visa to go anywhere in the world.*"

After a dangerous trip by sea, under the threat of a war that he was trying to leave behind, Goldschmidt arrived in Montevideo. He died a few months later, in June 1940, while he was preparing the third lecture he was to give at the Universidad de la República.

---

5 See in this connection A. Pellegrini Grinover, *O Magistério do Enrico Tullio Liebman no Brasil,* 1986, *Revista da Faculdade de Direito*, Universidade de São Paulo, www.revistas.usp.br/rfdusp/article/download/67069/69679 (last visited July 2016).

6 A summary of the relevance of Goldschmidt's work and its importance today may be seen in B. Hess. "Der Prozess als Rechtslage – James Goldschmidt 1925 Proceedings As a Sequence of Judicial Situations – A Critique of the Procedural Doctrine", in *Procedural Science at the Crossroads of Different Generations,* L. Cadiet, B. Hess, M. Requejo (eds.) Luxembourg, 2015, and A. Meroi, "James Goldshmidt y sus aportes a la cultura jurídica de América del Sur (trayectos intelectuales en un exilio)", in *Revista de Filosofía Jurídica y Social,* Rosario, 141-166 (2015, n. 36). In 1935 Goldschmidt had to leave Germany. He managed to work in Spain for a few years. The translation of his book *Derecho Procesal Civil* by L. Prieto-Castro, with additions on case law and Spanish law by N. Alcalá-Zamora y Castillo, was published in Madrid in 1936.

7 See the reprint of the Lecture given by Couture, on November 25, 1954, in *Homenaje a Eduardo J. Couture y James Goldschmidt,* published by Facultad de Derecho de la Universidad de la República, Fundación "Eduardo J. Couture", Comité Central Israelita del Uruguay, B´Naí B´rith del Uruguay y Fundación para la tolerancia "Dr. Carlos E. Miles", 2002.

In that lecture, Couture expresses his admiration for one of the salient figures of German procedural law of the first half of the 20th century. His words show his respect for the pain of exile and his condemnation of the intolerance suffered by a man persecuted for his religion.

The third letter was written to Couture, in 1941, by the philosopher Luis Recasens Siches,[8] to introduce Santiago Sentis Melendo,[9] who had recently arrived in Buenos Aires, fleeing from Spain following the end of the civil war. Sentís Melendo, to whom the Spanish-speaking community owes a debt of gratitude for his tireless work as a translator and for his acute production, was a disciple of Calamandrei, under whom he had studied in Florence.

Sentís Melendo's settlement in Argentina and that of Niceto Alcalá Zamora y Castillo[10] in Mexico had a deep impact in the procedural sphere throughout Latin America. In different ways, those two republicans who had to leave Spain paradoxically managed to help Latin Americans and Europeans strengthen their ties. Couture and Calamandrei contributed to that rapprochement as few others did.

The three letters referred to may be seen as anecdotal events. However, behind Couture's open-mindedness and generosity we can see the importance he had for his colleagues. These are the traces that endure. Follow-

---

8 It is interesting to read, in the above-mentioned issue of the *Revista de la Facultad de Derecho de México* (1956) the article by L. Recasens Siches, "Eduardo J. Couture y la filosofía del derecho" (*Eduardo J. Couture and the philosophy of law*). There he describes another instance of Couture´s hospitality before turning to the main subject of his article. He says: "*In a time of personal anguish for me, caused by the tragedy in Spain in 1937, Couture generously gave me a hand. Together with our common friend and colleague, Professor Juan Llambías de Azevedo, he got me an invitation from the Faculty of Law of the Universidad de Montevideo to give a number of lectures there.*"

9 See S. Sentís Melendo, *Teoría y práctica del proceso. Ensayos de Derecho Procesal Civil,* 148 (Buenos Aires 1959, vol. I). Reproduced in that issue is the tribute published in *La Ley* of May 20, 1956, entitled: "Eduardo J. Couture". A brief but eloquent summary of the life of Sentís Melendo is to be found in A.M. Morello, "Historia y obra de Santiago Sentís Melendo", *Procesalistas inolvidables,* 103 – 119 (Buenos Aires 2001).

10 Although Alcalá Zamora y Castillo lived in Buenos Aires from 1942 to 1946, his work is legitimately associated with Mexico, since he did most of it there.

ing them will take us to a mature moment in Couture's scientific work that contrasts with his youth.[11]

A cycle of three lectures on the *trajectory and future of Latin American law of civil procedure*,[12] given by Couture at the University of Córdoba, is one of the first enduring manifestations of his work. He begins the cycle by inquiring into the ideas that have conditioned the development of civil procedure in Latin America. Despite the fact that he refers to the evolution of the Spanish law of procedure, his line of inquiry seeks to gain an understanding of how the past, the main subject of the lecture, determines the present. There, to describe the fundamental character of the colonial law of civil procedure, he says that it is *written, desperately written*. That expression was so accurate that it is still used to describe the burdensome cultural heritage that dominates the practice of the Latin American law of civil procedure, which the various attempts to reform the process have sought to counteract, with uneven success. The second lecture is devoted to the present - the specific present of the first half of the 20th century. He believes that the basic matrix of civil procedure rests on the individualistic conception represented by the disposition of the parties on substantive law. Couture explains this conception through an analysis of the principles implementing it. He thus discusses the principles of equal opportunity to be heard, disposition by the parties, discretionary continuation of the case, reasonableness of the evidence and the principle of written pleading.[13] The third lecture deals with what was, in those years just before World War II, the future for Couture. He reviews the law of procedure in connection with the crisis of liberalism and its manifestations in democratic, totalitarian, fascist and communist governments, the tension between freedom and

---

11 It is not the purpose of this introduction to describe Couture's work. We will therefore only address some significant contributions of it.

12 First published in *Boletín de la Facultad de Derechos y Ciencias de la Universidad de Córdoba*, 233 – 287 (March – June 1940, vol. IV). The lectures were reprinted in E.J. Couture, *Estudios de Derecho Procesal Civil,* 289-341 (Buenos Aires 1948, vol. I).

13 In the aforementioned lecture, Couture makes a striking reference to the work of R.W. Wyness Millar, "The formative principles of Civil Procedure", in: A. Engelman, *A History of Civil Procedure* (Boston1927). Six years later he would write the prologue to the Spanish edition of that work. There are many quotations from Italian, French and German writers, but it is striking that he should resort to an Anglo-Saxon author to explain the principles of civil procedure at the time.

equality. He tries to understand how the basic ideas of due process could be preserved in a convulsed world.

An indication of the vitality of those lectures is the fact that they are included in Oquendo's casebook: *Latin American Law*,[14] in the section devoted to *Histories and Visions of Procedure.* Oquendo assigns Couture the well-deserved role of having been the most important procedural law specialist of the first half of the last century.

In 1942 Couture presented his *Fundamentos de Derecho Procesal*[15] *(Fundamentals of Procedural Law*). Sentís Melendo, in the magnificent prologue to the third edition,[16] says that the book sets forth the pillars, the foundations of Couture's thought. It is a fundamental work in his production which evolved with each edition.

A year later, the Uruguayan government commissioned Couture to draw up a draft code of civil procedure, which he delivered in 1945.[17] In the presentation, he stated that *the project thus aims to highlight the democratic nature of justice, to ensure it has the priority it should have in the republican system of government and to strengthen the free play of individual rights inherent in the civil system. With regard to this latter point, the only limitation to freedom is the one that arises from the concept that informs the Draft Code, that the process is not a duel between private parties but rather a legal relationship governed by public law, in which the State is an essential player...*

The proposed code was based on achieving three objectives: simplicity, probity and effectiveness. Despite the fact that it was never enacted it was one of the sources used for various Latin American legislations, and by the Preliminary Draft of the Model Code of Civil Procedure of the Instituto Iberoamericano de Derecho Procesal. The theoretical reference explained in the second of his lectures in Córdoba reflects an intelligent selection of the general principles on which he builds his proposed Code: conduct and prosecution of the case by the judge, equality, freedom of form, probity, economy and concentration, among others.[18]

---

14 A. R. Oquendo, 600-642 (New York, 2006).

15 The first edition, published in Buenos Aires, was followed by a second edition in 1950 and a third in 1958. In 1946 it was published in Portuguese.

16 S. Sentís Melendo, *Teoría y práctica del proceso*, supra n. 9, 203-211.

17 *Proyecto de Código de Procedimiento Civil*, 1945 (Montevideo and Buenos Aires).

18 *Proyecto,* 137 and 138.

In 1945 Couture wrote the introduction to two translations that had a significant impact on the law of procedure of Spanish-speaking countries. The first was the *Introduzione allo studio sistematico dei provvedimenti* by Calamandrei.[19] After some sharp comments on a book that manages to summarize the key points of provisional remedies, and following a description of the best contributions of the Italian procedural school, Couture shows his sensibility when he says: *The war interrupted this admirable work discipline. How much of all that effort will be left today? Which of all these teachers and young scholars have managed to survive the war? Which have fallen in it, or in the ardor of the civil war? At the time of writing these lines, we have not received a single page from Italy after the conflagration.* While there may have been other points of contact, the prologue witnesses the trust and the scientific respect Couture shows to Calamandrei.

The second was *The formative principles of Civil procedure* by Wyness Miller.[20] Couture found that Wyness Millar's work demonstrates a growing proximity between the common law and the civil law traditions. Couture says that in the book there is good evidence of some osmosis between the two traditions. The attention Couture pays to common law and the understanding he shows when discussing several of Wyness Millar's books bear witness to his search beyond the classic borders that limited the scholars of his time.

In 1945 Couture also published *Las garantías constitucionales del proceso civil (Constitutional Guarantees of Civil Procedure)*,[21] where he anticipated an approach that would be crucial in the natural assimilation between the law of procedure and constitutional law. Couture's analysis of the constitutional matrix of the right of action was especially highlighted

---

19 Padova, 1936, published in Spanish as *Introducción al estudio sistemático de las providencias cautelares* (Buenos Aires 1945). R. See Caponi, "*A Masterpiece at a Glance: Piero Calamandrei, Introduzione allo Studio Sistematico dei Provvedimenti Cautelari, Padova, Cedam 1936*", in https://papers.ssrn.com/sol3/papers.cfm?abstract_id=2693934 (last visited July 2016).

20 *Los principios formativos del procedimiento civil*, supra n. 13.

21 The text was first published in *Revista de Derecho, Jurisprudencia y Administración,* directed by Couture (Montevideo, vol. 43, at 353 *et seq.*) and later included in his *Estudios de Derecho Procesal Civil,* 18-95 (Buenos Aires 1948, vol. I).

by Piero Calamandrei[22] in his inauguration of the 1950 Florence Congress, a foundational milestone of the International Association of Procedural Law.[23] There, he said that: *We specialists in procedural law cannot resign ourselves to being merely patient and precise builders of precision clocks, whose work is limited to fine-tuning the needles, without asking ourselves whether the result that comes out of our hands will show the time of happiness or the time of death. That is the way in which the presence will be felt, as it has already begun to be, in a masterful essay of my Uruguayan friend Eduardo Couture - who it grieves me not to see among us -, the close links between procedural and constitutional law: in that fundamental part devoted, in the constitutions of all liberal States, to guaranteeing respect for the human being and the freedom of citizens, procedure is of paramount importance. All freedoms are meaningless unless they can be claimed and defended in court.*

The second Congress of the International Association of Procedural Law was held in Vienna in 1952. There, Couture presented his study on "*Due Process* as protection for human rights".[24] In this extraordinary essay, Couture anticipated the key problems that have caught the attention of procedural law specialists until our times. In developing his thesis on the scope of the notion of due process as a human right, Couture takes as a starting point Calamandrei's statements at the Florence Congress. Couture says: *At that meeting* (referring to the Florence Congress), *in his introductory speech, Calamandrei pointed out the links between procedural and constitutional law. All freedoms are in vain, he said, if they cannot be exercised and defended in court and if the procedure at that trial is not based on respect for the human person, which recognizes that every man has a free conscience that is only responsible to itself, and thus inviolable.*

---

22 P. Calamandrei. "Discorso inaugurale del prof. Piero Calamandrei, ordinario dell'Università di Firenze, sul tema: Processo e Giustizia" *Atti del Congresso Internazionale di Diritto Processuale Civile,* 9-23 (Padova 1953).

23 At the Florence Congress it was decided to entrust the organization of the International Association of Procedural Law to a group of "Americans" -Robert Wyness Millar (the United States and Anglo-Saxon countries), Niceto Alcalà Zamora (Mexico), Oscar de Cunha (Brazil) and Eduardo Couture (Uruguay)-, and "Europeans" - Enrico Redenti (Italy), Hans Schima (Austria), Adolf Schönke (Germany) and Victor Fairén-Guillen (Spain).

24 E.J. Couture, in *La Ley,* 802-813 (Buenos Aires 1953, vol. 72, section: legal authors).

The connection among procedural law, constitutional law and human rights conventions proposed by Couture was more than a merely acceptable theoretical view. It was a contribution that put procedural law in a dimension aligned with an era born under the shadow of World War II. There, Couture propounded a vision of procedural law without borders, that would be enriched by the coexistence and convergence of the civil law and the common law traditions, with its variations in each State. In concluding the aforementioned essay, Couture held that the law is, in a fashion, *the reflection of the social phenomena it aims to govern. It reflects what it plans and organizes. Perhaps that is why medieval legal scholars called their works Mirror: "Speculum Juris", the Saxon Mirror, the 13th century Spanish Speculum.*

Couture from Latin America, and Calamandrei from Europe, managed to build enduring links. The Instituto Iberoamericano de Derecho Procesal (*Ibero-American Institute of Procedural Law*), created at the Latin American Workshop on Procedural Law held in 1957 in Montevideo, convened in order to pay tribute to Couture on the first anniversary of his death; the International Association of Procedural Law, created in 1950, bears witness to the impetus that Calamandrei and Couture gave to scientific cooperation.

The notion of mirror includes the idea of reflection, and the latter may be applied both to Couture and to Calamandrei. Their lives are the echos of past times. They summarize an era that has repercussions in the present. Retracing their steps helps us understand current dilemmas. History as a permanent construction enlightens the present with explanations from the past, that are transformed when they make contact with a diversity that conditions them.

Arbitration and ADR/ODR

I. The Theory and Practice of Precedent in Convention on Contracts for the International Sale of Goods

Beata Fröhlich[*]

(I) Introduction

The Theory and Practice of Precedent in Convention on Contracts for the International Sale of Goods Arbitral precedent is a source of law in the transnational arbitral legal order.[1] Arbitral case law has a role to play in international commercial arbitration: when applying transnational rules of law, arbitrators tend to rely on arbitral precedents as it would be paradoxical to build non-national rules on national principles of law.[2] For that rea-

---

* Lecturer in law at Marbella International University Center. PhD and LLM from Vilnius University, LL.M. in Commercial Law from University College London (UCL). Visiting scholar at Columbia Law School. Postdoctoral fellow at McGill University (Canada) under the supervision of Professor Andrea Bjorklund. Recipient of the Swiss Arbitration Academy yearly Grant 2016, Zurich, Switzerland. Certificate of Advanced Studies in Arbitration of the Universities of Lucerne and Neuchâtel and the Swiss Arbitration Academy (SAA); Arbitration Practitioner (ArbP) diploma issued by the SAA. Regional Representative for YIAG 2016/2019.

1 For more information on the term "arbitral legal order" see E. Loquin, "L'application des règles nationales dans l'arbitrage commercial international", in: *L'apport de la jurisprudence arbitrale* 87, ICC Paris (1986); D. Cohen, *Arbitrage et société* 21 (Librairie générale de droit et de jurisprudence, 1993); E. Gaillard, "L'ordre juridique arbitral: réalité, utilité et specificité: conference commemorative John EC Brierley", 55:4 *McGill LJ* 891-892 (2010); E. Gaillard, *Legal theory of international arbitration* 66 (Martinus Nijhoff Publishers, 2010); Y. Dezalay and B. Garth, *Dealing in virtue, international commercial arbitration and the construction of a transnational legal order* 57, 312 (University of Chicago Press, 1996). F. Grisel, *L'arbitrage international ou le droit contre l'ordre juridique* (Fondation Varenne et LGDJ, 2011).

2 Moreover, transnational principles, for instance, *non venire contra factum proprium*, owe much to case law and scholars and not national law, see A. Mourre, "Precedent and Confidentiality in International Commercial Arbitration, The Case for the Publication of Arbitral Awards", in: E. Gaillard and Y Banifatemi (ed.) *Precedent in International Arbitration* 51, International Arbitration Institute, IAI Seminar (Juris Publishing, Inc., 2007).

son, the term "precedent" in international commercial arbitration should be treated as a distinct term; merely transferring a definition from a familiar common-law system is unsatisfactory.[3] Arbitral precedent differs from a common law precedent existing in national laws in terms of its content and authority.[4] And thus, I do not advocate the idea that one should disguise arbitral precedent by introducing new terminology. For instance, I do not share the expressed view that arbitral precedent in the context of the Convention on Contracts for the International Sale of Goods (CISG) should be denominated as "inspirational" precedent merely for the sake of semantics, or should be named as "shared uniform case law", which would make it more attractive to traditional common law benches.[5] A mere "relabeling" of arbitral precedent would not alter its essence.

A plausible definition of arbitral precedent recognising that international commercial arbitration is a transnational legal system has been proposed by *Legum*, who suggests addressing the term "precedent" from the relative different perspectives of the principal players in international commercial arbitration, i.e. counsel for the parties, arbitrators, academic commentators and other members of the public. He attempts a synthesis with a view towards a unified definition of precedent in international arbitration, i.e., a precedent is any decisional authority that is likely to affect the arbitrator's decision and that may reasonably serve to justify the arbitrator's decision to the principal audience for that decision.[6]

This article deals with the theory and practice of arbitral precedent in international sales of goods, where the CISG plays the major role. In the first chapter of the paper the special nature of CISG case law will be ad-

---

3 B. Legum, "The Definition of "Precedent" in International Arbitration", in: E. Gaillard and Y. Banifatemi (ed.) *Precedent in International Arbitration* 5, International Arbitration Institute, IAI Seminar (Juris Publishing, Inc., 2007). Also see G. Kaufmann-Kohler, "Arbitral Precedent: Dream, Necessity or Excuse?", 23 (3) *Arb. Int'l* 357, 358, 359 (2007).

4 The term "arbitral precedent" should be analyzed separately from a familiar common-law system precedent. For details, please refer to Section II of this paper.

5 P. Darbyshire, *Darbyshire on the English Legal System* (8th ed., Sweet & Maxwell. 2005), at paras. 2-030 and 2-037; C. Andersen, "The Global Jurisconsultorium of the CISG Revisited" 13 *Vindobona Journal of International Commercial Law & Arbitration* 43, 59-60 (1/2009). Also available at http://www.cisg.law.pace.edu/cisg/biblio/andersen7.html#2. NoA: all online pages have been last visited 2 February 2017.

6 Legum, *supra* n. 3, at 11.

dressed. I argue that arbitral precedent should ensure uniformity of interpretation and application of the CISG. An increase in the number of CISG cases that have referenced cases from other jurisdictions as persuasive or inspirational precedents has been noticed.[7]

In the second chapter, criteria for CISG precedent will be covered. The main purpose of uniformity is sound judgment, and scholars offer guidelines that would help to determine the persuasive weight of a foreign precedent.[8]

Last but not least, uniform application of the CISG will be analysed.

As can be observed, this article requires in-depth knowledge and expertise of arbitration. As primary source material, reference will be made to legal resources, especially primary law (cases, treaties, statutes, regulations, local ordinances, and related government information) as well as secondary sources (textbooks, treatises, monographs, articles, reviews, comments and others) which all are basically now available online through governmental websites and online databases (International Law Reports; European Journal of International Law; International Court of Justice; HeinOnline, LexisNexis; Quicklaw; Westlaw and others). A survey of CISG arbitral precedent will be conducted. Research reviewing arbitration awards applying the Vienna Sales Convention will be carried out based on Pace School of Law's online database of CISG cases.[9]

(II) The Special Nature of CISG Arbitration Case Law

International commercial arbitration is built on a network of transnational rules that, *inter alia*, governs international sales of good transactions. The nature of precedent in international law is similar to arbitral precedent under the CISG. The juridical discipline of uniform law - and the study of

---

7 Andersen, *supra* n. 5, at 50. For the proportion of CISG cases with references to foreign precedents as well as for the problems of foreign precedents in CISG cases see Andersen, *supra* n. 5, at 53-55.

8 H. Flechtner, H., "Recovering Attorneys' Fees as Damages under the U.N. Sales Convention: A Case Study on the New International Commercial Practice and the Role of Case Law in CISG Jurisprudence, with Comments on *Zapata Hermanos Sucesores, S.A. v Hearthside Baking Co.*" 22 *Northwestern Journal of International Law and Business* 121 (2002), available at: http://cisgw3.law.pace.edu/cisg/biblio/flechtner4.html#iv.

9 See http://cisgw3.law.pace.edu.

precedents in the context of the CISG - is unique, and scholars and practitioners should divorce themselves from domestic or regional notions of law.[10]

Some CISG cases show that courts now consider case law from other CISG jurisdictions and appear to feel bound by a duty to apply principles of uniform law[11] that would fit within the definition of persuasive precedent in civil law as well as in common law systems. CISG cases should have the same status amongst the courts of its Contracting States as decisions of Commonwealth courts have within common law countries.

Article 7(1) CISG establishes requirements for all CISG Contracting States and their courts for the interpretation of the entire Convention text: regard is to be had to the international character of the treaty and the need to promote its uniform application.[12] CISG commentators and national courts tend to agree that the command "to have regard" requires that consideration be given to CISG "foreign case law",[13] i.e. that having regard implies "a process or methodology involving awareness of and respect for, but not necessarily blind obedience to, interpretations of the CISG from outside one's own legal culture".[14] All in all, the majority of CISG scholars assume that Article 7(1) CISG provides the legal basis for a duty to aim for a uniform, transnational interpretation and commands national courts also to have (to a certain degree) "regard" to the international view.[15]

A judicial trend to take foreign scholars' views on the CISG and CISG rulings issued by tribunals of other jurisdictions into consideration has

---

10 Andersen, *supra* n. 5, at 56.

11 Andersen, *supra* n. 5, at 59.

12 J. Lookofsky, "Digesting CISG Case Law: How Much Regard Should We Have?", available at http://www.cisg.law.pace.edu/cisg/biblio/lookofsky9.html#jlfn21.

13 See, e.g., F. Ferrari, "International Sales Law and the Inevitability of Forum Shopping: A Comment on Tribunale Di Rimini, 26 November 2002", 23 *Journal of Law and Commerce* 169, 172 (2004)

14 H. Flechtner, "The Several Texts of the CISG in a Decentralized System: Observations on Translations, Reservations and other Challenges to the Uniformity Principle in Article 7(1)", 17 *Journal of Law and Commerce* 187, 211 (1998), available at http://cisgw3.law.pace.edu/cisg/biblio/flecht1.html.

15 J. Lookofsky, *Understanding the CISG*, (Kluwer, 2008), 34, 35; Lookofsky also points out the problematic issue of just how much 'regard' must be had.

been identified.[16] According to Italian jurisprudence on the CISG, foreign court case law *"merely* [has] persuasive, non-binding value",[17] i.e. foreign court judgements are not 'binding' in a *stare decisis* sense.[18] Thus, the requirement is that a CISG court must have "regard" to the Convention's international character and the requirement to promote its uniform application implies that the court should *consider* foreign case law, i.e. "take [it] into account".[19]

Given the *travaux préparatoires*, current practices of the CISG, and the aim of its drafters to create a level playing field in commercial law and remove barriers to international trade, a desire for a certain minimum level of applied uniformity must be assumed.[20] For that reason, courts should implement an autonomous and uniform transnational approach towards the application of the CISG. The notion that shared global law requires a shared global doctrine and jurisprudence has gained support in domestic courts (transnational shared case law is used to resolve disputes before domestic courts) and between transnational CISG academics: lawyers from around the globe consult with one another within scholarly contexts or by

---

16 Andersen, *supra* n. 5, at 50-53. A movement in courts applying CISG towards international precedent has been noticed – employment of a uniform transnational approach to foreign sources.

17 P. Schlechtriem, *Kommentar zum Einheitlichen UN-Kaufrecht – CISG* (3 d ed. Munich, 2000) and the English translation (of the 2 d ed.): *Commentary on the UN Convention on the International Sale of Goods (CISG)* (Oxford University Press, 1998). See United Nations document A/CN.9/SER.C/DIGEST/CISG and the official English version of UNCITRAL *Digest of case law on the United Nations Convention on the International Sales of Goods* at http://www.uncitral.org/english/clout/digest_cisg_e.htm of Article 7 at para. 4 in Lookofsky, *supra* n. 12, at 186.

18 See, e.g., Ferrari, *supra* n. 13 at 173 indicating agreement on this point between the decision of Tribunale di Vigevano (CLOUT case No. 378, available at http://cisgw3.law.pace.edu/cisg/text/000712i3italian.html, and the more recent decision of Tribunale di Rimini, 26 November 2002, English translation in 23 *J. Law & Comm.* 193, 197 (2004) (foreign case law 'can only have persuasive value and not binding value').

19 See United Nations document A/CN.9/SER.C/DIGEST/CISG and the official English version of UNCITRAL *Digest of case law on the United Nations Convention on the International Sales of Goods* at http://www.uncitral.org/english/clout/digest_cisg_e.htm of Article 7 at para 3.

20 For an in-depth analysis of the uniformity of the CISG, see Andersen, *supra* n. 5, at 46.

referring to each others' decisions and opinions across jurisdictional boundaries.[21]

Therefore, in order to develop a uniform approach towards an international convention, sources of uniform law should be shared: "[...] tribunals construing an international convention will appreciate that they are colleagues of a world-wide body of jurists with a common goal".[22] The duty to consider foreign sources or precedents is also based on the argument of comity. A duty to take relevant foreign judgments into account has long been supported by numerous CISG experts, including *DiMatteo,*[23] *Ferrari,*[24] *Zeller,*[25] *Flechtner,*[26] and *Schlechtriem.*[27]

International commercial law is especially reliant upon the efforts of a global judiciary and scholars. Firstly, the harmonisation[28] of commercial law gives immediate economic benefits to the community of states by re-

---

21 Andersen, *supra* n. 5, at 47.

22 J. Honnold, "Uniform Laws for International Trade: Early 'Care and Feeding' for Uniform Growth", in 1 *International Trade and Business Law Journal* 1 (2005).

23 L. DiMatteo, "The CISG and the Presumption of Enforceability: Unintended Contractual Liability in International Business Dealings" 22 *Yale Int. Law Journal* 111 (1997); *ibid.*, "The Interpretive Turn in International Sales Law: An Analysis of Fifteen Years of CISG Jurisprudence", 34 *Northwestern Journal of International Law and Business* 299(2004).

24 F. Ferrari, "CISG Case Law: A New Challenge for Interpreters?", 17 *Journal of Law and Commerce*, 246 (1999): "As many legal writers have pointed out, this means, above all, that one should not read the Convention through the lenses of domestic law, but rather in an autonomous manner."

25 B. Zeller, "Traversing international waters: With the growth of international trade, lawyers must become familiar with the terms of the Convention on Contracts for the International Sale of Goods", 78(9) *Law Institute Journal* 52 (2004).

26 See H. Flechtner, "The Several Texts of the CISG in a Decentralized System: Observations on Translations, Reservations and other Challenges to the Uniformity Principle in Article 7(1)", 17 *Journal of Law and Commerce* 187 (1998), available at http://cisgw3.law.pace.edu/cisg/biblio/flecht1.html.

27 P. Schlechtriem, "Uniform Sales Law - The Experience with Uniform Sales Laws in the Federal Republic of Germany", 2 *Juridisk Tidskrift* 1 (1991-92), available at http://cisgw3.law.pace.edu/cisg/biblio/schlech2.html, where he explains how consideration and critique of case law in other jurisdictions as well as help from scholars and comparative law centers smooth any divergent interpretations of uniform law.

28 For more information on the harmonization goal see G. Cordero-Moss, "Limits to Party Autonomy in International Commercial Arbitration", *Oslo Law Review* 47 (2014, 1); L. Meyer, "Soft Law for Solid Contracts? A Comparative Analysis of the Value of the UNIDROIT Principles of International Commercial Contracts and

moving barriers to international trade and the law being applied is a shared multi-jurisdictional law, which should be applied with a high degree of uniformity. Secondly, there is not one single body charged with the task of monitoring international commercial laws. To be more precise, there is no international commercial court that has the competence to monitor the application of shared global instruments like the CISG.[29]

Moreover, legal counsels and their clients tend to 'shop' for precedents as widely as possible to strengthen their position. There is no reason why a case or authority sharing common commercial values (on the assumption of similar values in international commercial law) should not be quoted merely because the scholar or commercial court deciding a dispute does not come from the same judicial system.[30] Judges and arbitrators should determine the persuasive weight of all available transnational sources: "Only a fool would refuse to seek guidance in the work of other judges confronted with similar problems."[31]

The number of CISG cases that have referenced cases from other jurisdictions as persuasive precedents has increased.[32] Moreover, on numerous occasions references to the case law of foreign jurisdictions are made in a

---

the Principles of European Contract Law to the Process of Contract Law Harmonization", *Denver Journal of International Law and Policy* 119 (Spring 2006); S. Gopalan, "From Cape Town to The Hague: Harmonization Has Taken Wing", 5 *U.Pa.J. Int'l L. & Pol'y.* (2006-2007).

29 H. Wehberg seems to have been the first to suggest such a tribunal; see H. Wehberg, *Ein Internationaler Gerichtshof für Privatklagen* 23 (Liebheit & Thiesen, 1911). Another suggestion was made in 1992: see also L. Sohn, "Uniform Laws Require Uniform Application: Proposals for an International Tribunal to Interpret Uniform Legal Texts", *Uniform Commercial Law in the Twenty-First Century: Proceedings of the Congress of the United Nations Commission on International Trade Law* 50-4, (1992, available at https://www.uncitral.org/pdf/english/texts/general/Uniform_Commercial_Law_Congress_1992_e.pdf). The latest official suggestion seems to have been made by F de Ly: see F de Ly, "Uniform Interpretation: What is Being Done? Official Efforts", in: F. Ferrari, F., (ed.), *The 1980 Uniform Sales Law* 346 (Sellier 2003).

30 This view has prevailed since 1974 when Otto Kahn-Freund first dared to state his point that commercial law is comparatively culture-free, see O. Freund, "On Uses and Misuses of Comparative Law" 37 *Modern Law Review* 1 (1974).

31 C. Koch, "Envisioning a Global Legal Culture", 25 *Michigan Journal of International* 51 *Law* (2003).

32 Andersen, *supra* n. 5, at 50. For the proportion of CISG cases with references to foreign precedents as well as for the problems of foreign precedents in CISG cases see pages 53-55.

'natural' manner, i.e. without justifying the reference to foreign cases. This highlights that domestic and foreign precedent are treated as equal.[33] Cross-referencing to other CISG precedents occurs, *inter alia*, due to the inertia of habit.[34] It is noteworthy that for various reasons, be it habits or traditions, courts in CISG cases taking into account CISG case law from foreign jurisdiction do so without express references to these foreign precedents.[35]

Despite the common belief that arbitral precedent is a self-referential system and courts do not rely on arbitration awards, there is the well-known Italian CISG *Vigevano* case, citing American, Austrian, Dutch, French, German, Italian, and Swiss CISG cases as well as arbitral awards.[36]

The arbitrator states the law, and the law of international trade is comprised of a set of rendered arbitral awards.[37] All in all, to modern CISG lawyers it is difficult to see why any judge, arbitrator or practitioner would not make use of foreign precedents when they are so readily available.

33 Andersen, *supra* n. 5, at 51-53.

34 D. Frisch, "Commercial Common Law, the United Nations Convention on the International Sale of Goods, and the Inertia of Habit", 74 *Tul. L. Rev.* 495, 522-23 (1999).

35 Andersen, *supra* n. 5, at 53-55.

36 District Court Vigevano, Italy, 12 July 2000, *Rheinland Versicherungen v. Atlarex*, available at: http://cisgw3.law.pace.edu/cases/000712i3.html. For instance, see para 22 of the Vigevano case, that refers to the decision of the International Chamber of Commerce Court of Arbitration, (arbitral decision) arbitration # 6653 [text and English translation available at http://cisgw3.law.pace.edu/cases/936653i1.html]): "the United Nations Convention does not govern the burden of proof issue'; see para 23 of the Vigevano case that refers to the decision of the International Chamber of Commerce Court of Arbitration, (arbitral decision), arbitration # 7660 [English text available at http://cisgw3.law.pace.edu/cases/947660i1.html] the issue of the validity of an assignment of rights arising from a sales contract, and the issue of the validity of a penalty clause limiting compensation for breach of a contract to an agreed amount (see the decision of the International Chamber of Commerce Court of Arbitration, (arbitral decision), arbitration # 7331 [English text available at http://cisgw3.law.pace.edu/cases/947331i1.html>].

37 M. Henry, "The contribution of Arbitral Case Law and National Laws in Towards a Uniform International Arbitration Law?", in: E. Gaillard (ed.), *IAI Series on International Arbitration*, n 3. 61.

(III) Criteria for CISG Arbitral Precedents

The main purpose of uniformity is to have a sound arbitral award. Guidelines that would help to determine the persuasive weight of precedent are offered below.[38] A reasonable scale to evaluate the weight of CISG precedent depends on a number of factors. These criteria should include the following:

- the authority of the arbitral tribunal rendering the decision and the level of experience arbitrators have with international trade;
- the extent to which the arbitral precedent complies with the interpretational guidelines of the CISG (i.e. good faith and uniformity);
- the extent of agreement on the issue amongst other tribunals, i.e. the CISG majority view: the well-reasoned[39] opinions previously rendered

---

38 Flechtner, *supra* n. 8 at 121. C. Andersen, "The Global Jurisconsultorium of the CISG Revisited', 13 *Vindobona Journal of International Commercial Law & Arbitration* 43, 59-60 (1/2009), available at http://www.cisg.law.pace.edu/cisg/biblio/andersen7.html#2.

39 W. Park, "Income Tax Treaty Arbitration", 10 *Geo. Mason L. Rev.* 803, 823(2002). For the functions that serve reasoned awards see W. Weidemaier, "Toward a Theory of Precedent in Arbitration" 51 *William and Mary Law Review* 1916, 1920 (2009-2010): "One benefit of reasoned awards is that losing parties may be more inclined to view them as legitimate and thus to comply voluntarily. [...] When voluntary compliance is not forthcoming, the winning party may seek to enforce the award through formal legal means. [...] Although judges do not review awards on the merits, the stringency of the review is likely to depend, in part, on whether the judge believes that the award resulted from a fair process. Here, a reasoned award may signal that the arbitrator made the decision and conducted the arbitration itself in a deliberate, unbiased way. [...] For arbitrators, reasoned awards may serve as a form of advertising; an award that demonstrates competence, neutrality, or expertise may enhance the value of the arbitrator's services. [...] Parties might fund this practice because it generates information about the arbitrator that can be used to improve future selection decisions. Parties might also pay for reasoned awards because they believe that arbitrators who must provide a written explanation are less likely to make careless or biased decisions. [...] Finally, and perhaps counter intuitively, parties may pay arbitrators to produce reasoned awards even when they do not want them. This is because public actors sometimes mandate the use of reasoned awards. For instance, in cases involving statutory rights, some U.S. courts will not enforce an arbitration agreement that does not provide for a reasoned award. [...] For all of these reasons, arbitration systems both within and outside of the United States commonly feature reasoned awards."

by an overwhelmingly large majority of arbitral tribunals;[40] the frequency of the rendering of similar arbitral awards, which brings case law closer to custom (i.e. precedent meaning a series of consistent decisions on a given question of law).[41] The availability of arbitral precedent in sufficient quantity (i.e. systematic publication), allowing trends to emerge is crucial, as arbitral precedent will arise if similar outcomes are repeated in a number of comparable cases. The persuasiveness of an argument or approach will often become more visible if it is repeatedly and frequently chosen.[42] Nonetheless, I would argue that isolated decisions can also be decisive in the absence of other relevant case law on the issue;

- the force of the reasoning in the arbitral award and the apparent soundness of the result.[43]

All in all, to develop a modern uniform autonomous approach and reach fair judgements in the CISG context, the whole picture should be considered. CISG arbitral precedents should be screened on a case-by-case basis, meaning that analogous case law is explored and applied by reference to the "reasoning which the decisions [...] bring to bear on the problem at hand."[44]

40 See the decision of Tribunale Civile di Monza, 14 January 1993, English translation available at http://cisgw3.law.pace.edu/cases/930114i3.html. For a well-founded criticism of the decision see F. Ferrari, "Specific Topics of the CISG in the Light of Judicial Application and Scholarly Writing", 15 *J. Law & Commerce* 1 (1995), also available at http://cisgw3.law.pace.edu/cisg/wais/db/editorial /ferrari 930329i3.html.

41 B. Starck, H. Roland, L. Boyer, *Introduction au droit* 327 (Litec, 5th ed. 2000).

42 A. Mourre, "Precedent and Confidentiality in International Commercial Arbitration, The Case for the Publication of Arbitral Awards", in: E. Gaillard and Y Banifatemi (ed.) *Precedent in International Arbitration* 48-49, International Arbitration Institute, IAI Seminar (Juris Publishing, Inc., 2007).

43 E.A. Farnsworth, *An Introduction to the Legal System of the United States* 52-57 (3 d ed. 1996).

44 J. Schwartze, "The Role of the European Court of Justice (ECJ) in the Interpretation of Uniform Law Among the Member States of the European Communities (EC)" in UNIDROIT (ed.), *International Uniform Law in Practice/Le droit uniforme international dans la pratique [Acts and Proceedings of the 3rd Congress on Private Law held by the International Institute for the Unification of Private Law (Rome 7-10 September 1987)]* 193-227, (Oceana, 1988).

(IV) Uniform Application of CISG

Research reviewing arbitration awards applying the Vienna Sales Convention has been carried out and can be found in Pace School of Law's online database of CISG cases.[45] An analysis of all electronically published arbitral awards prior to 20 February 2015 stored on this database has been conducted, i.e. 819 cases have been reviewed. Given that there is no data indicating how many CISG arbitration awards have been rendered, it is impossible to conduct a statistical analysis to find out what percentage of these actually contain arbitral precedent.

Moreover, contrary to existing opinion,[46] it seems that it is not possible to objectively determine the percentage of arbitration precedents in published CISG awards: usually only abstracts/excerpts of CISG arbitration awards are published without indicating that these are not entire awards. Thus, it is not possible to draw particular conclusion from that. Assuming that the existence of arbitral precedent is not confirmed in a particular case, advocates arguing for the existence of arbitral precedent would validly suggest that it is impossible to establish the presence of CISG arbitral precedent due to the fact that an award has not been published in sufficient detail. In contrast, opponents of the existence of arbitral precedent might find that less detailed arbitration awards are sufficient for establishing the absence of CISG arbitration precedent.

The existence of CISG arbitral precedent has been confirmed on several occasions, both in substantive and procedural issues. 31 arbitral cases referred to past awards (Table 1). Some scholars, presumably relying on common sense, state that "where a law other than the common law governs, precedent is less relevant to the award".[47] However, there is no data on CISG arbitral awards supporting that statement. To the contrary, in 31 CISG arbitral cases referring to past awards, the applicable law was continental law (Table 1). The aforementioned data reflects the stand-alone transnational approach to arbitral precedent that is detached from the differentiating aspect of common law and continental legal traditions, i.e. the absence of guiding historical precedent in continental law.

45 http://cisgw3.law.pace.edu.

46 Kaufmann-Kohler, *supra* n. 3, at 23.

47 B. Legum, "The Definition of "Precedent" in International Arbitration", in: E. Gaillard and Y Banifatemi (ed.) *Precedent in International Arbitration* 51, International Arbitration Institute, IAI Seminar 12 (Juris Publishing, Inc., 2007).

The survey confirms that reference to prior cases on substantive and procedural matters is made (Table 1). References to earlier cases were made with regard to matters of jurisdiction and procedure, in connection for instance with the determination of the law governing the merits,[48] and the applicability of CISG.[49] Reference to earlier cases was also made in connection with the determination of an interest rate,[50] the competence of the arbitral tribunal,[51] and interim measures.[52] Moreover, substantive issues prompt reference to arbitral awards in connection with the interpretation of: an exemption from liability,[53] the principle of *bona fide,*[54] *force majeure,*[55] the manner (methods) of examination of the goods,[56] and fundamental breach of contract.[57]

One might argue that while identifying the existence of arbitral precedent, reference should be made not to the applicable law but to the background of the arbitrator (common or civil law lawyer) as arbitral awards rely on past arbitral decisions with different applicable law. "Very often, this practice [reference to past awards] goes beyond the relevant applicable law of the dispute. It is almost second nature to invoke arbitral awards in support of one's argument, without even giving a second thought to the

---

48 ICC 9474 (1999), referring to ICC 5713 (1989) concerning choice of law rules.

49 ICC 5713 (1989), referring to ICC 7153 (1992); ICC 9781 (2000) referring to *inter alia* ICC 6653 (1993); ICC 11333 (2002) referring to *inter alia* ICC 9448 (1999).

50 ICC 7754 (1995), referring to *inter alia* ICC 5428 (1988); ICC 7331 (1994), referring to *inter alia* ICC 2375 (1975).

51 MKAC 125/2003 (2004), referring to Decisions of International Commercial Arbitral Tribunal at Chamber of Commerce and Industry of Russian Federation in 1999-2000 M., 2002. C. 67-72, 141-147.

52 MKAC 105/2005 (2006), referring to Practice of the International Commercial Arbitration Court at the Russian Federation Chamber of Commerce and Industry in 2003 […], p. 182-185.

53 AAA 50181T 0036406 (1997), referring *inter alia* to CIETAC 971130 (1997) as support for the interpretation of an exemption from liability.

54 ICC 8786 (1997), referring *inter alia* to ICC 4381(1986).

55 ICC 9978 (1999), referring *inter alia* to ICC 8486 (1998).

56 MKAC 54/1999 (2000) referring to Arbitration Practice of International Court of Commercial Arbitration at the Chamber of Commerce & Industry of the RF, 1998, Moscow: Statut, (1999), at 57; Netherlands Arbitration Institute 2319 (2002), referring to *inter alia* ICC 6653 (1993).

57 *Arbitral Tribunal Hamburg* (Chinese goods case) referring to ICC arbitral awards of 30 May 1979, nos. 2099-3100, summarized in Javin/Derains, *Collection of ICC Arbitral Awards*, 1986, nos. 5056, 5279; 1987, nos. 5255, 5318, 5418, 5558, summarized by Bühler, 87 *ZVglRWiss* 431, 443, 446, 448 (1988).

applicable law of the award that one is invoking.'[58] However, of the 31 CISG arbitral cases referring to past awards, only three disclosed the name of the arbitrator[59] and, interestingly, at least three out of four arbitrators are lawyers with a civil law background.

Moreover, nobody would argue that arbitrators referring to scholars' writings who in turn refer to arbitral awards apply precedents.[60] One might refer to the latter constellation as constituting 'indirect precedent'. In the conducted research on CISG arbitral precedent,[61] at least nine cases[62] refer to scholars' writings that in turn refer to arbitral precedents, both for substantive as well as procedural issues, and thus constitute indirect precedents (Table 2).

Furthermore, the aforementioned survey offers additional evidence for the existence of indirect arbitral precedent: at least on three occasions, arbitral cases[63] did not refer to concrete arbitral precedent but to arbitration case law and arbitration practice in general, confirming the existence of

---

58 E. Gaillard and Y Banifatemi (ed.) *Precedent in International Arbitration* 3, International Arbitration Institute, IAI Seminar (Juris Publishing, Inc., 2007).

59 Austria 15 June 1994 Vienna Arbitration proceeding SCH-4318 (*Rolled metal sheets case*) (http://cisgw3.law.pace.edu/cases/940615a4.html): M. Bonell (sole arbitrator); Netherlands 15 October 2002 Netherlands Arbitration Institute, Case No. 2319 (*Condensate crude oil mix case*): http://cisgw3.law.pace.edu/cases/021015n1.html: F. De Ly, Mr. E.J. van Sandick, Ir. L. Tjioe. Civil law lawyers: (http://www.unidroit.org/overview-principles-2010/309-instruments/commercial-contracts/unidroit-principles-2010/unidroit-principles-2010-history/780-michael-joachim-bonell-curriculum-vitae F. De Ly (http://www.esl.eur.nl/profile_az/?tx_eurliaatmetismis_pi1%5Bmetis_id%5D=1000487); Mr. E.J. van Sandick (http://cisgw3.law.pace.edu/cases/021015n1.html). The author has no information as to the background of Ir. L. Tijoe.

60 F. Ferrari, H. Flechtner and RA Brand (eds), *The Draft UNCITRAL Digest and Beyond: Cases, Analysis and Unresolved Issues in the U.N. Sales Convention* (2004); P. Schlechtriem and I. Schwenzer (eds), *Commentary on the UN Convention on the International Sale of Goods* (CISG) (2005).

61 Research reviewing arbitration awards applying the Vienna Sales Convention has been carried out and can be found in Pace School of Law's online database of CISG cases: http://cisgw3.law.pace.edu.

62 Please refer to Table 2 below.

63 1. Serbia 5 January 2009 Foreign Trade Court of Arbitration attached to the Serbian Chamber of Commerce (*Paper handkerchiefs production line case*) (http://cisgw3.law.pace.edu/cases/090105sb.html). The arbitral tribunal examining the validity of the arbitration clause stated: "This standpoint, based on similar formulations of parties agreement on dispute settlement, was previously taken by the

arbitral precedent. Furthermore, at least on one occasion, an arbitral case[64] relied on a past arbitral award without including an express reference to the arbitral precedent but by using the identical wording.[65]

Scholars also contribute to the uniformity of the CISG through, for example, the creation of databases, for instance the CISGW3 Database at Pace University[66] that helps unifying interpretations of the CISG, as well as study groups and panels, for instance the CISG Advisory Council, con-

---

Foreign Trade Court of Arbitration attached to the Serbian Chamber of Commerce for several times."; 2. Serbia 23 January 2008 Foreign Trade Court of Arbitration attached to the Serbian Chamber of Commerce (*White crystal sugar case*) (http://cisgw3.law.pace.edu/cases/080123sb.html). The arbitral tribunal on the application of lex mercatoria: "[...] practice of ICC: [...] Respectable Arbitral Tribunals in the world (especially the ICC Court of Arbitration) have long since made awards pursuant to these Principles [UNIDROIT Principles, UML on International Credit Transfers and Ole Lando Principles] and arbitrated disputes between Parties by applying these principles as lex mercatoria."; 3. Serbia 28 January 2009 Foreign Trade Court of Arbitration attached to the Serbian Chamber of Commerce (*Medicaments case*) (http://cisgw3.law.pace.edu/cases/090128sb.html). Reference to the choice of law clause applicable to the contract: "shall be governed and construed in accordance with applicable regulations and laws of the Republic of Serbia". [...] Since Serbia ratified [...] CISG, which thereby became an integral part of Serbian law, [...] the CISG should be primarily applied to the Contract [...]. This finding is in accordance with the foreign judicial and arbitral practice, which should be taken into consideration for the purpose of achieving uniform application of the CISG, [...]."

64 Internationales Schiedsgericht der Bundeskammer der gewerblichen Wirtschaft [Arbitral Tribunal - Vienna]. Austria 15 June 1994 Vienna Arbitration proceeding SCH-4318 (*Rolled metal sheets case*) (http://cisgw3.law.pace.edu/cases/940615a4.html). "The arbitrator awarded damages to the buyer for lack of conformity of the goods. With regard to interest, the arbitrator awarded interest at the average prime rate in the buyer's country (Germany) with respect to the currency of payment (US Dollars), giving the same reason mentioned in [CLOUT abstract] 93 [see: Austria: Arbitration 15 June 1994, SCH-4366]."

65 It might be possible that relying on a past arbitral award without reference to it but using the exactly same wording occurred due to the same arbitrator's ruling in earlier and later cases.

66 For more on the CISGW3 database as a source of law, see C. Andersen, "The Internet: Tool of Law, Source of Law or Tool for Sources - Use of the Internet in Legal Practice using Examples from International] Sales' in *Controlling Information on the Online Environment*, (2003), 18 BILETA Conference, available at http://www.bileta.ac.uk/03papers/baasch.html; see also C. Andersen, "Furthering the Uniform Application of the CISG: Sources of Law on the Internet", 10 *Pace International Law Review* 403 (1998).

ferences, or the UNCITRAL Digest.[67] Furthermore, international cross-referencing to other sources has increased significantly: scholars include more languages and international cases in their comments on the CISG. The notion of CISG has become a shared global law/instrument that purports to being uniform and global scholars contribute to the autonomous uniform interpretation of the CISG.[68]

All in all, after an initial period of less frequent reliance on arbitral precedents, commercial arbitration now demonstrates a greater degree of reliance on prior arbitral awards,[69] both in civil and common law jurisdictions.

(V) Conclusion

The system of international commercial arbitration is structurally compatible with the creation of CISG precedent as it produces reasoned awards that are accessible to the end-users and becoming even more so.

There is no CISG arbitral precedent on a *de jure* basis. However, it does exist on a *de facto* basis. The operation of arbitration community players reflects that there is a special role for arbitral precedent in international commercial arbitration. Arbitral case law exists in practice and it is not a mere academic fantasy. The CISG arbitration framework is a work in progress and this paper is intended to provide an indication of current development in the field.

67 Andersen, *supra* n. 5, at 62.

68 In addition, uniform law should be established as a separate discipline and a duty to look to uniform precedents has to be acknowledged. Andersen, *supra* n. 5, at 61.

69 Please refer to Table 1 below.

Table 1

No.	Arbitration Institution	Year	Case	Use of Arbitral Precedent	Applicable Law
1.	AAA[70]	1997	*Macromex Srl. v. Globex International Inc. Case* No. 50181T 0036406 (http://cisgw3.law.pace.edu/cases/071023a5.html)	Reference to arbitral cases[71] on the interpretation of an exemption from liability under Article 79 when a breach of the contract occurs.	CISG
2.	ICC[72]	1989	ICC Arbitration Case No. 5713 of 1989. (http://cisgw3.law.pace.edu/cases/895713i1.html)	Reference to arbitral cases[73] on the applicability of CISG (reflecting the trade usages) to non-signatories.	Turkish law
3.	ICC	1994	ICC Arbitration Case No. 7331 of 1994 (*Cowhides case*). (http://cisgw3.law.pace.edu/cases/947331i1.html)	Reference to arbitral cases[74] on the determination of an interest rate.	CISG
4.	ICC	1995	ICC Arbitration Case No. 7754 of January 1995 (*Computer hardware case*). (http://cisgw3.law.pace.edu/cases/957754i1.html)	Reference to arbitral cases[75] on the determination of an interest rate.	French law
5.	ICC	1997	ICC Arbitration Case No. 8786 of January 1997 (*Clothing case*). (http://cisgw3.law.pace.edu/cases/978786i1.html)	Reference to arbitral cases[76] on the interpretation of the principle of *bona fide* as expressed in Art. 7 para. 1 CISG.	CISG and Swiss substantive law
6.	ICC	1999	ICC Arbitration Case No. 9474 of February 1999 (*Printed banknotes case*) (http://cisgw3.law.pace.edu/cases/999474i1.html)	Reference to arbitral awards[77] concerning the choice of law rule.	The general standards and rules of international contracts.

70 American Arbitration Association.

71 Hungary, 10 December 1996 Budapest Arbitration Vb 96074 (*Caviar case*) <http://cisgw3.law.pace.edu/cases/961210h1.html>; China, 30 November 1997 CIETAC Arbitration proceeding (Canned oranges case) http://cisgw3.law.pace.edu/cases/971130c1.html.

72 International Chamber of Commerce.

73 ICC Case No. 7153 of 1992 Chambre de Commerce Internationale, Sentences Arbitrales *Journal du Droit International* 1992, at 1008.

74 ICC arbitration cases 2375 of 1975 and 5460 of 1987.

75 *Inter alia*, ICC Case No 5428-1988, ICC Case No 5440-1991.

76 Collection of ICC Arbitral Awards 1986-1990, Deventer/Boston 1994, Case no. 4381, at 272 and Case No. 5103, at 369.

77 Final Award in case no. 5713 of 1989, Collection of ICC Arbitral Awards 1986-1990, p. 223.

No.	Arbitration Institution	Year	Case	Use of Arbitral Precedent	Applicable Law
7.	ICC	1999	ICC Arbitration Case No. 9978 of March 1999 (http://cisgw3.law.pace.edu/cases/999978i1.html)	Reference to the constant practice of ICC[78] arbitrators who grant *force majeure* defences only in extreme cases.	CISG and German law
8.	ICC	2000	ICC Arbitration Case No. 9781 of 2000 (*Waste recycling plant case*) (http://cisgw3.law.pace.edu/cases/009781i1.html)	Reference to arbitral awards[79] concerning the choice of law rule, i.e. the applicability of the CISG.	CISG and Italian law
9.	ICC	2002	ICC Arbitration Case No. 11333 of 2002 (*Machine case*) (http://cisgw3.law.pace.edu/cases/021333i1.html)	Reference to arbitral awards[80] concerning the choice of law question, i.e. the applicability of the CISG.	CISG and French law
10.	MKAC[81]	2000	Russia 24 January 2000 Arbitration proceeding 54/1999 (http://cisgw3.law.pace.edu/cases/000124r1.html)	Reference to arbitral awards[82] on the determination of the manner (methods) of examination of the goods.	Russian law and CISG
11.	MKAC	2004	Russia 9 June 2004 Arbitration proceeding 125/2003 (http://cisgw3.law.pace.edu/cases/040609r1.html)	Reference to arbitral awards[83] concerning the issue of the competence of the Tribunal.	The Law of the Russian Federation
12.	MKAC	2006	Russia 13 April 2006 Arbitration proceeding 105/2005	Reference to arbitral awards[84] on the interpretation of Art. 71 CISG as unfounded ground	The CISG and Rus-

78 Sec. 1CC Award No. 8486, *Journal du Droit International* 1998, at 1047, 1048; No. 5485, Yearbook Commercial Arbitration 1989, at 156, 168; No. 5953, *Journal du Droit International* 1990, at 1056.

79 ICC Case No. 6653, 1993, JDI (1993) p. 1040, obs. JJA; ICC Case No. 7197, 1992, JDI (1993) p. 1029.

80 ICC Award No. 9448, in ICC International Court of Arbitration Bulletin, Vol. 11/no. 2, p. 105 [available online at http://cisgw3.law.pace.edu/cases/999448i1.html]; ICC Award no. 9187, in ICC International Court of Arbitration Bulletin, Vol. 11/no. 2, p. 95 [available online at http://cisgw3.law.pace.edu/cases/999187i1.html]; ICC Award no. 6653, in JDI 1993, p. 1040 [available online at http://cisgw3.law.pace.edu/cases/936653i1.html].

81 Tribunal of International Commercial Arbitration at the Russian Federation Chamber of Commerce and Industry.

82 Arbitration Practice of International Court of Commercial Arbitration at the Chamber of Commerce & Industry of the RF, 1998, Moscow: Statut, (1999), 57.

83 Practice of the International Commercial Arbitral Tribunal. Scientific and practical comments M., 1997. C. 9-12; Arbitration practice in 1996-1997 M., 1998. C. 162-163, 169-171, 234-239; Decisions of International Commercial Arbitral Tribunal at Chamber of Commerce and Industry of Russian Federation in 1999-2000 M., 2002. C. 67-72, 141-147.

No.	Arbitration Institution	Year	Case	Use of Arbitral Precedent	Applicable Law
			(http://cisgw3.law.pace.edu/cases/060413r1.html)	for retention of monetary funds as a measure ensuring performance of obligations.	sian substantive law
13.	Arbitral Tribunal - Vienna[85]	1994	Austria 15 June 1994 Vienna Arbitration proceeding SCH-4318 (*Rolled metal sheets case*) (http://cisgw3.law.pace.edu/cases/940615a4.html)	Reference to arbitral awards[86] concerning determination of the applicable interest rate.	Austrian law
14.	Arbitral Tribunal - Vienna	1994	Austria 15 June 1994 Vienna Arbitration proceeding SCH-4366 (*Rolled metal sheets case*) (http://cisgw3.law.pace.edu/cases/940615a3.html)	Reference to arbitral awards[87] concerning determination of the applicable interest rate.	Austrian law
15.	Bulgaria Bulgarian Chamber of Commerce and Industry[88]	1994	Case 39/1994 of 24 January 1994. Art. 71, (http://cisgw3.law.pace.edu/cases/940124bu.html)	Reference to arbitral awards[89] on the concerning the breach of contract and rights to damages.	CISG
16.	Bulgaria Bulgarian Chamber of Commerce and Industry	1998	Case 20/1997 of 2 February 1998. Art. 6, (http://cisgw3.law.pace.edu/cases/980202bu.html)	Reference to arbitral awards[90] concerning the competence of the arbitration tribunal.	CISG
17.	Bulgaria Bulgarian Chamber of Commerce and Industry	2000	Case 36/1999 of 24 July 2000. Art. 1(1), and 1(2), (http://cisgw3.law.pace.edu/cases/000724bu.html)	Reference to arbitral awards[91] concerning the choice of law clause.	Bulgarian law
18.	CIETAC[92]	1997	Award of 5 August 1997 [CISG/1997/25] (Cold rolled coils case). (http://cisgw3.law	Reference to arbitral awards[93] on the interpretation of the definition of the fundamental condition of the contract that	CISG

84 Practice of the International Commercial Arbitration Court at the Russian Federation Chamber of Commerce and Industry in 2003 […],182-185.

85 Internationales Schiedsgericht der Bundeskammer der gewerblichen Wirtschaft.

86 ICC Arbitral Award No. 6653 (1993), *Journal du Droit International* 1993, 1040.

87 ICC Arbitral Award No. 6653 (1993), *Journal du Droit International* 1993, 1040.

88 BTTP (Bulgarska turgosko-promishlena palata).

89 Case No. 1/93 and Case No. 30/93.

90 Arbitrate Tribunal of the BCCI case decisions No. 21/93, No. 32/93 and No. 37/93.

91 Practice of the Arbitrate Tribunal in Case No. 75/95. The practice of the Arbitral Tribunal of the Bulgarian Chamber of Commerce and Industry in Case No. 59/95.

92 China International Economic and Trade Arbitration Commission.

No.	Arbitration Institution	Year	Case	Use of Arbitral Precedent	Applicable Law
			.pace.edu/cases/970805c1.html)	would justify unilateral termination of the contract.	
19.	CIETAC	2002	Award of 23 July 2002 [CISG 2002/04] (*DVD HiFi case*) (http://cisgw3.law.pace.edu/cases/020723c1.html)	Reference to arbitral award[94] concerning the statement of facts established by prior arbitral award.	CISG
20.	CIETAC	2003	China 31 December 2003 CIETAC Arbitration proceeding (*Clothes case*) (http://cisgw3.law.pace.edu/cases/031231c1.html)	Reference to arbitral award[95] concerning the order of executing the former arbitration award between the parties.	CISG and law of the PRC.
21.	CIETAC	2004	China September 2004 CIETAC Arbitration proceeding (*Steel products case*) (http://cisgw3.law.pace.edu/cases/040900c1.html)	Reference to arbitral award[96] concerning an existence and validity of the penalty clause in the contract.	Chinese law
22.	CIETAC	2005	China 25 May 2005 CIETAC Arbitration proceeding (*Iron ore case*) (http://cisgw3.law.pace.edu/cases/050525c1.html)	Reference to arbitral award[97] concerning the choice of law clause, i.e. applicability of the CISG.	CISG
23.	Arbitral Tribunal Hamburg	1996	Germany 30 August 1996 Hamburg Arbitration Proceeding (http://cisgw3.law.pace.edu/cases/960830g1.html)	Reference to arbitral awards[98] concerning the choice of law clause, i.e. applicability of the CISG.	CISG and German law
24.	Arbitral Tribunal Hamburg[99]	1996	Germany 21 June 1996 Hamburg Arbitration proceeding (*Chinese goods case*) (http://cisgw3.law.pace.edu/cases/960621g1.html)	Reference to arbitral awards[100] concerning costs issue.	German law

93 Arbitration Decision R94190.

94 DVD HiFi case of 25 December 2001.

95 Case number SHEN G2002051, Clothes case of 3 June 2003.

96 ICC Arbitration Award of March 1999 (Case No 9978).

97 CIETAC Silicon case of 11 February 2000.

98 Hamburg Friendly Arbitration award [page 58] of 11 November 1975 (HSG D 3 a no. 6).

99 Schiedsgericht der Handelskammer.

100 *Supra*, n. 57.

No.	Arbitration Institution	Year	Case	Use of Arbitral Precedent	Applicable Law
25.	Arbitral Tribunal Hamburg[101]	1998	Germany 29 December 1998 Hamburg Arbitration proceeding (*Cheese case*) (http://cisgw3.law.pace.edu/cases/981229g1.html)	Reference to arbitral awards[102] concerning the choice of law clause.	German law (and CISG)
26.	Netherlands Arbitration Institute	2002	Netherlands 15 October 2002 Netherlands Arbitration Institute, Case No. 2319 (*Condensate crude oil mix case*): (http://cisgw3.law.pace.edu/cases/021015n1.html)	Reference to arbitral awards[103] concerning the interpretation of the standard of quality of goods.	Dutch law and CISG
27.	Foreign Trade Court of Arbitration attached to the Serbian Chamber of Commerce	2008	Serbia 23 January 2008 Foreign Trade Court of Arbitration attached to the Serbian Chamber of Commerce (*White crystal sugar case*) (http://cisgw3.law.pace.edu/cases/080123sb.html)	Reference to arbitral award[104] establishing the non-existence of identity of the claims between the same parties arising from the same contract.	Serbian law, lex mercatoria
28.	Foreign Trade Court of Arbitration attached to the Serbian Chamber of Commerce	2009	Serbia 28 January 2009 Foreign Trade Court of Arbitration attached to the Serbian Chamber of Commerce (*Medicaments case*) (http://cisgw3.law.pace.edu/cases/090128sb.html)	Reference to arbitral awards[105] concerning to the choice of law clause, i.e. applicability of CISG to a non-party. Reference by the seller to arbitral awards[106] regarding the determination of the interest rate.	Serbian law

101 Schiedsgericht Hamburger Freundschaftliche Arbitrage.

102 Arbitral Tribunal of the Hamburg Chamber of Commerce (Schiedsgericht der Handelskammer Hamburg - Arbitration Court of the Hamburg Chamber of Commerce)--SchiedsG HK-- 21 March 1996, *NJW* 1996, 3229, *RIW* 1996, 766, Cases of Commercial Arbitration (Rechtsprechung kaufmännischer Schiedsgerichte)--RKS--E 5 b Nr. 84.

103 Arbitral Award, June 5, 1998, Arbitration Institute, Stockholm Chamber of Commerce, Unilex database [see also English text available at http://cisgw3.law.pace.edu/cases/980605s5.html]; ICC arbitral award, Case 6653 (1993), Unilex database [see also English translation available at <http://cisgw3.law.pace.edu/cases/936653i1.html>], referring to Journal du Droit International 1993, 1040.

104 Cases No. T-10/06 (prior case) and No. T-9/07.

105 OLG Köln 22 February 1994; ICC case 7754 (1995), Tribunal of International Commercial Arbitration at the Russian Federation Chamber of Commerce and Industry, award of 9 February 2001.

106 CLOUT cases No. 93, SCH-4366 of 15 June 1994 and No. 94 SCH-4318 of 15 June 1994.

No.	Arbitration Institution	Year	Case	Use of Arbitral Precedent	Applicable Law
29.	Foreign Trade Court of Arbitration attached to the Serbian Chamber of Commerce	2009	Serbia 19 October 2009 Foreign Trade Court attached to the Serbian Chamber of Commerce (*Mineral water case*) (http://cisgw3.law.pace.edu/cases/091019sb.html)	Reference to arbitral awards[107] concerning the obligation to pay the interest rate on the value of the unreturned packaging, i.e. on damages suffered due to the breach of the Contract.	Serbian law
30.	Foreign Trade Court of Arbitration attached to the Serbian Chamber of Commerce	2009	10 November 2009 Foreign Trade Court of Arbitration, Serbian Chamber of Commerce (*Original DVD recordings case*) (http://cisgw3.law.pace.edu/cases/091110sb.html)	Reference to arbitral awards[108] concerning the choice of law clause to determine interest rate.	Serbian law
31.	Tribunal of International Commercial Arbitration at the Ukrainian Chamber of Commerce and Trade	2006	Ukraine 13 February 2006 Tribunal of International Commercial Arbitration, Ukrainian Chamber of Commerce & Trade (http://cisgw3.law.pace.edu/cases/060213u5.html)	In a case on the recovery of lost profit reference to the prior arbitral award[109] in the dispute between the same parties.	Ukrainian law

107 Arbitral decision SCH 4318, Schiedsgericht der Bundeskammer der gewerblichen Wirtschaft Wien from 15 June 1994, source: UNILEX, arbitral decision ICC Case no. 9187, source: CISG online, case no. 705 http://www.globalsaleslaw.org/content/api/cisg/urteile/705.htm.

108 Arbitral award Internationales Schiedsgericht der Bundeskammer der gewerblichen Wirstchaft – Wien, No. SCH 4318 from 15.06.1994.

109 Decision of 26 August 2005 the International Commercial Arbitration Court at the Ukrainian Chamber of Commerce and Industry.

Table 2

No.	Year	Arbitration Institution	Case	Reference to a scholar that refers to arbitral precedent (indirect precedent)
1.	2000	MKAC[110]	Russia 24 January 2000 Arbitration proceeding 54/1999 (http://cisgw3.law.pace.edu/cases/000124r1.html)	Reference to arbitral awards on the determination of the manner (methods) of examination of the goods.[111]
2.	1997	AAA	Macromex Srl. v. Globex International Inc. Case No. 50181T 0036406 Interim Award (http://cisgw3.law.pace.edu/cases/071023a5.html)	Reference to arbitral awards on the application of the common standard[112] and on the issue of fundamental breach of contract.[113]
3.	1997	ICC	ICC Arbitration Case No. 8786 of January 1997 (*Clothing case*). (http://cisgw3.law.pace.edu/cases/978786i1.html)	Reference to arbitral awards on interpretation of the Convention regarding the principles of good faith.[114]
4.	1995	ICC	ICC Arbitration Case No. 8324 of 1995 (*Magnesium case*)	Reference to the arbitral award on the establishment of market price.[115]

110 Tribunal of International Commercial Arbitration at the Russian Federation Chamber of Commerce and Industry.

111 M. Rozenberg, *International Sale of Goods* 94-95, (Yuridicheskaya literature, 1995), and decisions of the Arbitration Court, to which the present work refers.

112 http://www.cisg.law.pace.edu/cisg/biblio/visser.html. Id. Koneru refers with regard to this issue to Arbitral Award 7331 (Yugo. v. Italy), ICC Ct. Arb. (1994), 6 ICC *Int'l Ct. Arb. Bull.* 73 (1995).

113 http://www.cisg.law.pace.edu/cisg/biblio/visser.html: Many cases have appeared on the issue of fundamental breach of contract with regard to Article 64 CISG. See, for instance, ICC International Court of Arbitration, 7585/1992, reprinted in UNILEX, abstract in *Journal du Droit International* 1015-20 (1995); Oberster Gerichtshof, 6 Ob 187/97, 11 September 1997, abstract in *Zeitschrift für Rechtsvergleichung* 245 (1997); Bundesgerichthof, VIII. Zivilsenat, VIII ZR 306/95, 4 December 1996, reprinted in UNILEX, abstract in *Neue Juristische Wochenschrift Rechtsprechungs-Report Zivilrecht* 690 (1997); Landgericht Bielefeld, 15O 201/90, 18 January 1991, reprinted in UNILEX; Landgericht Kassel, 11O 4261/94, 21 September 1995, reprinted in UNILEX; Handelsgericht des Kantons Aargau, 26 September 1997, abstract in *Schweizerische Zeitschrift für International und Europäisches Recht* 78-80 (1998). Id., at 136-37. See, for instance, Internationales Schiedsgericht der Bundeskammer der gewerblichen Wirtschaft - Wien, SCH 4366, 15 June 1994, reprinted in UNILEX, abstract in CLOUT No. 94; ICC, International Court of Arbitration, 6653/1993, reprinted in UNILEX, abstract in CLOUT no. 103 etc.

114 Collection of ICC Arbitral Awards 1986-1990, Deventer/Boston 1994, Case no. 4381, at 272 and Case No. 5103, at 369; K.P. Berger, *International Economic Arbitration*, (Deventer/Boston 1993), page 141, 166, 184, 266.

No.	Year	Arbitration Institution	Case	Reference to a scholar that refers to arbitral precedent (indirect precedent)
			(http://cisgw3.law.pace.edu/cases/958324i1.html)	
5.	1996	ICC	ICC Arbitration Case No. 8740 of October 1996 (*Russian coal case*) (http://cisgw3.law.pace.edu/cases/968740i1.html)	Reference to the arbitral award on law applicable to interest rate.[116]
6.	2000	ICC	ICC Arbitration Case No. 9781 of 2000 (*Waste recycling plant case*) (http://cisgw3.law.pace.edu/cases/009781i1.html)	Reference to the arbitral award on the applicability of the CISG to the contract.[117]
7.	2004	MCKAC	Russia 9 June 2004 Arbitration proceeding 125/2003 (http://cisgw3.law.pace.edu/cases/040609r1.html)	Reference to the arbitral award on the applicable law.[118]
8.	2006	MKAC	Russia 13 April 2006 Arbitration proceeding 105/2005 (http://cisgw3.law.pace.edu/cases/060413r1.html)	Reference to the arbitral award on interim measures.[119]
9.	2002	Netherlands Arbitration Institute	Netherlands 15 October 2002 Netherlands Arbitration Institute, Case No. 2319 (*Condensate crude oil mix case*) [English text] [Cite as: http://cisgw3.law.pace.edu/cases/021015n1.html]	Reference to the arbitral award on burden of proof.[120]

115 L. DiMatteo et al., 34 *Northwestern Journal of International Law & Business* 299, 338-339 (2004), ICC Court of Arbitration - Paris 8324/1995 (Arbitral Award 1995), available at http://cisgw3.law.pace.edu/cases/958324i1.html.

116 H. van Houtte, ICAB (Fall 2000) 24 n.11 [choice of CISG by parties], 31 n.76 [interest], 83 [mitigation of loss]; L. Chengwei, *Recovery of interest*, (November 2003) n. 240, 264; I. Schwenzer and C. Fountoulakis ed., *International Sales Law* 544 (Routledge-Cavendish, 2007).

117 ICC Case No. 7153/93, JDI (1992) 1005, 1006.

118 M.M. Boguslavski, *Private International Law: Textbook* 125 (3rd ed. 1998) p. 125.

119 Practice of the International Commercial Arbitration Court at the Russian Federation Chamber of Commerce and Industry in 2003 […],182-185.

120 ICC arbitral award, Case 6653 (1993), Unilex database [see also English translation available at <http://cisgw3.law.pace.edu/cases/936653i1.html>], referring to Journal du Droit International 1993, 1040.

II. When Forward-Looking Aspect of Precedent Justifies Immediate Formally Binding Decisions

*Eduardo de Avelar Lamy**

(I) Introduction

In this paper, I demonstrate that the idea of the forward-looking aspect of precedent is misleading in any legal system. However, it now has been especially used in countries where the binding value of precedent does not naturally form part of legal culture, in order to justify immediate formally binding decisions.

The forward looking aspect of precedent ends up justifying judiciary policies that are built as a way to simplify what cannot be simplified, namely the analysis of facts. I show that the forward looking aspect is equivocated anywhere, but that in countries only developing stare *decisis* culture, it is used as a pretext to justify the existence of decisions that immediately rise as formally binding decisions to the future cases.

Professor Schauer's work is one of the most representative in this area, showing that the judicial lawmaking process differs from other legislative and agency ones. Criticizing Schauer's points, I state that the forward-looking aspect just increases the space for recharacterizations of precedents and that any judge is unable to foresee all kinds of new cases and to anticipate a general rule for them.

Finally, I argue that judges must be highly concerned with the facts of the case before the court. Instead of foreseeing what the facts will be, they should understand that the consequences of a judgment for future events must be weighed by other judges, when facing new disputes. Such a comprehension shows how misleading is the idea of decisions that arise and are already taken as formally binding decisions.

---

* Doctor (2007) in Law from the Pontifical Catholic University of São Paulo. Founding partner of Lamy & Faraco Lamy. Chairman of the OAB / SC Compliance and Compliance Committee.

(II) The Idea of the Forward-Looking Aspect

The basic idea of precedent, i.e. that similar cases must be decided similarly, guides not only American jurisprudence, but is true in many countries.[1] Even though there still is a caricature that, in civil law countries, the written law will contain in itself all the answers one may need and that the application process will be a simple subsumption, fitting the facts into a specific legal text, precedents play a large role in the judicial decision making process. Although "precedents [are] not thus formally binding, yet it is a fact that precedents are regularly followed by the courts".[2] However, one also needs to consider that in some legal systems, precedents are regulated as formally binding decisions and the whole precedent system is structured in that direction.[3]

Even someone who does not agree with the spread of precedents' usage in civil law countries cannot deny they have, at least, an important role: they become relevant when it is possible to extract a rule that solves the problem of structural (as gaps) and semantic indeterminacy of the Constitution or of the positive law in general.

In order to say that a previous case serves as precedent for a new one, the cases should be alike in fact and in law. In other words, when attorneys are constructing their arguments or when a judge is deciding a case, they must establish connections between the previous case they are referring to and the one before the court; that is why "The finding of similarity and difference is the key step in the legal process."[4]

In this context, various common law scholars share the view that the judge, in deciding a case, must not only rule a specific dispute of interests according to accepted legal standards, but also (and mainly) predict future uses of that judgment for new cases. This is the forward-looking aspect of precedent. MacCormick explains the idea of a forward-looking approach stating, "I cannot reasonably decide a case today without satisfying myself

---

1 About the importance of precedent in different countries, see N. MacCormick, R. Summers, "Interpreting Precedents: a comparative study" (Farnham, Ashgate Publishing, 1997).

2 A. Peczenik, "The Binding Force of Precedent", in: *Interpreting Precedents: a comparative study*, 461 (N. MacCormick, R. Summers ed., Farnham, Ashgate Publishing, 1997).

3 Brazilian 2015 Civil Procedure Code, articles 927, 947, 1036 and 1042.

4 E. Levi, *An Introduction to Legal Reasoning*, 501 (1948, vol. 15, number 3).

that the ground of my decisions would be satisfactorily applicable tomorrow or the day after, or in the future quite generally, in the event of a similar case recurring".[5]

It is important to make clear that when I am referring to the forward-looking aspect of precedent I mean the prognosis exercise that a judge does, trying to predict how other judges will use that decision as a precedent. That is the way that MacCormick, [6]Waldron[7] and Schauer[8] embrace this idea. Other scholars may use the same expression to designate different concepts, as, e.g., Caminker,[9] who refers to the forward-looking aspect as the prediction that inferior courts make about what would be the probable outcome given by their superior courts on appeal in a given case.

I will try to demonstrate that the idea of the forward-looking aspect of precedent is misleading. To do so, I will analyze Schauer's point of view, attacking his erroneous premise that judges, like legislators, should create law in as little a dispute-driven fashion as possible. Although he is not the only scholar who advances this idea, he is the one who made the clearest defense of the forward-looking aspect of precedent and developed it furthest, having the most radical view about it.

(III) Professor Schauer's Thesis

In 1987, Professor Schauer stated the premises of the forward-looking aspect of precedent, stressing two main arguments from precedent.[10] The first one is looking backward. This is the most traditional perspective about precedent, which is to focus "on the use of yesterday's precedents in today's decision."[11] The idea is that a judge must conform his or her decision to a previous settled principle instead of creating new rules and policies for each case before a court.

---

5 N. Maccormick, "The significance of precedent", *Acta Juridica*, 174, 175, (1998).
6 *Id.*
7 J. Waldron, "Stare decisis and the rule of law: a layered approach", 111 *Mich. L. Rev.* 1 (2012).
8 F. Schauer, "Precedent", *Stanford Law Review*, 571-605 (1987).
9 E. H. Caminker, "Precedent and prediction: the forward-looking aspects of inferior court decisionmaking", 73 *Tex. L. Rev.*, 1 (1994).
10 Schauer, *supra* n. 8, at 572.
11 *Id.*

The second is the forward-looking aspect of precedent. According to this perspective, a court, when deciding a case, should be highly concerned with how other courts will use that judgment as a precedent in the future. It means a commitment "to the future before we get there".[12] In other words, Schauer develops the idea that judges should be concerned not so much with the case before the court, but with the use of that decision in new cases.

Distinguishing what a court has *done* from what it has *said*, Schauer states that the forward-looking aspect would separate the decision's precedential effect from its canonical language or authoritative characterization.[13] By that he means that decisions that are not forward-looking precedents are going to be recharacterized over time. In other words, at each new application the future judge will find considerable space for different characterizations because there are "many directions in which it might be extended."[14] Schauer states that using this forward-looking approach "we remove the distraction of the canonical effect of simultaneous explanatory language"[15] and, in doing so, avoids the risk that tomorrow's judge will reach a decision that is seen today as both undesirable and distinguishable.[16]

Recently, analyzing Schauer's point, Waldron has said that "Disappointingly, Schauer did not do much with this. But it ought to be a promising perspective".[17] However, this conclusion is unwarranted. In other texts, Schauer continues to develop the forward-looking idea and, in doing so, make even more explicit and radical his view about this issue.

Developing the idea of a forward-looking approach, Schauer affirms that cases make bad law.[18] His main point is that concrete cases distort lawmaking, producing inferior law when compared to a less dispute-driv-

---

12 *Id.*, at 573.
13 *Id.*
14 *Id.*, at 574.
15 *Id.*, at 574-75.
16 *Id.*, at 585.
17 Waldron, *supra* n. 7, at 2.
18 Extending Holmes' idea that hard cases make bad law, Schauer affirms that "it is not just great cases and hard cases that make bad law, but simply the deciding of cases that makes bad law". F. Schauer, "Do cases make bad law?", 73 *U. Chi. L. Rev. 883*, 13 (2006).

en fashion.[19] Schauer takes the forward-looking aspect of precedent for granted,[20] explaining that the main goal of a lawmaker (judge, legislator or agency) is to set the rule not for one case, but rather, for a class of future events[21]. That is why a judges' task is "determining both how this case and also other cases of this kind ought to be decided".[22]

Schauer's assumption is that a case before a court is usually not representative of a class (the array of future events) and, as long as a judge must foresee the solutions for new cases, the influence of the concrete case is a substantial undue risk.[23] Therefore, the rulemaking from unrepresentative cases is a "pervasive pathology"[24] that gives a distorted view and, often, improper resolution for future cases.[25]

More recently, Schauer states that the best legal result may be something different from the best outcome in the immediate case and that is why appellate judges and law professors pose hypothetical situations for attorneys and students, respectively.[26] This concern explains why appellate

---

19 *Id.*, at 884: *"If in fact concrete cases are more often distorting than illuminating, then the very presence of such cases may produce inferior law whenever the concrete case is nonrepresentative of the full array of events that the ensuing rule or principle will encompass. Such distortion may rarely be seen or appreciated by the common law judge, who focuses, as she must, on the this-ness of this case. But the distortion of the immediate case may systematically condemn common law making not only to suboptimal results, but also to result predictably worse than those that would be reached by making law in a less dispute-driven fashion"* (emphasis added).

20 *Id.*, at 886: *"We no longer deny the creative and forward-looking aspect of common law decision-making, and we routinely brand those who do as 'formalists'"* (emphasis added).

21 *Id.*, at 890-91.

22 *Id.*

23 *Id.*, at 894.

24 *Id.*, at 904.

25 *Id.*, at 918: *"Holmes was partially right. Great cases and hard cases make bad law. But if the distorting effects produced by greatness and hardness are present in nongreat and nonhard cases as well just because of the very immediacy of those cases, then Holmes's insight about great cases and hard cases in not only broader than he thought, but also supports the proposition that cases simpliciter make bad law. And if that is so, then it may turn out to be more of a demerit than a merit that common law decides the case first and determines the principle after"* (emphasis added).

26 F. Schauer, "Is there a psychology on judging?" in: *The Psychology of Judicial Decision-Making* (D. Klein; G. Mitchell ed., 2010).

judges "focus as much on the effect of this ruling on future cases as with reaching the best result in the present case".[27]

When explaining the law professor's hypothetical situations, Schauer makes clear his most extreme point, i.e. that it is better to have an unjust outcome for a given case if, by doing that, a court can construct a better rule for the forthcoming ones. As he said, "the professor attempts to get the students to understand that the best legal rule may be one which produces an unjust result in the present case, but which will produce better results in a larger number of cases, the result in the present case notwithstanding."[28]

These are the main points of Professor Schauer's view of the forward-looking aspects of precedent. Despite his efforts, I argue that this theory is constructed under a misleading premise that it is not consistent with judicial decision-making.

(IV) Professor Schauer's Erroneous Premise

It is true that some courts, when judging, pay attention to the future consequences and are much more concerned about setting a rule for future events than solving the case before the court in the best way possible. In that sense, the forward-looking aspect of precedent may explain some courts' behaviour.

A good example is the opinion in *Moore v. The Regents of the University of California*, where the Supreme Court of California held that conversion was not a cause of action in a case where the defendants used the plaintiff's cells in lucrative medical research without his permission.[29] The forward-looking aspect is present here because the court's main reasoning was not about the case before it, but actually, the consequences of the decision in regard to medical research. If the court allowed recovery on the basis of conversion and other courts started using this decision as precedent, medical research could suffer serious limitations. As the court stated: "To impose such a duty, which would affect medical research of importance to all of society, implicates policy concerns far removed from the

---

27 *Id.*, at 105.

28 *Id.*

29 *Moore v. The Regents of the University of California*, 51 Cal.3 d 120, 124-25 (1990).

traditional, two-party ownership disputes in which the law of conversion arose".[30]

Although the forward-looking aspect may be empirically observed showing what some courts are doing, the normative question is not properly answered. The main problem is not what courts are doing, but what courts should do. In other words, is this forward-looking approach right? Is it consistent with the judicial role? My answer is no.

The first objection that one may raise against the forward-looking aspect of precedent is that it is inconsistent with the "case and controversy" requirement of Article III, § 2 of the Constitution. Even though the forward-looking aspect is highly inconsistent with this clause, I will not develop the argument here.[31] First, because Schauer agrees that it is a great trammel to his ideas, although he prefers to not discuss it, because, he argues, his concern is with lawmaking quality and not with lawmaking authority.[32] Therefore, to go straight to Schauer's concerns, it would not make sense to discuss here the "case and controversy" requirement, as well as the important question that forward-looking considerations would be nothing but *dicta* (as unnecessary to the result). Second, I will focus my critique on his premise, showing that the forward-looking aspect is a misleading idea even if the "case and controversy" did not exist, or if this kind of *dicta* could be authoritative.

The basis for Schauer's misleading idea is to equate the judicial, legislative and agencies lawmaking process. Schauer states that judges, legislators and agencies are lawmakers and, therefore, their main duty is establishing rules for future events. Even though there is no doubt about the creative function of judges[33] as lawmakers, their way of setting new rules differs from legislators and these differences are not consistent with the forward-looking aspect of precedent.

---

30 *Id.*, at. 154.

31 About this argument, see L. Weinreb, *Legal Reason: The Use of Analogy in The Legal Argument* 78-80 (2005).

32 Schauer, *supra* n. 18, at 893.

33 As it is not the main point here I will not develop the idea of judges as lawmakers. For a hermeneutic approach to the creative role of judges, see F. Vieira Luiz, "Teoria da Decisão Judicial: dos paradigmas de Ricardo Lorenzetti à resposta adequada à constituição de Lenio Streck" (Porto Alegre, Livraria do Advogado, 2012).

Basically, judges build the law from bottom-up and legislators from top-down.[34] Due to this structure, even though both construct the law, the way each one does it is quite different, as are their missions. Judges create law on a case-to-case basis. However, the judicial development of law will not operate by creations of general and abstracts standards (rules) extracted from each case.

Judicial lawmaking works in a micro-scale fashion, where, little by little, opinion after opinion, it develops the law, creating rules by the reinforcement of shared principles to each particular case. It is a tradition, a non-stopping interpretative task carried out over time, rather than a macro-scale fashion, as legislation, that tries to set a specific behavior for all persons at once. In this sense, Dworkin's idea of "the chains of law" explains better how judges develop law.[35]

Not taking these differences into account and taking for granted that the abstract rule created from each case will contain in itself all pre-conceived hypotheses of future application is a misconception in Schauer's forward-looking aspect. In the end, Schauer proposes an objective approach that assumes that the rule created by precedent reveals its own meaning, regardless of the facts that served as the base of its creation. It is important to stress that this plenipotentiary pretension is nothing but an erroneous metaphysical idea, because "the world of law does not exist as such, as 'posited' side-by-side with the social world."[36]

In other words, facts and law cannot be completely separate from each other. That is why professors use hypotheses when teaching. Their first aim is not to show that an unjust decision for a case may be the right answer as long as the rule inferred from it will be better for future cases. The main goal is to give concreteness to an abstract concept. It is impossible to work on a speculative level, where concepts just refer to other concepts

---

34 J. J. Rachlinsk, "Bottom-Up versus Top-Down Lawmaking", 73 *U. Chi. L. Rev.* 933, 934 (2006).

35 Dworkin compares law and literature, stating that judges should act as if they were writing a novel. Each author of a novel is responsible for writing a chapter; the following chapter should start from where the previous writer stopped and develop it so that in the end it has become a harmonious whole, coherent, as if it were the work of a single author. Therefore, each author must interpret everything that precedes it and, thereafter, propel the novel in this or that direction. R. Dworkin, *Law's Empire,* 229 (1986).

36 P. Nerhot, *Law, Writing, Meaning and Essay in legal hermeneutics,* 22 (Edinburgh University Press 1992).

and facticity has no place. The language itself is a set of inert landmarks[37] and just the application process can bring an abstract rule into life.

When a professor makes a hypothetical to explain the equal protection clause, for instance, it is not because a just or unjust decision will make a better law. It is simply because no one can do it without a set of facts. What does equal protection mean? It may be one thing in one context and another in a different one. Therefore, if a professor does not have a specific case to discuss in class, he or she has to create a hypothetical one in order to make the constitutional provision make sense. Trying to explain equal protection by just referring to abstract ideas would be misleading for students, and even really difficult for the professor because in the end what matters is not the abstract rule, but the meaning of a rule for a given set of facts.

By excluding the facticity and the temporality of the case, in a process of objectification of reality to create universal rules, Schauer's characterization of judicial lawmaking creates two problems. First, the possibility of applying a rule to a case that was not covered by it. Once one enforces an abstract concept to a new situation, the legal minimum requirement of the rule may be distorted and applied to an event that, by its uniqueness, is incompatible with the general standard. Second, in Schauer's model, judges are, paradoxically, giving answers before the questions.

In this first problem, if a precedent creates a rule that is disconnected from the case's facts, the future applications of this rule will be much more unpredictable. The facts of the previous case set a framework that will constrain the future uses of that case as a precedent. When one extirpates the factual basis, creating a general and abstract rule, the process of finding similarities and differences is over and, contrary to what Schauer says, it will give the future judge much more space for different characterizations.

This lack of guidance, represented by the lack of a fact basis, gives a judge a large space for different interpretations (because words are much more undetermined – as a semantic indeterminacy – than events or

37 R. Wollheim, *Art and its objects*, 104 (Cambridge University Press 2000).

facts).[38] In doing so, despite good intentions, the rule is more easily violated by an over-interpretation,[39] even bridging the semantic limits of rules.

Therefore, the judge's role is to decide the case properly, deeply concerned about its facts, and, in doing so, the holding of this case will constrain future judges when they face a similar situation. That is why "their mandate is to make a good decision in each individual case",[40] determining "the outcome of a specific, concrete controversy in all its particularity."[41]

Boomer v. Atlantic Cement Co. is a good example to compare to *Moore v. The Regents of the University of California.* There, the Court of Appeals of New York stated: "A court performs its essential function when it decides the rights of parties before it. In decision of private controversies may sometime greatly affect public issues. Large questions of law are often resolved by the manner in which private litigation is decided. But this is normally an incident to the court's main function to settle controversy."[42]

Judicial reasoning should present the answer to a case before a court. Judgments about prognosis or the consequences arising from the decision are not in play. The law should provide an answer to "the" case, not for future events. Its application to similar cases will be discussed later, again, according to the specifics of each new case and what could be taken as holding from the previous trial.

The prognosis is a proper activity of the legislature. In fact, one can say that the prognosis is something that states, particularly, to the structure of arguments of policy:[43] seeks to present projects that are intended to achieve greater collective welfare or improvement in socioeconomic conditions. That is why it is not a tradition (in the way that law is) and it can be discontinued over time, since the legislators can opt to change current

---

38 Even though a fact can be object of different interpretations, as shown in *Scott v. Harris* (550 U.S. 372, 2007), it is more likely that words suffer more from multiple meanings.

39 About over-interpretation, see J. Grondin, *Gadamer's basic understanding of understanding*, in: *The Cambridge Companion to Gadamer* 36, 43 (Robert J. Dostal ed., 2006).

40 Rachlinsk, *supra* n. 34, at 934.

41 Weinreb, *supra* n. 31, at 77-78 (2005).

42 *Boomer v. Atlantic Cement Co.* 26 N.Y.2 d 219, 222 (1970).

43 About the arguments of principles and arguments of policy see R.M. Dworkin, *Taking Rights Seriously* (London, Gerald Duckworth & Co. Ltd. 1977).

policies. Due to this distinction "judges neither should be nor are deputy legislators."[44]

Therefore, Schauer's idea must be turned upside down. It is not true that an unjust result for a case is good as long as a better rule is created for future events. The opposite is necessary. A court must use its best efforts to reach the right decision, analyzing a case in all its particularity, because just by doing that it can set a framework (from its holding) that can guide future judges in similar situations.

Regarding the problem of giving answers before the question, a judge simply cannot foresee – like a fortune teller – what the facts are going to be or what will happen before it happens, and, mainly, to what degree they may be distinguishable or not from another case before the court.

Schauer is worried that unrepresentative cases will make even worse law. However, we have examples that show the opposite. For instance, *Marbury v. Madison* can be regarded as the most unrepresentative case ever.[45] Its circumstances are far from trivial. Chief Justice Marshall's connection to the previous government and to the case content – as the former Secretary of State who blotched the commission's delivery – problems with judges' commission, or the historical context in general are far from being common, and neither can it be characterized as one case among others of its kind. Truly, *Marbury v. Madison* is better described as one of a kind.[46] Even with this set of circumstances, there is no doubt that *Marbury v. Madison* created an extremely powerful device for "checks and balances" between powers that is not just still good law, but became an important standard in contemporary world constitutionalism.

If Schauer is right, we are compelled to agree that Chief Justice Marshall should have been more concerned about how one court could use judicial review in the future. It means that Marshall should have been able to foresee all the kinds of cases where judicial review could be used and should have tried to narrow its possible analogies to make sure that any future application of judicial review would be made in a case not intended for that time.

---

44 *Id.*, at 82.

45 *Marbury v. Madison*, (5 U.S. 137, 1803).

46 About the historical context and particularities that make *Marbury v. Madson* one of a kind, see S. Levinson, "Why I Do Not Teach Marbury (Except to Eastern Europeans) and Why You Shouldn't Either", 38 *Wake Forest. L. Rev.* 553 (2003).

The complexity of social life makes it impossible to figure out all the kinds of events that any court will face. Courts today are deciding many disputes that would have been unimaginable in 1803. I have no doubt that Marshall never thought about whether it would be good a use of judicial review to restrain wheat crops plantation[47] or to avoid marijuana use,[48] or and even if he wanted to, I believe that he would not have been able to foresee all possible situations.

(V) When Forward-Looking Aspect of Precedent Justifies Formally Binding Immediate Decisions: The Brazilian Example

Especially in recent times, in countries that regard themselves as democratic ones, speech that defends the creation of a uniform and isonomic precedent system is well accepted by doctrine and scholars.[49]

However, the wide range of judicial powers and the traditional search for the maintenance of these powers reflect difficulties in creating a binding cultural value to precedent that is considerable. Judges are just not used to constructing their judgments according to precedent, still believing that their liberty of decision is beyond other colleague's decisions.

That is why there have been structural changes that some of these countries have experienced in their procedural norms. The problem is that all these legislative changes struggle to actually develop a precedent system once legislators have been mainly considering the misleading notion of the forward-looking aspect of precedent. They have not been aware that the judicial law-making process has its own particularities that differ from the legislative.

As an example, the 2015 Brazilian Civil Procedure Code creates a wide formal binding system for all the country's courts. Such legal innovation has frequently been named by the doctrine as a new "Precedent System".[50]

Even so, these legal changes did not even consider what a precedent is according to any legal theory concepts. They also did not really consider,

47 *Wickard v. Filburn* (317 U.S. 111, 1942).

48 *Gonzalez v. Raich*, (545 U.S. 1, 2005).

49 H. Krebs, *Sistemas de Precedentes e Direitos Fundamentais*,(São Paulo, RT, 2016).

50 R. Mancuso, *Sistema Brasileiro de precedentes* (São Paulo, RT, 2016).

through comparative studies, practical notions or experiences that could be useful.

According to the 2015 Brazilian Civil Procedure Code, articles 927, III, 985, II, 1036 and 1042, although the new law cherishes legal reasoning (article 489) a precedent is not generated by the evolution of legal reasoning over the years about a subject. It means that decisions may simply be taken as precedents. The new code simply establishes decisions that are immediate formally binding decisions.

In case a judge overrules or simply does not consider a formally binding decision, according to article 988 of that code, there will be a specific procedural remedy named "reclamação" that will formally guarantee the respect of the court's previous decision. So the formally binding decisions are the ones that challenge "reclamação" as a procedural means used by the parties to promote obedience to the so called "precedents".

Such a system is simply created by decisions that a specific court takes about a matter. So it is supposed to rise as a precedent, as if a precedent system could really be structured by immediate formally binding decisions. Decisions that are born as binding precedents.

As a result, one could say that the 2015 Brazilian Civil Procedure Code does not point to the idea of effectively constructing an actual precedent system, but a system that is already judging future cases (article 985, II). Judges will not only be judging actual cases, but mainly imagining future ones.

This scenario shows that what the 2015 Brazilian Civil Procedure Code actually builds is a binding decision system that protects the supposedly proper-functioning of the country's courts. A procedural structure that does not search for a system designed to protect and guarantee the citizen's rights, but guarantees less work, especially for the superior courts.

The elimination of the maturing process about all the different facts and theses using immediate formally binding decisions was supported by theoretical references in order to accomplish such a structure. I believe such marks state exactly and mainly the idea that the most definitive notion and aspect that defines a precedent is not the retrospective aspect of precedent, but the forward looking aspect defended by Professor Schauer.

(VI) Conclusion

The forward-looking aspect of precedent is inconsistent from the perspective of judicial decision-making and the function of law as a whole. Judges, legislators, and agencies all create new law while performing their duties. However, the judicial law-making process has its own particularities that differ from the legislative, or from agencies. In that sense, judges make law in a case by case fashion, prompted by particular circumstances, while legislators perform an abstract work of prognosis, trying to reach particular outcome.

Contrary to the position argued by Schauer, the forward-looking aspect does not make the application of law more uniform, or the judicial decision more predictable. Instead, it opens space for different interpretations and increases the different characterization of a precedent over time, also bringing the possibility of legal changes that consider immediate formally binding decisions as a "precedent system".

Deciding a case always involves a creative element, because the judge is not just declaring the law, but he is constructing it for that set of facts before him. Any attempt to anticipate this construction of meaning will fail. First, the creative element will be playing its role anyway in the new application (new decision). Second, it is impossible for a judge to foresee all the possibilities of future applications.

Therefore, the consequences of today's decision for tomorrow's cases are going to be weighed by future judges facing new cases with their particularities. Thus, those new judges will define if the previous decision – given the full facts and circumstances of both cases – is applicable to the present dispute.

Unfortunately, the 2015 Brazilian Civil Procedure Code has established a binding decision system that protects only the supposedly proper-functioning of the country's courts. It is a procedural structure that does not search for a system designed to protect and guarantee the citizen's rights, but guarantees less work, especially for the superior courts, through the elimination of the maturing process about different facts and theses that is the essence of legal reasoning and that is the main pillar of a precedent system.

III. Some Remarks about Collective Procedural Law and the New Brazilian Civil Procedure Code

*Aluisio Gonçalves de Castro Mendes**

(I) Introduction: a Brief Panorama of Collective Procedural Law

The history of collective redress began a long time ago:[1] It could be pointed out to popular action in Roman law or to the representative actions in England at the end of the 12th century.[2]

It is also important to highlight the huge development of class actions in the United States of America[3] since the 19th century and the role of the

---

* Professor of Law at Rio de Janeiro State University (UERJ) and at the Estácio de Sá University (Unesa). Appellate Judge of the Federal Court - Second Circuit - (Brazil). Director of the *Iberian American Institute of Procedural Law* and the *Brazilian Institute of Procedural Law*. Member of the *International Association of Procedural Law.* The author would like to thank Professor Burkhard Hess and the Max Planck Institute–Luxembourg (MPI-LU) for the invitation as a visiting researcher at MPI-LU and also for the opportunity to participate at this IAPL/MPI Summer School. The visit and research at MPI-LU was realized thanks to the support of the *Alexander von Humboldt Foundation* and the *Brazilian Federal Court – Second Circuit.* On behalf of the *Brazilian Institute of Procedural Law*, the *International Association of Procedural Law* and the *Iberian American Institute of Procedural Law* should be congratulated, represented by the Presidents Löic Cadiet and Eduardo Oteiza, for the organization and participation in this Summer School.

1 A. G. de C. Mendes, *Ações Coletivas e Meios de Resolução Coletiva de Conflitos no Direito Comparado e Nacional*, 49-64 (4th ed., Revista dos Tribunais, São Paulo, 2014).

2 In England, the first case occurred in 1199, in the Ecclesiastical Court of Canterbury, when parish priest Martin, from Barkway, sued parishioners of Nuthamstead, considered a group, to discuss offerings and daily services. S. C. Yeazell, *From Medieval Group Litigation to the Modern Class Action* (Yale University Press, New Heaven, 1987).

3 In the United States (US), the early studies about collective procedure were written by Joseph Story, Supreme Court Justice between 1811 and 1845. The first case, *West v. Randall*, occurred in 1820. In 1842, the Supreme Court edited Equity Rules, including the number 48 that was the first rule written about class action in the USA. In 1912, Equity Rules were changed and Equity Rule 48 was substituted by Equity Rule 38. In 1938, there was the first Federal Procedure Code in the USA,

Italian doctrine and scholars,[4] in the last century, around the subject of collective redress, both reflecting beyond their frontiers.

---

with Rule 23, that regulated the class actions. Rule 23 was changed substantially in 1966, and other changes were done in 1987, 1998, 2003, 2007 and 2009. In 2005 another important statute was edited, Class Action Fairness Act (CAFA), incorporating changes of the Title 28 of the United States' Code, with the scope to ensure fair and immediate benefits for the members of the class and to avoid abuses concerning the lawyer' fee, in case of success of the class action. A.G. de C. Mendes, *supra* n. 1, at 65 – 94. See about the American Class Actions, among other texts: A. Conte and H. B. Newberg, *Newberg on Class Actions* (4th ed., West, Denver, 2002); American Law Institute (ALI), *Principles of the Law: Aggregate Litigation* (American Law Institute Publishers, St. Paul, 2010); A. R. Miller, "Of Frankstein Monsters and Shining Knights: Myth, Reality, and the Class Action Problem", 92 *Harvard Law Review* (1979); B. Wolfman and A. B. Morrison, "Representing the Unrepresented in Class Actions Seeking Monetary Relief", 71 *New York University Law Review* (1996); E. H. Cooper. "Class-Action Advice in the Form of Questions", 11-2 *Duke Journal of Comparative and International Law* 215-248 (2001); G. P. Miller, "Overlapping Class Actions", 71 *New York University Law Review* (1996); G. Rutherglen, "Better Late than Never: Notice and Opt Out at the Settlement Stage of Class Actions", 71 *New York University Law Review* (1996); N. Morawetz, "Underinclusive Class Actions", 71 *New York University Law Review* (1996); R. A. Nagareda et al., *The Law of Class Actions and Other Aggregate Litigation* (2nd ed., Foundation Press, St. Paul, 2013); R. L. Marcus and E. F. Sherman, *Complex Litigation: Cases and Materials on Advanced Civil Procedure* (3rd ed., West, St. Paul, 1998); R. H. Klonoff, E. K. Bilich and S. M. Malveaux, *Class Actions and Other Multi-Party Litigation: Cases and Materials* (3rd ed., West, St. Paul, 2012); S. Estreicher, "Federal Class Actions after 30 Years", 71 *New York University Law Review* (1996); T. D. Rowe, "Beyond the Class Action Rule: an Inventory of Statutory Possibilities to Improve the Federal Class Action", 71 *New York University Law Review* (1996).

4 The precursors were, in the beginning of the last century, E. Bonaudi, *La tutela degli interessi collettivi*, 1911, and U. Ferrone, *Il processo civile moderno: fondamento, progresso e avvenire*, 1912. In 1974 and 1975, during the Congresses of Padua and Salerno, V. Denti, M. Cappelletti, G. Tarzia, A. Proto Pisani, V. Vigoriti, N. Trocker and M. Taruffo, among other jurists, were notable jurists that dealt with the issue of diffuse and collective rights. A. P. Grinover, "Significado social, político e jurídico da tutela dos interesses difusos", 97 *Revista de Processo* 9-15. (2000). See also: A. Giussani, *Studi sulle "class actions"* (Cedam, Milan, 1996); A. Angiuli, *Interessi collettivi e tutela giurisdizionale: le azioni comunali e surrogatorie*. (Jovene, Naples, 1986); C. Belli (org.), *Le azioni collettive in Italia: profili teorici ed aspetti applicativi* (Giuffrè, Milão, 2007); G. Alpa, "Interessi diffusi", 81 *Revista de Processo* (1996); L. Lanfranchi (org.), *La tutela giurisdizionale degli interessi collettivi e diffusi* (Giappichelli, Torino, 2003); M. Cappelletti, "Appunti sulla tutela giurisdizionale di interessi collettivi o diffusi", in *Le azioni a tutela di interessi collettivi: atti del convegno di studio* (Cedam, Pavia, 1976); U. Ruffolo, *In-*

Notwithstanding, the worldwide discussion about the theme has indeed increased significantly during the last 50 years.

The panorama shows that for a long period of time the collective procedural law was limited the subject to class actions, *Verbandsklagen* and collective actions, although the list of terms used to designate the phenomenon was wider: complex litigation, collective redress, mass torts, popular action, public civil action, group action, representative actions, amongst others.

Usually, three models of collective redress were or are indicated: a) American[5] class actions; b) "European"(?)[6] collective actions or *Verbandsklagen*; c) Latin American[7] collective actions.

---

teressi collettivi o diffusi e tutela del consumatore: il problema e il metodo – Legittimazione, azione e ruolo degli enti associativi esponenziali (Milão: Giuffrè, 1985).

5 The standard includes also other Common Law countries like Canada and Australia.

6 It is difficult to consider in the past and in the present a single European system of collective redress, because there are many different national standards and rules about it. For instance, England and Wales have traditional representative actions and since the Civil Procedure Rules, from 2000, a new instrument named Group Litigation Order (GLO). Germany has had for some time the Verbandsklagen (association suits), but also the Musterverfahren (Model Case Procedure), used by the administrative branch of the Judiciary in a practical way in the beginning and under the statute of the administrative courts since 1991. Since 2005 this procedure has been used for civil disputes under Capital Markets Law and as of 2008, for Social Benefits Conflicts. In Italy, the collective protection is particularly foreseen by the Consumer Law. In the current version, not only the associations, but also the members of the class, have standing to sue the *azione di classe* (article 140 *bis* of the Italian Consumer Law). In Portugal collective action is foreseen in the Constitution and by law, but it has not been often used before the courts; standing includes the members of the class. France has adopted the collective protection especially for consumers and the environment based on the standing of associations and unions. Spain has a general provision in the Constitution, in the Judiciary's Law, in the Civil Procedure Code and also in specific statutes, such as that of consumers' protection; groups' standing is foreseen besides standing of associations and other organizations. But the sense of a European Model is used to indicate the collective associations' suits (Verbandsklagen), that predominate in the majority of countries in Europe (Germany, France and Spain, for instance) and was adopted by the European Commission in the Recommendation in the year of 2013.

7 A.G. de C. Mendes, "Processos Coletivos na Ibero-América", In P. H. dos S. Lucon (eds.), *Processo em Jornadas: XI Jornadas Brasileiras de Direito Processual e XXV Jornadas Ibero-Americanas de Direito Processual* 1013-1045 (JusPodivm, Salvador, 2016); A.G. de C. Mendes, "Ações Coletivas nos Países Ibero-Americanos: Situação Atual, Código Modelo e Perspectivas", 153 *Revista de Processo* (2007);

The major, but not the only, difference is who has the standing to sue: a) the member of the affected class; b) the associations or groups (Spain);[8] c) state organs, like General Attorney, Public Defenders and agencies, but also associations and sometimes individuals.

Other important differences would be the requirements; (control of adequate representation by judge or by law; the role and the form of notice) and the binding system (opt-in, opt-out or by *res judicata secundum litis* or *secundum litis et probationis*).

There are some issues to note in the context of collective redress in the United States of America. The first is the importance of the notice, which, according to the situation and Rule 23 (c) (2) (A) or (B) of the Civil Procedure Rules, may or must be directed by the court to the class. Second, that the opt-out right is only possible if the claim is divisible according to Rule 23 (b) (3). Third, that initially the American Supreme Court edited in 1842 the Equity Rule 48,[9] permitting the representative actions, but adopted a *res judicata secundum litis* or only *pro* the represented class members, because "in such cases the decree shall be without prejudice to the rights and claims of all the absent parties". Nonetheless, only eleven years later, in *Smith v. Swormstedt*, the US Supreme Court did not consider the restriction of the last part of Rule 48 and, considering the adequate representation, decided that all the non-represented members were bound even if affected against their rights and claims. But formally, the Equity Rule 48 was only revoked in 1912 by the new Rule 38, without the before final re-

---

A.G. de C. Mendes, "O Código Modelo de Processos Coletivos para os Países Ibero-Americanos, in R. D. Nolasco (eds.), *Processo Civil Coletivo* (Quartier Latin, São Paulo, 2005); E. Oteiza (eds.), *Procesos Colectivos* (Rubinzal-Culzoni, Buenos Aires, 2006); E. Oteiza (eds.), *I International Conference & XXIII Iberoamerican Procedural Law Convention* (IAPL, AADP and IIDP, Buenos Aires, 2012); J.O. Favela (eds.), *Las acciones para la tutela de lós intereses colectivos y de grupo* (UNAM, México, 2004).

8 In Spain also, the public prosecutor (*Ministerio Fiscal*) has legal standing nowadays.

9 Equity Rule 48, "Where the parties on either side are very numerous, and cannot, without manifest inconvenience and oppressive delays, in the suit, be all brought before it, the court in its discretion may dispense with making all of them parties, and may proceed in the suit, having sufficient parties before it to represent all the adverse interests of the plaintiffs and the defendants in the suit properly before it. But in such cases the decree shall be without prejudice to the rights and claims of all the absent parties".

striction, to permit the *res judicata pro et contra* for the whole class, including the absent members.

(II) The Kind of Collective Protection

The first remark is the importance of establishing the kind of collective protection that is sought. *José Carlos Barbosa Moreira*[10] said 40 years ago that it may be an essential or accidentally collective protection.

If people are aiming at a material or legal indivisible good or claim, the feature of collective protection is essential and, for this reason, the devices and the solutions must be unique and uniform. Therefore, the *Civil Procedure Rules of the United States* states that "for any class certified under Rule 23(b)(1) or (b)(2), the court may", but not must, "direct appropriate notice to the class" and it's not possible for anyone to have an opt-out in these hypothesis according to the Rule 23 (c)(2) and (3).

Quite different is the situation if the rights are divisible. They are essentially not collective, but individual. Collective rights are only accidentally pursued in light of the commonality and the superiority of class actions in comparison to separate claims, as taught by the American doctrine.[11] Concerning the nature of the claims prescribed in Rule 23(b)(3), the class action's notice must be directed to the class members, who have the right to opt-out. A balance has to be found between the best notice as possible and its cost. The facilities and the lower cost of the new technologies should be considered and used by the courts such as online, internal and e-mail possibilities of communication. In addition, the mass media may help to inform the class members and the interested people, enabling them to track or participate in the suit.

It is important to look deeper into the concepts of divisible or indivisible claims and the respective legal treatment. The *Model Code of Collective Procedures for Iberian-America* and the procedure law of many Iberian-American countries,[12] like Brazil, Colombia and Portugal, have distin-

10 J.C.B. Moreira, "A ação popular do direito brasileiro como instrumento de tutela jurisdicional dos chamados interesses difusos", in *Studi in Onore di Enrico Tullio Liebman, v. IV* (Giufrè, Milano, 1979).

11 Rule 23 (a) (2): "There are questions of law or fact common to the class".

12 A.G. de C. Mendes, 'Ações Coletivas nos Países Ibero-Americanos: Situação Atual, Código Modelo e Perspectivas', 153, *Revista de Processo* 188-216 (2007).

guished these types of rights; however the respective statutes have not developed the necessary distinctions regarding the rules and the procedures.

(III) The Role of the Collective Procedure

The main role of the collective procedural instruments includes: a) access to justice; b) judicial economy; c) equality; d) effectiveness of the material law (if only few members of the affected group sue, it means that the offender may have success, if just the immediate profits are taken in consideration); and e) balance the situation of the parts in the process.

Of course, the necessity and the corresponding developments are not the same. Most probably, countries with a larger area or population density, with a larger scale economy, lower level of legal education, a greater amount of lawsuits, judicial backlog and culture of noncompliance may need the collective instruments more.

As regards to Brazil, three main issues stand out: a) a tremendous amount of lawsuits; b) a subsequent time delay in decisions; c) common matters are given unequal treatment due to a system that would privilege, to date, each judge's functional independence. After the strengthening of the Rule of Law, the number of prosecuted court proceedings skyrocketed. Numbers speak for themselves: at this moment, around 100.000.000 (one hundred million) lawsuits are being processed before all Judiciary sections. Back in 1950, 3.000 (three thousand) lawsuits a year were filed in the Supreme Court. However, in 2015, over 93.000 (ninety-three thousand) new lawsuits and appeals were filed in the Supreme Court.

(IV) The Collective Protection as a Fundamental or Constitutional Right

The necessity may vary, but the possibility to file claims for collective redress should be present, as part of the principle of access to justice. For this reason, many countries, like Portugal, Brazil and Argentina, have introduced the collective access to justice or specific collective devices in the Constitution, or it has been recognised by the courts as a guarantee. For instance, the decision, in 2001, of the Canadian Supreme Court in

Western Canadian Shopping Centres Inc. v. Dutton[13] could be mentioned as an example where the collective redress must be guaranteed by the federal and state courts, considering the role of the class actions as a fundamental right to access to justice.

Other recent examples of the worldwide importance of the collective procedural law could be mentioned: a) the reform of the American system: Rule 23 and *Class Action Fairness Act* (CAFA); b) the Iberian American Mode Code for Collective Procedures; c) Recommendations of the European Commission, in 2013,[14] and the respective innovations in the national legislations;[15] d) many new rules and statutes about collective redress around the world.

(V) Requirements, Protection of the Absent Members and Different Methods and Representation

The right to collective instruments does not mean that the collective claim should always be accepted. Each national system has its own legal requirements, especially to protect the absent members (for this reason, fair and adequate representation, even though by different ways, is basic) and to verify the superiority of the collective device, as taught in the United States.

In principle, the direct representation/participation in the process should be the best option. And the *opt-in* system, in light of this aspect, is perfect. Particularly, if there are no barriers to do that. But it is not always possible or easy. Other mechanisms, like opt-out right and *res judicata secundum eventum litis* or *secundum eventum probationis* may also be used. Perhaps, the national systems could be more flexible in offering the courts and parties the possibility to make the best choice according to each case.

Those issues could affect thousands or millions of people. The interested people or members of the class have difficulties (time, information and

13 *Western Canadian Shopping Centres Inc. v. Dutton*, 2001 SCC 46, [2001] 2 S.C.R. 534.

14 Recommendation 2013/396/EU on common principles for injunctive and compensatory collective redress mechanisms in the Member States concerning violations of rights granted under Union Law [2013].

15 A.G. de C. Mendes and L.C.P. da Silva, "A Recomendação da União Europeia, de 11.06.2013, sobre as Ações Coletivas", 239 *Revista de Processo* 195-211 (2015).

resources) to defend directly their rights. This is a problem of all the representative systems: legislative, executive and in the judicial process.

(VI) The Frame of the Collective Procedural Law and its Paths. A multi-door perspective

The collective procedural law has improved and enlarged the frame of procedure instruments beside the traditional way of the collective/class action in the last years especially toward three other devices:[16] a) Model Proceedings as *Musterverfahren*,[17] in Germany, Group Litigation Order, in England and Wales; Judgment of representative appeals and the common questions, in Brazil; b) Alternative Dispute Resolutions (ADRs), On Line Dispute Resolutions (ODRs) and other consensual methods of resolution could be more focused, conceived and regulated for collective conflicts, as made in the *Class Action Fairness Act* or in the last reform of the KapMuG (the statute for *Musterverfahren* in the capital market); and c) also a systematic approach to the system of precedents and *stare decisis* in the civil law countries, with the eventual and necessary adjustments in order to adapt it to the national culture and rules, to solve common questions with binding effect, as is the case in the recent *Brazilian Civil Procedure Code*, in force since March, 2016. It may be a new aim or possibility for the new devices: the resolution of common questions even though there are differences in the claims. For example, procedure issues or common issues in different claims.

In the past most countries adopted one kind of collective redress type. Usually, the respective systems were compared and the positive and negative aspects emphasized. It can be questioned whether some legal devices

---

16 A.G. de C. Mendes, "Resolução coletiva de conflitos" in A.G. de C. Mendes and T.A.A. Wambier (eds.), *O Processo em Perspectiva – Jornadas Brasileiras de Direito Processual* 47-70 (Revista dos Tribunais, São Paulo, 2013), and A.G. de C. Mendes and L.C.P. da Silva, "Ações Coletivas e Incidente de Resolução de Demandas Repetitivas: algumas Considerações sobre a Solução Coletiva de Conflitos', in F. Didier Jr and H. Zaneti Jr (eds.), *Coleção Repercussões do novo CPC – Processo Coletivo* 535, 536-545 (Juspodivm, Salvador, 2016).

17 See B. Hess, F. Reuschle und B. Rimmelspacher, *Kölner Kommentar zum KapMuG (Gezetz über Musterverfahren in kapitalmarktrechtlichen Streitigkeiten (Kapitalanleger-Musterverfahrensgesezt)* (2nd ed., Carl Hezmanns, Köln, 2014).

would not be compatible and could not be joined and disposed, for the best appropriate use, according to the case and people involved.

This multi-door perspective may be presented in many ways. For example, with regards to class actions or collective actions, the procedural law system could provide standing capacity for the members of the class and also for the associations, groups and public organizations. Then, each party could have the initiative to sue when the case had more relation with the procedural body or person. For instance, processes for substantial damages may attract more law firms and consequently the members of the class could be the plaintiff. On the other hand, preventive environmental litigation may be more attractive to governmental agencies or associations for environmental protection. Among the guidelines it should be emphasized that (*i*) the system must offer a broad list of possibilities in terms of standing capacity to guarantee the access of justice; (*ii*) the ideal, for economic and political reasons, is that the society organizations or members of the affected class are stimulated to have the prominent role, as it has been professed by Mauro Cappelletti.[18]

For many reasons, such as the absence of mass litigation culture, praxis or specialized lawyers, or dispersion of the affected people, a collective action may not be sued. In order to avoid many individual claims involving the same question or similar facts, the procedural law system should have other possibilities to solve the situation efficiently. Test claims or model cases are alternative dispute resolutions that may be offered and applied in those circumstances.

The contemporary procedure law stresses on the consensual devices. The adjudication solution should not be the only possibility of collective litigation resolution. The procedural system should offer the possibility to resolve disputes by an agreement between the interested parties, either without or during judicial processes. Otherwise, the risks of fraud by collective arrangements are even larger than by individual deals. Therefore, special mechanisms of proposed agreements' control and guaranties for

18 "Appunti sulla tutela giurisdizionale di interessi colletiti o diffusi", in *Le azioni a tutela di interessi collettivi : atti del convegno di studio (Pavia, 11-12 giugno 1974)* 201-206 (Pádua: Cedam, 1972).

the parties must be created or strengthened as it happened in relatively recently through procedural reforms in the USA[19] and Germany.[20]

(VII) The New Brazilian Civil Procedure Code

The Federal[21] Law n. 13.105 was published on the 17.03.2015, introducing the new Brazilian Civil Procedure Code, with a period of one year of *vacatio legis*, coming into force on the 18.03.2016 and revoking the 1973 Code.

---

19 Concerning the class actions, two important changes were introduced in 2003 and 2005. The first was in the Rule 23 (c) and (e) of the Federal Rules of Civil Procedures by adding requirements to approve the collective settlement, especially the mandatory notice to the class members and the possibility that they opt out of the agreement. The second was the edition of the *Class Action Fairness Act* (CAFA), adapting rules of the Title 28 of the United States Code, with national enforcement and purpose to assure fair and immediate benefits to the member of the class in case of success, establishing limits to the lawyers' fees aiming to avoid abuses.

20 The German legislator amended in 2012 the Act on Model Case Proceeding in Disputes under Capital Markets Law (Capital Markets Model Case Act) (*Gesetz über Musterverfahren in kapitalmarktrechtlichen Streitigkeiten – Kapitalanleger-Musterverfahrensgesetz – KapMuG*). In relation to the consensual solution, the Sections 17, 18 and 19 concerning settlement were introduced, foreseeing that the model case plaintiff and the model case defendant may conclude a litigation settlement agreement by submitting to the court a written settlement proposal ending the model case proceedings and the main case proceedings or by accepting a written settlement proposal from the court through a written pleading to the court. It shall be granted for the interested parties the opportunity to comment on the matter. The settlement shall require the approval of the court. The approved settlement shall take effect if fewer than 30 per cent of the interested parties summoned declare their withdrawal from the settlement. The approved settlement shall be served on the interested parties summoned. The interested parties summoned may declare their withdrawal from the settlement within a period of one month after the serving of the settlement. The interested parties summoned shall be informed of their right to withdraw from the settlement, of the required conditions and time limit, and of the effect of the settlement. In a certain way it may be said that the German Law introduced a kind of the American opt-out right system with some innovations in the Model Case Proceedings in Disputes under Capital Markets Law.

21 The State Members of the Brazilian Federation don't have competence to legislate in procedural law matters according to the Federal Constitution of 1988. Therefore, the Brazilian Civil Procedure Code is applied in Federal and State Courts.

The main goals of the new Brazilian Code include: encouraging consensual litigation settlement, seeking more cost-effectiveness and reasonable-enduring procedures, as well as reinforcing equality and legal certainty.[22]

Three innovations[23] that have been brought by the new code are central and connected to mass litigation and to the new devices indicated above include; a) the refinement of a system of common issues or repetitive cases; b) the establishment of the *stare decisis* in the Brazilian procedural law, with some constraints, while reinforcing its binding authority; c) the judges' power duty to inform the standing persons about the existence of a great number of repetitive individual claims sued, in order to be proposed a class action, if the standing person or entity consider that it should be done.[24]

The number of lawsuits being processed in Brazil, as mentioned, is extremely high, around 100.000.000 (one hundred million) nationwide, which means nearly 6.000 (six thousand) per judge.[25]

---

22 A.G. de C. Mendes and T. A. A. Wambier, "Le Nouveau Code de Procédure Civile Brésilien", 5 *International Journal of Procedural Law* 337-345 (2015).

23 A.G. de C. Mendes, L. C. P. da Silva and M. P. de Almeida, *Novo Código de Processo Civil Comparado e Anotado* 595-599 (GZ, Rio de Janeiro, 2016).

24 Brazilian Civil Procedure Code, art. 139, X.

25 Brazilian courts' data is available at http://www.cnj.jus.br/files/conteudo/arquivo/2015/11/491328c33144833370f375278683f955.pdf.

Improvement of collective actions[26] has been sought. However, because such actions have not been sufficient to address the issue,[27] they may now rely on a complementary system of decisions concentrated in common law matters with the new Code of Civil Procedure.

The system comprises two instruments in respect of common or repetitive matter decisions: a) repetitive appeals, on superior courts level; and b) the new Incidental Resolution of Repetitive Demands,[28] inspired by the German *Musterverfahren* (model proceeding).

Therefore, in the appeals filed to superior courts, it is possible since 2007 for the *Supreme Court*[29] and since 2008 for the *Superior Court of Justice*[30] to select only a few controversial representative appeals. Mean-

---

26 Specific statutes were edited during the second half of the last century that foresaw the possibility of associations and organizations to sue defending collective rights. In 1985 a wide statute called "Lei da Ação Civil Pública" was approved, regulating a new proceeding about claims to defend the environment; consumers; artistic, esthetic, historic, touristic and landscape rights and properties; and, since 1990, also other diffused rights or interest. The new Constitution from 1988 included the protection of many collective rights and foresees that associations, unions, public agencies and the public prosecutors have to sue collective actions and injunctions. In 1990, the Consumer Protection Code was edited with rules that integrated the collective actions' statute from 1985 and were enforceable not only in the consumer subject, but almost in general, because only tax and public funds claims were accepted. Since 2007, the public defenders have the standing to sue collective actions in favor of people without enough resources. The use and culture of collective actions strengthened a lot during the last decades. In 2016, only 61.546 new collective actions were sued in Brazil. The number of new cases is available on the National Council of Justice's website at http://paineis.cnj.jus.br/QvAJAXZfc/opendoc.htm?document=qvw_l%2FPainelCNJ.qvw&host=QVS%40neodimio03&anonymous=true&sheet=shResumoDespFT (last visited February 2017).

27 The author believes that some changes could improve the Brazilian collective action system. Among these measures, some can be highlighted: a) the expansion of the standing to sue, including the members of the class; b) the necessity to notice the members of the class; c) the possibility to opt out; and d) the *res judicata pro et contra*.

28 A.G. de C. Mendes and S. Temer, "O Incidente de Resolução de Demandas Repetitivas no Novo Código de Processo Civil", 243 *Revista de Processo* 283-331 (2015).

29 The Brazilian Supreme Court has the competence to know and decide only the appeals against final decisions concerning federal constitutional law matters.

30 The Brazilian Superior Court of Justice decides the appeals against final decisions concerning federal non constitutional law matters.

while, the other lawsuits[31] discussing the same legal issues are put on hold. Hence, there is a clear procedural economy, as the *Supreme Court* or the *Superior Court of Justice* will try only a few appeals, which shall set forth legal arguments, with binding effect, to be applied to the cases that were on hold, and will be then tried by lower judicial bodies.

The technique applied by the Incidental Resolution of Repetitive Demands is quite similar to the one applied by repetitive appeals. Whenever a common matter of law (not about facts) exists in different lawsuits being processed before first instance judges or appeal courts, this instrument may be raised before the appeal court in terms of legal admissibility and merit. This means that every lawsuit in the area of court that is found pending, will be put on hold. After the judgment, the decision on the incidental may be directly challenged via a special or extraordinary appeal before the Superior Court of Justice or the Supreme Court, if there is a federal law question or a federal constitutional law question respectively. Afterwards, the judicial bodies connected with the decision-rendering court will enforce the legal thesis to every single case.

The judgment of each proceeding, the repetitive incidental or appeal, must happen within a year. The interested parties from the parallel lawsuits may intervene in the repetitive incidental or appeal. The legal thesis fixed may be reviewed through a specific proceeding before the same court that had set the final decision about the legal question.

Finally, the previous Brazilian procedural law did not provide binding effect to precedents. This caused great disorder in the legal system. Judges were not liable to precedents, as a rule, due to their respective independence.

This situation started to change in 1993, when the binding effect *erga omnes* was established through a constitutional amendment in respect of decisions rendered by the Supreme Court for direct constitutional review.

Later, in 2004, other constitutional amendment passed, bringing the so-called *Supreme Court's Binding Summary Statement*.[32]

---

31 Before the new Civil Procedure Code only the appeals were put on hold.

32 The Brazilian Courts have traditionally a *Summary Statement* (*Súmula*), that contains the statement of meanings fixed in cases previously decided. In 2004, the binding effect was established only for the *Supreme Court's Binding Summary Statement*. Between 2004 and 2016, the *Supreme Court* maintained two different *Summary Statements*, one with persuasive effect and the other being the *Binding Summary Statement*. Both *Summary Statements* still coexist, but the statements in

Now, the new Code of Civil Procedure, which came into force March 2016, includes additional binding effect provisions for judicial bodies besides the two previously referred, namely: 1. For decisions rendered in Repetitive Appeals and Incidental Resolution of Repetitive Demands, as mentioned; 2. In the so-called Incidental Competence Assumption, whenever there is a relevant matter of law with social impact, or a potential or real disagreement in internal bodies, these suits may be judged by a most comprehensive Panel, which then binds every internal body; 3. The wording of every Supreme Court summary statement in constitutional matters is now binding, and also of the Superior Court of Justice in federal sub-constitutional matters; and 4. Bodies and judges are now expressly and formally bound to the decisions of the Court Plenary which they are tied to.

Some Brazilian scholars criticized the introduction of the binding effect especially by an ordinary law and not by a constitutional rule. However, many authors think that in other countries it is not necessary. Moreover, the constitutional system, rules and principles foresee this function and role for the courts, as well as the legality, equality and legal certainty.

Its recent entry into force has not offered enough time yet to evaluate the success of the new measures. Of course more time will be needed for the new devices to be used by judges and lawyers. It is expected that the procedural actors will be inclined to collaborate for a more harmonic judicial system. It seems to be possible or easier with the introduced hybrid precedent or Brazilian's *stare decisis* system. It may be the beginning or the continuation of an approach between the civil and the common law in Brazil. Cultural difficulties were and are forecasted, although the choice for a non-pure precedent system may soften the modification.

The controversial system's problems will not be entirely solved by the new Civil Procedure Code and its innovations. There are many other historical difficulties to overcome, like structural problems, cultural addictions amongst others. Still, there is much hope and expectancy that the new rules will contribute for the modernization, stability, certainty and efficiency of the Brazilian judicial system.

---

constitutional matters of the first (normal *Summary Statement*) have been given binding effect since the entrance into force of the new Civil Procedure Code.

(VIII) Final Questions

The global frame of collective redress has been characterized until now by a dispute of continental or national systems. But could a new panorama with pluralism or a combination of methods and devices be considered? Would a multi-door model for collective procedural law not be possible and should it not be stimulated? Could the scholars and students of Civil Procedure dream of a broader set of collective protection in the national law? The author thinks affirmatively about these interrogative sentences. But for all these questions, the new generation will give the final answers!

Meeting Points: International, European, Domestic Procedural Law

I. Judicial Review of Administrative Decisions in Domestic Courts – Union Law Requirements on the *locus standi* of Individuals

*Hilde K. Ellingsen**

(I) Presentation and Legal Framework

It is a widely shared procedural principle that judicial proceedings are initiated by the parties rather than by the judge.[1] Whether an applicant has standing to make a claim in court – *locus standi* – is critical to whether he may seize the court and obtain redress. The idea that every person should have the right to bring an action in the collective interest – an *actio popularis* – is not fully recognized in any of the member states of the EU.[2] Most states require an applicant to demonstrate either a right or an interest in order to be granted access to court.[3] What this implies more precisely varies between legal systems, and it may also vary depending on the type of proceedings at stake.[4] For present purposes the important point is that the standing rules applicable in proceedings of a wholly domestic charac-

* PhD candidate, Centre for European Law, University of Oslo. The author would like to thank Halvard Haukeland Fredriksen, Finn Arnesen, Tarjei Bekkedal, Sofie A. E. Høgestøl, Stian Øby Johansen, Edilson Vitorelli and the participants at the MPI-AIPL summer school for helpful comments on earlier drafts of this chapter.

1 J. Zekoll, "Comparative Civil Procedure", in: M. Reimann and R. Zimmermann (eds.), *The Oxford Handbook of Comparative Law* 1335 (Oxford, Oxford University Press, 2006).

2 There are, however, Member States operating with an *actio popularis* in environmental cases, cf. J. Ebbesson, "Comparative Introduction", in: J. Ebbesson (ed), *Access to Justice in Environmental Matters in the EU* 28 (The Hague, Kluwer Law International, 2002).

3 Sacha Beljin, "Rights in EU Law", in: S. Prechal and B. Roermund (eds.), *The Coherence of EU Law. The Search for Unity in divergent Concepts* 105 (Oxford, Oxford Univeristy Press, 2008).

4 See further M. Eliantonio et al., *Standing Up for Your Right(s) in Europe - A Comparative Study on Legal Standing (Locus Standi) before the EU and Member States' Courts* (Cambridge Intersentia, 2013).

ter will not necessarily be decisive where the proceedings engage issues of EU law.

This article presents the requirements that Union law sets for the standing of individuals in the context of judicial review proceedings.[5] It will be submitted that individuals whose Union rights are adversely affected cannot be denied standing if they have a personal stake in the outcome of a case. Phrased differently, Union law requires the Member States to furnish an applicant with standing when three criteria are met: *First*, the applicant is the holder of a Union right; *second*, this right is adversely affected by the state measure; and *third*, the applicant demonstrates a vested and present interest in the proceedings. These three criteria together constitute the *Union law doctrine on standing*. This doctrine only constitutes a floor, below which the Member States cannot go; but they are free to operate with a more liberal approach to standing.[6]

This article is limited to addressing judicial review of public acts,[7] but its conclusions will have relevance also to standing in civil proceedings. The Court has made clear that Union law may affect standing doctrines also when proceedings are brought against private parties.[8] This contribution seeks to shed light on the *right to judicial proceedings* as an aspect of the wider principle of effective judicial protection, which means that it feeds into the broader debate on how Union law affects the procedural and remedial structures in the Member States.

This contribution is structured as follows: *Section 2* describes the legal framework governing the domestic enforcement of Union law, with particular emphasis on the principle of effective judicial protection. *Section 3* addresses the range of persons entitled to challenge individual administrative decisions for Union law compatibility. It sets out to highlight the ex-

5 The right to standing must not be conflated with the "invocation right", which is the right to invoke Union law provisions in the course of an ongoing proceeding, see further N. Poltorak, *European Union Rights in National Courts* 128 (Alphen aan den Rijn, Wolters Kluwer, 2015).

6 Applicants seeking to engage in abusive litigation cannot rely on the principle of effective judicial protection, see further Poltorak *supra* n. 5, at 141-142.

7 Decisive is whether the state (or exceptionally a private party) exercises public powers, that is "powers derogating from the rules of law applicable to relations between private individuals", cf. Case C-167/00, *Henkel* [2002], ECLI:EU:C:2002:555.

8 See Case C-253/00, *Muñoz*, [2002] ECLI:EU:C:2002:497.

tent to which addressees and third parties must be granted standing as a matter of EU law. *Section 4* contains discussions and final remarks.

(II) The Principles at Play: Equivalence, Effectiveness, and Effective Judicial Protection

Although the enforcement of substantive EU law lies largely with the Member States, Union law can influence procedural and remedial rules in two different ways: *First*, through explicit rules in secondary legislation, and *secondly* through general principles of Union law.[9] There are a growing number of Directives and Regulations that contain explicit enforcement provisions. In fact, there has been an increased tendency to specify not only the national remedies available for breaches of Union law but also to list the range of persons that should be granted standing.[10] Conflicting national provisions have to yield, due to the principle of primacy.[11]

In the absence of explicit enforcement provisions, the division of competences between the Union and the Member States is determined by the principles of national procedural autonomy, equivalence, effectiveness, and effective judicial protection. As the Court spelled out in *Mono Car Styling*:

> *"[Whilst] it is, in principle, for national law to determine an individual's standing and legal interest in bringing proceedings, Community law nevertheless requires, in addition to observance of the principles of equivalence and effectiveness, that the national legislation does not undermine the right to effective judicial protection."*[12]

---

9 It should also be added that domestic procedural rules must comply with the substantive rules of the Treaty (such as Article 18 TFEU prohibiting discrimination on grounds of nationality), see M. Dougan, *National Remedies before the Court of Justice: Issues of Harmonisation and Differentiation* 20-23 (Oxford, Hart, 2004).

10 See, *inter alia*, Article 11(1) of the Posted Workers Enforcement Directive (Directive 2014/67/EU).
For an overview of enforcement provisions in secondary law, see F. Wilman, *Private Enforcement of EU Law before National Courts: The EU Legislative Framework* (Cheltenham, Edward Elgar, 2015).

11 See *inter alia*, Case C-462/99, *Connect Austria* [2003], ECLI:EU:C:2003:297, Rec. 40.

12 Case C-12/08, *Mono Car Styling* [2009], ECLI:EU:C:2009:466, Rec. 49. See also joined Cases C-87/90, C-88/90 and C-89/90, *Verholen* [1991], ECLI:EU:C:1991:314, Rec. 24.

The Court had already held in the seventies, in *Rewe* and *Comet*, that in the absence of Union rules on the subject "it is for the domestic legal system of each Member State to designate the courts having jurisdiction and to determine the procedural conditions governing actions at law intended to ensure the protection of the rights which citizens have from the direct effect of Community law."[13] Although the freedom to determine the procedural conditions governing actions involving Union law is often referred to as the principle of national *procedural autonomy,*[14] it covers not only strictly procedural rules, but also the remedies granted to a successful plaintiff.[15]

The premise underlying this autonomy is that "states based on the rule of law will organize their national legal systems in such a way as to ensure proper application of the law and adequate legal protection for their subjects."[16] Still, acknowledging that an unfettered procedural autonomy could jeopardize the uniform and effective application of Union law and undermine the protection of Union rights, the Court has required that "such conditions cannot be less favourable than those relating to similar actions of a domestic nature … [and must not make it] impossible in practice to exercise the right which the national courts are obliged to protect."[17] These two conditions – commonly referred to as the principles of equivalence and effectiveness, respectively – are cumulative, in the sense that they both need to be fulfilled in order for national procedural law to live up to the demands of EU law.[18]

The principles of effectiveness and equivalence are derived from the duty of loyal cooperation laid down in Article 4(3) TEU.[19] The *principle of equivalence* is in essence a non-discrimination principle, requiring that a procedure or remedy available to enforce domestic law must also be

---

13 Case 33/76 *Rewe* [1976] ECLI:EU:C:1976:188. See also Case 45/76, *Comet* [1976], ECLI:EU:C:1976:191.

14 See, *inter alia*, case C-201/02, *Wells* [2004], ECLI:EU:C:2004:12, and case C-93/12, *ET Agrokonsulting* [2013], ECLI:EU:C:2013:432.

15 See *inter alia* Case 130/79 [1980], *Express Diary Foods*, ECLI:EU:C:1980:155.

16 Advocate General Jacobs in joined Cases C-430/93 and 431/93, *Van Schijndel* [1995], ECLI:EU:C:1995:185, para. 30.

17 Case 33/76 [1976], *Rewe*, ECLI:EU:C:1976:188, Rec. 5. See also case 45/76, *Comet* [1976], ECLI:EU:C:1976:191.

18 S. Prechal, *Directives in EC Law* 138 (2nd edition Oxford, Oxford University Press, 2005).

19 See, *inter alia*, Case C-93/12, *ET Agroconsulting* [2013], ECLI:EU:C:2013:432.

available if equivalent Union law is infringed.[20] The *principle of effectiveness*, having been reformulated since the Court's seminal ruling in *Rewe*, implies that national procedural or remedial rules should not make the application of Union law "impossible or excessively difficult".[21]

The procedural autonomy of the Member States is also restricted by the right to effective judicial protection enshrined in Article 47(1) of the Charter of Fundamental Rights.[22] Here it is stated that "[e]veryone whose rights and freedoms guaranteed by the Union are violated has the right to an effective remedy before a tribunal…" Article 47(1) corresponds largely to Article 13 of the European Convention on Human Rights (ECHR) providing for the 'right to an effective remedy before a national authority'.[23] This provision must be seen in connection with Article 19(1) TEU, which requires the Member States to "provide remedies sufficient to ensure effective legal protection in the fields covered by Union law." The two mentioned provisions codify the general principle of effective judicial protection as it has been developed in the Court's case law.[24]

Although the principles of effectiveness and effective judicial protection are similar in some respects, they have a different legal basis and underlying rationale: The principle of effective judicial protection seeks to ensure that individuals are able to enforce the rights conferred on them by

---

20 See Case C-63/08, *Pontin* [2009], ECLI:EU:C:2009:666, Rec. 45.

21 See joined Cases C-430/93 and C-431/93, *Van Schijndel* [1995], ECLI:EU:C:1995:441, Rec. 19, and Case C-312/93, *Peterbroeck* [1995], ECLI:EU:C:1995:437.

22 The Charter applies to the Member States when they are "implementing Union law", see Article 51(1), which has been interpreted broadly, see, *inter alia*, Case C-617/10, *Åkeberg Fransson* [2013], ECLI:EU:C:2013:105, Rec. 21. For a detailed analysis, see M. Dougan, "Judicial Review of Member State Action under the General Principles and the Charter: Defining the Scope of Union Law" 52 *Common Market Law Review* 1201 (2015).

23 Explanations relating to the Charter of Fundamental Rights (2007/C 303/02), at p 29. Article 47(2) on the right to a fair trial, corresponds in essence to Article 6(1) of the ECHR, cf. Explanations at 30.

24 See Case C-93/12, *ET Agroconsulting* [2013], ECLI:EU:C:2013:432, Rec. 59, where the Court held that Article 47 "constitutes a reaffirmation of the principle of effective judicial protection, a general principle of European Union law stemming from the constitutional traditions common to the Member States, which has been enshrined in Articles 6 and 13 of the European Convention for the Protection of Human Rights and Fundamental Freedoms…" The principle was first laid down in Case 222/84, *Johnston* [1986], ECLI:EU:C:1986:206, and Case 222/86, *Heylens* [1987], ECLI:EU:C:1987:442.

Union law and obtain effective redress, whereas the effectiveness principle is geared towards ensuring that national rules do not impede the effective application of Union law.[25] The Court applies the latter principle also when Union law is enforced against an individual,[26] and it can thus be regarded as an aspect of the wider principle of *effet utile*.

The Member States are required to organize their legal systems so as to comply with these principles. The primary responsibility for implementation lies with the Member States' legislatures, and they need to provide rules that afford effective enforcement of Union law and effective judicial protection of Union rights. But the principles are also binding on the courts in pending cases. When it comes to the impact on national *standing rules*, it is primarily the principle of effective judicial protection that is of interest.[27] The principle of effectiveness will be overshadowed by that of effective judicial protection where Union rights are at stake. The principle of effective judicial protection enshrined in Article 47 of the Charter is not only a yardstick against which national procedures must be assessed; it is also a right vested in individuals. Hence, the principle does not merely require the setting aside of domestic procedural rules that fail to provide sufficient protection, but to a certain extent it also *dictates the means* by which to provide such protection. In that sense it imposes a new EU-wide standard of judicial protection that will have to be implemented in the Member States.[28]

---

25 To the same effect, S. Prechal and R. Widdershoven, "Redefining the Relationship between `Rewe-Effectiveness´ and Effective Judicial Protection" 4 *Review of European Administrative Law* 31, 46 (2011). *A contrario*, Wilman, *supra* n. 10, at 39.

26 See, *inter alia*, Case C-74/14, *Eturas* [2016], ECLI:EU:C:2016:42, para. 35, where the Court held that "[t]he principle of effectiveness requires … that national rules governing the assessment of evidence and the standard of proof must not render the implementation of EU competition rules impossible or excessively difficult and, in particular, must not jeopardise the effective application of Articles 101 TFEU and 102 TFEU."

27 Still, effectiveness concerns "come in through the back door" since individual rights are partly instrumental in ensuring the effective application of EU law in the Member States, see further section III(b).

28 See further P. Van Cleynenbreugel, "National Procedural Choices before the Court of Justice of the European Union", in L. Gruszczynski and W. Werner (eds.), *Deference in International Courts and Tribunals: Standard of Review and Margin of Appreciation* 183-184 (Oxford, Oxford University Press, 2014). He calls this approach "positive comprehensive review", and holds that "the Court itself crafts a

In order to comply with the principle of effective judicial protection it is first necessary that individuals have *access to a national court*, in other words a right to judicial process. Secondly, the national court must have at their disposal *effective remedies* by which to prevent and redress violations of Union law.[29] The focus in the following will be on the first aspect, in that it sets out to spell out the category of persons that have administrative measures assessed for Union law compliance.

(III) Standing to Challenge Administrative Decisions

(a) Introduction

It is primarily through administrative decisions that public authorities affect the legal position of individuals, and hence primarily against these decisions that the individual needs protection.[30] If necessary, the illegality of a legislative measure can be pleaded incidentally in the course of proceedings. Still, legislative acts may also affect individuals directly in the absence of implementing measures. The Court seems to have required the availability of a free-standing action to have assessed the Union law compatibility of legislative acts in exceptional circumstances, where alternative routes of enforcement are lacking.[31]

The Court has on several occasions stated that the Member States' courts are to control the Union law compatibility of administrative decisions.[32] The category of persons that can initiate judicial review proceedings is, however, not clearly delineated. Both the *addressee* of an un-

---

standard of adequate procedure that will subsequently have to be implemented at all national levels."

29 These two aspects can be referred to as the *formal* and *substantive* aspects of judicial protection respectively, see R. Widdershoven, "The Principle of Loyal Cooperation: Lawmaking by the European Court of Justice and the Dutch Courts", in: F. Stroink and E. van der Linden (eds.), *Judicial Lawmaking and Administrative Law* 17-18 (Antwerpen Intersentia, 2005).

30 J. Engström, *The Europeanisation of Remedies and Procedures Through Judge-Made Law: Can a Trojan Horse Achieve Effectiveness? Experiences of the Swedish Judiciary* 169 (PhD thesis on file at the EUI, Florence).

31 See Case C-432/05, *Unibet* [2007], ECLI:EU:C:2007:163.

32 Union law may also affect the type of acts open to challenge, see Case C-97/91, *Borelli* [1992], ECLI:EU:C:1992:491, and Case C-269/99, *Kühne* [2001], ECLI:EU:C:2001:659.

favourable decision (such a decision imposing a sanction or denying a potential advantageous position) and *third parties* adversely affected by a decision may want to seize the court. An addressee of an administrative decision will usually be granted standing as a matter of domestic law, which means that it is primarily with respect to third parties that Union law will have a role to play.[33] In the following, the intention is to take a closer look at the requirements that Union law sets for the standing of private parties.

(b) Standing of Private Parties – Rights Protection or Effectiveness?

The category of persons being entitled to initiate proceedings against the state is closely linked to what is seen as the function of a court in administrative proceedings. A court's function can either be tuned towards the protection of individual rights and interests, or it can be a means of keeping public authorities within their powers. These functions are often referred to as *recours subjectif* and *recours objectif* respectively.[34] These two conceptions of legal control tend to result in different rules on legal standing. Where the courts have a wider responsibility for controlling the legality of governmental action and ensuring public accountability, this militates against restricting access to the judicial procedure, since it could prevent a matter from being brought before a court, and render public action immune from challenge.[35] When spelling out the requirements that EU law sets for the domestic standing rules, it is paramount to determine whether the primary focus is on the protection of individuals, or whether it is rather about private parties policing the Member States' Union law compliance.

The Court seems to have adopted a doctrine whereby a private party must be *adversely affected in his Union law rights* in order to be granted standing. The case law is primarily based on the principle of effective ju-

33 For a comparative overview of domestic standing doctrines, see Eliantonio *supra* n. 4, at 61-84.

34 See further Beljin *supra* n. 3, at 97.

35 Still, as Beljin points out, neither of these two models exist in its purest form in any of the Member States; most judicial systems acknowledge the complementary nature of the two approaches and seek to combine elements of both: "[I]n models that prioritize the protection of rights, not only rights and not all rights can be enforced by legal action … [and] in systems of judicial control of legality not everybody can sue for everything.", cf. Beljin, *supra* n. 3, at 97-98.

dicial protection, now codified in Article 47 of the Charter.[36] Individuals must be entitled to enforce their Union rights before a domestic court. As the Court held in Heylens, "the existence of a remedy of a judicial nature against any decision of a national authority refusing the benefit of that right [free access to employment] is essential in order to secure for the individual effective protection of this right".[37]

A mere interest in the application of an EU law norm seems, however, insufficient to ground standing as a matter of Union law.[38] The clearest expression to this effect is found in the Court's ruling in *Zuchtverband für Ponys*.[39] The questions that arose in this case were whether a breeding association was entitled to demand the refusal of recognition of a new association, and whether it had standing to contest before the court an administrative decision recognizing the new association. The criteria for the approval or recognition of associations which maintain or establish studbooks for registered equidae are laid down in Commission Decision 92/353. In order to be officially approved or recognized, an association has to meet certain conditions, such as having a "sufficient number of equidae to carry out an improvement or selection programme or to preserve the breed where this is considered necessary".[40] According to Article 2(2), a Member State can refuse to recognise a new organization if it "endangers the preservation of the breed or jeopardises the operation or the improvement or selection programme of an existing organisation or association".

With reference to the discretion possessed by the authority, the Court held that Union law cannot be interpreted as creating a right for existing associations to have the recognition of a new association refused. Consequently, the Court held that the Member State was not required to grant

36 See, in particular, Case C-104/13, *Olainfarm* [2014], ECLI:EU:C:2014:2316, and Case C-510/13, *E.ON Földgáz Trade* [2015] ECLI:EU:C:2015:189.

37 Case 222/86, *Heylens* [1987], ECLI:EU:C:1987:442, Rec. 14.

38 In legal scholarship, there is support for the position that standing extends beyond right-holders, to those who have a "direct interest" in the application of the norms. The ruling primarily relied on to support a wide category of enforcers is joined Cases C-87/90, C-88/90 and C-89/90, *Verholen* [1991] ECLI:EU:C:1991:314. Although cast in the language of standing, this ruling did in fact concern the "invocation right", see *supra* n. 5.

39 Case C-216/02, *Zuchtverband für Ponys* [2004], ECLI:EU:C:2004:703.

40 See Article 2(1) and point 2 (d) of the Annex to the decision.

the plaintiff standing in order to contest the decision.[41] The Court did not address whether the plaintiff was *factually* concerned or whether the association should be allowed to enforce the law in the public interest.[42] The ruling supports the view that the Court is tuned towards a *recours subjectif*, where rights protection is the primary concern.[43]

A caveat is still in order: Although the Court's case law is based on the need to ensure effective rights protection, this rationale is closely intertwined with that of *rendering Union law effective* in the Member States. By initiating court proceedings, a plaintiff also contributes to ensuring that the behaviour of the Member States is in conformity with Union law.[44] The instrumental role of private enforcement was highlighted already in *Van Gend en Loos*, where the Court stated that "the vigilance of individuals concerned to protect their rights amounts to an effective supervision in addition to the supervision entrusted by [now Articles 258 and 259] to the diligence of the Commission and the Member States".

Aspects of rights protection and effectiveness become intertwined, due to the way policy making in the Union works. The particularities of the dominating mode of governance are captured in Kelemen's notion of *eurolegalism*.[45] This notion denotes a type of regulatory style that is characterized, *inter alia*, by detailed, prescriptive norms, subject to strict en-

41 The decision has been criticized for being restrictive as regards standing to challenge decisions addressed to third parties. Jurgens makes the argument that the relevant Union law provision was intended also to protect the interests of competing organizations, and therefore finds the conclusion "remarkable", cf. G. Jurgens, "Introduction of a Relativity-Related Requirement in Dutch Administrative Law", 4 *Journal for European Environmental & Planning Law* 260, 264 (2007). It is, however, not the case that Article 2 grants individual rights, as this provision is merely an *exception* from the duty to grant approval.

42 As pointed out by Engström, if the Court had wanted to ensure the effectiveness of EU law, it could have allowed the organization to initiate proceedings to ensure that the administration had complied with the conditions laid down in the Annex. The consequence of the ruling is that no one can bring proceedings to control that the administration complies with these criteria, see J. Engström, "Rättsskyddsprincipens Krav På Talerätt I Nationell Domstol I Ljuset Av RÅ 2006 Ref 9 Och C-216/02", 3 *Europarättslig tidsskrift* 511, 525-526 (2006) .

43 Similarly Enström *supra* n. 42, at 526.

44 J. H. Jans, "Legal Protection in European Environmental Law: An Overview", in H. Somsen (ed.), *Protecting the European Environment: Enforcing EC Environmental Law* 75 (London, Blackstone 1996).

45 R.D. Kelemen, *Eurolegalism: The Transformation of Law and Regulation in the European Union* (Cambridge Harvard University Press 2011).

forcement, often by private actors. As an aspect of this governing mode, the EU is increasingly pursuing policy objectives through the creation of individual rights, thereby encouraging private enforcement.[46] As Kelemen explains:

> *"Repeatedly, and in a diverse range of policy areas, EU policy makers have created individual rights, framed policies in the language of rights, and encouraged private parties to enforce their rights. Policy makers have relied on this individual rights model even in areas where rights-based approaches were clearly not the norm at the national level."*[47]

Empowering the individual can be seen as serving a dual function: Protecting a claimant's rights and at the same time empowering him to serve as a guardian of the effective implementation and application of Union law.[48] The value of private enforcement for ensuring the "full effectiveness" of Union law has been stressed by the Court on several occasions.[49] Even so, there are no examples of the Court requiring Member States to afford standing to individuals to function as 'private attorney generals' strictly in the public interest.

(c) The Existence of a Right Deriving From Union Law

The right to effective judicial protection accrues to those holding a Union law right.[50] There is consequently a need to determine what constitutes a 'right' under EU law. The Court has never been explicit as to what it

---

46 This particular mode of governance is due, inter alia, to a weak administration at the Union level and principal-agent problems, see Kelemen, *supra* n. 45, at 8.

47 Ibid., at 45.

48 In the words of Craig: "[D]irect effect creates a large number of "private attorney-generals", who operate not only to vindicate their own private rights, but also to ensure that the norms of the ... Treaty are correctly applied by the Member States.", cf. P.P. Craig, "Once Upon a Time in the West: Direct Effect and the Federalization of EEC Law" 12 *Oxford Journal of Legal Studies* 453, 455 (1992).

49 The value of private enforcement for ensuring the "full effectiveness" of Union law has been stressed by the Court primarily in "horizontal" cases, see in particular Case C-453/99, *Courage* [2001], ECLI:EU:C:2001:465, Rec. 26; Case C-253/00, *Muñoz* [2002], ECLI:EU:C:2002:497, Rec. 30, and joined Cases C-295/04 to C-298/04, *Manfredi* [2006], ECLI:EU:C:2006:461, Rec. 60.

50 Considering the close connection to Article 13 ECHR, it is presumably only those having an arguable claim who can benefit from the protection of Article 47 of the Charter, see for comparison Boyle and Rice v. The United Kingdom,

means when speaking of a ‘right’ and the term seems to be used rather indiscriminately.[51] Eilmannsberger has called the notion of rights “the missing link” in the Court’s jurisprudence relating to national remedies and procedures.[52] The Court has primarily discussed the issue of whether a provision confers rights (or, in the case of Directives, intends to confer rights) in the context of correct implementation of Union Acts or as one of the preconditions for Member State liability. The issue of rights has also figured in the debate on direct effect, but it now seems to be widely agreed that the conferral of individual rights is no precondition for direct effect. It may be that we are not dealing with a uniform ‘rights’ concept, but that the content varies, depending of the context in which it is used.[53] For present purposes, it suffices to note that the in relation to *standing*, the concept is construed broadly.[54]

There is a vast range of Union rights, both procedural and substantive, and these may arise in all sectors covered by Union law and can potentially be conferred by all rules of Union law. Rights can be granted either explicitly or as a ‘reflex’ of a duty. As the Court held already in *Van Gend en Loos*:

> “*Rights arise not only where they are expressly granted by the Treaty, but also by reasons of obligations which the Treaty imposes in a clearly defined way upon individuals as well as upon the Member States and upon the Institutions of the Community.*”[55]

19/1986/117/165-166, Council of Europe: European Court of Human Rights, 24 March 1988.

51 S. Prechal, “Does Direct Effect Still Matter”, 37 *Common Market Law Review* 1047, 1057 (2000). For a thorough analysis of the concept of Union rights, see Bjarte Thorson, Individual Rights in EU Law (Cham, Springer 2016).

52 T. Eilmansberger, “The Relationship between Rights and Remedies in EC Law: In Search of the Missing Link” 41 *Common Market Law Review* 1199 (2004).

53 To that effect, see Prechal, *supra* n. 18, at 119 and J. H. Jans and A. P. W. Duijkersloot, State Liability in J. H. Jans et al. (eds) , *Europeanisation of Public Law* 453 (2nd. Edition, Groningen, Europa Law Publishing 2015).

54 Within the framework of Member State liability in damages, the concept is arguably construed more narrowly, see particularly Case C-222/02, *Peter Paul* [2004]. Jurgens claims that the Court seems to “seek more concrete provisions which can provide an entitlement for individuals to pursue a certain course of conduct with a view to their own interests.” Jurgens, *supra* n. 41 at 267-268.

55 Case 26/62, *Van Gend en Loos* [1963], ECLI:EU:C:1963:1.

These two forms of rights can be labelled directly and indirectly conferred rights, respectively.[56] As to the latter, the Court seems to examine the protective scope of the norm to determine whether the norm in question exists to protect an individual, as opposed to merely a public, interest. The Court's ruling in *E.ON Földgáz Trade* can illustrate. The Court addressed the locus standi of a company to challenge a decision of a regulatory authority amending the criteria for deciding on applications for the long-term reserve capacity in a gas pipeline. The Court held that Article 5 of Regulation No 1775/2005 sets out the principles that a regulatory authority is required to respect in order to ensure that the access of market participants to the transmission network takes place in non-discriminatory and transparent conditions. The Court held that this provision "must be interpreted as constituting protective measures adopted in the interests of users wishing to gain access to the network and therefore capable of conferring rights on them."[57]

This means that an awareness of the underlying interest pursued by a Union law provision is important to determine whether – and to whom – a right is granted. A provision must be construed paying due regard not only to its wording, but also to its object and purpose.[58] Importantly though, effectiveness concerns also have a role to play in determining the protective scope of Union law norms.[59] The Court has construed the concept of Union law rights broadly, and acknowledged that provisions protecting diffuse interest may give rise to Union rights. Examples can be found in the environmental sphere, where the Court has held that environmental Directives that aim, inter alia, at protecting public health grant rights to indi-

---

56 Eilmannsberger *supra* n. 52, at 1238-1243. Although the distinction between directly and indirectly conferred rights may be useful for thinking clearly about the issue, there is no watershed between the two categories. The circle of beneficiaries can be more or less explicit, depending on the wording of the relevant Union provision.

57 See Case C-510/13, *E.ON Földgáz Trade* [2015], Rec. 40. See also joined Cases C-178/94, C-179/94, C-188/94, C-189/94 and C-190/94, *Dillenkofer* [1996], Rec. 36. This protective scope approach is also pointed out by other authors, such as S. Prechal, "Protection of Rights: How Far", *The Coherence of EU Law. The Search for Unity in Divergent Concepts* 164 (Oxford, Oxford University Press 2008).

58 On the criteria for determining EU rights, see Beljin, *supra* n. 3, at 113-120 and Prechal, *supra* n. 18, at 111-130.

59 Similarly Prechal, *supra* n. 57, at 181, who points out that "the full effectiveness dimension implies that the protective scope requirement should not be too stringent."

viduals.[60] Similarly, competition rules do not only protect market integrity through preserving a competitive market place, but also have a protective element with respect to individual market participants, which means that they may give rise to rights.[61]

As the Court held in *Van Gend en Loos*, the obligations giving rise to corresponding rights must be "clearly defined". In the words of Prechal and Hancher: "the ascertainability of the scope of the right is a criterion which helps to decide whether a provision confers rights as such. The content of the alleged right must be sufficiently concrete or delineated. Hence, provisions involving discretion may not give rise to rights."[62] Provided that this criterion is fulfilled, the right is a mirror image of a duty – it is the right to have individuals or public authorities conduct themselves in accordance with the law.[63]

(d) Adverse Effects on the Applicant

Determining whether an applicant falls within the protective scope of the norm invoked is important for the standing inquiry. Still, alleging the existence of a Union right is not sufficient in order to be granted standing as a matter of Union law. The protective scope of a Union norm is determined

60 See Cases C-361/88, *Commission v Germany* [1991], ECLI:EU:C:1991:224, C-58/89, *Commission v Germany* [1991], ECLI:EU:C:1991:391, C-59/89, *Commission v Germany* [1991], ECLI:EU:C:1991:225, C-13/90, *Commission v France* [1991], ECLI:EU:C:1991:358, C-14/90, *Commission v France* [1991], ECLI:EU:C:1991:359. Environmental directives that seek to protect the environment as such are found not to confer rights, see Case C-115/09, *Bund für Umwelt und Naturschutz Deutschland* [2011], ECLI:EU:C:2011:289. For a critical analysis, see S. Prechal and L. Hancher, "Individual Environmental Rights: Conceptual Pollution in EU Environmental Law?" 2002 *Yearbook of European Environmental Law* 89.

61 N. Reich, "The *Courage* Doctrine: Encouraging or Discouraging Compensation for Antitrust Injuries" 42 *Common Market Law Review* 35, 54 (2005). The Court expressed this dual rationale in Joined Cases C-501/06 P, C-513/06 P, C-515/06 P and C-519/06 P, *GlaxoSmithKline Services Unlimited* [2009], ECLI:EU:C:2009:610.

62 Prechal and Hancher *supra* n. 57, at 102.

63 See Advocate General Szpunar in *T-Mobile*, who stresses the importance of protecting "individual rights under public law, understood as the possibility of compelling a regulatory authority to conduct itself in accordance with the law", cf. Case C-282/13 [2014], ECLI:EU:C:2014:2179, para. 72.

in the abstract, whereas the issue of standing concerns the question of whether a plaintiff is sufficiently affected by the breach having taken place.[64] The Court seems to require that a plaintiff is *adversely affected* by a Union law infringement in order to be granted standing.[65] If that is the case he may initiate proceedings, provided that his interest is *vested and present*.

As argued by Prechal, persons falling within the personal scope of a Union law provision will normally be sufficiently affected by the misapplication or non-application of the provisions protecting them, and they will have an interest in the judicial decision they are seeking to obtain. They should consequently be given standing.[66] The Court has on occasion presumed that such an interest exists, without further discussion. In *Olainfarm*, the Court found that the holder of a marketing authorization for a medical product had standing to challenge the grant of a marketing authorization for a generic product, where his product was used as a reference product.[67] Referring to Article 47 of the Charter, the Court held that the plaintiff had the right to a judicial remedy enabling him to challenge the decision of the competent authority which granted the approval of the generic, provided that he was seeking judicial protection of a right conferred on him by Article 10 of Directive 2001/83/EC (Medicines Directive). This was the case because the holder demanded that his medicinal product was not to be used for the purpose of obtaining a marketing authorization for a product in relation to which his own product could not be regarded as a reference product within the meaning of the Directive. The Court did not address whether the undertaking was sufficiently affected by the alleged breach or what he stood to gain from the proceedings, as this was rather obvious from the circumstances of the case. Olainfarm's would be put at a competitive disadvantage by placing on the market a generic product.[68]

---

64 N. Fenger, *Forvaltning Og Fællesskab: Om EU-Rettens Betydning for Den Almindelige Forvaltningsret: Konfrontation Og Frugtbar Sameksistens* 709 (Copenhagen, Jurist- og økonomforbundets forlag 2004).

65 See, *inter alia*, Case C-426/05, *Tele2* [2008], ECLI:EU:C:2008:103, Rec. 48.

66 Prechal, *supra* n. 18, at 149.

67 C-104/13, *Olainfarm* [2014], ECLI:EU:C:2014:2316.

68 Advocate General Wahl explicitly stated that "it seems justified to assume that the placing on the market of a generic will have an impact on sales of the reference product and competitive conditions in its regard", see his opinion in case C-104/13, *Olainfarm* [2014], ECLI:EU:C:2014:342, para. 48.

The need to narrow down the category of enforcers is particularly pressing in the case of provisions protecting collective or diffuse interests, since Union rights may pertain to large classes of persons.[69] A breach of such provisions may potentially affect a wide category of people, and to avoid an *actio popularis*, assessing the specific interest of a plaintiff becomes paramount. I endorse Beljin, who holds that "[t]he following rule should apply in EU law …: the *less* one can derive from the norm, the greater the significance of being concerned *factually*", or phrased differently "[t]he more vaguely [the protected group of people] is defined, the more the entitlement depends on factual aspects of concern."[70]

A measure's actual effect on the claimant's position is also the approach adopted by the Court in annulment proceedings under Article 263(4) TFEU. In order to be granted standing before the Union courts, a plaintiff must demonstrate that an act is of 'direct and individual concern' to him (or as regards regulatory acts not entailing implementing measures, that an act is of 'direct concern' to him). In *Plaumann*, the Court held that persons other than those to whom a decision is addressed may only claim to be individually concerned if that decision

> "*affects them by reasons of certain attributes which are peculiar to them or by reason of circumstances in which they are differentiated from all other persons and by virtue of these factors distinguishes them individually just as in the case of the person addressed.*"[71]

This has become a standard formulation of the Court. Although this line of case law serves to illustrate the issue of factual concern, the *Plaumann* doctrine is not directly transferable to a domestic context.[72] Since private

---

69 Whereas collective interests are the aligned, identical interests of many people, diffuse interests are characterized by their indivisible nature and their attribution to an indeterminate number of people, cf. C. Godt, "Enforcement of Environmental Law by Individuals and Interest Groups: Reconceptualizing Standing" 23 *Journal of Consumer Policy* 79, 81 (2000). By way of illustration, the consumer interest is primarily a collective interest, whereas the environmental interest can be considered diffuse, cf. p. 86.

70 Beljin, *supra* n. 3, at 118 and 122 respectively (italics in original).

71 Case 25/62, *Plaumann* [1963], ECLI:EU:C:1963:17.

72 To the same effect, see T. Tridimas, *The General Principles of EU Law* 454 (2nd ed, Oxford, Oxford University Press 2006), and Ebbesson, *supra* n. 2, at 27.

parties' access to the Union courts is severely restricted, the national courts are the primary venue for ensuring effective judicial protection.[73]

The Court's case law indicates that it is seeking to align the judicial safeguards operating at Union and domestic level.[74] There are, however, no indications that the Court requires that a plaintiff is affected in a way that distinguishes him from all others to be entitled to standing before domestic courts. In fact the Court seems implicitly to have rejected this strict approach in *Muñoz*, despite Advocate General Geelhoed's suggestion that domestic standing criteria should mirror those laid down in Article 263(4) TFEU.[75] A plaintiff adversely affected by an infringement has a need for judicial protection, regardless of whether and how other private parties are affected.[76] It can even be argued that the need for judicial control increases when a measure affects a large number of people.[77] This militates against a requirement that a plaintiff is 'individually concerned' in the sense that his situation can be differentiated from that of all others.

At the same time, a mere abstract interest in seeing Union law enforced is insufficient for the purpose of meeting the requirements for standing. Boch argues individuals should be regarded as "guardians of the [Union] interest, in so far as overseeing actions by member states, ensuring that member states comply with the [Union] obligations and fulfil their duties, in turn guarantees that individuals are not deprived of the benefits what would accrue to them" in the case of compliance.[78] Still, it is submitted that the general interest that all individuals have in the government duly

---

73 See Case C-50/00 P, *UPA* [2002], ECLI:EU:C:2002:462, Rec. 41, where the Court held that "it is for the Member States to establish a system of legal remedies and procedures which ensure respect for the right to effective judicial protection." This division of competences has now found its expression in Article 19(1) TEU.

74 The Court has sought to achieve equal standards of protection both as regards liability in damages (see Joined Cases C-46/93 and C-48/93, *Brasserie du Pêcheur* [1996], ECLI:EU:C:1996:79, Rec. 42 and Case C-352/98 P *Bergaderm v Commission* [2000], ECLI:EU:C:2000:361, Rec. 41) and the scope and intensity of judicial review, (see Case C-120/97, *Upjohn* [1999], ECLI:EU:C:1999:14, Rec. 35).

75 Advocate General Geelhoed in case C-253/00 *Muñoz* [2001], ECLI:EU:C:2001:697, para. 68.

76 Fenger, *supra* n. 64, at 694.

77 Fenger, *supra* n. 64, at 694. This argument was also (futilely) made by Advocate General Jacobs in his opinion in Case C-50/00 P, *UPA* [2002], ECLI:EU:C:2002:197, see para. 59.

78 See C. Boch, "The Iroquois at the Kirchberg; Or, Some Naïve Remaks on the Status and Relevance of Direct Effect", *The State of the European Union: Structure,*

observing Union law is not sufficient to ground standing as a matter of EU law.[79] This does not mean that the harm cannot be widely shared, which is often the case for instance in environmental disputes.

As to the magnitude of adverse effects a private party must demonstrate in order to benefit from the right to judicial protection, the Court has been rather laconic. In *Kühne*, the Court held that the right to judicial control extended to administrative measures "capable of *adversely affecting* the rights of third parties under Community law."[80] Moreover, in *Tele2*, the Court held that the requirement to provide effective judicial protection applies to those deriving rights from the Union legal order and "whose rights are *adversely affected*" by a decision taken by a national regulatory authority.[81]

How to delineate the category of enforcers depends on the type of violation pursued. The Court has held that the right to contest a decision granting state aid in violation of the stand-still provision (Article 108(2) TFEU) accrues to "parties affected by the distortion of competition caused by the grant of the unlawful aid".[82] Presumably it must be required that the effect on their market position reaches a certain threshold. The situation in the market needs to be assessed, taking into account, *inter alia*, the number of actors operating in the market. In *T-Mobile Austria*, concerning the transfer of rights to use radio frequencies, the Court stressed that the applicant was in direct competition in the electronic communications services market with the parties to the transaction. The Court concluded that:

> *"T-Mobile Austria must therefore be regarded as being 'affected' by a decision of an NRA, such as that at issue in the main proceedings, since the trans-*

---

enlargement and economic union 32 (Harlow, Longman 2000. She does, however, not advocate an *actio popularis*.

79 As held by Advocate General Jacobs "[T]he public at large, as well as ecologist and environmental pressure groups, have a general interest in water quality an indeed the respect of Community law. It does not, however, automatically follow that enforceable rights must be made available to them in national courts", see Advocate General Jacobs in Case C-58/89, *Commission v Germany* [1991], ECLI:EU:C:1991:197, para 34.

80 Case C-269/99, *Kühne* [2001], ECLI:EU:C:2001:659 (emphasis added).

81 Case C-426/05, *Tele2* [2008], ECLI:EU:C:2008:103 (emphasis added).

82 See Case C-199/06, CELF I [2008], ECLI:EU:C:2008:79. See also Case C-368/04 *Transalpine Ölleitung* [2006], ECLI:EU:C:2006:644. In other cases, the Court simply refers to "persons concerned" without specifying the range of individuals protected against infringements (see, inter alia, Joined Cases C-261/01 and C-262/01 *Van Calster & Cleeren* [2003], ECLI:EU:C:2003:571.

> *fer of rights to use radio frequencies (...) modifies the respective shares of radio frequencies granted to those undertakings and, consequently, has an impact on T-Mobile Austria's position on that market.*"[83]

Environmental rights are also granted generously. Arguably, the Union legal order not only grants procedural environmental rights[84] but also *substantive environmental rights* – meaning rights "intended to protect a given level of environmental quality"[85] The Court has held that environmental directives that aim, inter alia, at the protection of human health are to be interpreted as granting rights, even if they concern a potentially wide range of persons.[86] Still, it is not the case that everyone is entitled to seize a court in the event of an infringement of such norms. I subscribe to the view of Ebbesson, who holds that "[p]ersons may invoke the right to human health in a particular case, basically because they are likely to be affected by the violation in question; that is what makes them 'concerned'."[87] In *Janecek*, the Court has held that persons *"directly concerned by a risk that the limit values or alert thresholds [enshrined in the Air Quality Framework Directive] may be exceeded"* must be entitled to initiate proceedings.[88] A possible distinguishing criterion when it comes to environmental interventions – which the Court arguably hinted to in

83 Case C-282/13, *T-Mobile Austria* [2014], ECLI:EU:C:2015:24, Rec. 47. Advocate General Szpunar stressed not only that the applicant was in "direct competition" with the parties to the transaction involving the transfer of frequencies, but also that the competitors were "operating on an oligopolistic market characterised, inter alia, by substantial barriers to entry", cf. Advocate General Szpunar in case C-282/13, *T-Mobile Austria* [2014], ECLI:EU:C:2014:2179, para. 100.

84 The obligations to carry out an environmental impact assessment under the EIA Directive (Directive 2011/92/EU), for instance, confers on individuals concerned a corresponding right to have environmental effects assessed, see Case C-420/11, Leth [2013], ECLI:EU:C:2013:166, Rec. 32. The range of procedural environmental rights expanded with the accession of the EU to the Aarhus Convention (the Convention on Access to Information, Public Participation in Decision-Making and Access to Justice in Environmental Matters, signed on 25 June 1998) which establishes various rights of the public with regard to the environment.

85 Godt, *supra* n. 69, at 85.

86 See n. 62.

87 J. Ebbesson, "European Community", in: J. Ebbesson (ed.), *Access to Justice in Environmental Matters in the EU* 61 (The Hague, Kluwer Law International 2002).

88 Case C-237/07, *Janecek* [2008], ECLI:EU:C:2008:447, Rec. 39.

Janecek – is geographical proximity.[89] As Advocate General Cosmas argued in his opinion in *Stichting Greenpeace*:

> "*An intervention in the environment ... is located in a specific geographical area, and the extent of its impact is lessened the further away one is from the area of intervention. Accordingly, persons close to the construction works suffer its consequences in a different, more intense manner than persons farther away, the latter being at a greater radius from the epicenter of the intervention in the environment.*"[90]

In *Stichting Greenpeace*, Advocate General Cosmas was not able to convince the Court to afford environmental plaintiffs with standing under Article 263(4) TFEU by referring to the actual effects on the applicants. This may, however, be a viable line of argumentation in a domestic context, due to the fact that the threshold for establishing sufficient adverse effect is lower than that established following the Court's *Plaumann* formula.[91]

The criterion of being adversely affected raises particular challenges in the event of procedural infringements, since not every procedural defect will affect the content of a decision. *Altrip* lends support to the view that standing need not be granted where the procedural error has not affected the decision subject to challenge. The applicants in the case sought the annulment of a decision approving plans to construct a flood retention scheme, claiming that the environmental impact assessment carried out was inadequate. The Court stated that it could be permissible for national law not to recognise *locus standi* if it is established that it is conceivable that the contested decision would not have been different without the procedural defect.[92] Where that is the case, an applicant's rights are not impaired by the illegality. However, shifting the burden of proof onto the applicant is capable of making the exercise of the rights conferred by the Directive excessively difficult.[93] Hence, a plaintiff cannot be required to demonstrate that the agency certainly or probably would have reached a different result in the absence of the procedural defect.

---

89 The Court stressed that the applicant lived on Munich's central ring road, approximately 900 meters north of the air quality measuring station.

90 Advocate General Cosmas in case C-321/95 P, *Stichting Greenpeace*, [1997], ECLI:EU:C:1997:421, para 104. He also suggested that the gravity of the impact which a measure has or may have on a person may bring about a situation which distinguishes that person from others, cf. para. 106.

91 See *supra* n. 71.

92 Case C-72/12, *Altrip* [2013], ECLI:EU:C:2013:712.

93 Cf. Rec. 53.

(e) Vested and Present Interest

The Member States are presumably not required to provide for standing unless a plaintiff has a *vested and present interest* in bringing a case to court. In other words, an applicant must have a personal stake in the outcome of the proceedings. The Court has seldom addressed this issue, largely due to the fact that this criterion is most often satisfied. As a rule, an applicant who can demonstrate that his Union rights are adversely affected by an administrative measure will have an interest in initiating judicial proceedings. The interest requirement was, however, made evident in *Streekgewest*, where the court was asked whether a breach of the standstill provision (now) enshrined in the last sentence of Article 108(3) of the Treaty may be relied on by a litigant who is not affected by distortion of cross-border competition arising from an aid measure. The Court stated that:

> "*[a]n individual may have an interest in relying before the national court on the direct effect of the prohibition on implementation referred to in the last sentence of [Article 108(3)] of the Treaty not only in order to erase the negative effects of the distortion of competition created by the grant of unlawful aid, but also in order to obtain a refund of a tax levied in breach of that provision.*"[94]

In its case law pertaining to standing under Article 263(4) TFEU the Court has repeatedly held that an action for annulment brought by a natural or legal person is not admissible unless the applicant has a vested and present interest in the proceedings, which means that the action must be capable of procuring him an advantage.[95] The interest must not only exist at the time when the application is lodged, but must also persist during the proceedings. If the interest upon which the applicant relies relates to a future legal situation, he must demonstrate that the prejudice to that situation is already certain.[96]

Although one should be cautious when drawing parallels to Article 263(4) TFEU, it is submitted that the requirement of a vested and present interest must apply also in the domestic context. As the Court held in

---

94 Case C-174/02, *Streekgewest* [2005], ECLI:EU:C:2005:10, Rec. 19.

95 See *inter alia* Case C-133/12 P, *Stichting Woonlinie* [2014], ECLI:EU:C:2014:105, Rec. 54.

96 See, *inter alia*, Case T-138/89, Nederlandse Bankiersvereniging, [1992], ECLI:EU:T:1992:95, Rec. 33.

Mory, Mory Team and Superga Invest, "[having an] interest in bringing proceedings is an essential and fundamental prerequisite for any legal proceedings."[97] The interest criterion is closely linked to the one of being directly affected. Still, since the action *through its outcome* must be capable of procuring an advantage to an applicant, it is relevant what the applicant seeks to achieve with the proceedings. The interest requirement must be assessed with reference to the remedy sought.

As a starting point, an applicant is not, as a matter of EU law, entitled to challenge a decision before it is issued.[98] Still, it cannot be required that the effects of the Union law infringement have manifested themselves. In *CELF II*, the Court addressed the obligation of national courts to adopt safeguard measures in the form of interim relief with a view to enforcing the stand-still provision in Article 108(2) TFEU. The Court held that there is an obligation to adopt safeguard measures provided inter alia that the aid "*is about to be*, or has been, implemented".[99] Generally speaking, it is preferable to prevent the adverse effects from occurring. To cite Advocate General Geelhoed in *British American Tobacco* "A system of legal remedies should be established in such a way that it makes provision to prevent, so far as possible, damage arising or at least to limit the extent of the damage."[100]

An applicant will rarely have an interest in seeking review where a decision is no longer in force or where he has achieved what he sought prior to or in the course of the proceedings. But such an interest cannot be ruled out from the outset, and an assessment must be done on a case-by-case basis. Having an infringement recognized by a court may cause the Member State to change its course of conduct, which may benefit an applicant in the future.[101] The interest of an applicant can thus vary depending on

97 Case C-33/14 P, *Mory, Mory Team and Superga Invest* [2015], ECLI:EU:C:2015:609.

98 Still, a right of action to prevent an imminent breach cannot necessarily be excluded, where the applicant can demonstrate that the prejudice to his legal situation is already certain.

99 Case C-1/09, *CELF II* [2010], ECLI:EU:C:2010:136.

100 Advocate General Geelhoed in Case C-491/01, *British American Tobacco* [2002], ECLI:EU:C:2002:476, para. 57. Although the case concerned the question whether the Court could rule on the validity and interpretation of a directive before the period for its implementation has expired, the argument is of broader relevance.

101 By implication, Case C-432/05, *Unibet* [2007], ECLI:EU:C:2007:163.

whether he is a one one-shot player or a repeat player. Having a court recognize a breach can also be of relevance for later proceedings for monetary damages. In its case law relating to Article 263(4) TFEU, the Court has also acknowledged that having the illegality of the contested act recognized can constitute a form of reparation for the non-material harm which he has suffered by reason of that illegality.[102] Considerations of moral redress can possibly – depending on the area – also be of relevance in relation to judicial protection before domestic courts.[103] The decisive criterion is whether this interest is protected by the provision invoked.

When it comes to procedural infringements, it is not always easily determined whether an applicant will benefit if a court grants relief. Having gone through all the right procedures, a government may still decide not to change its substantive decision. In section III(d) above, it was made clear that an applicant cannot be perceived as 'affected' by a procedural violation if it is conceivable that the contested decision would not have been different without the procedural defect, but the burden of proof cannot be shifted onto the applicant. Building on the same line of thought, requiring an applicant to establish that the contested decision will be altered following an annulment would render the enforcement of such rights 'virtually impossible or excessively difficult'. Rather standing should be granted provided there is a *real possibility* that the state will reconsider the decision.

(IV) Discussion and Final Remarks

The criteria for standing that can be deduced from the principle of effective judicial protection focus on an applicant's legal interests. At the same time, by pursuing his own interest, a private party contributes to furthering the goals of the Union. Through legal proceedings in the domestic courts, private parties become "part of the implementation process".[104] Although

---

102 See Case T-290/14, *Portnov* [2015], ECLI:EU:T:2015:806, Rec. 30.

103 This would primarily be relevant in the case of social rights, such as for instance the right to non-discrimination under the Racial Equality Directive (2000/43/EC) and Equality Framework Directive (2000/78/EC).

104 M. Ruffert, "Rights and Remedies in European Community Law: A Comparative View", 34 *CML Rev* 307, 316 (1997). He uses the term "functional subjectivation".

the right to effective judicial protection is based on Article 13 of the European Convention on Human Rights, this right takes on a different form in the Union law context. Rights protection is not only of intrinsic value, but it is also a means of rendering Union law effective in the Member States.[105] Acknowledging the (partly) instrumental nature of Union rights, means accepting that considerations of *effet utile* influence the requirements deriving from Union law. Too lenient requirements can prevent matters from being brought before a court, and this may hamper a court from performing its function to ensure compliance with the Treaty.

Whereas generous access rights will enhance the prospect of judicial control of governmental acts, there is also the potential of unduly disrupting national standing doctrines. Circumscribed standing rules may serve, inter alia, to avoid courts being flooded with claims, overloading their dockets, and may also hinder courts from being converted into political platforms, which subverts democratic processes. It must be kept in mind that national standing rules operate within a broader constitutional and cultural context.[106] In the words of Rehbinder: "rules relating to standing are deeply imbedded in the respective domestic system of judicial review, they are an expression of basic constitutional concepts and function in the framework of domestic political-administrative and social cultures."[107] The Court must ensure respect for the principles of subsidiarity and proportionality, as laid down in Article 5(3) and (4) TEU.

---

105 It should be noted that the European Convention on Human Rights also has a certain "objective" aspect, meaning that human rights observance is beneficial to other private persons and society in general, see M. Emberland, *The Human Rights of Companies* 58-59 (Oxford, Oxford University Press 2006). This wider objective finds its expression, inter alia, in Article 37(1) which states that the Court may pursue a case in the public interest, even if the applicant withdraws his application "if respect for human rights … so requires". On the individualistic and communitarian models of rights enforcement, see further J. Miles, "Standing under the Human Rights Act 1998: Theories of Rights Enforcement & the Nature of Public Law Adjudication", 59 *The Cambridge Law Journal* 133, 148- 152 (2000).

106 M. Dougan, "Who Exactly Benefits from the Treaties? The Murky Interaction Between Union and National Competence over the Capacity to Enforce EU Law", 12 *Cambridge Yearbook Of European Legal Studies* 73, 78 (2009).

107 E. Rehbinder, "Locus Standi, Community Law and the Case for Harmonization", in: H. Somsen (ed.), *Protecting the European Environment. Enforcing EC Environmental Law* 162 (London, Blackstone 1996).

The right to effective judicial protection under Article 47 of the Charter is not absolute, but can be subject to limitations, provided that these respect the essence of the right, they pursue a legitimate purpose, and are proportionate with regard to the objectives pursued in accordance with Article 52(1) of the Charter.[108] When doubts are raised as to whether a national procedural provision is compatible with the right to effective legal protection, the issue must be analysed by reference to the role of that provision in the procedure, its progress and its special features. In that context, it is necessary to take into consideration the principles forming the basis of the national legal system.[109] Such a balancing approach ensures that domestic procedural ideals are not sacrificed at the altar of effectiveness. Interestingly, though, in the Court's case law pertaining to *locus standi*, there are no signs of the Court resorting to this objective justification approach. The Court's view seems to be that applicants who derive rights from the Union legal order and whose rights are adversely affected should be granted standing.[110] This stands in contrast to other types of procedural rules hampering the domestic exercise of Union law rights.[111] The reason why the Court does not resort to this objective justification-approach in its case law on standing can be explained by the fact that a denial of locus standi would easily undermine the very essence of the right to effective judicial protection, since it would constitute an absolute obstacle to enforcement.

The right to effective judicial protection comes into play where an applicant seeks to enforce a *right* stemming from Union law. Where Union rights are not at stake, the Member States have considerable leeway when

108 Case C-300/11, *ZZ* [2013], ECLI:EU:C:2013:363, Rec. 51, and Joined Cases C-317-320/08 *Alassini* [2010], ECLI:EU:C:2010:146, Rec. 63.

109 This "procedural rule of reason" test was first laid down by the Court in Joined Cases C-430/93 and C-431/93, *Van Schijndel* [1995], ECLI:EU:C:1995:441, and Case C-312/93, *Peterbroeck* [1995], ECLI:EU:C:1995:437 in the context of the principle of effectiveness. Still, the elements of the test seems equally applicable in relation to Article 47 of the Charter, see *inter alia* Advocate General Cruz Villalón in Case C-510/13, *E.ON. Földgáz Trade* [2014], ECLI:EU:C:2014:2325, para. 46. It may, however, be the case that the test will be stricter when the fundamental right of judicial protection is at stake, see Prechal and Widdershoven, *supra* n. 25, at 44.

110 See, inter alia, Case C-426/05, *Tele2* [2008], ECLI:EU:C:2008:103, Rec. 32-33.

111 Joined Cases C-317-320/08, *Alassini* [2010], ECLI:EU:C:2010:146, Rec. 63-65 (concerning a mandatory out-of-court settlement procedure.)

crafting and applying their domestic rules on standing. It must, however, be kept in mind that they are still bound by the principles of equivalence and effectiveness, and – more generally – the duty of loyal cooperation enshrined in Article 4(3) TEU. Enabling and encouraging private parties to pursue infringements may be a way of ensuring that Union law is rendered effective in the Member States. The 'Union standard' of effective judicial protection is only a minimum standard, and the Member States may adopt more lenient standing rules, to ensure that public organs can be held to account for Union law violations. Private parties are thereby enlisted as 'watchdogs' of the Union interest, aiding the Commission in its enforcement efforts.

II. Procedural Law and Global Governance: Exploring and Mapping a New Research Field

*Remo Caponi**

(I) "Sentry"

The final part of "Sentry", a short story by Fredric Brown, a classic of science fiction published in the United States in 1954, reads as follows:

> "He stayed alert, gun ready. Fifty thousand light-years from home, fighting on a strange world and wondering if he'd ever live to see home again. And then he saw one of them crawling toward him. He drew a bead and fired. The alien made that strange horrible sound they all make, then lay still. He shuddered at the sound and sight of the alien lying there. One ought to be able to get used to them after a while, but he'd never been able to. Such repulsive creatures they were, with only two arms and two legs, ghastly white skins and no scales."

The main character of this story is a soldier at war against aliens on a remote planet. The plot urges the reader to identify herself with the soldier, but in the last passage there is a *coup de théâtre*: as the soldier describes the appearance of the enemy, the reader realizes she has identified herself with an alien who has just killed a human.

---

* Professor of Civil Procedure, School of Law, University of Florence, Fellow of the Alexander von Humboldt Foundation, Senior Hauser Global Research Fellow at the New York University (2014-2015). The studies leading to this contribution have received funding in the framework of the research project of national interest (PRIN) 2012 (2012SAM3KM) on Codification of EU Administrative Procedures, financed by the Italian Ministry of Universities. The reserch project on "Procedural Law and Global Governance" was triggered by the exciting atmosphere at NYU School of Law, where I stayed as a senior Global Hauser research fellow in the academic year 2014-2015. I am very grateful to Oscar Chase, Gráinne de Búrca, Kevin Davis, Franco Ferrari, Samuel Issacharoff, Benedict Kinsbury, Linda Silberman for the great opportunity of intellectual exchange.

(II) With the Eyes of a Stranger

Drawing a moral from this tale, we should perhaps look at our daily reality a bit through the eyes of a stranger, discover oddities in things that look normal, consider with surprise aspects of our country and culture that seem obvious to us, build on changes occurring in our way of seeing the world and ourselves, experience our own otherness.[1]

These attitudes are essential now, since the conquest of territories almost at the borders of Europe by an enemy power is causing a dramatic increase in the stream of refugees, and terrorist attacks in the heart of Europe are considerably challenging European security policies. In addition, the victory of the Brexit campaign is a warning to the liberal international order.[2]

But in situations that typically urge us to focus on the exceptional, immediate event, we should instead take a long-term perspective.[3] In 2001, there were already more (domestic and international) migrants than ever before,[4] so that the twenty-first century could be labelled as the "century of the migrant".[5] To look at immigration requirements in liberal democracies is a prominent way of dealing with our identity and value choices.

---

1 Timely enough, the overarching theme of the third annual meeting of the International Society of Public Law (Berlin, Germany, on 17-19 June 2016) is "Borders, Otherness and Public Law", while underlining that "Today, more than ever before, questions of movement, displacement and belonging, equality and inequality, borders and otherness have become hot-button issues, passionately debated worldwide, and are likely to remain at the forefront of public discourse and scholarly research for the foreseeable future. Line-drawing, practices of inclusion and exclusion, borders and boundaries of many kinds raise persistent questions within contemporary domestic, transnational and international public law" (s. https://icon-society.org/previous-conferences/2016-conference/call_2016, last visited 1 July 2016). However, one could advocate the same for private law, as it "inevitably affects the structure of a society (its "system building", public side) as well as the private relations of people living in that society": cf. G. Calabresi, "The Italian Law Journal: Challenges and Opportunities", 1 *Italian Law Journal* 1 (2015). Finally, one could advocate exactly the same for procedural law, as it is at the crossroads between private and public law.

2 "The Politics of Anger", *The Economist*, July 2, 2016.

3 Cf. for this approach, K. Loevy, *Emergencies in Public Law. The Legal Politics of Containment* (Cambridge University Press, 2016).

4 Cf. the data of the International Organisation for Migration (IOM), available at *www.iom.int.*

5 So T. Nail, *The Figure of The Migrant* (Stanford University Press, 2015), at 1.

The problem is how we should cope with the current emergency. It is awkward that the usual reaction is to introduce immigration and citizenship policies aimed at protecting the majority culture.[6] We should instead seek to promote sustainable diversity among the cultural traditions of the world,[7] which are now converging through the remarkable migration movements.

There are plenty of ways to pursue this aim. The changes that are occurring day by day in the capillary fabric of our lives are more and more frequently triggered by the transnational circulation of ideas. This phenomenon is one of the key features of the contemporary world. As Saskia Sassen put it:

> "*The epochal transformation we call globalization is taking place inside the national to a far larger extent than is usually recognized. It is here that the most complex meanings of the global are being constituted, and the national is also often one of the key enablers and enactors of the emergent global scale. A good part of globalization consists of an enormous variety of micro-processes that begin to denationalize what had been constructed as national — whether policies, capital, political subjectivities, urban spaces, temporal frames, or any other of a variety of dynamics and domains. Sometimes these processes of denationalization allow, enable, or push the construction of new types of global scalings of dynamics and institutions; other times they continue to inhabit the realm of what is still largely national.*"[8]

Such phenomena trace out fragmented or reticular lines and develop rather independently of the political process. National governments have to put up with, more than being promoter of, them. The drivers are primarily the cultural attitudes and open-mindedness of the people, then economy, finance, science and technology.

---

6 Cf. L. Orgad, *The Cultural Defense of Nations. A Liberal Theory of Majority Rights* (Oxford University Press, 2015), arguing that a narrow defence of the majority culture may often be justified.

7 As regards law, cf. H. P. Glenn, *Legal Traditions of the World. Sustainable Diversity in Law* (5th ed., Oxford University Press, 2014).

8 S. Sassen, *Territory, Authority, Rights. From Medieval to Global Assemblages* (Princeton University Press, 2008), at 1.

(III) A View from Procedural Law

One may wonder what procedural law has to do with all that. Quite a lot, actually. First, some key features of procedural law that build the civil procedure scholars' cast of mind and way of thinking – the purpose of protecting rights effectively, the right to be heard, the duty to give reasons, the review of decisions (in other words: the fair trial guarantee) as well as, in recent decades, the advancement of mediation and other "alternative" dispute resolution methods – prove critical to understanding other people's reasons, and aim at finding out the sustainable diversities among different cultural traditions and attitudes.

(IV) Procedural Law and Global Governance: Towards a Workable Research Agenda

This is not the only reason why scholars in procedural law ought to get even more involved in dealing with somc key issues arising from the globalization. The objective of this paper is to assess to what extent procedural law (in particular: civil procedure) scholarship may contribute to the framing of issues concerning transnational regulatory regimes in the European and global arenas, with a view to setting up a workable research agenda.

The expected outcome is to create the conditions for increased dialogue and exchange between scholars in procedural law and other legal scholars (and social scientists at large) dealing with transnational governance, as well as to contribute to a better understanding of the procedural components of transnational law and the regulatory functions of dispute resolution in this context.

This research project is closely linked to some topics procedural law scholars normally deal with: transnational litigation and the elements of fair trial; the shift to alternative dispute resolution methods in transnational transactions; judicial cooperation and the dialogue between judges; the pros, cons, feasibility and limits of harmonization of civil procedure in Europe; the use of indicators as a tool to evaluate and compare judicial systems. The research idea is to link at least some of these topics to each other with a view to identifying some elements of an overarching scheme that could help in discovering a common framework for scholarly reflection and the advancement of knowledge in these fields.

I have chosen this approach for it is particularly challenging in terms of the methodology of academics dealing with procedural law: it requires an advanced awareness of the functional connections among different societal sectors touched upon by procedural law, and suggests multi- and interdisciplinary perspectives to be adopted. This topic seems to me to be appropriate for a summer school focusing on the pluralism of methods in procedural law. It might indeed be tricky to be confronted with methodological issues in abstract terms: as you know, "the proof of the pudding is in the eating". One is better advised to link methodological issues to an inquiry into the merits. That might well be the first rule of methodology.

(V) The Silence of Procedural Law Literature

To take a first glance at transnational regulatory regimes, a simple observation can serve as a starting point. Recent decades have witnessed a growth of global administrative law in response to the need for accountability in global regulatory governance through increased transparency, participation, reason-giving, and review. As Richard B. Stewart put it:

> "*A wide variety of global regulatory authorities, including international and transnational organizations, private regulators, and hybrid public-private bodies [...] generate and apply a flood of regulatory norms and decisions in such diverse fields as banking, financial services, monetary policy, telecommunications, intellectual property, competition law, international trade, international investment, environment, labor, intellectual property, development assistance, international security, and human rights [...]. Many of the cases now brought before international and domestic courts and tribunals concern these bodies and their decisions. This expansion of global regulation responds to functional necessities created by economic integration and other forms of interdependency associated with globalization. States can no longer deal adequately with these interdependences and secure the welfare of their citizens through uncoordinated domestic regulatory measures*".[9]

Against this backdrop, one might have expected that scholars focusing on judicial process (particularly civil procedure), which possibly represents in any legal system the most sophisticated body of legal knowledge on the legitimacy of the exercise of public power, as well as the interplay be-

9 R. B. Stewart, "Part I Courts, Institutions and Access to Justice: Legitimacy and Accountability in Global Regulatory Governance: Global Administrative Law and Developing Countries", 1 *Jindal Global L. Rev.* 41 (2009).

tween public (judicial) power and private powers of the parties to a proceedings, would powerfully contribute to frame legal issues related to transnational governance. Quite the opposite holds true. Academics whose primary field of expertise is civil procedure currently examine, besides their own national judicial systems, issues either relating to transnational litigation or comparative civil procedure, but they seldom address the 'big picture' concerning the theoretical dimensions of the interplay between national law (especially judicial systems) and transnational regulatory regimes. Conversely, scholars dealing with transnational law seldom take into consideration procedural law scholarship.

A similar issue has been raised as regards private international law. As H. Muir Watt and D. P. Fernández Arroyo put it: "*Despite the contemporary juridification of international politics, private international law has contributed very little to the global governance debate, remaining remarkably silent before the increasingly unequal distribution of wealth and authority in the world.*"[10]

This holds even truer for procedural law. The increase of wealth and power imbalances caused by the globalization of economy and finance does not stop at national borders. Systems, like civil procedure, aimed at ensuring "justice", simply because they are about achieving justice through the means of law enforcement, are affected by these phenomena in a very incisive way.

(VI) Misleading Perceptions

In the first place, one has to consider the reasons for the lack of communication and dialogue between scholars in civil procedure and scholars in transnational legal theory. They are primarily found in the way civil procedure scholarship and practice are normally perceived. First, the widespread conception of mainstream research in the field of civil procedure today still mirrors the frightening assessment of Friedrich Stein: "civil procedure is technical law par excellence".[11] Second, particularly from the perspective of civil law systems, the distinction between substantive law and procedural law has fostered the view that procedural law is 'neu-

10 Cf. H. Muir Watt, D. P. Fernández Arroyo, *Private International Law and Global Governance* (Oxford University Press, 2014), "Introduction".

11 F. Stein, *Grundriß des Zivilprozeßrechts* (2nd, Mohr, Tübingen,1924), XIV.

tral' as regards substantive law, i.e. any particular procedural law could implement any substantive law. Third, consequently, civil procedure is perceived as a rather technical and professional field of law. Finally, procedural law is regarded as more closely linked to State authority than other branches of the law: justice being administered primarily in courthouses and not just through written words in legal provisions, it depends on considerable financial resources invested by governments. Therefore, procedural law can be studied as a purely national product. Nineteenth- and twentieth-century nationalism contributed to an entirely national approach to law possibly nowhere more than in the field of civil procedure. It is no huge surprise, then, that the report of the German Council of Science and Humanities "Prospects of Legal Scholarship in Germany" (2013), reflecting on how to adapt legal education and legal scholarship to the challenges of increasing internationalization of the law, seems to neglect the role of procedural law.[12]

(VII) Janus-Faced Civil Procedure

This perception is misleading.

Civil procedure has suffered, probably more than other fields of law, from the fixing of boundaries among branches of law, in particular from the great divide between private and public law, historically peculiar to European continental law. In this context, civil procedure was Janus-faced or acted as an interface: one face looked to public law, as civil proceedings are mainly set up by the State; the other looked to private law, as civil proceedings aim to protect individual rights. The divide between private and public law caused (and still causes) the theory and practice of judicial protection of rights to be affected by a sort of 'magnetic field' and to oscillate between these two opposite conceptual poles. Although firmly grounded on the terrain of public law, civil procedure bears traces, in its basic structures (from standing to sue to adjudication), of its historical foundations in natural-law theory which aimed at protecting the 'new bourgeois individual' and his economic freedom in a fragmented and individualistic view of social relationships.

12 Available at http://www.wissenschaftsrat.de/download/archiv/2558-12_engl.pdf, at 63 (last visited 1 July 2016).

This longstanding tension meant procedural law could not be fully absorbed into either private law or public law. However, this in-built opposition between different conceptual poles can be beneficial for procedural law scholarship, because it gives procedural law the flexibility to address certain key issues concerning transnational governance.

(VIII) The Case for Procedural Law

The case for increasing the involvement of procedural law scholarship in the discussion concerning European and global governance is indeed compelling.

First, a key feature of the juridification of the global arena is the development of judicial dispute settlement,[13] and, in particular, the broadening of the exercise of individuals' right to sue in national or international courts, pursuing matters relating to transnational regulatory regimes. Thus, procedural devices and principles play a major role in the European and global arena. Consider, for example, the procedure for preliminary reference to the Court of Justice of the European Union, the weight of the right to be heard in the *Kadi* ruling (ECLI:EU:C:2008:461), the epistemic community currently working on European Principles of Civil Procedure in the framework of a ELI-UNIDROIT joint project, and the discussion on the regulation of investment dispute resolution during the negotiations about the transatlantic trade and investment partnership.

Second, procedural principles and safeguards are called on to play a major role in the activity of global regulatory authorities. As already mentioned, in the last two decades principles pertaining to (procedural) due process, like the right to a hearing, the duty to provide a reasoned decision, and the duty to disclose all relevant information have developed and have been enforced in the area of global regulation.[14]

---

13 Cf. K. Alter, *The New Terrain of International Law. Courts, Politics, Rights* (Princeton University Press, 2014); A. von Bogdandy, I. Venzke, *In Whose Name? A Public Law Theory of International Adjudication* (Oxford University Press, 2014); C. Romano, K. Alter, Y. Shany (eds.), *The Oxford Handbook of International Adjudication* (Oxford University Press, 2014).

14 Cf. S. Cassese, *The Global Polity. Global Dimension of Democracy and the Rule of Law* (Global Press, 2012), 48; G. Della Cananea, "Procedural Due Process of Law Beyond the State", in A. von Bogdandy, *The Exercise of Public Authority by International Institutions* (Dordrecht, Springer, 2010), 965.

Thus, some key features of procedural law heavily affect transnational governance.

There is however the other side of the coin: tools of European and global governance influence the domestic regulation of judicial proceedings more widely than is often acknowledged. Consider, for example, the far-reaching reforms of the national procedural laws and court systems of the Member States of the European Union that have been ensured in the context of the troika process, e.g. in Ireland, Portugal and Greece, and the remarkable impact of the World Bank's Doing Business Reports on the reforms of national judicial systems.

The issues common to both sides of the coin are precisely those at the core of the necessity of enhancing global regulation, i.e. standing, legitimacy and accountability of the actors concerned (private actors, national and international courts, public agencies, etc.).

(IX) Roadmap of the Research Project

The roadmap of the research is divided into two sections, mirroring the relationship of mutual influence between procedural law and global governance:

a) Aspects of procedural law affecting transnational governance;
b) Tools of transnational governance affecting the regulation of civil proceedings.

Both sections will deal with problems that are well known in transnational legal theory, but which are normally addressed in different research fields. It is the purpose of this research proposal to explore this research area and to map the topics belonging to it, including:

(a) Domestic and international courts and transnational governance. The working hypothesis aims to establish whether there are symptoms of an 'over-judicialization'.

A key feature of the juridification of the global arena is the development of judicial dispute settlement and, in particular, the broadening of the exercise of individual rights to sue in national or international courts, for matters relating to transnational regulatory regimes.

To put this phenomenon into perspective, one needs to recall the developments of the right of judicial action in national settings. It is, indeed, a time-honoured achievement of procedural law scholarship to have been able to establish a link in public law between violations of rights and a right-holder's power to resort to judicial protection. However, the traditional structure of judicial systems leaves unchanged in civil proceedings the imbalances of wealth and power occurring in the daily life of people. Thus, the primary function of a right of action is to guarantee the right to sue in court in the context of a liberal concept of equal protection under the law (formal equality). In the global arena, the different positions of individuals, regarding wealth and power, might be even more pronounced than in a purely national setting. Individual access to the courts might amplify distributional differences.

Consider the *Kadi* case. The right of judicial action, the right to be heard, and the right to an effective remedy had possibly their most remarkable impact on the international legal order through the judgment of the European Court of Justice in this case (ECJ, 3 September 2008, joined cases C-402 & 415/05P). One can hardly conceive of an individual other than a multi-millionaire from Jeddah or an individual with equivalent resources, capable of the huge financial effort needed to obtain judicial protection of his assets from U.N. Security Council resolutions. His lawsuits might have induced the U.N. bodies to adopt changes - such as the establishment of an ombudsman, which can be beneficial to other individuals affected by U.N. targeted sanctions. However, one cannot rely only on initiatives of Kadi-like litigants as systemic incentives for introducing changes in the architecture of global governance.

Further reasons to avoid over-emphasizing access to the courts as a tool of governance come from recent developments concerning the relationship between civil adjudication and out-of-court dispute resolution methods. These developments may reveal the link between diplomatic and political negotiation and judicial dispute settlement in the global arena. Consider the tension between international customary law on State immunity and the constitutional principle of access to the courts arising from lawsuits filed against Germany by Italian citizens seeking compensation for international law crimes committed by Nazi military forces in Italy during World War II. The working hypothesis aims to advance the case for coordinating inter-State diplomatic negotiations on the one hand, and access to the courts by the victims, on the other.

(b) *Use of indicators (and big data) as a tool to evaluate and compare judicial systems.*

Using indicators for the evaluation of legal systems is for the jurist a 'risky business', as there is often no control over the criteria for collection, selection and presentation of data. However, the jurist cannot remain silent because the use of indicators for evaluating and comparing the performance of national legal systems has been spreading at a remarkable pace since the beginning of the twenty-first century. Indicators have attracted the attention of policy makers and government officials, and thus are having a powerful impact as a tool of European and global governance.

Most influential are data about the performance of judicial systems produced within the context of wider comparisons including rankings regarding the attractiveness of different legal systems for doing business: the Doing Business project (World Bank Group). In light of the ongoing success of the Doing Business annual reports, it is easy to explain why the European Commission for the Efficiency of Justice (CEPEJ) report, a detailed report published bi-annually since 2006, has come to prominence. The report aims at measuring and comparing the efficiency and effectiveness of European countries' judicial systems and has been used since 2013 as a data base to create a simplified and more appealing information tool. The EU Justice Scoreboard published by the EU Commission, intends to shed light on the quality, independence and efficiency of justice systems as co-determinants of economic growth in the Member States of the European Union.

The working hypothesis is that the EU Justice Scoreboard might overcome the fragmentation of the legal framework concerning the harmonization of civil procedure in Europe (cf. mainly Art. 81 and 114 TFEU, but also Art. 118 TFEU as well as Art. 102 TFEU), by way of supervising the national judicial systems and comparing their performances, with the aim of harmonization *de facto*, under a functional perspective.

Although the complexity and distinctive features of each national judicial system cannot be entirely captured by quantitative indicators, they can be beneficial for fostering comparative knowledge of judicial systems and for promoting reforms. Dealing with them can be fascinating and rewarding for the lawyer, particularly the scholar in civil procedure, as it helps in dispelling the sense of distinctiveness of civil procedure from other fields of the law, to say nothing of the sense of remoteness of civil procedure from the society.

Indicators are also tremendously successful in attracting the attention of policy makers and government officials, thus prompting critical amounts of benchmarking, dialogue and reform.[15] Indicators can be beneficial to fostering comparative knowledge of legal systems and promoting reforms. Information gathered through the creation and use of indicators needs, however, to be integrated and corrected, both on the descriptive and the prescriptive side, far more than currently happens, through the knowledge of lawyers and social scientists living and working in the targeted countries.[16]

(X) Aim of the Research Project

It is the aim of this research project to address issues common to both aspects of procedural law impacting on transnational governance and tools of transnational governance impacting on the regulation of civil proceedings strands, such as the problems of standing, legitimacy and accountability of the actors involved (individual plaintiffs in 'international public interest litigation', national courts dealing with issues related to transnational governance, international courts, agencies producing and implementing indicators, etc.), through a parallel analysis, that might be mutually beneficial.

15 K. Davis, B. Kingsbury, S.E. Merry, "Indicators as a Technology of Global Governance", 46 *Law & Society Review* 71, 92 (2012).

16 This approach also reflects a certain methodological focus, which is best expressed by Clifford Geertz' words: "*Like sailing, gardening, politics and poetry, law and ethnography are crafts of place: they work by the light of local knowledge*". Cf. C. Geertz, "Local Knowledge: Fact and Law in Comparative Perspective", in *Local Knowledge: Further Essays in Interpretive Anthropology* (Basic Books, New York, 1983), at 167.

Index